LIVING COMMUNION

**The Official Report of the 13th Meeting
of the Anglican Consultative Council,
Nottingham 2005**

Compiled by James M. Rosenthal and Susan T. Erdey
with the daily Bible studies
of Archbishop of Canterbury Rowan Williams
and the Special Report on Human Sexuality:
Presentations by the Anglican Church of Canada
and the Episcopal Church USA

CHURCH PUBLISHING
an imprint of
Church Publishing Incorporated, New York

Published for the Anglican Communion Office
Saint Andrew's House
16 Tavistock Crescent
London W11 1AP
England
Tel: +44 (0) 207 313 3900
FAX: +44 (0) 207 313 3999
e-mail: aco@aco.org
www.anglicancommunion.org

Printed in the United States of America

10-digit ISBN 0-89869-522-8
13-digit ISBN 978-0-89869-522-9

Library of Congress Cataloging-in-Publication Data

Anglican Consultative Council. Meeting (13th : 2005 : Nottingham,
England)
Living communion : the official report of the 13th Meeting of the
Anglican Consultative Council, Nottingham 2005 / compiled by James M.
Rosenthal and Susan T. Erdey ; with the daily Bible studies of Archbishop
of Canterbury,Rowan Williams and the special report on human sexuality
presentations by the Anglican Church of Canada and the Episcopal Church
USA.
p. cm.
ISBN-13: 978-0-89869-522-9
ISBN-10: 0-89869-522-8
1. Anglican Consultative Council. 2. Anglican Communion--Con-
gresses. I. Rosenthal, James. II. Erdey, Susan T. III. Title.
BX5002.A6326 2005
262'.53--dc22

2006016026

Cover design by 3+Company
Interior design by Beth Oberholtzer Design

Church Publishing Incorporated
445 Fifth Avenue
New York, NY 10016
www.churchpublishing.org
5 4 3 2 1

Contents

Acknowledgements vi
The Church of England vii

THE REPORT

The Resolutions

The Resolutions of ACC-13 5

Archbishop of Canterbury's Daily Bible Studies

20 June 2005 35
21 June 2005 39
22 June 2005 43
23 June 2005 47
24 June 2005 53
25 June 2005 57
27 June 2005 62
28 June 2005 66

Sermons, Lectures, and Addresses

Archbishop of Canterbury's Presidential Address 71
     The Most Reverend and Right Hon. Rowan Williams,
     Archbishop of Canterbury
Chairman's Address 82
     The Right Reverend John Paterson, Bishop of Auckland, New
     Zealand
Address on the Millennium Development Goals 92
     Hilary Benn, Member of Parliament
Secretary General's Address 96
     The Reverend Canon Kenneth Kearon
Sermon at the Diocesan Celebration 102
     The Most Reverend and Right Hon. Rowan Williams,
     Archbishop of Canterbury
Closing Address to ACC-13 106
     The Right Reverend Dr. N.T. Wright, Bishop of Durham

Departmental and Commission Reports

Department of Communications 121
Department of Ecumenical Affairs 126
Inter-Anglican Standing Commission on Mission and Evangelism .191
Department of Telecommunications 381
Anglican Observer at the United Nations .385
    Archdeacon Taimalelagi Fagamalama Tuatagaloa-Matalavea

Ecumenical Greetings

From the Baptist World Alliance 457
From the Ecumenical Patriarch Bartholomew 459
From the Churches Together in England .461
From the Churches of the Union of Utrecht 463
From the Lutheran World Federation 465
From the Mar Thoma Church of Malabar 467
From the Methodist Church Conference .469
From the Pontifical Council for Promoting Christian Unity 472
From the World Council of Churches 475

Provincial and Network Reports

Provincial Reports

Province of the Anglican Church of Congo 481
Melanesian Brotherhood 484

Network Reports

Anglican Indigenous Network 501
Anglican Peace and Justice Network 519
Anglican Communion Environmental Network 550
International Anglican Family Network 555
Global Anglicanism Project 557
International Anglican Women's Network 561
International Anglican Youth Network 588
International Anglican Liturgical Consultation 590
Network for Inter-Faith Concerns 592
Theological Education for the Anglican Communion 607

FINANCIAL REPORTS

Report of Financial and Administration Committee 627
Inter-Anglican Budget 643

CONSTITUTION

Constitution 661

The New ACC Constitution: Explanatory Notes 675

ACC MEMBERSHIP

ACC-13 Participants List 681

SPECIAL REPORT: HUMAN SEXUALITY

Presentation by the Anglican Church of Canada

Introductory letter from the Primate of Canada 689
The Most Reverend Andrew S. Hutchinson,
Archbishop and Primate

The Conversation in the Canadian Church 690

Presentation by the Episcopal Church USA

The Right Reverend J. Neil Alexander, Bishop of Atlanta 694

The Reverend Dr. Michael Battle, Associate Dean of
  Academic Affairs and Vice President, Virginia Theolgoical Seminary . . .698

The Right Reverend Charles E. Jenkins, Bishop of Louisiana 703

The Reverend Susan Russell, All Saints Episcopal Church,
  Pasadena, California 706

Mrs. Jane Tully, Clergy Families and Friends of Lesbians and Gays,
  New York, New York 710

PROVINCIAL SECRETARIES

Directory of Provincial Secretaries of the Anglican Communion . . .717

ADDITIONAL MATERIAL

Photographs from ACC-13 729

Prayers for the Anglican Communion 735

Letter to the Children of Anglican Communion 737

List of Child Artists in the Compass Rose Competition 738

The Compass Rose 739

Acknowledgements

Our thanks to Kenneth Arnold, Amy Davis, Ryan Masteller, Beth Oberholtzer, and Church Publishing Incorporated, New York, for their commitment to this report at this important time in the life of the Anglican Communion; and to Gill Harris Hogarth, Liza Grant, and the volunteer staff in Nottingham for their invaluable assistance in making this report a reality.

A note from Canon James Rosenthal: This volume has been compiled from the papers, speeches, and addresses of ACC-13 "as presented" (spoken or written), with the minimum of editing. This is to preserve the integrity of the presentations as they, by their very nature, reflect the global character of our Communion.

The Church of England

Covering all of England, including the Isle of Man and the Channel Islands, the Church is the ancient national Church of the land. Its structures emerged from the missionary work of St Augustine of Canterbury, sent from Rome in 597, and from the work of Celtic missionaries in the north. Throughout the Middle Ages, the Church was in Communion with the See of Rome, but in the sixteenth century it separated from Rome and rejected the authority of the Pope. The Church of England is the established Church, with the administration governed by a General Synod that meets twice a year. There are 44 dioceses and two provinces, York and Canterbury (www.anglicancommunion.org).

The Church of England Today

The Church of England plays a vital role in the life of the nation, proclaiming the Christian gospel in words and actions and providing services of Christian worship and praise.

Its network of parishes cover the country, bringing a vital Christian dimension to the nation as well as strengthening community life in numerous urban, suburban and rural settings. Its cathedrals are centres of spirituality and service, and its network of chaplaincies across continental Europe meet important local needs.

The Church of England plays an active role in national life with its members involved in a wide range of public bodies. Twenty-six bishops are members of the House of Lords and are engaged in debates about legislation and national and international affairs.

Key facts about the Church of England:

- More than **1.7 million** people take part in a Church of England service each month.

- More than **2.6** million participate in a Church of England service on Christmas Day or Christmas Eve.

- The Church of England conducts more than **440,000** 'rites of passage' each year. This includes more than **158,000** baptisms and thanksgivings, around **60,000** marriages and blessings of civil marriages, and some **224,000** funerals.

- Every year, around **12.5 million** people visit Church of England cathedrals, including **300,000** pupils on school visits. Three of England's top five historic 'visitor attractions' are York Minster, Canterbury Cathedral, and Westminster Abbey.

- The Church of England directly supports more than **4,700** schools. **One in four** primary schools and **one in 16** secondary schools in England are Church of England schools. Approaching **one million pupils** are educated in Church of England schools.

- The Church of England has more than **27,000** licensed ministers—including more than **9,000** paid clergy; more than **2,000** non-stipendiary ministers; more than **10,000** Readers; around **5,000** active retired clergy; and **1,100** chaplains in colleges, universities, hospitals, schools, prisons and the armed forces.

- An average of **510** men and women have been ordained each year over the last three years.

- Forty-five per cent of the country's Grade I listed buildings are maintained by the Church of England. These churches and cathedrals are largely supported by the efforts and financial support of local communities. Often, they are the focus of community life and service.

- In total, some **13,000** of the Church of England's **16,000** buildings are listed by the government as being of special architectural or historic interest.

- A 2003 survey showed that **86 per cent** of the population had visited a church building or place of worship in the previous twelve months, for reasons ranging from participating in worship to attending concerts or simply wanting a quiet space.

THE REPORT

The Resolutions

The Resolutions of ACC-13

1. The Appointment of the Archbishop of York

The Anglican Consultative Council:

notes with pleasure the news of the appointment of the Bishop of Birmingham, Dr John Sentamu, as Archbishop of York, and offers its prayers and good wishes for a fruitful and happy ministry.

2. The Instruments of Unity (Communion)

The Anglican Consultative Council:

(a) notes with approval the suggestion of the Windsor Report that the Archbishop of Canterbury be regarded as the focus for unity and that the Primates' Meeting, the Lambeth Conference, the Anglican Consultative Council be regarded more appropriately as the "Instruments of Communion"

(b) resolves that henceforth it will use this terminology for those bodies currently known as "the Instruments of Unity".

3. ACC Constitution (Change of Status to charitable company)

The Anglican Consultative Council:

(a) notes and approves the draft memorandum and articles proposed by the Standing Committee in order to reconstitute the work of the Council within the framework of a limited liability company as requested by ACC 11 and ACC 12

(b) authorises the Standing Committee to make such final amendments to the documentation as may be needed in the light of this Council's discussions and the views of the Primates Meeting, and in accordance with legal advice and any further comments received from the Charity Commissioners

(c) requests the Standing Committee to establish such a body with charitable status in accordance with the such approved draft Memorandum and Articles as amended as a result of any such views, advice or comments

(d) resolves to transfer to the new charitable company all the Council's assets and liabilities in due course and to wind up the affairs of the existing legal entity once the new arrangements are in place.

4. ACC Constitution (Recommendations of the Windsor Report)

The Anglican Consultative Council:

(a) takes note that the Secretary General has taken appropriate steps to implement and respond to the recommendations of Appendix One of the Windsor Report insofar as they relate to the administration of the Anglican Communion Office, and thanks him for this work

(b) requests that the Standing Committee of the Council and the Archbishop of Canterbury give consideration to convening a meeting of the Standing Committee at the same time and in the same place as the next meeting of the Primates, and that they facilitate the opportunity for joint sessions of business and consultation

(c) requests that the Schedule of Membership of the Council be amended to make the members of the Primates' Standing Committee for the time being *ex officio* members of the Anglican Consultative Council in accordance with the text set out in *Appendix One*

(d) resolves that the Constitution of the Council be amended by the deletion of existing Article 7(a) and replacing it with the text set out in *Appendix Two;*

(e) requests that the Schedule of Membership of the Council be amended to provide that the Primates and Moderators of the Churches of the Provinces of the Anglican Communion shall be additional ex officio members of the Council, and that in order to achieve appropriate balance between the orders of bishops, clergy and laity in the Council that the representative members shall thereafter be only from either the priestly and diaconal orders or from the laity of the appropriate Provinces as set out in *Appendix Three,* the execution of this amendment being subject to

    (i) the Primates' assent to such a change at their next meeting

    (ii) two thirds of the Provinces of the Anglican Communion giving their approval of such a change by resolution of the appropriate constitutional body

    (iii) final amendment (if any) and approval by the Standing Committee in the light of such deliberations

    (iv) such provisions taking effect in relation to existing members of the Council only upon the occasion of the next vacancy arising in the membership.

Appendix One

The Schedule of Membership shall be amended by adding the new category:

> "(e) *Ex officio* members
> Five members of the body known as the Standing Committee of the Primates of the Anglican Communion in each case for so long as they shall remain members of such Standing Committee."

and that the remaining categories in the schedule be redesignated accordingly.

Appendix Two

Article 7(a) of the Constitution shall be amended to read as follows:

> "7(a) The Council shall appoint a Standing Committee of fourteen members, which shall include the Chairman and the Vice-Chairman of the Council, and the members listed in category (e) to the schedule to the Constitution. The Secretary General shall be the Secretary of the Standing Committee."

Appendix Three

The Schedule of Membership shall be amended as follows:

> "(b) Three from each of the following, either two clergy (priests or deacons) and one lay person, or one priest or deacon and two lay persons."

> "(c) Two from each of the following, consisting of one priest or deacon and one lay person."

> "(d) one lay person from each of the following:"

5. ACC Procedures

The Anglican Consultative Council, within the context of the present review of the Constitution and Procedures of the Council, requests the Standing Committee to:

(a) examine circumstances in which it might be appropriate for the Council to vote by Orders

(b) clarify the circumstances in which it might be appropriate to use secret ballots and to require majorities other than a simple majority

(c) examine means by which, for the time being, those Provinces which appoint only one member in addition to their Primate may be persuaded to regard the appointment of lay members as normative

(d) ensure that for the appointments of Chair and Vice-Chair one shall be clerical and one lay

(e) bring forward suggestions and proposals regarding these matters to ACC-14

(f) provide that there be a meeting of the Lay Members early in each meeting of the Council, as part of the introductory process.

6. Standing Committee Procedures

The Anglican Consultative Council:

requests the Standing Committee to circulate the agendas of Standing Committee meetings to all members of the Council prior to meetings, and the minutes of the Standing Committee meetings to all members of the Council as soon as possible following the meetings.

7. & 8. Inter-Anglican Finance and Administration Committee

The Anglican Consultative Council:

adopts and approves the Statement of Accounts for the fifteen months ending 31 December 2003 and the year ending 31 December 2004.

The Anglican Consultative Council:

adopts and approves the Budgets presented to the meeting for the years 2006–2008.

9. Provisions at Meetings of the ACC

The Anglican Consultative Council resolves, at all future plenary meetings of the Council, the Joint Standing Committee and the Inter-Anglican Finance and Administration Committee, where possible and practicable:

(a) to serve only fairly-traded beverages, fruit and other products

(b) to provide drinking water only from suppliers offering financial support for water-supply and irrigation projects in the developing world.

10. Response to the Primates' Statement at Dromantine

The Anglican Consultative Council:

(a) takes note of the decisions taken by the Primates at their recent meeting in Dromantine, Northern Ireland, in connection with the recommendations of the Windsor Report 2004

(b) notes further that the Primates there reaffirmed "the standard of Christian teaching on matters of human sexuality expressed in the 1998 Lambeth Resolution 1.10, which should command respect as the position overwhelmingly adopted by the bishops of the Anglican Communion"

(c) endorses and affirms those decisions

(d) consequently endorses the Primates' request that "in order to recognise the integrity of all parties, the Episcopal Church (USA) and the Anglican Church of Canada voluntarily withdraw their members from the Anglican Consultative Council, for the period leading up to the next Lambeth Conference"

(e) interprets reference to the Anglican Consultative Council to include its Standing Committee and the Inter-Anglican Finance and Administration Committee.

11. Supplementary Resolution of Thanks

The Anglican Consultative Council:

(a) notes with appreciation the response of the Episcopal Church (USA) and the Anglican Church of Canada to the request of the Primates' Dromantine Statement

(b) expresses its thanks for the presentations made on Tuesday, 21st June; and requests the observers from those Provinces to convey those thanks back to their Provinces

(c) reminds all parties to have regard for the admonitions in paragraphs 156 and 157 of the Windsor Report.

The Windsor Report, paragraphs 156 and 157

156. We call upon all parties to the current dispute to seek ways of reconciliation, and to heal our divisions. We have already indicated (paragraphs 134 and 144) some ways in which the Episcopal Church (USA) and the Diocese of New Westminster could begin to speak with the Communion in a way which would foster reconciliation. We have appealed to those intervening in provinces and dioceses similarly to act with renewed respect. We would expect all provinces to respond with generosity and charity to any such actions. It may well be that there need to be formal discussions about the path to reconciliation, and a symbolic Act of Reconciliation, which would mark a new beginning for the Communion, and a common commitment to proclaim the Gospel of Christ to a broken and needy world.

157. There remains a very real danger that we will not choose to walk together. Should the call to halt and find ways of continuing in our present communion not be heeded, then we shall have to begin to learn to walk apart. We would much rather not speculate on actions that might need to be taken if, after acceptance by the primates, our recommendations are not implemented. However, we note that there are, in any human dispute, courses that may be followed: processes of mediation and arbitration; non-invitation to relevant representative bodies and meetings; invitation, but to observer status only; and, as an absolute last resort, withdrawal from membership. We earnestly hope that none of these will prove necessary. Our aim throughout has been to work not for division but for healing and restoration. The real challenge of the gospel is whether we live deeply enough in the love of Christ, and care sufficiently for our joint work to bring that love to the world, that we will "make every effort to maintain the unity of the Spirit in the bond of peace" (Eph. 4.3). As the primates stated in 2000, "to turn from one another would be to turn away from the Cross", and indeed from serving the world which God loves and for which Jesus Christ died.

12. Listening Process

In response to the request of the bishops attending the Lambeth Conference in 1998 in Resolution 1.10 to establish "a means of monitoring the work done on the subject of human sexuality in the Communion" and to honour the process of *mutual* listening, including "listening to the experience of homosexual persons" and the experience of local churches around the world in reflecting on these matters in the light of Scripture, Tradition and Reason, the Anglican Consultative Council encourages such listening in each Province and requests the Secretary General:

(a) to collate relevant research studies, statements, resolutions and other material on these matters from the various Provinces and other interested bodies within those Provinces

(b) to make such material available for study, discussion and reflection within each member Church of the Communion

(c) to identify and allocate adequate resources for this work, and to report progress on it to the Archbishop of Canterbury, to the next Lambeth Conference and the next meeting of this Council, and to copy such reports to the Provinces.

13. The Anglican Gathering

The Anglican Consultative Council:

(a) remains enthusiastic about the concept of holding an Anglican Gathering

(b) thanks the Design Group for the proposed Anglican Gathering in 2008, and all others involved, for their work for the proposed gathering in association with the Lambeth Conference

(c) acknowledge that they have followed the advice of the Joint Standing Committee in October 2004 and acted responsibly with their decision that plans for the Anglican Gathering should be cancelled

(d) offers sincere thanks to the Archbishop of Cape Town and the South African team for all their work in preparation for the Gathering, and are sorry that it was not possible to proceed

(e) asks the Standing Committee to consider the viability, concept and funding for a future Anglican Gathering.

14. Anglican–Baptist Relations

The Anglican Consultative Council:

(a) welcomes the publication *"Conversations Around the World"* as the report of the conversations between representatives of the Anglican Communion and the Baptist World Alliance, and commends it to the parishes, dioceses and provinces of the Anglican Communion as a resource for study and reflection on the nature of mission and of the way in which Baptists and Anglicans can co-operate

(b) encourages Anglicans to meet with Baptists at the appropriate level and locality and reflect on this report and on their common mission to bear witness to the salvation found in Christ

(c) offers its congratulations to the members of the Continuation Committee, especially the co-chairs, Professor Paul Fiddes and Professor Bruce Matthews, on the completion of their work, and to all those who contributed to the regional meetings

(d) requests the Director of Ecumenical Affairs to explore ways in which the conversation at international level may be developed in the future.

15. Anglican–Roman Catholic Relations

The Anglican Consultative Council:

(a) welcomes the publication of the Agreed Statement of the Anglican–Roman Catholic International Commission (ARCIC), *Mary: Grace and Hope in Christ,* and the completion of the second phase of the Commission's work

(b) expresses its gratitude to all the members of ARCIC over the last thirty-five years for their outstanding contribution to Anglican–Roman Catholic dialogue

(c) offers its thanks for the ongoing work of the members of the International Anglican–Roman Catholic Commission on Unity and Mission (IARCCUM), and encourages them to proceed with the work of drafting a Common Statement of Faith (which can represent the 'harvesting' of the convergence in faith discerned in the work of ARCIC) and with the other initiatives of common witness being developed by IARCCUM

(d) asks the Director of Ecumenical Studies to ensure that Provinces are invited to undertake a process of study of all the Agreed Statements of the second phase of ARCIC, and, in particular, that they have the opportunity to evaluate the way in which any Common Statement of Faith produced by IARCCUM might represent an appropriate manner in which to recognise the convergence of Christian Faith between the Anglican Communion and the Roman Catholic Church expressed in the work of ARCIC

(e) respectfully requests His Holiness the Pope and His Grace the Archbishop of Canterbury to proceed to the commissioning of a third phase of ARCIC and of theological dialogue between the Anglican Communion and the Roman Catholic Church in pursuit of the full visible unity of Christ's Body here on earth, which is the stated goal for the ecumenical quest in both traditions.

16. Anglican–Lutheran Relations

The Anglican Consultative Council:

(a) welcomes the news of the continuing establishment of closer relations between Anglican and Lutheran churches across the globe, contained in the Report of the Director of Ecumenical Affairs

(b) offers its encouragement to the newly established Anglican–Lutheran International Commission as it begins its work

(c) encourages the All Africa Anglican–Lutheran Commission to resume its work at the earliest opportunity.

17. Anglican–Methodist Relations

The Anglican Consultative Council:

(a) welcomes the news of the establishment of closer relations between Anglican and Methodist churches across the globe, and particularly in England, contained in the Report of the Director of Ecumenical Affairs

(b) requests the Director of Ecumenical Affairs to pursue the establishment of an appropriate instrument of dialogue between the Anglican Communion and the World Methodist Council.

18. Anglican–Old Catholic Relations

The Anglican Consultative Council:

(a) extends its greetings to the Archbishop of Utrecht on behalf of all the churches of the Union

(b) gives thanks to God for seventy-five years of shared life in communion with the Churches of the Union of Utrecht

(c) celebrates the seventy-fifth anniversary of the Bonn Agreement

(d) offers its thanks to all the members of the outgoing Anglican–Old Catholic International Co-ordinating Council for the work over the past five years, and welcomes the establishment of a new Council.

19. Anglican–Oriental Orthodox Relations

The Anglican Consultative Council:

(a) gives thanks to God for the work already achieved by the Anglican–Oriental Orthodox International Commission (AOOIC) in their draft Christological Agreement, and urgently requests those Provinces which have not done so to offer their reflections upon it to the Inter-Anglican Standing Commission for Ecumenical Relations, in order to enable its ratification by the Lambeth Conference in 2008

(b) receives with regret the news that the work of the AOOIC is currently suspended

(c) asks the Director of Ecumenical Affairs to report to the representatives of the Oriental Orthodox churches that the Primates have now twice reaffirmed the 1998 Resolution of the Lambeth Conference 1.10 as "the standard of Christian teaching on matters of human sexuality...", which should command respect as the position overwhelmingly adopted by the bishops of the Anglican Communion" together with the affirmation of this Council, presently meeting in Nottingham, and trusts that this will provide a sufficient basis for the resumption of the work of the AOOIC

(d) asks the AOOIC to consider whether it might examine the relationship between universal and local churches, and the processes of decision making in the life of the churches.

20. Anglican–Eastern Orthodox Relations

The Anglican Consultative Council:

(a) receives with pleasure the news in the Director's Report of the forth-coming completion of the work of the International Commission for Anglican–Orthodox Theological Dialogue (ICAOTD), and thanks its members for their long-standing contribution to the quest for the full visible unity of the Church of Christ

(b) encourages the ICAOTD to move towards the publication of their Agreed Statements at the earliest convenient moment.

21. Regional Ecumenical Developments

The Anglican Consultative Council:

(a) welcomes the establishment of the Communion of Churches in India, and looks forward to seeing the fruits of further co-operation between the United Churches of North and South India and the Mar Thoma Syrian Church of Malabar

(b) welcomes the covenant and Agreed Statement commitments made in Papua New Guinea between the Anglican Church of Papua New Guinea, the Roman Catholic Church and the Evangelical Lutheran Church in Papua New Guinea, and believes that they have offered a benchmark in ecumenical relations

(c) welcomes the recent covenant between the Church of the Province of Southern Africa (CPSA) and the Ethiopian Episcopal Church (EEC), and

   (i) awaits further developments in this relationship with interest
   (ii) encourages CPSA to continue to develop its links with EEC
   (iii) looks forward to the time when CPSA may be able to recommend that EEC become a church in communion with the wider Anglican Communion.

22. Multilateral Ecumenical Instruments

The Anglican Consultative Council:

(a) sends its greetings to the World Council of Churches, which will meet in plenary Assembly in February 2006 in Porto Alegre, Brazil, and its congratulations to its new General Secretary, Dr Samuel Kobia

(b) adopts the Message to the World Council of Churches drafted by IASCER, meeting in Jamaica in 2004, which stresses the priority of Faith and Order work in the ecumenical movement

(c) requests the World Council of Churches to find ways by which the Anglican Communion can enhance its participation as a Communion in the life of the World Council, and in which Anglicans can play a full part in its life and work

(d) affirms the work of the Global Christian Forum, and encourages all Provinces to support the programme being developed by it for mutual listening across the whole breadth of the Christian family.

23. The Inter-Anglican Standing Commission on Ecumenical Relations

The Anglican Consultative Council:

receives the Report of the Director of Ecumenical Affairs on the work of the Inter-Anglican Standing Commission on Ecumenical Relations (IASCER), adopts its resolutions as set out in Appendix Five (pages 27–41) of the Report, particularly the Guidelines on Ecumenical Participation in Ordinations, and commends these resolutions to the Provinces for study and reflection.

24. The Inter-Anglican Theological and Doctrinal Commission

The Anglican Consultative Council:

(a) receives the Report of the Director of Ecumenical Affairs and Theological Studies on the work of the Inter-Anglican Theological and Doctrinal Commission (IATDC), and thanks the Commission for its ongoing study of Communion

(b) encourages the Inter-Anglican Finance and Administration Committee to provide the resources to enable IATDC to meet again in 2006

(c) asks IATDC to integrate an evaluation of the Windsor Report 2004 into its continuing studies and work, and to complete its work in time to be able to report to the Lambeth Conference in 2008

(d) commends the fruitful interactive process adopted by IATDC to the Communion, and encourages full participation in its future work.

25. The Department of Ecumenical Affairs and Theological Studies

The Anglican Consultative Council:

(a) expresses its heartfelt thanks to those who have in past years dedicated themselves on its behalf in the area of Ecumenical Affairs, gratefully recalling the work of Bishop David Hamid, Bishop John Baycroft and Ms Frances Hillier

(b) offers its gratitude to Canon Gregory K Cameron, Director of Ecumenical Affairs since 2003, for his Report to the Council, and its good wishes for his ongoing work

(c) offers thanks and good wishes to Mrs Christine Codner and to the Revd Terrie Robinson for their continuing work in the Department.

26. Inter-Anglican Standing Commission on Mission and Evangelism

The Anglican Consultative Council:

(a) receives the report from the Inter-Anglican Standing Commission on Mission and Evangelism (IASCOME) entitled "Communion in Mission"

(b) expresses its appreciation to IASCOME and thanks its members for their work and dedication

(c) adopts as the mandate for the next IASCOME the text set out in their Report

(d) encourages IASCOME in its work over its next term.

27. The Covenant for Communion in Mission

The Anglican Consultative Council:

(a) commends the *Covenant for Communion in Mission* to the churches of the Anglican Communion for study and application as a vision for Anglican faithfulness to the mission of God

(b) forwards the *Covenant for Communion in Mission* to those bodies of the Anglican Communion tasked to consider an Anglican Covenant as commended by the Windsor Report and the Statement of the February 2005 Primates' Meeting

(c) requests the next Inter-Anglican Standing Commission on Mission and Evangelism to monitor responses to the *Covenant for Communion in Mission* and evaluate its effectiveness across the Communion.

28. Resolution on recommendations from IASCOME

The Anglican Consultative Council:

(a) receives the *Guidelines for Evangelism Co-ordinators* and recommends them to the Provinces for their use and guidance

(b) gives thanks for the Consultation of Provincial Co-ordinators of Mission and Evangelism held in Nairobi, Kenya, in 2002, and the Second Anglican Conference for Mission Organisations held in Larnaca, Cyprus, in 2003, and asks IASCOME to give consideration to holding further consultations of this kind in the future

(c) asks IASCOME to address the question of the colonial and post-colonial past and present of Anglican mission in its future work, and advise on how Anglicans may be helped to explore such issues in mission relationships

(d) receives the recommendations of IASCOME for a Mission Consultation for Network representatives, and asks the Standing Committee to explore how best to take forward this suggestion

(e) encourages IASCOME and TEAC to discern together ways in which their work may be integrated and mutually supported.

29. The Anglican Communion Observer at the UN

The Anglican Consultative Council:

(a) gratefully receives the Report of the Office of the Anglican Observer at the United Nations (ACC-UN)

(b) seeks the full implementation of the Millennium Development Goals (MDGs) within the Provinces of the Anglican Communion

(c) encourages the churches of the Anglican Communion to identify link provincial contacts for the ACC-UN office.

30. The Office of the UN Observer

The Anglican Consultative Council:

(a) expresses its gratitude to Archdeacon Taimalelagi Fagamalama Tuatagaloa-Matalavea for her dedicated service over the last four years as Anglican Observer at the United Nations and to the members of the Advisory Council for their invaluable work in support of the Office of the Anglican Observer at the United Nations

(b) asks the Secretary General and the Chairman of the ACC to explore whether the Office of the Anglican Observer at the UN can be continued, and in particular to consider the following matters:

  (i) the role of the Observer, the number of staff and the location of the Office

  (ii) an agreed job description for the appointment of the next Observer·

   (iii) clear lines of accountability and line management arrangements through the Secretary General of the Communion

   (iv) possible ecumenical cooperation

   (v) the role of the Advisory Council, and appointment by the Standing Committee of the Chairperson of that Council

   (vi) a working budget for the next five years, and

   (vii) contributions to that budget

(c) authorises an Appointment Committee consisting of representatives of the Archbishop of Canterbury, the Chair of the ACC, the Secretary General and a representative of the Advisory Council to select and appoint a new Observer for a term not to exceed five years, subject to the Standing Committee being satisfied on the matters set out in clause (b) above, and

(d) requests that budgetary provision for the Office should be continued on the basis of the recommendation of the Inter Anglican Finance and Administration Committee.

31. The 49th Session of the UN Commission on the Status of Women

The Anglican Consultative Council:

(a) receives and adopts the Report of the ACC Provincial Delegation to the 49th UN Commission on the Status of Women (UNCSW), and affirms the work of the International Anglican Women's Network (IAWN) in responding to the Beijing Platform for Action and the Millennium Developments Goals (MDG), thereby carrying forward the full flourishing of God's Creation

(b) acknowledges the MDG goal for equal representation of women in decision making at all levels, and so requests

   (i) the Standing Committee to identify ways in which this goal may appropriately be adapted for incorporation into the structures of the Instruments of Unity, and other bodies to which the Anglican Consultative Council nominates or appoints

   (ii) all member churches to work towards the realisation of this goal in their own structures of governance, and in other bodies to which they nominate or appoint

and to report on progress to ACC-14

(c) recommends that a study of the place and role of women in the structures of the Anglican Communion be undertaken by the Standing Committee in line with the objects of the ACC "to keep in review the needs that may arise for further study, and, where necessary, to promote inquiry and research"

(d) requests that each Province give consideration to the establishment of a women's desk for that Province

(e) thanks those Provinces which sent participants to the 49th Session of UNCSW, and encourages those who did not to review their decision in time for the 50th Session in 2006 in solidarity with all women of the Anglican Communion.

32. Anglican Communion Environmental Network

The Anglican Consultative Council notes the Statement to the Anglican Communion from the ACEN, and

(a) endorses its recommendation that all Anglicans be encouraged to:

   (i) recognise that global climatic change is real and that we are contributing to the despoiling of creation

   (ii) commend initiatives that address the moral transformation needed for environmentally sustainable economic practices such as the Contraction and Convergence process championed by the Archbishop of Canterbury

   (iii) understand that, for the sake of future generations and the good of God's creation, those of us in the rich nations need to be ready to make sacrifices in the level of comfort and luxury we have come to enjoy

   (iv) expect mission, vision and value statements to contain commitment to environmental responsibility at all levels of church activity

   (v) educate all church members about the Christian mandate to care for creation

   (vi) work on these issues ecumenically and with all faith communities and people of good will everywhere

   (vii) ensure that the voices of women, indigenous peoples and youth are heard

   (viii) press government, industry and civil society on the moral imperative of taking practical steps towards building sustainable communities.

(b) asks Provinces to take the following steps urgently:

   (i) include environmental education as an integral part of all theological training.

   (ii) take targeted and specific actions to assess and reduce our environmental footprint, particularly greenhouse gas emissions. Such actions could include energy and resource audits, land management, just trading and purchasing, socially and ethically responsible investment.

(iii) promote and commit ourselves to use renewable energy wherever possible.

(iv) revise our liturgies and our calendar and lectionaries in ways that more fully reflect the role and work of God as Creator.

(v) press for urgent initiation of discussions, which should include all nations, leading to a just and effective development beyond the Kyoto Protocol.

(vi) support the work of the World Council of Churches Climate Change Action Group.

(vii) bring before governments the imperative to use all means, including legislation and removal of subsidies, to reduce greenhouse gases.

33. International Anglican Family Network

The Anglican Consultative Council:

(a) receives the report of the International Anglican Family Network

(b) thanks the members of the Network for their ongoing contribution to the life of the Anglican Communion.

34. Anglican Indigenous Network

The Anglican Consultative Council

(a) gratefully receives the report of the Anglican Indigenous Network [AIN]

(b) notes the AIN resolutions for its own work, contained in the Report of the AIN Gathering at Pala in 2005

(c) requests the Provinces of the Communion to support those resolutions where appropriate.

35. The Network for Inter Faith Concerns

The Anglican Consultative Council:

(a) receives the report of the Network for Inter Faith Concerns

(b) commends its insights to the Provinces for reflection in the period leading up to the Lambeth Conference 2008

(c) asks the Standing Committee to give consideration to the NIFCON request for Commission status.

36. The Israeli Palestinian Conflict (APJN)

The Anglican Consultative Council:

(a) welcomes the September 22nd 2004 statement by the Anglican Peace and Justice Network on the Israeli/Palestinian Conflict

(b) commends the resolve of the Episcopal Church (USA) to take appropriate action where it finds that its corporate investments support the occupation of Palestinian lands or violence against innocent Israelis, and

    (i) commends such a process to other Provinces having such investments, to be considered in line with their adopted ethical investment strategies

    (ii) encourages investment strategies that support the infrastructure of a future Palestinian State

(c) requests the Office of the Anglican Observer to the United Nations, through or in association with the UN Working Committee on Peace in the Middle East, as well as through this Council, and as a priority of that Office, to support and advocate the implementation of UN Resolutions 242 and 338 directed towards peace, justice and co-existence in the Holy Land.

37. Refugee Situations in Africa (APJN)

The Anglican Consultative Council:

(a) supports initiatives aimed at ensuring that Burundian refugees returning from the Democratic Republic of the Congo, Tanzania and elsewhere, as well as displaced persons within Burundi, are assisted and cared for during their rehabilitation and integration by agencies of the United Nations, the European Union, the African Union and other appropriate governmental and non-governmental organisations

(b) supports the peacemaking process in Burundi, and assures the people of Burundi of our prayers during the period of their ongoing elections

(c) calls for the provision of necessary care from the international community to Congolese refugees gathered in Burundi and Rwanda border areas and other countries of Africa, and calls upon those involved in the conflict to end the killing of civilians.

38. Conflict Resolution (APJN)

The Anglican Consultative Council:

(a) encourages representatives of the Communion to effect pastoral visits to regions of conflict and instability, especially the African Great Lakes

Region, central Asian States and South Asia, Sri Lanka, West Africa, Sudan, the Korean Peninsula, and the Middle East in order to encourage the Churches in those regions to carry on with the mission of peacemaking and reconciliation, and providing care for persons displaced by conflict in those regions

(b) requests that the training of Church leaders in peace and justice and conflict transformation throughout the Communion be made a priority theological education project.

39. Theological Education (APJN)

The Anglican Consultative Council:

notes the recommendations of the Anglican Peace and Justice Network on Theological Education set out at paragraphs G, H, I, J and K of its 2004 report and refers them to the Theological Education for the Anglican Communion Network (TEAC) for consideration and appropriate action, taking gender into serious consideration.

40. Inter Faith Relations (APJN)

The Anglican Consultative Council:

notes the recommendations of the Anglican Peace and Justice Network on Interfaith Relations set out at paragraphs L, M, N, O, P and Q of its 2004 report and refers them to the Network for Interfaith Concerns for the Anglican Communion (NIFCON) for consideration and appropriate action.

41. The Environment (APJN)

The Anglican Consultative Council:

notes the recommendations of the Anglican Peace and Justice Network on the environment set out at paragraphs R, S and T of its 2004 report and refers them to the Anglican Communion Environmental Network for consideration and appropriate action.

42. International Anglican Women's Network

The Anglican Consultative Council:

(a) receives the Report of the International Anglican Women's Network

(b) affirms the developing work of the Network

(c) encourages each Primate to maintain regular communication with the woman or team appointed as a link with the region in which his Province is located.

43. International Anglican Youth Network

The Anglican Consultative Council:

(a) receives the Report of the International Anglican Youth Network, and thanks the Network for its ongoing work in support of the witness of young people across the Communion

(b) recommends that dioceses and Provinces review their provision for ministry amongst young people and ensure appropriate budgetary provision

(c) asks the Standing Committee in consultation with the Secretary General to consider ways of funding the work of the Network and providing part-time administrative assistance at the Anglican Communion Office.

44. The Province of the Anglican Church of the Congo

The Anglican Consultative Council:

(a) receives the report of the Province of the Anglican Church of the Congo

(b) recognises that the Province faces a grave social crisis which deserves the special attention of all Churches of the Communion, and especially the Networks of this Council

(c) encourages the Province to pursue its mission of evangelisation in Congo Brazzaville as a new step in the growth of Anglican faith in the francophone world.

45. The Extra-Provincial Diocese of Cuba

The Anglican Consultative Council:

(a) notes with pleasure the presence for the first time at a meeting of the Council of a member from the Extra-Provincial Diocese of Cuba

(b) resolves to assist that Diocese in its missionary work by making available to it resource materials on the history of Anglicanism, theological education and Anglican liturgy

(c) calls on all Provinces of the Communion to contribute, as their resources allow, to the development of Anglicanism in Cuba.

46. Corruption

The Anglican Consultative Council:

(a) notes with concern the fact that corruption in all its forms is still present in many governments, corporations and organisations

(b) commends those governments, corporations and organisations which have taken steps to tackle the issue of corruption

(c) supports the position that no person or organisation is above the law

(d) encourages all governments to fight corruption at all levels and to strive for good governance

(e) to that end calls on them to take appropriate measures including removing statutory immunities and other legal barriers which prevent those guilty of corruption from being called to account

(f) recognises with shame incidents of corrupt behaviour within the church, commits itself to the highest standards of integrity in church government and encourages Provinces of the Communion to identify and strive to eradicate corruption from church, state and society.

47. Drought in Africa

The Anglican Consultative Council:

(a) notes with concern the ongoing serious drought in Central and South Africa and the effect of this on populations of the region

(b) offers its prayers to the communities thus affected

(c) asks Provinces to consider ways in which aid and support can be offered.

48. Fair Trade

The Anglican Consultative Council:

(a) gratefully recognises the efforts so far made by developed countries, in particular the G8 states, to assist developing countries with their programmes aimed at providing better health and education, as well as clean water, to their populations

(b) believes however that developed countries can assist further in the realisation of these objectives by the establishment and promotion of fair terms of trade between developed and developing countries

(c) requests the Archbishop of Canterbury, in his capacity as President of the Council, to convey to the leaders of the G8 states prior to their meeting in July 2005, a reminder of their responsibility towards the eradication of poverty in the world and the promotion of fair terms of international trade.

49. Korea

The Anglican Consultative Council:

(a) expresses its profound concern about the deepening crisis in the Korean peninsula, consequent upon the announcements by the Democratic People's Republic of Korea [DPRK] that it is developing nuclear weapons and by the United States of America [USA] that it is contemplating the use of military force against the DPRK in order to prevent this

(b) believes that, for the sake of peace in North East Asia and the world, armed conflict in the Korean peninsula must be prevented, and to that end the DPRK and the USA should renounce the acquisition of nuclear weapons and the use of military force respectively, and endeavour to resolve the present crisis through dialogue and negotiation

(c) recognises that the origin of the present crisis threatening peace in the Korean peninsula and North East Asia lies in the division of the Korean peninsula into two states, and therefore supports and encourages the Anglican Church in Korea and other churches and organisations in Korea in their work for reunification of the two Koreas

(d) asks Anglican Church leaders in nations with influence on the North East Asia situation to consider visiting the DPRK and the Republic of Korea and contribute in whatever ways they can to the reunification of the two Koreas.

50. Protection of Children and Vulnerable Adults

The Anglican Consultative Council:

(a) takes to heart the admonition in Matthew 18.6 and the priority given in Jesus' ministry to children and to the vulnerable of society; and therefore

(b) commits itself to the highest standards of care for all young and vulnerable people, seeking to ensure their protection, safety and well-being, and requests similar pledges of commitment from all the Provinces and churches of the Communion

(c) notes the recommendation from the Anglican Church of Australia that ACC establish a Safe Ministry Task Force to promote the physical, emotional and spiritual welfare and safety of all people, especially children, young people and vulnerable adults, within the member churches of the Anglican Communion, and

(d) refers the recommendation and proposed action plan to the Standing Committee for evaluation and recommendations on the further action that may be taken by this Council and the Provinces of the Communion.

(Matthew 18.6 reads: Whoever causes the downfall of one of these little ones who believe in me, it would be better for him if a heavy millstone were hung around his neck and he were drowned in the depths of the sea!)

51. Zimbabwe

The Anglican Consultative Council acknowledges the social and historical imbalances that the people of Zimbabwe have experienced in the tenure of their land, their implications for the current crisis and the need for them to be addressed. However, the Council:

(a) notes with profound sorrow and concern, and condemns, the recent political developments in Zimbabwe where hundreds of thousands of persons have had their homes destroyed and have become displaced persons within their own country, and where:

   (i) after up to two years of drought many families are dependent on relief but food distribution is often refused to those who do not support the political party in power

   (ii) those suffering from HIV/AIDS and orphans do not receive appropriate help from the government

   (iii) there are serious restrictions on democracy

   (iv) there is little freedom of speech or tolerance, and human rights are denied

   (v) politicians and uniformed forces act as if they are above the law

   (vi) people are arrested, imprisoned without fair trial, and tortured.

(b) asks the government of Zimbabwe to reverse its policies of destruction and begin to engage in development that eradicates poverty

(c) calls upon the leadership of the African Union to persuade the government of Zimbabwe to consider the humanitarian aspects of the situation in that country, and to act to remedy the suffering of the people of Zimbabwe

(d) supports the Church of England in its approaches to the government of the United Kingdom to reconsider its policy of repatriation of refugees to Zimbabwe

(e) welcomes the proposed pastoral visit of church leaders from South Africa to Zimbabwe to take place in the near future

(f) assures the Christian churches and the people of Zimbabwe of its prayers in this time of national disaster.

52. The Compass Rose Society

The Anglican Consultative Council:

(a) gratefully acknowledges the excellent fundraising and mission support work of the Compass Rose Society

(b) thanks the Society for its generous financial support of the Council

(c) assures the Society of its prayers in its continued work.

53. Regional Episcopal Meetings

The Anglican Consultative Council:

(a) applauds the initiative taken in 2004 by the Africa Anglican Bishop's Conference to hold a conference of African bishops in Nigeria in order to discuss problems faced by the African dioceses and to find local solutions thereto

(b) recommends this initiative to other regions.

54. Prayers and Greetings

This Anglican Consultative Council sends its greetings and assurances of prayer to:

The Bishop of Rome, His Holiness Pope Benedict XVI, with prayers for his apostolic, evangelical and ecumenical ministry among Christians everywhere, and with thanks for the greetings from Cardinal Walter Kasper, President of the Pontifical Council for Promoting Christian Unity, delivered on his behalf by the Revd Don Bolen.

The Ecumenical Patriarch, His All Holiness Bartholomew I, with prayers for the apostolic See of Constantinople New Rome, and with thanks for the long-standing fraternal relationships between the Orthodox Churches and the Churches of the Anglican Communion and the presence of His Grace Bishop Kallistos of Diokleia, who delivered the greetings of the Ecumenical Patriarchate.

The General Secretary of the Lutheran World Federation, the Revd Dr Ishmael Noko, and with thanks for the greetings delivered on his behalf by the Rt Revd Walter Jagucki.

The Most Revd Joris Vercammen, Archbishop of Utrecht, and the Most Revd Dr Philipose Mar Chrysosstom for ensuring the presence of representatives from Churches in Communion—The Revd Wietse Van der Velde and the Rt Revd Dr Euyakim Mar Coorilos, who delivered greetings on their behalf.

Dr Samuel Kobia, General Secretary of the World Council of Churches, with thanks for the representation from Ms Teny Simonian from the WCC Office of Church and Ecumenical Relations.

The Revd Esme Beswick President of Churches Together in England, and the Revd Mark Fisher; The Revd William R. Morrey, President of the Conference of the Methodist Church of Britain; The Revd Dr Paul Fiddes, Principal, Regent's Park College in the University of Oxford, and representative of the Baptist World Alliance.

55. Resolution of Thanks

The Anglican Consultative Council thanks God for the ministry of so many whose dedication and service have enabled the Council to do the work of the Church:

For our President the Most Revd and Rt Hon Dr Rowan Williams, Archbishop of Canterbury; for His Grace's confident proclamation of the Word; his love, vision and scholarship, and we express our heartfelt gratitude for his stimulating reflections upon the Acts of the Apostles at our daily Bible Studies.

For Mrs Jane Williams' presence among us in Nottingham and the Archbishop's involvement in the daily life of the Council which constantly inspires the Communion which looks forward to his continued spiritual support and example.

For the invaluable presence of members of the Primates' Standing Committee: the Most Revd Peter Kwong, the Most Revd Bernard Malango, the Most Revd Barry Morgan, the Most Revd Orlando Santos de Oliveira and the Most Revd James Terom.

For our Chair, the Rt Revd John Paterson, Bishop of Auckland, who also chairs the Inter-Anglican Finance and Administration Committee; for his irenic and encouraging guidance of our debates; for his vigilant and proficient stewardship of the successful refurbishment of St Andrews House, the headquarters of the Anglican Communion Office.

For our Vice-Chair Professor George Koshy whose enthusiastic commitment to the work of the Council has helped shape our deliberations.

For the Design Group led by Professor George Koshy, assisted by the Rt Revd John Paterson, the Rt Revd James Tengatenga, the Rt Revd Robert Thompson and Ms Fung-Yi Wong, who enabled us diligently to discharge our responsibility to the Communion in addressing the agenda before us.

For the Standing Committee, the Most Revd Peter Akinola, Mrs Jolly Bambirukamu, the Rt Revd Riah Abu El-Assal, the Very Revd John Moses, the Rt Revd James Tengatenga, the Rt Revd Robert Thompson and Ms Fung-Yi Wong.

For the Inter-Anglican Finance and Administration Committee, formerly chaired by the Most Revd Robin Eames and presently chaired by the Rt Revd John Paterson, assisted by the Most Revd Peter Kwong the Most Revd Peter Akinola, the Most Revd Clive Handford, Canon Elizabeth Paver, the Revd Bob Sessum and Ms Fung-Yi Wong for their conscientiousness and insights on financial matters.

For the Nomination Committee led by the Rt Revd James Tengatenga, assisted by the Very Revd John Moses and Ms Candice Payne who helped us discern our future leaders.

For the Resolutions Committee led by Mr Bernard Georges, assisted by Mrs Philippa Amable, the Very Revd Michael Burrows, Dr Tony Fitchett, the Rt Revd David Vunagi and Ms Fung-Yi Wong who helped us express our minds and priorities clearly, and for the staff support offered through the Revd Canon Gregory Cameron.

For the Bible Studies group leaders: the Rt Revd Mauricio de Andrade, the Rt Revd Riah Abu El-Assal, the Ven Kay Goldsworthy, the Very Revd Dr David Chidiebele Okeke, Mr Humphrey Peters, Miss Sylvia Scarf, the Rt Revd James Tengatenga, Miss Kate Turner, and Mr Luis Roberto Vallee.

For the dedication and service of those members for whom ACC-13 is their last meeting.

The Anglican Communion Office

For the Secretary General, the Revd Canon Kenneth Kearon who, at his first Meeting of the Council, has led a dedicated and professional team of colleagues from the Anglican Communion Office with outstanding leadership and diplomacy.

For the Director of Ecumenical Affairs and Deputy Secretary General, the Revd Canon Gregory K Cameron, for assisting the ACC with the work of the Council and leading us through its ecumenical and doctrinal agenda, with astonishing grasp of detail.

For the Communications team led by Canon Jim Rosenthal with assistance from Mr Rob Bergner, and from the Church of England, Gavin Drake, Steve Jenkins and David Johnson, together with Rachel Farmer from the Diocese of Southwell, and the international team of Alex Allotey, Joe Mdhela, Lynn Ross, and the Revd Alistair Macdonald Radcliffe.

For the United Nations Observer for the Anglican Communion, Archdeacon Taimalelagi Fagamalama Tuatagaloa-Matalavavea, and her presentation of our mission and opportunities for service at this international organisation.

For the Executive Assistant to the Secretary General, Mrs Deirdre Martin, and for Marjorie Murphy, Director of Mission and Evangelism, who not only supported the presentation of the work of IASCOME, but also undertook the management of the Meeting of the Council.

For Mr Andrew Franklin, Director of Finance and Administration, and the team who attended Nottingham from the Anglican Communion Office, Ms Lynne Butt, Mrs Christine Codner, Mrs Gill Harris-Hogarth, Mr Ian Harvey, and the Revd Dorothy Penniecooke.

For Mrs Clare Amos, the Revd Eric Beresford, Mrs Susanne Mitchell, Ms Sue Parks, and Dr Sally Thompson, who assist the Networks and meetings of the Communion.

For the other staff at the Anglican Communion Office, and their support: for Mr Michael Ade, Ms Maggie Anderson, Mrs Clara Giraldo, Ms Ann Quirke and the Revd Terrie Robinson.

For the Legal Adviser, the Revd Canon John Rees, for his counsel and assistance on legal and constitutional matters.

For the Archbishop of Canterbury's staff: Mr Chris Smith, Chief of Staff, the Revd John Corrie, the Revd Jonathan Jennings, Miss Fiona Millican, the Revd Andrew Norman, the Revd David Peck, and Mrs Sarah Walker.

For Our Guest Speakers and Presenters

The Rt Hon Hilary Benn MP, the Revd Joel Edwards, the Rt Revd Malcolm McMahon, the Rt Revd Sebastian Bakare, the Rt Revd Michael Jackson, the Rt Revd Michael Nazir-Ali, and the Rt Revd Tom Wright, Mr William Anderson, Dr Albert Gooch, the Revd Alice Medcof, the Revd Canon Robert Paterson, Dr Bill Sachs, and Dr Jennie Te Paa.

For Our Hosts

Bishop George Cassidy and the Diocese of Southwell, the Lord Mayor and Council of the City of Nottingham; for their warm hospitality and the reception at the Council House on Sunday 26th June 2005.

For the Volunteers and Local Organising Committee, splendidly organised by the Revd Canon Andrew Deuchar; for Wendy Pearce and all the office Staff, the Revd Helen Walker, Dr Esther Eliot, the Revd Alison Maddocks and all the volunteers, and for Carol and all the Brownies of the 1st Wollaton St Leonard Brownies for the wonderful banner of welcome that greeted us when we arrived at Newark Hall.

For the Worship team, the Revd Ian Tarrant, Mr Adam Pullen, Mr Peter Price, the musicians, and all those others involved with the services here on the campus and at St Mary's, St Peters and the Minster.

For Mr Peter Siepmann and other volunteers who assisted with the technical and administrative support.

For the Organisers of the Local Visits to Capital One, The Malt Cross project, Emmanuel Church of England Secondary School, Thorney Abbey Farm, and Mansfield Woodhouse on Thursday and for the Dean and Chapter of Southwell Minster for their hospitality in the evening.

For the local Parishes who so warmly welcomed us on Sunday 26th June: The Revd Chris Moody at the World Mission Day, Diocese of Leicester; the Revd David Bignell and Holy Rood, Edwalton; the Ven Ian Russsell, and the Southern Cluster of the Southwell Deanery; the Revd Graham Burton and Hyson Green Ecumenical Group; the Revd Philip Thomas and St Mark's Woodthorpe; the Revd George Butler and St Mark's Mansfield; the Revd Graham Pigott and St Paul's Wilford Hill; the Revd Tony Cardwell and St Mary's Eastwood; the Revd Canon Janet Henderson and St Patrick's Nuthall; the Revd Simon Cansdale and St Giles' West Bridgeford; the Revd Glynis Hetherington and St Mary's East Leake; the Revd Jerry Lepine and St Leonards Wollaton; the Revd Michael Knight and St Mary's Chesterfield; the Revd Canon Robert Parsons and St Peter's Belper; the Revd John Fisher and St Helen's Burton Joyce; the Revd Philip Nott and St Martha's Broxtowe.

For the interpreters: Ben Andréo, Katie Attwood, Karine Orbaum, Carissa Richards and Judy Rous.

For the staff of Nottingham University and all who assisted in the Chapel, plenary hall, dining room, the Bible study foyer, the corridors, and shepherding us to the correct venues, the amenities and facilities rooms.

Archbishop of Canterbury's Daily Bible Studies

Daily Bible Study

Monday 20 June 2005

In these reflections on the Acts of the Apostles, what I would like us to focus upon is the picture given in the Acts of the Apostles of the Church as the community that makes Christ visible. The Church is the community that makes Christ visible. And in the readings that we share morning by morning, we will be looking at different dimensions of that process in which Christ becomes visible. Because it has rightly been said that the Book the Acts of the Apostles might more accurately be called the Acts of the Holy Spirit. We begin with the gift of the Holy Spirit, or rather we begin with the Disciples waiting for the Spirit to gift them, and then in this memorable second chapter, the Spirit comes in power and splendour, and the Church's reality unfolds and the fact of Christ's work becomes manifest. 'Acts of the Holy Spirit'—because as St Paul tells us more than once, it is the Holy Spirit that makes us call Jesus Lord and God the Father. And when the Church learns to call God Father with all its heart and conviction, the Church shows who and what Jesus is. In this second chapter of Acts, the great explosion happens and the Disciples spill out into the street looking drunk (a problem which has not all that often afflicted the Church since—the confusion between the joy and exuberance of the Spirit and a bad Saturday night in Nottingham!). But there it is—an explosion of joy and exuberance so dramatic that it can't be ignored. And Peter stands up and tells us (because <u>we</u> are part of the audience immediately told this) what is going on. And the first thing—the central thing—he says is, 'This is God fulfilling his promise'. Look carefully through Chapter 2 and see how many times that idea recurs. God has promised and now God honours his promise. God has promised that the Spirit will be poured out and visions of joy will be given to sustain people through the last days of their terrible trials. God's Holy Spirit is to be given. Here is the mystery. And the Spirit is given somehow through a human being, through one who was a descendant of King David. In the life and death of that human being the Holy Spirit is set free on them, and God's promise can be fulfilled. So within the great promise of the outpouring of the Holy Spirit is this other promise, and Peter quotes the Psalms: David foresees ones of his descendants being given an eternal throne. The kingship of the Son of David becomes the means by which the Holy Spirit is poured out. The Son of David is lifted to God's right hand and the Father gives him authority to pour out the Spirit.

So the first thing we hear in this chapter is that God is a God who keeps his promises, a faithful God, a God so determined to pour out his Spirit upon all flesh. That he does this even at the unimaginable cost involved in the Cross of Jesus. I think it helps us sometimes to see the Cross of Jesus within that wider context. Not just the Cross where our sin is cancelled— our guilt taken away—but also the Cross as part of that longer story which is God's giving of the Holy Spirit. The Cross itself as opening the way for the Spirit to be given, which of course you find not only here but so frequently in St John's Gospel. In Chapter 7 St John says the Spirit is not yet given because Jesus has not yet been glorified. Jesus' Glorification is the Cross, and that is the moment when the Spirit is released. And one particular dimension of this that is worth reflecting on a bit further is: if this is how God is and how God has acted what do we need to do? Peter says 'Each one of you must turn away from your sins and be baptised in the name of Jesus Christ so that your sins will be forgiven and you will receive God's gift of the Holy Spirit.' Here again is a moment when St Luke in the Acts comes very close to St John. The gift of forgiveness and the gift of the Holy Spirit belong together. And why is this? Think what forgiveness is about, or rather what sin is about. If there's no forgiveness we are trapped. Trapped in a pattern of repetition. We go round and round and round the same territory. We can't forgive and we can't let ourselves be forgiven. Nothing new breaks in. And due to our own failure and our own guilt towards God, we think: no act of mine can lift me up. All my acts and all my hopes are infected by the same selfishness, the same rebellion. What can I do? I don't feel forgiven and I don't feel I'm free to forgive. What happens is simply that I'm trapped. Nothing new can break in. And we know in our own lives as individuals, and in our life as communities what it is to be trapped: a situation where there is no forgiveness and all anyone can do is repeat the pattern. A lack of forgiveness is being stuck in a place where there is no movement forward. And that of course is a very familiar part of our human experience. We come to what seems to be a dead end. We don't know how to change ourselves, to change our relations with others, or with God.

And when forgiveness comes what happens is newness. Not just a signature at the bottom of a piece of paper from God saying, I've written this off, but much more than that. It is the introduction into our situation of something new, something unexpected. Why? Because the Holy Spirit is the creative Spirit. In the first chapter of the Bible the Holy Spirit breathes over the waters and life comes to birth. Ages later, at the pivot on which the whole history of the universe turns—the incarnation—the Holy Spirit overshadows the Virgin Mary so that Christ, who makes all things new, can be born from her. Through the spirit of newness the world that is stale and tired and dying and starved is refreshed. When we ask for the forgiveness of sins, and when we declare our faith in the Creed in the forgiveness of sins we are asking for the gift of the Spirit; we are proclaiming our belief in the promise of the Spirit. And when we find ourselves stuck, paralysed, unable to change, it is the Spirit that makes the difference.

But the Spirit makes a particular <u>kind</u> of difference. It is tempting sometimes to think that the Spirit equals renewal, renewal equals change, and change equals anything that's different from yesterday. And as we're all aware, it's not quite as simple as that, because the change that the Holy Spirit brings is a Christ-shaped change. Because what the Spirit does in order to break through our paralysis, our stuckness, is to bring Christ into us, into our lives, so that we can create change in a Christ-like way. We begin to learn the words that Jesus himself speaks to God so that we can pray Abba, Father—the first, greatest gift of the Spirit. And we begin to change in our understanding of one another—our fear and resentment of each other falls away as we stand before God. We sense in ourselves as a community of believers the freedom and the power for healing and proclamation, for bringing change to others, bringing Christ-shaped change to others. The fulfilment of God's promise in this chapter is that we should be forgiven so that we may move in Christ's steps, in Christ's rhythm you might say. That is what the Spirit is. When we are forgiven, when the trap is broken, when, as the Psalm says, the snare is broken and we are set free, Christ becomes visible. If our lives can conform to Christ's, if we can pray in a Christ-like way, relating to each other in a Christ-like way, the world sees that we mean what we say when we talk about Jesus Christ.

We are an 'apostolic' Church, we hope and trust, wondering what God will do with us, what the Acts of <u>these</u> Apostles will be, the Acts of Anglican Apostles; or perhaps we should say (back to the beginning) the Acts of the Holy Spirit among Anglican Apostles. That is no distinctive, no different task from that which belongs to any of us. It is the task which, once again, the second Chapter of Acts, spells out of witnessing that God has raised Jesus from death, and we are all witnesses to this fact. At the very beginning of our time together, let us simply think about what it is for us to be witnesses of <u>this</u> fact—the fact that God has kept his promise, the fact that God has dealt with our sins, that Christ-shaped renewal and change is real. When Christians gather together whether for worship or for reflection, they are, whether they like it or not, a Church—that is to say an assembly convened by God in the power of the Spirit; so that even when we are voting on procedural resolutions, we are an assembly convened by God here, and that means we expect the Holy Spirit to be around—even in what feel like the most boring moments of this meeting (and I daresay there will be one or two!) We remember quite simply that we are as a community called together in Christ here to make Jesus visible. And we remember, each of us in our hearts where and how <u>we</u> have found the renewing strength of the Holy Spirit; where in our situations as individuals, as nations, as communities or as local churches, something has broken in that we could not have expected, getting us out of the trap of unforgiveness.

Being faced with so many and so great problems, we are aware of the divisions between us, and the bitterness and the fear that that can bring us, let us spend a moment thinking about the Holy Spirit as the one who brings Christ into the situation to make a Christ-like difference. We don't know what that will be; but we pray for it very earnestly and we trust the God who keeps his promises. In the Bible Study groups this morning, I will leave you simply with one question to reflect on, and that is the question I have just put to each of us. Where have I found that in-breaking, renewing work of the Spirit most present and most evident? Perhaps we can share with one another just a little of what we have found of renewal in the Holy Spirit.

To conclude: we go back to our reading this morning, 'God's promise was made to you and your children and to all who are far away, all whom the Lord God calls to himself. It's a fascinating way for St Peter to speak. He has been talking about the promise made in prophesies, a promise found in Joel, a promise that the Psalms mention. And then he says that this is a promise for <u>you</u>, a promise for the future, for you and your children. God's promise doesn't change; it's made equally unchanging in every generation, so that whenever anyone reads these words—the second chapter of Acts—'God's promise was made to you and your children'—it is contemporary. We don't say, oh God's promised something to Joel and David and it's been fulfilled in the second Chapter of Acts and it's all over. The process continues, and we still need to hear the promise of God, the will of God to pour out his Spirit so that we relate to him in freedom and joy. God keeps his promises.

Let us pray. Faithful God, you are faithful to your word in every age, faithful to your cross, committed to your eternal promise, your purpose from all eternity to bring us in Christ to call you Father and so be reconciled to you and one another. When our trust is weak when our vision is unclear, when our strength fails, when our hope falters, grant us by your Holy Spirit to have a right judgement in all things, and as you grant forgiveness, pour out the Holy Spirit for our renewal. We gather this week in debate and discussion, airing our deep and painful concerns for the Church into which Jesus has called us. Keep before our eyes day after day the hope to which you have called us, so that our whole life as Church and Communion throughout the world may reveal the love and the gift of the one in whose precious name we make our prayer, Jesus Christ our Lord. Amen.

Daily Bible Study

Tuesday 21 June 2005

Yesterday we reflected on the Church as a place where Christ becomes visible; and in today's reading from Acts we see that theme of visibility coming through very strongly. The leaders of the council see Peter and John's boldness, and they see they've been with Jesus; and they can't deny what's claimed because there is the man who was healed, and Peter and John say, 'We cannot stop speaking of what we ourselves have seen and heard.' So this reading is a very powerful affirmation of the <u>visibility</u> of Jesus Christ in his Church. And working through this passage is another rather subtler, but very profound theme. Listen to the words at the very beginning of this morning's reading—the first part of chapter 4:

> 'The next day the Jewish leaders, the elders, and the teachers of the Law gathered in Jerusalem.'

Why on earth does St Luke mention Jerusalem at this point? Of course it's Jerusalem; Everything that's happened so far has been in Jerusalem. That's where Annas and Caiiaphas and the others live. So is this just a casual remark? I think not, for two reasons. One is the clue that's given in the Gospel reading we heard this morning. The whole of Luke's Gospel focuses very strongly on the journey to Jerusalem—the great city Luke's Jesus sets his face to is Jerusalem. Jerusalem is where it's all going to happen, and we are reminded this is the very place where the whole story of Jesus' work is coming to its climax. But behind that again is a still deeper resonance in the Bible. In the Old Testament God tells his people repeatedly that he will find a place where he will 'set his name'. Jerusalem is the place where God becomes <u>identifiable</u>, so that the God of Hebrew Scripture chooses to identify himself as the God of <u>this</u> place and <u>these</u> people. Now as we move into the New Covenant, God identifies himself as the God of Jesus—the God of the Jesus who was crucified and raised from death in Jerusalem, because this is the place where God makes his name dwell. Here in Jerusalem is the place where God becomes recognisable, where God says, '<u>This</u> is who I am', and so behind this passage lies the extraordinary affirmation God makes, displaying to us Jesus crucified and arisen and saying, 'This is who I am. I am eternally the God of Jesus.' All that's bound up in the Old Covenant, with God saying, 'I am the God of this shrine, this temple, this people, this place,' all of that now explodes into the new recognition of God saying, 'I am the God of Jesus crucified, and I will be recognised because of the resurrection of Jesus.'

So you can see why the theme of the <u>name</u> appears so often in this passage. The leaders of the council ask rather nervously, 'How did you do this? What power have you got, or what name did you use?' The leaders of the council are probing to see if the apostles are magicians of some kind. Have they got hold of some very powerful angelic spell? It's very much the world of Judaism at the time of Jesus, where the powers of angelic names were of great influence in performing mighty works. The apostles reply, 'Yes, we have power, and we have a name; it's the name of Jesus the anointed from Nazareth; and that is not the name of any angelic power or any magic force. It is the name given by God for salvation, and there is no other.' In other words, this name is God's name; God is Jesus crucified and risen in Jerusalem. God has said once and for all, this is who I am, this is where I am to be found, this is my name. So if you think of what it is for the Church to make Jesus visible, we have to ponder on what this chapter is telling us about how God has told us who he is. How can we make God recognisable as we show that God has identified himself in the Cross and the Resurrection? And we say, with Peter and John, that belonging with the God of the Cross and Resurrection is something so complete, so universal, that no human society, no human opinion, no human traits are more important. And when the council invite Peter and John to stop making a nuisance of themselves, they say, 'We can't. It's not who we are. We are bound to the God who has said 'Here I am in Jesus of Nazareth'.' And that is not just a matter of obedience to a great teacher; it's not just a matter of faithfulness to a group committed to the memory of Jesus; it is being taken into the life of Jesus, the <u>new world</u> we were thinking about yesterday.

Now that gives us a little bit of perspective, perhaps, on those sometimes quite difficult words, 'There is no other name under heaven.' What terrible arrogance, people will say to us in our world; what shocking Christian exclusiveness this is, 'no other name'. There are lots of names of God in the world. Why should we claim to have a bigger and better? But we can perhaps hear Peter and John saying in reply: 'We're not talking about a human system or human allegiances; we're not talking about the memory and example and teaching of a famous dead man. We're talking about the world we have come to live in. And we simply know that that world is a world held in the hands of the God of Jesus, and no one else.' So far from being exclusive, this is the most <u>inclusive</u> thing that Peter and John or anyone else can say. In the hands of Jesus the world belongs to God. How God works that out, you might say, is God's plan. But we know where we stand and what we have been given. We know that the new world comes into existence and holds together in the crucified and risen One, nowhere else. And the heart, the sense, the logic of all this is that we cannot stop speaking of what we ourselves have seen and heard. Difficult isn't it, in a world that loves pluralism and variety, and is very cautious about 'absolute truth'. And yet, what we have to bear in mind is that this is not a matter of claiming, 'We've got the system; we've got the answer.' It's more like saying, 'The answer has got us; the truth has taken hold of us; the world is different.' And Jesus is not a teacher, an example, a leader; Jesus is the new world, the name of God transforming all reality.

This is an exciting chapter of Acts. It's one of the first great moments of collision between Peter and John, and those who are powerful and secure in their belief. And here they are, these ordinary men of no education, as Luke says of them (I sometimes wonder if Peter would have been a little indignant if he'd ever read this chapter!), confronting the most influential and the most unscrupulous masters of their world, and saying, 'Sorry, our world is different. You run this world, and you can do what you like with us; you can threaten us as much as you like. Fine. That's your privilege, that's your freedom. It's just that we happen to live somewhere else. We live in the world that is held by and in Jesus of Nazareth.' And the members of the council realise then that they have been companions of Jesus. We see the solemn headdresses moving together, the beards being stroked, as the elders of the council whisper to one another, 'Jesus of Nazareth.' And for us? Do the mighty of the world look at us and realise we have been with Jesus of Nazareth? Do they look at us and think we belong in a bigger world? Well, all great Christian martyrs, all great Christian witnesses have in one way or another said exactly that. They've said to their persecutors, to their enemies, 'Your world is too small. Do what you like with me, but my world is greater.' And that is why the martyrs go to their deaths praising God, forgiving their enemies, showing their world is bigger. They don't accept the terms of the argument. They blithely ignore what can be done to them as they step among the dangers of the world. And they do it in so many different ways. They do it like Thomas More, whose commemoration comes up quite soon in our Church, going to the scaffold to have his head cut off with a joke, telling the executioner, 'Help me up the steps, I'll be all right coming down,' and saying, as he prepares for death 'Of course I am the King's good servant—but God's first.' A very simple affirmation that the world of the King, like the world of the council and the high priests here, is too small, for God will show his name in Jesus and make his name dwell in the city of Jesus' Cross and Resurrection. That's the God in whom we breathe the full and free air of the real universe.

So, as we think about this in our groups this morning, and in the days ahead, let's hold a couple of themes in our minds for our reflection. Maybe a question we might like to consider in the groups this morning will be this: what are the stories that we tell in our own setting about those who have shown the light of Jesus—who have shown they've been with Jesus? They may be stories of martyrdom, literal martyrdom; they may be stories of resistance and struggle; they may be very simple stories about ordinary people choosing Jesus against all the other things that pressed upon them. But, more widely during this week, let us remember the contrast here between the two worlds—the world of the council, the world of the professionals, the people who run things, the people who make decisions, those people with their flowing beards and their enormous headdresses and their fringed robes, or in these days, their smart suits and their electronic communications—and the world of the ordinary, uneducated people of faith who face them and say, 'Your world is too small.'

Let us pray. Father, we thank you because you have planted your holy name within our hearts. You have given us knowledge and truth and life immortal. We thank you that the world is in the hands of your Son, crucified and raised from the dead, so that all people, all things, all worlds may find life in Him. Father, keep us alive in this great, expansive world, which is the world Christ has created anew. Keep our eyes and ears open to all those things in us and in the world around which strives to keep us captive in a world of power and control, of wealth and violence. Help us day by day to open doors out of that world into the glorious truth of yourself. And above all, Father, let it be known that we have been companions of Jesus. Amen.

Daily Bible Study

Wednesday 22 June 2005

To be a place where Christ is visible. To be a place where the Holy Spirit is active. These, we have seen, are the characteristics of the Church at its beginnings as the Acts of the Apostles disclose it. And yesterday our attention was turned towards that deeply rooted biblical idea that God chooses to put his name on the earth and make a place where he can be recognised. His name is spoken, his reality is present. We have seen that in the Old Testament where the shrine of Jerusalem is that place where his name is set; and in the New Testament his name is fixed in Jesus Christ. From now on the God of Israel is the God of Jesus Christ. He is recognised in that relation to Jesus.

I suggested yesterday that, when we read those words about there being 'no other name under heaven by which human beings may be healed and saved', this should not be read simply as claiming that Christianity is another but better philosophy excluding everything else, but quite simply that our relation with Jesus is not a relation with a great teacher, a great example. It is like our relation to the air that we breathe. And, if it is like our relation to the air we breathe, we can't just say, 'well of course, there are alternatives'. This is our world, this is the truth we know.

But we turn now to a story which shows once again the conflict that can arise between the new world and the old, a degree of conflict still worse than that we were thinking about yesterday—Stephen's great speech to the council. And in this speech, Stephen returns more than once to the theme of where God is to be found. At the beginning of Israel's history, God was to be found in the tent, dismantled and rebuilt as the people wondered through the wilderness. Later on, the Ark of the Covenant, the sign of God's presence, was in one place. Later on again, Solomon built a house for God. But where is God truly to be found? Stephen, confronting the leaders of his people in the very heart of the holy place, the holy city, says, "The most high God does not live in houses built by human hands. As the prophet says, 'heaven is my throne, says the Lord, and the earth is my footstool. What kind of house would you build for me?'" Naturally, we again and again build houses where we hope to meet God; and again and again we have to resist the temptation to imagine that when we have closed the doors of those houses, we have God shut in with us. As St Paul will say later in the Acts, it is not so much that God dwells in what we make, but that we dwell in Him.

So where is God to be found, where will God live? Stephen's answer is that God lives in Jesus. He is the holy place, where he is is the sanctuary of God. So "The members of the council listened and became furious, and ground their teeth at him in anger, but Stephen, full of the Holy Spirit, looked up to heaven and saw God's glory and Jesus standing at the right hand side of God. 'Look,' he said, 'I see heaven opened and the Son of Man at the right-hand side of God.'"

There, in the middle of everything, is heaven laid open, the sanctuary of God. There is the throne of God, and there, next to the throne, like the high priest in the temple, stands Jesus, offering the world and its needs to God's throne. As Stephen speaks, heaven—the sanctuary—is there in the midst, no longer a 'house made with hands' but the dynamic, living reality of Jesus, gathering together our prayers and our needs, offering them to the throne of God the Father. So the answer to the question of where God can live is that God lives in Jesus. Where the prayer and the work of Jesus is alive <u>now</u>, there God lives.

Stephen is taken out and killed. And "as he died, he said, 'Lord Jesus, receive my spirit'. Then he knelt down and cried in a loud voice, 'Lord, do not remember this sin against them.'" He gives his spirit into the hands of the high priest who stands in God's sanctuary—to Jesus who stands at God's right hand in heaven, who takes Stephen and makes Stephen a gift to God the Father. And at the same moment Stephen repeats the words of Jesus, 'Lord, do not remember this sin against them'—'Father, forgive them, they do not know what they do.' In the moment when Stephen dies, Jesus lives in Stephen, because in Stephen that great act of forgiveness which happens on the cross happens in Stephen. The words Jesus says as he is crucified—'forgive them'—are said <u>in</u> Stephen. Stephen grows up into Jesus, and so it's Stephen who is now part of the holy place, the sanctuary; it is the dying, forgiving Stephen, where God is seen.

Which helps to explain why, from the beginning of the Church, the martyrs were so important. They were not just examples of heroic suffering. The martyr was a place where God's power was at work. When the martyr had completed his or her suffering and forgiveness, there was Jesus in the midst. St Ignatius of Antioch, at the very beginning of the 2nd Christian Century, facing his execution, says 'When I have come to my martyrdom, then I shall have become human; then I shall grow up—grow up into Jesus.' And so, through the centuries, the places where martyrs died and the relics of martyrs became places of power for Christians, places where Jesus had been seen. For so many of us here, the memories of martyrdom are part of the sense of where the power of the Church comes from. When, three years ago I visited Uganda, I remember visiting the two great shrines of the Ugandan Martyrs—the Roman Catholic and the Anglican shrines—and in the

Roman Catholic church the altar is on the very spot where Charles, the first of the Roman Catholic martyrs, was killed; and I thought that this is exactly what martyrdom is about. Here is the place where Jesus sees his people. Here is the place where the martyr dies in peace and forgiveness. And to see the table of the Lord there on the site of a terrible death—there you see somehow how heaven and earth come together in the discipleship of the martyr, growing up into Jesus like Stephen. Places like those two shrines in Uganda, places like Namogongo, other places that all of us know locally in our churches, places where Jesus has been seen in suffering and forgiveness, those are the places where it seems the veil is taken away and we see what the Church truly is—a place of the cross and a place of mercy; a place where Jesus is visible.

Now by God's grace, not many of us are called to that kind of public witness in suffering; and if you are at all like me, when you read these stories, you think, 'these cannot have been men and women like myself'. And yet of course, the frightening truth is that they were; and, thank God, we none of us know what we are capable of or not capable of before the moment of trial comes. Yet it's good for us to tell these stories over again, to tell ourselves, the way for a Christian to die is with words of mercy and words of reconciliation on their lips. Because the Christian work of risk and suffering for the sake of faith is the work of growing up into Jesus.

So perhaps it matters less to ask ourselves, 'How would I cope if I faced martyrdom?'—because that's a frightening question and most of us would shrink away from it—than to ask, 'Can I make mercy and reconciliation so much part of my natural response day by day that if it ever came to trial and test, my instinctive response would be Christ-like, would be mercy and reconciliation?'

Like many of you I have children who learn musical instruments, and many of you will know the real stress and terror of practicing a musical instrument, and the great revolts and anger, misery and fears that happen when you try and get children to practice their musical instruments. Yet we know, we trust, that one day the music flows out of the fingers; one day it just comes. And so we do our little exercises daily of mercy and reconciliation in the smallest, most apparently trivial contexts, we play our scales. Sometimes our fingers ache and sometimes we don't very much want to do our practice, and like our children, we whine and complain, and we put it off. But, moment by moment, that's what we <u>have</u> to do—to get used to mercy and reconciliation as the natural, the instinctive thing for us to do. So that perhaps amazingly one day, if it came to trial, if it came to the ultimate test, Christ's music would flow from our finger ends. Because they were ordinary men and women after all. They'd just got used to practicing. Somehow or other, unobtrusively, year after year, they'd got used to Jesus as a living presence in them. And so in their deaths the martyrs became places where God was and is alive.

In the text, at the end of the story of Stephen's martyrdom, 'when he had said this he fell asleep'—that great Christian contribution to the world's vocabulary, 'he fell asleep'. It has become almost trivial now to talk about people sleeping or resting in Christ, but at that time it was a sharp new metaphor. The martyr falls asleep—and God will wake them. Stephen fell asleep, rested in the Christ into whose life he had grown. And in Christ he lives.

Perhaps this morning in our reflections we can look at holy places. What are the holy places in our lives? We were thinking yesterday of Christ-like people. What about the places in our lives where Jesus has come alive? Why and where have certain places mattered like that to us? They may be just ordinary places, we remember, houses, gardens. They may be churches; they may be the site of some great event. What are those stories of the places that have been holy to us, and what personal associations do they have? Do they help us into thinking about how and why the tombs of the martyrs in the earliest church were the places where people wanted to gather and worship because they knew Christ lived there?

Glorious, all powerful God, almighty and immortal, no place can contain, no words can capture your beauty. Out of your free will you have made your life to live on this earth in Jesus Our Lord. And by His Spirit you have made your life to live in us, in our brothers and sisters across the ages and across the world. We thank you especially today for those who have risked and given their lives for your sake, who by their deaths have made the good news real. We thank you for those who today risk their lives for faith, for love and for justice. We pray for those whose lives are under threat because of persecution. Father, teach us day by day the habits of mercy and of trust. Do not bring us unprepared to test and trial, but give us the strength we need should we ever be called on to witness and bear the cost. We make our prayer through our great high priest, into whose hands all our spirits are surrendered. May he present us to you, a holy, reconciled offering in the sanctuary of heaven. Amen.

Daily Bible Study

Thursday 23 June 2005

Yesterday our attention was on Stephen the martyr, who in his death and in the forgiveness that flowed from him as he died became a sanctuary, a holy place where God's glory was visible. And in the chapter of Acts that follows, we see the immediate effect of Stephen's martyrdom: this effect is mission. What happens after he dies is that persecution deepens—'That very day the Church in Jerusalem began to suffer'. The apostles are scattered, but when they are scattered, what do they do? They tell the Gospel for which Stephen had died. So martyrdom and mission at the beginning of this 8th chapter of Acts are held together. You might say that in God's hands the meaning of Stephen's suffering becomes mission. His death becomes a powerful word that changes things.

There's a great deal we could say about that, and some of that was in our reflection yesterday in the Bible Study groups. But specifically in this 8th chapter of Acts, there are two stages of mission. First of all, the Gospel is proclaimed to the Samaritans. That in itself is remarkable enough, given the attitude of Jews to Samaritans. St Luke in his Gospel has underlined time and again how very difficult it is for Jews to speak to Samaritans. We find it in all the Gospels (you will remember John chapter 4 as well). And then, it's as if the Gospel makes what in science people call a quantum leap. Not only is the Gospel proclaimed to alienated neighbours, it suddenly leaps a whole continent, because the reading we had this morning is about the planting of the Gospel in Africa—the biggest cultural leap that we have yet encountered in the story of the young church, and it's a very remarkable story; dramatic and rather picturesque (when I was a little boy, one of my favourite pictures in the Bible Study book was the picture of the Ethiopian eunuch in his chariot; I don't think that the person who drew the picture had any idea what a historical Ethiopian eunuch might have looked like, but he had draped him in furs and feathers in a very dramatic way). The story is very carefully constructed. He's reading the Prophet Isaiah in his carriage—and well he might, because in Isaiah 18 we read about the Ethiopians: 'They will come to Mount Zion where the Lord Almighty is worshipped'. And in Isaiah 56, we read that a eunuch should never think that because he cannot have children, he cannot be part of God's people. St Luke is directing our attention not just to one passage of Isaiah, but to the whole thrust, the whole logic of that book, where the Gospel reaches out to the most unlikely of people. Here is an Ethiopian who has come to join himself to God's people in Jerusalem. Here is a eunuch, who is acceptable in God's sight.

Let's pursue this a little further. In Isaiah 56, the prophet is alluding to that general disapproval in ancient Israel of people who don't have children. Eunuchs, men incapable of having children, could not be priests, so we read in Leviticus. But that's only part of the broad unease, discontent, and disapproval directed towards people who don't do their bit for keeping the nation going. It's about progeny, children. And Isaiah in his chapter 56 says that 'The childless person who honours God will have his name remembered longer than if he had sons and daughters.' So already in Isaiah there's a hint of something very new. The value of a person now no longer rests on whether they are contributing to keeping the people, the tribe, going. In ancient Israel generally, your value (your virtue almost) depended on doing your part to keep God's people alive; making a future, generating new members of God's people. Isaiah says that God sees people not just in those terms of increasing the numbers of the tribe. God sees people one by one; and the childless person in Isaiah 56, the eunuch who can't have children, is precious in God's sight, and his name will be remembered because of his love and service.

So, as we move into the New Testament, the new covenant, the story of the new people of God, this is a point underlined. The church is not a tribe. It's not a natural extended family where your importance depends on having children and preserving the tribe. The church is a community of persons called by God to love and service, and the value and the virtue of someone called by Christ is far more than the value that simply belongs to being a valued member of the tribe. All this in the background here; it's not just a picturesque accident that the Ethiopian official is a eunuch, a person who cannot have children.

Luke is very interested in his Gospel as well in people who can't have children. He begins, you remember, with two great miracles—the miracle of a child being given to the ageing Zachariah and his wife who is supposed to be beyond the age of childbearing, and the greater miracle of the gift to the Virgin Mary of a child. Luke is saying right at the start, 'Put out of your mind the old system of value and virtue depending on having lots of children for the sake of the tribe. God is dealing with people differently, not in big collective patterns, not through the ongoing history of a nation, but in persons called into communion with each other—'living communion', as you might say.

Just in passing, I think it's worth reflecting on the way in which Christianity throughout its history has had a slightly mixed attitude to the family. It has stressed the value of the family; it has imposed a creative, constructive morality on family life. It has understood family life as reflecting something of God. It has also valued the single life, and it has treated those who take vows of single life as deeply important in the church. And, something we often forget, it has also loved and valued those who can't have children. It has treated with respect and compassion those who because of sickness or disability are not going to have families. And that is a very significant aspect of the Gospel, so I believe. When I look today at the work done in the L'Arche communities where what we call 'ordinary' people and people with disabilities live together, I realise that for many of these people with disabilities who are never going to have families, <u>this</u> is their family, and this is where they are valued and loved as deeply precious and important, with wisdom and joy to share. I put that in as a reminder in passing of one of the great things Christianity has done to make us value persons of that sort.

But back to our text. If we're reading with attention, with other Bible passages ringing in our ears, by the time Philip gets up into the carriage we ought to be expecting something to happen, because here is an Ethiopian who has come as prophesied in Isaiah, here is an Ethiopian <u>eunuch</u> who has come as prophesied in Isaiah—surely something's going to happen. And the queen's treasurer is reading—reading out loud, as people always did in those days, and reading a very significant passage:

> 'Like a sheep that is taken to be slaughtered, like a lamb that makes no sound when its wool is cut off, he did not say a word. He was humiliated, and justice was denied him. No one will be able to tell about his descendants, because his life on earth has come to an end.'

Is it any wonder that the Ethiopian eunuch was struck and halted in his tracks by these words. Here is a saving figure, a hero, a saint depicted in Isaiah, and yet 'he was humiliated and justice was denied him'. 'No one will be able to tell about his descendants.' Here is someone else who has no family, no successors, quite isolated and cut off. But here is the one in whom above all God's power is at work. Imagine for a moment the eunuch reading those words and thinking 'So God can use a person, childless, humiliated, excluded? Of whom does the prophet speak? Who is this about?' And Philip jumps up from the foliage by the roadside and says, 'I know', and leaps into the chariot. Evangelism by hitchhiking! He says, 'I can tell you.' Philip began to speak; starting from this passage, he told him the Good News about Jesus. Jesus, humiliated, shut out; Jesus turned into a foreigner, pushed out of the life of his people. No one will be able to tell about his descendants, no one will 'declare his generation', in the old translation. He's not somebody who's remembered because he's the patriarch of a long line of descendants. No, Jesus is standing with those who are excluded, humiliated, denied justice; those who don't have status among their people. And Jesus is the one in whom God is at work.

So all sorts of things converge on this passage—it's not just a wonderfully dramatic story, the occasion for a nice picture in the Sunday School book, not even just a story of the Gospel, leaping contents, but a story about the newness of the church, which is not an ethnic or a tribal group where your importance depends on having lots of children and keeping the tribe going. The church is a place where, in relation to the humiliated suffering Jesus, all the lonely and the humiliated of the earth may find a family. So it's again a deeply exciting passage. It's about the church, as (to use a phrase of a great New Testament scholar some twenty years or so ago) 'a home for the homeless'. The church is a family for those outside the tribe. The church is a challenge to all our assumptions about race and tribe, ethnic division, even loyalty. We are asked to be loyal to God and to God's children. The church is a community where that loyalty is alive—loyalty to God and loyalty to God's children, not just a great big extended loyalty to a racial group, an ethnic group. The church is a new community centred on this haunting figure that the eunuch reads about in Isaiah: 'He was humiliated, and justice was denied him. No one will be able to tell about his descendants, because his life on earth has come to an end.' And yet he lives, this humiliated suffering servant, he lives and he calls to him a new people, the new family of God. And from the ends of the earth they come flocking to him, especially the humiliated, the rejected, the forgotten, and the oppressed, knowing that in him, in his community and his kinship, his kindred, which is the church, they have hope.

Sometimes I have an incurable novelist's mind when I read the Bible, and I wonder further about the Ethiopian eunuch. Eunuchs were almost always slaves, and slaves were almost always people who had been kidnapped from their own folk. I suspect that the Ethiopian official, powerful though he is—like many slaves in the ancient world he has risen to a high office—is still someone 'taken away from his people', cut off from his own folk. He is someone who has been humiliated, deeply, by his status; and underneath the fur and the feathers and the grandeur of being the court treasurer, he remains a slave and a foreigner, childless, unloved. And it is he who is centre-stage here, he is the sort of person to whom the suffering servant speaks. Perhaps as we think forward to the celebrations in two years' time of the second centenary of the abolition of the slave trade in the British Empire, we might think of the Ethiopian eunuch and the millions and millions of people who shared his fate and were cut off from their people, humiliated, and silenced across the world, and who yet found community and family in their faith in Jesus Christ. And God forgive the church for taking so long to wake up to the fact that it was complicit in this terror.

The church, the family of God: so often that is a term that sounds rather cosy. We can snuggle up to each other, as we do in a family. But in fact this is a family where strangers find a home, where the homeless find a home. This is not a family of 'people like us', and as we look around this room, I hope we're aware of that fact. This family is full of ethnic diversity and educational diversity and diversity of opinion, and God has called us together to be a family of strangers; that's why to belong in such a family is so much deeper and richer than belonging just with 'people like us'. That's why this is a family where the homeless ought to know there is a home for them, where the forgotten and the humiliated ought to know that they will be taken seriously and loved, treated as precious. So it's not surprising, once again, that the Ethiopian eunuch, hearing all this explained to him, and being clearly a man of both insight and impulse, says, 'Well, here's water. This baptism you've been talking about—why not just do it?' And Philip, being a man who also acts on impulse, says, 'Fine.' They get down, out of the chariot, and the first African is baptised, and the church is never quite the same again.

And my mind starts running again—what happened afterwards to the Ethiopian eunuch? Did he go back to Ethiopia and start a church? I don't know, and I don't really need to know. All I need to know at this point is that the Ethiopian eunuch heard Good News and he knew that being associated with Jesus would make all the difference. In a way, that's all he needs to know in this story; and when I start asking these curious questions, 'So what happened next?', St Luke looks up from his page and says, 'None of your business. Leave that to God. All you need to know is that a humiliated foreigner has found hope in Jesus Christ.' 'Now,' says Luke to me, 'go and do likewise. Go and see what you can do about all this. Go and see how the church can become the sort of church where humiliated foreigners may be valued and find a home.' I expect Philip too quite wanted to take it further. Maybe, after the baptism Philip said, 'Well, now let me tell you about all the obligations of membership in the church. Let me have your covenant form, give me a list of addresses of your friends to contact.' But no, no, the Spirit of the Lord took Philip away before Philip had even started on the follow-up. The Spirit of the Lord takes him away and leaves the eunuch going on his way rejoicing, back to Queen Candace, and Philip 'found himself in Azotus'. A lovely phrase again. I imagine Philip standing at the door of the City of Ashdod, scratching his head and saying, 'Now what was that all about? Was that a dream? I thought I was walking along the desert road and there was a strange man and we talked and there was something about a river.' And on he goes with his work. 'And he went on to Caesarea, and on the way he preached the Good News in every town.'

And, like anyone engaged in sharing the Gospel with the humiliated, the lost, and the injured, he too has heard Good News for himself, and he is reinforced and strengthened in the news he is taking to Caesarea and the other towns on the Palestinian coast.

In our reflections this morning, perhaps we can think a bit about where we've seen the Gospel making a quantum link, jumping boundaries. Where have we been surprised by the spread of the Gospel? We may have seen the Good News taking root in a person or in a community we would never have expected to turn to Christ. Where have we been surprised by the Gospel touching the life of strangers?

Lord God of the whole earth, God of all creation, you are the father of the fatherless and defend the cause of the widows. You speak to those who are alone, humiliated, and isolated, you give a family to those who have none. You value each of us, irrespective of our success and our productivity, our contribution to the society we're in, our place in the life of the tribe. You value each of us for who we are, made in your image, called to live with your Son. May our churches truly be homes for the homeless, places where the forgotten and the humiliated may be remembered and honoured. Father, may the Gospel of your Son continue to leap over all the boundaries of race and country and class that we can think of; help us to carry it to the ends of the earth, because we know that we, lost as we are, have been found by you; that we, lonely as we are, have been brought into community by you, and that we have a gift to share, the gift of fellowship and communion with our Lord and Saviour Jesus Christ. Amen.

Daily Bible Study

Friday 24 June 2005

Yesterday we were reflecting on the story where the Gospel leaps from continent to continent, from heart to heart, and the Gospel crosses visible boundaries. But today, as we think about the conversion of Saul, it's another kind of boundary that the Gospel is crossing, a boundary within the human heart, a boundary between hostility to Christ and friendship through Christ. How very vividly St Luke depicts Saul the persecutor. The knock upon the door at 5 o'clock in the morning, people shouldering their way in, dragging folk out of bed off to prison. No explanation. People never heard of again, disappearing mysteriously into the gaols in the rocks under Jerusalem. It's a picture which is not by any means unfamiliar in the modern age, and not at all unfamiliar to many of you in your own contexts. And here is a story of the chief of the security services suddenly realising that he is going to have to join the group whose persecution he has been organising. That in itself is dramatic enough. But how much more dramatic is the mode of his conversion, and what he sees in it.

Paul, as he tells us in his own letters, was not a corrupt, bullying sadist. He was a man who loved God and had 'advanced' in the love of God and the keeping of the Law, he says, more than most people of his generation. It's not difficult to believe that as he rode to Damascus, his mind and his heart were turning in meditation on the God he loved and the Law he kept. And what happens then? It's as if three quite different pictures suddenly come together at a thunderclap. Can you imagine, as if on a screen, three pictures, in different kinds of focus, or different places on the screen—and suddenly something turns a dial, and they come together. Saul is riding along, and, let us imagine, his mind is fixed on his Lord, the Lord of heavenly glory. And in his mind there is another picture, a picture of Jesus, whom perhaps he never met, the source of all his trouble, the man who is tormenting him, the man who is causing him to behave in this violent and dreadful way. Perhaps we can imagine the anger and the furious resentment he feels at this heretic, this sinner, this accursed figure who has so corrupted the religion he loves. Then there's a third picture, and I wonder what Saul felt about this—the picture of Stephen's face streaming blood under the stones that were flung at it.

And then, they come together. The Lord of glory speaks the word from Sinai in the voice of the crucified cursed sinner, and in the voice of the martyr Saul helped to kill. 'Who are you?', says Saul. 'I am Jesus. It is me you are persecuting. I am your Lord, I, the crucified sinner. I am the man you have murdered.'

Saul falls to the ground, he is blind, he is silent. Are we surprised? To me the very heart of this story, this terrifying story of a man whose life is utterly turned around like that, is in these words: 'For three days he was not able to see, and during that time he did not eat or drink anything.' This is first of all a story about the loneliness of the convert. Paul has stepped into that new world we have being reflecting about—or rather he has been pushed into it violently—and he doesn't know where he is, he doesn't know any Christians except the ones he's been killing. It's not as if he can go to the local vicarage and say, 'I think I'd like to start a course of instruction.' He is about to alienate himself from everything he has ever known, all those people who have ever admired and valued him. He is utterly alone. 'For three days he was not able to see. During that time he did not eat or drink anything.' He is, we might say, three days with Jesus in the tomb. He can see nothing and he can say nothing. It is as if by God's providence he has returned to the darkness and chaos of all creation. He has to be made again out of nothing. 'For I am new begot, Of silence, darkness, death, things that are not', wrote the poet and priest John Donne. And here is Paul being newly begotten, in silence, darkness, and death. Things that are not.

Scholars of the New Testament have said that you can deduce the whole of St Paul's theology from that moment on the Damascus road. Can you see how that is? First of all, there is his vision that Jesus is his Body, that the suffering struggling body of believers really is Jesus in our midst. All of Paul's doctrine of the body of Christ was revealed to him in a flash on the road to Damascus, when he saw that Jesus is his people. And those who despise, persecute, and reject the poor struggling body of believers are rejecting Jesus; and those within the body, who, as he says in 1 Corinthians, don't 'discern the body, don't discern the nature of community', they too turn their back on Jesus by turning their backs on the responsibility of love and the care they owe to each other. All of that in one moment on the Damascus road.

And secondly, the Paul who writes about justification by faith, about the fact that we are renewed and renamed not by our effort or our achievement, but by the pure gift of God, is the Paul who for three days was not able to see—newly begot from darkness and death. But then the focus of the story shifts to Ananias, about whom we know absolutely nothing except that he baptised Paul. I have a picture of Ananias in heaven wandering amiably among the crowds and, falling into conversation, someone says, 'Why are you here? You don't seem to have done anything much.' And Ananias says, 'Well, there was this man I visited in Damascus one day, and he turned out to be quite important. I think that's probably why I'm here.' I suspect, you know, that sometimes we may by God's grace get into heaven, not because of the Christians we have been, but because of the Christians we have made. Maybe we have been allowed to touch something in another person that has brought them to life, in a way quite outside our own capacity and our own strength and skill; we get there on their coat-tails, because they have become much greater than we. Perhaps John the Baptist felt something like that also, when he spoke about the Saviour whose sandals he wasn't worthy to untie.

The call of Ananias strikes me as a wonderful example of divine tact. 'Ananias,' says the Lord. 'Yes,' says Ananias, looking surprised—what has he done to deserve this? 'I'd like you to go to Straight Street,' says the Lord, 'and look for somebody called Saul of Tarsus at the House of Judas.' 'Because,' says the Lord, 'he's had a vision of a man called Ananias coming to visit him.' An enormous hint thrown at Ananias; it's not that God directly says, 'You go and convert him'.

Ananias panics; he is the second lonely man in this chapter, a chapter about lonely people. He has been told to go and baptise the greatest enemy of the faith. Is this a trap? It could well be. But he goes, he takes the risk, and we know what follows. But Ananias, as he makes his way through the crowded streets of Damascus, his heart beating rather fast—what does he think? 'What would my fellow Christians think of me? I'm putting my head in a noose; perhaps I'm being followed. Perhaps they've found my house, and the police will be round in the morning to arrest the Christians. Perhaps I'm putting my fellow Christians at risk by doing this. There'll be blood on my hands. All I know is what terrible things this man has done to God's people.'

Two lonely men taking risks—Ananias going to meet the man he has no reason to trust or love, to make him a brother, and Saul leaving all he has ever known. When Saul, Paul, becomes a Christian, more than one person takes a risk for him. Saul or Paul has a difficult personality—anyone who has read his Epistles knows he must have been a very difficult man! I don't imagine that he was particularly easy to befriend or to defend. But Ananias takes a risk; and when Saul turns up in Jerusalem, Barnabas takes a risk—'he took him by the hand and introduced him to the Apostles'; and it sounds from Galatians as though Peter and James and John took a risk as well in receiving him. Paul gets into the church because lots of people take risks for him and put their reputations on the line for him. And that's perhaps another thing about our sharing of the Gospel—that at times we have to take risks to go to meet people before we're sure, before we know what will happen. Yet we go there, we meet them, we give them time.

It is an astonishing story. It's not surprising that it's right at the heart, it's a pivot of the story of the Acts of Apostles. It's as if this is really, truly where we see what the 'Acts of the Holy Spirit' can be like—that explosive moment when the images come together, the new begetting out of darkness and silence; the new creation in Paul's life, and the astonishing risks that people then take for the Gospel, because the whole new world has been revealed.

Perhaps for now I can leave you with an invitation to think in the Bible Study groups a little bit about your own moments of loneliness, those times in your Christian journey when you have felt deeply alone, whether because of events outside or because you feel you've been called on to take a step that is unclear and dangerous for the sake of Jesus Christ. And think of those two lonely men in the story—Saul and Ananias—each one stepping out of their familiar world so that they can touch, the Holy Spirit bringing Jesus alive in that encounter in two lonely, brave figures stepping out to meet, as strangers become brothers in that moment.

Father, thank you for touching the heart of Saul, because our debt to him is so enormous. Thank you for making him our Apostle, a preacher to the Gentiles. Thank you for the new birth that you gave him, in darkness and silence, so that he knew faith to be a gift and a grace, not a reward. Father, thank you for Ananias, who stepped out of his safety, stepped away from what he was familiar with to make a disciple of Saul. Grant us, Father, the gifts of Paul and of Ananias—the gift to know that we are all renewed by your grace and love for them, the courage to go to all those who need to hear your word, however risky and strange it seems, however lonely we feel. In our moments of loneliness, in the moments when we take great risks, Father let us know that you are with us, leading us forward step by step, and in the darkness that we sometimes enter, when we suffer alone for your sake, remind us that with the three days' darkness comes the risen life of your Son, our Saviour Jesus Christ. Amen.

Daily Bible Study

Saturday 25 June 2005

The death of Stephen, as we've seen, prompted the spread of the Gospel, and in the 11th and 12th chapters of Acts we've read something about that as the leaders begin to move to Jewish colonies abroad. They go to the Jewish groups in Phoenicia and Cyprus, and they meet members of the great synagogues of North Africa in places like Cyrene. Antioch becomes the centre of the Christian community of this time. But the Holy Spirit has still further plans, and they begin to unfold in this 13th chapter. Right from the beginning of the 13th chapter we see the hints of those further plans, already spelled out in the names of the prophets and teachers of Antioch. Barnabas we've already met, a Cypriot Jew. 'Simeon called the Black' sounds like a Jewish convert from one of the North African synagogues; here he is alongside Lucius from Cyrene, a North African Jew. And then, even more surprisingly, Manaen, or Menachem, 'who had been brought up with King Herod', somebody from the highest levels of the ruling class. There they are, converts, foreigners, people of different races and different classes, gathering in Antioch. And the Holy Spirit tells them to 'set aside Barnabas and Saul', to take that kind of community, a community of all races and classes, outside the world they are familiar with; and off they go to begin what generations of schoolchildren have learned to know, if not to love, as 'St Paul's first missionary journey'. Many of us spent a lot of time drawing maps of this in our religious studies lessons at school, which undoubtedly made a great difference to our future grasp of the Christian faith . . .

The mission abroad begins, not just as a reaction, but as a deliberate policy, a policy of the Holy Spirit—an act of the Holy Spirit. And here, as in the other crucial and transition moments in the Book of Acts, we have mention of the Holy Spirit prompting, urging, deliberately shaping the policy of the church. Being sent by the Holy Spirit are Barnabas and Saul, who went to Seleucia and sailed from there to the island of Cyprus. And there follows a very odd little story about the conflict which Saul and Barnabas had to confront as soon as they arrived in Cyprus. It seems they found a very sympathetic Roman administrator. 'An intelligent man', says St Luke, but clearly one of those Romans who is fascinated by odd religions, by magic, by what we might call the New Age of the first Christian century. There were many like him in the Roman administration who enjoyed exotic gurus, soothsayers, fortune-tellers, magicians, prophets, and self-styled mystics around them to make them feel better. The Gospel here has its first encounter, not with classical paganism, not with the Jewish faith, but with that strange and persistent underworld of magic, which always stands alongside religion—its shadow, its counterpart, true faith, which resigns power into the hands of God, and magic, which tries to seize power in order to control the world. They can look so much alike sometimes. There are ways of being religious, ways of expressing faith, which sadly come very close to magic, when we use our faith as if it were a means of controlling the world. There are kinds of magic which suggest solemnity and seriousness and can look very like real faith; but there's all the difference in the world—as both the Roman governor and Elymas, the magician, are about to discover.

A word about two interesting details here. One is, of course, that this is the first place where we learn Saul's other name. He is 'also known as Paul'. Why does Luke choose this point to tell us? Goodness knows—but I do have a theory. Indulge me for a moment, because it's not completely irrelevant to what the chapter is about. Jews who were Roman citizens naturally adopted Roman names. Paul's Hebrew name we know was the name of the first King of Israel; but he had adopted a Roman family name, Paulus, perhaps because of an association (professional or personal) with a Roman family back in Tarsus; and now, the governor of the island is Sergius <u>Paulus</u>. I imagine Paul introducing himself to the governor by saying, 'You won't believe this, but I am actually Paulus as well. My family is associated with yours.' And the governor looks with some amazement at this dishevelled Jewish traveller, wondering what on earth his business is, but expecting something quite important, and discovering to his astonishment—it is the word at the end of our reading—and to his embarrassment there is a family connection. Here is somebody who clearly has some connection with the Paulus family in Tarsus, with cousin Gaius so to speak, and yet he is involved with this strange sect he's talking about, in which people of all classes and races are mixed up, whereas the dignified Paulus family have spent their lives alongside the privileged. I'm not surprised the governor was astonished about the teaching about the Lord, and I think that is why Luke chooses this point to tell us, perhaps with a broad smile in brackets, that Saul was 'also a Paulus'.

The second point is that what happens to Elymas or Bar-Jesus, the prophet magician is a kind of reflection of what has happened to Paul himself. He's been resisting the truth, and suddenly he's lost, he's blind. '"The Lord's hand will come down on you now, you will be blind and will not see the light of day for a time." And Elymas at once felt mist and darkness covering his eyes.' Paul knew what it was to have the Lord's hand come down upon him, and I would like to think that this little detail of the story was meant to tell us that perhaps Elymas, resisting the truth, just as Paul had done, may also be given a chance as the Lord's hand comes on him, and in blindness be able has to rediscover the truth. It's one of those stories where so many different details come together that we think, yes, that somehow fits in to the whole pattern of the story we're being told in the Acts of the Apostles, the Acts of the Holy Spirit.

But the main thing to come out of this story is in that last line. 'The governor was greatly amazed, was astonished at the teaching about the Lord.' Luke in telling the story has carefully laid the foundations of why the governor might have been astonished. 'Teaching about the Lord' is teaching about the One who has become visible in our midst alone, and has established this community in which His work and His reality are visible—the church. That community we have already seen at work in the first twelve chapters of Acts is an 'astonishing' community, not just because signs and wonders happen, though they do, but because it grows through loss and suffering. It is 'astonishing' because it draws together people from the royal court and people from the streets: Ethiopian eunuchs and Jewish priests and rabbis. It is astonishing because it refuses to sit still and behave itself in the place where it is born. It leaps boundaries and continents, and it makes what could be a supremely arrogant, and yet is in a way a supremely humble claim, 'We have bread for the whole world; we have something everyone needs, and so there is nowhere we will not go.'

'The governor was greatly astonished.' All of these things, you see, we may take for granted. We know that the faith is meant to be universal. We know that the faith is meant to draw together people of different races and classes. We have learned how the faith grows through loss and suffering. In the ancient world, none of this was obvious, none of this was conventional. Nations and peoples had their religions, their gods, and that was perfectly straightforward, and up to a point you didn't worry very much about what people believed, so long as they were good citizens within the realm of the Roman Empire. The Roman Empire, like most of the ancient world, took for granted, in a way we can scarcely imagine, that there was no real community between free people and slaves, between the civilised and the barbarians. It took for granted, without question, the deepest divisions between human beings, and while it could make sense of heroic death for the sake of a great cause, it could not make sense of dying for love of a divine saviour. 'He was greatly astonished at the teaching about the Lord', because at that time it was amazing—it was new.

We all now take for granted something different. We do understand, don't we, what sort of thing the church is, what kind of community it's meant to be? We do understand, don't we, that martyrdom for the sake of the Gospel is the seed of the church, and we do understand, don't we, that we have something for everyone, we have bread for everyone's hunger. So why aren't people amazed? Because in fact, we're slipping back fast into something like the ancient world. We are slipping back towards a world of narrow tunnel vision of religious and superstitious practice, a world where common religious beliefs united with common social practice seem very unlikely. We're slipping into a world where lots and lots of people have their lords and their gods, their practices and their mysticisms, that don't really relate to each other. We're slipping away from the idea that there might be a faith that would bring all human beings together. We're slipping back socially and internationally into the assumption that there really are such differences in human beings that we can forget about God's universal righteousness. We can treat whole continents as if they were dispensable. Can the church be 'amazing' in this world, as it was there, saying, 'Yes, there is one truth in Jesus Christ, a truth which sets everyone free. Yes, there is one family of God into which all may be re-born. And yes, the cost of living this out is very terrible, and through that cost God is at work.' If the life of our church were astonishing like that, who knows what might be possible.

But then, as now, we face competition. We face the various magicians who are whispering into the ears of the world today. And they're probably whispering pretty much what Elymas whispered into the ear of Sergius Paulus. They're whispering that it is possible to control our environment, whether by magic or by technology. They're whispering that you can forget about transfiguring faith, and that what you need is the technical skills to make yourself feel better and to get on top of the environment, to control it. And sometimes, when I read about the aspirations of technologists these days, I think this really is magic. It's as fantastic and unreal as any magical aspirations in past centuries. 'Of course we have a great environmental challenge—but don't worry, technology will sort it out.' 'Of course, we have a great moral problem about bioethics and experimentation with embryos, and genetic manipulation, but don't worry. Technology will sort it out.' If that's not believing in magic, I don't know what is. Elymas is still busy whispering.

It may be that in our groups this morning, we might like to think about magic in the world today as a rival faith. For many of us, and I don't just mean people in the Global South, real literal magic is a problem. Most of our cultures have superstition rampant within them, and lots of claims by pseudo-mystics, false prophets, magicians. The fact is that the occult is a reality in every country of the world. We in Britain are not without our occultists, our magicians. But we might think, too, of those other 'magic' faiths, like the faith that, by some mysterious process, technology will solve our problems and make us happy and free. Think about how those things apply in the various context that we come from, and then think once more of the astonishing truth. Sergius Paulus, the governor, looking at an alarming, astonishing stranger, who might be distantly connected to him, talking about this different world, this revolutionary society—which means freedom for everyone, bread for all people, in which the leaders may be as diverse as Manaen the prince and Simeon the African convert.

Father, teach us again and again to be surprised by your work, amazed by your generosity, astonished by the love that has brought us together in this miracle which is the Body of Christ. May our Communion, our love and fellowship with each other, our care for all, surprise and amaze the world around us, so that they will ask 'What power is this?' Father, keep us from turning our faith into magic, looking for quick answers, ways of solving our problems that are not according to your will. Give us patience to find you, even in loss and suffering, knowing that only through Christ is resurrection possible. And Father, bring us to be fully of one mind with your Holy Spirit. May our policy for the church be the policy of the Holy Spirit, so that our acts may be the Spirit's acts, which honour Jesus Christ our Lord. Amen.

Daily Bible Study

Monday 27 June 2005

'The Holy Spirit did not let them preach the message in the province of Asia.' So far the acts of the Holy Spirit seems to have been a story of the Holy Spirit giving positive encouragement, opening new doors. Suddenly, we meet the Holy Spirit putting up barriers. 'The Holy Spirit did not let them preach the message in the province of Asia. When they reached the border of Mysia, they tried to go in to the province of Bithynia, but the Spirit of Jesus did not allow them.' Suddenly the Holy Spirit is getting very directive and rather difficult. All the plans that seemed obvious about the mission that Christ had entrusted to his church, the Holy Spirit seems to be blocking. Looking at the map, it's fairly clear what Paul and his friends had intended to do—they intended to make a circuit of Asia Minor and then probably head back towards Jerusalem. But something gets in the way.

It's a reminder in the most general terms of two things about the work of the Spirit; one is the familiar point that, when God closes some doors, he opens others. But the other is just a recognition of how the Holy Sprit works in each of us. The Holy Spirit is changing us, the Holy Spirit is making us different people. And that means that we sometimes get to the point where we sense, 'I can't go that way. I don't know why it is, but there's something that doesn't fit about this course of action. It makes perfect sense in human terms, but it somehow doesn't seem quite to be what God wants.' Some of us who are bishops have sat with clergy talking with them about their plans and their hopes. And sometimes I find myself offering a position to someone that seems perfectly obvious given their gifts and their experience. And they'll pray about it and they'll say, 'Yes, I know it seems perfectly obvious, but somehow it just doesn't seem to be from God.' And one of the hardest problems that we have as Christians is just keeping a little bit of distance between those two things—the something that seems perfectly obvious, and the something that comes from God. Sometimes they coincide, and sometimes they don't, and when they don't, it's difficult. Going back to the bishop's study and the job being offered, 'But for goodness sake,' say I, 'here is a parish that needs your gifts. Here is a parish where you can give your best for the next ten years. Here is a post which stretches you just the way you need to be stretched at this particular point in your career.' And if the priest I'm talking to has any sense or depth, they will say, 'It's not about career, it's not about stretching me for my benefit, and it's not about the right step in a neat story. It's about God. Sorry Bishop, you'll have to wait.' And if the Bishop has got any sense or depth, the Bishop ought to say, 'Amen.' I have to tell you in the strictest confidence that not everybody does!

And there we are—it happens not only in the lives of ministers, but in the lives of church members—things that look obvious, but may not be from God. And now here is this challenge in the ministry of Paul. The next step seems clear, but there's something not quite right about it, and I can imagine Paul and his travelling companions sitting underneath the table rather late at night, and Paul saying, 'Yes, I know that seems the next place to go, but there's something telling me it's not quite right.' The Holy Spirit, or the Spirit of Jesus, steers away from what is obvious towards a very remarkable next step. The next door that God is to open is of course the Gospel leaping yet another continent—this time to the benighted continent of Europe. Just as they had left, that very night, says the text, Paul dreams of a figure on the further shore saying, 'Come to Macedonia.' Suddenly, that is right, that is clear. It may not be obvious, but it's what God wants: God bringing into the situation something quite new in that prophetic dream. Then Paul knows and the pieces fall into place. So that's a first theme in today's reading: the Holy Spirit who can set up frustrations and barriers, in order to take us away from what we think is the obvious and clear, simple next step and lead us to where the creative new opportunities lie.

Then comes one of the most striking moments in the whole of the Acts. You hardly noticed it if you weren't listening carefully. Suddenly the text changes from 'they' to 'we'. This is the moment when the author of the Acts of the Apostles slips onto the scene unobtrusively. *They* travel from the region of Phrygia, and when *they* reach the border of Mysia *they* try to go to the Province of Bithynia. *They* travel right on, and, as soon as Paul has his vision, we got ready to leave for Macedonia. And what makes it so wonderful is that St Luke doesn't say, 'This is the moment when I arrived at 9 o'clock in the morning and said, 'I'd like to speak to Paul, please' and he said, 'I'd love to have you with us—will you join us on our trip to Macedonia?'.' Luke doesn't say anything. Luke just slips quietly into the picture as part of the *we* that is the Body of Christ. He doesn't underscore his part in it; he just signals very quietly, 'I am now part of the story, I am now part of that great corporate activity that is the Body of Christ.' And, as I read Acts, I feel that that's how we should all come into the story—no great dramas about how we join in, what we bring, but just that quiet slipping into the stream, God's action in the Holy Spirit, joining in something that's already unfolding; what was once grain is now wheat. I am part of this book. It's something which we often need to remember in worship, because sometimes, when we approach our worship, we feel it is us doing something new, making an approach to God, starting a new event; whereas in fact, we're slipping quietly into the great stream of worship and praise that exists throughout the whole universe, into which we are brought as we start worshipping. It's simply the moment when *they* becomes *we*. We join in the great act of all creation, offering praise through the Son to the Father. It's a fact about worship—but surely it's also a fact about all of our mission, the 'Acts of the Holy Spirit'. God works through his creation, God working in mission, in history, in the world, and we slip in to work in what God is doing.

One of the phrases about mission that seems to have rung most bells for a lot of people in the Church of England in recent years is that it is about 'finding out what God is doing and joining in'. Something like that comes through in this unobtrusive moment as St Luke slips into the story, as much as to say, 'I've found what God is doing—can I join in?' No big drama, no great story to be told there, 'But,' says Luke, 'I became part of the story of what God was doing.' So the Acts of the Apostles is no longer about *them*, but about *us*.

Today then, two thoughts perhaps for our reflection. They're rather different, but there are some connections, as I'll say in a moment. One is, that we might like to think about our own experience of moments when the Holy Spirit has apparently said no to what is obvious. Perhaps in our own vocation, our own service—moments when we have thought we had a plan, and God somehow corrected us in another way, we ran into a brick wall, we found the possibilities we thought clear were not there. What for us have been the doors God has closed in order to open others? I suspect we all have some experience of that. The second is just to reflect a little bit on people with whom we have shared in our mission—the people who've been alongside us in mission, the people who have formed us and been with us. Who are the people who drew us in to God's mission? Who are the people who laid the foundations and made us see what God is doing? Because the thing that holds these two themes together is that it's only together in the Holy Spirit that we really find discernment—and here is of course one of the great themes of all our reflection on Communion. Together in the Holy Spirit we find discernment. We think, we pray, and we feel our way forward as a Church, as *we*, not *them* and *us*, not *me* and *him* or *her*, but *we*. Together our sense of where the Holy Spirit is leading me to others, into the global Church, into communion together is sharper and more spirit-filled. Together it is easier to interpret the brick walls, easier to search and open all the doors that God has opened—the new opportunities that God has set before us.

Father, by the gift of your Holy Spirit you make us different people. Perhaps what once seemed clear is now not clear at all; what once seemed strange or dangerous is now the path we have before us. Help us to trust you when we are frustrated, when our plans do not go as we want them to, and help us together to discern the open door that in every situation you have prepared for us. Thank you that because of Paul's dream the Gospel came to Europe. Thank you for the ministry and witness of Luke, who joined in Paul's mission, and recorded his words and his views—your Acts in him. By the same Spirit, teach us to see ourselves together as one Body, drawn into the great eternal act of worship which all creation offers to you, the great act of mission, which flows from your eternal work. Help us find our place in that great co-operative work. In the name of Jesus Christ our Saviour. Amen.

Daily Bible Study

Tuesday 28 June 2005

'He had been instructed in the Way of the Lord and with great enthusiasm he proclaimed and taught correctly the facts about Jesus. However, he knew only the baptism of John.' That is what we're told about Apollos in the reading we had this morning, a little vignette, a little picture of Apollos the missionary, which relates to the story told at the beginning of Chapter 19—the chapter that follows—where Paul in Ephesus meets some disciples who only know about the baptism of John, and they don't know about the Holy Spirit. Apollos, like these believers, knows all there is to know, it seems, about the life and death of Jesus. He even knows that there is baptism for the forgiveness of sins. But he doesn't know that point which we began with in these Bible Studies ten days ago, and that is that forgiveness is only the opening of the door to the life of the Holy Spirit. In other words, Apollos is still looking backwards. There's a sort of echo here of the disciples on the road to Emmaus. You remember as they walk along, Jesus explains to them the things about himself, and it's exactly the same phrase here—'the things about Jesus.' And like those disciples on the road to Emmaus, Apollos is filled with enthusiasm. His heart burns, like the disciples on the Emmaus road. But when the Emmaus disciples return to Jerusalem, they, with all the others, have to sit and wait for the Holy Spirit.

So it's as if here, in this passage, many of the themes we've been thinking about in these last days come together. The facts about Jesus—yes; the forgiveness of sins—yes; but most important of all, the present action of the Holy Spirit, who makes the facts about Jesus the facts about us, who makes the life of Jesus our life, or rather makes our life the life of Jesus, makes Jesus live in us and act in us. That is what Apollos doesn't know. And actually a lot of the time most Christians, like Apollos, don't fully seem to know. We talk a great deal about Jesus; we remember Jesus with gratitude; we express the warmth of our feelings towards him; we believe that because of Jesus our sins are forgiven, and yet there is something trembling on the edge of our vision that is so much greater, which is the Jesus who is alive gloriously in our midst, not only promising, but present in his Spirit, working for the transformation of all things in Him.

What would the Church be like if we knew only the facts about Jesus and the forgiveness of sins? I suspect that we would think very differently about baptism and about the Holy Communion. Baptism would be a mark of our allegiance to Jesus. The Holy Communion would be a reminder of his saving death. But baptism as the gift of the Holy Spirit, and Holy Communion as the moment when the Holy Spirit comes down on the bread and the wine and fuses us into the life of Jesus in the fire of his love—we'd miss that. And yet that is the spring, the source of all we are and all we do.

This morning, I'm not actually going to suggest any questions in the Bible Study groups. I think it might be fruitful for us simply to reflect on what we've heard and learned in the whole of this conference, to make our farewells, to appreciate one another in God's presence for a while. But I think it is a gift of God's providence that the reading on this last morning should so clearly take us back to where we began in the 2nd chapter of the Acts. 'Each one of you must turn away from your sins and be baptised in the name of Jesus Christ, so that your sins will be forgiven and you will receive God's gift of the Holy Spirit.' It's not only, you see, baptism and Holy Communion that would be different if we only believed in the facts about Jesus and the forgiveness of sins. Meetings like this would be different, because with a great deal of boldness, we have prayed for the Holy Spirit to be here between us. And we have, please God, met the Holy Spirit here between us in these days. We have not simply been a society meeting in the memory of Jesus, not even a society celebrating the forgiveness of sins given in Jesus. We have been a church—that is people gathered by the present action and life and call and gift of Jesus—looking for Jesus alive in one another. And when in any meeting, the smallest meeting for worship, the biggest gathering of Christians, we come, looking and listening for the living Jesus in each other, we meet differently.

Somebody mentioned yesterday that favourite quote of Archbishop Michael Peers of Canada who used to tell us of Desmond Tutu saying that Anglicans were defined simply by the fact that they meet. Well, so we do, a lot; but we don't only meet. We meet as church; we meet looking and listening for the living Jesus; we meet in the Holy Spirit. And again, whether it's a formal session, whether it's a Bible Study group, or whether it's a conversation over coffee, we meet in the Holy Spirit. So we really have a lot to be thankful for in that Apollos was wrong—or rather that Apollos was only partly right. It's very good that Priscilla and Aquila were able to spend the time with him putting him straight. As usual, a vivid picture comes to mind—the brilliant, sparkling young preacher from Alexandria, riveting his audience with his eloquence, and at the end of the meeting an elderly couple coming up to him and saying, 'That was wonderful, but only half the truth. So, come back to lunch and we'll tell you.' And the brilliant Apollos, perhaps thinking, 'Who on earth are these dinosaurs?' As Aquila and Priscilla gently say, 'It's all wonderful, it's all true—but the most important thing is missing, and that is the Spirit, the awareness of the <u>living</u> Jesus.'

The 'Acts of the Holy Spirit': the Acts of the Apostles is a history of the church as if Jesus were really alive—and that's the history of the church we hope and pray will be written—our church, anybody's church, the history of the church as if Jesus were really alive. That's what we need to know, and in one sense that is all you need to know. It doesn't solve our problems straight away, it's not a programme for action; it's just true, it's just there: the fact that we are baptised not only into the forgiveness of sins, but into the life of the Holy Spirit. So, in Study Groups this morning, just give thanks for the living Jesus in each other, the living Jesus you will have met in these days together. And make space in your heart for meeting the living Jesus when you return among your churches. Ask, in whatever church context you find yourself, how will the history of this church become a story of the acts of the Holy Spirit? Not only the acts of this person or that person, this group, this bishop, this committee, but a story of the Spirit bringing Jesus alive in all the ways we've been thinking about in these days, alive in leaping the boundaries of race and class, alive in drawing us together, collaborating in mission, alive in common discernment and shared hope: because that is the real story of the church, then and now, and in the future. May God grant that that will be the story to be written of the Anglican Communion.

Beloved Lord, in your Son made flesh among us, You have brought healing and wiped away our sin by the blood of the cross. You have raised him from the dead and exalted Him to your right hand in glory; but so that nothing should be left undone, you have poured upon us, through him the gift of your Spirit. We thank you that because of that Spirit, He lives in us and we in Him. Thank you that by the light and power of that Spirit, we may see Jesus in each other. Thank you that in the strength and hope of the Spirit, we see your mercy reaching out always before us to the ends of the earth. Bless this, your Anglican family, enrich and deepen our awareness of the Holy Spirit, that, as we share with each other and with the world the facts about Jesus, it will be a living Jesus who speaks and acts in us. In His name we make our prayer. Amen.

Sermons, Lectures, and Addresses

Archbishop of Canterbury's Presidential Address

Monday 20 June 2005

I

Who are we talking to in this meeting? To be a Christian is to believe we are commanded and authorised to say certain things to the world; to *say* things that will make disciples of all nations. Our words matter. We have to think with care about them and to try and know something of how they will be heard. If they are not heard as good news from God, as words that change the world and release people from various sorts of prison, what has gone wrong? Are we talking only to ourselves?

This week it will be of the greatest importance that we remember to ask, whenever we say anything, whether we are doing more than talking to ourselves—and to ask what will be heard in what we say here and how far it helps or hinders the communicating of the gospel of Jesus. A gathering like this always attracts a degree of media attention, and we can guess already what the pattern of this is likely to be—'The Communion is in great trouble; conservatives and liberals are going to split from each other'. Different people will have different stories to tell, with different interests to serve. These stories will be the subject of still more stories, and the rapid fire of exchanges will continue to stream across the electronic pathways. That is the way of the world. And however unworldly we may like to think ourselves, somehow we remain the world's captives in this connection.

But meanwhile the bulk of the media's attention will probably be focused elsewhere—on the meeting that will take place just after we have finished, the meeting of the G8 leaders. Grief, anger and frustration at the injustice of the world's trade systems and at the sluggishness of wealthy nations in addressing the menace of systematic environmental degradation is boiling over, here in the UK and in many other places. The report of the Africa Commission here a couple of months ago outlined the challenges and opportunities that face the wealthy nations, and the continuing horror of disease and violence and corrupt, dysfunctional government that imprisons millions. Africa is the focus, but it is not a challenge in relation to Africa alone. Debt and poverty and oppression are realities for other continents. Corrupt government afflicts supposedly 'developed' nations too. And the environmental crisis confronts us all with growing urgency. But at the moment, the question most sharply in focus is, 'What do the most powerful nations in the world intend to do to reduce even a little the burden of suffering that afflicts those over whom their power is exercised in various ways?'

This is what a large part of the general public at least in this country will be thinking about this week. Some of those, especially those who are most committed to the ending of poverty and injustice, will be people who speak the same language as us; they will be people of faith, often Christian faith. And we have to ask what if anything they will hear from us that is good news for them and for the poor for whom they burn with Christ-like indignation. Are we talking to them at all? What have we to say?

The chances are that they will hear a little of what we say—like a set of noises off, a bit of background buzz. Here is a group of Christians talking to each other, they will think, arguing over matters that seem quite a long way from the plight of a child soldier in Northern Uganda or a mother with HIV/AIDS in Lesotho or a sweatshop worker or fisherman in South Asia. Some will react with contempt—what a parade of foolish anger and bigotry or self-importance, what a fuss over the 'rights' of the prosperous; some with indifference; some with real sorrow that we are not speaking to them and the world they know.

And for at least some of those—indeed, for many, I suspect—it is not that they are wanting us to abandon talking about our faith so as to talk about the world's crisis. They are wanting us to talk about Jesus and what Jesus has to say to this crisis. They know the economics and the politics, even the ethics; they don't need us for that. But they do want to hear a word from the one we call our saviour. Are we speaking to them about him?

II

I shall come back to what we might be saying about Jesus in a moment. Because some may object that I am trying to distract the meeting from addressing the immediate issue that needs resolution in our church, the questions around the limits of our diversity, the location of our authority and the rightness of certain developments in attitudes to sex. Let me say that I have no intention of making any distracting manoeuvre; I want only to point out where and when we are meeting and thus the way in which what we say may well be heard. I point this out also so that we can ourselves remember the background to our debates on these matters—since they are not just about morality and biblical authority but about perceptions of how power is used in church and world, how agendas are set. The political and economic world in which the prosperous set the agenda is the same world that is at work in the Church, so many feel, a world where discussions are held and priorities agreed and decisions taken in ways that exclude those who don't have the language or the leverage. North-South inequality is a real issue in this context, however hard it is for the 'North' to hear this.

But since some may challenge whether all this is about taking our eyes off the immediate problem, I shall say a few words about our present crisis—hoping that these reflections will in fact lead us back to the fundamental question of what we are saying and to whom. The debate over sexuality is a story that can be told more than one way. One story is this. The churches of the 'North' are tired and confused, losing evangelistic energy. For a variety of reasons, they have been trying to reclaim their credibility by accepting and seeking to domesticate the moral values of their culture, even though this is a culture that is practically defined by the rejection of the living God. A history of over-intellectual approaches to the Bible and the communication of the faith has led to a disregard of the Bible's call to transformation. The revolt against the plain meaning of Scripture's condemnation of same-sex activity is a symptom of this general malaise.

Another story is this. The churches of the North have been made aware of how much their life and work has been sustained in the past by insensitive and oppressive social patterns, with the Bible being used to justify great evils. Whether they like it or not, they inhabit a world where authority is regarded with much suspicion; it has to earn respect. In recent decades there has been a huge change in the general understanding of sexual activity. Can the gospel be heard in such a world if it seems to cling to ways of understanding sexuality that have no correspondence to what the most apparently responsible people in our culture believe? It is not enough, some have said, to stick to the words of the Bible; we have to go deeper and ask about the logic and direction of the Bible as a whole. And when we do that, we may find that it is not so impossible to reach a position that can be taken seriously in contemporary culture.

So for some we have a problem of the Church accepting a set of false premises, a wrong and unbiblical picture of human nature; for others a problem of communicating with human beings where they actually are, in terms they can grasp. Many issues are involved here, not only the presenting question about homosexuality. Perhaps the most difficult is how we make a moral assessment of modern culture in the developed world. And for many of us this is complicated. Modernity has brought great goods; yet in vital respects it has promoted a picture of humanity that is deeply flawed—individualistic, obsessed with rights and claims and uninterested in bonds of obligation or the need for sacrifice for the good of others: the world that has produced our current nightmare of international injustice. So the question is how far the concern for reaching an understanding with the world about sexual ethics is based on uncritical acceptance of the values of a culture like this.

I don't think that this question is quickly resolved. There are those who say, 'This is an issue of justice, comparable to the rights of black people in the Western world, or the rights of women. Our church must be inclusive of all, committed to liberation for all from the burden of prejudice and hatred'. There are those who say, 'The Bible is clear; there is no argument to be had'. Yet the latter often in practice find they are themselves interpreting Scripture more flexibly in other areas. And the former may have to recognise that there is a difference between campaigning for civil equality and declaring discipline or defining holiness for the Church of Christ, a difference between including all who come to Christ and being indifferent to how human lives are actually challenged and altered by him.

Very tentatively, I believe that this is how we should see our situation. Christian teaching about sex is not a set of isolated prohibitions; it is an integral part of what the Bible has to say about living in such a way that our lives communicate the character of God. Marriage has a unique place because it speaks of an absolute faithfulness, a covenant between radically different persons, male and female; and so it echoes the absolute covenant of God with his chosen, a covenant between radically different partners. Those who have criticised the blessing of same-sex partnerships have been trying, I think, to say that we cannot change what we say about marriage without seriously upsetting what you might call the ecology of our teaching, the balance of how we show and speak of God. They would say that blessing same-sex unions has this effect, and that without such blessing people living in such unions are at least in tension with the common language of the Church. And living in this tension is not a good basis for taking on the responsibilities of leadership, especially episcopal leadership, whatever latitude we allow to conscience and pastoral discretion in particular instances among our people. This, incidentally, is broadly the view of the authors of the 'St Andrew's Day Statement' of 1997, which remains a helpful reference point, managing to avoid a bitter politicising of the dispute. Its method deserves more imitation than it has received.

So there are two issues coming out of this that need patient study. What is the nature of a holy and Christ-like life for someone who has consistent homosexual desires? And what is the appropriate discipline to be applied to the personal life of the pastor in the Church? The last Lambeth Conference concluded that the reasons just outlined made it impossible to justify a change in existing practice and discipline; and the majority voice of the Communion holds firmly to this decision. It is possible to uphold this decision and still say that there are many unanswered questions in the theological picture just outlined, and that a full discussion of these needs a far more careful attention to how homosexual people see themselves and their relations. The Lambeth Resolution called for just this. It also condemned in clear terms, as did earlier Lambeth Conferences, the Windsor Report and the Primates' Dromantine statement, violent and bigoted language about homosexual people—and this cannot be repeated too often. It is possible to uphold Lambeth '98 and to oppose the shocking persecution of homosexuals in some countries, to defend measures that guarantee their civil liberties. The question is not about that level of acceptance, but about what the Church requires in its ordained leaders and what patterns of relationship it will explicitly recognise as unquestionably revealing of God. On these matters, the Church is not persuaded that change is right. And where there is a strong scriptural presumption against change, a long consensus of teaching in Christian history, and a widespread ecumenical agreement, it may well be thought that change would need an exceptionally strong critical mass to justify it.

That, I think, is where the Communion as a whole stands. That is why actions by some provinces have caused outrage and hurt. To invite, as does the Windsor document, those provinces to reconsider is not to say that there are no issues to be resolved, no prejudice to be repented of (because there unquestionably is much of this); it is not to reject the idea of an 'inclusive' Church or to canonise an unintelligent reading of the Bible. It is to say that actions taken in sensitive matters against the mind of the Church cannot go unchallenged while the Church's overall discernment is as it is without injuring the delicate fabric of relations within the Church and so compromising its character.

It is said that there are times when Christians must act prophetically, ahead of the consensus, and that this is such a time for some of our number. We should listen with respect to what motivates this conviction. But we also have to say that it is in the very nature of a would-be prophetic act that we do not yet know whether it is an act of true prophecy or an expression of human feeling only. To claim to act prophetically is to take a risk. It would be strange if we claimed the right to act in a risky way and then protested because that risky act was not universally endorsed by the Church straight away. If truth is put before unity—to use the language that is now common in discussing this—you must not be surprised if unity truly and acutely suffers.

III

But what is this teaching us about our character as a church? There is one deeply uncomfortable lesson to ponder, which is best expressed in shorthand by saying that we are in danger of falling into exactly the trap that St Paul lays for his readers in the beginning of his letter to the Romans. He has begun by defining 'God's way of righting wrong' (1.17), which is by faith; and he then gives a vivid account of the wrong that needs to be righted. Human beings are in revolt against the creator, exchanging (he repeats the word) what is natural for what is unnatural. He lists those things which for Jewish readers and sympathetic Gentiles would most obviously suggest revolt against God's will. People know what is natural yet invent alternatives—whether it is intercourse with the same sex, worship of material things, breaking promises or using their God-given skills of speech to spread evil reports. But, says Paul as he begins chapter 2, this is not about some distant 'they'; it is about 'you', his readers, then and now. *You* know what is natural but do not do it, and you pass judgment on others, so condemning yourself. Paul does not say that the sins he has listed in ch.1 are not sins at all; he simply points out that he has been egging us on in recognising the sins of others so as to expose our own deadly lack of self-knowledge. This is terrible, he says, isn't it? And this and this? And we eagerly say yes; so that he can turn on us and say, 'So now you know how terrible is the lack in your own heart of the recognition of *your* rebellion, whatever it is.'

'Whenever you erect yourself upon a pedestal, you do wrong; whenever you say 'I' or 'we' or 'it is so', you exchange the glory of the incorruptible for the image of the corruptible . . . By striding ahead of others, even though it be for their assistance, as though the secret of God were known to you, you manifest yourself ignorant of His secret . . . Even 'brokenness'; even the behaviour of the 'Biblical Man'—if these proceed from the adoption of a point of view, of a method, of a system, or of a particular kind of behaviour, by which men distinguish themselves from other men—are no more than the righteousness of men'. These are words from the greatest commentary on Romans in the modern era, Karl Barth's early masterpiece (pp. 56-57); and they should drive us to some very hard questions. When we call on others to repent, can we hear God calling us to recognise our own rebellion, whatever it is? If not, have we understood faith? We are always in danger of the easiest religious technique of all, the search for the scapegoat; Paul insists without any shadow of compromise upon our solidarity in rebellion against God, and so tells us that we shall not achieve peace and virtue by creating a community we believe to be pure. And these words are spoken both to the Jew and the Gentile, both to the prophetic radical and the loyal traditionalist. The prophet, says Barth, 'knows the catastrophe of the Church to be inevitable' and he knows also that there is no friendly lifeboat into which he can clamber and row clear of the imminent disaster' (336).

'We are all butchers pretending to be sacrificers. When we understand this, the *skandalon* that we had always managed to discharge upon some scapegoat becomes our own responsibility, a stone as unbearably heavy upon our hearts as Jesus himself upon the saint's shoulders in the Christopher legend'. Not Barth this time, but Rene Girard, the French philosopher (*A Theatre of Envy: William Shakespeare*, p. 341), once again paraphrasing Paul's central theme. When we have said all there is to say about our discipline and how we reinforce it, about the practical crises of deciding what degree of communion we can enjoy with some of our brothers and sisters—and no doubt these things have to be settled—we had better remember this level of solidarity with whoever it is we have separated from. The deepest spiritual problem is *not* resolved by separating ourselves from the sinner, whatever has to be done in the short term (and Paul of course exercises discipline robustly); God's word to us remains the challenge of Romans 2. And what grieves me about so much of our current debate is that I see few signs of awareness of this deeper level, and a good deal of the effort to 'distinguish ourselves' from each other, in Barth's terms, whether we call ourselves radicals or traditionalists. Even for me to say this in these terms opens me to the same charge—*I* am 'grieved' by the failings of *others*. I too have to accept that I am part of this failing or 'catastrophic' church.

So that we are driven back to the place where Paul started: *God's* way of righting wrong. Can we allow this present crisis to teach us something basic about the good news? Because of the cross of Jesus and his resurrection, we may trust that God has acted to overcome our rebellion and more, to bring us into a renewed world. In that world, we live in gratitude to God and in a pervasive sense of involvement in and responsibility for each other. We acknowledge that we shall none of us be healed alone. We confess that each of us is made poor and sick by the poverty and sickness of our brothers and sisters. So we do not shrink from fellow believers who have erred and reconstruct ourselves as a pure remnant; we admit that we are all now suffering. Likewise we need each other's life and hope, each other's positive experience—which is why the life of the churches of the 'North' would be so deprived if they separated from the life of the 'South' (and vice versa, since there is good news to be had in the North too).

So the answer to the question, 'What is this teaching us about our character and our life as a church?' seems to be this. If we have understood what Paul says about faith we shall understand that we all stand together in sin and need. When we acknowledge our sin and our need of God's grace, we also begin to see our need of each other in the Body of Christ. What we have to do is to work hard to see that—whatever else happens to us as a Communion—we don't lose the sense of our dependence upon grace, not on success or human virtue.

IV

Who are we talking to? What we have to say to the world—a world that is concentrating on what we too must address, the challenge to the world's wealthy—is just this: God calls human persons to a life in which poverty is everyone's poverty and wealth is everyone's wealth. This is how St Paul in II Corinthians describes Christian life. This is the life that makes the Church the way it is. This doesn't mean that the Church is an agency or a movement for political change. It simply *is* new life, new creation. When human life is renewed in this way, so that poverty and wealth are re-imagined like this, the result is something like the Church; and Christians will insist that only through the act and call of God is any of this ever possible, and only in conscious relation with Jesus is it fully realised. When we celebrate the Holy Communion, we are not awarding each other points for good behaviour or orthodox teaching but showing what it will be like in the Kingdom of Heaven—Christ's life given equally to all as all share in one bread; every communicant called by name to God's table, so that we have to look at every other communicant as God's beloved guest. Out of this flows the vision of a renewed world that keeps alive our hope and our anger at a system that treats so many as unwelcome in the world, nameless statistics, making no contribution to the life of others, dispensable.

Now the more we live and speak—this week and every week—as Church in this sense, the more we shall have to say to the real world. Christians should emphatically be campaigning for justice for the poor—but the Church is not a campaign. Sometimes I have been challenged to state 'my' vision or agenda for the Church. But we need real caution in using such language. The Church is the new creation, it is life and joy, it is the sacramental fellowship in which we share the ultimate purpose of God, made real for us now in our hearing the Word and sharing the Sacrament. What has this to do with anyone's 'agenda'? The Church is always greater than this, and the vision we most deeply need is the vision of new creation.

The Russian Orthodox theologian Alexander Schmemann distinguishes the Church from a sect very simply by saying that a sect is always transforming itself into an 'agency', committed to a succession of causes, and so 'easily mobilizes people *against* and not *for*', creating a typically modern sense of pervasive guilt for not being radical enough (*The Journals of Fr Alexander Schmemann,* p. 203). But the Church is just life in the new world which is the old one transfigured in Christ's light. The Church does not have to be defined by its activism, justified by its good causes. 'Dead end of the world with its "progress." Dead end of religion with its laws and therapeutics. Christ has taken us out of both these dead ends. The Church eternally celebrates it, and people as eternally reject it and are deaf to it' (p. 292). So if we ask what we need to be heard saying, perhaps it is this—that the new world is a reality here in the Church, not by our activism and our anxious struggles to keep up with an agenda, but in the gift of presence in the Eucharist and in every moment when we meet our Father through Jesus. The possibility of a world differently organised, where poverty and wealth, joy and suffering, are everyone's, where every person is not just a possessor of 'rights' but a precious and unique friend, is a fact among us. It may and will move us to action, to the fullest share in the struggle to change things; but the Church is not there in order to change things—if it were, it would disappear when injustices disappear, instead of being fully itself when injustices disappear. When we start defining the Church by campaigns and struggles, God help us; we have lost the one thing only the Church can give, the *fact* of God's future made real. That is why Schmemann can say that our biggest problem as a Church is that we have lost *joy* (p. 291); and this is not because *we* fail to feel or look happy enough, which really has nothing at all to do with anything and could be the most blasphemous and stupid of ideas, given the tragedy of the world. It is about the fact that joy exists, that God's blissful enjoyment of his own loving being is open to the world he has created. Will this week's proceedings suggest to anyone that joy exists and is offered us by God?

V

We can't guarantee anything at this point. We can't ignore the seriousness of what divides us. But if there is no easy solution, we can at least think about this simple suggestion. If it is difficult for us to stand together at the Lord's Table as we might wish, can we continue to be friends? Its sounds very weak; but I think it is actually of great significance. It is a way of saying that we do not know how to go on being visibly full brothers and sisters, that we can find no clear visible way of expressing any sense of being together in the Body of Christ. But this is the case already with a number of other Christian bodies, and several other Christian bodies view us in this way, notably the Roman Catholic and Orthodox Churches. Yet we maintain respect and often something more than respect. Friendship in Christ, it seems, is possible even when sacramental communion isn't.

Friendship is something that creates equality and mutuality, not a reward for finding equality or a way of intensifying existing mutuality. That's why we can talk—astonishingly, when you think about it—of friendship between us and God, the friendship Jesus speaks of. It is why St Teresa can write about friendship as the most radical mark of Christian community, as we find our common ground simply in God's invitation to us to be his friends. And so, alongside the wearisome and saddening divisions of the Church, common ground stubbornly persists.

What are we prepared to do to nourish this sort of friendship? My sense of where we now are is that this is not high on our agenda. The debates are so close to us, so emotionally involving, that we can hardly conceive of being friends in Christ. Yet it may be that many of our difficulties have their roots in a failure to give enough energy to friendship in the past across cultures and theologies. If we can correct this, we at least lay some foundations for the reconciliation that we shall have to go on praying for, though who knows how or when it will happen? Friendship in Christ is a willingness to share prayer, to listen without rancour to one another, to respect and even enjoy difference, to be patient with each other, not expecting quick healing of divisions but not walking out every time difference raises its head. It is best and most creative when it is linked with sacramental fellowship; but if that fellowship is hard or controversial, we need to remember from our ecumenical experience that this need not and should not mean a spirit of bitter contempt towards each other. It has taken the great churches of the world centuries to make this sort of friendship a routine matter, but, thank God, it is so now for the most part. Can we make a resolution that it will not take so long to confirm these bonds between us? Of course it is harder in some ways: direct conflict and even rivalry darkens the sky so much. But when we cannot witness together as fully as we long to do, this is something of real witness nonetheless. We can look at and listen to the language we use of each other and watch how easily we are ready to let it slip from proper and honest disagreement towards contempt and mutual exclusion. Yet as baptised believers, we still have something to offer each other; and the friendship of the baptised should remain, whatever else divides.

And it may be that as we work on what our friendship through Christ and in Christ's presence demands, we shall find ourselves able to step back from things that make our divisions deeper, ways of relating to each other with respect and integrity that stop any of us pushing a local agenda too far and too fast (and I am not speaking only of one issue or one locality here). We already see signs of this in some places. Who knows what might be possible for us with patience and—simply—love?

VI

While I have been speaking, on a conservative estimate, twelve hundred children have died of poverty-related causes. By the end of our meeting, the number will be some 300,000. I say this not to induce guilt, but to remind us of the world to which we have to speak, the world in which we have to make the good news sound credible. Too often, even when we speak of things we know we can't avoid speaking about—some of the things I have touched on here—we must surely realise that we sound as though we lived in a quite unreal world, where the passions that moved us made no sense to most people. We can remedy this not by ignoring the need for honest talk among ourselves but by resolutely bringing all our speaking back to the *fact* of what we have been given, which is finally so infinitely more important than our debates—the fact that God's future is real now because of the cross and resurrection of Jesus and the coming of the Holy Spirit. In that context, as we struggle to find ways of understanding and responding to each other that are in every way and every sense faithful to the gospel, let us at least try to remember what a church is and what the nature of a church requires of us—that it is not a pressure group of right or left. If we treat it like that, we fall under Barth's heavy strictures, acting as if the secret of God were ours. We shall not manifest to the world anything other than a religious version of the world's own quarrels and tensions. And if we are not showing the triumphant work of Christ, we are saying to the world that we have no real word to speak that the world doesn't know already; we are just echoing the anger or the compassion or the generosity of the human heart. There are worse things; but Christ did not die and rise for that.

If this time together can be a true experience of the Church, what may not be possible for us by God's grace? We shall have found again the sources from which we can confront the deep evils of our world with resolution and passion. We may be just a little less likely to seem an embarrassing, even insulting, set of noises off in a time when serious moral attention is on those evils and how they are to be ended. What, I wonder, do we imagine God saying to us at the end of things? Not, I think, 'Did you successfully negotiate the structural and ethical problems of the Anglican Communion?' but perhaps, 'Did you so live in the experience of the Church, the Body of my Son, that a tormented world saw the possibility of hope and of joy?' 'Did you focus afresh on the one task the Church *has* to perform—living Christ in such a way that his news, his call, is compelling?' The Orthodox Church at the Liturgy prays for 'a good answer before the terrible judgement seat of Christ'; we might well pray the same, as we pray for the wisdom to know how to speak to each other in this meeting so that we speak at the same time to the world Christ loves and longs for.

Chairman's Address

THE RIGHT REVEREND JOHN PATERSON
21 June 2005

Your Grace, Archbishop Rowan—President of the Anglican Consultative Council—members of the Primates' Standing Committee, Ecumenical Guests and Observers, and fellow members of the ACC, I greet you all warmly and sincerely as the Chair of the ACC. I have now been a member of this Council since ACC-8 met in 1990 in Cardiff, Wales. That means I have fifteen years of ACC experience on which to reflect, and I think that only two of the longer serving Staff members have anything like that number of memories, that number of meetings, that number of years. Little did I realise, however, when so narrowly elected to this post three years ago in Hong Kong, what the ensuing three years would hold. They have been eventful years, they have been difficult years, and now more than ever before, the Anglican Communion needs the solidarity and the sound common sense which the Anglican Consultative Council offers, to be brought to bear in its affairs.

As the Chair of the ACC I have been at times privileged, at times burdened, to be involved in events in and around the Anglican Communion, and I hold it to be my responsibility to report on some of those matters to this Thirteenth Meeting of the Council.

Inter-relationships of the Instruments of Communion

For a six year term from 1998 to 2004 I served as Primate and Presiding Bishop of the Anglican Church in Aotearoa, New Zealand, and Polynesia, which meant that I have experienced at first hand membership of three of the four 'Instruments of Unity' or as the Windsor Report suggests they might better be called 'Instruments of Communion'—namely the Lambeth Conference, the Primates' Meeting, and what I like to refer to as the most representative body in the Anglican Communion, the Anglican Consultative Council.

I make that point because my being part of the Primates' Meeting gave the ACC a presence and a voice within that Instrument which it otherwise does not have. For some years now the ACC has welcomed the presence of members of the Primates' Standing Committee at the full Council meeting, although they do not have a vote, but most certainly they have a voice and a presence which is helpful to all. Those Primates, however, do not have a mandate to represent the concerns of the ACC at the Primates' Meeting, and the recent request of the Primates concerning the participation of the representatives of ECUSA and the Anglican Church of Canada at this meeting of the ACC, throws up in sharp contrast that lack of reciprocal membership, and certainly the lack of at least an ACC voice at the Primates' Meeting. I shall return to this matter when touching on the Lambeth Commission and the Windsor Report.

The Reverend Canon John Peterson

When ACC-12 met in Hong Kong it was clear to many of us that it would be the last full meeting of the ACC that Canon John Peterson would serve in his role as Secretary General of the Anglican Communion. John, however, was adamant that he should not be thanked and farewelled at that point as he still had two years to serve in office, and I am sure that decision was correct. In 2004 his term of office, which had already been extended twice, came to an end. The Joint Standing Committee of the ACC and the Primates met in October 2004, and took the opportunity to thank John and Kirsten for the selfless manner in which they had served the Communion for more than ten years. Subsequently the Archbishop of Canterbury very generously hosted a Dinner at Lambeth Palace for the express purpose of thanking and farewelling John and Kirsten, and a number of people from around the Communion attended on that occasion to wish them well. At the October meeting I expressed the thanks of the ACC in particular, and we presented the Peterson family with some furniture, on your behalf, for their new home near Kanuga in the USA. The idea was that John might occasionally be able to literally 'put his feet up' but those of us who know John well, realise that to be a forlorn hope. He is now busily engaged as a Canon for Global Justice and Reconciliation at the National Cathedral in Washington, and I hope that this meeting of the ACC might send him an assurance of our gratitude and good wishes for his new ministry.

St Andrew's House, London

One of the matters which concerned John greatly during the latter years of his work as Secretary General was the cramped working conditions for the staff of the Anglican Communion Office in Partnership House, Waterloo Road, London. John examined a number of possible alternative locations, and then entered into negotiations with the Tavistock Trustees, the Community of St Andrew and the London Diocesan Order of Deaconesses for the use of St Andrew's House, Westbourne Park in London. We have been grateful for the helpful assistance of the Bishop of London in this matter, who is Visitor to the St Andrew's Trust, and the gracious encouragement of the remaining Sisters of the Order.

We do not own the building at Westbourne Park, but have entered into a long term leasing arrangement with the Tavistock Trustees at very advantageous rates. However, the building required extensive renovations before being able to be used for our purposes, and this proved to be a very expensive exercise. Despite the Joint Standing Committee placing a limit on the extent of the costs involved, there was a serious overrun. Canon John Peterson worked tirelessly to attract donors to assist with these costs, and many parts of the Church, including numerous individuals, responded generously. Details of the financing arrangements will be presented when we examine our accounts later in the meeting. We still have a way to go on clearing our indebtedness over St Andrew's House, but the positive side of the story is that we now have an attractive and welcoming base for the work of the Communion, and much improved working conditions for our staff. There are a small number of ensuite guest bedrooms for visitors to London to use, and Ann Quirke ensures an efficient and welcoming homely atmosphere as House Manager. The use of that form of accommodation reduces the costs of meetings, and also provides a small but useful income stream.

The Compass Rose Society

Another of the enduring legacies of John Peterson's tenure of office is his initiation and nurturing of the Compass Rose Society. The Society has already become a very important part of the Anglican Communion, and through the journeyings of groups of members to various parts of the Communion to learn and share in our global mission, and through its very generous sharing of resources and contributions to the Inter Anglican Budget, it has become a very valuable ally and partner in the work of the Communion. In particular, I am thankful that representatives of the Compass Rose Society have been able to observe meetings of the Inter Anglican Finance and Administration Committee, and in return the Secretary General and other representatives of the ACC have been consulted and included in various activities and meetings of the Society. That close interaction and good communication needs to continue, so that understanding, trust and co-operation will realise the enormous benefits to us of the existence in our midst of the Society.

The Compass Rose Society is particularly active in the United States of America, in Hong Kong and in Canada, and its current Chairman, Philip Poole has recently been episcopally ordained and we wish him well in his new ministry within the Diocese of Toronto.

The Compass Rose Society has worked hard to establish an Endowment Fund for the work of the Communion, at a time when the cohesiveness and commonality of the Communion itself has been called into question, and thus their work has been made much more difficult. The Society has also made great efforts to assist in the financing of the renovations to St Andrew's House, as a more immediate call upon their fund raising activities. The Council will have an opportunity to hear directly from representatives of the Compass Rose Society later in this meeting. At this point I simply wish to place on record our gratitude for their tremendous work amongst us, and on our behalf.

Appointment of the new Secretary General

During the year prior to the completion of Canon John Peterson's term of office, I consulted Archbishop Rowan as the President of the ACC, and brought a paper before the March 2004 meeting of the Joint Standing Committees of the ACC and the Primates, suggesting a process for us to follow in the matter of the appointment of a new Secretary General. The Joint Standing Committee duly appointed two Primates and two ACC representatives to form a Committee to conduct the search and interview process. Ms Fung-Yi Wong of Hong Kong and myself were the two ACC members, and The Most Reverends Dr Bernard Malango of Central Africa and Dr Barry Morgan of Wales were the two Primates. The process was very well administered by Chris Smith from Lambeth Palace, and I wish to record here my personal gratitude to Chris and the staff of Lambeth Palace for the expert help and advice given to the search and interview group. We are also indebted to the members of the search and interview group for a task done with care and prayer and great sensitivity.

The position was widely advertised, the Primates were invited to comment and nominate suitable persons, and we received a very healthy number of applications from several Provinces of the Communion. These were reduced to a short list and interviews took place at Lambeth Palace. We nominated three of the applicants for final interview and decision by the Archbishop of Canterbury who then announced that The Reverend Canon Kenneth Kearon, Director of the Irish School of Ecumenics in the Church of Ireland, had been duly appointed.

One of the factors we had to take into consideration was the need for close cooperation and constant communication with both the Archbishop of Canterbury and the staff of Lambeth Palace, particularly with regard to the Archbishop's critical role in the Anglican Communion. There has been noticeable improvement in these matters in recent years, and with the Secretary General being enabled to occupy a flat at Lambeth Palace, another step forward has been taken.

Kenneth was commissioned by Archbishop Rowan in the Chapel at St Andrew's House in January of this year, and in his first six months in the position has already arranged, administered and survived a meeting of the Primates, and now comes face to face with the whole ACC. I am sure the ACC will want to join me in welcoming Kenneth, ably supported by his wife Jennifer, to this aspect of his work, and to assure him that what Archbishop Robert Runcie once described as the 'bonds of affection' which have kept the Anglican Communion together, are elastic enough to enclose the Kearon family carefully, prayerfully and with equal affection.

The Most Reverend Dr RHA Eames

The Lambeth Commission on Communion was chaired by Dr Robin Eames, Primate of All Ireland. In fact one of the reasons it was called the 'Lambeth Commission' was because there had already been two entities known as the 'Eames Commission'. Archbishop Eames has also served the Communion as Chair of the Inter Anglican Finance and Administration Committee and retired from that position in 2004. We owe Archbishop Robin a tremendous debt of gratitude for his enormous contribution to the life and mission of the Anglican Communion. The Joint Standing Committee mounted an appeal for funds to assist in the completion and naming of an area in St Andrew's House in order to honour the senior Primate of the Communion, and I am pleased to report that some generous responses have come to hand, and that there is room for more!

The Lambeth Commission on Communion

For some decades now questions surrounding the issue of authority in the Anglican Communion have been addressed by some of our best minds. Since the last meeting of the Anglican Consultative Council, this matter has been given intense scrutiny because of differences over human sexuality in various parts of the Communion. A special meeting of the Primates of the Communion in October 2003 requested the Archbishop of Canterbury to appoint a Commission on Communion, and this was duly done. I was asked to serve as a member of the Commission, and I accepted the task as I believed it to be important that the ACC could have a voice there. Although the Commission was established at the request of the Primates' Meeting, the Mandate of the Commission is clear in that it was to report to the Archbishop in time for this meeting. I therefore wish to quote in full the Mandate of the Commission, so that it becomes written into the record of this meeting of ACC-13.

"The Archbishop of Canterbury requests the Commission:

1. *To examine and report to him by 30th September 2004, in preparation for the ensuing meetings of the Primates and the Anglican Consultative Council, on the legal and theological implications flowing from the decisions of the Episcopal Church (USA) to appoint a priest in a committed same-sex relationship as one of its bishops, and of the Diocese of New Westminster to authorise services for use in connection with same-sex unions, and specifically on the canonical understandings of communion, impaired and broken communion, and the ways in which provinces of the Anglican Communion may relate to one another in situations where the ecclesiastical authorities of one province feel unable to maintain the fullness of communion with another part of the Anglican Communion;*

2. *Within their report, to include practical recommendations (including reflection on emerging patterns of provision for episcopal oversight for those Anglicans within a particular jurisdiction, where full communion within a province is under threat) for maintaining the highest degree of communion that may be possible in the circumstances resulting from these decisions, both within and between the churches of the Anglican Communion;*

3. *Thereafter, as soon as practicable, and with particular reference to the issues raised in Section IV of the Report of the Lambeth Conference 1998, to make recommendations to the Primates and the Anglican Consultative Council, as to the exceptional circumstances and conditions under which, and the means by which, it would be appropriate for the Archbishop of Canterbury to exercise an extraordinary ministry of episcope (pastoral oversight), support and reconciliation with regard to the internal affairs of a province other than his own for the sake of maintaining communion with the said province and between the said province and the rest of the Anglican Communion;*

4. *In its deliberations, to take due account of the work already undertaken on issues of communion by the Lambeth Conferences of 1988 and 1998, as well as the views expressed by the Primates of the Anglican Communion in the communiques and pastoral letters arising from their meetings since 2000."*

The sixteen members of the Commission worked well together both in the course of the three actual meetings of the full Commission, and individually in coping with the enormous amount of reading, preparation and writing that was required. I wish to acknowledge the way in which our own ACC staff worked to support the Commission. The Reverend Terrie Robinson and Mrs Christine Codner worked long hours as Administrative Assistants. Canon Gregory Cameron brought his extraordinary skills and knowledge as the Secretary of the Commission, and our Legal Advisor, Canon John Rees contributed wit, wisdom and learning to the work.

The documents circulated prior to this ACC meeting contain excerpts from the Windsor Report, as the published report of the Commission has become known, which have a bearing on the ACC in particular. This full meeting of the Council will have to devise a way of dealing with the various recommendations about our own membership, about the frequency and timing of meetings of the Standing Committee to coincide with meetings of the Primates, about the *ex officio* membership of the Primates' Standing Committee on the ACC and our own Standing Committee and therefore trustees. Further, the recommendations about the Anglican Communion Office require urgent consideration, and of course all these matters have significant budgetary implications, as do the recent recommendations from the Primates' Meeting.

We are in fact experiencing changes in the inter-relationships of the Instruments of Unity as we speak. The Primates' Meeting met for years without making any recommendations or passing resolutions, with the one exception in the late 1980's expressing reservations about constitutional changes in the Anglican Church in Aotearoa, New Zealand and Polynesia. But that is now changing, and the 'enhanced responsibility' which successive Lambeth Conferences and the Inter Anglican Doctrinal and Theological Commission recommended is finally being taken on board. Yet the ACC needs to take care lest such enhanced responsibility on the part of one of the Instruments of Unity move from the art of gentle persuasion to what has been called 'institutional coercion'. The fact that the Lambeth Commission on Communion was asked to report to the Archbishop of Canterbury, whose office is itself one of the Instruments of Unity, 'in preparation for the ensuing meetings of the Primates and the Anglican Consultative Council' yet has found that the Instrument which happened to meet first, has taken steps to recommend that the Instrument which was to meet subsequently can only meet without its full membership, is at least slightly premature, if not coercive and somewhat punitive. A body which exists by means of a constitution agreed to by all the member churches of the Anglican Communion, and that is required by that constitution to be 'consultative' cannot consult fully or properly if all of its members are not sitting at the same table. It is surely not for one Instrument of Unity to disempower another?

Similarly there is a constitutional and legal difficulty in that both the Lambeth Conference and the Primates' Meeting are able to resolve that certain work be undertaken, that certain bodies be established, yet are not able to provide the funding necessary for those things to be accomplished. At present, the members of the ACC Standing Committee are constituted as the Trustees of the assets and funds of the Anglican Communion, and bear a degree of personal liability for the decisions on income and expenditure, but are not consulted when some of those decisions or recommendations are being made. The Anglican Communion Office and its staff are thus sometimes placed in invidious positions by being asked to ensure that these matters are administered, arranged or otherwise organised. Unless the Bishops who come to the Lambeth Conference, or the Primates who make those recommendations are able to stand behind them by ensuring an increased level of contributions to the Inter Anglican Budget, or the Primates' Standing Committee assumes responsibility as joint Trustees, then the present arrangements cannot hold. In this respect members will note that our papers contain a report from a small sub-committee established as a result of recommendations from both ACC-11 and ACC-12 on a new Constitution and structure which will go some way towards meeting the concerns I have identified. However, that work was largely completed before the publication of the Windsor Report, and we will have to take care that the recommendations in that Report are considered before a revised structure and constitutional framework are put in place. Since writing the first draft of this Address, the Joint Standing Committee of the Primates and the ACC has met here in Nottingham, and spent some very useful time in considering these matters. As a result, the recommendations of the Windsor Report have now been incorporated in the constitutional amendments which the ACC has already been able to consider, particularly with regard to the membership of the Standing Committee, and the inclusion of the Primates as members of the ACC itself.

The Anglican Consultative Council as an Instrument of Unity

Those who care deeply about their membership of the Anglican Communion, this world-wide faith community characterised since the 1963 Toronto Congress by mutual responsibility and interdependence and held together by little more than those 'bonds of affection' will have been concerned at the somewhat dismissive comments that have abounded in recent times about the effectiveness of this body, and particularly by some of those voices which have been raised in support of an enhanced role to be played by the Primates' Meeting.

A careful reading of the papers already circulated for ACC members, and those reports still to come before us, will reveal a consensus of concern and care for our continuing cohesiveness as a Communion. And it is not only present amongst those Commissions and Networks which report to the Consultative Council. The meeting last year of the Provincial Secretaries and Treasurers of the Anglican Communion clearly stated a strong desire for the Anglican Communion to remain together and united. The Network reports seem to me to share an underlying concern that the important and often pioneering work that they undertake is given strength and coherency and significance because of the international nature of our constituency.

A considered look through the expanded description of the 'Object' of the ACC in the Report of the Constitutional Review sub-committee identifies our role clearly. And it is not that the ACC is important because we have identified its role in that manner, but rather that those important elements of tasks and responsibilities do not belong anywhere else. A worldwide Communion that consists of 39 autonomous Member Churches plus a number of associated dioceses and areas which takes our international membership to perhaps 43, has to have some way of working together and relating to each other and to other major Christian Churches and a host of other organisations.

The ACC gives voice and hope and strength and dignity to those 80 million or more Anglicans who say they belong to us, and look to us to represent them, but who are not themselves Primates, Archbishops, Bishops, Priests, Deacons or ACC members. They are the *laos*, they are the people of God, and they are our people, and they are importantly and impressively represented in the ACC, and I believe they want us to stay together, to live with difference, and not have difference forced upon them. Many Anglicans know what it is to have been colonised, and have no wish to repeat that experience in a new colonising of the mind and heart. Let ACC-13 declare to our watching and rather anxious church that our Communion is indeed a living Communion, that God lives, that God loves, and that we can continue to worship and serve God from our many different perspectives, while still proudly calling ourselves 'Anglicans'.

My personal hope is that this ACC-13 can express sufficient confidence in our 'Living Communion' that we can mark Anglican Communion Sunday in every parish, in every ministry unit, in every diocese, in every Province with a real celebration of our unity, and by remitting to the Anglican Communion Office a suitable donation of whatever size, for the express purpose of endowing our Communion, of ensuring our future.

Conclusion

It is an honour to serve the Communion as Chair of the ACC. I look forward to three or might it be four more years working with the Standing Committee, with the Archbishop of Canterbury, and with the Primates' Standing Committee. More immediately I look forward to the work of ACC-13 with members both new and experienced, and to what our time together in Nottingham might mean for the unity and strength of the Anglican Communion.

Address on the Millennium Development Goals

THE RT HON HILARY BENN, MEMBER OF PARLIAMENT
Wednesday 22 June 2005

Good morning.

What an honour to be asked to speak to you today on such an important subject. Because making poverty history is the moral issue of our generation.

As the Archbishop of Canterbury said just two days ago: *"Grief, anger and frustration at the injustice of the world's trade systems and at the sluggishness of wealthy nations in addressing the menace of systematic environmental degradation is boiling over"*.

St Paul reminds us of the importance of "Faith, hope and charity".

Faith, hope and charity are cornerstones in the lives of the people, whom I am lucky enough to meet—day in and day out, in rich countries and poor, fighting to rid this world of poverty. It is Faith which nourishes the many Christian, Jewish, Muslim and Hindu groups with whom the Department for International Development works. It was Charity in its fullest expression when people all over the world responded to the Boxing Day Asian Tsunami. They saw that in an increasingly globalised and inter-dependent world, there is a moral imperative to help our fellow human beings. People whose names and faces we may not know, but whose humanity we share. But it is Hope that inspires us to create a better world. This is no distant hope: it's well within our grasp. We can make poverty history.

No less than 125 million people have been lifted out of poverty in the last decade.

- Average life expectancy in developing countries has increased from 46 years to 64 in the last generation.

- Thirty years ago, one in five children in the world died before their fifth birthday. Now, the figure is one in ten.

- Both the adult literacy rate and the proportion of people in developing countries with access to safe water have increased by 75% in the last 20 years.

But it's not enough, we need to do more because:

- One in five of the world's population are still living on less than $1 a day.

- 1.1 billion people still lack access to safe drinking water,

- 104 million children are not enrolled in school and,

- Some 10 million children die each year before their fifth birthday, largely from preventable diseases.

The fight against poverty must remain the moral imperative for us all.

Faith groups have a unique and important role in making poverty history. You don't need me to tell you that churches and other faith groups are often poor people's most trusted institutions. They are often the first to which the poor turn in times of need and crisis, and to which they give in times of plenty. As a result you are closely embedded and committed to local communities.

Faith groups provide crucial services to the poor. They often run the only schools and health clinics in rural communities. In Sub-Saharan African, faith groups provide more than 50% of all health and education services. You can and do reach poor people largely untouched by other institutions. In the Democratic Republic of the Congo, for instance, we are supporting CAFOD to work with the Catholic Church. This is bringing local voices into the process of national reconciliation across the Great Lakes region. One result is that every single parish in the country will carry out a programme of education about human rights. In Pakistan and Yemen, we have also seen Islamic schools starting to go well beyond their religious roles, in teaching literacy and numeracy.

As you all know, this year, 2005, offers a unique opportunity to make real gains that improve the lives of millions of poor people. The British government has a huge responsibility, through our Presidencies of the G8 and the EU and at the Millennium Review Summit in September when it will represent the EU.

The UK is taking a lead by calling on the international community to take action on:

- more and better aid,

- debt relief, and

- trade justice.

More aid. Donors need to give more aid. Without a significant increase in aid, the MDG targets will not be met. We need to double the current aid flows from $50 to $100 billion a year to meet the MDGs. We in the UK are doing just that. On present plans, the UK will meet the UN target of providing 0.7% of our national income as aid by 2013. And I'm delighted that the EU agreed on 24 May to meet this target by 2015. It also agreed to double aid flows by 2010 to over £45 billion. As you will have seen daily on the news we are pressing the G8 to support a doubling of aid to Africa. The International Finance Facility—a proposal initiated by the UK Chancellor Gordon Brown—is designed to do this: to double aid now, when poor countries need it most.

And aid works. So it was spectacularly unhelpful for NGOs like Christian Aid to publish reports saying that UK aid had led to the suicide of Indian farmers, or that 70% of aid was phantom.

Aid does work. £10 million of UK money given to the government of Kenya in 2002 making free primary schooling possible for all. No less than 1.2 million additional children turned up to enroll during the school year, and in so doing transformed their possibilities for a better life. After all, the best possible start that life can offer—apart from the love of our families— is an education.

Better Aid. Money alone is not enough. We need better aid. We must enable countries to take the lead in their own development.

Aid works if it is spent in countries where there is a commitment to poverty reduction and sound economic management. Donors have a responsibility to ensure that aid is allocated to countries that need it most, and who can use it best. Partner countries have a responsibility to spend aid monies wisely. And donors need to co-ordinate their aid. Mozambique is a good example of donors working together. Twelve bilateral donors plus the EC and World Bank are providing general budget support to back up the Government's own poverty reduction plan.

Debt. There are three key areas of work on debt:

- Major progress has already been made on the first. A couple of weeks ago, a historic debt deal was agreed by the G8 Finance Ministers to cancel up to $55 billion worth of debt stock for up to 38 countries.

- Secondly, we are now working hard to ensure that non G8 donors also join.

- Finally, the UK still remains committed to debt relief through full and generous implementation of the **Heavily Indebted Poor Countries (HIPC) Initiative.** $70 billion of debt relief has already been agreed for 27 countries so far.

Trade. Aid and debt relief are only part of the answer. Oxfam estimates that an increase in Africa's share of world exports of just 1% would be worth five times as much as the continent's share of aid and debt relief. We need to reform the international trading system.

Too many products from developing countries are still denied access to the rich world's markets. These barriers must be removed and quickly. Agricultural trade is key for many developing countries. In 2000, support to farmers in the EU, US and Japan was $250 billion. That's five times the amount spent on aid. The key to this is the World Trade Organisation (WTO) talks in December. These talks could produce annual global benefits of up to $600 billion. This may sound very dry but in human terms, it means 144 million people lifted out of poverty. We recognise that poor countries need to manage their trade liberalisation to fit with their poverty goals.

Developing countries need assistance to make sure they maximise the gains and, for some, deal with the costs in adjusting to more open trade patterns.

How the churches can help. 2005 is unique year of opportunity in the fight to eliminate poverty. We are already seeing the makings of a new compact between the rich countries and the poor. It took faith to persuade us that slavery was an unimaginable evil, that had to be stopped and yet they succeeded. Perhaps ending poverty sounds about as distant a goal today as did ending slavery, but we can do it. Today, it is the same hope that drives the churches and the global movement to make poverty history. It's that belief and action that has made such a difference.

The historic G8 debt deal and the EU commitment to meet the UN target of 0.7% is evidence that we can really change things. However this campaigning needs to be based on solid evidence and coherent positions. People joining together to demand change can and do make a real difference. Campaigning works. Aid works. Let 2005 be the turning point for us all. Let it be the year when we put into action all our good words and promises. Let's together make poverty history!

Secretary General's Address

THE REVEREND CANON KENNETH KEARON
Friday 24 June 2005

As most of you will realise it is less than six months since I took up this position of Secretary General, so it is invidious for me to attempt to review the activities of the Anglican Communion Office for the last three years since I was not in post for most of them, and I certainly don't wish to find myself reporting on the work of my predecessor. However, I must begin by paying a very warm tribute to my predecessor Canon John Peterson. I am only the fourth Secretary General and each Secretary General in turn has made a very different and distinctive contribution to the life of our Communion, and none more so than Canon John Peterson. Most of you will know, far better than I do, the contribution he has made to the life of our Communion over his ten years of ministry with us. It falls to me, however, simply to pay tribute to those ten years work, to thank him on behalf of us all, for all that he has done for us and to wish him every blessing in his new sphere of ministry.

One, and only one, of his lasting achievements for the Anglican Communion is the transformation of St. Andrew's House into the modern and convenient headquarters for the Anglican Communion Office. Those of you who have visited the building, and I hope all of you will eventually have the opportunity to visit, will know what a useful, attractive and excellent working environment it is for all of us who work there, and also a wonderful facility for the many, many meetings that take place there, and of course the accommodation aspect of it is an added bonus to our work there. It is one of the many lasting benefits which John Peterson will leave to the Communion. We should all acknowledge his contribution to that and what a wonderful facility it is for us all.

In paying tribute to John Peterson and his work, I would also like to thank him for the welcome he gave me from the time of the announcement of my appointment, and the encouragement and help he has given me in transition, but I would also like to thank our Chairman, Bishop John Paterson, for the way in which he has overseen the process of the appointment of a new Secretary General and also the work he has done in easing me into the post, particularly in the early stages. I am very grateful. I would also like to pay tribute to our own staff at the Anglican Communion Office for the way in which they have patiently encouraged and eased me in to the post, corrected my early mistakes and hid their embarrassment when I made some fairly obvious blunders in the early stages. I am grateful to them, they are a hard working staff and they are deeply committed to serving the life of our Communion. I would also like to pay tribute to you, Archbishop Rowan for the way in which you have welcomed me into this new post and through your advice and through our many meetings you have helped me to understand the role of Secretary General as it relates to the Communion today. I am also grateful to your staff at Lambeth Palace and particularly the Chief of Staff, Mr Chris Smith for the way in which he has opened his resources to me and to our office and the way in which he has worked tirelessly to enable a good relationship to exist between our two offices for the sake of the Communion and for the sake of the Church as a whole. I am also grateful to the Reverend Andrew Norman for his work in this area. The appointment of Canon Gregory Cameron, Director of Ecumenical Affairs to the additional responsibility of Deputy Secretary General was a welcome move, and has served to strengthen the structures within the office. I am grateful to him for his personal support of me.

I wasn't very long in post before I realised that two very, very large and important meetings were looming on the horizon. The first one was the Primates in Dromantine in Northern Ireland last February. The second one, of course, is this meeting of the Anglican Consultative Council. Each of those meetings are an enormous logistical effort in their own right. They are extraordinarily taxing on the resources of a very small staff at St Andrew's House. In both cases we were enormously helped by support from the local church and the way in which the local church welcomed us and supported us on the ground in very practical ways. In one case it was the Church of Ireland and particularly the work of Archbishop Eames and his office and here at the Anglican Consultative Council here meeting in Nottingham we are tremendously supported by the local parishes and the local Diocese. Mention of meetings of course, calls to mind the fact that in the last few weeks the Lambeth Conference Manager has taken up her office. I very much welcome Sue Parks, who is originally from Australia, as the new Lambeth Conference Manager. I do assure her of the support, not only of myself, but of the whole Anglican Communion Office as she takes responsibility for the organisation of what is now a huge logistical exercise of the Lambeth Conference of 2008.

I have already mentioned the Primates Meeting. That was an extraordinary important meeting in the life of our Communion. There were huge concerns beforehand, particularly expressed in the various media about how the issues before us would be handled, and they certainly were difficult days for our Communion. But remarkably, and I think this must be remarked on, the Primates did end up with a unanimous communiqué and in so doing the unity of our Communion took a major step forward. It is not my place here to dwell upon the content of that meeting or on the Communiqué but simply to remark on a valuable lesson that we can all learn from that event. The lesson is that when we as Anglicans meet together in a context of prayer and bible study, and mutual respect it is possible for us to discern a way forward together. The Primates Meeting demonstrated that and I believe that that way of handling issues is open to all of our meetings as Anglicans.

We are a community of faith, we belong to local parishes, we belong to dioceses, we belong to provinces, we belong to a world-wide Anglican Communion. In our various communities we are not just simply groups of individuals, we believe that as Christians our exploration of the Christian faith is taken on more effectively when we meet together. Either when we meet together on a Sunday morning for worship and prayer or when we meet together in a meeting which is supported by prayer and worship. Such was the Primates Meeting, such is the Anglican Consultative Council, such will be the Lambeth Conference. We meet here as Christians not in isolation, not just simply a meeting that could happen anywhere, but in arriving here in Nottingham we are entering into the life of the local Christian community who are supporting us by their practical actions as well as by their prayers. I am very grateful to the local vicar here, The Revd Andrew Deuchar, and his parishioners and many people from the Diocese of Southwell for their practical support in the organisation of this event and in the day to day management of it which you can see all around you.

As a community of faith we recognise that our partners in that community are not just simply our fellow Anglicans, the presence of our ecumenical partners and their representatives here at our meeting of the Council is a tangible sign of the maturity of our ecumenical relations today. I very much welcome the presence of significant figures from our fellow Christians in our other communities among us. They are very, very welcome among us, but they do reflect and express the modern reality of ecumenical relations; the fact that as Christians we need one another in our various Christian traditions to enrich and to support one another in good times and in bad.

So we meet together as Christians, as Anglicans, we meet as a community of faith and recognising the enrichment of faith that comes from our engagement with each other. The fact is we need each other for our growth in the faith. That's what the word interdependence really means: the word that is used in the Windsor Report but also has been used within Anglicanism for very, very many decades now. Interdependence is not just a desirable feature of Anglicanism, it is about sharing, it is about depending on our fellow Christians in the various communities of faith so that together we can work together, we can come together to share and enrich our faith.

As partners in a community of faith we need to ensure that we genuinely communicate with one another.

Many years ago I worked as a university chaplain, we had decided that we would have a campaign to raise the profile of the Bible within the university community; as you can imagine we had the usual events, exhibitions, talks, displays and so on, and at the heart of all of that we decided that we would have what we called a Bible reading marathon, in other words in a public place, in the chapel, which was right in the middle of the university we would advertise the fact that we were going to read the Bible cover to cover. Let the scriptures simply stand by themselves to be heard by others. Of course you can't simply have a reading marathon, the Bible must be heard as well as read, so the role of listeners became very important in our Bible reading marathon. It was amazing how the numbers of listeners grew, even during the night. There were always people there to listen, to hear and in fact the hearing became more important than the reading.

Our communications department within the Communion must fit into this model of communications. The Communications Department of our Office is about communicating from one part of the Communion to another and also from the Communion to the wider Christian community and to the wider world. Its role is to enable us not just to speak to one another, but to hear what is happening in other parts of the Communion and it must serve that role through the use of its website, through the printed media, Anglican World, and so on. Need for communications is rooted in our need to share not just though lectures and sermons, not simply to communicate, but to listen to each other.

I remember many years ago taking part in a seminar with that well known missionary bishop and writer on evangelism, Bishop Leslie Newbigin. During the seminar Bishop Newbigin was exploring the meaning of the word evangelism and he was particularly rooting it in a study of the great commission in St Matthew's Gospel: "Go forth into all the world and preach". He was exploring the meaning of the word "preach". The command that Jesus gave to his disciples, he said, was to preach the Gospel, not to convert people. The Church is called to preach, the work of conversion is the work of the Holy Spirit. Conversion isn't just an experience for those who are new to the faith, conversion is also an ongoing experience for us all. Finding and exploring ways of enabling the Gospel to be preached, to be heard and to enable the ongoing work of conversion both within the life of the community of faith and outside of it is the work of IASACOME— Inter-Anglican Standing Committee on Mission and Evangelism. That body is seeking to further the work of evangelism in partnership with the various Mission Agencies of our Communion.

Interdependence, ecumenism, communication and evangelism. These are the three central areas of work in our office. Each area looks, attends and seeks to engage with others within or on behalf of the Communion. When Christians are asked to explain what they mean by truth they point, not to a set of propositions, not to a series of statements, but they point instead to a person, to a figure hanging on a cross. That's Christian truth, that is where truth lies, and through that cross, Christians believe that we are enabled to enter into a relationship with God as Father, Son and Holy Spirit. We are also called to model the relationship which exists within the Godhead in the relationships we have with each other. Ecumenism, communication and evangelism are about enabling our relationships one with another and in the end of the day they are the ideals that the Anglican Communion Office tries to hold to.

Let me now make a few brief comments about the Windsor Report. We have made some important decisions this week about the Windsor Process, the setting up of the listening process, in the long term is going to be one of the most important things we have done this week. The Primates Meeting was a private meeting, but I share with you one thing that was said on a number of occasions during that meeting. In the current difficulties in our Communion we must remember, all of us, that there is integrity on both sides of this debate. There is integrity on both sides of this debate. If we don't recognise that fact then there is no point in having a listening process, because the listening simply won't happen if one side is already deaf to what the other has to share. So let us, as we go forward in this process remember that basic statement, there is integrity on both sides.

A second comment I would like to make, which is if you like almost a side issue from the Windsor Report. The Windsor Report reported to the Archbishop of Canterbury in October 2004 and to the Joint Standing Committee of the Primates and of the ACC. Immediately after that there began a brief but intensive consultative process which was reported to the Primates Meeting in February 2005. That is a very brief period for a consultative process, but during that time all of the Provinces of our Communion were contacted and almost all of them responded with a responsible analysis of the Windsor Report. That consultative process whereby each Province decided for itself what body within its structure was the most appropriate body to deal with this issue was an important discovery within Anglicanism. I believe that in so doing we discovered a consultative process within our Communion which is effective and has integrity within it. I believe that we should use that consultative process more often as we work to develop systems of communication within the Communion.

A third point which I think we are in danger of overlooking. The Windsor Report made a number of structural recommendations for changes within the Communion: changes to the role of the Archbishop of Canterbury; changes to the Primates Meeting; changes to the ACC and also a proposal for a covenant within the Communion. On some issues we have taken decisive steps forward at this meeting. The response to other proposals through that consultative process has been uneven, and I sense that many parts of our Communion are decidedly lukewarm to some of these proposals. However, behind all of this is the fact that the Windsor Report has uncovered a weakness in our ecclesiology at the international level. I believe we have a strong and clear ecclesiology within each of our Provinces, but we do run into grave difficulties as a Communion when we try to work at the level above that of a Province. Other Christian traditions have dealt with this by means of some form of universal jurisdiction, but I think there is a great unwillingness among Anglicans to develop any form of universal jurisdiction. However, in rejecting some of the practical proposals for structural reorganisation within the Windsor Report, we mustn't lose sight of the big picture, that is that we do have this weakness in our ecclesiology and we must address it if we are not to go from crisis to crisis. These are difficult times for our Communion, I think you all realise that that is an understatement, but we have taken important steps to maintain and develop and strengthen our Communion. Like the grit which gets into an oyster shell and that ultimately becomes a pearl, we do have the opportunity to turn our current difficulties into lasting benefits provided there is respect on all sides.

Like many of you here, this is my first ACC meeting. I have met and spoken to many of the extraordinarily talented people sitting here before me. We need to harness these resources for the well being of our Communion.

I believe we have within the ACC the potential for a global body capable of guiding our Communion through difficult waters. I support warmly the decision to consider involving Primates in our body. They are a strong and influential body, and will strengthen the ACC. But how do we at the same time, enable and strengthen the voice of clergy and laity who are already members? If Primates do join us, it's already been said that they will be a powerful voice among us. But the existing members, those of you in front of me, will be a powerful voice to the Primates as well. Together, both will represent a very powerful and representative voice to the Communion as a whole.

I am honoured to have been called to serve the Communion in this post. I look forward, with God's will, to fulfilling the mandate I have been given. I thank you all for your prayers, support and encouragement.

Sermon at the Diocesan Celebration

ARCHBISHOP OF CANTERBURY
Sunday 26 June 2005

Let me begin by giving you a summary of the sermon that I'm not going to preach. It's very tempting when we hear the New Testament lesson today to use it as a way of thinking about the Church including strangers. The Church moves from one ethnic group to another and proves that it is adaptable for new people. The Church is always changing itself so as to be a welcoming place for the stranger, the unfamiliar neighbour. And that wouldn't be a bad sermon, but I have a suspicion that it's not quite what the Acts of the Apostles wants us to think about. I have a suspicion that the Acts of the Apostles is here telling us something rather deeper and more central about our faith.

The relation between Jews and Gentiles in the Acts is not simply that of one racial group to another. As the story is presented to us, it's a story about a great crisis over what faith really is, and what salvation really is. The strict believers who challenge Paul and Barnabas and have no small dissension and debate with them—one of Luke's wonderfully tactful phrases— those strict believers are in effect saying it is possible to know that you are in the favour of God. Be circumcised, keep the law, and when you are alone in the silence of your room, you will know where to turn to be sure; you will know what your record is. You will know that you have the signs that make you acceptable to God. To which Paul and Barnabas, and the Church ever since have replied, 'There is no sign by which you can tell in and of yourself that you are acceptable to God. There is nothing about you that guarantees love, salvation, healing, and peace. But there is everything about God in Jesus Christ that assures you, and so if you want to know where your certainty lies, look to God, not to yourself.' Don't tick off the conditions that might possible make God love you, scoring highly, perhaps, and thinking, 'So God must love me after all.' Begin rather by looking into the face of the love of God in Jesus Christ, and then, as it were, out of your bewilderment and your speechlessness at that love, thinking, 'And yes, I am loved.' Not just one episode, you see, in the history of the Church, but almost another Pentecost.

About half way through the Acts of the Apostles, here comes this great event in which the Church together, in a difficult and painful discernment, comes to say, 'It is not in us, but in God, that our security lies, because we cannot assure ourselves, and we cannot heal ourselves, and we cannot feed ourselves. We can only come to God empty-handed, looking into his face, depending absolutely on Him.' We believe that we will be saved through the grace of the Lord Jesus, just as they will. The grace of the Lord Jesus, which is what the Gospel story is about today. Once again, the strict make their challenge. What is Jesus doing in the company of tax collectors and sinners? Jesus' reply is wonderfully ironic. 'If you don't think you need me,' he says to the strict believers, 'feel free to go.' And we might think he looks each one of them in the eye and says, 'If you don't think you need, you can go.' And there's our challenge. As Christ looks at each one of us, which of us is able to say, 'All right, I don't need you, I'll go.' 'Those who are well have no need of a physician.' So says Jesus to his critics and to us. 'So if you are healthy, you don't need me. If you are whole, at peace with yourself, satisfied in your skin, happy in the world, you don't need me.' And again, which of us will say, 'I am whole. I have finished my work. I am at peace in the world.'

The difficulty of the Gospel is perhaps this: that it gives comfort neither to the legalist nor to the libertine. It doesn't say, 'You can win the grace of God by being good', and it doesn't say, 'The grace of God makes no difference to you.' It sweeps away the cobwebs and the veils, and makes us face a Jesus who says, 'So, do you need me or not? Are you hungry? Are you sick? Is your work, your life unfinished? Because, if you are whole and not hungry, and finished, go.'

Here we are then, this morning, the people who have not found the nerve to walk away. And is that perhaps the best definition we could have of the Church? We are the people who have not had the nerve to walk away; who have not had the nerve to say in the face of Jesus, 'All right, I'm healthy, I'm not hungry. I've finished, I've done.' We have, thank God, not found it in us to lie to that extent. For all the lies we tell ourselves day after day, that fundamental lie has been impossible for us. Thank God. We're here as hungry people, we are here because we cannot heal and complete ourselves; we're here to eat together at the table of the Lord, as he sits at dinner in this house, and is surrounded by these disreputable, unfinished, unhealthy, hungry, sinful, but at the end of the day almost honest people, gathered with him to find renewal, to be converted, and to change. Because the hard secret of our humanity is that while the body has the capacity to heal itself, the soul it seems doesn't. The soul can only be loved into life— and love is always something that we cannot generate out of our own insides—where we have to come with hands and hearts open to receive.

The people who didn't have the nerve to walk away. And because they didn't have the nerve to walk away, the people who not always in an easy or welcome way, find they have more in common than they might have thought. What do we all have in common this morning in this church? We are hungry for God's love, God's truth, and God's healing, and we have recognised that we cannot heal our own spirits, but must come to one another and to God for that healing. Hungry together, reaching out our empty hands together, we discover something about our humanity that we could in no other way discover, and we as an Anglican Communion, a world-wide fellowship of believers, we are saying that from country to country and language to language, and culture to culture, there is always the hunger, there is always the need for love, and at that level our human solidarity is revealed to us as it is in no other way.

Just theology? Just pulpit talk? No. No, in a world where human solidarity doesn't seem so obvious. Next weekend, and the week after that, the wealthy nations of the world will be considering what particular crumbs from their table might fall somewhere in the direction of the needy of the world. In a world where such a meeting is even necessary, we need witnesses to solidarity. We need to remember that those who starve and struggle in terrible violence and deprivation are us, not them—part of one human community, loved equally with the passion of God, invited equally to the table of Jesus Christ. We are part of the civilisation which has somehow got used to the idea that what is good for us in the wealthy part of the world has no connection with what is good for anyone else. We have somehow got used to this, and we as Christians are all too seldom pained and angered enough by this. I spoke during the meeting last week of the vision of the Church as that of a community where the poverty of one is the poverty of all, where the wealth of one is the wealth of all. Where because we recognise our solidarity as human beings, our active compassion for one another is kindled. And in a civilisation that is deeply sick, we need the Body of Christ to be alive and well. And that too is what we celebrate this morning. Invited into the Body of Christ, into those who recognise together their need and their hunger, we proclaim to the world that it is God's purpose that we should live with and for each other; that it is God's purpose that each of us here to be a gift to the neighbour of whatever background, whatever race. 'Those who are well have no need of a physician, but those who are sick.' And Jesus says to us, not only as individuals, but as a whole civilisation here in the northern world, the western world, 'So, you don't need me; so you are well?' God help us if we try to turn away from that challenge.

So our being together here, at the table of the Lord, recognising that it is not about us but about Him, that our security lies not in the signs of our virtue and achievement, but in God's generosity—being here on that basis is itself a mark of hope. And those of us who care about our Anglican Communion worldwide—its unity, its life, and its peace—care for it not in order to keep an ecclesiastical institution more or less upright, propping it up with more and more crumbling pillars and struts and buttresses. We care about it because we are part of the Body of Christ and the world needs the Body of Christ. It is hungry for truth and for love. We are here to be fed with that truth and that love in the body and the blood of the Lord in His Holy Sacrament. As we open our hands to receive that gift, so we open them to one another and to the world. We do not have the nerve to walk away. So much the better for us. The appetite for truth is still alive. So much the better for us. May truth and love, the truth and love of Jesus as he sits with sinners, be the motive power of all we do and say in our meetings as Church, in our witness to the world, in our protest against division and violence and hunger. May we say to the whole world that we believe that we will be save through the grace of the Lord Jesus, just as they will.

Amen.

© Rowan D. Williams 2005

Closing Address

THE RIGHT REVEREND DR N.T. WRIGHT
28 June 2005

Shipwreck and Kingdom:
Acts and the Anglican Communion

When I heard that you had been studying Acts in your time together, my mind went, for some reason, to acronyms. I imagined myself coming to address the Anglican Communion Theological Society, or perhaps the Anglican Council for Tea and Sympathy, which goodness knows you may be in need of by this stage of your meeting. And I have finally come up with an answer to a question which Archbishop Rowan asked me a year or two ago, whether there might be an organisation whose acronym would be ACRONYM: I propose that we set up the Anglican Communion Renewal Of New Youth Ministries—and in fact I think that's just what we need right now, certainly where I come from. But actually I was delighted when I heard that you had been mulling over Acts, because I've been doing that as well; and I believe there are fresh things to be heard from within this great book, which comprises roughly one-eighth of the whole New Testament and yet is often neglected as we analyse the gospels and squabble over Paul.

Acts, in its own way, is all about what books such as Daniel and Revelation, in their very different ways, are all about: the kingdoms of the world and the kingdom of God. And we who live in the swirling seas of world history, with all kinds of political winds blowing this way and that, could do worse than chart our own course by that which Luke marks out as he tells his tale, in which he is not simply telling us a story for antiquarian interest but in order to sketch a model of the calling of the church. In fact, as I shall point out later, the fact that his tale takes his hero right into the swirling seas and stormy winds is enormously significant both for his story and for ours—not least since that is the route by which Paul finally arrives in Rome, to announce under the very nose of Caesar himself that God is King and that Jesus is Lord. If we can get our heads around the twin themes of shipwreck and kingdom, and the way they actually go together, we may be able not only to understand something of what Luke was trying to say but also something of what our living and loving God may be saying to us today, this week, at this moment in the history of that battered little ship we call the Anglican Communion.

1. Jesus as King and Lord

It is hard to tie down a single theme and declare that it is the main one in a book as large and sprawling as Acts, but if we look to the key passages at the very beginning and the very end we are struck by Luke's dramatic insistence that Jesus is the true King of Israel and the true Lord of the world. The Ascension has been woefully misunderstood, both by the literal-minded, who suppose that Luke imagines Jesus engaging in a primitive form of space travel to another location within our space-time universe, and by the Deists, who suppose that if Jesus is now in heaven (whatever that means) he is of little immediate relevance to earth. Few first-century readers would have made either of those mistakes. As any reader of the book of Daniel could have told you (and Daniel was very popular in the first century AD), the one who dwells in heaven is the one who rules on the earth. As any watcher of the Roman Imperial cult could have told you (and the Imperial cult was the fastest-growing religion in the first-century Mediterranean world), the one who is seen being taken up into heaven is the one who is thereby revealed as divine, as the ruler of the present cosmos. That was how Augustus made out that Julius Caesar was divine. On the triumphal arch of Titus in Rome there is a carving of Titus ascending to heaven. For the Jew, the Ascension story speaks of the Son of Man being exalted to the right hand of the Ancient of Days, sovereign over the beasts of pagan empire. For the Roman, the Ascension offers a sudden and unexpected rival to Caesar.

Luke draws these effortlessly together: the Ascension happens as the real answer to the disciples' question, 'Lord, will you at this time restore the kingdom to Israel?' Jesus' verbal answer, to promise them the Spirit and to commission them to be his witnesses to the ends of the earth, should not be understood as a cryptic answer 'No'. It is, rather, the pointer to the real answer, which is, as so often in the New Testament, 'Yes, but not in the way you imagined.' 'You will receive power when the Spirit comes upon you, and you will be my witnesses to the ends of the earth': and immediately he is taken into heaven. From the Jewish point of view, they are to declare that in Jesus the resurrection of the dead has already begun; the new age has broken in; Jesus is the Messiah, already ruling in his kingdom. From the pagan point of view, if the story means anything it means an implicit challenge to Caesar. The first thing we have to get our heads and hearts around as we read Acts is its unequivocal declaration and celebration of the fact that Jesus, the King of Israel, is the world's rightful Lord.

Before we ponder what it means to say this today, we glance ahead to the very end of the book. There we find exactly the same point. The proclamation of the gospel has at last reached Rome itself—not that Paul was the first Christian in Rome, but that within the narrative logic of the book he is completing the command to witness to Jesus as King and Lord to the ends of the earth. Get the message to Rome and it will go everywhere else. And notice how Luke ends the book. Paul is under house arrest, yes, but the gospel is not bound. Some of you will remember Bishop Stephen Neill, that great missionary statesman who knew a great deal about shipwreck and the kingdom of God. Once, a long time ago, when we were in conversation I mentioned something about Acts, and Stephen became excited. 'Do you know,' he asked me, 'what the very last word of Acts is?' At that time, I did not. 'Akōlytōs!', he exclaimed. 'Unhindered!' Paul is under arrest and awaiting trial, but nothing can stop him announcing that God is King, and teaching about Jesus the King as Lord, *with all boldness, and unhindered.* This is the framework within which Luke has told his tale: that Jesus is Israel's Messiah and the world's true Lord, and that in and through him the one true and living God has become king of the world, king in a way which ought to make Caesar shiver in his shoes, king in a way which sends his heralds scurrying out into the world, or for that matter languishing in prison as a direct result of their work, but still announcing his kingship with full, complete boldness and with unstoppable, Spirit-given power.

We know all this, and it's good to be reminded that Luke says it so firmly, and yet if we're honest it sounds . . . well, somehow rather unAnglican. It's a bit too enthusiastic, too definite, too many hard edges. What has happened, of course, is that our Anglicanism has often become just a bit too much inculturated into the world of western Deism, where all beliefs are simply opinions, where all statements of theological truth are reduced to statements of personal likes and dislikes (remember Ronald Knox's splendid line about 'suave politeness tempering bigot zeal' and correcting 'I believe' to 'one does feel'?). But the cooling of ardour which some have embraced as a virtue, leaving room for tolerance, for generosity of heart and mind, for openness to fresh truth—that is all very well when you apply it, as we have often done, in the world precisely of private opinion. But when you are in Caesar's world, where truth comes out of the barrel of a gun, or in his day the sheath of a sword, tolerance is a fancy name for cowardice. The claim that 'Jesus is Lord' was never, in the first century, what we would call a *religious* claim pure and simple. There was no such thing as religion pure and simple. It was a claim about an ultimate reality which included politics, culture, commerce, family life and everything else you could think of. And if you stop saying 'Jesus is Lord' out of deference to the private opinions of your friends and neighbours, Caesar smiles his grim smile and extends his empire by one more street. After all, the great eighteenth-century virtue of tolerance was developed not least by those who were keen on extending their geographical or industrial empires, and who didn't want God breathing down their necks to stop them. Keep religion in the private sphere and we'll run the public square. And to that idea Luke says a clear No; and so must we.

The joke at the moment, of course, is that in America the people who want to keep religion out of the public square are on the left, frightened of the New Right that sustains the present White House. Here in Britain it's the other way around; those of us who go around saying that Jesus is Lord and Caesar isn't, so it's time to remit global debts and look after our planet before it becomes uninhabitable, are accused by a sneering right-wing press of shoving our religion where it's not wanted. That just shows how shallow much contemporary analysis actually is. But my point is this. It is becoming increasingly clear in our society—you only have to look at France to see the point—that under the superficial smile of tolerance is the hard fist of secular power. And the task of the church in this day, as in Luke's day, is to find the appropriate ways of declaring that Jesus is Lord, openly and unhindered, recognising that this is a statement about the real, public world as well as the world of private religious experience, indeed that it is only truly the latter, about me and my religion, because it is truly the former, about God and his created world. And this is part of the point of Acts as a whole: that whatever troubles the church may get itself into, whatever divisions and persecutions and disputes there may be, we must end up, whether in Rome in the first century or in Edinburgh this next weekend, saying to the powers of the world that Jesus is Lord and that they are not. That is our primary calling; it is for this task, not in order to wallow in our own spiritual experiences, that the church must pray for the fresh wind of the Holy Spirit.

Luke leaves us no choice. Let's look now at how he has structured his whole book, and see how it works out and how his other themes fit within this overarching one.

2. King of the Jews, Lord of the World

The book of Acts divides fairly obviously into two. The first half, chapters 1–12, sees the early Christians announcing that Jesus is Israel's Messiah, the true King, great David's greater Son. That is the message of the early sermons, demonstrating from scripture that the resurrection constitutes Jesus as Messiah, as King. But this is no mere 'religious' message. The Chief Priests are furious that the disciples are 'proclaiming, in Jesus, the resurrection of the dead' (4.2); and the reason they're furious is not because they are theological liberals who don't believe in resurrection but because they are political and theological conservatives who know very well that resurrection is an extremely dangerous doctrine, because it speaks about Israel's God turning everything upside down and creating a new world, a world full of a new kind of justice (rather than the kind which they operate and which always works to their advantage), a Magnificat world in which the poor get their rights at last and the rich are sent empty away. All sorts of other people as well are angry with the apostles, not least those who sense that the Jerusalem Temple and the Mosaic Law seem to have been upstaged by Jesus coming as the new place of meeting between God and his people. That is what generates the stoning of Stephen. And standing behind both Chief Priests and Pharisees is the one who supposes himself to be King of the Jews, and who is not going to be best pleased with rival claimants: Herod Agrippa, another descendant of Herod the Great, another would-be king of the Jews who finds himself facing the claim that Jesus is the true Messiah. Herod kills James, and wants to kill Peter; but Peter is rescued, and Herod puffs himself up like a pagan monarch, claiming to be divine— and is suddenly smitten down and dies a horrible death. Josephus, the first-century Jewish historian, confirms the account. But, says Luke, the word of God continued to advance and gain adherents. That is the end of the first half of the book: Jesus is announced as the true King of Israel, and the fake one is overthrown while the message about Jesus speeds on and flourishes.

The second half of the book, chapters 13-28, follows an interestingly similar course. This time the theme is the announcement of Jesus as the true Lord of the whole world, as of course the ancient psalms and prophecies had claimed about the coming Messiah of Israel. It has already become clear in chapters 10 and 11 that the message is for all people, Gentile as well as Jew; now we see what that is going to mean. Off goes Paul around Turkey and Greece, developing as he goes an apologia before the watching pagan world, a simultaneous celebration of the goodness of creation and a denunciation of the idolatry of that created order. He runs into trouble from his fellow Jews, but also from the pagan world—not, again, primarily for what we would call 'religious' reasons, but for nakedly economic, social and political ones. In Philippi Paul exorcises a slave-girl who has been making money for her owners by fortune-telling; and those whose income is hit by God's liberating act of healing quickly seize on political charges. 'These men,' they say, 'are advocating customs that are not lawful for us Romans to adopt or observe'. At last the shadow of Caesar falls across the page; ambiguously, of course, because Paul is himself a Roman citizen and uses that status to get out of jail and extract a public apology from the magistrates who have beaten and jailed him.

The hint becomes more explicit in the next chapter (17.7): 'these men,' say the accusers, 'who have been turning the world upside down have come here also; they are acting contrary to the decrees of the Emperor, saying that there is another King, named Jesus.' Well, precisely. That is what Acts is all about, because that was what the early Christians were all about. How refreshing—at least, I hope you find it refreshing—to discover that early Christianity was not a matter of teaching people a new way to be religious. It was not about reconnecting with your own inner self. It was not even about a new means of securing a place in heaven after you died—since the new world, the new creation, and the resurrection which would bring you to share in it, was far more important. No: the central thing was this, that Jesus, the Jewish Messiah, was the true Lord and King of the world, and was calling everyone to account. That is why Paul's wonderful philosophical *tour de force* in Athens later in the same chapter ends with the news, the good news, that the one true God has fixed a day on which he will judge the world by a man whom he has appointed, and of this he has given assurance to all by raising him from the dead. The resurrection constitutes Jesus as Israel's Messiah, the world's true Lord, and hence as the one through whom God will put everything to rights, bringing peace and justice to the world at last. Just as the resurrection was rightly seen by the Sadducean Chief Priests as a highly dangerous doctrine, so the Athenians mocked at it, not just because they knew people didn't get raised from the dead but because if it had happened it would mean that a whole new world had been born. And once more, looking with Luke's eyes, we say: well, precisely.

But then, in Luke's larger scheme, Paul gradually gets to the point where he has to go to Rome; and his clashes with the authorities become more and more frequent until several of the later chapters consist of little else. As in Philippi, so in Ephesus: the gospel message, this time denouncing idolatry, is threatening to put some people out of business, so they raise a political charge against Paul from which he has a narrow escape. Finally he arrives in Rome; and if we have kept Luke's framework in mind we will realise with a shock what he intends us to think. In the first half of the book, Jesus is announced as King of Israel, and the would-be but idolatrous king of the Jews opposes him and comes to a bad end. Now, says Luke, Jesus is Lord of the world, and here he is arriving in Caesar's capital, proclaiming the kingdom of God and teaching about Jesus the Messiah as Lord, openly and unhindered; and what do we suppose will happen next? Most of Luke's readers will have known what happened next, albeit after Paul's death: Nero's suicide, the year of the four emperors, chaos come again. Once more Luke would say: well, precisely.

Jesus as Israel's Messiah; Jesus as the world's true Lord; and the apostolic task, in the power of the Spirit, is to announce him as such, to watch his kingdom come in power in lives and communities, and to risk the consequences. And among those consequences are of course the controversies that the early church had to face, the greatest among them being the integration of Jew and Gentile into a single family. Notice how it's done, in the famous chapter 15. The issue is faced. The scriptures are searched. The decision is made: *of course* the kingdom of God welcomes people from every family under heaven; but *of course* that family must renounce the twin dehumanizing evils of idolatry and sexual immorality. It is, after all, supposed to be the model of a new way of being human, a way inaugurated by Jesus and now enabled by the Spirit, a way which anticipates the way of being human which will obtain when Jesus comes again to put all things to rights.

Let me reflect for a few moments on where we've got to so far before we move to consider what, for me, is the most powerful lesson in Acts, full of meaning for us today and in the days we now face. It is sometimes proposed today that in order to grasp the political meaning of the New Testament, you have to downgrade the theology; as though, for instance, a high Christology would lead you off in the direction of 'religion' rather than politics, or as though talk of the bodily resurrection would project you out into the world of 'pie in the sky when you die' rather than the hard, real world in which we are called to work for justice and peace. In fact, as Paul or Revelation would make just as clear as Luke, the opposite is the case. It is because Jesus is bodily risen from the dead, because Jesus is Israel's Messiah, because he is the one and only Lord of the world, that the Sadducees are worried, Herod is worried, the Athenians are worried, the idol-makers of Ephesus are furious, and ultimately, if he knew his business, Caesar should be making his will. The point about Jesus going to heaven is not that we'll go there to be with him one day, away from this wicked old world at last. The point is that from heaven he is ruling the world, ruling it through the faithful lives, the suffering and the witness of his Spirit-driven apostolic followers, calling it to account, demonstrating that there is a new way of living, a way which upstages all Caesar's pretensions to have saved the world, or united it, or brought it genuine justice, freedom and peace. (All those claims, by the way, are the standard things that all empires have claimed, whether in the first century or the twenty-first.)

And this brings us back once more to the collusion between certain types of theology and certain modes of operating in the world. Ever since the eighteenth century, western protestantism has been pulled more and more towards a denial, explicit or implicit, of the great central truths of Christian faith—sometimes, indeed, towards watering them down while still saying the words, sometimes actually to open mockery of the idea of the Trinity or the resurrection or the full meaning of the cross. And what has happened, exactly as the eighteenth-century Deists intended it should, is that God is no longer a player on the world scene; Jesus is Lord far away in heaven, or in the secret places of my heart, perhaps, but he can't tell me how to run my business or which way to vote. And when that happens Caesar smiles his grim smile and pulls in the rope, and the worlds of money and sex and power all dance to his tune, exhibiting that tell-tale imperial pattern, the pagan pattern, the pattern that says there is no resurrection, that Herod is King of the Jews and Caesar is Lord of the world, that Mammon, the money-god, is divine and rules our pockets, that Aphrodite, the goddess of erotic love, is divine and rules our loins, that Mars the god of war is divine and doesn't mind who wins as long as people keep fighting each other. My brothers and sisters, is it surprising that, when every doctrine from the Trinity to the divinity of Jesus to his saving death and bodily resurrection and ascension has been dismissed as outdated, disproved or irrelevant, the church should then have no means of protesting against massive economic injustice, against the erosion and inversion of sexual morality, against rampant militarism—in other words, against Caesar and all his weapons? Is it not time to be grasped once more by the real authority of scripture, which is not about quoting a verse here and a line there but about being reshaped by the full story, the whole narrative, the entire drama of a book like Acts until the picture becomes clear and we see who Caesar is and how he works, who Jesus is and how he rescues God's lovely world from corruption and slavery, and who we are called to be as his Spirit-led witnesses to the ends of the earth?

When, and only when, we are fired by that vision, we may be able to see more clearly the truth which is waiting for us in the great drama of the closing chapters of Acts, which bring us, I believe, very close to hearing God's word to the Anglican Communion in the year of grace 2005.

3. The Storm and the Gospel

It has often been remarked that in both volumes of Luke's work, the gospel and the Acts, we find the motif of a journey. Ten full chapters out of the twenty-four in Luke's gospel have Jesus on the road, going up to Jerusalem, from the moment when we are told that this is to happen in chapter 9 to the moment when he finally enters the city in tears in chapter 19. Of course, plenty of things happen on the way, and Luke has used the motif of the journey both as a framework for a whole range of material he wants to place there and as a way of telling us that to be a disciple of Jesus is to learn to follow him on that journey, ultimately the journey to the cross and then to Emmaus and then to the ends of the earth. But the story is so familiar to us that we easily miss the way in which it works as a drama: the long journey (through which we know from early on that Jesus is going to redeem Israel, is going to become king indeed) comes at last to the place of darkness, the place where the forces of evil gather together and do their worst, the place where Jesus is mocked and beaten and crucified, where the sun goes dark at noon. We had hoped, say the two on the road to Emmaus, that he was the one to redeem Israel; but he can't have been, because they crucified him. Foolish ones, says the risen Jesus, and slow of heart to believe all that the prophets had foretold. *Was it not necessary* that the Messiah should suffer these things and enter into his glory? And he expounds the scriptures, breaks the bread, and their eyes are opened and they recognise him; and he sends them out to announce the new way of life, the way of repentance and forgiveness, to all nations, beginning from Jerusalem, clothed with power from on high.

All this, as I say, is well known, though still deep and true and powerful. But now come with me to the equivalent climax of the Acts of the Apostles. You need to remember that for most Jews of the day the sea was a powerful symbol of untameable danger and evil. Think of the watery chaos before creation. Think of the Red Sea, and the Psalms which celebrate YHWH's kingship over the mighty waters. Think of Jonah. Think of the monsters in Daniel, coming up out of the sea in a ghastly parody of the creation story, until they are brought to order by the exalted Son of Man. Think of the storm on Galilee. And now notice how Luke tells us, just as he tells us of Jesus setting his face to go to Jerusalem, that Paul has decided it is time to go to Rome (19.21f.). From then on, the scene is set. Messengers are sent ahead. Paul must get to Rome because his message—that the crucified and risen Jesus is the world's true Lord—must be announced under Caesar's nose, openly and unhindered. And almost at once all hell breaks loose. That's what happens when the gospel begins to challenge the principalities and powers. The riot in Ephesus. The warnings of prophets on the way. Paul beaten and arrested in the Temple. Trial before the Sanhedrin. The plot against his life. Trial before Felix. A two-year imprisonment. At this point the alert reader who knew Luke, but not how Paul's story worked out, might suppose that Paul, like his master before him, was on his way, via trials before Jewish and Roman courts, to crucifixion. But no; that isn't how Christian theology, or for that matter history, works. Jesus' crucifixion was and is unique; he died once for all, and our sufferings, though as Paul himself says they fill up the measure of Christ's sufferings, cannot and do not repeat his unique achievement. Rather, Luke with consummate artistry has something different in store. At the equivalent point where, in the gospel, we come to the crucifixion itself, we come in Acts to the shipwreck, the moment when the forces of wind and wave do their worst and it looks as though Paul will be drowned at sea, or smashed on the rocks, or killed by the soldiers, or finally, in an almost comic touch, poisoned by a Maltese snake. The darkness and hopelessness of the storm at sea mirror the dark hopelessness of Gethsemane and Calvary iself. And then, finally, after the sailors have used one anchor after another to slow the boat down and prevent it simply accelerating into the waiting rocks, they manage to steer close enough in to land so that when the ship finally runs aground and starts to break up, everyone on board comes safe to shore.

And the point of it all is that God's kingdom and Jesus' Lordship must be announced before Caesar, openly and unhindered; and at this point it seems as though the cosmos itself has joined forces with the pagan world to prevent Paul getting there, to stop Caesar's world from being challenged by the message of the crucified and risen Lord. We might imagine Paul arriving in Rome; Oh, Paul, we heard you'd been shipwrecked. Fancy having to go through such a thing. In fact, that's exactly what they said on Malta: he's obviously done something wrong, so blind justice is determined to kill him, whether by sea or by snakebite. Foolish ones, Paul would reply, and slow of heart to believe; was it not necessary that the gospel and its carriers should follow their Master, should pass through the dark waters, in order to come to Caesar's city, Caesar who kills but cannot make alive, Caesar in whose empire Mammon, Aphrodite and Mars reign unchecked and unchallenged? Did you expect that the gospel would stroll in to Rome of all places with its hands in its pockets and whistling a cheerful tune? Was it not necessary that it should arrive having gone through fire and water, embodying the truth it comes to tell, the truth that you only live if first you die, that you only celebrate if first you suffer, that you only preach if first you drown. God forgive us for our pseudo-gospels of cheap grace, of cossetting self-fulfilment, of a Christ without a cross and a church which never got its feet wet.

And it is only now, now that we have the full sweep of Acts before us, that we can see where we are today in the Anglican Communion, why we have arrived at this point, and perhaps even where we must go from here. We know we've got to get to Rome with the gospel. That is, we know in our bones, and more explicitly in this generation than ever before, that the task of the church is not to save souls for a disembodied heaven but to save whole human beings for God's new creation, and so to be agents in the present time of that salvation and renewal which was accomplished when Jesus died on the cross and rose from the tomb to launch God's new world. We know today better than for many generations that we have to announce to the principalities and powers that their time is up, that Jesus is Lord and that they are not, that the unchecked power of Mammon is an idol that has to be named and shamed, that the seductive blandishments of Aphrodite are a ghastly lie which has to be refuted and resisted, that the horrid trumpets of the war-god Mars appeal to all that is worst in us and will make the world a worse place. We know all this. We know we must resist paganism in all these forms in the name of Jesus the crucified and risen Lord. And we are eager to bring this message to bear, at the G8 summit next week, in working for peace in the Middle East, in sustaining healthy and appropriate human relationships, in supporting our brothers and sisters who live in daily fear and suffering because of their faith in several countries, and in many other ways. We are not a complacent church. We are struggling to be a faithful church.

So why are we surprised that we have been asked to go through fire and water? Why are we surprised that, just when our journey to bring the gospel before the powers is getting near some very significant achievements, the powers of the world would strike back at the very heart of our Communion? Is this not utterly typical of the way things always happen when the gospel is going forward in individual lives, in vocations, in local churches, in all kinds of Christian groupings? Was it not necessary that we should pass through these things and so declare, openly and unhindered, that Jesus is Lord and Caesar is not? Might we not have expected that one at least of the three standard themes of paganism, money, sex and power, would blow up a storm that might threaten to shipwreck us?

And might we not develop the theme a bit further? The sailors, as was the custom of the time, let down from the stern of the boat one anchor after another, slowing down the rush of the boat while bringing it in closer and closer to land. When we were faced, it seemed, with imminent shipwreck two years ago, we put down one anchor, a Primates' meeting, in November 2003. We then put down another one, the Eames Commission. We then put down another, the Primates' meeting earlier this spring. We have now put down another one this last week. None of them, perhaps, was or is sufficient in itself to prevent us coming to shore in a different manner than we might have wanted. But each has done its part. And now, even if we are going to run aground, there may at least be a chance that we may all come safely to land.

No doubt the picture could be developed and applied in several different ways, and we should not press it too far. We cannot tell if the good ship *Ecclesia Anglicana* may yet break up on a reef, or find its way, battered but still whole, onto a sandy beach. But that is not my point. My point is this: that we have in our day the greatest opportunity for the wholistic proclamation of the gospel of Jesus Christ that has occurred in our world for many a year. We are getting stuck in and getting our hands dirty with this multi-level gospel work. And we should not be surprised that all the forces in the cosmos seem to rage against us to prevent the message getting out, to prevent us even getting to the point where we can announce the message, because we are so taken up with surviving the storm at sea.

Let me just spell this out a bit as I close. We are living through a set of massive cultural shifts which, in different ways, affect the whole world. The old certainties by which the western world ordered its life over the last two centuries have been shaken to the core. Easy travel and communication have brought great blessings and great dangers. Many in the western world are looking once more for spirituality, for justice, for beauty, for relationship—all of which the church ought to know something about, though ironically people are looking everywhere except the church to find them. Many in the former communist countries are looking for something which is neither the communism they knew nor the western consumerism they are getting in its place. Many in the so-called two-thirds world are looking for freedom and justice and recognising that they are much more elusive than they had been led to believe. And in this context the church is finding its voice in new ways. We are reaching out and grasping again the wholistic gospel of Jesus Christ, a gospel not just for souls and not just for bodies but for whole persons and the whole world, the whole cosmos which is groaning in travail. We are working in new ways for Christian unity and refusing to connive at the scandal of separation. We are learning from one another, and discovering that we have more in common than we had imagined. We are asking the hard questions about how the gospel applies to the real world and refusing to be put off by the sneers of the media and the threats of some politicians. We are starting to realise that the lies put out by the Enlightenment—that Christianity was disproved, outdated, and bad for your health—were the childish taunts of those who were anxious in case God's kingdom might call them after all to costly obedience. *We are on the threshold* of a great new work of God, a work of wholistic mission and evangelism in which God's kingdom will be announced, and Jesus will be named as Lord, openly and unhindered. And it is precisely at such points that we should expect the strongest winds and the fiercest waves to blow us off course, to turn the ship upside down, and to drown us all in the dark sea of postmodern amorality and factious in-fighting.

And the answer is that we must keep up our courage and see the thing through. Don't be afraid, said the Lord to Paul in Corinth (18.9); speak and do not be silent, for I am with you. Keep up your courage, said the Lord to Paul after the hearing before the Council (23.11); as you have testified for me in Jerusalem, so you must bear witness also in Rome. Don't be afraid, said the angel to Paul on the boat (27.24); you must stand before the emperor, and God has granted safety to all who are sailing with you. We must keep our nerve. We must say our prayers. We must hold fast to the risen and ascended Lord, at whose name every knee shall bow, not least Caesar, Mammon, Aphrodite and Mars. We are on our way with the gospel,

Departmental and Commission Reports

Department of Communications

Canon James M. Rosenthal

[A PowerPoint presentation of images from around the Communion was shown throughout the presentation. In a prelude to the presentation, communications intern Robert Bergner, Anglican Church of Canada, sang the aria "Comfort Ye" from *The Messiah* by Handel to mark St John the Baptist Day.]

The voice of him that crieth in the wilderness; prepare ye the way of the Lord; make straight in the desert, a highway for our God...every valley shall be exalted and every mountain and hill made low...the crooked straight...the rough places plain...

Today is the great Prayer Book feast of John the Baptizer, June 24, celebrated in all of the churches of the Anglican Episcopal world, as a major feast, a red letter day. But the resounding words of the Baptist are also brought home to us each Advent when we sing "On Jordan's banks the Baptist's cry, announcing that the Lord is nigh, awake and hearken for he brings glad tidings from the King of Kings."

Now we think John the Baptist was a bit of a character, we know about the loin cloths and the locusts and wild honey. Well, I chose not to emulate the great saint in either vesture or dare I say diet, but I trust that my performance as the one often crying in the media communications cyber wilderness telling people that the good news abounds in this our global family. Yet I must say, like in the days of the Baptist, often finds the transmission and reception of news and information a challenge. I ask—then shall the eyes of the blind be open and the ears of the deaf unstopped...I wait for this day with hopes and expectations as well as a pledge to try to facilitate the accomplishment of the same.

Today instantaneous news, breaking news, one voice tells one gruesome story, while the screen shares another as bad or worse as rolling text on the screen. They bombard us, at least those who find television a means of obtaining information, or dare I say the internet where news of football stars and film divas eradicate news of famine, disaster, and community welfare.

But what of the church—locally, nationally, internationally. Resources shrink and so does the work of communications. Communications is not magic, even though advertising can mesmerize us totally, but the vast array of professional modes of presenting one's case makes the competitive nature of what we do a stark reality.

Yet if we do not tell the story, meaning us, those entrusted with the care and facilitating of the work of the Communion, let me say undoubtedly, others will, and do, as many of you know full well.

What of the director? Is he propagandist? Journalist? Photographer? PR manager? Publisher? What is required? Dare I say, all . . . and sometimes all at once.

The print media is alive and well and even flourishing. Visit your corner shop, your bookstore or train station, the magazines are proudly presented and the buyer buys with eager anticipation of obtaining some gratification in return for spending their money.

Our website is visited often and thousands subscribe to our ACNS, but funding is a continuing issue. Dare we not have active presence on the phenomena called the internet.

Like print, books, magazines, the dark side is made manifest, at many levels, and especially in this genre in sadly unexpected and dangerous ways. A simple search can find one exposed to things most shocking to say the very least, especially for the very young.

I believe, however, that communication with a purpose makes a great impact, if everyone is playing from the same cards or as we say in church circles, singing from the same hymn sheet. Are we singing from the same hymn sheet is my question, my dilemma, and my concern.

In a recent sermon at the Russian Orthodox Cathedral in London our Archbishop Rowan spoke of how the church is or might be seen, in the light of the current rhetoric. He said, "In our attempts at excellence in communication we have tried to maintain a sense of who we are as Communion in a way that could be seen as a way that avoided much of the difficult banter that was shared freely on the websites of interest groups and concerned people, especially in North America. Fund raising does not relish controversy."

But the Communion we share, or indeed living Communion, means setting goals and proclaim a vision that echoes that of John the Baptist whom we honour today. The message and the messengers need to claim the high calling the communication can inspire and enable.

What is the most frequently asked question we get at the ACO in my office—how can we get in touch with Desmond Tutu, why, because he has been a voice crying in the world for truth and justice in the name of Christ who is our truth, our way, our life. An image, a person, whether in miter or not, that evokes confidence, and might I say joy and smile, to the beholder.

The prophet asked, what shall we cry?

What is our response?

As a global church we present immediate obstacles to the seeker or observer, or even the press and media. Who are we? In one place we are Anglicans, in another Episcopalians, in another the Church of Somewhere ...as if there were no others churches around.

When I visit a city I immediately look at the local telephone directory. I check Anglican/Episcopal and I find numerous churches listed that are simply not part of the Communion. One ACC member from the global south on arrival on this campus said to me, change that sign from Anglican to Anglican Communion. "There are too many Anglicans churches around these days," she said.

The faithful Anglican trying to find fellowship in a new city can be at the least misled by this clever means of communication or miscommunication.

One diocesan communications officer told, we simply don't have the money to advertise. Can we actually afford not to? That is my question.

But again, when we do commit the money and energy then we need to offer a purposeful challenge to the reader or recipient of our own communications.

We can not nor should we want to rely on the secular media or interest groups to carry our message to the greater world. It is not their job or responsibility, and in this day and age the newspapers seem to have their own raison d'etre and if what the church is saying doesn't match that criteria, then we (the church) receive negative or even no coverage at all.

Need I say why this ACC meeting has received more attention that any since my first meeting in 1991 in Wales? Or why the last Primates meeting had media and press interest from around the world, even though we were in the far reaches of rural Ireland?

But what does the communication operation look like?

There are two full time persons. I have been 17 years in post, after coming for 3 years—more of that over coffee—and Michael Ade whose chief job is database manager though now filling several gaps. We answer endless information questions especially in England as we are the only Anglican entry in the phone system; all else are C of E, I presume. We welcome a large number of visitors and much of our time is spent in the Benedictine mode of hospitality and care. This provides great interaction and learning. I for one find this important as over the years I have been welcomed so lavishly when visiting your many provinces and experiencing your incredible hospitality and gift giving. You will see many photos of the Archbishop of Canterbury's most recent visit to Ghana and Melanesia, lands of faith, as well as celebration, colour and faithfulness.

Anglican World is designed by Andy Day in Canterbury and well under market rates for sure. He is a dedicated Anglican to say the least. Occasional freelance and stringers help, usually at very moderate costs, such as the incredible series I hope you have all read on Audacious Anglicans. The Family Network pages are done by the staff person for the network, Sally Thompson, and AEW picks up the printing costs.

Another question to ponder—why (at great expense to us) have so many thousands downloaded the Windsor Report from our website while only some few have downloaded the ARCIC Mary: Hope and Grace in Christ?

If I can turn your attention to the telecommunications work and firstly thank the Reverend Clement Lee from the Episcopal Church USA who serves very part time as Director, after his retirement from the communications department at ECUSA. Again through Trinity Grants he is able to give us his time and share expertise in this growing aspect of our work, growing while resources diminish or run out. There is a small telecommunications commission that serves as a resource when called upon, led by Fr Philip Sallis from New Zealand.

The post once offered for an on-site person is no longer funded, leaving a huge gap.

A renewal with the communications of our Communion is a must, and I believe we can generate the same, with your help and determination in making our work—work for you and your province, as well as for the whole Communion.

Look at us, look at the true living communion we are . . . the pictures say so much.

Our needs are exacerbated by the need to offer all our official documents in the languages of our people.

It would be wrong for me to speak to you without telling the incredible work that is being carried out in your name by a tiny staff that involves communication. Though on the admin staff, Ian Harvey responds to the call of the Ecumenical Department as he designs the many documents coming from them; Michael Ade the same, though not his "job" he fills the gap created by the completion of the Trinity Grant and works above and beyond the call. Our most recent assistant Michael Craske, like his predecessor Matthew Davies, after learning from the old man, has gone on to higher paying and excellent jobs. Makes us proud, but at a loss. An intern is with us for two months that has been a godsend.

So we have a chance from this moment in time to make a statement to a weary yet wonderful world that needs to hear the audacity of the Baptizer's cry to move us on. In my prayer I try when time allows to listen to the voice of the Baptizer's, the saints of old, that I believe urge me on my way, or us on our way, share the stories, who they are in God's plan so we too can be inspired to tell our story, with boldness and in thanksgiving for the Christian faith received, explored and invigorated by the tradition we call Anglican.

As the person who you have given much to as your voice enabler, I pledge to continue that ministry as you each, in the places of your ministry, makes us among the first to know so that our living communion can be examples to others as we share faith and news with our ecumenical partners (and I am so grateful to our friends in places like the Vatican that treat me with such respect on so many occasions) and our interfaith friends. We can only come to the table when we have something to share.

Some of you know of my work with charity for children through the tradition of my favorite saint. All I can say is look to the brightness and creativity expressed in the coloring pages that decorate our hall . . . their message is one of pride and will certainly find a place of honour in Anglican Episcopal World.

But I wonder, is it too late in our plans to share a response to these young Anglicans, a message that is as bright and clear as their art displays, yes, even from this meeting to show them where our priorities lie rather than reacting to those who cry louder or shout the loudest.

Dr. Silvio Waisbord of the Academy of Educational Development said recently in print, "Communications professionals are hardly in the driver's seat of development programmes". Sometimes I moan in the office, I am the last to know but am responsible to make whatever it is to be known. Why hasn't this diocese or that bishop let us know what has happened or better yet about to happen, so we can give intelligent responses, as trust me, we will be asked. "No comment" to a journalist is not the best way to gain friends! For a true communications person will have as his or her vision statement and part of its strategy, to quote Dr Waisbord, is a distinctive and central characteristic of the contemporary world and it has much to contribute to improve the lives of people around the world.

It seems like that is an indication to us especially, to make communications happen in the best way we can. Communication is more than information, it is more than countering perceived negatives. Remember what I face daily is one group's negative clamour can be another's positive energy released.

Department of Ecumenical Affairs

Personnel

The last three years have seen a significant change in personnel in the Department, and, of course, in its location and configuration. The move to Saint Andrew's House undoubtedly helped the working environment, since the Ecumenical Department now has a dedicated area on the World Mission Floor (the ground floor).

Bishop David Hamid
Director of Ecumenical Affairs, 1996–2002

When ACC met in Hong Kong, it was already known that David had been appointed as Assistant Bishop in the Church of England Diocese of Gibraltar in Europe. David left to take up his new ministry in November 2002, following his consecration in the previous month. He was highly successful in his ministry at ACO, bringing many dialogues to a successful culmination, including the completion of *Growth in Communion* (Anglican–Lutheran International Working Group, 2002) and *The Gift of Authority* (ARCIC, 1999).

Bishop John Baycroft
Acting Director of Ecumenical Affairs, 2002–2003

Bishop John took care of the Department for some seven months, until the appointment of David's successor. Bishop John was an old hand when it came to ecumenical matters, having been a long-standing member of ARCIC, and highly involved in ecumenical affairs during his time as Bishop of Ottawa. We are grateful to him for being willing to live a transatlantic life for the period of the interregnum, and for ensuring that none of the work of the department failed for want of a hand on the tiller.

Canon Gregory K Cameron
Director of Ecumenical Affairs from 2003,
Deputy Secretary General from 2004

Gregory came to the Anglican Communion Office from the Church in Wales, where he had worked alongside Archbishop Rowan Williams. Gregory had had a varied ministry before joining ACO, having worked in parish and schools ministry, as well as participating in the ecumenical life of the Church in Wales, and being trained as a canon lawyer. He enjoys the work of the Ecumenical Department, which he believes to be at a time of critical juncture at the beginning of the twenty-first century.

Ms Frances Hiller
Programme/Research Assistant, 2000–2002

Frances had joined ACO in 1998 as receptionist and then transferred to the Ecumenical Department in 2000 before eventually leaving in 2002 to continue working alongside David Hamid in his new ministry. Frances showed great commitment and service to the work of the Ecumenical Department during her two years' service.

Mrs Christine Codner
Senior Personal Assistant

Christine is one of the "old faithfuls" of the ACO, having joined the staff in 1983. She worked in the Secretary General's Department for ten years, before joining the Ecumenical Department in 1993. Her knowledge of the bilateral dialogues and ecumenical networks is invaluable. Christine has not been blessed with fullness of good health in recent years, and had to take a period of extended leave in early 2003 to recuperate from surgery, but continues to work with cheerfulness, and competence.

The Revd Terrie Robinson
Personal Assistant and Research Officer

Terrie is an NSM priest of the Diocese of Oxford. Before joining ACO, Terrie worked with the Save the Children charity based in London, and brings a wealth of diverse experience and talent to her post. She has willingly joined in the huge variety of activities which the department demands, and has brought unfailing dedication, talent and good sense to its work.

The Work of the Department

The principal work of the Department is to carry forward the ecumenical and doctrinal commissions of the Communion on behalf of the Consultative Council, and to resource, staff and service the international dialogues. This means that in the period since the last meeting of ACC, the Department has had responsibility for some twelve commissions: the Inter-Anglican Theological and Doctrinal Commission (IATDC), the Inter-Anglican

Standing Commission on Ecumenical Relations (IASCER), the Lambeth Commission on Communion (LCC), and the Reception Reference Group for the Windsor Report (RRG), in addition to dialogue commissions with the Baptist World Alliance, the Lutheran World Federation, the World Methodist Council, the Old Catholic Churches of the Union of Utrecht, the Oriental Orthodox Churches, the Orthodox Churches, and the Roman Catholic Church.

In addition, the Department carries out a great deal of ambassadorial and representative work for the Communion: at the World Council of Churches, the Faith and Order Commission, the Global Christian Forum, the Conference of Secretaries of the Christian World Communions, with the Holy Synod of the Ecumenical Patriarchate and the Pontifical Council for Promoting Christian Unity. It was in connection with this last that the Director was part of substantial Anglican delegations to both the funeral of Pope John Paul II and the Inaugural Mass of Pope Benedict XVI. There is also the full range of speaking, teaching and preaching engagements in addition to the work of reviewing and advising upon national and regional ecumenical developments.

Finally, the Department provides a service to the Churches and Provinces of the Anglican Communion and the Instruments of Unity as requested or required and, in co-operation with the Communications and Telecommunications Departments, maintains the ecumenical and other pages of the Anglican Communion website, and oversees the publication and distribution of the fruits of the commissions and bodies with which it is associated.

Ecumenical Relations

Anglican–Baptist Relations

Since 2000, the Anglican Consultative Council has been joint sponsor with the Baptist World Alliance of a series of regional conversations intended to facilitate a global dialogue between the member churches of these two traditions. The conversations have not been a formal theological dialogue, in the sense that such dialogues are often oriented towards the goal of full, visible unity, but have rather been an attempt to explore how Anglicans and Baptists relate in their understanding of the Christian faith, and to map the ways in which Anglicans and Baptists share in common witness to Jesus Christ across the globe.

The report of these conversations is now laid before the Anglican Consultative Council in the publication, *Conversations Around the World* (which will be circulated to all members of ACC). This report has been published by the Anglican Communion Office on behalf of the Anglican

---

Anglican Communion–Baptist World Alliance International Conversations

MEETINGS

2000	European round, Norwich, England
2001	Asian round, Yangon, Myanmar
2002	African round, Nairobi, Kenya
2003	Latin American round, Santiago, Chile
2003	Caribbean round, Nassau, Bahamas
2003	North American round, Wolfville, Canada
2004	Continuation Committee, Oxford, England

CONTINUATION COMMITTEE 2000–2004

Anglicans
The Revd Professor Bruce Matthews, Canada (Co-Chair)
The Revd Canon David Hamid, ACO, 2000–2002 (Co-Secretary)
The Revd Canon Gregory Cameron, ACO, from 2003 (Co-Secretary)
The Revd Prebendary Dr Paul Avis, England
Chancellor Rubie Nottage, West Indies, from 2003
The Most Revd Samuel San Si Htay, Myanmar, 2000–2002

Baptists
The Revd Prof. Paul Fiddes, England (Co-Chair)
The Revd Tony Cupit, BWA (Co-Secretary)
The Revd Dr Ken Manley, Australia
The Revd Dr Malcolm Yarnell, USA

Consultative Council and the Baptist World Alliance, and represents a new departure for such international ecumenical reports. In its main section, it offers an account, largely developed by the Baptist Co-Chair, Professor Paul Fiddes, of the main themes of the various conversations, and explores the major subjects of Christian faith as they are lived out by the two traditions. The report also contains an extensive section setting out the various ways in which Anglicans and Baptists share in common witness to Jesus Christ, ranging from partnership in specific projects to the ministry of bishops in United Churches from Baptist and Anglican backgrounds.

The Baptist World Alliance has been facing problems in its own life recently, with the withdrawal of the Southern Baptist Convention from the Alliance following the admission of the Co-operative Baptist Fellowship to membership. The Co-operative Baptist Fellowship is a group that has broken away from the Southern Baptist Convention on the grounds of the increasing fundamentalism they believe is exhibited within the Convention, and the Southern Baptist Convention objected to its admission to membership within the Baptist World Alliance.

The Anglican Consultative Council:

- welcomes the publication *Conversations Around the World* as the report of the conversations between representatives of the Anglican Communion and the Baptist World Alliance, and commends it to the parishes, dioceses and provinces of the Anglican Communion as a resource for study and reflection on the nature of mission and of the way in which Baptists and Anglicans can co-operate.
- encourages Anglicans to meet with Baptists at the appropriate level and locality and reflect on this report and on their common mission to bear witness to the salvation found in Christ.
- offers its congratulations to the members of the Continuation Committee, especially the co-chairs, Professor Paul Fiddes and Professor Bruce Matthews, on the completion of their work, and to all those who contributed to the regional meetings.
- requests the Director of Ecumenical Affairs to explore ways in which the conversation at international level may be developed in the future.

Anglican–Lutheran Relations

The report of the Anglican–Lutheran International Working Group, *Growth in Communion,* was received by ACC-12 in Hong Kong. Since then, the report has been published by the Lutheran World Federation, and included in a comprehensive collection of Anglican–Lutheran Agreements at regional and global level published together by the Anglican Communion Office and the Lutheran World Federation as part of the Lutheran Documentary Series, Volume 49. This publication is available to all members of ACC at the meeting in Nottingham.

At their meeting in 2002, IASCER expressed some reservations about part of the approach adopted by the Anglican–Lutheran International Working Group, and you can find these qualifications reproduced in Appendix 5, Resolution 2.02 of IASCER. Whilst IASCER welcomed the report as a whole, they expressed some concern about whether the concept of "transitivity" could adequately sustain all that was asked of it in the report, and suggested some clarifications about the way in which the matter should be approached.

In the light of the welcome given to *Growth in Communion* at ACC-12, the Joint Standing Committee subsequently authorised a mandate for a new Anglican–Lutheran International Commission (ALIC), which is reproduced in Appendix 1. This commission will meet in early 2006, under the leadership of the Bishop of Nova Scotia, Fred Hiltz. A primary task for the new ALIC will be to discern how the highly successful regional agreements of (full) communion between Anglican and Lutheran churches in North America and northern Europe can be translated into a universal relationship.

Members of ACC will also be aware of the existence of the All Africa Anglican–Lutheran Commission (AAALC), which was set up in 2000 to look specifically at the ecumenical relations between the churches of the Anglican Communion and the Lutheran World Federation within Africa. This body has not managed to resolve some of the difficulties surrounding its meetings, and has not met since 2001.

The Anglican Consultative Council:

- welcomes the news of the continuing establishment of closer relations between Anglican and Lutheran churches across the globe, contained in the Report of the Director of Ecumenical Affairs;
- offers its encouragement to the newly established Anglican–Lutheran International Commission as it begins its work;
- encourages the All Africa Anglican–Lutheran Commission to resume its work at the earliest opportunity.

Anglican–Methodist Relations

The Report of the Anglican–Methodist International Commission, *Sharing in the Apostolic Communion,* had been received at ACC-11. At the Lambeth Conference 1998, a resolution was passed requesting that steps should be taken for the establishment of a new Anglican–Methodist International Commission. Unfortunately, progress has been difficult. After a period of inactivity on the Anglican side, recent approaches to the World Methodist Council have been met with hesitation. It appears that the World Methodist Council is fully committed elsewhere in its ecumenical programme at present, and recent tensions within the Anglican Communion about developments in North America have made the representatives of the Council less sure that now is the appropriate moment to proceed to the establishment of an Anglican–Methodist Commission.

At the same time relations remain warm on a personal and regional level. 2003 saw the signing of a Covenant between the Church of England and the Methodist Church of Great Britain and Ireland. This represents a major development in ecumenical relationship between these two bodies and it has translated swiftly and easily into ecumenical commitment and shared mission at grassroots level. ACC will be delighted to receive Mr Will Morrey, the current President of the Methodist Church of Great Britain and Northern Ireland as an ecumenical delegate to their meeting in Nottingham, and to hear from him something about this new level of ecumenical action.

The Anglican Consultative Council:

- welcomes the news of the establishment of closer relations between Anglican and Methodist churches across the globe, and particularly in England, contained in the Report of the Director of Ecumenical Affairs;
- requests the Director of Ecumenical Affairs to pursue the establishment of an appropriate instrument of dialogue between the Anglican Communion and the World Methodist Council.

Anglican–Old Catholic Relations

2006 will see the 75th Anniversary of the signing of the Bonn Agreement in 1931, which created a relationship of (full) communion between all the churches of the Anglican Communion and the churches of the Union of Utrecht. This anniversary therefore marks one of the earliest, and one of the most straightforward, ecumenical agreements of the twentieth century, and it will be rightly celebrated in a number of ways, including a joint the-

---

Anglican–Old Catholic International Co-ordination Council (AOCICC) 1998–2004

MEETINGS

1998	Frankfurt, Germany	2001	Ely, England
1999	Norwich, England	2002	Prague, Czech Republic
2000	Rotterdam, Netherlands	2004	Canterbury, England

ANGLICANS

The Rt Revd Jonathan Gledhill, England (Co-Chair)
The Revd Canon Gregory K Cameron, ACO, from 2003 (Co-Secretary)
The Revd Canon David Hamid, ACO, 1998–2002 (Co-Secretary)
The Revd Gabriel Amat, Switzerland
Mrs Gillian Ratcliff, Sweden
The Revd Sarah Rowland-Jones, Wales
The Revd Canon Dr J Robert Wright, USA
The Revd Dr Charles Hill, C of E CCU, from 2001 (Observer)

OLD CATHOLICS

The Right Revd Joachim Vobbe, Germany, 1998–2003 (Co-Chair)
The Rt Revd Dr Jan-Lambert Wirix-Speetjens, Netherlands, 2004 (Co-Chair)
The Revd Dr Thaddeus A. Schnitker, Germany, 1998–1999 (Co-Secretary)
The Revd Dr Angela Berlis, Netherlands, from 2000 (Co-Secretary)
The Reverend Jerzy Bajorek, Poland, 1998
The Revd Dr Harald Rein, Switzerland, 1998
The Revd Canon Wietse van der Velde, Netherlands
Professor Dr Urs von Arx, Switzerland, from 2000

ological conference held in the United Kingdom in September this year, a shared pilgrimage to the Shrine of St Willibrord, and celebrations at the Old Catholic Congress in 2006.

The Anglican–Old Catholic International Co-ordinating Committee (AOCICC) has recently completed a five year phase, and has been reconstituted under a new mandate approved by the Joint Standing Committee last year. It will meet in autumn this year. The mandate, which concentrates on understanding questions of parallel jurisdiction and initiatives of common mission, is reproduced in Appendix 2.

The Union of Utrecht has faced difficulties recently with the break of communion between the Polish National Catholic Church which operates in the United States of America and the remainder of the churches of the Union, ostensibly over the issue of the ordination of women to the priesthood.

The Anglican Consultative Council:

- extends its greetings to the Archbishop of Utrecht on behalf of all the churches of the Union;
- gives thanks to God for seventy-five years of shared life in communion with the Churches of the Union of Utrecht;
- celebrates the seventy-fifth anniversary of the Bonn Agreement;
- offers its thanks to all the members of the outgoing Anglican–Old Catholic International Co-ordinating Council for the work over the past five years, and welcomes the establishment of a new Council.

Anglican–Oriental Orthodox Relations

Negative reaction to the developments in Anglican life in North America amongst the churches of the Oriental Orthodox family has meant that the work of the Anglican–Oriental Orthodox International Commission (AOOIC) has been suspended. This is most unfortunate, given the substantial work achieved by the Commission in the very short time since its establishment in 2001.

The draft agreement on Christology offered to the Anglican Communion by this Commission is highly significant, since it builds on work already undertaken in relations between the Oriental Orthodox family of churches with the Orthodox and Roman Catholic churches. These agreements taken together heal the schism between the Oriental Orthodox churches and the churches which accepted the Christological Definitions of the Council of Chalcedon in AD 451, and therefore represent a huge step forward in ecumenical relations. The healing of a division which has afflicted the Christian household of faith for over fifteen hundred years in

The Anglican–Oriental Orthodox International Commission (AOOIC)

MEETINGS

2001   Midhurst, England (preparatory)
2002   Holy Etchmiadzin, Armenia

ANGLICANS

The Rt Revd Dr Geoffrey Rowell (Co-Chair), Europe
The Revd Canon Gregory K Cameron, ACO, from 2003 (Co-Secretary)
The Revd Canon David Hamid, ACO, to 2002 (Co-Secretary)
The Rt Revd Duleep de Chickera, Sri Lanka
The Revd Canon Jonathan Gough, Archbishop of Canterbury's
    Representative
The Most Revd George Clive Handford, Jerusalem and the Middle East
The Rt Revd Michael Jackson, Ireland
The Revd Canon Harold J. Nahabedian, Canada
The Rt Revd John Craig Stewart, Australia
The Revd William Taylor, England
The Revd Canon Professor J Robert Wright, USA

ORIENTAL ORTHODOX

His Eminence Metropolitan Bishoy (Co-Chair), Coptic Orthodox Church
His Grace Bishop Nareg Alemezian (Co-Secretary), Armenian
    Catholicosate of Cilicia
His Grace Bishop Mikael Ajapahyan, Armenian Catholicosate of All
    Armenians
His Grace Bishop Angaelos, Coptic Orthodox Church
His Grace Bishop Geevarghese Mar Coorilos, Malankara Syrian
    Orthodox Church
The Revd Dr K M George, Malankara Syrian Orthodox Church
The Revd Kaleab Ghebreslassie, Eritrean Orthodox Tewahdo Church
His Eminence Metropolitan Mor Gregorios Youhanna Ibrahim, Syrian
    Orthodox Church
His Grace Bishop Kegham Khatcherian, Armenian Catholicosate of Cilicia
His Grace Bishop Yeznik Petrossian, Armenian Catholicosate of All
    Armenians
His Eminence Metropolitan Mor Eustathius Matta Roham, Syrian Orthodox
    Church of Antioch
The Revd Seife-Sellassie Yohannes, Ethiopian Orthodox Church

no small matter, even in parts of the world where direct contact between Anglicans and Oriental Orthodox is limited.

It is disappointing therefore that not only has the work of the Commission been delayed by recent developments, but Provinces of the Anglican Communion have been slow or even reluctant to offer their assessment of the draft Agreement.

The Anglican Consultative Council:

- gives thanks to God for the work already achieved by the Anglican–Oriental Orthodox International Commission (AOOIC) in their draft Christological Agreement, and urgently requests those Provinces which have not done so to offer their reflections upon it to the Inter-Anglican Standing Commission for Ecumenical Relations, in order to enable its ratification by the Lambeth Conference in 2008;
- receives with regret the news that the work of the AOOIC is currently suspended;
- asks the Director of Ecumenical Affairs to report to the representatives of the Oriental Orthodox churches that the Primates have now twice reaffirmed the 1998 Resolution of the Lambeth Conference 1.10 as "the standard of Christian teaching on matters of human sexuality ..., which should command respect as the position overwhelmingly adopted by the bishops of the Anglican Communion" together with the affirmation of this Council, presently meeting in Nottingham, and trusts that this will provide a sufficient basis for the resumption of the work of the AOOIC;
- asks the AOOIC to consider whether it might examine the relationship between universal and local churches, and the processes of decision making in the life of the churches.

Anglican–Orthodox Relations

The International Commission for Anglican–Orthodox Theological Dialogue (ICAOTD) has been working in its current phase since 1989. The focus of our current discussions has been the theology of the Church and ministry in the Church, including the question of the ordination of women. Between the writing of this report and its presentation at ACC-13, the ICAOTD will have held a meeting in Cyprus as guests of the Monastery of Kikkou. It is hoped that this meeting will have seen the completion of work on the Agreed Statements in this area, in preparation for their final approval and publication next year in preparation for the Lambeth Conference of 2008.

The reports will provide a comprehensive treatment of our common understanding of the nature of the Church, and is likely to represent a high degree of convergence.

The family of Orthodox churches has reacted variously to the developments in North America, but international Anglican–Orthodox relations remain warm, and ACO has been grateful for the warmth and hospitality of the Holy Synod of the Ecumenical Patriarchate on several occasions.

International Commission for Anglican–Orthodox Theological Dialogue (ICAOTD)

MEETINGS

1999   Salisbury, England
2001   Volos, Greece
2002   Abergavenny, Wales
2003   Addis Ababa, Ethiopia
2004   Canterbury, England

ANGLICANS

The Rt Revd Mark Dyer (Co-Chair)
The Revd Canon Gregory K Cameron, ACO, from 2003 (Co-Secretary)
The Revd Canon David Hamid, ACO, to 2002 (Co-Secretary)
The Rt Revd Riah Abu El-Assal, Palestine
The Rt Revd John Baycroft, Canada
The Revd Dr Timothy Bradshaw, England
The Revd Dr Donald Edwards, Australia
The Revd Dr John Gibaut, Canada
The Revd Canon Jonathan Gough, Lambeth Palace
The Rt Revd Dr William Gregg, USA
The Revd Dr Professor William Green, USA
The Revd Canon Dr John McNab, Canada, to 2003
The Revd Canon Livingstone Ngewu, South Africa
The Revd Dr Duncan Reid, Australia
The Revd Canon Professor John Riches, Scotland
The Ven Joy Tetley, England
The Rt Revd Dr Maxwell Thomas, Australia
The Revd Canon Hugh Wybrew, England

ORTHODOX

Metropolitan John of Pergamon, Constantinople (Co-Chair)
The Revd Dr Christos Christakis, USA, (Co-Secretary)
Metropolitan Ambrosius of Helsinki, Finland
Metropolitan Petros of Aksum, Alexandria
Bishop Basil of Sergievo, Moscow
Fr Alexander Haig, Antioch
Fr Michael Harper, Antioch
Professor Dr Mircea Ielciu, Romania
The Revd Dr Vaclav Jezek, Czech Lands and Slovakia
Fr Matthias Palli, Estonia
Bishop Ilia of Philomelion, Albania
Archbishop Niphon of Targoviste, Romania
Professor Constantine Scouteris, Greece
Bishop Gerasim Sharashenidze, Georgia
Bishop Vasilios of Trimithus, Cyprus
Archpriest Giorgi Zviadadze, Georgia

The Anglican Consultative Council:

* receives with pleasure the news in the Director's Report of the forthcoming completion of the work of the International Commission for Anglican–Orthodox Theological Dialogue (ICAOTD), and thanks its members for their long-standing contribution to the quest for the full visible unity of the Church of Christ;
* encourages the ICAOTD to move towards the publication of their Agreed Statements at the earliest convenient moment.

Anglican–Roman Catholic Relations

May 2005 will have seen the publication of the final Agreed Statement of the second phase of the Anglican–Roman Catholic International Commission (ARCIC), with the Seattle Statement on the place and understanding of the Blessed Virgin Mary in the Christian Faith, *Mary: Grace and Hope in Christ.* This document is now being offered by ARCIC for study and evaluation by the Roman Catholic Church and the churches of the Anglican Communion. It follows the Agreed Statements on *Salvation and the Church* (1986), *The Church as Communion* (1990), *Life in Christ: Morals, Communion and the Church* (1993), and *The Gift of Authority* (1999).

ACO is also extremely grateful to Dr Timothy Bradshaw of Regent's Park College, Oxford, for writing a commentary to go alongside the publication of the Mary document, and which introduces its contents to an Anglican readership.

The production of the Mary document brings to a close the round of dialogue on subjects outlined in the Malta Report of 1968, and at the heart of the mandate for ARCIC II established by Archbishop Robert Runcie and Pope John Paul II.

At ACC-11 in Dundee, ACC specifically requested that there should be a debate on the earlier report of ARCIC, *The Gift of Authority.* Such a debate now would be premature. IASCER has continually monitored the reception process for this document, accompanied as it was by the 'Auxiliary Resources for Cross-Reference' and the 'Questions for Study by the Provinces'. To date, IASCER has had the opportunity to evaluate the responses of some eight provinces.

Part of the reason for this patchy response is the more diverse nature of the documents and subject matters that have been generated as part of the process of ARCIC II. There has not been a Final Report, such as was produced by the first phase of ARCIC, and the churches of the Anglican Communion may have been waiting for such a drawing together of the work of

Anglican–Roman Catholic International Commission (ARCIC)

MEETINGS

1998	Rome	2001	Dublin, Ireland
1999	Mississauga, Canada	2002	Vienna, Austria
2000	Paris, France	2003	Delray Beach, Florida, USA

ANGLICANS

The Most Revd Peter Carnley, Australia, from 2004 (Co-Chair)

The Most Revd Frank Griswold, to 2004 (Co-Chair)

The Revd Canon Gregory K Cameron, ACO, from 2003 (Co-Secretary)

The Revd Canon David Hamid, ACO, to 2002 (Co-Secretary)

The Rt Revd John Baycroft, Canada

Dr E Rozanne Elder, USA

The Revd Professor Jaci Maraschin, Brazil

The Revd Dr John Muddiman, England

The Rt Revd Michael Nazir-Ali, England

The Revd Canon Dr Nicholas Sagovsky, England

The Revd Canon Dr Charles Sherlock, Australia

Archbishop of Canterbury's Observer:

The Revd Canon Jonathan Gough, from 2002

The Revd Dr Herman Browne, 2000–2001

The Revd Canon Dr Richard Marsh, to 1999

ROMAN CATHOLICS

The Most Revd Alexander J Brunett, USA, from 2000 (Co-Chair)

The Rt Revd Cormac Murphy-O'Connor, UK, to 2000 (Co-Chair)

The Revd Canon Donald Bolen, PCPCU, from 2001 (Co-Secretary)

The Revd Monsignor Timothy Galligan, PCPCU, until 2001 (Co-Secretary)

Sister Sara Butler, MSBT, USA

The Revd Dr Peter Cross, Australia

The Revd Dr Adelbert Denaux, Belgium

The Most Revd Brian Farrell, LC, Vatican City, from 2003

Dom Emmanuel Lanne, OSB, Belgium, from 2001 (Consultant)

The Rt Revd Malcolm McMahon, OP, UK, from 2001

The Revd Professor Charles Morerod, OP, Italy, from 2002

The Rt Revd Marc Ouellet, PSS, Vatican City, 2001–2002

The Revd Jean Tillard, Canada, to 2000, deceased

The Revd Professor Liam Walsh, OP, Switzerland

ARCIC II before proceeding to evaluation and response. In the light of this, ACO has commissioned a study on the reception of all the Agreed Statements of ARCIC II from Dr Mary Tanner, a member of the Church of England and former Moderator of the Faith and Order Commission of the World Council of Churches. It is hoped that this study will be available to members of ACC at their meeting in June. Such a study, when it is produced may indicate more clearly the way in which to proceed.

In May, 2000 at Mississauga, a conference of Anglican and Roman Catholic bishops encouraged the establishment of a new commission for Anglican–Roman Catholic dialogue; a request which became the foundation of the commission now known as the International Anglican–Roman

---

International Anglican–Roman Catholic Commission for Unity and Mission (IARCCUM)

MEETINGS

2001   London and Rome
2002   Malta
2003   Dromantine, Northern Ireland

ANGLICANS

The Rt Revd David Beetge, South Africa (Co-Chair)
The Revd Canon Gregory K Cameron, ACO, from 2003 (Co-Secretary)
The Revd Canon David Hamid, ACO, to 2002 (Co-Secretary)
The Most Revd Peter Carnley, Australia
The Rt Revd Edwin Gulick, USA
The Most Revd Peter Kwong, Hong Kong
The Rt Revd Michael Nazir-Ali, England
The Revd Canon Jonathan Gough, Archbishop of Canterbury's Office
Dr Mary Tanner, England

CONSULTANTS

Bishop John Baycroft, Canada
Bishop David Hamid, C of E in Europe

ROMAN CATHOLICS

Archbishop John Bathersby, Australia (Co-Chair)
The Revd Donald Bolen, PCPCU (Co-Secretary)
Archbishop Alexander Brunett, USA
The Revd Dr Peter Cross, Australia
Bishop Anthony Farquhar, Ireland
Sr Dr Donna Geernaert, Canada
Bishop Crispian Hollis, UK
Bishop Lucius Ugorji, Nigeria

CONSULTANTS

Monsignor Timothy Galligan, UK
The Revd Dr Paul McPartlan, UK

Catholic Commission for Unity and Mission (IARCCUM). The intention for this new commission is that it would complement the theological process of ARCIC, and provide a more ecclesiologically and practically based process of dialogue between our two traditions.

The work of IARCCUM has proceeded along three major threads. The first has been to examine the possibility of practical initiatives of co-operation between Anglicans and Roman Catholics. The Canonists Colloquium, and the developing joint Bishops' Training Programme in North America are examples of practical initiatives being undertaken in co-operation with IARCCUM. Also, there is the work of the regional and national ARCs.

Secondly, IARCCUM has taken some responsibility for fostering the reception of the corpus of ARCIC's work across the globe. It notes with satisfaction therefore, the production of study resources such as 'Church as Communion—A Discussion Resource for Anglicans and Roman Catholics' in Australia. A careful programme for study and reflection will undoubtedly be the fruit of IARCCUM's future work.

Thirdly, and most ambitiously, IARCCUM initiated a process whereby the fruits of thirty years of theological dialogue can be harvested. The nature of this process has subsisted in the development of a draft text for a Common Statement of Faith for the Anglican and Roman Catholic churches. This work is still very much in progress, and it would be inappropriate to bring a text before ACC for its consideration at present. Nor is it clear what status of authority could be given to the text, and the way in which it will be offered to the churches for reception. However the aim is to produce a condensation of the broad sweep of theological agreement discerned by both ARCIC I and ARCIC II, and to offer that for evaluation by the authorities in both families of churches as a foundation for future co-operation in mission and in ecumenical work. It may be that the approach of IARCCUM to this project offers the most effective and accessible way to ground the reception of *The Gift of Authority* and the other fruits of this highly successful dialogue.

Informal relations with the Vatican remain strong. The presence of the Anglican Centre in Rome is an added blessing, and a foundation which sustains day-to-day liaison and fellowship between Anglicans and Roman Catholics in Rome. Our colleagues in the Pontifical Council for Promoting Christian Unity have been generous in their time and efforts to further relations. The fruit of this relationship could be discerned in the place given to ecumenical delegates at the funeral of Pope John Paul II and in the Inaugural Mass of Pope Benedict XVI. It is surely of significance that significant delegations of Anglicans were invited, alongside other ecumenical representatives, to take a prominent place both at the mourning for John Paul II, and the welcome for the ministry of Benedict XVI.

The Anglican Consultative Council:

- welcomes the publication of the Agreed Statement of the Anglican–Roman Catholic International Commission (ARCIC), *Mary, Grace and Hope in Christ*, and the completion of the second phase of the Commission's work;
- expresses its gratitude to all the members of ARCIC over the last thirty-five years for their outstanding contribution to Anglican–Roman Catholic dialogue;
- offers its thanks for the ongoing work of the members of the International Anglican–Roman Catholic Commission on Unity and Mission (IARCCUM), and encourages them to proceed with the work of drafting a Common Statement of Faith (which can represent the 'harvesting' of the convergence in faith discerned in the work of ARCIC) and with the other initiatives of common witness being developed by IARCCUM;
- asks the Director of Ecumenical Studies to ensure that Provinces are invited to undertake a process of study of all the Agreed Statements of the second phase of ARCIC, and, in particular, that they have the opportunity to evaluate the way in which any Common Statement of Faith produced by IARCCUM might represent an appropriate manner in which to recognise the convergence of Christian Faith between the Anglican Communion and the Roman Catholic Church expressed in the work of ARCIC;
- respectfully requests His Holiness the Pope and His Grace the Archbishop of Canterbury to proceed to the commissioning of a third phase of ARCIC and of theological dialogue between the Anglican Communion and the Roman Catholic Church in pursuit of the full visible unity of Christ's Body here on earth, which is the stated goal for the ecumenical quest in both traditions.

Regional Developments

The Ecumenical Department also keeps an eye on the progress made by the Provinces and Churches of the Anglican Communion in the ecumenical quest. ACC may wish to take note of the following developments.

In South Asia, the United Churches of North India and South India have joined with the Mar Thoma Syrian Church of Malabar, a Church which has long been (since 1974) a church in communion with the Anglican Communion, in a Communion of Churches in India. In many ways this new development, which was inaugurated in 2004, formalises much of the co-operation that has already been evident in India, but it assists in Christian witness in the sub-continent by presenting ever more clearly the ecumenical commitment of these churches.

In Australia, Anglican and Lutheran churches have entered into a covenantal relationship founded upon the document *Common Ground* published in 2001. This covenant parallels the agreements established elsewhere across the globe, including, for example, the Meissen Agreement between Anglican, Lutheran and Reformed churches in central Europe.

Mention has already been made of the Church of England–Methodist Church of Great Britain Covenant signed in December 2003. One particular feature of this covenant of which ACC may wish to take note is the practical initiatives sustained by the Joint Implementation Commission, which exists to ensure that the Covenant is more than a formal commitment, but something which touches the lives of the churches at grassroots level.

Of considerable significance is the Covenant in Papua New Guinea between the Anglicans of that Province and the Roman Catholic Church in Papua New Guinea. The mission relationship is expressed in two documents, a formal Covenant recognising a common faith (see Appendix 3), and a specific commitment, which includes the Evangelical Lutheran Church, to recognise and respect each other's baptisms.

Ecumenism takes many forms, and the pattern of the churches changes as they evolve their lives in the local context. In 1998, the Order of Ethiopia,[1] a body of South African Christians which had retained a distinct character within the Church of the Province of Southern Africa (CPSA) decided to withdraw to establish a separate Ethiopian Episcopal Church (EEC) in South Africa.

Relations with CPSA, and indeed, the wider Anglican Communion remain strong however, and the EEC has entered into a formal covenant with CPSA, and wishes to formalise links with the Communion as a whole.

Relations with the Iglesia Filipina Independiente (IFI), the third of the churches to be in (full) communion with the Anglican Communion, remain strong, and in particular, the link with the Episcopal Church (USA) is in the process of being renewed and enhanced at present.

The Anglican Consultative Council:

1. welcomes the establishment of the Communion of Churches in India, and looks forward to seeing the fruits of further co-operation between the United Churches of North and South India and the Mar Thoma Syrian Church of Malabar;

2. welcomes the covenant and Agreed Statement commitments made in Papua New Guinea between the Anglican Church of Papua New Guinea, the Roman Catholic Church and the Evangelical Lutheran Church in Papua New Guinea, and believes that they have offered a benchmark in ecumenical relations;

3. welcomes the recent covenant between the Church of the Province of Southern Africa (CPSA) and the Ethiopian Episcopal Church (EEC), and
   (i) awaits further developments in this relationship with interest,
   (ii) encourages CPSA to continue to develop its links with EEC, and
   (iii) looks forward to the time when CPSA may be able to recommend that EEC become a church in communion with the wider Anglican Communion.

Multilateral Ecumenical Bodies

The Ecumenical Department continues to engage not only with our ecumenical partners in the different churches of the *oikumene,* but also with bodies that work in the ecumenical quest across the denominational frontiers.

Chief amongst these is the World Council of Churches (WCC). The ACO has a limited role in the life of the World Council, being invited to send an observer to meetings of the Central Committee and meetings of the Faith and Order Plenary Commission. Recently, the World Council has been underwriting a number of interesting developments which are changing the face of multi-lateral work; chief amongst them being the formation of the Global Christian Forum and the Reconfiguration of the Ecumenical Movement Process.

The Global Christian Forum (GCF) is an initiative which emerged from conversations within the WCC but is now served by its own committee. It was set up as a way of reaching out to those parts of the Christian family who, through reasons of conviction or temperament, had not engaged with membership of the WCC. In particular, neither the Roman Catholic Church nor large sections of the Pentecostal and house church movements feel able to participate fully in the life of the WCC because it does not fit with their ecclesiological understandings. The GCF was conceived as an informal forum where the whole range of the *oikumene* could meet at an affective level, in contrast to formal theological or structural dialogue. The process adopted has been one of regional meetings with representatives of all Christian traditions being invited to come to share their stories and experience of Christian faith. An international consultation in the USA in 2002 was followed in 2004 by the first of the regional consultations in Hong Kong. Two more consultations are planned for Africa and Europe and these will culminate in what is hoped to be a truly global gathering of Christian leaders in 2007. The Anglican Communion has been represented on the ongoing work of the Forum by the Revd Sarah Rowland-Jones, a priest of CPSA, and a member of IASCER.

Towards the end of the twentieth century, discussion developed about the way in which to carry the ecumenical movement into the next century. The twentieth century had been a century of sea change with respect to the quest for unity amongst Christians, but as the churches moved into the new millennium questions needed to be asked about the adequacy of the instruments which carried ecumenism forward. In this process the WCC was an active and willing participant, asking questions about its own role and how best to serve Christ's Body. The process of evaluation and rethinking which developed has become known—perhaps inadequately—as the "Reconfiguration of the Ecumenical Movement Process". WCC has facilitated a number of conferences on this subject now, and the current state of thinking is represented in Appendix 4. You may wish to read this alongside the statement by IASCER in 2004 (Resolution 6.04 in Appendix 5) which touches upon the same subject.

Finally, mention ought to be made of the work of the Conference of Secretaries of Christian World Communions. This is also an informal body, which brings the General Secretaries of all those Christian bodies which can claim a global presence in an annual meeting to exchange information and co-ordinate the work which their various offices undertake. The Director of Ecumenical Affairs assists the Secretary General in his work with this body. The Conference is not a formal body—it has neither constitution nor membership as such, but allows for fellowship, co-operation and mutual understanding across the world communions.

The Anglican Consultative Council:

- sends its greetings to the World Council of Churches, which will meet in plenary Assembly in February 2006 in Porto Alegre, Brazil, and its congratulations to its new General Secretary, Dr Samuel Kobia;
- adopts the Message to the World Council of Churches drafted by IASCER, meeting in Jamaica in 2004, which stresses the priority of Faith and Order work in the ecumenical movement;
- requests the World Council of Churches to find ways by which the Anglican Communion can enhance its participation as a Communion in the life of the World Council, and in which Anglicans can play a full part in its life and work;
- affirms the work of the Global Christian Forum, and encourages all Provinces to support the programme being developed by it for mutual listening across the whole breadth of the Christian family.

The Inter-Anglican Standing Commission on Ecumenical Relations

In 1998, the Lambeth Conference proposed the formation of a Standing

Commission which could offer advice to Provinces on ecumenical projects and agreements. In addition, it would be able to co-ordinate the various dialogues of the Anglican Communion with ecumenical partners, so that by holding a watching and advisory brief, the Commission could assist coherence and integrity amongst the many-faceted aspects of Anglican engagement across the *oikumene*.

The Inter-Anglican Standing Commission on Ecumenical Relations (IASCER) met for the first time in 2000, under the chairmanship of the Primate of the West Indies, Archbishop Drexel Gomez. Since then it has met annually in the discharge of its mandate, receiving reports of all the inter-

---

Inter-Anglican Standing Commission on Ecumenical Relations (IASCER)

MEETINGS

2000	Nassau, Bahamas
2001	Cape Town, South Africa
2002	Bose, Italy
2003	Delray Beach, Florida, USA
2004	Montego Bay, Jamaica

MEMBERS

The Most Revd Drexel W Gomez (Chair)
The Revd Canon Gregory K Cameron, from 2003 (Secretary)
The Revd Canon David Hamid, to 2002 (Secretary)
The Revd Prebendary Dr Paul Avis
The Revd Canon Alyson Barnett-Cowan
The Revd Dr William Crockett
The Rt Revd Mark Dyer, to 2003
The Rt Revd Christopher Epting, from 2001
The Revd Dr John Gibaut, from 2004
The Rt Revd Dr John Gladstone
The Revd Canon Jonathan Gough, to 2004
The Rt Revd John Hind
The Revd Dr John Jae Joung Lee
The Rt Revd Justus Marcus, to 2003 (deceased)
The Revd Jane Namugenyi
The Revd Canon Luke Pato
The Revd Dr George Pothen, The Mar Thoma Church, India,
    2002–2003 (Observer)
The Rt Revd Dr Geoffrey Rowell
The Revd Sarah Rowland-Jones
The Revd Dr Charles Sherlock, to 2003
The Revd Canon Professor J Robert Wright

national dialogues, and commenting, where appropriate, on ecumenical developments across the globe. This significant work is incorporated every year into a set of resolutions which reflect the advice and thinking of IASCER to, and occasionally, on behalf of, the Communion. The formal resolutions made by IASCER in the period since ACC-12 may be found in Appendix 5.

The Anglican Consultative Council:

- receives the Report of the Director of Ecumenical Affairs on the work of the Inter-Anglican Standing Commission on Ecumenical Relations (IASCER), adopts its resolutions as set out in Appendix 5 of the Report, particularly the Guidelines on Ecumenical Participation in Ordinations, and commends these resolutions to the Provinces for study and reflection.

The Inter-Anglican Theological and Doctrinal Commission

The Inter-Anglican Theological and Doctrinal Commission (IATDC) was set up following the 1998 Lambeth Conference, in order to continue reflection and study on the basis, nature and sustaining of Communion, building on the work of the Virginia Report (1997) and to study such other documents, such as *To Mend the Net*, which were referred to it. The Commission adopted an inter-active study approach, seeking to engage the Communion at large with these important issues, and an ambitious series of mailings were undertaken to all diocesan bishops and theological institutions.

The first meeting of the Commission was in fact disrupted by the events of 9.11, but the Commission still managed to formulate Four Key Questions on Communion which were circulated for comment and response. On the basis of responses received from across the Communion, the Commission then proceeded to formulate Six Propositions, which again were circulated for comment and study (see Appendix 6). Responses received to this second phase of consultation have then formed the basis of further reflection. A full account of the process, and of the current thinking of the Commission can be found on the IATDC section of the Anglican Communion website. In early 2004, a member of the Commission, the Revd Philip Thomas, enjoyed a Visiting Fellowship provided by Virginia Theological Seminary (who have provided substantial ongoing support to the life of the Commission), which enabled him to collate and integrate much of the material received and generated by the Commission as a basis for ongoing study.

In 2004, the meetings of the Commission were suspended for two years, largely because finance had to be found from within the Inter-Anglican budget

---

Inter-Anglican Theological and Doctrinal Commission (IATDC)

MEETINGS

2001 Wimbledon, England
2002 Virginia Theological Seminary, USA
2003 Virginia Theological Seminary, USA

MEMBERS

The Rt Revd Professor Stephen W Sykes (Chair)
The Revd Dr Philip H E Thomas (Assistant to the Chair)
The Revd Canon Gregory K Cameron, from 2003 (Secretary)
The Revd Canon David Hamid, to 2002 (Secretary)
The Revd Victor R Atta-Baffoe
The Rt Revd Dr Samuel R Cutting
The Revd Professor Kortright Davis
The Rt Revd J Mark Dyer
The Rt Revd Tan Sri Dr Lim Cheng Ean
The Revd Dr Katherine Grieb (Observer)

The Revd Dr Bruce N Kaye
Dr Esther M Mombo
The Rt Revd Dr Matthew Oluremi Owadayo
The Revd Canon Luke Pato
The Revd Dr Stephen Pickard
Dr Jenny Te Paa
The Rt Revd Paul Richardson
The Revd Dr Nicholas Sagovsky
Dr Eileen Scully
The Rt Revd Dr N Thomas Wright
The Very Revd Paul F M Zahl
The Rt Revd Tito Zavala

---

for the work of the Lambeth Commission. The Commission's life, however, has not entirely halted, and work has continued to be undertaken, both by members of the Commission, and through electronic means. The Commission intends to meet in 2006 to begin the process of bringing together the fruits of its studies for presentation at the 2008 Lambeth Conference.

The Windsor Report 2004 will undoubtedly itself be a contribution to the reflection of the Anglican Communion on its nature and future, and IATDC is well placed to carry the process of further reflection forward.

The Anglican Consultative Council:

- receives the Report of the Director of Ecumenical Affairs and Theological Studies on the work of the Inter-Anglican Theological and Doctrinal Commission (IATDC), and thanks the Commission for its ongoing study of Communion;
- encourages the Inter-Anglican Finance and Administration Committee to provide the resources to enable IATDC to meet again in 2006;
- asks IATDC to integrate an evaluation of the Windsor Report 2004 into its continuing studies and work, and to complete its work in time to be able

to report to the Lambeth Conference in 2008;

- commends the fruitful interactive process adopted by IATDC to the Communion, and encourages full participation in its future work.

The Lambeth Process

After the Primates' Meeting in May 2003, there were the now well-known developments in the dioceses of New Westminster in Canada and New Hampshire in the USA which have been the focus of so much attention since then. At the Primates' Meeting in October 2003 to consider these developments, the Archbishop of Canterbury was asked to set up the Lambeth Commission on Communion, which was staffed and serviced by the Ecumenical Department.

The work and meetings of the Commission, and the subsequent publication of the Windsor Report 2004, took up a great deal of the energies of the Ecumenical Department through the year of its operation, and the Ecumenical Department was also asked to staff and service the work of the Reception Reference Group set up by the Primates' Standing Committee after the publication of the Windsor Report and intended to oversee reactions to the report from the Provinces and our ecumenical partners.

The Lambeth Process continues with the establishment of the Panel of Reference at the request of the Primates' Meeting in Dromantine this year. The Ecumenical Department has risen to the challenge of staffing this body, and stands ready to serve the Communion and the Consultative Council as requested.

Conclusion

As will be observed from this report, the work of the Ecumenical Department is highly varied and demanding. However, it is also central to the international life of the Anglican Communion. As we move into the twenty-first century, the challenge to make our Christian witness and the preaching of the Gospel more effective by the witness of all the churches united in love and service to the world becomes ever more pressing. Whilst the heartbeat of the Church's life will always be at the local level, the international dimension is one which helps to fashion a positive environment in which that fundamental element of life in Christ can be lived out.

It is a privileged ministry with the whole *oikumene* that members of the Ecumenical Department carry out in their service to the Anglican Consultative Council, and to the hundreds of volunteers who actually carry the work of ecumenism forward by their service on the committees and commissions of the councils of the Communion. May God bless us in His service and guide the Church into the fullness of life which is his gift to us.

Gregory K Cameron
Deputy Secretary General
London, May 2005

The Anglican Consultative Council:

- expresses its heartfelt thanks to those who have in past years dedicated themselves on its behalf in the area of Ecumenical Affairs, gratefully recalling the work of Bishop David Hamid, Bishop John Baycroft and Ms Frances Hillier;
- offers its gratitude to Canon Gregory K Cameron, Director of Ecumenical Affairs since 2003, for his Report to the Council, and its good wishes for his ongoing work;
- offers thanks and good wishes to Mrs Christine Codner and to the Revd Terrie Robinson for their continuing work in the Department.

Appendices

Appendix 1:
Anglican–Lutheran International Commission—Mandate 2004

The Anglican Consultative Council and the Lutheran World Federation, in accordance with the resolutions of the Twelfth Meeting of the Anglican Consultative Council in Hong Kong in September 2002, and the commitments of the Tenth Assembly of the Lutheran World Federation in Winnipeg in July 2003, approve the establishment of a new Anglican-Lutheran International Commission (ALIC), with the following mandate.

That the Commission shall

1. provide guidance regarding the evaluation and implementation of the Report of the Anglican-Lutheran Working Group (1999-2002), *Growth in Communion,* with a view to co-ordinated decisions by the governing bodies of both communions, in co-operation with their member churches

2. continue to monitor and advise upon the development of Anglican–Lutheran relations around the world, having regard to their consistency with each other and with the self-understanding of the two communions, give attention to the impact of different ecumenical

methodologies, and to clarify questions of transitivity (i.e. the conse-quences that an agreement reached in one ecumenical relationship may be seen to have for other relationships)

3. explore the possibility of common actions and statements, and, in particular, seek ways to promote joint study projects of issues rele-vant to Anglican–Lutheran relations

4. consider ways to engage with and promote the wider ecumenical movement, and, in particular, give consideration to the ecumenical role and contribution of Christian world communions

5. report to the relevant bodies on both sides on the progress of work, and to ensure consultation on emerging developments in regional Anglican–Lutheran relations.

Approved, Joint Standing Committee, 3 March 2004

Appendix 2:
Anglican–Old Catholic International Co-ordinating Council— Mandate 2005

The Archbishops of Canterbury and Utrecht, on behalf of the Anglican Con-sultative Council, and the International Bishops' Conference of the Union of Utrecht, commission a new body for a period of four years to consult on Anglican Old Catholic relations in succession to the work of the Anglican Old Catholic International Co-ordinating Council, whose mandate expired with their final meeting in Canterbury in March 2004. This new body will:

- assist the Council of Anglican Bishops in Continental Europe and the International Bishops' Conference to develop a common definition and understanding of shared mission for their work in Europe, and to advise on the establishment of appropriate mechanisms to carry for-ward that mission

- promote the drafting of a common statement of ecclesiological under-standing to assist in exploring the shape of the future relationship between the churches of Anglican Communion and the Union of Utrecht, and to advise the Anglican Consultative Council and the International Bishops' Conference on the future development of that relationship

- review the nature and content of ecumenical agreements by the churches of the Anglican Communion and the Union of Utrecht with regard to their impact on ecumenical progress

- explore concrete proposals for joint initiatives in mission work in continental Europe.

Approved by the Archbishop of Canterbury, and the JSC, 3 March 2004

Appendix 3:
Anglican–Roman Catholic Covenant and Agreed Statement, Papua New Guinea

A Covenant between the Anglican Church of Papua New Guinea and the Roman Catholic Church in Papua New Guinea

In the name of the Father, the Son and the Holy Spirit.

Believing in the will of God that all Christians are called to be one so that the world will believe in the Lord Jesus Christ, recognizing our common baptism in the name of the Holy Trinity, encouraged by many years of dialogue, co-operation and friendship between our communities, wishing to respond to the pastoral needs of our people and be an effective evangelistic witness to the nation, we the bishops of the Anglican Church of PNG and the Catholic Bishops Conference, in the name of our clergy and people, enter into this covenant.

We affirm:

1. that the source of true ecclesial unity in Christ is the unity of the Triune God: Father, Son and Holy Spirit;

2. that Jesus Christ, the living centre of our faith, is the Saviour and Lord of the world;

3. that the desire of Christ is that the Church be one people brought together from all races, languages and cultures;

4. that the life of grace is nourished by the Word of God we receive through the Scripture, Sacraments and the action of the Holy Spirit within the Church;

5. that the Holy Spirit, having revealed a rich diversity of gifts in the Anglican and Roman Catholic communions while never ceasing to draw these communions into the fullness of ecclesial unity in Christ, and having enabled us internationally through ARCIC to achieve substantial agreement on the Eucharist, Ministry and Authority, now prompts us to overcome the separation which exists in doctrine and ecclesial life, in order to achieve that full visible unity which Christ wills for his Church.

We resolve:

1. to strengthen our unity in Christ and maintain our commitment to eventual full communion by:
   - pursuing theological dialogue on matters that still separate us: for example, authority and freedom, unity and pluriformity, setting limits and respecting differences, inter-communion and the validity of Anglican Orders, married priests and women's ordinations;
   - having standing invitations for the attendance of one episcopal representative of the sister-Church at the yearly meeting of the Catholic Bishops' Conference and the Anglican Bishops' Meeting;
   - holding an annual ARC–PNG meeting of the Ecumenical Commission of the two Churches; and
   - making an act of re-dedication to the goal of unity each Pentecost.

2. to do together whatever does not have to be done separately:
   - working together on matters of social concern and undertaking joint programmes to strengthen family life and other Christian relationships; and
   - giving mutual support in educational ministries in seminaries such as through an exchange of staff and students in specific areas of study, mutual visits, encouragement of research papers relating to Anglican/Roman Catholic issues and occasional shared prayer.

3. to give witness to our growing unity by:
   - responding to the appropriate openings of closer relationships which emerge naturally between religious orders of the two Churches, such as participation in workshops together (Xavier Institute, the National Formators Workshop), sharing in common outreach programmes (Aitape), cooperation in various ministries (Family Life, Word Publishing, the Melanesian Institute) and an exchange of retreat and workshop directors;
   - working together to strengthen wider ecumenical activity, particularly through the PNG Council of Churches;
   - encouraging prayer for a wider unity, especially through the Week of Prayer for Christian Unity from Ascension to Pentecost; and
   - making joint witness to the claims of Christ to the lapsed and to those in particular spiritual need.

19 July 2003. St. Martin's Church. East Boroko. Port Moresby

(Signed) For the Anglican Church: Archbishop James Ayong
(Signed) For the Roman Catholic Church: Bishop John Ribat

An Agreed Statement on Baptism between the Anglican Church, the Evangelical Lutheran Church and the Roman Catholic Church

in Papua New Guinea

We confess together that in the sacrament of baptism the Holy Spirit truly incorporates us into Christ and into his Church, justifies and truly renews us, hence we are reborn to a sharing of divine life.

We confess together that baptism is the effective sign of our participation in the passion, death and resurrection of our Lord whereby the baptised receives adoption by the Father and becomes a child of God, receives the gift of the Holy Spirit, obtains the forgiveness of sins, shares in Christ's eternal priesthood, participates in his messianic mission in the world, and becomes an inheritor of God's Kingdom.

Therefore together we recognise the necessity of baptism and affirming our common doctrine and practice in respect to this sacrament, do declare;

1. That we mutually recognise and respect each other's rite of baptism as contained in the Book of Common Prayer, the Lutheran Book of Worship and the Roman Catholic rite of Baptism;

2. That the rite of baptism performed by our churches is valid and therefore not to be repeated even conditionally;

3. That although our churches have always recognised the sacrament of baptism administered according to the New Testament, this present declaration constitutes an act whereby our churches mutually give guarantee of the validity of the baptism administered by their respective ministers;

4. That our churches accept the baptism of infants where the faith of the parents and of the eccesial community supplies for the child's inability to profess a personal faith and represents a commitment to raise the child in the Christian faith;

5. That baptism administered by our respective ministers are to be duly recorded in the proper registry books, and certificates of baptism delivered to all who are baptised. The presentation of the said certificate of baptism shall be deemed sufficient evidence of the fact and validity of baptism. We agree, in cases of real doubt to consult each other in these matters;

6. That we commit ourselves to earnest continual prayer, consultation and working together so that we may come to the fullness of our unity in Christ of which baptism is the foundation, the impetus and the pledge.

In testimony thereof, we affix our signatures this 19th day of July in the year of our Lord 2003 at St. Mary's Cathedral, Port Moresby.

(Signed) For the Anglican Church in PNG: Archbishop James Ayong
(Signed) For the Evangelical Lutheran Church of PNG: Assistant Bishop
Kiage Motoro
(Signed) For the Roman Catholic Church in PNG: Bishop John Ribat

Appendix 4: Statement from the WCC Consultation, *'Ecumenism in the 21st Century'*

30 November–3 December 2004

Introduction

> "For the peace of the whole world,
> the stability of the Holy Churches of God
> and for the Union of All,
> Let us pray to the Lord."
> (St. John Chrysostom)

1. In the spirit of this prayer, the World Council of Churches invited a group of 106 representatives from churches, agencies/specialised ministries, regional and national councils of churches, Christian World Communions and international ecumenical organisations to a consultation on "Ecumenism in the 21st Century," held at Chavannes-de-Bogis, Switzerland from 30 November to 3 December 2004.

2. The need for such a consultation comes from the fact that Christians face new challenges in the world and that new and effective ways of working together are required in order to respond to the demands of the world from the perspective of the Gospel of Jesus Christ.

The Ecumenical Movement

3. There is a rich history of ecumenical traditions and achievements which served as the starting point for these discussions. The term 'ecumenical' embraces the quest for visible Christian unity, which is undertaken in theological study, in common witness in the worldwide task of mission and evangelism as well as in diakonia and the promotion of justice and peace.[2]

4. Participation in the ecumenical movement follows from and leads toward shared faith in the Triune God and common Christian values. Before his crucifixion Jesus Christ prayed for his disciples and all Christians: "that they may all be one, just as you, Father, are in me, and I in you, that they also may be in us, so that the world may believe that you have sent me" (John 17:21). Thus Christian unity is related to the unity of the Triune God. We are therefore urgently called to

transform our self-centred mentality into selfless love for the other and the society of which we are a part. As Christ is one with his father we too as Christians have the vocation to be one. We have the duty to make evident that Christianity is a unity in which the many form a unique whole. Their belonging together is based on the unity of the work of God the Father through the Son and the Holy Spirit. Accordingly the renewal of the ecumenical movement is an invitation to all involved to go beyond the present boundaries, to interact with each other and with society. "It is a call to bear witness to unity by making an optimum use of the abilities, history, experience, commitment and spiritual tradition of everyone involved. This includes submission to one another and the search to understand the will of the Lord in a spirit of repentance and reconciliation."[3]

5. The ecumenical movement today is carried out at different levels by churches acting through conciliar bodies (e.g. WCC, regional ecumenical organizations, sub-regional fellowships and national councils of churches), Christian World Communions, ecumenical communities, mission agencies, theological colleges and associations, ecumenical academies and lay training centers as well as agencies/specialized ministries, international ecumenical organizations and many other ecumenical bodies. It is obvious that the ecumenical movement is far wider than any one institution and includes all those who yearn for unity and all those who dream of a common Christian voice on the burning issues of the day.

A Time of Change

6. The ecumenical movement is living and operating in a world which is constantly changing. The political constellation is very different from what it was during the 20th century. The world today is dominated by a concentration of extreme power and wealth. As people seek to affirm their identities in the light of globalizing forces, increasingly many are identifying themselves in terms of their religion.

7. It is a world of brilliant new technologies and a world in which millions of people suffer from hunger and die from rampant violence. The environment is threatened with destruction because of disrespect for creation.

8. People in many regions are increasingly embracing the view that another world is possible. They are seeking a world undergirded by a deep sense of spiritual discernment. The growth of civil society is transforming communities and nations. Those who have traditionally been marginalized and excluded are struggling to make a more

just and peaceful world possible.

9. These changes are also affecting the churches. Declining membership in some European and North American churches will have consequences for the material resourcing of ecumenical bodies in the future, while at the same time prompting new relationships of genuine partnership between churches of the North and those of the South. The proliferation of non-governmental organizations has created a more competitive environment in which churches and their related organizations sometimes struggle for survival, but also opens up new possibilities of partnerships and coalitions in the cause of peace, justice and the care of creation.

10. This has changed the ecumenical life of the churches. There are important new ecumenical actors who are not formally included in the existing structures and there are some in the ecumenical family who do not feel valued by others. Many new ecumenical organizations have been created, giving rise to fears that all of these ecumenical bodies cannot be sustained. Churches complain that there are too many levels of "belonging." Insufficient programme coordination by confessional and ecumenical bodies may represent duplication of efforts. There are questions around membership and around funding of the ecumenical movement.

11. The primary structures of the ecumenical movement were established decades ago, when both the world and the churches were in a very different place. Today the world challenges us in ways that we have not known before.

Ecumenism in the 21st Century

12. In recent years, discussions about the effects of the changing world on the ecumenical movement have taken place in different fora. In November 2003, a consultation on "Reconfiguration of the Ecumenical Movement" in Antelias/Lebanon affirmed the urgency of the issues and called for further discussions to "re-vitalize the ecumenical movement and to ensure that our structures and our actions respond to the changing global realities." In this line, the meeting in Chavannes-de-Bogis continued the work and looked into the question of how to find a new configuration or re-shaping which strengthens ecumenical relationships and structures in face of the new challenges mentioned above. The new study of current ecumenical structures and relationships *(Mapping the Oikoumene),* the *Reflections on Ecumenism in the 21st century,* both published by the WCC (2004) and the reactions from the churches to the report

of the Antelias Consultation (2003) provided insightful resources in the deliberations of this consultation.

Recognizing that any discussion of structures must be guided by the values and *vision* of the ecumenical movement, the following vision was identified:

13. We hope that the ecumenical movement in the 21st century will be a special space:
    - where more and more Christians are involved in the work of Christian unity, and the fellowship among the churches is strengthened
    - where open and ecumenically-minded culture is fostered in the everyday lives of people in their own contexts and where ecumenical formation is a central focus at all levels of church life, from the local to the global
    - where spirituality is the basis of the life of Christians together and where, as individuals, churches and organizations, Christians can pray together and can encourage each other to discern God's will for their lives
    - where all, including the marginalized and excluded, are welcomed into inclusive and loving communities
    - where relationships, built on mutual trust, are strengthened between all parts of the ecumenical family
    - where each Christian can be supported in practising responsible stewardship and where churches and Christian organizations can be mutually accountable to each other
    - where diversity of cultures and traditions is recognized as a source of creativity
    - where hospitality is manifest towards those of different faiths and where dialogue is encouraged
    - where young people are encouraged to join in and to lead
    - where women's visions of being church are shared
    - where the ministry of healing is carried out in shared actions
    - where the healing of memories leads to reconciliation
    - where, together, we are enabled to be prophetic in confronting the injustices and violence of the world and to take risks in our commitment to justice and peace when Christ calls us to do so.

14. We recognize that there are still many issues that divide us which need to be overcome. But we still hope that the Holy Spirit leads us to the end that one day we can celebrate the Eucharist together as the sign of our unity.

15. The process of moving towards a new configuration of the ecumeni-

cal movement is urgent. Financial difficulties in many churches put pressure on the ecumenical movement to reconsider how it works. But the needs coming from a changing world also ask for a common agenda which harnesses collective energies to work together for the healing of the world. Moreover, a need is felt for more effective instruments in the quest for Christian unity given the changing landscape of Christianity.

16. A new configuration of the ecumenical movement will require *change* from our churches and our organizations. Structures are needed which are less rigid, more flexible, and which lead us to develop more collaborative initiatives with each other. Beyond structures, we seek to change the way we work and to find more creative and innovative opportunities for working together.

17. Participants expressed their hopes that the Global Christian Forum would provide an opportunity for broadening the ecumenical movement. Cooperation in the area of diakonia and mission was considered as a way to strengthen relationships between Pentecostal and other churches.

18. With any new configuration, WCC has a leading role to play in facilitating, networking, coordinating and challenging churches and organisations within the ecumenical movement.

19. The following section presents specific *recommendations* to the churches, the WCC, the REOs and NCCs, the Christian World Communions, the international ecumenical organizations, and the agencies/ specialised ministries.

Recommendations

Participants celebrated the fact that this diverse group of representatives from the broader ecumenical movement had come together at Chavannes-de-Bogis to reflect together on a new configuration of the ecumenical movement. This was a special event and participants expressed their joy at being together. In fact, some felt that WCC's role in facilitating such a gathering is a model for its future work in creating ecumenical space. While the recommendations below focus largely on issues of structures and relationships, participants affirmed the need for renewal, for "re-freshing" the ecumenical movement in a way which focuses less on institutional interests and more on fostering a spirit of collaboration. The need to develop more effective ways of working in order to witness to the world—in areas such as justice, reconciliation, and inter-faith dialogue—is a strong motivation for grappling with many and diverse structural issues.

Working groups during the meeting made many recommendations on specific issues which are incorporated into the summary report of this meeting. These provide broad and important suggestions for the work of the churches and other participants in the ecumenical movement. In particular participants recognized the essential role of ecumenical formation for the future ecumenical movement and urged all churches and organizations to make this a priority, for example in religious education and in selecting representatives to ecumenical events. Churches are encouraged to ensure that their members who have ecumenical experiences are able to share these experiences with their Church.

The recommendations presented below focus on only a few concrete steps which can be taken in the immediate future. At the same time, it was recognized that the process of developing a new configuration of the ecumenical movement is a long-term one which will require discussion and reflection by the churches and indeed by confessional and ecumenical bodies.

1. A Reaffirmation of the Theological Basis of the Ecumenical Movement

We affirm that theological dialogue about the nature of unity and the church is a priority for all ecumenical work and should be revitalized. The WCC's Faith and Order has a central role to play in shaping the multilateral dialogue on issues (both theological and social) uniting and dividing the churches today, and in monitoring and mapping the many bilateral dialogues on church unity. A statement on the church as local/universal, living in unity/diversity is now being prepared for the 2006 WCC Assembly. We strongly recommend that the WCC and its member churches continue theological reflection on the nature of the church, particularly on the biblical understandings and different theological interpretations of the church.

2. Mapping of Programmatic Work

WCC is asked to facilitate a mapping study of existing programmatic work of ecumenical and denominational bodies, identifying who is doing what in which area of work and the financial resources which support these programmes. This is intended to serve as a tool for avoiding duplication and fostering cooperation and could build on the annual WCC Ecumenical Partner Survey. Such a mapping exercise could also provide opportunities for mutual learning. As this is a substantial task, it may be necessary to limit the scope of the study.

This mapping could be supplemented by case studies by appropriate bodies, in which a small group of people analyze and learn from specific examples of programmatic collaboration or overlap.

3. Clarifying the Respective Roles of WCC, REOs, and NCCs

We see a need for the WCC, the regional ecumenical organizations (REOs), and national councils of churches (NCCs) to clarify their programmatic roles, to discuss and formulate a common agenda and to stimulate collaborative action in order to achieve greater ecumenical coherence. WCC is asked to work with REOs and NCCs to develop an appropriate process for furthering these discussions, by building on work carried out through the Common Understanding and Vision process.

The principle of subsidiarity—ensuring that decisions are made closest to the people affected—may be helpful in delineating roles. Greater coherence could also be fostered by:

- Linking governing bodies (for example, the REOs could organize joint meetings in each region)

- Clearer accountability of representatives participating in ecumenical bodies to the churches they represent

- Clearly formulated agendas for regular meetings between WCC, REOs and NCCs

- Organizing meetings between REOs and Christian World Communions

REOs and NCCs also have a responsibility to encourage ecumenical formation among their constituencies and they are asked to work with theological institutions in their regions to organize seminars on ecumenical formation.

4. Clarifying the Role and Space of Agencies/Specialized Ministries Within the Ecumenical Movement

As diakonia is an essential part of being church, and as agencies/specialized ministries are recognized as an integral and indispensable part of the ecumenical movement, the Consultation agreed to ask:

- WCC to invite the agencies/specialized ministries to discuss together the shape and form of their institutional space

- WCC to include agencies/specialized ministries in its strategic planning and on-going work in the field of diakonia and development, relief and advocacy

- Similarly, agencies/specialized ministries to share their plans with WCC which in turn will seek to share them more broadly with ecumenical partners.

5. Towards Enhanced Collaboration with Christian World Communions

WCC is asked to facilitate a consultative process to explore the nature and form of a common Assembly or process that will draw the Christian World Communions, international ecumenical organizations, REOs and the WCC into a common ecumenical agenda. The possibility can also be explored of working with WCC's Faith and Order Plenary Commission and the Commission on World Mission and Evangelism in planning future meetings.

Further work is also needed to discuss ways in which Christian World Communions can more effectively participate in the work and life of WCC.

6. Exploring Possibilities for Greater Financial Stability

In light of the financial difficulties being faced by many ecumenical organisations, WCC is asked to facilitate a task force in which representatives from different ecumenical bodies, including from agencies/specialized ministries, can explore together additional and new ways of funding ecumenical work. Collaboration between churches, NCCs, REOs and WCC is needed in the regions to increase possibilities of raising funds for the common ecumenical movement. The Consultation stressed that building relationships is essential to efforts to increase financial support for ecumenical work.

7. The Role of WCC

Participants affirmed that WCC is a privileged instrument, entrusted with ensuring the coherence of the ecumenical movement. As a fellowship of churches it has an important prophetic role.

All organisations within the ecumenical movement, including WCC, need to change to address the challenges of today. The consultation recommends that in setting its priorities, WCC includes the following:

- Providing space for the ecumenical movement to formulate a common ecumenical vision for the 21st century

- Considering comprehensively the results and significance of bilateral theological dialogue at national, regional and international levels

- Facilitating a common theological understanding of diakonia among churches and agencies/specialized ministries

- Providing a forum for exchange of information and common advocacy against injustice, perhaps through coordinating advocacy vis-à-vis the UN

- Facilitating constructive cooperation and accountability between different partners in the ecumenical movement

- Facilitating a process of bringing the specialised staff of ecumenical organisations into regular and systematic conversation and information-sharing in order to develop common work plans.

In terms of structures it is recommended that WCC consider a balance between permanent tasks and time-limited, urgent projects.

8. Establishment of a Continuation Group

In order to continue this process, a continuation group will be established as soon as possible and will be composed of 15 representatives of different constituencies, as follows:

- 5 representatives of member churches (to be selected by the WCC Executive Committee)

- 1 representative of the Roman Catholic church

- 1 representative of Pentecostal churches

- 2 representatives from ecumenical youth organizations

- 1 each from REOs, CWCs, NCCs, agencies/specialized ministries, international ecumenical organizations and ecumenical renewal communities.

Each of these constituencies will name their own representatives by 14 February 2005 and the names will be shared with the WCC Central Committee for information.

WCC will convene this group and a first meeting will take place in the first half of 2005.

Terms of reference for the Continuation Group:

- Review the recommendations from this meeting, establish timelines and monitor their implementation to determine which can be implemented in the short and long term

- Set priorities among the recommendations, and

- Decide and accompany the process of working towards a new configuration of the ecumenical movement. (This may include, at some point in time, another consultation.)

9. The Need for Inclusive Participation

The continuing process of developing a new configuration of the ecumenical movement must include the increased participation by women and youth and priority should be given to participation from the South.

10. Going Forth

As only 106 representatives participated in this consultation, *Ecumenism in the 21st Century*, participants agreed to discuss the issue of a new ecumenical configuration with their churches and constituencies and to refer relevant measures to their respective governing bodies. The continuation group is asked to provide regular updates on this process to participants in this consultation as well as to the broader ecumenical constituency.

Appendix 5:
Inter-Anglican Standing Commission on Ecumenical Relations— Decisions and Resolutions 2002 to 2004

The following Resolutions were passed by the Inter-Anglican Standing Commission on Ecumenical Relations (IASCER), meeting in Bose, Italy, 2002

Resolution 1.02: AOCICC
IASCER:

- receives the report from the Revd Sarah Rowland Jones and the verbal report from Canon Wright and notes the progress made and expresses its appreciation for the work of the Co-ordinating Council

- reaffirms its support for plans for a 75th anniversary celebration, and

- asks Bishop Rowell to investigate some possibilities for further work in Europe during the coming year and to report back to IASCER in 2003.

Resolution 2.02: Growth in Communion
IASCER:

a) expresses its deep appreciation for the quality of this report, not only as to the range and detail of the data presented about Anglican–Lutheran dialogues around the globe, but also as to the synthesis of the issues raised

b) acknowledges the report as a significant contribution to the deepening of relationships between the member churches of the Anglican Communion and of the Lutheran World Federation

c) encourages responses to the report, especially from regions of the Communion where renewed Anglican–Lutheran relationships have been inaugurated or are proposed

d) notes that Recommendation 7 has already been endorsed by the ACC 12 meeting in Hong Kong, and recommends to the ACC Ecumenical office that such a Commission be established

e) endorses Recommendation 1, noting that the necessary administrative support implied may not be present in parts of the Anglican Communion

f) in relation to Recommendation 2, notes that 'the appropriate bodies of the Anglican Communion' include IASCER, which, while unable to give unqualified endorsement to the Report's evaluation of the theological consistency of the various agreements, commits itself to further study and response

g) endorses Recommendation 3 warmly

h) advises a cautious approach to Recommendation 4, calls for a further exploration within the Anglican Communion of 'transitivity' (see paragraphs 157–159) and the implications of 'extending interchangeability', and refers this Recommendation both to the new *Anglican–Lutheran International Commission* and to those Anglican Provinces which have reached agreements with Lutheran churches, asking them to make responses to IASCER

i) advises some caution regarding Recommendation 5, noting that sacramental hospitality in relation to lay persons already exists, and while affirming the positive intention of the Recommendation for churches working towards an agreement, IASCER believes that extending ministerial functions to individual ordained ministers raises fundamental matters which can only be rightly considered in the context of a particular ecclesial agreement

j) endorses Recommendation 6 warmly, noting that resources for theological education (both prior to and following ordination) have been developed in seminaries of ECUSA, which IASCER encourages to be made available more widely, possibly using the Anglican Communion website

k) recommends that the report be published, whether separately or together with the proposed collection of all Anglican–Lutheran documents, but in either case only if this Resolution and the attached comments from IASCER (and any made by the Lutheran World Federation) are included.

Resolution 3.02: Anglican–Methodist Covenant

IASCER welcomes the report "An Anglican–Methodist Covenant: Common Statement of the Formal Conversations between the Methodist Church of Great Britain and the Church of England" and commends the members of the formal conversations for this report, particularly for its fine sections on the history of the relationship and the healing of memories necessary along the way toward unity.

The Commission acknowledges the importance of this dialogue, finds it consistent with the Anglican Communion's ecumenical agreements at similar stages, and awaits with interest the decisions to be taken by the Methodist Conference and the General Synod of the Church of England.

IASCER reiterates its endorsement of the establishment of an international working group with the World Methodist Council and hopes to receive a report of progress next year.

IASCER noted with approval the beginning of a new bilateral dialogue between the United Methodist Church and the Episcopal Church of the United Church of America.

Resolution 4.02: Anglican–Oriental Orthodox International Commission
IASCER:

thanks the A-OOIC for its important work on the Christological Agreement to be submitted to the Anglican Communion and the Oriental Orthodox Churches and:

- draws the attention of the Primates' Meeting to this significant development;

- requests the provinces of the Anglican Communion to submit the text of the Agreement together with a note from the Anglican Co-Chair of A-OOIC for study by those who have responsibility for monitoring faith and order issues in their provinces requesting them to offer any comments they may have to IASCER by 30 October 2003;

- intends to give further consideration to the agreement at a future meeting in the light of comments received from the Communion.

Attached Note to Resolution 4.02:

A Note from the Co-Chairman of the Anglican–Oriental Orthodox International Commission (The Rt Revd Dr Geoffrey Rowell, Bishop of Gibraltar in Europe)

At the beginning of November 2002 bishops and theologians of the Anglican Communion and of the Oriental Orthodox churches, the ancient Christian churches of Egypt, Armenia, Syria, Ethiopia and the Malabar coast of India met in Armenia. Anglicans have had long and close relations with these churches, which have now spread beyond their ancient heartlands to a diaspora in the Western world. Our meeting was the first of an official dialogue to work towards a deeper unity and even closer relations.

The separate development of these ancient churches was bound up with some of the earliest Christian divisions. Political and cultural factors not surprisingly played a part, for these were all Christian communities on the fringe of, or beyond, the Eastern Roman Empire. The Council of Chalcedon in 451, which spoke of two natures in Christ, was not accepted by these churches, whose understanding was shaped by the teaching of Cyril of Alexandria, who taught that in Christ there was 'one nature of the incarnate Word of God'. For these churches the language of two natures, divinity and humanity, seemed to come dangerously close to a schizoid Christ, keeping God at a distance. In recent decades ecumenical conversations have gone a long way to resolving this ancient difference of understanding, and we rejoiced that in our own meeting Anglicans and Oriental Orthodox were able to agree a common statement on our understanding of Christ, and reach out to heal what is one of the most ancient Christian divisions.

Such theological divisions and arguments can easily seem remote and distant from our contemporary world. They can be mocked, as the historian Gibbon mocked the dispute over different terms of Christ in the Arian controversy, when, noting the different terms used, he said that Christendom was split over an iota. But in that controversy it was an important iota. What was at issue was whether Christ was a supernatural being but not fully God, or, as the Nicene Creed was to confess, he was fully and completely God. The ancient debates about the person of Christ have something of the same character, the point at issue being the unity of the person of Christ, the reality of his human nature and, centrally, the affirmation that God gave himself fully and completely into our human condition. In a world in which Platonist philosophy spoke of a God remote from the flux and change of history, the Christian affirmation of the incarnation, of God taking human nature, was bound to be offensive. The struggles of the early Church with the nature of Christ are in the end struggles to say that the God with whom we have to do is a God who does not stand aside from his creation, but, in the words of the fourteenth century English mystic, the Lady Julian of Norwich, is a God who "comes down to the very lowest part of our need." In Christ God freely chooses to know our humanity from the inside. In Jesus we encounter no less than God incarnate. That is the radical, wonderful and challenging reality that is at the heart of the Christian faith.

This is not just a theological dispute of long ago. The remote, distant and uninvolved God, repudiated in the theological battles of the early Church, is always in danger of creeping back. The deists of the eighteenth century, who turned God into the abstraction of a first cause, setting the universe going and then remaining all but absent from it, is one instance of this. It is often such a God who is denied by atheists and tilted at by critics. But that is not the Christian God, who is uniquely revealed in Christ.

This agreed statement, as the Commission notes, builds on much ecumenical work to heal this ancient Christian division, Anglicans along with Christians from the Reformed, Roman Catholic and Orthodox traditions, have seen agreement on who Christ is as at the very heart of Christian faith and mission, as we note in §8 of the agreed statement. Our citation of words of Richard Hooker show that what we have said is rooted in our Anglican theological tradition. We recognise that what we attempt to express is a saving mystery, the person of Jesus Christ to whom in the end our response is one of worship and adoration not the technicalities of theological statement. Our creed is part of our worship, and words fail us in the face of the love of God who gives himself to us in Christ (§4).

In §7 we speak of the will of Christ. In him there is a perfect union of divine and human will. Every time we pray 'Your will be done in earth as it is in heaven' we are praying for that to be true in our own lives which was found perfectly in Christ. What we see in him, his grace makes possible for us also.

The Oriental Orthodox Churches have been often and wrongly represented as teaching a 'monophysite' Christology. They point out that *monos* means isolated and alone; Saint Cyril spoke of *mia* meaning united, and therefore they should be referred to as holding a 'miaphysite' understanding of Christ.

In §9 there is reference to the discussion in the early twentieth century between Anglicans and the Assyrian Church of the East, originating in East Syrian Christianity associated with the name of Nestorius. In 1911, referring to in the text of the Agreement, the Patriarch of the Church of the East, replied to our Anglican request for a statement of their faith in relation to Christ and the Blessed Virgin Mary by writing to Archbishop Randall Davidson in the following terms:

> "Some time ago, brother, you asked us two questions, namely concerning whether we accept the Creed of [Mar] Athanasius, and concerning [Mart] Mariam the bearer of Christ our Lord. And on these questions of yours we answer as follows. We believe and confess that our Lord Jesus Christ Son of God, is God and man, God of the same substance of his Father, born before the worlds, and man of the same substance of his mother, born in the world; perfect God and perfect man, of a rational soul and body united; equal to his Father in respect of deity, and less than his Father in respect of humanity. Being thus God and man, he is not two but one Christ: [one,] not by the change of deity into flesh but by taking humanity into God: one completely, not by the mixture of substance but by the union of person *(parsopa)*. For just as a rational soul and body are one man, so God and man are one Christ, for ever.
>
> Then, about the Blessed [Mart] Mariam: we confess that she is Bearer of Jesus Christ our Lord and our God: him with whom, at the beginning of the formation of our Lord's manhood *(barnasha),* God the Word the second person of the Holy Trinity, was united and became one Christ, one Son, in one person *(parsopa)* for ever and ever.

And this faith, after enquiry and examination we have found to resemble and be at one with the faith of our Eastern Chaldean church; and there is nothing in it opposed to the teaching of our fathers and to the faith of our church. And therefore we accept and confirm it, because we too believe and confess according to the orthodox teaching handed down to us by our fathers, the holy teachers; and for this we honour them and commemorate their names."

Anglicans have long had cordial relations with the Church of the East. It is in this spirit that we have asked that the regional discussions with the Assyrian Church of the East commended by Lambeth 1998, should take place in the light of this Agreed Statement and with reference to the concerns expressed by the Oriental Orthodox.

06/12/2002

Resolution 5.02: Anglican–Orthodox Relations—International Commission of the Anglican–Orthodox Theological Dialogue (ICAOTD)
IASCER:

- welcomes the continuing progress of ICAOTD in its preparation of its interim agreed statements

- asks that the interim agreed statements be made available confidentially to IASCER in order to facilitate IASCER's work of monitoring Anglican participation in multilateral and bilateral dialogues with a view to ensuring consistency and coherence.

Resolution 6.02: Anglican–Roman Catholic—International Anglican-Roman Catholic Commission on Unity and Mission (IARCCUM) & Anglican–Roman Catholic International Commission (ARCIC)
IASCER:

- was encouraged by the report from IARCCUM of its progress in the preparation of a common declaration of agreement, plans for the next steps in furthering ecumenical reception, and proposals for pastoral and practical strategies to help our two communions do together whatever is now possible

- endorses the proposal, conveyed verbally by the Anglican Co-Secretary, that the collected ARCIC texts, including the anticipated statement on the place of Mary in the faith and life of the Church, be published together

- believes that our communions would benefit if IARCCUM's communiqués could in future convey more detailed information about its plans

- requests that the permission of IARCCUM be sought to provide documentation and details of its deliberations confidentially to IASCER in order to facilitate IASCER's work of monitoring Anglican participation in multilateral and bilateral dialogues with a view to ensuring consistency and coherence.

Resolution 7.02: General Work
IASCER:

a) asks Bishop Geoffrey Rowell, Canon Robert Wright and Prebendary Paul Avis to continue work for IASCER on the meaning of 'communion' in Anglican external relationships, keeping in contact with the Inter-Anglican Theological and Doctrinal Commission (IATDC) in their work on 'communion' from an internal Anglican perspective;

b) recognizes that work needs to be done on the range and function of doctrinal formularies, including the forms of Assent, in the various Provinces and member churches of the Anglican Communion, and asks Dr Paul Avis to report to the next meeting (noting that such work may already be under way by people who may be consulted);

c) asks Dr Charles Sherlock and Canon Alison Barnett-Cowan to prepare a paper on 'mapping' the language used to describe 'church', the goal of our endeavours to make visible the unity which is Christ's gift, and the various stages which may lead towards it, in order to promote mutual clarity but not necessarily uniformity of terminology.

Reaffirmed Resolutions from 2001
IASCER also reaffirmed three resolutions of its 2001 meeting:

1. Joint Declaration on the Doctrine of Justification

IASCER rejoices at the achievement of agreement between the LWF and the Roman Catholic Church in the Joint Declaration on the Doctrine of Justification. Anglicans have addressed the doctrine of justification and related issues both within our own Communion and in our ecumenical dialogues with Lutherans and Roman Catholics. The Anglican Roman Catholic International Commission (ARCIC) in its 1986 statement Salvation and the Church affirmed that our two Communions "are agreed on the essential aspects of the doctrine of salvation and on the Church's role within it." The Niagara Report (1987) of the Anglican–Lutheran International Continuation Committee cites among the truths shared by Anglicans and Lutherans "a common understanding of God's justifying grace". Therefore, it would not be necessary or appropriate for the Anglican Communion to adhere formally to this bilateral agreement which arises out of a particular theological history and context.

2. Unilateral Changes to Bilateral Agreements

IASCER is concerned about unilaterally altering agreements after they are signed, in light of the developments in Anglican–Lutheran relations in the USA, namely the implications of the ELCA bylaw concerning ordination "in unusual circumstances", which contradicts the agreement in Called to Common Mission. Such a development seems to undermine ecumenical method and could potentially hinder progress in dialogue between Anglicans and Lutherans in other parts of the world. IASCER maintains that the ordination by pastors in Lutheran Churches which have entered binding agreements with Anglican Churches is an inconsistency which would be difficult to explain to other ecumenical partners, especially the Orthodox and Oriental Churches and the Roman Catholic Church. Anglicans do not consider ordination solely by pastors/presbyters to be an acceptable practice within an agreement of this nature which is intended to bring about a fully interchangeable ministry. IASCER has a similar concern about the continuing practice of ordination by Deans in the Church of Norway, which Anglicans had anticipated would be phased out in the light of the Porvoo Agreement.

3. Lay Presidency of the Eucharist—Sydney Diocese

IASCER concurs most strongly with the view expressed in the Report of the 1998 Lambeth Conference concerning lay presidency of the eucharist, that:

> "Such a development would challenge the tradition of the church catholic that ordained ministry serves the church by uniting word and sacrament, pastoral care and oversight of the Christian community. Presiding at the Eucharist is the most obvious expression of this unity. Lay presidency would also create major difficulties with many of our ecumenical partners as well as within the Anglican Communion. We are not able to endorse this proposal". (Lambeth Conference 1998 Official Report p. 202)

The Commission is aware that among ecumenical agreements which have been formally received by the Churches of the Anglican Communion is the ARCIC elucidation on Ministry (1979), which the 1988 Lambeth Conference recognised as "consonant in substance with the faith of Anglicans". That statement asserts that:

> "At the Eucharist Christ's people do what he commanded in memory of himself and Christ unites them sacramentally with himself in his self-offering. But in this action it is only the ordained minister who presides at the Eucharist, in which, in the name of Christ and on behalf of his Church, he

recites the narrative of the institution of the Last Supper, and invokes the Holy Spirit upon the gifts." (ARCIC The Final Report, Elucidation on Ministry 1979, paragraph 2)

The Faith and Order text Baptism, Eucharist and Ministry, about which the Lambeth Conference of 1988 stated "Anglicans can recognise to a large extent the faith of the Church through the ages", states that:

> "The minister of the Eucharist is the ambassador who represents the divine initiative and expresses the connection of the local community with other local communities in the universal Church." (BEM, Eucharist, paragraph 29)

It is the consensus of this Commission then, that a diocese or province which endorses lay presidency of the Eucharist would be departing from the doctrine of the ministry as Anglicans have received it, and from the practice of the undivided Church. Such action would jeopardise existing ecumenical agreements and seriously call into question the relation of such a diocese or province to the Anglican Communion.

The Following Resolutions were passed by the Inter-Anglican Standing Commission on Ecumenical Relations (IASCER), meeting in Delray Beach, Florida, USA, 2003

Resolution 1.03: Recent Developments in the Anglican Communion
IASCER:

- deeply regrets the ecumenical consequences for Anglican international ecumenical dialogue resulting from the consecration in the Episcopal Church (USA) of a non-celibate priest in a committed same-sex relationship as Bishop Co-adjutor of New Hampshire, noting with particular concern the impairment of the work of the Anglican-Oriental Orthodox International Commission (AOOIC) and of the International Anglican-Roman Catholic Commission for Unity and Mission (IARCCUM) and the declaration of the Russian Orthodox Church, which severed ties with ECUSA whilst "wanting to maintain contacts and co-operation with the members of the Episcopal Church in the USA who clearly declared their loyalty to the moral teaching of the Holy Gospel and the Ancient Undivided Church"

- acknowledges the urgent need to address the ecclesiological and practical issues for the Communion and its ecumenical relations that arise from a province of the Communion taking unilateral action involving a substantive matter of faith, order or morals

- welcomes the establishment by the Archbishop of Canterbury at the request of the Primates of the Anglican Communion of a Commission to address the ecclesiological questions concerning the unity and working together of the Communion

- notes that in the past Anglican participation in global ecumenical dialogues with other world communions has been predicated on the assumption of common faith and practice, and

- therefore urges the Commission to find ways of reasserting and maintaining common faith and practice so that such world-wide ecumenical dialogue may proceed with confidence in the future.

Resolution 2.03: Ongoing Studies—Direct Ordination
IASCER:

- notes with concern the suggestion in the IALC statement *Anglican Ordination Rites* that 'provinces may wish to consider the possibility of direct ordination'

- observes that the invariable practice of Anglican churches has been sequential ordination and that this is presupposed in the ecumenical agreements that they have made.

Resolution 3.03: Ongoing Studies—Use of Language
IASCER:

- recognising that the language of the methods and goals of ecumenical dialogue is complex and that there is a danger that different parts of the Anglican Communion may mean different things by the same terms, and may sometimes describe the same reality by different terms, recommends that a glossary be produced of this language.

Resolution 4.03: Anglican–Old Catholic Relations
IASCER:

- reaffirms its support for an international celebration of the 75th anniversary of the Bonn Agreement in the year 2006, to be held either in continental Europe or in England, or both, to consist of a major theological conference and of a major liturgical celebration held either together or separately

- further suggests that the theological conference be held in conjunction with the regular conference of Old Catholic theologians and either immediately before or after the next regular meeting of AOCICC, and that Prebendary Paul Avis serve as the liaison of

IASCER for this purpose

- also recommends that the major liturgical celebration of the Bonn Agreement be timed to coincide with a meeting of the Primates of the Anglican Communion in the same year, and that consideration be given to holding such a meeting in an appropriate location on continental Europe.

Resolution 5.03: Iglesia Filipina Independiente
IASCER:

- encourages the Episcopal Church in the United States of America to resume negotiations with its full communion partner, Iglesia Filipina Independiente, to establish a formal body to co-ordinate ECUSA-IFI relations and to report on its progress at the 2004 meeting of IASCER.

Resolution 6.03: All Africa Anglican–Lutheran Commission
IASCER:

- having noted with regret the lack of recent progress by AAALC, encourages Anglican churches in Africa to advance their relations with their Lutheran counterparts, acknowledging that it must be for the Anglican and Lutheran churches involved to determine the most appropriate regional contexts for such ecumenical initiatives. IASCER looks forward to receiving reports on progress at their meeting in 2004.

Resolution 7.03: Papua New Guinea
IASCER:

- welcomes the Covenant between the Anglican Church in Papua New Guinea and the Roman Catholic Church in New Guinea, and the Agreed Statement on Baptism between the Anglican, the Evangelical Lutheran and the Catholic Churches in Papua New Guinea, and regards both as notable ecumenical advances

- in welcoming both developments, IASCER expresses the hope that the Anglican Communion Office might be given the earliest possible notice of similar proposed developments in order that IASCER and the other competent bodies of the Anglican Communion might give due consideration to such proposals.

Resolution 8.03: Reception of Agreed Statements in the Communion
IASCER:

- requests the Joint Standing Committee of the Anglican Consultative

Council and the Primates' Meeting to clarify the procedures by which agreed statements from bilateral commissions may be received in the Anglican Communion.

Resolution 9.03: Churches Uniting in Christ (United States of America)
IASCER:

- is generally encouraged by recent progress within CUIC on the reconciliation of ministries

- is, however, concerned about the extensive use of functional, as opposed to sacramental, language for ministry

- advises that the tendency to use "ministry" as a synonym for Christian life and discipleship should be avoided

- points out that the sufficiency of "servant" language to describe the diaconate is being widely reconsidered in the light of fresh New Testament scholarship

- expresses the hope that some of this material may be recast to reflect a theology of ministry and holy order that is more clearly focussed on the nature and purpose of the Church.

Resolution 10.03: Reconfiguration of the Ecumenical Movement
IASCER:

- re-affirms Resolution IV.7 of the 1998 Lambeth Conference that called for the reform of the WCC in such wise that the Orthodox Churches would wish to remain within the WCC and the Roman Catholic Church would wish to participate more fully in its work

- believes that rediscovering the founding vision of the WCC as a 'fellowship of churches' is the key to a viable future for the WCC

- welcomes the recommendations of the Special Commission on Orthodox Participation in the WCC

- questions the wisdom of planning a full Global Christian Forum event in 2007 without considering its relationship to the next Assembly of the WCC in 2006

- believes that the reform of the WCC, including a degree of devolution to global regions and national councils of churches, could make the idea of a global forum largely redundant.

The Following Resolutions were passed by the Inter-Anglican Standing Commission on Ecumenical Relations (IASCER), meeting in Montego Bay,

Jamaica, 2004

Resolution 1.04: Ecumenical Participation in Ordinations
IASCER:

- adopts the attached statement on the participation of Anglican bishops and clergy in ordinations outside the Anglican Communion, and of the clergy of other churches in Anglican ordinations, and refers these guidelines to primates and provincial secretaries, and to the Primates' Meeting.

The Anglican Communion Guidelines on Ecumenical Participation in Ordinations

The following guidelines are addressed to situations in which Anglican bishops and priests are invited to participate in ordinations of clergy in churches outside the Anglican Communion, or in which clergy of churches outside the Anglican Communion are invited to participate in Anglican ordinations.

Recognising that such acts can have wider consequences than originally intended, and in response to many requests from bishops and others for guidelines and clarifications concerning the standards for individual Anglican bishops or priests participating in such ordinations, or clergy of other churches desiring to participate in Anglican ordinations, IASCER commends the following guidelines for adoption throughout the churches of the Anglican Communion.

These guidelines are not intended to address situations in which a church of the Anglican Communion is engaged in a process leading toward the establishment of communion with another church or churches. In these cases, Anglican churches are requested to consult with IASCER in advance of such participation.

Guidelines:

1(a) It is appropriate for Anglican bishops, when invited, to participate in episcopal ordinations or consecrations in churches with which their own churches are in communion, including the laying on of hands. Within this ecclesial context, the laying on of hands is an indication of the intent to confer holy orders, and a sign of the communion that we share.

1(b) Anglican bishops should refrain from participating in the laying on of hands at the ordination or consecration of a bishop for a church with which their own church is not in communion. Ordination is always an act of God in and through the church, which from the Anglican perspective means that bishops are representative ministers of their own churches. Ordination is not the individual act of bishops in their own persons.

1(c) Similarly, bishops from other churches not in communion should not take part in the laying on of hands at the ordination or consecration of Anglican bishops, for the collegial and sacramental sign of the laying on the hands by bishops belongs within the context of ecclesial communion.

1(d) Anglicans welcome the participation of bishops from other churches in the Liturgy of the Word and elsewhere in celebrations of episcopal ordination or consecration. Their very presence and prayers are valued ecumenical signs, even when the present state of ecclesial relations does not permit the interchangeability of sacramental ministries.

2(a) It is appropriate for Anglican priests, when invited, to participate in ordinations of presbyters in churches with which their church is in communion, including the laying on of hands. Such acts are a sign of the communion that we share.

2(b) Anglican priests should not take part in the laying on of hands in the ordinations of ministers of word and sacrament in churches with which their own church is not in communion, because such an act belongs within the context of ecclesial communion.

2(c) Similarly, ministers from churches not in communion should not take part in the laying on of hands at the ordination of Anglican priests, because this too belongs within the context of ecclesial communion.

2(d) Anglicans welcome the participation of presbyters and other ministers of word and sacrament from other churches in the Liturgy of the Word and elsewhere in celebrations of priestly ordination. The very presence and prayers of such ministers are valued ecumenical signs, even when the present state of ecclesial relations does not permit the interchangeability of sacramental ministries.

NB: This version of the guidelines is as approved by the Primates and Moderators of the Anglican Communion at their meeting in Northern Ireland in February 2005.

Resolution 2.04: The Windsor Report
IASCER:

- adopts the attached statement as a summary of its reflections on the Windsor Report, as requested by the Reception Reference Group established by the Primates' Standing Committee, and submits the document to the Reception Group for consideration by the Primates at their meeting in February 2005.

Response to the Windsor Report

IASCER has been asked to respond to the Windsor Report in preparation for the meeting of the Primates in February 2005. Below are the initial reflections on the Report and its ecumenical implications, agreed at IASCER's meeting in December 2004.

The Windsor Report is a rich resource for ecumenical endeavours, offering mature consideration of Anglican self-understanding, grounded in Scripture, which invites partners to engage with the fundamental issues that it addresses.

These issues, and the Communion's response, have major ecumenical implications.

Reception of the Windsor Report: Implications for Ecumenical Relations

IASCER hopes the Communion will pursue the Report's recommendations, as this will significantly assist ecumenical relations. Not following this course is likely to complicate and further impair relations.

Provinces should note that ecumenical partners will follow their responses in close detail.

IASCER welcomes in principle the proposal for a Council of Advice for the Archbishop of Canterbury (§111,112). This should contain ecumenical expertise and be charged with considering ecumenical dimensions of the matters before it, in conjunction with appropriate advice from IASCER.

IASCER also welcomes in principle the proposal for an Anglican Covenant (§118-120). This could have major implications for the conduct of ecumenical relations, as a covenant might clarify the process by which the Anglican Communion makes decisions about proposed ecumenical agreements.

IASCER believes the recognition and articulation of the body of shared principles of Canon Law could strengthen the ecclesial character of the Anglican Communion (§113-117).

In their legislation, Anglican provinces should always be mindful of their local and global ecumenical responsibilities (§47, 79, 130).

Associated Developments in Ecumenical Relations

Several ecumenical partners have reacted strongly to the developments behind the Windsor Report (§28, 130).

Consequentially, there is a slow-down in some bilateral dialogues during what partners see as this unstable period prior to provinces' responses to the Report. Some have questioned whether we are a reliable and consistent ecumenical partner.

Nevertheless, partners have appreciated our ecumenical intent, shown by seeking their contributions to the Lambeth Commission, and now inviting their responses to the Report.

IASCER looks forward to studying these responses, as a further contribution to our ecumenical relations.

The Windsor Report as a Resource for Ecumenical Relations

Many of the Report's themes are prominent in ecumenical relations, e.g. the nature of the Church and local, regional and international ecclesial bodies, and relationships between them; authority; the instruments of unity; and episkopé, including primacy.

Koinonia refers primarily to the life of the one Church of Christ. Its theological principles therefore are relevant both to the life of the Anglican Communion and to ecumenical relations (Section B in particular). Fractures in communion are always serious and care should be exercised in using such expressions as 'impaired communion.'

The report also articulates a vision of the nature of Anglicanism which can be offered in ecumenical relations. Whatever we say about the Anglican Communion and its ecumenical relations should be brought to the touchstone of the four credal marks of the Church—One, Holy, Catholic and Apostolic (§49).

Issues for Further Consideration

Many partner churches experience similar tensions over human sexuality. They also face the legislative redefinition of marriage in many countries (§28). We might profitably share with each other our continuing work on the theological understanding of human sexuality, and its grounding in Scripture, tradition and reason.

Many provinces have entered various Covenants with partners: fuller theological reflection on the meaning of Covenant might help our understanding of our interdependence.

IASCER considers that ecumenical relations would be assisted by further careful clarification of terminology (e.g. distinguishing between homosexual orientation and practice; also clarifying usage of 'church' between the Universal Church and its Anglican expressions).

Ecumenical relations would similarly be helped by fuller exploration and articulation of the following matters to which the Windsor Report refers:

- The role of the Archbishop of Canterbury—noting the Communion-wide ministry of the Archbishop of Canterbury as an Instrument of Unity, and in the service of the other Instruments of Unity (§108-110). Baptism, Eucharist and Ministry speaks of personal, collegial and communal dimensions of ministry operating at every level of the Church's life (BEM: Ministry, III.B.27)

- Adiaphora—noting that Hooker spoke rather of 'things accessory to salvation' (§36,37)

- The 'common good'—noting this applies within the Anglican Communion, and within the Universal Church and wider world (§51,80)

- Covenant—noting that several provinces have entered various types of covenant with ecumenical partners, and that fuller theological reflection on the meaning and expression of covenant may help our understanding of our familial relationship (§119)
- Language used to describe interdependence within the Anglican Communion, which may help us, and our partners, better understand and live out the autonomy within mutual commitments.

Resolution 3.04: Anglican–Lutheran Relations in Australia
IASCER:

- welcomes the resolution of the General Synod of the Anglican Church of Australia 2004 concerning the Anglican/Lutheran Dialogue and notes the Report of their Doctrine Commission which "states that 'Common Ground', as supplemented by the Second Report of the Dialogue, is in conformity with Anglican doctrine and other agreed ecumenical statements"

- while celebrating the adoption of a covenant between the Anglican Church of Australia and the Lutheran Church of Australia, urges greater clarity in the use of the terms "recognition" of ministry (as a basis for eucharistic hospitality between the two churches), and "reconciliation" of ministries (on the way to full communion).

Resolution 4.04: Anglican–Oriental Orthodox Dialogue
IASCER:

- welcomes the responses that have been received, following the request of IASCER in 2002, to the Agreed Statement on Christology produced by the International Dialogue between the churches of the Anglican Communion and the Oriental Orthodox churches until now divided over the Christological Definition of the Council of Chalcedon in 451

- in the light of the full and positive responses from the provinces of Canada, Ireland and North India, and the need for the Lambeth Conference 2008 to consider the Agreed Statement on Christology, urges those provinces who have not so far responded, or who have not regarded such a response as a matter that concerns them, to respond to this agreement touching the central theological question of our understanding of the Lord Jesus Christ, and encourages such responses to be made by Easter 2006

- notes the response of the Standing Committee of the Oriental Orthodox churches of the Middle East regarding the Windsor Report and the postponed dialogue; and encourages a response to be sought from the whole family of Oriental Orthodox churches. In seeking such a response IASCER recognises that there is a need to explain carefully to the Oriental Orthodox churches the processes by which the provinces of the Anglican Communion are responding to the Windsor Report, and also to address some of their expressed concerns by drawing their attention to the Statement of the Primates' Meeting in October, 2003

- hopes that a resumption of the dialogue may be possible, with a consideration of 'The life of the Holy Spirit in the Church' and 'Living together as a family of churches', in which the understanding and experience of Anglicans and Oriental Orthodox may be reflected on together.

Resolution 5.04: Christian World Communions
IASCER:

- welcomes the general direction of the draft resolutions of the meeting of Secretaries of Christian World Communions (attached below), in the spirit of the Lund principle that churches should do together all those things that deep differences of conviction do not compel them to do separately

- encourages the Secretaries of the CWCs to consult each other prior to advising their communions on any proposed communion-wide initiatives and to take ecumenical considerations into account at an early stage

- wishes to see the CWCs taking a more prominent role in the ecumenical movement generally and in the WCC in particular.

Concerning the Role of the Christian World Communions in the Search for Christian Unity

Proposals from Group I of the Conference of Secretaries of Christian World Communions, Buenos Aires, 23–28 October 2004

Group I invites the 2004 meeting of the CS/CWCs to consider the following seven proposals and whether they should be sent to the CWCs for comment by March 2005:

As the Christian world communions consider the ways in which they contribute to Christian unity, it is proposed that the CWCs:

1. be guided by the "Lund dictum"—to do separately what can only be done separately, and do ecumenically what can be done ecumenically

2. invite the participation of ecumenical representatives and advisers in their own commissions and governing bodies

3. welcome a representative of the WCC in bilateral dialogues and other ecumenical relations

4. use fully the opportunities given to them in the WCC bylaws for various forms of participation in the life of the WCC, such as sending advisers to the meetings of the Central Committee

5. seek to avoid "pillarization" of the ecumenical movement, with the various problematic consequences it entails—e.g. in the area of dual membership by churches in CWCs

6. open up for deeper forms of mutual questioning and listening in matters of faith and Christian life

7. explore whether the time has come for world presidents/representatives of governing bodies of the CWCs to meet in the context of the Conference of Secretaries, as was originally envisaged.

Resolution 6.04: The World Council of Churches
IASCER:

- adopts the message to the World Council of Churches (attached below) and requests the Director of Ecumenical Affairs to forward it to the Secretary General of the World Council

- requests the Deputy Secretary General of the Anglican Communion to establish an electronic meeting that would enable Anglican delegates and advisers to the World Council of Churches in Porto Alegre, Brazil, in February 2006 to exchange information and Anglican perspectives as part of their preparation for that meeting

- requests the member churches of the Anglican Communion to send contact information about their participants in the Assembly to the Anglican Communion Office as soon as possible.

Message to the World Council of Churches

Members of the Inter-Anglican Standing Commission on Ecumenical Relations (IASCER), meeting in Jamaica December 5–10, 2004, received reports of the Kuala Lumpur meeting of the Faith and Order Plenary Commission of the World Council of Churches, and of the Geneva meeting on Reconfiguring the Ecumenical Movement.

IASCER wishes to express some concern about the present situation of the World Council of Churches. We recognize that there has been a steady diminution of money and staff over the past decade. This situation should lead to a serious scrutiny of the Council's activity, with a view to discontinuing any work that is more appropriately done regionally or locally. Without such scrutiny, undertaken in consultation with member churches, we fear that the Council will continue some programmes because of their history rather than because of their necessity in the present moment and for the future.

IASCER also has a concern that meetings of the WCC do not always make the most of the opportunities for the work of the ecumenical movement when representatives of member churches come together. There is sometimes not enough attention paid to questions of process design that would facilitate every participant making their best contribution and meeting with people from other traditions in a way that promotes ecumenical friendship and furthers understanding.

Despite the warm hospitality of local hosts, the joy of meeting, and some significant contributions, IASCER notes with concern some negative reports of the Plenary Commission of Faith and Order meeting in Kuala Lumpur in July/August 2004.

Anglicans bear a particular concern for the welfare of Faith and Order, having been strongly committed to the movement from its beginning. Indeed, for many Anglican churches, Faith and Order remains the most privileged instrument for serving the quest for the full visible unity of the Church. We thus regret the tendencies in recent years to weaken the role and particular focus of Faith and Order within the World Council of Churches as a whole. While we welcome the way in which its theological support is often sought for other programmes, we think this should not be allowed to distract Faith and Order from its core responsibilities in the area of ecumenical ecclesiology.

Anglican priorities lead us to insist that in any reconfiguring of the ecumenical movement, the central place of Faith and Order should be maintained and strengthened. Without this, we consider the future of the World Council of Churches may look increasingly vulnerable and the churches' quest for unity may be compromised.

At the same time as we offer these critical points, we want to affirm the new ways of working undertaken by the Council in response to the Special Commission on Orthodox Participation, particularly in making decisions as much as possible by consensus. We believe that this will strengthen the Council's ability to be a fellowship of churches and to serve the member churches in their ecumenical endeavours.

Montego Bay
December 2004

Appendix 6:
Six Propositions from the Inter-Anglican Theological and Doctrinal Commission

Anglicans and Communion

When the Commission began its work we posed four questions to Anglicans world-wide. A summary of the answers received can be found in *'The Communion Study, 2002'* (which can also be seen on www.anglicancommunion.org.uk) and our discussion has continued in response to what has been said. A summary of the conversation so far—in deliberately non-technical language—has been expressed like this:

- Communion is God's gift—and it is good for you. Human beings are not meant to exist on their own. It is in fellowship with God and neighbour that we find lasting fulfilment and real life.

- This 'communion' is offered to everyone in the Gospel, to be received by faith, sealed in baptism, and sustained by faithful participation in the family of God's thankful people.

- It is not easy to love your neighbour. In our world it is difficult enough to even meet one. And at times disputes and controversies can threaten to disrupt even the most Christian communities.

- What enables Christian people to walk together in the footsteps of Jesus is their common Faith, which is intimately linked with their shared calling to a corporate life of holiness.

- You cannot often specify in advance what distortions of belief or behaviour could disable the Christian fellowship, but listening to God's Word together, entering in to the story and actions of His salvation, and keeping in touch with other parts of the family, helps sensitise it to things which could be really damaging.

- Anglicans share a 'family likeness' with other families around the world. They do not look much like each other, but when they do happen to get together they realise how much they have in common.

- They all face different problems—although even the same problem can look different when it is viewed from another angle. Some communities are especially worried about personal issues, like homosexuality or whether gender determines who is competent to lead the churches. Most are more concerned about how their fellow Christians and fellow citizens possibly survive under the threat of prejudice, poverty, violence or the enormity of human suffering.

- Each church has to face its own problems, but in a communion there must always be ways for them to help each other with their tasks. After all, communion is God's gift—and no one church has ever unearthed the full extent of all his promises!

- What many people are wondering at the moment is whether there might be some better ways for Anglican churches to support each other as they discover the significance of their life together. It is not just a matter of money (although that can certainly make a difference). The biggest help we can offer each other is the chance see <u>ourselves</u> in a new way. We can learn from each other about good things that God offers his people. We have insights, ideas, convictions to share that can help us on the way, and clarify our sense of common purpose in God's service together. (Philip Thomas, England)

To continue the study process the Commission would like to test SIX PROPOSITIONS, arising from these discussions, which follow. We want to encourage churches, theologians, and individual Anglicans to share something of their own experience, and tell us as frankly as possible how they see the theological issues confronting the Anglican Communion today. Details of how you can do this can be found overleaf.

+ Stephen Sykes (Chairman)

Proposition 1

The koinonia of the Anglican Communion is both greatly enriched, and at times challenged and confused, by the variety of ways of encountering scripture. We bring our whole lives, in our different cultural and personal contexts, to scripture, and from those places open ourselves to 'being read by' scripture.

A passage for reflection: Luke 24.13–35

> As particular members of the Anglican Communion, we bring our contextual, cultural, and personal situations to bear upon the task of 'reading in communion' with others across space and time. Private reading and study of scripture takes place, by implication, within the larger framework of the church's praise of God and proclamation of the Word in common prayer and eucharist.
>
> The Anglican tradition of reading the Bible carries an historic deep respect for biblical scholarship, taking seriously the integrity of the canon, historical contextuality and original languages of the Bible. 'Historical' studies are well complemented by 'theological' interpretations and 'literary' readings. In addition, theologians in many parts of the world have called attention to issues of power and privilege in biblical interpretation and the

need for Christians to listen to one another across cultural differences and economic divisions.

The rich variety of material within the canon resists all human attempts to reduce it a flat or uniform agenda. At the same time, the biblical writings are consistent witnesses to the trustworthiness of the triune God and, for all their differences of style, content, and opinion, they are clearly part of one conversation that intends to be open to hear the Word of that one God. A Ghanian parable of individuals and community within the village helps us here: from a distance one sees the people of the village like a forest; only in closer proximity does one see the particular features of each tree. So the art of reading and living under a scripture which is both unified and diverse is an organic part of the vocation to live together within our single, yet richly variegated, Communion. It is within this context that our ongoing and vital debates about the 'authority' of scripture must take place.

A. Katherine Grieb (USA)
Esther M. Mombo (Kenya)
N. Thomas Wright (England)

How does the Bible function as a source of authority in setting priorities and resolving disputes in your church?

Proposition 2

Dividing doctrine from ethics not only creates the possibility for serious mistakes in Christian thinking but also diminishes the coherence of the life of holiness which is the Christian vocation.

A passage for reflection: Ephesians 4.1–6

In our initial questions to the churches, we asked in what way Christian teachings about moral behaviour are integral to the maintenance of communion. The answers we received were overwhelmingly affirmative. And this indeed is our view. What we call ethical teachings are woven into the fabric of Christian doctrine. Christians are called to die to sin and to rise again with Christ into newness of life (Romans 6.4). The doctrines of the resurrection and of baptism contain a teaching about personal transformation. Indeed the very idea of communion is inseparable from holiness of life, a sharing in the very being of God (II Peter 1.4). It belongs to the integrity of the Church that it teaches the truth that is in Christ Jesus, which is a new way of life (Mark 10.21). That life is no easy option. It involves personal struggle against temptation and a commitment to freedom from oppression. It is taken up truly as a taking-up of the cross (Ephesians 4.20–24). It is simply a mistake to think that 'core doctrine' does not include such teaching (as apparently the Righter Judgement of 1994 does).

+ Stephen Sykes (England)

Where do you see Christian doctrine informing or challenging ethical questions arising in your own situation?

Proposition 3

The reality of the incarnation implies that the Gospel is always proclaimed in specific cultures. Inculturation always runs the risk of syncretism, in all cultures without exception. One of the gifts which comes from membership of the Anglican Communion is that other Provinces hold up a mirror to each of us, enabling us to question whether the gospel has been compromised among us.

A passage for reflection: Acts 17.16–34

The Incarnation of Jesus Christ is God's Self-revelation to the world. Jesus' ministry on earth included both the acceptance of a particular culture and a moral confrontation with elements in that culture. When Jesus in turn commissioned his disciples, they too were to pursue the mission, which the Holy Spirit would give them by relating to their society incarnationally.

The theological concept of inculturation denotes the process whereby the church becomes incarnated in a particular culture of a people.

Inculturation occur when dialogue is sought at the level of trust between Christian message and praxis *vis-à-vis* local beliefs and values. Thus, as Christianity carries the structures and theology of the church into the conversation, so the same must grow out of local symbols, and, in so doing maintain the cultural and spiritual integrity of the local people. Inculturation, well understood, is openness to a process whereby the Christian gospel is interpreted and reinterpreted in an ongoing process of faithful reciprocity among peoples in the different contexts and cultures of the global church.

However, inculturation is not limited to religious cultural beliefs and practices. In its broadest sense, it includes all endeavours aimed at making the Christian message relevant to the local context. It is also an interaction and integration of the Christian message and socio-political and economic reality. True inculturation entails a willingness to incorporate what is positive, and to challenge what is alien to the truth of the Christian faith. It has to make contact with the psychological as well as the intellectual feelings of the people. This is achieved through openness to innovation and experimentation, an encouragement of local creativity, and a readiness to reflect critically at each stage of the process—a process that, in principle is never ending.

Victor Atta-Bafoe (Ghana)
Luke Pato (South Africa)

What are the issues in your own cultural situation which need to be reconsidered in the light of the gospel?

Proposition 4

Since the beginning of Christianity disputes have arisen in which the truth of the Gospel is seen to be at stake. Not all disputes are of such significance, but some are. In a Communion made up of many different churches, discernment is required to identify what in any particular context are the crucial issues for the life of the Church.

A passage for reflection: Acts 15.1-35

> The Scriptures themselves bear witness to varieties of understanding within the people of God. This diversity of interpretation has sometimes given rise to lively disputes: for instance, in the Hebrew Scriptures, about the obligations of the covenant, both for God and for Israel, or in the New Testament about the demand that Gentile converts to faith in Christ should be circumcised in accord with the Law. In some such conflicts, fidelity to the covenant, or to the Gospel, was seen to be at stake. In others, legitimate diversity of interpretation is reflected in the diversity of Scriptural witness: for instance, in the Hebrew Scriptures there are two versions, with differing emphases, of the pre-Exilic history of Israel, and in the New Testament there are four Gospels, which give four distinctive perspectives on Jesus and the Gospel. We can therefore expect diversity of practice and of theological interpretation to continue within a communion of churches, especially when the individual churches are reading the Scriptures and practising the Christian faith in hugely different contexts and circumstances. Even within the New Testament, it is clear that some Christians thought others were not being faithful to the Gospel and, on the issue of circumcision, a council was held at Jerusalem to resolve the issue. From the beginning, conciliar processes and conciliar decision-making have enabled the Church to identify those issues on which unity must be maintained and to reaffirm its faith in Father, Son and Holy Spirit, often in innovative ways. Within the conciliar process, an openness to the fresh reading of Scripture and of Christian tradition, together with a willingness to listen to one another and so to what the Spirit may now be saying to the churches, has been vital to the faithful proclamation of the Gospel in changing circumstances.
>
> +Paul Richardson (Papua New Guinea and England)
> Nicholas Sagovsky (England)

In what ways can church councils, synods, bishops and theologians be seen to maintain a balance between faithfulness to common belief and effective engagement with changing local circumstances?

Proposition 5

Disputes in the Church may be on many issues. Issues of discipline, such as Church teaching on sexuality or the recognition of ministerial orders may be important in some contexts: specific issues of poverty, justice and peace in others. Attention to the concerns of other churches within the Communion is important for putting those of each local church into a proper perspective.

A passage for reflection: II Corinthians 1.23–2.11

> We recognise the importance of addressing together the issue of human sexuality, and of homosexual practice in particular. It has become for many a church-dividing issue. For others the ordination of women to the priesthood and episcopate still lingers as a crisis of faith. For still others, the persistence of white supremacy stifles the spirit of Communion. We also weigh the importance of the world-wide distribution of wealth, issues of justice in varying contexts, and the goals of peace and the cessation of violence. Often the developed world puts its own hot-button issues in the forefront and misses other equally important issues, such as global warming. Our Communion serves us when it puts all the issues on the table, omitting none.
>
> Paul Zahl (U.S.)
>
> Kortright Davis (West Indies)

How far can membership of a Communion of churches help a local church to discern what are the crucial issues in its own situation?

Proposition 6

At every level the practice of koinonia requires that there are those who have the responsibility to arbitrate in disputes and conflicts vital to our shared life. Such arbitration gains its force from the ties that bind us together in a voluntary communion. The church then, needs to develop structures for testing, reconciliation and restraint.

A passage for reflection: Matthew 18.15–17

> We should not be surprised when conflicts and disputes occur in the church. Such things arise for many reasons, for example, failure of communication, misunderstandings, jealousy etc. Conflict also occurs because of the sheer richness of the gospel of Christ and the difficulty of deciding amidst a number of possibilities what is the faithful way forward in a particular situation.
>
> In a voluntary society like the church we rely heavily on the ties that bind us together as the body of Christ as a way if resolving our differences and disputes. The church places a high premium on face-to-face relations as the natural means through which it tries to discern what is right, test disputed practices and exercise discipline. Conflict resolution and the kinds of sanctions exercised in the church are thus primarily persuasive compared with those of a coercive and judicial kind. However, this does not mean that arbitration can be avoided in disputed areas at a level appropriate to the strength and extent of the disputed. Indeed, the church would be failing in its duty if it did not work hard at all levels of its life—parish, diocese, province, region and beyond—to deal with disputed matters, striving for reconciliation and implementing appropriate sanctions when necessary.
>
> The church needs those who will exercise a ministry by which disputes are resolved and structures which allow such arbitration to take place. These

structures will be both formal and informal and involve face-to-face relations as befits the community of Jesus Christ.

Stephen Pickard (Australia)

+ Matthew Owadayo (Nigeria)

Bruce Kaye (Australia)

How are disputes addressed and conflicts resolved in the practice of your church?

Notes

[1] "Ethiopia" in this context refers not to the nation state in north east Africa, but to the aspirational concept of Ethiopia as providing a distinctively African and indigenous form of Christianity.

[2] cf. World Council of Churches *Towards a Common Understanding and Vision of the World Council of Churches* Policy Statement, 1998

[3] World Council of Churches *Report of the Special Commission on Orthodox Participation in the World Council of Churches,* August 2002

Inter-Anglican Standing Commission on Mission and Evangelism: Communion in Mission

Section I IASCOME Final Report to ACC-13 2005

List of Contents

Foreword	195
Five Marks of Mission	196
Introduction	196
Chapter 1 A Covenant for Communion in Mission English, Spanish, Portuguese, French, Swahili	204
Chapter 2 Communion in Mission	224
Chapter 3 New Developments in Mission Relationships	232
Chapter 4 Evangelism	247
Chapter 5 Mission in the Context of our Blessed but Broken and Hurting World	257
Chapter 6 Mission and Theological Education	268
Chapter 7 IASCOME (II) and Anglican Communion Office Mission and Evangelism Desk	280
Chapter 8 Stories	283
ACC-13 Resolutions	306

Section II Travelling Together in God's Mission:
IASCOME Interim Report to ACC-12 2002

List of Contents

Foreword   308

A. Introduction   308

B. Our Mandate and Summary of Action so far   309
   1 Reporting
   2 To oversee mission relationships
   3 Reflection
   4 Priority of Mission and Evangelism
   5 New Structures
   6 Ecumenical Expressions

C. Major Meetings and Conferences Held and Forthcoming   311
   1 'Encounters on the Road': Nairobi, Kenya, 6–13 May 2002
   2 'Transformation and Tradition in Global Mission':
     Cyprus 12–18 February 2003
   3 All-Africa HIV/AIDS Consultation: Johannesburg,
     South Africa, 14–22 August 2001

D. Tasks Remitted to IASCOME   314
   1 'Mission 21'
   2 Proposal from the GEM Network
   3 Network for Anglicans in Mission and Evangelism
   4 The South to South Movement
   5 The Anglican Gathering
   6 CWME—Conference for World Mission and Evangelism
   7 The Partners in Mission process—a comment
   8 Companion Diocesan Links

E. Equipping and Formation for Mission   317

F. Some Areas of Concern and Continuing Work   320
   1 Islam and Islamisation
   2 Developing Anglicanism: A Communion in Mission
   3 The Journey towards Wholeness and Fullness of Life
   4 Mission as Justice-Making and Peace-Building
   5 Money, Power and Christian Mission
   6 Evangelism

G. ACC-12 Resolution   332

Section III   Appendices

Appendix 1   The Journey So Far   333

Appendix 2   Anglican Contextual Theologians Network (ACTs)   338

Appendix 3   The Global Anglicanism Project Report to the
IASCOME, March 2005   339

Appendix 4   Provincial Evangelism Co-ordinators Consultation   342

Appendix 5   Mission Organisations Conference   349

Appendix 6   Guidelines for Misson and Evangelism Co-ordinators   351

Appendix 7   The Anglican Gathering   355

Appendix 8   'Our Vision, Our Hope, The First Step':   357
Statement from the All Africa Anglican
HIV/AIDS Planning Framework

Appendix 9   Mission Focus Expressed by Commission Members   361

Appendix 10 Global Reporting Initiative   365

Appendix 11 An agreement for dialogue between the
Anglican Communion and al-Azhar al-Sharif   368

Appendix 12 Mission 21   370

Appendix 13 ACO Books on Mission   374

SECTION I

IASCOME Final Report to ACC-13 2005

FOREWORD

This is an immensely helpful book which charts the recent history of our Communion's engagement with mission and evangelism. The initials MISAG, MISSIO and IASCOME do not immediately bring to our minds the heart of the Church's life. But the commissions and standing committee work on mission and evangelism which these initials represent certainly do.

In reading this material it is clear how much both the global nature of the conversation and local contexts of encounter inform how we understand not only our missionary work, but the apostolic purpose of our communion. The particular stories of how church planting is done in Egypt, or how the church emerges from genocidal civil war in Burundi to minister to a nation takes us into the heart of the work of the body of Christ. The discussion of leadership challenges us to ask what kinds of ministers—lay and ordained—does the church require and how shall we to equip them? The Guidelines for Mission and Evangelism Co-ordinators offer concrete advice on appointing individuals who can challenge and resource our work of holistic mission and evangelism.

This book is a resource, and I hope the questions set at the end of each chapter will be taken very seriously, as the issues and answers that arise from them will determine key aspects of the shape of our Communion. Our unity comes from Jesus Christ alone. We exist not for ourselves or for a unity that is our will, but rather for the sake of the unity that is God's will in Christ. As the Father sent his Son, so we are equipped by his Spirit and sent into the world he made. He sends us to encounter and engage those he loves and those he longs to see living with us a life whose full abundance only Christ can bring. It is in that communion with the God of mission that we discover the deepest sources of our own communion in the church.

The Most Reverend Dr Rowan Williams
Archbishop of Canterbury

THE FIVE MARKS OF MISSION

(ACC, 1984 & 1990)

- To proclaim the Good News of the Kingdom of God.
- To teach, baptise and nurture new believers.
- To respond to human need by loving service.
- To seek to transform unjust structures of society.
- To strive to safeguard the integrity of creation, and sustain and renew the life of the earth.

INTRODUCTION

After a very busy ten day meeting in Cyprus, I looked for a very quiet corner in the transit hall at Larnaca International Airport in order to reflect on the insights gained at the meeting. As I read through our communiqué, a fellow traveller stood behind me without my noticing. The title: INTERANGLICAN STANDING COMMISSION ON MISSION AND EVANGELISM drew his attention, and he said to me, "So you are a bishop on church business, and where do you come from?" I said, "Yes, I am a bishop from Zimbabwe in Africa". I did put more emphasis on Africa because Zimbabwe is such a small country and whenever I mention Zimbabwe in the North, I very often end up giving a geography lesson. So when I said Zimbabwe–Africa he seemed to be satisfied with my identity.

It was his turn to introduce himself and what work he was doing. He said that he worked for a shipping company in Europe but he went on to mention that he was a Christian and a lay reader in his church. One thing he did not disclose to me was his denomination and I did not think it proper to ask for that extra bit of information. In the course of a very brief discussion my fellow traveller made it very clear to me that the church had no mission anymore because there are more Christians in the South than in the North. I was quick to inform him that my commission covered both South and North because the Anglican Communion is a worldwide family. My reply concluded the short discussion. I resumed my reading of the IASCOME communiqué but the view of my fellow traveller that the church has no mission anymore raised a lot of questions in my mind as to how much the ordinary person in the pew understands the work of the church and its worldwide mission. In so far as my friend was concerned, the church was in the North and that church had the responsibility to engage in mission out there. The thought that kept coming to my mind was, if a lay reader still has such an antiquated idea of mission, then no better understanding could be expected from ordinary church goers.

The primary task of IASCOME is to find ways to remind all members of the Communion that the church's understanding of mission today has shifted from mere expansion to individual conversion regardless of geographical location. As members of the Commission we constantly reminded ourselves about the local as well as worldwide context challenging the mission and evangelism of the church.

Mission and evangelism are two sides of the same coin. There is no mission without evangelism. The respective context determines the expression of mission and evangelism.

Living as members of the Anglican Communion in a global village we need to find new ways for the church to participate meaningfully in God's Mission.

The Communion therefore has to deal with the questions raised by current realities such as:

HIV and AIDS
Conflicts and wars
Unfair distribution of resources
Religious conflicts
Misuse of power and authority
Challenges in the context of human sexuality
Corruption
Human rights and gender equality
Abject poverty to mention but a few.

The mission and evangelism of the church therefore has to be kenotic and self-sacrificing (Phil. 2) and has to be understood by the local community through its involvement in social activities where the unreached encounter Jesus (Mt. 25 cf. spiritual motif in Luke 4).

During the Commission's meetings in different locations, we reminded ourselves again and again that the purpose of mission and evangelism is to bear witness to a ravaged humanity in a broken world as well as to offer healing and reconciliation. Thus we shared stories from our various contexts in the Communion. We also listened and witnessed to the ways in which the host church was engaged in mission. We were encouraged to discover that there is an increased interest and zeal for mission in the Communion.

We also acknowledged the need for the Communion to come up with an effective language to evangelise the unreached and to re-evangelise those who live in a so-called Christian culture but who have become strangers to the Christian faith.

We hope that this report with all the issues raised in it will inspire new ways of doing mission in our time and context where the challenges are formidable and demand constant evaluation of our work in mission and evangelism.

As chair of the Commission, I would like to express my appreciation to the members whose individual contributions made a difference to the work reflected in this report. I pray that the successor to IASCOME will develop ways of dealing with the emerging new challenges to mission and evangelism in our ever-changing world.

The Rt Revd Dr Sebastian Bakare, Bishop of the Diocese of Manicaland
Chair of IASCOME

INTER-ANGLICAN STANDING COMMISSION ON MISSION AND EVANGELISM

The Anglican Consultative Council, at its 11th meeting in Dundee, Scotland in 1999, established the Inter-Anglican Standing Commission on Mission and Evangelism (IASCOME). It further instructed its Standing Committee to appoint members to IASCOME for a five-year term of service. IASCOME is the latest in a series of commissions, committees and working groups with responsibility to maintain a global overview and provide some international co-ordination of mission and evangelism in the Anglican Communion.[1] It is accountable to the Anglican Consultative Council, to which it submitted an Interim Report, 'Travelling together in God's Mission', at its 12th meeting held in Hong Kong in 2002.[2] This is the final report of the work of IASCOME, submitted to the 13th meeting of the Anglican Consultative Council in Nottingham, England, 2005.

MANDATE

Tasks and Functions:
Report to the Anglican Consultative Council.

To report to and receive reports/tasks from ACC.

Oversee Mission Relationships.
To facilitate Companion Diocese and other companionship links throughout the Communion, in accordance with the Guidelines for such links.
To work with Anglican networks for mission and evangelism as they currently exist or might emerge in the future.
To facilitate the sharing of resources, both human and financial, throughout the Communion.
To link, share and critique experiences of capacity-building for mission and evangelism.

Reflection.

To engage in theological reflection on mission. This would include but not be limited to, reflections on Gospel and Culture, on the Missio Dei, on the Transformation of the Church, on the implications of the changing profile of the Anglican Communion, on the Good News in situations of poverty, displacement, war and conflict.

To be a forum where the Provinces and the Voluntary and Synodical Mission Agencies of the Communion share and reflect on their practices, experiences and learnings of mission and evangelism.

Priority of Mission and Evangelism.

To continue the momentum of the Decade of Evangelism, in accordance with the learnings described elsewhere in this report. This includes encouraging the Anglican Communion to see mission and evangelism as a Gospel imperative, not an optional activity.

New Structures.

To encourage the emergence of new and appropriate structures for mission and evangelism.

To liaise with the South-to-South Movement.

Ecumenical Expressions.

To encourage, monitor and learn from ecumenical expressions of mission.

MEMBERSHIP 2000–2005

The membership of IASCOME intentionally includes representatives of different regions of the Anglican Communion and different mission boards and agencies. To ensure a mix of gender, skills and experience, Provinces were asked to nominate a slate of names from which the Standing Committee of the Anglican Consultative Council selected the final Commission.

The following is a list of members of the Commission, giving their positions within their churches at the time of appointment and also subsequent changes.

*The Rt Revd Maurício José Araújo de Andrade
Formerly Provincial Secretary; (2003) Bishop of Brasilia; **Igreja Episcopal Anglicana do Brasil.**

*The Most Revd Joseph Akinfenwa
Formerly Bishop of Ibadan, (2003) Archbishop of Ibadan Province and Bishop of Ibadan; **Church of Nigeria (Anglican Communion).**

The Rt Revd Dr Sebastian Bakare (Chair)
Bishop of Manicaland, Zimbabwe; **The Church of the Province of Central Africa.**

The Rt Revd Dr John Chew Hiang Chew
  Bishop of Singapore; **The Church of the Province of South East Asia.**
Mr John Clark (Continuing Member)
  Formerly, Secretary of PWM (2003) Director: Mission and Public
  Affairs, Archbishops' Council; **The Church of England.**
The Revd Canon Tim Dakin
  General Secretary of Church Mission Society Britain; **The Church
  of England.**
The Rt Revd Dr Harold Daniel (Continuing member)
  Formerly, Church Army, Jamaica (2002) Bishop of Mandeville,
  Jamaica; **The Church in the Province of the West Indies.**
*The Revd J W Kofi deGraft-Johnson
  Formerly, Director of Programs, Christian Council of Ghana, (2003)
  Regional Manager CMS West Africa; **The Church of the Province of
  West Africa.**
The Revd Dr Ian T Douglas
  Professor of Mission and World Christianity, Episcopal Divinity
  School; **The Episcopal Church USA.**
Mrs Joy Kwaje Eluzai
  Sudan Council of Churches; **The Episcopal Church of the Sudan.**
The Rt Revd Armando Guerra-Soria
  Bishop of Guatemala; **Iglesia Anglicana de la Region Central
  de America.**
The Very Revd Muhindo Ise-Somo
  Mission and Evangelism Co-ordinator; **La Province de L'Eglise
  Anglicane Du Congo.**
Dr Eleanor Johnson (Continuing Member)
  Director of Partnerships; **The Anglican Church of Canada.**
The Revd Joseph K Kopapa
  Formerly, Acting Principal of Newton Theological College, 2003
  Chaplain of Martyrs Secondary School; **The Anglican Church
  of Papua New Guinea.**
The Rt Revd Edward P Malecdan
  Bishop of the Episcopal Diocese of Northern Philippines; **The
  Episcopal Church in the Philippines.**
Ms Pat McBryde
  Formerly, Deputy Secretary, Council, General Synod; **The Scottish
  Episcopal Church.** 2001 Retired.
Ms Shirley Moulder
  Community Development Worker, **The Church of the Province of
  Southern Africa.**

*The Rt Revd Richard Naramana
    Formerly, Secretary of Melanesian Board of Mission: 2003, Bishop of
    Ysabel; **The Church of the Province of Melanesia.**
Sister Chandrani Peiris
    Chair of National Christian Council in Mission and Evangelism,
    Church of Ceylon, Extra Provincial to Canterbury.
Mrs Lynlea Rodger
    St Mark's National Theological Centre, Canberra; **The Anglican
    Church of Australia.**
The Revd Pearl Prashad
    Parish Priest, **The Church of North India** (United).
The Revd Canon Fareth S N Sendegeya
    Corresponding Secretary of ANITEPAM, (2003) Rural Dean Diocese
    of Kagera; **The Anglican Church of Tanzania.**
Staff to IASCOME listed below:
Miss Marjorie Murphy
    Director for Mission and Evangelism; Anglican Communion Office
The Revd Canon John L. Peterson
    Formerly, Secretary General; Anglican Communion Office (2004)
Mrs Jenny Clark
    Secretariat Support

*Appointed archbishop, bishop or clergy during IASCOME period.

MEETING IN THE LOCAL CONTEXT

Following the pattern and recommendation of the previous Commission,
IASCOME chose to hold each of its meetings in a different country, thus
enabling exposure to four different contexts during the five-year life of the
Commission. The importance of experiencing some aspects of local mission brought a living dimension to our thinking. Each venue brought its
own unique contribution to our understanding of mission throughout the
Anglican Communion.

Kempton Park, South Africa, 2001

In our first meeting in South Africa from 7–18 May 2001, members of the
commission were exposed to the impact of the HIV and AIDS pandemic.
Lynn Coull, a deacon of the Highveld Diocese highlighted the work being
done in the diocese and the critical role the Church was playing in ministry to
those infected and affected by HIV and AIDS in the context of post-apartheid
South Africa where 4.5 million, or one out of every ten, people are HIV positive. Lynn pointed out that in the year 2000, 250,000 South Africans died

from AIDS. This number will double in six years. Children and young adults are especially hard hit by the pandemic and it is estimated that 50% of current young people under 15 will succumb to the disease. These statistics were given a face when the Commissioners accompanied local Home Based Care givers as they ministered to persons living with AIDS in the sprawling townships that ring Johannesburg. At the end of our meeting each member of the Commission received the challenge to address the HIV and AIDS situations in their own country. Commission member Sister Chandrani Peiris said, "Having considered mission and evangelism in the midst of HIV and AIDS, I am prepared to go home and challenge my community as to how we will reach out to those with HIV and AIDS in Sri Lanka, strengthened by the love and life we have found here in South Africa."

St Andrew's, Scotland 2002

Our second meeting took place in the historic city of St. Andrew's, Scotland, from 16–25 June 2002. The Rt Revd Ted Luscom, former Primus of the Scottish Episcopal Church, gave us a detailed overview of the Church's history, which was new to most members of the Commission. The present Primus, the Most Revd Bruce Cameron, continued the story-telling about the seven dioceses of the Province, many of them very rural and small in number. The program "Mission 21: Making Your Church More Inviting", which is used by parishes to attract new members, has helped the Province in recent years. IASCOME members were sent out in pairs to all the dioceses for weekend visits, during which time they experienced warm hospitality and also had first hand encounters with the church's work across the country. Many inter-Anglican links, both diocesan and personal, were formed during this meeting.

Runaway Bay, Jamaica 2003

Our third meeting, from 1–11 December 2003, was held in the small town of Runaway Bay, Jamaica, so named because many slaves used this bay as an escape route. A history of Jamaica, and of the Anglican Church in Jamaica, was provided by the Rt Revd Harold Daniel, IASCOME member and area Bishop of Mandeville. The diocesan bishop, the Rt Revd Alfred Charles Reid, who hosted the Commission at a lunch in his home, further explained this history. Members went out on weekend visits to various parishes across the island, enjoying warm hospitality, seeing first-hand how the church is addressing various social issues, and participating in Sunday worship with parishioners, including confirmations which the Episcopal members of IASCOME were asked to administer.

Larnaca, Cyprus 2005

Our final meeting was held in Larnaca, Cyprus, from 28 February–9 March 2005. The Most Revd Clive Handford explained to us that the Province of

Jerusalem and the Middle East spreads across three continents, Asia, Africa and Europe. Apart from Jerusalem, the Anglican Church ministers mainly to expatriates from many countries around the world, who are seeking a home away from home. In many parts of the Province, the Anglican Church is one of very few Christian denominations registered for worship, and therefore extends hospitality to other Christian groups who are thankful to find safe places to meet within its walls. Visiting some of the Christian historical places of St Paul's journeys highlighted our sense of calling to the mission of the Church. We visited the ancient Roman ruins at Salamis, where Paul, Barnabas and John Mark first set foot on the shore of Cyprus. The journey they took across the island to Paphos took on a new meaning, as we understood the distance and terrain they travelled. The burial places of Barnabas and Lazarus also spoke of the persecution of the early Christians. The many Orthodox churches are testimony to the enduring influence of Orthodox Christianity in the Greek section of the Cyprus.

SHARING OUR OWN MISSION CONTEXTS

Listening to each other's stories

Each time we came together, we spent a significant amount of time sharing our own mission stories and relating what was happening in our provinces, churches and regions. This intentional listening focussed our attention on the realities of our mission contexts in the Anglican Communion today. Storytelling was a critical methodology out of which our agenda emerged. For example, members told of their own situations of war in the Sudan, the Democratic Republic of the Congo, Liberia and Sierra Leone, Christian/Moslem conflict in Nigeria, effects of globalisation in Brazil, Guatemala and Jamaica, interfaith tensions in India, poverty and the impact of HIV and AIDS in South Africa and Papua New Guinea, secularism in Britain, Australia, and the USA, the struggles of Aboriginal peoples in Canada and Tribal peoples in the Philippines, political and economic instability in Zimbabwe and the tsunami disaster in Sri Lanka. These personal challenges deepened and sharpened our discussions as we sought to discern God's will for mission in the world. Many of our stories are included in this report.

The language barrier of English

Although English was the communicating language of the Commission, many members struggled with English as a second or third language. Unfortunately translation facilities were not available to us, so we eventually adopted a practice of breaking into small groups and reading aloud the texts of some of our documents, allowing time for questions and discussion. This method helped ensure a more equitable level of participation by all members of the Commission.

CHAPTER 1

A COVENANT FOR COMMUNION IN MISSION

English

The Lambeth Commission in its *Windsor Report* 'recommended and urged the primates to consider the adoption by the churches of the Communion of a common Anglican Covenant which would make explicit and forceful the loyalty and bonds of affection which govern the relationships between the Churches of the Communion'.[3]

IASCOME has discussed ways to take forward mission imperatives in the Communion following the Partners in Mission process and the Decade of Evangelism. The idea of a Covenant for Communion in Mission has emerged as a key proposal. We believe that a Covenant enshrining the values of common mission that could be used as a basis for outward-looking relationships among the churches, mission organisations and societies, and networks of the Communion would provide a significant focus of unity in mission for the Anglican Communion.

In Scripture, covenants are central in the Old Testament to God's relationship to Noah, Abraham, Moses, and to the people of Israel. Jeremiah and Ezekiel foretell the coming of a new covenant—in which God will give God's people a new heart and new life and will walk with them, and they with him. In the New Testament Jesus inaugurates this New Covenant. It was marked by the breaking of his body and the shedding of his blood, celebrated in the central Christian meal of the Eucharist and effected through the Resurrection of Jesus the Christ for all people for all time.

IASCOME considered in depth the nature of covenant. We recognised that within our cultures a covenant is a serious and significant agreement. Covenants are fundamentally about relationships to which one gives oneself voluntarily, while contracts can be seen as a legally binding document under a body of governing principle. Covenants are free-will voluntary offerings from one to another while contracts are binding entities whose locus of authority is external to oneself. Covenants are relational: relational between those who are making the covenant and relational with and before God.

As Anglican churches, we have a tradition of covenants that help to clarify our relationships with other ecumenical churches, such as the Porvoo Agreement between the Church of England and the Baltic Lutheran churches, and Called to Common Mission between the Episcopal Church and the Evangelical Lutheran Church in America.

We recommend for consideration by the ACC and testing within the Communion the following nine-point covenant. We believe it provides a basis for agreements between Anglican churches at the national level—but local parish/congregations, mission movements and networks, companion diocese links, etc, may also use it. We believe the Covenant for Communion in Mission can provide a focus for binding the Communion together in a way rather different from that envisaged by the Windsor Report.

A Covenant For Communion In Mission

This Covenant signifies our common call to share in God's healing and reconciling mission for our blessed but broken and hurting world.

In our relationships as Anglican sisters and brothers in Christ, we live in the hope of the unity that God has brought about through Jesus in the power of the Holy Spirit.

The preamble recognises that the world is one that has been graced by God but that God's work through Jesus, empowered by the Holy Spirit, is to seek to heal its hurts and reconcile its brokenness. The preamble reminds us that as Christians we are called to share our relationships in the mission of God to the wider world, bearing witness to the kingdom of love, justice and joy that Jesus inaugurated.

The nine points of the covenant are predicated on Scripture and the Sacraments providing the nourishment, guidance and strength for the journey of the covenant partners together.

Nourished by Scripture and Sacrament, we pledge ourselves to:

1 Recognise Jesus in each other's contexts and lives
The nine points begin with Jesus Christ, the source and inspiration of our faith and calls for those covenanting for mission to look for, recognise, learn from and rejoice in the presence of Christ at work in the lives and situations of the other.

2 Support one another in our participation in God's mission
Point two acknowledges that we cannot serve God's mission in isolation and calls for mutual support and encouragement in our efforts.

3 Encourage expressions of our new life in Christ
Point three asks those who enter into the covenant to encourage one another as we develop new understandings of our identities in Christ.

4 Meet to share common purpose and explore differences and disagreements

Point four provides for face-to-face meetings at which insights and learnings can be shared and difficulties worked through.

5 **Be willing to change in response to critique and challenge from others**
Point five recognises that as challenges arise changes will be needed as discipleship in Christ is deepened as a result of both experience in mission and encounters with those with whom we are in covenant.

6 **Celebrate our strengths and mourn over our failures**
Point six calls for honouring and celebrating our successes and acknowledging and naming our sadness and failures in the hopes of restitution and reconciliation.

7 **Share equitably our God-given resources**
Point seven emphasises that there are resources to share—not just money and people, but ideas, prayers, excitement, challenge, enthusiasm. It calls for a move to an equitable sharing of such resources particularly when one participant in the Covenant has more than the other.

8 **Work together for the sustainability of God's creation**
Point eight underscores that God's concern is for the whole of life—not just people, but the whole created order—and so we are called to strive to safeguard the integrity of creation and to sustain and renew the life of the earth.

9 **Live into the promise of God's reconciliation for ourselves and for the world**
This last point speaks of the future hope towards which we are living, the hope of a reconciled universe—in which 'God's will be done on earth as it is in heaven' for which Jesus taught us to pray.

We make this covenant in the promise of our mutual responsibility and interdependence in the Body of Christ.

The conclusion provides a strong reminder that we need each other. We are responsible for each other and we are mutually interdependent in the Body of Christ.

IASCOME proposes that the ACC commend the Covenant for Communion in Mission to the churches of the Communion for study and action and remits it to the next IASCOME for evaluation of its reception in the Anglican Communion. IASCOME further proposes that the ACC advance the Covenant for Communion in Mission to the bodies of the Anglican Communion tasked to continue consideration of covenants for the Anglican Communion as commended by the Windsor Report and the "Communiqué" of the February 2005 Primates' Meeting. To that end, IASCOME presents the following resolution for adoption by ACC-13:

ACC RESOLUTION—This Anglican Consultative Council:

1. Commends the Covenant for Communion in Mission to the churches of the Anglican Communion for study and application as a vision for Anglican faithfulness to the mission of God;
2. Advances the Covenant for Communion in Mission to the bodies of the Anglican Communion tasked to continue consideration of covenants for the Anglican Communion as commended by the Windsor Report and the "Communiqué" of the February 2005 Primates' Meeting;
3. Remits the Covenant for Communion in Mission to the next Inter-Anglican Standing Commission on Mission and Evangelism for monitoring responses to and evaluating effectiveness of the Covenant for Communion in Mission across the Anglican Communion.

The covenant is deliberately general in its principles. In its understanding of mission it builds on the Five Marks of Mission of the 1984 and 1990 Anglican Consultative Councils.[4] It provides a framework within which those entering into the covenant can identify specific tasks and learnings that relate to their particular situations.

UN CONVENIO PARA LA COMUNIÓN EN MISIÓN

Spanish

La Comisión de Lambeth en el Reporte Windsor, «recomendó y urgió a los primados a considerar la adopción, por parte de la iglesias de la Comunión de un Convenio Anglicano Común que haría explícita y obligatoria la lealtad y los lazos de afecto que rigen las relaciones entre las Iglesias de la Comunión».

IASCOME ha considerado formas de impulsar los Imperativos de Misión en la Comunión siguiendo los procesos de Compañerismo en Misión y la Década de Evangelización. La idea de la propuesta de un Convenio para la Comunión en Misión ha surgido como algo clave para la Comisión. Creemos que un Convenio destaca los valores comunes de misión que podrían ser usados como base para examinar las relaciones entre iglesias, por su parte, los movimientos y redes de la Comunión podrían proveer un enfoque significativo de unidad en misión para las iglesias de la Comunión.

En las Escrituras los Convenios ocupan un lugar central, ejemplos de esta centralidad se encuentran en el Antiguo Testamento, en la relación que Dios establece por medio de Alianzas con Noé, Abraham y con la gente de Israel. Jeremías y Ezequiel anticipan la realización de una nuevo Convenio—en el que Dios dará a su pueblo un nuevo corazón y nueva vida y caminará con ellos, y ellos con Él. En el Nuevo Testamento Jesús inaugura este nuevo Pacto. Este fue marcado por el partimiento de su cuerpo y el derramamiento de su sangre y es conmemorado en la celebración de la comida central cristiana que es la Eucaristía.

En nuestras culturas un Convenio (Pacto/Alianza) es un acuerdo serio y de gran importancia. En África los Convenios pueden hacerse para transferir propiedades; para poner fin a un conflicto; en relaciones familiares (ej. matrimonio); provisión de protección (ej. por una familia para la protección de las mujeres de otra familia); apoyo en tiempos de crisis. El sello visible del Convenio puede tomar diversas formas—muy a menudo incluye la mezcla de un pequeño elemento de sangre de aquellos que entran en el Convenio y una comida para celebrar en la que las partes comen y beben juntos. La celebración de un Convenio incluye el coincidir alrededor de un acuerdo, el establecimiento de confianza y relaciones donde antes hubo disputa y desacuerdo poniéndole fin de esta manera—es un nuevo comienzo. En el Occidente un Convenio es un acuerdo solemne en el que se entra y en el que se estampa la firma de las partes.

Recomendamos para su consideración por la ACC y para que sea puesto a prueba por la Comunión los siguientes nueve puntos de Convenio. Creemos que éste provee las bases para acuerdos entre las Iglesias Anglicanas en el nivel nacional—pero también para ser usado por parroquias/congregaciones locales, movimientos misioneros, redes, y diócesis en relación de compañerismo, etc. Creemos que el Convenio para la Comunión en Misión provee un enfoque para unir la Comunión en una manera un tanto diferente a la concebida por el Reporte Windsor.

El Convenio de forma deliberada es general en sus principios. Provee un marco en el cual aquellos que entran en Convenio pueden identificar tareas específicas y aprendizajes que refieren a sus situaciones particulares.

El preámbulo a el Convenio nos recuerda que como Cristianos somos llamados a compartir en la misión de Dios en un mundo vasto, dando testimonio del reino de amor, justicia y gozo que Jesús inauguró. Para los Anglicanos tal entendimiento de misión ha sido bien sintetizado en la Cinco Marcas de la Misión. El preámbulo también reconoce que el mundo ha sido bendecido con la gracia de Dios y que por el trabajo que El hace a través de Jesús busca reconciliar sus divisiones y sanar sus heridas.

Los nueve puntos del Convenios son afirmados por la Escritura y los Sacramentos proveyendo el alimento, guía y fortaleza para el viaje que realizan juntos los hermanos y hermanas en relación de Convenio.

Un Convenio para la Comunión en Misión

Este Convenio representa nuestro llamado común a compartir en la misión sanadora y reconciliadora de Dios para nuestro bendecido, quebrantado y lastimado mundo.

En nuestra relación como Anglicanos hermanas y hermanos en Cristo, creemos en la esperanza de la unidad que Dios trajo por medio de Jesús en el poder del Espíritu Santo.

Nutridos por la Escritura y Sacramentos nos comprometemos a:

Reconocer a Jesús en el contexto y vida del otro
Los nueve puntos comienzan con Jesucristo, la fuente e inspiración de nuestra fe, llama a aquellos entrando en convenio para la misión a mirar, reconocer, aprender de y regocijarse en, la presencia de Cristo actuando en las vidas y en las situaciones del otro.

Apoyarnos mutuamente en nuestra participación en la misión de Dios
El punto dos reconoce la necesidad de apoyo y animación mutuos en los esfuerzos para alcanzar el cumplimiento de nuestro llamado en la misión de Dios.

Animar expresiones de nueva identidad en Cristo

El punto tres pide a aquellos que entran en un Convenio alentarse mutuamente en el proceso de desarrollo de nuevos entendimientos e identidades en Cristo. El reto que muchos podrían enfrentar es tener que ver sus identidades primariamente como Cristianos y no como ciudadanos cuya primera lealtad es a una comunidad étnica, o nación estado.

Encontrarse para compartir una meta común y explorar diferencias y desacuerdos

El punto cuatro provee encuentros cara a cara en los que aspectos de la vida espiritual y aprendizajes pueden ser compartidos y las dificultades pueden ser solucionadas.

Tener la voluntad a cambiar en respuesta a la crítica y desafíos presentados por otros

El punto cinco, reconoce que en la medida que surgen los retos será necesario introducir cambios como resultado de la profundización de nuestra experiencia de discipulado cristiano tanto en la misión, como en nuestro encuentro con quienes estamos en Convenio.

Celebrar nuestras fortalezas y llorar nuestros fracasos

El punto seis hace un llamado a celebrar nuestros triunfos y a manifestar tristeza por nuestros fracasos.

Compartir de forma equitativa los recursos que hemos recibidos de Dios

El punto siete reconoce que existen recursos para compartir—no solo dinero y gente, sino también ideas, emociones, oraciones, desafíos y entusiasmos. Llama a compartir recursos de manera justa particularmente cuando uno que participa en el Convenio tiene más que el otro.

Trabajar juntos por la sustentación de la creación de Dios

La preocupación de Dios por la vida—no sólo de gente sino también de todo el orden de lo creado—de este modo el punto ocho recoge las Cinco Marcas de la Misión que nos llaman a «luchar por salvaguardar la integridad de la creación y sostener y renovar la vida de la tierra».

Vivir en la promesa de la reconciliación de Dios para nosotros y para el mundo

El último punto habla sobre la esperanza futura en la que nuestra vida se desenvuelve, la esperanza de un universo reconciliado—en el que «la voluntad de Dios será hecha así en la tierra como en el cielo» y por la que Jesús nos enseñó a orar.

Hacemos este Convenio en la confianza de nuestra mutua responsabilidad e interdependencia en el Cuerpo de Cristo.

La conclusión provee un fuerte llamado a que recordemos que como miembros del Cuerpo de Cristo no podemos caminar en el Convenio solos. Nos necesitamos mutuamente, somos responsables y interdependientes uno del otro.

ISCOME propone que el ACC recomiende el Convenio para la Comunión en Misión a las Iglesias de la Comunión Anglicana para su estudio y acción y remita este a la próxima IASCOME para su evaluación y recepción en la Comunión Anglicana. Además, IASCOME propone que la ACC promueva el Convenio para la Comunión en Misión a los cuerpos de la Comunión Anglicana requiriéndoles su continua consideración de convenios para la Comunión Anglicana tal como se recomendó por el Reporte de Windsor y el «Communiqué» de la reunión de los Primados de fecha Febrero 2005. Por tal motivo, IASCOME presenta para su adopción por el ACC-13 la siguiente resolución:

ACC RESOLUTION—Este Concilio Consultivo Anglicano:

Recomienda el Convenio para la Comunión en Misión a las iglesias de la Comunión Anglicana para su estudio y aplicación como una visión de la fidelidad Anglicana a la misión de Dios;

Ofrece el Convenio para la Comunión en Misión a los cuerpos de la Comunión Anglicana requiriéndoles su continua consideración de convenios para la Comunión Anglicana tal como lo recomienda el Reporte de Windsor y el «Communiqué» de la reunión de Primados de Febrero 2005;

Somete el Convenio para la Comunión en Misión a la consideración de la próxima Comisión Permanente Inter(Anglicana sobre Misión y Evangelismo para que monitoree las respuestas y evalúe la efectividad del Convenio en Misión a lo largo y ancho de la Comunión Anglicana.

ACORDO PARA COMUNHÃO NA MISSÃO

Portuguese

A Comissão Lambeth no seu Relatório Windsor recomendou e insistiu que os bispos primazes considerassem a adoção pelas igrejas da Comunhão Anglicana de um Acordo anglicano comum, que poderia explicitar e fortalecer a lealdade e os vínculos de afeição que governam as relações entre as igrejas da Comunhão Anglicana.[5]

IASCOME tem discutido formas de incrementar os imperativos de missão na Comunhão Anglicana, seguindo o processo dos Companheiros em Missão e a Década de Evangelização. A idéia de um Acordo para a Comunhão na Missão surgiu como uma proposta chave. Nós acreditamos que um Acordo, reunindo os valores da missão comum, que poderiam ser usados como base na busca de relações formais entre as igrejas, sociedades, organizações missionárias e redes da Comunhão Anglicana, poderia fornecer um *focus* significativo de unidade na missão para a Comunhão Anglicana.

Nas Escrituras, os acordos são centrais no Velho Testamento na relação de Deus com Noé, com Abraão, com Moisés e com o povo de Israel. Jeremias e Ezequiel profetizaram a vinda de uma nova aliança—em que Deus dará ao seu povo um coração novo e uma nova vida, e andará com eles e eles com Ele. No Novo Testamento, Jesus inaugura esta Nova Aliança. Ela foi marcada pela quebradura de seu corpo e pelo derramamento de seu sangue, e celebrada na refeição cristã central da Eucaristia e efetivada através da Ressurreição de Jesus Cristo para todos os povos em todos os tempos.

IASCOME considerou em profundidade a natureza do acordo. Reconhecemos que em nossas culturas um acordo é um pacto sério e significativo. Os acordos se referem fundamentalmente às relações em que alguém participa voluntariamente, enquanto os contratos podem ser vistos como um documento legal sob o princípio de um organismo governamental. Os acordos são oferecimentos voluntários e de livre vontade de um para com o outro, ao passo que os contratos são entidades unidas cujo focus de autoridade é externamente unilateral. Os acordos são relacionais: relacionais entre aqueles que participam do acordo e relacionais com e diante de Deus.

Como igrejas anglicanas, temos uma tradição de acordos que ajuda a esclarecer nossas relações com outras igrejas ecumênicas, como o Acordo Porvoo entre a Igreja da Inglaterra e as Igrejas Luteranas Bálticas, e o Chamados Para a Missão Comum entre a Igreja Episcopal e a Igreja Evangélica Luterana na América.

Recomendamos para consideração pelo Conselho Consultivo Anglicano e para teste dentro da Comunhão Anglicana os seguintes nove pontos do Acordo. Acreditamos que ele proporcionará a base para um acordo entre as igrejas anglicanas em nível nacional—mas também poderá ser usado pelas paróquias e congregações locais, movimentos de missão, redes, dioceses companheiras, etc. Acreditamos que o Acordo Para Comunhão na Missão proporcionará dessa forma um *focus* unindo a Comunhão Anglicana de uma maneira diferente daquela que está prevista no Relatório Windsor.

O Acordo é deliberadamente genérico em seus princípios. Na sua compreensão de missão, está baseado nas Cinco Marcas de Missão do Conselho Consultivo Anglicano de 1984 e 1990.[5] Fornece uma estrutura dentro da qual aqueles que entram no Acordo podem identificar tarefas específicas e aprendizagem que se relacionam com as suas situações particulares.[6]

Acordo Para Comunhão Na Missão

Este convênio significa o nosso chamado comum para participar na missão reconciliadora e pastoral em favor de nosso abençoado mas alquebrado e ferido mundo.

Em nossas relações como irmãos e irmãs em Cristo, vivemos na esperança da unidade que Deus realizou em Jesus Cristo pelo poder do Espírito Santo.

O preâmbulo reconhece que o mundo é um mundo que foi abençoado por Deus, mas este trabalho de Deus por meio de Jesus, fortalecido pelo Espírito Santo, foi dado para curar suas feridas e reconciliar o mundo alquebrado. O preâmbulo nos lembra que como cristãos somos chamados a compartilhar nossas relações na missão de Deus a um mundo mais amplo, dando testemunho do reino de amor, de justiça e de alegria que Jesus inaugurou.

Nutridos pelas Escrituras e Sacramentos, comprometemo-nos a
Os nove pontos do acordo estão baseados nas Escrituras e nos Sacramentos, proporcionando nutrição, direção e força para a jornada dos participantes do Acordo em conjunto.

Reconhecer a Jesus nas vidas e nos contextos de uns e de outros.
Os nove pontos começam com Jesus Cristo, a fonte e inspiração de nossa fé, e conclama os signatários do acordo na missão para procurar, reconhecer, aprender e se alegrar na presença de Jesus agindo nas vidas e situações do outro.

Apoiar um ao outro em nossa participação na missão de Deus
O ponto dois reconhece que não podemos servir a missão de Deus de maneira isolada e solicita mútuo apoio e encorajamento em nossos esforços.

Encorajar expressões de nossa vida nova em Cristo

O ponto três solicita àqueles que entram no acordo a encorajar uns aos outros, na medida em que desenvolvemos uma nova compreensão de nossas identidades em Cristo.

Compartilhar propósitos comuns e explorar as diferenças e as divergências

O ponto quatro proporciona reuniões francas e abertas em que o discernimento e a aprendizagem podem ser compartilhados e as dificuldades superadas.

Desejar mudar como resultado das críticas e desafios dos outros

O ponto cinco reconhece que assim como os desafios surgem assim também as mudanças serão necessárias à medida que o discipulado de Cristo é aprofundado, resultando ambos da experiência na missão e do acometimento com aqueles com os quais estamos acordados.

Celebrar nossas forças e lamentar nossos fracassos

O ponto seis solicita honrar e celebrar nossos sucessos, e reconhecer e registrar nossa tristeza e fracassos na esperança da restauração e reconciliação.

Compartilhar eqüitativamente nossos recursos dados por Deus

O ponto sete enfatiza que há recursos a compartilhar—não só dinheiro e recursos humanos, mas idéias, orações, estímulos, desafios, entusiasmo, e conclama à iniciativa de uma ampla participação de tais recursos, especialmente quando um dos participantes deste acordo tem mais do que o outro.

Trabalhar unidos pela sustentabilidade da criação de Deus

O ponto oito sublinha que a preocupação de Deus é pela totalidade da vida—não só pelos seres humanos, mas por toda a ordem criada— e por isso somos chamados a salvaguardar a integridade da criação e sustentar e renovar a vida na terra.

Viver na promessa da reconciliação de Deus por nós mesmos e pelo mundo

O último ponto fala da futura esperança pela qual estamos vivendo, a esperança de um universo reconciliado—em que a vontade de Deus será feita assim na terra como no céu, pela qual Jesus nos ensinou a orar.

Fazemos este acordo na promessa de nossa mútua responsabilidade e interdependência no Corpo de Cristo.

A conclusão proporciona uma forte lembrança de que precisamos uns dos outros, que somos responsáveis uns pelos outros e que somos mutuamente interdependentes no Corpo de Cristo.

IASCOME propõe que o CCA recomende o Acordo Para Comunhão na Missão às igrejas da Comunhão Anglicana para estudo e implementação e o submeta ao próximo IASCOME para avaliação de sua aceitação na Comunhão Anglicana. IASCOME propõe também que o CCA envie o Acordo Para Comunhão na Missão aos organismos da Comunhão Anglicana para continuarem as considerações do Acordo para a Comunhão Anglicana, como foi recomendado pelo Relatório Windsor e pelo Comunicado da Reunião dos Primazes de fevereiro de 2005. Para esse fim, IASCOME apresenta a seguinte resolução para adoção pelo CCA-13:

Resolução do CCA—Este Conselho Consultivo Anglicano:

1 Recomenda o Acordo Para Comunhão na Missão às igrejas da Comunhão Anglicana para estudo e implementação como uma visão da fidelidade anglicana para a missão de Deus;

2 Enviar o Acordo Para Comunhão na Missão aos organismos da Comunhão Anglicana, encarregados de continuar as considerações do acordo para a Comunhão Anglicana, nos termos recomendados pelo Relatório Windsor e pelo Comunicado dos Bispos Primazes de fevereiro de 2005.

3 Submete o Acordo Para Comunhão na Missão a próxima Comissão Permanente Inter-Anglicana sobre Missão e Evangelismo para monitorar as respostas e avaliar a eficácia do Acordo Para Comunhão na Missão em toda a Comunhão Anglicana.

UNE ALLIANCE POUR LA COMMUNION DANS LA MISSION

French

La *Commission de Lambeth,* dans le *Rapport Windsor* a recommandé et exhorté les primats à considérer l'adoption par les églises de la Communion d'une alliance anglicane commune qui rendrait explicite et énergique la loyauté et les liens d'affections qui gouvernent les relations entre les églises de la communion.

IASCOME a discuté des façons pour faire avancer les impératifs missionnaires de la Communion suivant le processus de Partenaires-en-Mission (PIM), et de la Décennie sur l'Évangélisation. L'idée d'une alliance sur la mission dans la Communion a émergé comme une proposition-clé. Nous croyons qu'une alliance qui enchâsserait des valeurs de la mission commune qui pourraient être utilisées comme une base pour des relations entre les églises, les organisations les sociétés missionnaires, et les réseaux de la Communion, et serait un important foyer d'unité dans la mission pour la Communion Anglicane.

Dans la Bible, les alliances sont centrales dans l'Ancien Testament dans la relation de Dieu avec Noé, Abraham, Moïse, et le peuple d'Israël. Jérémie et Ezéchiel prédisent la venue d'une nouvelle alliance—dans laquelle Dieu donnera à son peuple un nouveau cœur et une nouvelle vie, et marchera avec eux, et eux avec lui. Dans le Nouveau Testament, Jésus inaugure cette nouvelle alliance. Elle a été marquée par le sacrifice de la Croix, célébrée dans le repas chrétien central de l'Eucharistie, et rendue effective par la résurrection de Jésus le Christ pour tous les peuples et une fois pour toutes.

IASCOME a considéré en profondeur la nature de l'alliance. Nous avons reconnu que dans nos cultures une alliance est un accord sérieux et significatif. Les alliances sont fondamentalement des relations dans laquelle l'on se donne soi-même volontairement, alors que les contrats peuvent être vus comme des documents légalement contraignants. Dans les alliances, les parties s'offrent volontairement, tandis que les contrats lient des entités sous la supervision d'une autorité extérieure. Les alliances sont relationnelles, relations entre les parties, relations avec et devant Dieu.

Comme églises anglicanes, nous avons une tradition d'alliance qui aide à définir nos relations œcuméniques avec d'autres églises, tels que l'accord de Porvoo entre l'église d'Angleterre et les églises luthériennes Baltes, et celui entre l'Église Épiscopale des Etats-Unis d'Amérique et l'Église Luthérienne Évangélique de l'Amérique.

Nous recommandons pour considération par le Conseil Consultatif Anglican et expérimentation dans la Communion l'alliance suivante avec ses neuf points. Nous croyons qu'elle fournit la base pour les accords entre les églises anglicanes au niveau national—mais peut-être aussi utilisée par les paroisses/congrégations locales, les mouvements de mission, les réseaux, et les liens diocèses compagnons de la Communion, etc. Nous croyons que cette Alliance pour la Mission dans la Communion liera la Communion d'une façon plutôt différente que ce qui est envisagé par le rapport de Windsor.

L'alliance est délibérément générale dans ses principes. Dans sa compréhension de la mission qu'elle construit sur les Cinq Marques de la Mission de 1984 et 1990 du Conseil Consultatifs Anglican, elle fournit un cadre à l'intérieur duquel ceux qui y entrent peuvent identifier des tâches et priorités spécifiques à leurs situations particulières.

Une Alliance pour la Mission dans la Communion

Cette alliance donne du sens à notre appel commun de prendre part à la mission de guérison et réconciliation de Dieu pour un monde béni, mais blessé et meurtri.

Dans nos relations en tant que sœurs et frères anglicans dans le Christ, nous vivons dans l'espérance de l'unité apportée par Dieu à travers Jésus, par le pouvoir de l'Esprit Saint.

Le préambule reconnaît que le monde,tout en étant une grâce de Dieu, est aussi troublé et bouleversé ; mais Dieu, à travers Jésus Christ et par la puissance du Saint Esprit, cherche sans cesse à guérir ses plaies et refaire son unité. Le préambule nous rappelle qu' en tant que chrétiens, nous sommes appelés à partager la Bonne Nouvelle avec le monde entier comme témoins du royaume d'amour, de justice et de joie inauguré par Jésus.

Nourris par l'Ecriture et les Sacrements, nous nous engageons à:
A faire reposer cette alliance de neuf points l'Écriture et les sacrements donnant la direction et la force nécessaires aux partenaires de l'alliance dans leur cheminement.

Reconnaître la présence Jésus dans le contexte et la vie de l'autre:
L'alliance commence avec Jésus Christ, la source et l'inspiration de notre foi et vocation pour travailler ensemble dans la mission, chercher, reconnaître, apprendre les uns des autres, et se réjouir ensemble de la présence du Christ dans le travail, la vie et situation de l'autre.

Se soutenir mutuellement dans notre participation à la mission de Dieu:
Nous ne pouvons pas servir la mission de Dieu dans l'isolement et appelons le soutien et l'encouragement mutuels dans nos efforts.

Encourager les expressions de notre nouvelle vie dans le Christ:
Ceux qui entrent dans l'alliance doivent s'encourager les uns les autres pendant qu' ils développent de nouvelles compréhensions de leur identité dans le Christ.

Se rencontrer pour célébrer ce que nous avons en commun et é chercher à nous entendre sur nos divergences et désaccords:
Organiser des réunions face-à-face dans lesquelles perspicacité et expérience peuvent être partagées et les difficultés surmontées.

Etre prêt à changer en réponse aux critiques et aux défis des autres:
U fur et à mesure que les défis se présentent, nous aurons besoin de changer, car l'appartenance au Christ est profondément ancrée dans l'expérience de la mission et la rencontre avec ceux-là avec qui sont dans l'alliance.

Célébrer nos forces et porter le deuil par-dessus nos échecs :
Honorer et célébrer nos succès, mais aussi reconnaître et nommer notre tristesse et nos échecs dans l'espérance de réparer et de réconcilier.

Partager équitablement nos ressources que Dieu nous a données:
Pas seulement l'argent et des missionnaires, mais aussi les idées, prières, réussites, défis, l'enthousiasme.

Travailler ensemble pour la durabilité de la création de Dieu:
Dieu se préoccupe non seulement des humains mais aussi de la création tout entière. Aussi sommes nous appelés à lutter pour l'intégrité de la création, à soutenir et renouveler la vie dans notre environement.

Vivre dans la promesse de la réconciliation de Dieu pour nous et pour le monde:
Vivre dans l'espérance d'un monde réconcilié, une espérance qui fait en sorte que la volonté se manifeste sur la terre et dans les cieux, comme Jésus nous l' a enseigné

Nous faisons cette alliance dans la promesse de notre responsabilité mutuelle et d'interdépendance dans le corps du Christ.

La conclusion fournit un rappel fort que nous avons besoin que chacun soit responsable de l'autre, et soit mutuellement entre protégé dans le corps du Christ.

IASCOME propose que le ACC recommande l'Alliance pour la Communion dans la Mission aux églises de la Communion Anglicane, pour étude et action, et la remet au prochain IASCOME pour évaluer l'accueil qui lui est fait à travers la Communion et son exécution. IASCOME propose également que le ACC avance l'alliance pour la communion dans la mission de l'ensemble des tâches de la communion anglicane, pour continuer la considération d'alliances pour la communion anglicane comme recommandée par le rapport de Windsor et le communiqué des primates en février 2005. Rencontrer à cette fin, IASCOME présente la résolution suivante pour l'adoption par ACC-13 :

La résolution de ACC—Le Conseil Consultatif Anglican :

1. Recommande l'Alliance pour la Mission dans la Communion aux églises de la Communion Anglicane pour étude et application, comme une vision pour la fidélité anglicane à la mission de Dieu.

2. Fait la promotion de cette alliance telle que recommandée par le rapport de Windsor et le communiqué des primats de février 2005.

3. Remet cette alliance au prochain IASCOME pour contrôler les réponses et évaluer l'efficacité de son application pour la Communion dans la mission à travers le monde.

AGANO LA USHIRIKA KATIKA
UMISHENI

Kiswahili

Tume ya Lambeth katika *Windsor Report* "ilipendekeza na kuwahimiza viongozi wa majimbo kufikiria jinsi makanis ya Ushirika wa Kianglikana, yatakavyochukua na kufuatilia Agano sawa, ambalo litaonyesha waziwazi na kwa dhati, uaminifu, na ushikamano wa upendo, unaoendeleza uhusiano kati ya makanisa ya ushirika.[7]

IASCOME imejadili njia za kutekeleza sehemu muhimu za umisheni katika Ushirika wa Kianglikana kufuatia miaka kumi ya uijilisti na harakati ya Washirika Umusheni. Wazo la Agano Katika UMission lililzuka kuwa kipengele cha mbele. Twaamini ya kwamba Agano linaloshirikisha umuhimu wa umoja katika umisheni, lingeweza kuwa msingi wa husiano kati ya makanisa, mashirika ya umisheni na mitandao ya Ushirika huu zikatoa shabaha adhimu ya umoja katika umisheni kwa Ushirika wa Kianglikana (Anglican Communion).

Kwenye Maandiko, maagano ni muhimu hasa katika Agano La Kale kwa uhusano wa Mungu na Nuhu, Ibrahimu, Musa na uma wa Israeli. Jeremia na Ezekieli wanatabiri kuja kwa agano jipya- ambamo Mungu anawapa watu wake mioyo mipya na maisha mapya, naye atatembea nao, nao watatembea naye. Katika Agano Jipya, Yesu yuanzisha Agano hilo Jipya. Lilianzishwa na kuvunjwa kwa mwili wake na kumwagika kwa damu yake nalo lasherehekewa katika karamu muhimu ya Ushirika Utakatifu na kudhihirishwa kupitia Ufufuo wa Jesu Kristo kwa watu wote kwa nyakati zote.

IASCOME ilifikiria kwa undani Jinsi ya kubuni hulka ya agano. Tulitambua ya kwamba katika tamaduni zetu, agano ni makubaliano ya uzito na adhimu. Msingi wa maagano ni husiano ambamo watu hujitolea kwa hairi, hali mikataba yaweza kuwa mapatano ya kisheria chini ya Kanuni tawala. Maagano ni matoleo ya hairi mmoja kwa mwingine, hali mkataba unashikamanisha kwa utawala wa nje. Maagano ni ya kiuhusiano kati ya wanaofanya mapatano hayo na Kiuhusiano na Mungu na mbele ya Mungu.

Kwa vile sisi, Makanisa ya Kianglikana tuna desturi ya maagano yanayosaidia kufafanua uhusiano wetu na makanisa mengine, kwa mfano mapatano ya Porvoo kati ya Kanisa La Vingereza (Church of England) na makanisa ya Kilutheri eneo la bahari ya Baltic, na pia Wito kwa Umoja wa Umisheni, kati ya Kanisa la Episkopeli na Kanisa la uijilisti la kilutheri la Amerika.

Tunapendekeza kwa shauri ya ACC na majaribio ndani ya Ushirika, agano lifuatalo lenye vipengele tisa.Twaamini linatoa chanzo cha mapatano kati ya Makanisa ya Kianglikana kitaifa—bali pia yaweza kutumiwa katika parokia/makanisa, mashirika na mitandao ya umisheni, wenzi kati ya madiyosisi n.k. Twaamini Agano kwa Ushirika wa Kianglikana katika umisheni unatoa mwelekeo wa kushikamanisha huu ushirika pamoja kwa hali tofauti na ile ya 'The Windsor Report'.

Agano Kwa Ushirika Katika Umisheni

Agano hili la bainisha umoja wa mwito wetu kushiriki katika Kazi ya Mungu ya uponyaji na upatanisho kwa ulimwengu wetu uliobarikiwa walakini hali ya kuvunjika na wenye maumivu.

Katika uhusiano wetu kama ndugu na dada wa Kianglikana dani ya Kristo, tunaamini katika tumaini la umoja ambalo Mungu ameleta kupitia Yesu katika nguvu za Roho Mtakatifu.

Utangulizi huu unatambua ya kwamba, Ulimwengu ni mmoja ulioneemeshwa na Mungu lakini Kazi ya Mungu kupitia Kristo, inayoofulizwa na roho Mtakatifu, ni ya kutafuta kuponya daumivu ya dunia na kupatanisha matengano. Utangulizi huu, watukumbusha ya kwamba sisi wakristo tumeitwa kushirikisha husiano zetu katika umisheni wa Mungu ulimwenguni, tukishuhudia ufalme wa upendo, haki na furaha ulioanzishwa na Yesu Mwenyewe.

Tukijengwa na Maadika na Sakramenti tunajitolea kwa:
Vipengele tisa via agano vimesimama katika maandiko na sakramenti panapopatikana chakula rohoni, wongozi na nguvu za safari kwa wenzi agano pamoja

Kutambua Yesu katika hali na maisha ya Kila Mmoja.
Vipengele tisa viaanzo na Yesu Kristo, chanzo na ufulizo wa imani yetu, na kutuelekeza kwa wale tunaopatana nao katika umisheni, kutafuta, kutambua na kujifunza kwao na kufurahia mbele za kazi ya kristo ndani ya maisha na hali za wenzetu.

Kusaidiana Katika Kushiriki Kwetu Katika Kazi ya Mungu.
Kipengele cha pili chatambua ya kwamba hatuwezi kutumika kwa kazi ya Mungu peke yetu na yahimiza kusaidiana, kujengana na kutiana moyo katika bidii zetu.

Kukutana na Kushirikiana yanagotuungawisha na Kutafakari yanayo tugawanya.
Kipengele cha nne chaelekeza kwa mikutano ya ana kwa ana ambamo mapya yaweza kushirikiwa na magumu kusawazishwa.

Kuwa Tayari Kubadilika Wenzentu wanapo dhihirisha makosa kwetu.
Kipengelecha tano chatambua ya kwamba chenga moto zinapotokea bas mabakiliko yatahitajika mamna ya wanafunzi wa Yesu unapokuwa kutokana na mapitoyetu katika umisheni na kukabiliand na wale tulio nao Agano.

Kusherekea Nguvu zetu na kuomboleza unyonge wetu.
Kipengele cha sita cha tuita kuheshimu na kusherekea tunayofaulu na kutambua fadhaa na unyonge wetu kwa tumaini la kurekebisha na kupatanishwa.

Kushirikishana kwa usawa rasli mali Mungu alizotukirimia.
Kipengele cha saba kinasisitiza ya kwamba kuna rasli mali za kugawana—sio pesa na watu tuu, bali mawazo, maolbi, uchangamfu, chengamoto, msisimko na kutuita kugawana rasli mali hizo hasa iwapo mmoja wa mshirki katika agano akiwa na zaidi ya mwingine.

Kufanya kazi pamoja Kustawisha viote alivyo viumba Mungu.
Kipengele cha nane cha bainisha Mungu anavyojali alivyoviumba—sio binadamu tuu, bali vyote vilivyoumbwa—kwa hivyo twaitwa kufanya bidii kulinda vyote na kustawisha na kufanya upya maisha ya dunia.

Kuishi na kuingia ndani ya ahadi ya Mungu ya Upatanisho wetu na wa ulimwengu.
Kipengele cha mwisho chazungumza kuhusu tumaini la baadaye tunawishi kwalo, tumaini ya Ulimwengu—ambamo "mapenzi ya Mungu yatatimizwa duniani kama yalivyo mbinguni" ambavyo yesu alitufunza kuomba.

Tunafnya Agano hili kwa ahadi ya jukumu letu kwa kila mmoja na kutegemeana kuliko ndani ya Mwili wa Kristo.

Mwisho huu watukumbusha ya kwamba tunahitajiana, tuna jukumu mmoja kwa mwingine na tunategemeana katika Mwili wa Kristo.

IASCOME inapendekeza ya kwamba ACC iweke Agano la Ushirika Katika Umisheni ya Ushirika wa Kianglikana waliotunukiwa kuendelea Kuangalia maagano kwa niaba ya Ushirika, kama ilivyopendekezwa na Windsor Report na "Communique" ya Februari 2005 ya mkutano wa viongozi. Kumaliza, IASCOME inatoa makubaliano haya kubainishwa na ACC-13:

MAAZIMIO YA ACC-

Hii kamati:

Yapendekeza Agano ya Ushirika katika umisheni kwa makanisa ya Ushirika wa Kianglikana kwa kuangalia na kutekeleza kama Maono ya uaminifu wa kianglikana kwa kazi ya Mungu.

Yaendeleza Agano ya UshirIka Katika Umisheni Kwa Mashirika mbali mbali ya Kianglikana yaliyojukumishwa kuendelea kufikiria maagano kwa ushirika wa kianglikana kama ilivyo pendekezwa na Windsor Report na "Communique" ya mkutano wa viongozi Februari 2005.

Inaachia Agano ya ushirika katika umisheni kwa kongamano lijalo la Inter-Anglican Standing commission on Mission and Evangelism, kote katika Ushirika wa Kianglikana.

Agano limewakwa kwa ujumla makusudi. Katika kuelewa umisheni linajenga juu ya vipengele Vitano Vya Umisheni vya 1984 na 1990 Anglican consultative Council.[8] Linatoa muelekeo ambamo wanaoingia waweza kuona na kuchagua kazi na maelezo maalum yanayo fuatana na hali zao hususa.

CHAPTER 2

COMMUNION IN MISSION

DEVELOPING ANGLICANISM

The Anglican Communion grew out of a vision for world mission.[9] The recent Decade of Evangelism highlighted this founding perspective and encouraged churches of the Communion to explore what this perspective might mean for a new era. Today we see signs of many different kinds of mission in the Communion, leading to growth and development in terms of both the size and the nature of Anglicanism.

One way of expressing this re-emerging perspective is to say that we are a family of churches who find their *communion in mission*. Within our Communion there are *structures*, which express our *unity, marks*, which identify our *mission* and *relationships*, which create our fellowship. Yet we are a communion in mission in so far as our identifiable mission is relational and our structures serve those mission relationships.

A *communion in mission* is characterised at one and the same time by a celebration of commonality and difference. As Anglicans we believe that both commonality and difference are sustained by apostolic truth and the hope of the final unity of all things as expressed in our worship.

As an Anglican *communion in mission*, led forward by the Holy Spirit, we acknowledge (as sister churches) that we are God's pilgrim people. Therefore, whilst affirming the patterns and traditions of our past, we realise that such historic arrangements are provisional, and that our Communion is developing as it is being transformed in Christ.

TRANSFORMATION AND TRADITION

So at the heart of the Anglican Communion is a living tradition that is in constant transformation. Historically this dynamic of transformation was generated not just by the Reformation but also by the changes resulting from the missionary movement that emerged at the turn of the 18th century and subsequently developed into worldwide outreach.

But, of course, the fountain-head of transformation is found in the Biblical tradition itself. The root word for tradition, *traditio*, which means handing over, is the word used of Jesus when he was handed over to the Roman soldiers for execution.[10] Yet out of this *traditio* a transformation took place through our Lord's passion and resurrection.[11] When the Lord commissioned his disciples to share and teach the Gospel he handed over this transforming tradition.

So when Paul talks of passing on what he has learnt about the Lord's Supper (1 Cor. 11:23) we should see a handing over of the dynamic of transformation. "For I received from the Lord that which I also delivered to you, that the Lord Jesus in the night in which he was betrayed (handed over) . . .". In the mission of Jesus, tradition becomes transformation and transformation becomes tradition.

It is as we find communion in this transforming tradition that we are drawn into the mission of Jesus. Our communion in this transforming tradition is a communion realised through our lived-out participation in Jesus' *traditio* and nurtured by discerning his mission in the Bible and the Lord's Supper. But what is the nature of this *communion in mission?*

AFFECTION AND ASSOCIATION

One way of describing the relationships in the Anglican Communion, that have emerged out of the mission of previous generations, is as 'bonds of *affection*'. Furthermore, the recent Windsor Report also refers to a paramount model of the Communion, to "the voluntary *association* of churches bound together in their love of the Lord of the Church, in their discipleship and in their common inheritance" (p. 64).

As the Anglican Communion has slowly developed, so new ways have emerged for how bonds of affection and the voluntary association of the churches are shaped and supported. Four ways of doing this have been recognised or introduced in the Anglican Communion. In historical order they are: the Archbishop of Canterbury, the Lambeth Conference, the Anglican Consultative Council, and the Primates' Meeting. Yet it could be suggested that these four have themselves grown out of the mission relationships that first generated the Anglican Communion.[12] So perhaps the four Instruments are like musical instruments as, in their leadership role, they 'play the music' of the Anglican Communion's mission relationships.[13]

The importance of both giving and receiving in relationships has been recognised for a long while in the Anglican Communion, at least since the principle of mutual responsibility and interdependence (MRI) was first proposed in 1963 and was worked out in the Partners in Mission process.[14] Yet the nature and reality of MRI, as bonds of affection and association, needs to be continually articulated and redefind to express what these relationships are as the glue that holds the Communion together.

Christian communion has its roots in the divine communion[15]. But there are many ways of defining the concept of communion and, as Nicholas Healy notes, "what governs the use of 'communion' is not so much the model as such but the respective imaginative judgements and agendas of the theologians".[16] The imaginative judgement at play in this Report is to bring together, but still distinguish, communion and mission so as to explore the transforming tradition of Jesus as *communion in mission*. This means that whatever understanding we have of relationships in the Church or mission in a communion of churches, communion is inseparable from and indeed is expressed in Christian mission. We discover our communion with others in mission and our mission is to spread communion in Christ, ultimately with the whole of creation.

Whilst Biblical images like the Body of Christ or People of God can be used to describe the Church as a whole, it is other Biblical terms that can help us explore what these images mean for relationships in the Communion. These other images or metaphors include partners, pilgrims, companions, brothers and sisters, and friends. Each of these has been used at different times and in different contexts to explore how our relationships express our mission in the wider world.[17] Chapter Three traces some of the dynamics and developments within relationships in the Communion; Chapter Five outlines challenges faced by the relationships of the Communion in its wider context.

"The closest analogy between the triune God and human existence created in the image of this God is not persons but the personal relationships themselves."

Paul Fiddes: *Participating in God*

DEEPENING PARTNERSHIP

One of the most significant metaphors for *communion in mission* has been partnership. In fact one could say that, for the last 50 years, there has almost been a partnership paradigm for interpreting communion in mission.[18] But there are indications, suggested in the report from the previous Anglican Communion Mission Commission (MISSIO) that we now need to move on in our understanding of partnership.[19]

Companion

We are being called to build on, and deepen, the partnership in our relationships as a communion in mission.[20] An alternative metaphor, explored by the previous Commission, (MISSIO) was companion. This metaphor appears again in this Report as part of the way members of IASCOME described their mission relationships with each other and as a description of formal diocese-to-diocese links (see Chapter Three). Companion is a metaphor that is particularly popular in the South American context. It has connotations of sharing and equality in a relationship that has been given a wider purpose and direction. The picture of Christians as companions on a pilgrimage of discovery and witness can be found in the story (in Luke 24) where Jesus walks, unbeknown, with two disciples to Emmaus. As he listens to their disappointments and fears, and then shares from scripture and breaks bread, they discover with whom they have been travelling. The two then return to Jerusalem, full of joy, to witness to the risen Lord.[21]

Brother-Sister

Another metaphor for the depths of mission relationships is brother-sister. This is a common form of address in the New Testament, but it is also implied by Jesus' use of Father for his relationship with God. When Mary met the resurrected Lord, as she wept near his tomb in the garden, he told her to "go to my *brethren* and say to them 'I ascend to my *Father* and your *Father*, to my God and your God'" (John 20:17). Jesus' disciples and his wider followers are his brothers and sisters bound together in a family relationship with God the Father.

The power of this metaphor for conveying the depth of communion in mission relationships can be gauged when the place of the family in African cultures is considered. Writing on the traditional African understandings of human nature, Joe Kapolyo stresses that to be human is to be family. But this is not the Northern pattern of nuclear family. "My nuclear family that is the immediate family to which I belong as a son, at the moment comprises sixty-eight people (three have died: my father, one niece and a nephew)"![22]

In acknowledging the challenge faced by African Christians to not just adopt surface cultural changes but find deep cultural change arising from the Gospel, he says, "One thing that stands out strongly is the African sense of community. This value is close to biblical emphases as seen in the use of collective metaphors to describe the people of God, such as the 'body' of Christ".

Friend

In John's Gospel Jesus gives his disciples a new commandment and later reiterates it: "love one another as I have loved you". He then says what this means: "Greater love has no one than this, that one lay down his life for his friends" (John 15:12-13). Friend is the way Jesus describes his disciples when he reiterates this new commandment.

So another metaphor, which may help us to explore our mission relationships, is that of friend. To understand ourselves as Christians, in terms of being friends of Jesus, may open us anew to rediscover our friendship with God, with each other and with the world.[23]

Jesus made friends of his disciples by loving them. Christian mission is the call to love others the way Jesus did, so that we, and they, can discover the loving friendship of Jesus. The story of Christian mission includes the discovery of friendship in Jesus. This is the story of finding friendship across differences of culture, age, gender and viewpoint. It is the story of discovering the Jesus who befriends people who are excluded from their own community or are from another community. It is the ongoing story of the greatness of Jesus' befriending-love across differences and despite difficulties. The metaphor of friend may have particular relevance in the Northern context where there has been an erosion of community and a breakdown in family life.

As we look at the past and present of the Communion we can see that there have been fruitful mission outcomes, not least in the growth of mission relationships. And perhaps the emergence of networks and gatherings for mission (official or otherwise) in the Anglican Communion may also suggest a growth in companion/sister-brother/friend-type relationships in which there is a deepening of receiving and giving. These could be seen as a re-emergence of the network-kind of mission relationships that first generated the Communion. But some of those past relationships reflected the dysfunctional patterns of imperialism. Much more needs to be said about this dark side of mission.[24]

The covenant for *communion in mission* is a call to recommit ourselves anew: to find ways of deepening partnership by rededicating ourselves to each other as companion, brother-sister, friend. "You did not choose me but I chose you, and appointed you that you would go and bear fruit . . . This I command you, that you love one another." (John 15:16–17).

"Pure friendship is an image of that original and perfect friendship which belongs to the Trinity and which is the very essence of God".

Simone Weil: *Waiting on God*

THE FULLNESS OF CHRIST

The emergence of a new emphasis on mission as the mission of God *(missio dei)*, arising out of the ecumenical movement and other perspectives in the 1950s, was an important corrective to the view that mission was a human enterprise. Having said this, the Christian way of understanding God's mission is given shape by the story of the One who was with God and has made him known. So the place of Jesus in the *Missio Dei* must be an important focus for the Anglican Communion. As John Taylor writes in his booklet *The Uncancelled Mandate* (London: Church House Publishing, 1998):

"For the mission that has been laid upon the Christian community from its inception arose out of, and is forever focused upon, the historical event of Jesus Christ and the task he believed he was sent to undertake as the means of bringing the purposes of God to fruition." (p. 2)

Andrew Walls offers one way of exploring how this focus might also highlight the importance of valuing relationships in mission. Reflecting on the mission significance of the relationships between Jews and gentiles in *Ephesians*, he suggests that: "If I understand what Paul says in Ephesians correctly, it is as though Christ himself is growing as the different cultures are brought together."[25]

Yet, as Walls also says elsewhere, "the Ephesian moment—the social coming together of people of two cultures to experience Christ—was quite brief". But as he goes on to comment,

"In our day the Ephesian moment has come again, and come in a richer mode than has every happened since the first century. Developments over several centuries, reaching a climax in the twentieth, mean that we no longer have two, but innumerable, major cultures in the church."[26]

Mission relationships across diverse contexts and cultures are therefore essential for discovering who Jesus is. For Jews, Jesus was the Messiah; for gentiles, he was the Lord, but together they discovered more of Jesus. Because of the decline of Northern Christianity and the growth of Southern centres, we have the opportunity today to know, in a way never possible before, "the fullness of him who fills all in all" (Eph. 1:23). It is in the mutual enrichment of our mission relationships, as companions, brothers-sisters and friends, that we discover the fullness of Christ. And it is this greater Jesus we seek to share with others;[27] and the One whom we shall one day all worship as that great throng around the throne from all tribes, languages and nations (Rev. 7:9-17).

The vision that we may know the fullness of Jesus as we share, in our mission relationships, what he means to us in our different contexts, releases insights that can inform new and different kinds of mission initiatives.

We need to move from a programatic approach to mission towards one that is values-based.[28] This alternative approach would be rooted in those values that grow out of mission relationships that cross cultures and contexts and through which the fullness of Christ is unfolded. It is these values that are encapsulated in the proposed mission covenant. Thus through study and action arising from the Covenant a values-approach would be taken forward, as the values of the vision of the fullness of Christ are used, to recognise and encourage mission relationships that reflect the depths of this communion in mission.

DEBATES AND CHALLENGES

The word partner may now need to be qualified, where the imbalance in power between a shrinking minority in the North and a growing majority in the South, has become obvious. Perhaps other metaphors are better at expressing the aspiration for something deeper as is required by the new commandment: the willingness to lay down one's life for another.

Some might say that the name we have given to our bonds of affection and the association of our churches, the Communion *(koinonia)* is enough. But the need to say more about the nature of this communion has become necessary in recent years. It is only as the bonds of affection have been stretched, by changes and events in the Anglican Communion, that the nature of the relationships in the Communion has become clear. There can be little doubt now that we really do need to be Jesus' kind of friends, to really love each other as he loved us.

Perhaps only companions, sister-brothers or friends can truly talk about deeply difficult things: like disagreements, imbalance of resources, and differences in power. If mission is about the sharing of the Gospel in relational terms, then the quality of the relationships modelled and sought after in the Church, and more widely, are crucial.

Thus the metaphors for communion in mission need to be related not only to the vision but also to the challenges of mission in the Anglican Communion (for more detail on this see the early sections of the next chapter). The first challenge is the change in the nature of global Christianity[29]. Yet not only is there now a clear shift from centres in the North to centres in the South, but there is also, secondly, a growing awareness of the challenge of the power of globalisation: an economic and cultural order that frames all our international relationships.

There is a need for the Communion to address the reality of the colonial and post-colonial past, and the present neo-colonial context, of Anglican mission. If Anglican mission is sometimes a hidden side of the Communion's story, then the dark side of this mission remains largely unspoken. Whilst the simplistic equation, that modern mission equals colonial imperialism, is now being challenged,[30] Anglicans need to be able to share colonial, post-colonial and neo-colonial experience[31] and to do so with reference to questions of power, resources and disagreement (see Chapter Eight of this Report for a story from Canada). One focus for this exploration could be the bicentennial, in 2007, of the abolition of the slave trade in the British Empire (1807).[32]

Samuel Adjai Crowther was the first African Bishop in the Anglican Communion (and should be included in our liturgical calendar). He became Bishop on the Niger in 1864. Crowther came to faith as a freed slave who had been rescued off the West African coast having been taken captive in Yorubaland (part of present-day Nigeria). About his conversion he says: "about the third year of my liberation from the slavery of man, I was convinced of another worse state of slavery, namely, that of sin & Satan." Crowther was educated as a teacher and minister in Sierra Leone (that extraordinary reconstructed country populated by freed slaves and African returnees from the Americas) and in England.

His remarkable ministry included not only a commitment to evangelistic mission—in the most difficult of circumstances—but also to translation work, dialogue with Muslims and establishing an indigenous ministry. Unfortunately he died a broken man, following a resurgence of European leadership, which did not share the vision of those who had first realised that only in a truly indigenous Church, can the greater Jesus be known.

Yet Crowther stands as a figure not only of personal transformation, but also as someone who foreshadows the coming emancipation of the African peoples. His commitment to indigenous languages and customs made him a symbol for those who came after seeking greater social freedom.

Unfortunately slavery is not at an end. In today's world we still see disturbing reports that tell us that, for example, there are 211 million children in slavery around the world. A most vicious form of child slavery is the abuse of girl-children as sex slaves in war zones. Rape as a policy of war has now become rampant in central Africa. Young girls are the most vulnerable victims, often suffering multiple forms of abuse.

One victim who has felt able to talk about her captivity is Acayo Concy. She has bravely shared her story of abduction and sex slavery with CMS Britain. Despite being very young, she has already had three children from the terrible experience of being used as a 'wife' of soldiers bent on demeaning and dehumanising their own people.

Acayo's experience in Northern Uganda is, unfortunately, replicated in many parts of the world; be that in war zones, mega-cities with sex-trade centres or porn sites on the internet. The challenge for today's church is how to liberate these children from a modern form of slavery.

Recommendation:

That any subsequent mission and evangelism commission be tasked to address the question of the colonial and postcolonial past and present of Anglican mission, and consider how Anglicans might be helped to explore this through mission relationships.

Questions

What Biblical or other metaphor best expresses your experience of mission relationships?

What have you learnt about Jesus by listening to other people's experience, especially those from another part of the world?

In what way would you like to get to know people from other churches in the Communion?

What forms of slavery do you know of in your region and what can the church do about them?

CHAPTER 3

NEW DEVELOPMENTS IN MISSION RELATIONSHIPS

'Flourishing in a myriad of ways'

The Anglican Communion is "connected through a web of relationships—of bishops, consultative bodies, companion dioceses, projects of common mission, engagement with ecumenical partners, that are the means and signs of common life. This continues to flourish in a myriad of ways at the local as well as the national and international level."[33] These words from the Windsor Report summarise all too briefly what in fact gives the Communion life and energy—namely the connections and relationships that result from people meeting and engaging in mission in their local situations, supporting each other through prayer and presence.

With the increase in travel and the growth of the Communion, there has been a remarkable multiplication in the web of connections that contribute to the sharing of the Gospel and building of the kingdom. A report like this can only highlight changes and trends and suggest ways in which they may be enhanced. In particular it can suggest ways in which the threads of the web can be developed and strengthened.

This chapter provides an analysis of the changes that have taken place in the contexts of global and Anglican Communion development over the past two decades, outlines major responses to these developments and concludes with suggestions for the future.

The Church's agenda has always been set in the wider world because our Creator God is at work through the Spirit in the world calling for responses from a missionary church. The Church is called to discern where God is at work and to incarnate the Gospel of the kingdom. That discernment will include assessing when and where the Gospel affirms, challenges or seeks to transform culture. Thus a Church (whether internationally, regionally or locally) that sees its calling to carry forward the work of Christ will need to listen to what God is saying and respond to that agenda. This chapter therefore begins with a brief outline of recent major changes and developments in the global context.

CHANGES IN THE GLOBAL CONTEXT

Over the last quarter century, there have been major changes in the global context which can be listed as follows:

Globalisation reflected in increased speed of communication (in all forms) and movement of resources of people, goods and money. It has also increased the gap within and across nations between the economically and technologically rich and poor. The role of the internet *for those with access to it* has eased communication dramatically;

Global warming and humanity's impact on the environment, exacerbated by the demands of industrially developed and developing countries, has made climate change and humankind's care of the planet a long-term priority issue;

The rapid growth of cities and particularly the rise of mega cities (population of over ten million) pose great challenges for churches which originated from rural settings;

HIV and AIDS is spreading with increased rapidity (and its effects have been compounded by the incidence of malaria and tuberculosis);

The increase in internal conflicts often arising in contexts of poverty and ethnic difference, the starkest example being the 1994 genocide in Rwanda;

The continuation of extreme poverty with over one billion people living on less than one US dollar a day;

The rise of extremist Islam, highlighted by the terrorist attacks on the USA (September 11, 2001) has emphasised the significance of religion and faith in world affairs, but also has raised fears of international terrorism associated with religious ideology;

The USA has become the single global power, following the collapse of the Soviet Union, although new economic power blocs are emerging in the European Union, China, India and South East Asia.

These changes are having their impact on the Anglican Communion, for example in increased travel and electronic-communication; the movement of peoples; the emergence of Communion level task priorities and networks to share information and co-ordinate action (e.g. on HIV and AIDS and the environment); in raising peace and justice issues to which responses are required and in influencing the whole mission agenda of the Communion.

CHANGES IN THE ANGLICAN CONTEXT

The most substantial change has been the significant growth in size, sense of identity and autonomy of the Anglican and United Churches in

Africa, Asia, Oceania and Latin America. This has been reflected in increased meetings of the leadership of what are known as the 'churches of the global South'. Examples of this include: the way responses to issues were co-ordinated in preparation for the 1998 Lambeth Conference; the organising of the All Africa Conference on HIV and AIDS; the organising of the first All-Africa meeting of African Bishops in 2004; various consultations organised by the Council of Anglican Provinces in Africa (CAPA); and meetings that have developed around issues of sexuality in the Communion.

At a pan-Anglican level the two most sustained and imaginative Communion-wide initiatives of the last twenty-five years were the Partners in Mission Consultation process and the Decade of Evangelism. Although both have formally ended now, their influence still continues. The following sections examine the development of formal and informal networks within the Communion arising out of these two initiatives.

The Partners in Mission (PIM) Consultation process

Partners in Mission was a continuing process by which the Churches of the Communion contributed to each other's local mission. It assisted churches in sharpening their mission priorities and setting goals. Each Province or Church of the Communion invited Anglican and ecumenical partners to a formal consultation in order to assist them to set their mission priorities and the help they would need from others. Lessons learned at these consultations also helped the partners in their own planning processes. These large-scale consultations died out for several reasons. Provinces are now much larger (at least in the global south) and consultations would be too complicated and expensive to organise and co-ordinate. Secondly, a new generation of leaders has taken over within the Communion who were not part of the development of the original PIM process.

The agencies which largely drove Partners in Mission (national structures of churches like the Episcopal Church USA and the Anglican Church of Canada, and the mission agencies of churches like the Church of England) have found that their resources have decreased and their own policies have changed, as a number, at least, have put more stress on mission 'from everywhere to everywhere' and recognised that their own countries in the 'north' should be included in their mission activities. More importantly, a wide range of other connections has grown up linking parishes, dioceses and individuals across the Communion. Many of these new links, which have made very positive impacts on the church's mission, were established as a result of the PIM process.

The Decade of Evangelism

The 1988 Lambeth Conference call to make the 1990s a Decade of Evangelism was taken up with energy right across the Communion and at grass root levels. The Decade helped to refocus the Communion on its missionary calling to build the kingdom and share the Gospel. It led to the highly significant Communion-wide gathering in Kanuga (USA) at the mid-point of the Decade in 1995. It also added to the move away from the PIM process. Other issues, most notably, concerns about human sexuality, have consumed much of the Communion leadership's energy in recent times.[34]

In summary the world has changed. Times have moved on but the call to mission, the call to Christians to participate in Christ's mission of justice and joy has not changed. What has changed is the way this call is expressed and the way connections are developing across the Communion.

COMPANION DIOCESE LINKS

Diocesan Companion Links have expanded greatly. The 1998 Lambeth Conference called for every diocese of the communion to have some link with another part of the communion by 2008. Their purpose may be expressed in different ways but at the heart, the aim is to help members of the linked dioceses to grow in their discipleship of Christ, by getting to know and learn from each other through experience of each other's situations, through prayer and friendship. These diocesan companion links have led to a greater exchange of people in short-term visits, in mission teams, in prayer and in fellowship. The following stories illustrate the power of Companion Diocese Links.

Link between the Church of Melanesia and the Diocese of Chester, Church of England

There are many positive features of our partnership relations. We have come to learn and appreciate one another as we are. Chester Diocese has supported the Church of Melanesia more than ever before. Visits both ways have become more frequent. Recently a few English parishes have begun links with parishes in Melanesia. We hope there will be many more in the future. The Church of Melanesia has benefited from this link and would like to continue in the future. To foster the relationship we have sent Bishop Willie Pwaisiho to work as a Rector in one of the parishes of Chester Diocese. Also, teams of Melanesian Brothers continue to visit Chester Diocese on mission from time to time.

Some people in Chester Diocese have become Companions of the Melanesian Brothers (Friends of the Brothers) and have helped raise funds for them as well as sponsoring a few Brothers to study theology in Chester. Another tangible result has been Chester's funding of the Rest House for the Melanesian Brothers in Honiara (capital of the Solomon Islands). Income from this property has greatly enhanced the ministry and mission work of the Brothers, both in the islands and overseas.

The Church of Melanesia in our simple, humble way offers Chester Diocese an open field for studies. Recently there have been theological students who have come to study about spirituality in our four Religious Communities (the Melanesian Brotherhood; the Sisters of Melanesia; the Sisters of the Church and the Franciscan Friars). Some have come to learn why our Religious Communities are thriving, while those in the North are closing down. There have been other people who have come to learn about high church liturgy in our local context.

We are now so privileged and are encouraged to host many more clergy, lay people and students coming to the Church of Melanesia. They come to see a young vibrant church, which they are proud to have supported. From this link we now realise that we are not isolated, forgotten and lost in the Anglican Communion, but we are a part of the wide Anglican family.

The Rt Revd Richard Naramana, Bishop of Ysabel, Solomon Islands

South-North-South: A New Experience of Companionship

In 2000, a three-way companionship in mission began between the Diocese of Bor, Sudan, the Diocese of Brasília, Brazil and the Diocese of Indianapolis, United States. This companionship has created the possibility for these three dioceses, two from the Global South and one from the Global North, to share their experiences of hope and their dreams of mission. It has deepened their relationship of mutual understanding.

The first contacts happened during the visit in April 2000 of the Bishops of Brasília and Indianapolis, together with people from these two dioceses, to the Diocese of Bor. In July of the same year the Bishops of Bor and Indianapolis visited the Diocese of Brasília. On each visit they had opportunities to know and to live the reality of the different churches in their local contexts.

The July visit was intended to take the form of a ten-day "Encounter of Young People" from the three dioceses. Unfortunately the Sudanese were not able to obtain entry visas to Brazil. Nevertheless for ten days young people from Indianapolis and Brasília, with their bishops, gathered to study the Bible, share the Eucharist, celebrate the happiness of life, engage in mission, share life-changing experiences and build bonds of affection and unity.

Particularly special were the three days that the young people and their bishops spent in a settlement for landless people. They accompanied the people in their search for justice and their struggle for land, and at the end celebrated together. This experience, a new engagement in mission, left a mark on the lives of all who took part.

The new companionship between Bor-Indianapolis-Brasília has strengthened our understanding that we are part of Christ's Body. The mutuality of our relationship, our respect for each other, our honesty with each other and our common service have deepened our understanding of what it means to be one in Christ.

The Rt Revd Maurício Andrade, Bishop of Brasília, Brazil

Companionship between the Dioceses of Manicaland and Lebombo

The link between the Dioceses of Lebombo (Mozambique) and Manicaland (Zimbabwe) has been established in recognition of the pioneer missionary evangelist, Bernard Mizeki, who came to Zimbabwe from Mozambique via South Africa in 1890. Bernard was martyred by the local people who did not accept his mission. More than a century later, Christians in Zimbabwe have realised and come to appreciate that Bernard was a gift of God from Mozambique. The two dioceses border each other.

The Diocese of Manicaland organised a pilgrimage to visit Bernard Mizeki's birth place. Eighty Zimbabwean Christians were hosted by the Diocese of Lebombo. In return an equal number of Christians from Lebombo have been coming to Manicaland to participate in the yearly June 18th festival to remember and celebrate Bernard Mizeki. As a result of this contact, local parishes have taken up contacts among themselves, especially where illegal border crossing have created hostility between the two nations. The border crossing hostilities have presented the church with a great opportunity for mission in working to reconcile those caught up in the conflicts.

The Rt Revd Sebastian Bakare, Bishop of Manicaland, Zimbabwe

Virtual Bible Study though Diocesan Links

In June 2004, Christians in the Dioceses of Bradford and Salisbury (England) joined with others from the Episcopal Church of Sudan and the Diocese of Southwestern Virginia (USA) to form a 'virtual Bible study'—a unique way of studying a Bible passage that gave each group the perspective of different cultures.

Both English dioceses have close links with the Dioceses of Northern Sudan and Southwestern Virginia. Bridget Rees, the Links Officer for Bradford says, "The Virtual Bible Study is an excellent example of what our diocesan links with the world church are about—people in different situations exploring separately and together what God is saying to us in our own situations as well as together in the world. This method of Bible Study is used much in the so-called 'third world'—ordinary people reading the text and letting it speak to them directly—emotionally as well as intellectually—rather than worrying too much about what theologians have said about the passage."

She added, "The groups studied Acts 2 during the week which began with Pentecost Sunday. They reflected on what God is saying to us here and now in this passage in our particular situation. Then a summary of each group's study was circulated among the other groups who then read it again having seen how others read God's word."

Diocese of Bradford, England

Cross Border Links in East Africa

In the early 1960s, thousands of Rwandan Tutsi refugees crossed into Tanzania and settled in what is today the Diocese of Kagera. They were educated and naturalised in the country. The Tanzanian Church ministered to them, including providing training for clergy.

In 1994 following the genocide the Rwandan Government was overthrown by the Rwandan Patriotic Front (RPF), and the refugees returned home. The Diocese of Kagera lost 16 clergy among those who returned to Rwanda. However, the crossing over of these clergy has helped to develop a link between the Dioceses of Kagera (Tanzania) and Kibungo (Rwanda). Bishops and clergy visit and invite each other to participate in formal and informal ministries.

In addition the Diocese of Kagera has been helping with theological training and even ordaining clergy who eventually return to lead parishes in Rwanda.

The Revd Canon Fareth Sendegeya, Tanzania

Alongside the formal diocesan links like those described above, informal connections between dioceses and parishes have also increased as people have met.

NETWORKS IN THE ANGLICAN COMMUNION

Networks within the Communion, linking those working on common issues, began to develop in the early 1980s and were originally intended to be self-funding. There are a number of networks, both official[35] and informal. They have taken particular aspects of mission to a more focussed and detailed level than would be possible for IASCOME, which was established to maintain a comprehensive overview of mission within the Communion.

The networks are intended to link the Anglican Communion Office staff and other interested members of churches engaged on the relevant issues.

Formerly the Director for Mission and Evangelism (then titled Director for Mission and Social Concerns) provided some staff support for many of the networks.

The formal networks recognised by the Anglican Consultative Council include:

The Anglican Peace and Justice Network (APJN)

The Anglican Indigenous Network (AIN)

The Network for Inter Faith Concerns in the Anglican Communion (NIFCON) with a part-time staff based in the Anglican Communion Office.

The Inter Anglican Family Network (IAFN) with a budget and part-time staff member and a quarterly newsletter circulated through Anglican World.

The Inter-Anglican Women's Network (IAWN)

Colleges and Universities of the Anglican Communion (CUAC)

The Anglican Communion Environmental Network (ACEN) which met before the 2002 Johannesburg summit on the environment and set up a continuing body with a further meeting in April 2005.

The networks not accountable to the Anglican Consultative Council include:

HIV and AIDS network in Africa. It includes all thirteen provinces in Africa (including the Diocese of Egypt).

MEGAN—Mission and Evangelism Global Action Networking—an electronic network (e-network) communicating through the internet.

The Network for Anglicans in Mission and Evangelism (NAME) established particularly for bishops in Section II of the 1998 Lambeth Conference to encourage bishops in mission and evangelism, and to assist in building capacity in dioceses and provinces.

The Anglican Contextual Theologians Network, theologians from around the Communion interested in the diverse cultural and geographic contexts of contemporary Anglicanism.[36]

ANITEPAM (the African Network of Institutions of Theological Education Preparing Anglicans for Ministry).

The Task Group on Trade and Poverty.

PITOT—a youth electronic network that meets online and so far has representatives from ten provinces.

A number of mission agencies have developed networks of co-ordination among themselves. Some campaign networks have also developed around issues in human sexuality prior to and following the consecration of Bishop Robinson of New Hampshire.

Ecumenical networking developments—an example from India

The Church of South India was formed out of 11 different denominations in 1947 to be followed by the Church of North India, formed from six denominations in November 1971. Efforts are now being made to bring the CSI, CNI and Mar Thoma Church together under one name. This has not yet succeeded but there are increased joint efforts.

One of the recent developments is that the three Churches are planning to bring into one fold mission organisations like the Friends Missionary Prayer Band, the National Missionary Society, the Evangelical Fellowship and others. A small group met in Delhi in February 2005 to plan a large mission conference scheduled for July 2005. This conference will include representation from CMS (Britain); the USA and other parts of the world.

The Revd Pearl Prashad, Church of North India

Other forms of networking

It is also worth noting that email, the internet and the Anglican Cycle of Prayer all help develop Anglican relationships and interconnectedness thus contributing to a sense of Anglican identity.

OTHER WAYS MISSION RELATIONSHIPS ARE FORMED IN THE ANGLICAN COMMUNION

Day to day life

The heart of the witness of the Church is the day-to-day presence, life and witness of lay Christians in their places of residence, work and the neighbourhoods where they live, and the networks with which they are associated. The Christian faith is a way of life rather than an organisation and Christians live out that life in the wider society. The resources of the organised Church, its worship and teaching, need to focus on strengthening and enabling Christians to witness in their daily lives.

Congregational life and other forms of Christian gathering

The lives of individual Christians are strengthened and resourced by their lives together in many different forms of Christian community focused around the Bible and the Eucharist. Rowan Williams, the Archbishop of Canterbury, has spoken in Britain of the 'mixed economy' Church—one in which the life of the parish congregation is held alongside the many other ways in which Christians meet to sustain and nourish their faith and discipleship of Jesus Christ—for as he puts it: "'If 'church' is what happens when people encounter the Risen Jesus and commit themselves to sustaining and deepening that encounter in their encounter with each other, there is plenty of rhythm and style, so long as we have ways of identifying the same living Christ at the heart of every expression of Christian life in common."[37]

Movements of people

Movements of people have always been of great significance in the spread of the faith from the day of Pentecost and the scattering of the Church following the martyrdom of Stephen in the Book of Acts.[38] Movements may be forced or natural.

Forced movements are caused by civil war, famine and natural disaster, and have displaced growing numbers of people, both within countries and across borders. Sudanese Christians, for example, have migrated to many countries, setting up congregations in Uganda, Congo, Canada, the USA and Britain, to name just a few countries. In Britain many refugees seek asylum because of fear of persecution in their home countries. Government policy has been to disperse them to different parts of the country. Often local churches have come to assist them and as a result have had to engage for the first time with people from other countries—a good number of them Christian.

Natural movements include Christians drawn to other countries for reasons of economics. One example is Filipinos employed as domestic workers in households in many parts of the world including Saudi Arabia, Britain, the USA, Japan, Hong Kong and Cyprus. This is part of a national policy to use the people resource of the Philippines to produce foreign currency for the development of the Philippines and to meet interest payments on international debt. Other examples are the mass internal movement of Southern Africans to cities like Johannesburg to find work, the movement of various European nationalities across Europe, and the flow of migrant workers across European borders to undertake menial tasks in agriculture and food production. Alongside such movements there are also the world-wide movements of people with professional skills.

Christians are caught up in these wider people movements and take their faith with them, establishing new Christian communities in the places where they settle.

Missionary bishops and new dioceses

One of the notable features of the growth of the Church in Africa south of the Sahara has been the consecration of bishops charged with starting new missionary dioceses, often with no resources other than themselves and their people.[39] The trend has been most prolific in Nigeria, which has started 21 more dioceses since the original ten missionary dioceses were formed at the beginning of the Decade of Evangelism. And there are other examples in Kenya, Sudan, Uganda, Tanzania, Congo, Central Africa and Southern Africa.

Responding to social need and injustice.

Although not new, a feature of the last twenty years has been coalitions formed to address serious issues of social need. Many of these are ecumenical or inter agency. A good example is the response to the crisis caused by the spread of HIV and AIDS. In many countries, issues of injustice and social need lead to Christian action. In Zimbabwe, for example, there has been a marked increase in social commitment over the past ten years with congregations sourcing food aid, money and clothing to assist the destitute and those displaced for political reasons. In the Democratic Republic of Congo, a country racked by civil war, the Church at a national level is involved in health, education and agricultural development in so far as it can be, but it has found that with the withdrawal of foreign missionaries, financial support from overseas sources has dropped significantly. The Sudan Relief Aid (SUDRA) is the development agency of the Episcopal Church operating as a fully Sudanese organisation co-ordinating the Church's relief work in the South, in Khartoum, and most recently in Darfur. Stories of some of this work can be found in Chapter Four.

Pastoral chaplaincy work among peoples who have moved.

One of the features of the movement of peoples is that it often proves difficult for new arrivals to be assimilated into the congregations and structures of churches in the receiving country. Barriers of language and culture have led to the growth of separate Anglican congregations such as Congolese French-speaking congregations in England, French-speaking Rwanda, Burundi and Haitian congregations in Canada, Nigerian congregations in the USA, Cantonese-speaking congregations in Canada, and English-speaking chaplaincy congregations in a number of non-English speaking countries, (the latter being the latest phase in the long history of chaplaincy to expatriates and their descendants carried out first by the Church of England[40]). Different patterns emerge in these situations, including separate congregations based on language or culture: fellowships of people who are integrated into local congregations but wish to meet from time with those of their own language group, cultural or national groups; and chaplains invited by a local bishop to pastor a distinct language congregation.

These developments raise significant questions about our understanding of church mission policy, which we recommend should be explored by the next IASCOME.

New mission movements and programs

If one of the historical impetuses driving the evolution of the Anglican Communion was the role of voluntary mission societies, so new, contemporary societies and patterns of voluntary initiative are emerging and will continue to emerge within the Communion. Voluntary initiatives represent the coming together of Christian people to undertake specific tasks. Recent examples include the Bangladeshi Mission Church, and the Anglican Village Mission Movement in Malaysia, to name just two. In Sudan, Revival Movements of lay people from the Episcopal Church, particularly those involving the Mothers' Union and young people, arising from the Decade of Evangelism, have formed churches in new areas particularly in northern Sudan, to be followed by clergy and bishops.

Following the Provincial Mission and Evangelism Co-ordinators Consultation in May 2002 and the Mission Organisations Conference in Cyprus in February 2003 a network of mission organisations and practitioners was established under the acronym MEGAN (Mission and Evangelism Global Action and Networking) to share information and stories electronically. There is scope for further developing MEGAN.

Mission 21, a mission program of the Scottish Episcopal Church, has opened up new opportunities for mission throughout Scotland. The program has been adapted for use in the Diocese of Meath and Kildare (Church of Ireland), the Diocese of Kumi (Uganda),[41] the Diocese of Guatemala, and most recently, the Episcopal Church in the Philippines.

Projects for sharing and structures for co-ordination

Effective witness is determined by the local context in which the church is situated. Although there are global trends, the call to incarnational presence and mission means that congregations, dioceses, national churches and mission movements and organisations shaped by their understanding of their Christian calling, will be responding to needs and opportunities in their local contexts. That makes for rich variety. The Global Anglicanism Project (GAP) is engaged in a survey of the provinces of the Communion to identify some of the richness and characteristics of the Anglican Communion and make that available for sharing.[42]

As movements and mission organisations multiply, structures are needed to encourage co-ordination, sharing of information and decisions about joint action. In England, the Partnership for World Mission (PWM) has provided that forum since 1978. A significant development has been a covenant of co-operation signed by the heads of the ten mission agencies in the presence of the Archbishop of Canterbury as witness. In the United States, the Episcopal Partnership for Global Mission (EPGM) provides a forum not just for mission agencies, but also for dioceses, parishes and canonical bodies of the church, and is greatly assisted by electronic communication between annual meetings.

In countries that lack those forums bishops have a key role to play. As leaders in mission their task includes the facilitation, co-ordination and direction for mission in their dioceses and provinces, and to ensure that mission agencies and voluntary movements are included in that co-ordination.[43]

Regional and Communion-wide gatherings

Occasional Communion-wide gatherings provide key opportunities for networking and reflection. They also support and supplement the informal networking that can take place by email and other means of communication. Recent examples include the mid-point Review of the Decade of Evangelism at Kanuga, USA in 1995, which helped develop links between provinces in the Global South: the Provincial Mission and Evangelism Co-ordinators Conference in Nairobi in 2002: the Mission Organisations Conference in Cyprus in 2003[44]: and the mission conferences for bishops that NAME has held in different parts of the world. One of the roles of a future mission commission would be to continue to sponsor such gatherings as key moments for the establishment of links and connections of many sorts.

Mission links resulting from IASCOME meetings

The meetings of IASCOME in Kempton Park, South Africa, (2001), St Andrews, Scotland (2002), Runaway Bay, Jamaica (2003) and Larnaca, Cyprus (2005) each bore fruit with regard to the emergence and blossoming of relations between individuals, groups, congregations and dioceses within the Anglican Communion.

At the Johannesburg meeting the Commission was exposed to work being done among people with HIV and AIDS. As a result, 2000 AIDS badges were bought for $1.00 each and sold for £2.00 each in Britain. All income from this project went to the township where the badges were made.

The St Andrews meeting led to connections between the Dioceses of Cape Coast (Ghana) and Edinburgh (Scotland). The Scottish Mothers' Union links with Manicaland in Zimbabwe were strengthened through increased information, commitment to prayer and financial support for widows' projects. Following the 2004 South Asian Tsunami, the Scottish Episcopal Church focused its 2005 Lent Appeal on children's work in Sri Lanka about which it had heard during the Commission visit.

Following the Runaway Bay (Jamaica) meeting the Franciscan Friars of Melanesia began to build closer links with the Church in Jamaica. Two brothers have since travelled to join the sole Franciscan already living on the island to form a community. The Church in Papua New Guinea (PNG) invited an HIV and AIDS worker from Zimbabwe to lead seminars in PNG as a result of conversations held in Jamaica. The Diocese of Ysabel, in Melanesia, is establishing a link with the Diocese of Northern Luzon in the Philippines to share personnel, prayer and experience.

PROPOSALS

A Covenant for Communion in Mission

Although the Partners in Mission process and the Decade of Evangelism have come to an end, they gave cohesion to the Communion and identified principles[45] to guide relationships in mission. Their influence and effects continue. While there does not seem to be much interest in communion-wide programs at the present time, what can be helpful is a fresh articulation of the principles and values that can serve to guide our cross-cultural and cross boundary relationships in mission and undergird our mission life as a Communion. This is what our proposal for a Covenant for Communion in Mission offers.

The appointment of IASCOME II[46]

The Anglican Communion has been well served over the years by its various mission and evangelism oversight bodies, beginning with the first Mission Issues & Strategies Group, MISAG I, followed by MISAG II, MISSIO, and IASCOME.[47] These groups, committees and commissions have enabled the Anglican Communion to follow the changing patterns of mission relationships over the years, to appreciate the breadth and depth of our mission response to God's call, and to offer some measure of guidance in an ever-changing world context. In order for this work to continue, we recommend that new members be appointed, to serve under a revised mandate.

Communion-wide Consultations on Mission and Evangelism

A key role for the Anglican Consultative Council is to maintain an overview of the ways in which the many different parts of the Communion are expressing their relationships in mission, encouraging wider engagement with society and sharing learnings. It is through the struggles of such engagement with the wider world, participating in the mission of God to all people, that the Spirit gives new life and energy. That is why gatherings that include a wide range of people are important milestones and generators of new initiatives in the life of the Communion. We propose that there be further Consultations of Provincial Evangelism Co-ordinators and of Mission Organisations during the term of the next IASCOME.

A Pan-Anglican Gathering

IASCOME and its predecessor MISSIO both viewed the proposal for an Anglican Gathering in 2008 in association with the Lambeth Conference as a highly significant and worthwhile development. While understanding the reasons for the cancellation of the proposed 2008 gathering in Cape Town, the Commission was saddened by the decision and strongly commends that consideration be given for a gathering in 2013.[48]

Questions for Discussion

What cross-cultural or cross-border links are you aware of in your church? What has been the influence of these relationships in the life of your church?

In what ways is your church connected to any of the formal or less formal networks named in this chapter, and how have these connections affected the life of your church?

Discuss any other networks, coalitions or other mission relationships that are important in the life of your church.

CHAPTER 4

EVANGELISM

Therefore go and make disciples of all nations, baptising them in the name of the Father and of the Son and of the Holy Spirit. . . . Matthew 28:19

INTRODUCTION

At the 1988 Lambeth Conference, the bishops of the Anglican Communion called for a Decade of Evangelism to call the attention of the church to the important task of "making new Christians" within the Anglican community. The Decade of Evangelism launched officially in 1991, motivated many people across our Communion to new evangelistic efforts, many of which have continued beyond the official ending of the Decade in 2000.

This chapter provides a definition and discussion of evangelism, outlines various aspects of evangelism, and includes stories of a several of models of evangelism, as told and collected by members of IASCOME.

DEFINITIONS

The World Council of Churches, in its 1982 document *Mission and Evangelism in Unity Today,* defined mission as:

> *The proclamation and sharing of the Good News of the Gospel by word, deed, prayer and worship and the everyday witness of the Christian life; teaching as building up and strengthening people in their relationship with God and each other, and healing as wholeness and reconciliation into communion with God, communion with people and communion with creation as a whole.*[49]

Evangelism, on the other hand, is defined in the same document as:

> *Explicit and intentional voicing of the Gospel, including the invitation to personal conversion to a new life in Christ and to discipleship.*

The Anglican Consultative Council in 1990 approved the following Five Marks of Mission[50]

To proclaim the Good News of the Kingdom of God
To teach, baptise and nurture new believers
To respond to human need by loving service
To seek to transform unjust structures of society and
To strive to safeguard the integrity of creation and sustain and renew the life of the earth.

Thus both the World Council and the Anglican Consultative Council position mission as the broader concept, with evangelism conceptualised as one part of the larger whole. For Anglicans, evangelism is the first of the Five Marks, and is understood to be an essential part of the total mission in which the church participates.

Raymond Fung, in his address to the 1995 Global Conference on Dynamic Evangelism[51], marking the midpoint of the Anglican Communion's Decade of Evangelism, stressed the importance of evangelism but also clarified its limitations. He cautioned against both the temptation to marginalise evangelism, and also the temptation to overload it.

Mission without evangelism loses its authenticity. Accordingly evangelism cannot be marginalised in the life and identity of the church. It is for every Christian person and it is for every Christian ministry and for every office in the church. While there are full time evangelists, all believers share in the task of evangelism, for example as Christian teachers, homemakers, business people, civil servants, doctors, lawyers, policemen, farmers, craft workers, etc. Evangelism is also given to every office and ministry, to bishops, pastors, to development workers and chaplaincy ministries, to the laity in their everyday lives.

While evangelism is essential, and while evangelism must not be marginalised, evangelists ought not be overloaded either. Evangelism is one, albeit essential, aspect of mission. Raymond Fung expresses it this way.

> *Don't put too much into evangelism, don't expect it to bring the second coming of Jesus, and don't expect it to bring justice and peace to the whole world. It is but one ministry . . . I think in a way we expect too much of evangelism, we will overload it, we will break its back, we would domesticate it, and we would destroy its power.*
>
> *Given that I want to reject temptations to overload evangelism, I want to say that evangelism is not mission; evangelism rather is the sharpest point of mission. It is the cutting edge in the church's encounter with the world . . . And therefore without this cutting edge, without this evangelistic context our missionary encounter with the world cannot be complete.*

While evangelism is not the whole of mission, mission without evangelism is incomplete. More than this, evangelism is the cutting edge of mission. This is a point of key importance to us in the Anglican Communion. This is because evangelism, this cutting edge of mission, brings a profound challenge as well as opportunity to the church. This happens in at least three ways.

First, new believers coming into the church from various ethnic, racial and social backgrounds bring new challenges to the church. New questions are asked, different experiences are shared, new gifts are offered within the life of the church. Old allegiances are tested and new allegiances are introduced. It was evangelism, which caused many of the troubles of the early church. It was when Gentiles became Christians that the Council of Jerusalem was called to resolve the first great missiological controversy in the church. It was and is evangelism, which poses challenges to established understandings of theology and to social relationships within the life of the church.

This creates the second profound challenge and opportunity. Like conversion, evangelism compels creative, life bringing change. Evangelism creates a response. Proclamation speaks to another. A person or community listens and hears the message of God within their context. Fruitful and powerful evangelism invokes a response from individual human hearts and lives and also from communities. Proclamation meets a response of articulation. It is new believers who, in turn, become some of the most powerful evangelists for their neighbours and their communities.

This in turn creates a third challenge. New conversations about God emerge. New questions about worship, discipleship, Christian teaching, and appropriate behaviour for Christians in local contexts arise. The church discovers that evangelism has a key role to play in the engagement of the church in theological reflection. Evangelism compels the church to seek and to develop new directions. Evangelism, therefore, both initiates and results in new understandings of theology.

ASPECTS OF EVANGELISM

Evangelism, the proclamation of the Good News of God's grace and abundant life as promised and demonstrated through Jesus Christ, is characterised by the following:

It is intentional. As such it requires evangelists to speak boldly about how God is working in their own lives, and about the reason for their hope. This bold and public intentionality works well for Members of the Anglican Evangelistic Association in Tanzania who are succeeding in bringing many people to confess Jesus Christ as their Lord and Saviour and to become active members of Christian communities. On the other hand, the intentionality of the evangelistic task also requires sensitivity to the cultural context and to the particular circumstances of the hearer or audience. We heard about the care that must be taken in India at the present time so as not to be seen to be breaking the law by actively proselytising. This means sometimes choosing to baptise new believers privately in their homes rather than publicly in the church.

It is an invitation. Jesus invited his disciples into fellowship, but never threatened or coerced them into joining him. The invitation to the new life in Christ must be freely offered, but not forced upon people. We heard about how the House-to-House visitation ministry in the Diocese of Kagera in Tanzania succeeds in bringing people to faith in Christ Jesus. In this simple process, small bands of Anglicans are invited to visit individuals in their homes to bring a message about the Good News of Jesus, followed by evening worship and prayers.

It is founded in grace. Our invitation should be a testimony to the grace that we have found, not a promise of specific benefits such as material wealth or protection from illness. Grace is a gift from God. Our invitation is an offer to accept this gift as a new way of seeing and experiencing the world. The following example from Burundi illustrates the grace, the hope, and the life Jesus the Christ offers in the most challenging circumstances.

> *The civil war, which has been ongoing for many years, has caused incredible damage to the country's infrastructure, eroded trust among its people, and displaced millions. In such an environment, you would expect the church to crumble; but through the constant efforts of its congregations and leaders, the Anglican Church has been at the forefront of many social initiatives, giving people reasons to stay together, and offering opportunities for reconciliation.*[52]

It is a process. We understand God to be continually calling us to new understandings and new challenges. Conversion happens repeatedly in our lives. So the task of the evangelist is both to proclaim to those who have not heard, but also to encourage and edify those who are already in Christ. This is the reciprocal encouragement that Paul spoke about in Romans 1:12, that all Christians, both old and new, are built up in their faith. An example from Central America illustrates this process of evangelism.

The story began with a call made by some non-Anglican Christians to the Anglican Church in the area. They requested pastoral assistance because they felt that they were in the process of losing their Christian faith due to the strong witness of Mayan traditionalists amongst them. The local Anglican priest then accompanied a representative group from the community to a meeting with the bishop.

The bishop explained to them that the process of becoming Anglican was not simply accepting a number of beliefs, but rather sharing a common life and hope in Jesus Christ as Saviour. He told them that this was a process of learning and living together in the faith, and was to be followed by the next step of communicating to others the Good News of salvation. They accepted the bishop's terms, designed an educational program, and proposed a date by which they hoped to be ready to be received as faithful Anglicans. The implementation of this process was left in the hands of the priest in charge of the area and four lay readers from the nearby mission. Nine months later the community invited the bishop to receive the people into the Church. That day the bishop received and confirmed 60 adult people and officially commissioned them to evangelisation and outreach ministries. One month later the leaders of the new Anglican community requested official recognition as an organised mission within the diocese. The bishop accepted them and approved their evangelism plan to establish two new congregations in the area.

MODELS OF EVANGELISM

There are many different ways in which the Good News can be effectively proclaimed. The challenge for the evangelist is to find a method or model that fits the local context, speaks to local cultural realities, and can be adapted to changing circumstances. The models that follow are by no means comprehensive, but are examples of how evangelism is being expressed as the cutting edge of mission in the Communion today.

'He sent them out two by two' (Mark 6:7)

The Episcopal Church of the Sudan, in their "Send Me" evangelism program, has used the model described in Mark 6:7. Teams of evangelists are sent out to rural areas to intentionally proclaim the Good News and to invite people to personal conversion. This program has been highly successful.

A similar model has been successfully used in the Democratic Republic of the Congo. Teams of between 15 and 20 evangelists have been trained in each diocese. Each team is sent out to a new area for a two-week period, with each evangelist assigned to a village where he or she preaches the Gospel each morning and each evening. Once a community has come to faith in Christ, the villagers are asked to choose one of their number who is then given a month-long basic training, and is then sent back to serve as the village catechist. All the village catechists from the given area then choose one village that is easily accessible to which they make a commitment to travel each Sunday, along with some of their villagers. At these Sunday meetings a priest from a nearby parish preaches and further instructs them. Eventually, a new church is planted at this preaching point.

'Come over and help us' (Acts 16:9)

Just as Paul answered God's call to travel to Macedonia in order to preach the Good News and help establish a church among the people, so too we heard how this model has been used by the Melanesian Brothers who have responded to a call from the Episcopal Church of the Philippines to "come over" and establish a new branch of their Order.

The story from Egypt also illustrates this model of coming over to help. The evangelist began his work in Alexandria where he established an Arabic-speaking congregation. He was then sent to Suez where he encountered a group of young people who gathered regularly for prayer. The group requested the use of the Anglican church building for their meetings. The request was granted and a positive outcome resulted. "All these people came along to the church and belong to the church, and now we have three prayer meetings. These are very important prayer meetings, believe me this is the foundation of the church.'[53]

'The harvest is plentiful but the labourers are few' (Matt. 9:37)

One of the dioceses in the Province of Central America became concerned about the great need for outreach among the people of the country, but also about the tremendous shortage of personnel willing to serve as evangelists. In a context of poverty and high unemployment, the bishop decided to advertise in the local newspaper that the Episcopal Church was seeking to hire evangelists for modest payment, and with the following prerequisites:

proof of their Christian baptism;
a sense of being called to serve in the spreading of the Good News;
proof of godly life (letters, note from their pastor, recommendations
    from former employers);
a written biography tracing their spiritual journey;
proof of undergraduate studies;
proof of theological or biblical studies if any, and a willingness to take
    an intensive course of preparation.

More than one hundred men and women applied. The diocese carefully selected ten, and signed a three-year contract with them. At the time of writing (September 2003), these ten were being trained and were designing a strategic plan for evangelism in the diocese in the years to come.

This story recognises the fact that there is a desperate need to bring labourers into God's vineyard. Secondly, the method recognises that there are people from other Christian denominations willing to serve the Lord as evangelists who have not received a call from their own church. Thirdly, offering paid employment is a positive response to the situation of high unemployment in the area.

'My message and my preaching were not with wise and persuasive words, but with a demonstration of the Spirit's power . . .' (1 Cor. 2:4)

This verse speaks to those churches dominated by rationality, and encourages an approach in which the Spirit has demonstrated power over worldly powers. A story from the USA illustrates the working of the Spirit where there is a hunger and search for evangelism, and an outward spiritual focus.

'Something is happening in the Episcopal Church. It started as a restlessness some of us began to notice that doing and being the church was not the way it used to be. . . . As a church we are becoming uncomfortable; it is an anxious restlessness. It is exactly the kind of discomfort that often leads to a change of behaviour. . . . Personal faith and spirituality are a high priority for us. We have learned to pray, we have sought out spiritual directors, we have tended ourselves as spiritual beings. In a world where increasing numbers of people do not know how to name God and do not know Jesus Christ, perhaps our inner work now has an outward focus. Is it time to learn how to share our personal faith with others—even with our children, even with strangers?'[54]

'I eagerly expect and hope that I will in no way be ashamed, but will have sufficient courage so that now as always Christ will be exalted in my body, whether by life or by death.' (Phil. 1:20)
Paul's letter to the saints at Philippi was written from his prison cell where he was held in chains for preaching the Good News. Today too there can be a cost to evangelism. During the civil conflict in the Solomon Islands, members of the Melanesian Brothers and other religious orders risked their lives trying to bring God's peace. Some of them were murdered in the process, thus paying the ultimate price. 'At the height of the tension, the Melanesian Brothers and the other religious orders stood together between the two warring parties, trying to bring peace between the two sides. What was outstanding was that the religious communities remained faithful to their vows and did not side with either of the warring parties.'[55]

Reaching the outcasts
Jesus' encounter with the Samaritan woman at the well in John 4:1–41 provides us with another model for evangelism. By initiating contact with a Samaritan woman, asking her to attend to his needs, and engaging her in dialogue about the nature of God, Jesus openly challenged two strongly held social conventions of his time, namely, the barrier between 'chosen people' (Jews) and 'rejected people' (Samaritans), and the barrier between 'male' and 'female'. His respectful acceptance of the Samaritan woman as a worthy recipient of God's grace enabled her to hear and receive the Good News. While we did not hear an example that parallels this biblical story, we did hear of one-on-one Christian trauma counselling being done by workers among refugee populations in camps in the Sudan, where outcast people are in despair and are struggling to survive in deplorable conditions.

LEARNING AND CONSULTING ABOUT EVANGELISM

Not wanting to lose the momentum created by the Decade of Evangelism, the Advisory Group of the former MISSIO recommended that IASCOME sponsor two inter-Anglican gatherings, one for Provincial Mission and Evangelism Co-ordinators and the other for Anglican Mission Organisations working cross-culturally. These consultations were held in Nairobi in May 2002 and in Cyprus in February 2003, respectively.[56]

Provincial Mission and Evangelism Co-ordinators Consultation

For the first time in the history of the Anglican Communion, Provincial Evangelism Co-ordinators met to share their experiences of evangelism. At this conference[57] almost every province was represented. Participants shared together in Bible study, prayer and worship, and also exchanged information about goals, strategies, programs and problems. This shared fellowship brought a real sense of understanding and exuberant joy. Many Evangelism Co-ordinators were new to the job and so the chance to exchange ideas and discuss problems released a buzz of energy. From this exchange came a request for Guidelines for Mission and Evangelism Co-ordinators that have been put together by IASCOME and are included in this report.[58] The second request was for another gathering in the future, to enable further exchange of ideas and programs, as well as practical training in the task of drawing others into fellowship with Jesus.

In the years since the conference, several Anglican provinces have been inspired to gather together their diocesan mission co-ordinators to look at their own strategies and exchange ideas, discuss problems, strengths and weakness. For example, before leaving Nairobi the Africans delegates began planning their follow-up. The Council of Anglican Provinces of Africa (CAPA), sponsored an inter-African Consultation that took place in 2003 and was held alongside the CAPA Primates' meeting. Significant conferences have been held in Uganda which resulted in careful strategic planning for evangelism in the province. Tanzania brought together evangelism co-ordinators and bishops both of whom play key evangelistic roles in their dioceses. Other consultations are planned in other African provinces.

The delegate from Canada, encouraged that God is at work in the world, was stimulated to press for more awareness of the need for evangelism, resulting in a consultation in her own diocese. The diocese has since appointed a diocesan evangelism co-ordinator who is working with local parishes to help them find ways to make their churches more appealing to their unchurched neighbours.

From Scotland, the delegate reported that the Nairobi Consultation was a valuable catalyst in the adoption by their General Synod of the vision for mission contained in the document *Journey of the Baptised: the Mission Strategy of the Scottish Episcopal Church for the 5 years from 2003–2008.*

Missions Organisations Conference

Entitled, *Transformation and Tradition in Global Mission,* the Mission Organisations Conference[59], held in Cyprus from 12–18 February 2003, brought together both the traditional mission agencies from the Global North and the new mission organisations and initiatives from the Global South. The fact that the conference was attended by 100 delegates from all 39 province of the Communion, attested to the transformation in global mission since the previous Mission Agencies Conference of 1987, which was held for Northern mission agencies only, with those from the South invited only as 'external partners'. The 2003 conference noted this major shift in mission leadership as well as the move towards more equal partnerships than had been the case in 1987.

One delegate from Guatemala offered the following reflection. '*I believe that for all the representatives of mission organisations attending the conference, including myself from this new Province in Central America, the vision of the mission of the Church for the present century has been reshaped. Our globalised world requires a strategy somewhat different from the traditional one. At present the Church faces many new challenges but also thousands of mission opportunities. In my opinion the participants in the conference experienced a transformation in vision and a transformation in the appreciation of our Anglican tradition. However, we also experienced a transformation in our understanding of the world and its present need.*'

Another delegate from West Malaysia commented: '*The Cyprus conference has inspired me and has greatly influenced the strategic mission planning of the diocese. We had our first diocesan mission conference with seminars and workshops about the challenging opportunities in Cambodia, Laos, Vietnam, Nepal, Thailand and Indonesia. The diocese has set up a Diocesan Mission Fund to send workers to these areas and beyond. This conference has become an annual event along with our Prayer Summit.*'

Feedback from participants stressed the invaluable opportunity to meet people who share the same vision, the same responsibility and focus of work, and most importantly, people who share the same Anglican faith. Contacts were established and are still maintained around which a number of collaborative ventures are taking place, including one involving youth. Thus the opportunity to meet and spend time together is an essential part of any gathering.

The main outcome of both conferences was the energy, stimulation and visioning arising from the face-to-face meetings and exchanges of ideas. Results include ongoing networking among delegates and important strategic planning for evangelism within provinces and dioceses. The energy generated by these two conferences continues to have a ripple effect across our Communion.

Guidelines for Evangelism Co-ordinators[60]

The encouragement of the Decade of Evangelism and the added momentum to the witness of the church in its mission has been strengthened in the years that have followed. Mission and evangelism haves taken a higher place on the agendas of provinces and dioceses of the Communion. As the ministry of mission and evangelism is developing the need for guidelines for evangelism co-ordinators has become more apparent.

In Mission Commissions and ACC meetings of the past, guidelines for partnership in mission, networks, companion diocesan links, principles of partnership, development programs, partnership visits and priorities in evangelism have been put together to encourage and assist the work of mission in the provinces, dioceses and mission organisations. These guidelines have been gathered together into one booklet that has been distributed widely in the Communion.[61]

These guidelines are the result of research into the practice of mission and evangelism through the years, evaluating what has been both successful and difficult. They have been distilled from the experience of people involved in mission who have seen the usefulness of having a guide to help those starting new programs and ventures in mission. The Guidelines for Companion Link Relationships in particular have proved a great asset to dioceses and have been adapted by some provinces to suit their own needs.

The Guidelines for Evangelism Co-ordinators have been put together using the same process of sharing the experiences of those co-ordinating mission and evangelism in their provinces and dioceses. The research for these guidelines has particularly drawn upon the experiences of the participants at the Inter Anglican Provincial Evangelism Co-ordinators Consultation in Nairobi, and other Provincial Consultations.

Recommendation

We recommend that during the next decade, IASCOME sponsor a second consultation of provincial co-ordinators of mission and evangelism and a third conference of mission agencies and organisations.

We recommend that the Guidelines for Evangelism Co-ordinators be accepted and recommended and distributed, through the ACO Mission and Evangelism Desk, to the Provinces of the Anglican Communion for implementation.

Questions for Discussion

Raymond Fung suggests that evangelism is the cutting edge of mission and that mission activity is most likely to challenge established understandings of God. What challenges to established theology and practices has the church in your area faced from new-comers?

Four aspects of evangelism are described. Do you agree with these? Can you think of others?

Six models of evangelism are named and illustrated. Are there other models used in your area? Does your church have a preferred model? Are there models which you think would not succeed in your culture? Why?

CHAPTER 5

MISSION IN THE CONTEXT OF OUR BLESSED BUT BROKEN AND HURTING WORLD

I have come that they may have life and have it to the full. (John 10:10)

Jesus ultimately gave up his life by being crucified on the cross so that all might have life in abundance. However, we live in a world that is dominated by wars and conflict caused by a greedy minority. We live in a global village, with systems that create wars, conflicts, poverty and violence, systems that dehumanise the majority of people by denying them the opportunity to live purposeful and peaceful lives.

The God we proclaim is a God of love and justice. The world in which we live, however, is characterised by injustice, greed, poverty, terrorism, abuse of power and exclusion. It is in this broken world that we are called to joyful participation in God's mission of love and justice for all.

This chapter outlines some of the many contexts in which the church in mission is responding to unjust and inhuman systems. God is calling Christians, Anglicans among them, to respond to the mission challenges of today's world. Thankful for God's blessings, Anglicans throughout the Communion are responding to God's call to be bearers of the Good News. In the following stories, the members of IASCOME describe their own mission contexts. Other stories can be found in Chapter 8 of this report.

Mission as solidarity with the dispossessed

Marginalised, minority groups are found in all societies. Many of these are Indigenous Peoples who have been dispossessed of their traditional lands by newcomers or by multinational corporations wanting to exploit natural resources. IASCOME members told moving stories of how local churches are supporting these groups in their struggles for justice, often with successful outcomes.

In Guatemala, foreign mining companies are being allowed to extract mineral resources in ways that destroy the agricultural base of local communities. The churches, working ecumenically, are advocating in solidarity with the local people.

In the Amazonia region of Brazil, the Indigenous Peoples have been forced off their land by pressure from foreign multinational corporations who want to exploit the resources of the land. In 2004 a National Indigenous Forum came into being as a result of co-operation between churches

and other non-governmental organisations, working in solidarity with
Indigenous Peoples. These advocacy efforts have been very costly. For
example, the Krao-Kanela people, a group of 85 families, failed in their
efforts to re-occupy their traditional lands. An Anglican priest, Father Bras
Rodrigues, encouraged their efforts, and now lives with the families in a
home supported by the church. The members of this small community are
living in crowded and undignified conditions. Father Rodrigues' name has
been added to a list of people targeted to be killed for activism. The murder
of Chico Mendes in 1988 was reported around the world, as was the recent
murder, in February 2005, of Sister Dorothy Stang. Between 1994 and
2003, 1,349 people have been killed in land conflicts in Brazil.

In Botswana, despite the existence of a stable democratic government,
the minority rights of the Indigenous San people are not being honoured.
Non-governmental organisations and the churches are advocating in support of the San people, providing encouragement and affirmation to this
marginalised group.

"Tribal Filipinos" is the term used to refer to Indigenous Peoples in the
Philippines. They live mainly in the mountainous regions, especially in the
cordillera region of Northern Luzon. At present, multinational mining and
logging companies are victimising them. It is a common occurrence for
people to be evicted from their homes and land, these evictions being carried out by company employees backed by the military. The Tribal Filipinos
are branded as people against development, if not as outright "insurgents".
Many have died in defence of their lands and ancestral domains. The Episcopal Church of the Philippines is in solidarity with the Tribal Filipinos and
is directly involved in two ways. Firstly, it issues statements opposing illegal
logging and mining. Secondly, it helps to organise the people so that they
can express their sentiments effectively to the government which supports
the mining and logging activities without consideration of the environmental and social effects. "Tribal Filipino Sunday", a yearly event, draws the
attention of the nation to these issues, building empathy and support among
the wider church membership.

In Canada, the churches have long been strong advocates for the rights
of Indigenous Peoples, particularly land rights. First Nations, Inuit and
Métis Peoples now have strong national political organisations, and are
achieving considerable success in securing rights over their traditional lands,
and over the development of their natural resources. The churches continue
to support these efforts, working ecumenically.

Mission as peace-building and conflict resolution

There are many places in the Anglican Communion where people are struggling to survive in the midst of war and violence. In such contexts, God

calls us to search for ways to bring an end to violence, and to support efforts at peace-building.

In the Solomon Islands, the religious orders have played a key role in stopping the violence between warring factions. Melanesian Brothers and Sisters have courageously stood between armed fighters, successfully persuading them to lay down their arms. The Brothers gained the trust of the fighters to the extent that they were seen as providing a safe place for warriors to surrender their weapons. At a later stage in the conflict, six Melanesian Brothers were martyred during their efforts to secure information about the murder of one of their members. Peace cannot be achieved without sacrifice—there is a cost to the mission of peace-building.

The Episcopal Church of the Sudan, in an effort to address the issues of conflict and the civil war in the Sudan, have set up a Justice and Peace Commission which has been actively involved in peace-building and conflict transformation training in affected communities throughout the country. In addition to this, the Sudan Council of Churches has played a key role by rallying the ecumenical efforts for peace advocacy and human rights issues through its national peace building and civic education programs, and at the international level through the Sudan Ecumenical Forum.

In the Democratic Republic of Congo, priests and pastors struggle to provide basic pastoral care and sacramental ministry to people traumatised by years of war. They lack the most basic resources to support their ministry, namely sufficient food to feed their own families, and any means of transport to move from place to place in their vast country. Church properties and belongings have been looted, and houses and schools burned. Thousands of church members are still in exile having lost property and family members. We learned of the murder of Revd Basimaki Byabasaija, who was killed while setting out to attend the Anglican Consultative Council meeting in Hong Kong in 2003. Nonetheless, we rejoiced to hear that church leaders continue to work towards peace and reconciliation, providing trauma counselling, comforting the bereaved, and looking for ways to rebuild church properties.

Mission in interfaith contexts

Building relationships with believers of other faith communities can be challenging. The challenges vary depending on the specific context, and bearing witness to God's love and salvation through Jesus Christ often requires great patience, sensitivity and caution. During its five-year term, IASCOME did not deal in any depth with relations between Christians and those of other faiths. However, our membership included people who are living and working in contexts where interfaith relations are difficult and highly charged.

In Nigeria, relations between Christians and Muslims can be hostile and violent, with Christian evangelising efforts being firmly rejected by the Moslem population. Nonetheless, in some areas, the Church of Nigeria (Anglican Communion) has chosen to provide social services to people regardless of religious affiliation. These services are appreciated, and have led to improved relations in some religiously mixed neighbourhoods.

In India, Christians are a small minority and are associated with the former colonial power. A past history of aggressive evangelism, as well as the resurgence of Hindu nationalism, has resulted in negative attitudes towards Christians at the present time. The 1999 murder of an Australian missionary, along with his two young sons, illustrates the risk of Christian witness in this hostile environment. Christians, who find themselves a persecuted minority in parts of India, now witness most effectively by their actions and lifestyles.

The situation in the Middle East is extremely complex and volatile. The Episcopal Church of Jerusalem and the Middle East must adopt a variety of strategies according to each local situation. In many parts of the Province, the Anglican Church provides chaplaincy ministry to refugees and migrants from neighbouring countries. An important mission of the church is to provide hospitality to other Christian communities by enabling them to meet and worship in Anglican buildings. Anglicans provide safe meeting places, but also offer material resources and social and medical assistance.

Mission as humanitarian relief

The humanitarian needs of people the world over are enormous. Meeting basic human needs is a Christian responsibility. The first story cited below comes from Sri Lanka where, following the Decemer 2004 South Asian Tsunami disaster, the Diocese of Colombo has been very active in responding to the need for relief and reconstruction, particularly in the north of the island. Additionally, the Sisters of St. Margaret are engaged in the mission of humanitarian relief in their own locale.

"Our task today more than ever before is to rebuild the country which was destroyed by the tsunami. Shelter is not merely having a roof over one's head, it is also an expression of an individual's concept of life, it reflects his ambitions and hope. Our people have shown their commitment and willingness to forge ahead to build a nation. After concentrated and thoughtful prayer, we Sisters of St. Margaret came together as a team to help twenty-five families without any religious barriers. We came together as a team in order to bring love and care for those most affected. Our aim is to create a new society where justice prevails."[62]

Sister Chandrani Peiris

The second story is of the courageous efforts of women in the Sudan, who despite their desperate plight, continue to work at providing for the needs of their families.

"Women in Sudan like anywhere in conflict situations have endured untold sufferings as a result of the long and protracted war. They have had to cope with the unprecedented situation of displacement and uprooted-ness, being household heads without the necessary resources, living in poverty and deprivation; being discriminated against and marginalised, being victims of violence. Yet they struggle to uphold their dignity and integrity despite suffering and turbulence.

"It is a reality that the Sudanese women in general (women in the church included) have been very active particularly at the grassroots level during the war, empowering themselves through various activities such as small income-generating ventures, skills promotion, spiritual fellowship, conflict resolution and peace-building initiatives, literacy campaigns and higher education etc. This has been very important and crucial for livelihood sustainability, hope and resilience, not only of the women themselves, but also of families and communities throughout the conflict period."[63]

Mrs Joy Kwaje Eluzai

Mission as ministering to migrants and displaced persons

Movement of peoples is a common feature of our world. More people are on the move than ever before. Some of these are voluntary migrants, some have been driven out of their homes, and some are fleeing conflict. In all cases, people are experiencing dislocation, bewilderment, anxiety and loneliness. In many Anglican Provinces, mission expressed in offering support, services and ministry to such people.

The Philippines is the largest exporter of labour to almost all parts of the world, and the Episcopal Church of the Philippines extends assistance to overseas migrant workers, providing legal assistance to victims of fake job recruiters, and seeking the co-operation of Anglican churches in the recipient countries to deal with maltreatment and abuse of workers.

The Anglican Church in Central America is working to assist the many thousands of Central Americans in the United States, many of whom have migrated illegally and are thus subject to exploitation and abuse. The same story is told from Brazil, and also from Zimbabwe where huge numbers have left in search of a better life, only to be disappointed by unemployment and dislocation.

The migration of Sudanese people is massive, both from Southern Sudan, and more recently from Darfur. In addition to the huge numbers of people living in refugee camps outside of the country, there are also about 4.5 million internally displaced persons in camps within the Sudan. The conditions in many of these camps are deplorable. The Sudan Council of Churches has a plan to help the internally displaced persons return to their homes, and to receive back refugees from outside the country, but can help only a portion of those needing assistance

Mission as the alleviation of poverty and debt

Most Anglicans live in countries that are struggling with the burden of poverty. Christ's ministry was directed largely to the poor and dispossessed. In the same way, many faithful Christians, Anglicans among them, are devoted to serving the poor and advocating for and with them. We heard stories of local level mission and ministry in service to God's mission, from all parts of the world, with churches being planted in urban shantytowns, and income-generating projects being supported in both rural and urban areas.

In late September 2001, within days of the terrorist attacks on the United States, the House of Bishops of the Episcopal Church (USA) met to consider the effects of globalisation. This meeting resulted in the Bishops' statement and commitment to 'Waging Reconciliation.' In January 2003, a core group of bishops and presenters from the 2001 bishops' meeting re-convened with lay and ordained economists, business people, students, social organisers, theologians, attorneys, labour activists, and advocates to imagine the next steps in the Episcopal Church's efforts to wage global reconciliation. Soon a growing community of mobilisation developed around a core vision for God's mission of reconciliation. After considerable reflection they organised themselves as a network of prayer, reflection and action known as Episcopalians for Global Reconciliation (www.e4gr.org).

Episcopalians for Global Reconciliation chose the Millennium Development Goals (MDGs) as a focus for their action, and committed 0.7% of their personal budgets towards these goals as a central organising action. With the leadership of Episcopalians for Global Reconciliation, close to thirty dioceses in the Episcopal Church have committed 0.7% of their budgets to alleviate suffering and poverty globally. Episcopalians for Global Reconciliation is a dynamic broad-based movement that unites American Episcopalians and congregations to understand and address global issues while engaging and deploying human and financial resources to effect structural changes.

At the global level the churches were at the forefront of the Jubilee 2000 Campaign calling for debt relief for the highly indebted countries of the world, and for economic justice so that all might share in the richness of God's creation. Networks of churches worldwide are currently campaigning for the implementation of the Millennium Development Goals and have called on the G8 countries to release the promised resources so that these goals can be met. It is also appropriate to remember that at the 1998 Lambeth Conference all the dioceses of the Anglican Communion were asked to allocate 0.7% of their resources to address poverty. The Anglican Communion's Task Force on Trade and Poverty is surveying all Provinces to learn to what extent this goal has been achieved. The results of this survey will be presented to the Anglican Consultative Council's 13th meeting in Nottingham in June 2005.

Mission as truth telling and the search for healing and wholeness

The work of reconciliation is at the heart of Christian mission. Where there have been serious conflicts and betrayals, this is long and difficult work. The Anglican Communion is largely a result of British colonialism, so there is much work to be done in the mission of truth telling and healing. But there are also other examples of colonial domination that Anglicans are trying to redress, and other contexts of brokenness in which Anglicans are engaged in truth telling and the search for wholeness.

In South Africa the churches, played a key role in the Truth and Reconciliation process following the peaceful change from the apartheid regime to a democratically elected government. Archbishop Desmond Tutu chaired this Commission. The work of reconciliation and reparation continues, with the churches still fully engaged in this process, even as they take up the mission work associated with the HIV and AIDS pandemic.

In Canada, white Anglicans are working to acknowledge and repent for the church's past complicity in the assimilationist policies of the Canadian government towards Indigenous First Nations, Inuit and Métis Peoples. This involves reparation and apology. The long-term goal is reconciliation.[64] The Anglican Churches in Australia and New Zealand are engaged in a similar mission.

In the Solomon Islands the Anglican Church is working with long-term reconciliation programs between the warring factions, by encouraging people to meet together in peaceful dialogue.

In Rwanda ten years after the genocide, the work of repentance and the rebuilding of society is just beginning, with healing and wholeness still a distant goal. The same can be said for Burundi. The cycle of violence continues in both countries and also in the refugee camps in neighbouring countries such as Tanzania, largely due to external factors. There is, however, some basic ministry going on in the camps in Tanzania, where hope is beginning to take root.

Mission as bearing witness to injustice and suffering

The stories of human suffering and injustice are overwhelming. Efforts at peace-building and conflict resolution often fail. Nonetheless, the church needs to continue to be present to bear witness, even when no other action is possible. Peoples' experiences need to be witnessed, recorded and honoured. Then, those who have borne witness need to name the injustices and speak the truth to those in power. Often this means speaking to international bodies, national bodies, and even to the powers in our own churches. Those who take up this mission often put their own jobs, and sometimes their lives, at risk.

Mission as addressing the HIV and AIDS pandemic

As we shared our stories we were often reduced to silence as we heard of the suffering and pain of God's people affected by and infected with HIV and AIDS. We shared how we as Anglicans, often in partnership with our ecumenical sisters and brothers, were participating in God's mission to bring some form of Good News in the midst of this disaster. The HIV and AIDS pandemic is decimating Africa, Asia, Latin America, and Oceania.

The current inter-Anglican effort to combat the pandemic of HIV and AIDS in Africa south of the Sahara is an inspiring mission story. In August of 2001, a first-ever All Africa Anglican Conference on HIV and AIDS was held in Johannesburg, South Africa to address how the Church could be more effective in combating the pandemic. Over 130 delegates from 34 countries attended the conference, including church, business and government leaders. By the end of the four-day meeting, church and secular leaders alike had dedicated themselves to a multipoint 'planning framework' for: 'securing the human rights of those infected by HIV and AIDS, and giving unconditional support; improving the health and prolonging the lives of infected people; accompanying the dying, those who mourn and those who live on; celebrating life; nurturing community; and advocating for justice.'[65] The co-operation of many agencies and churches to address AIDS in Africa resulted in new relationships in service to God's healing mission. Included at the Conference were representatives from every Anglican province in Africa as well as a variety of other Anglican churches and non-governmental agencies including: Christian Aid from Britain, Episcopal Relief and Development from the United States, the Mothers' Union, the Compass Rose Society, The United Society for the Propagation of the Gospel, The Anglican Church of Canada, The United Nations Agency for International Development, Tear Fund, Africa Alive, and the World Bank.

The ambitious plans and early hopes of the All Africa Anglican Conference on HIV and AIDS have been owned and implemented in varying degrees across the Anglican churches in Africa, and new relationships in mission continue to be forged to fight the pandemic. Co-operation between many African Anglican churches and the Episcopal Church in the United States continues in life-affirming relationships in mission. Dr. Douglas Huber, a specialist in women's health and HIV and AIDS prevention who is

Principal Medical officer for the international NGO Management Sciences for Health, has been a special Volunteer for Mission from the Episcopal Church helping the CAPA AIDS Board to plan and implement its programs. He is supported in his work, for CAPA and other individual Anglican churches such as the Anglican churches in Uganda and Nigeria, by the Diocese of Massachusetts Jubilee Ministry. The Jubilee Ministry is an organisation of the Diocese of Massachusetts in the Episcopal Church that receives and disburses funds for development and relief related to HIV and AIDS, particularly in Africa, and also provides technical support to Church groups engaged in HIV and AIDS related activities.

On September 26, 2003, a major conference was held by CAPA in Nairobi, in conjunction with the 13th International Conference for AIDS and Sexually Transmitted Infections in Africa (ICASA) to evaluate and plan CAPA's next steps in addressing the HIV and AIDS pandemic. In addition to CAPA's leaders, present at the consultation were representatives of the Diocese of Massachusetts Jubilee Ministry, Episcopal Relief and Development, the United Thank Offering, Trinity Church Grants Program in New York, The Episcopal Church Centre in New York, the Diocese of Washington DC, the Anglican Communion Office, and a host of individuals from Communities Responding to the HIV and AIDS Epidemic Initiative, known by its acronym the CORE Initiative (a non-governmental organisation working with CAPA that is funded by the United States Agency for International Development, and working in partnership with CARE International, the World Council of Churches, the International Centre on Research on Women and the Johns Hopkins Bloomberg School of Public Health.) All of these individuals and agencies met to consider how, drawing on their own particular strengths, they could work together more effectively to advance African Anglican efforts to overcome HIV and AIDS. The Conference Proceedings with Recommendations emphasised that: "Working together, CAPA and the Provinces of the Anglican Churches are demonstrating how the Church in partnership with donors, local and national authorities, and other faith groups, can presents new opportunities for communion in mission relationships."[66]

We listened to stories that told of the campaigns in South Africa to raise awareness and break the stigma of silence around the disease. The Mothers' Union is building up a network of home-based care, and ministering to those infected and affected by HIV and AIDS, as well as organising funerals for bereaved families. Faithful people minister to the sick, the dying and to those left behind. The enormity of the disaster came home to IASCOME when a priest in the Diocese of the Highveld took us to a cemetery to witness 20 funerals taking place at 20 gravesites, this being a "normal" part of the church's daily ministry.

The Province of Papua New Guinea and the Diocese of Manicaland in Zimbabwe have embarked on a project of raising awareness about HIV and AIDS among high school students. A Zimbabwean priest has run workshops in Papua New Guinea. Education and prevention are critically important to stop the pandemic.

In Tanzania, there is a partnership between the Anglican Church of Tanzania and the Provincial Department of Health to raise awareness in all the dioceses, as well as to minister to those living positively with the virus. The work being done also includes caring for the increasing number of orphans, encouraging young people to participate in sporting activities to encourage a healthy lifestyle, and delivering programs to supplement incomes.

In all the areas affected by HIV and AIDS there are important ministries to the sick, the dying and those left behind, including children heading households, and grieving aged grandparents who have buried their children and taken on the economic burden of raising their grandchildren.

The HIV and AIDS stories of pain and suffering are threaded through with love, hope, compassion and caring.

Communications failures

The importance of communication dominated many of our discussions and we recognise how, within our own church community, we have excluded some by failing to translate key documents from English into the other languages of the Communion. While acknowledging that translation costs money, nonetheless innovative solutions are possible. For example, the Brazilian church uses a network of volunteer translators to help them in this task. They succeeded in translating the Windsor Report into Portuguese within one month of its release, thus enabling the entire Province to participate in the debate. Another suggestion was to read news releases and documents onto tapes and CDs, in local languages.

The Commission recognises that information and communication technology has made communication easier. However many have no access to these this technology, and are thus excluded from the "information highway". Full participation is thus compromised.

Conflict and abuse of power within our churches

Stories were shared of the way power is abused in our own Anglican structures. Sometimes the model of servant leadership is abandoned by bishops in favour of authoritarian models. Sometimes lay leaders in local congregations bully the clergy to achieve their own ends. Stories about the misuse of church resources were also mentioned. Although the abuses were not violent or spectacular there was a cost; the mission of God was compromised, people were hurt and distrust was sown.

On a positive note, we also heard from a new bishop who succeeded in gently persuading the laity of his diocese to come into his house, as they had never been allowed in during the time of his predecessor.

Recommendation

IASCOME appreciates that others connected to various networks of the Anglican Communion, both formal and informal, are engaged in focused ways with particular contexts of injustice and brokenness, and with particular constituencies and interest groups. While we have done some consulting with some members of some of these networks, we recognise the need for more intentional connections to support the missiological commitment of their work.

We recommend, therefore, that IASCOME, during the next five-year term of office, sponsor a Mission Consultation for Network Representatives, to better understand and co-ordinate pan-Anglican information and action in service to God's mission.

Questions for Discussion

Discuss the ways in which your church is participating in God's mission in some of the contexts identified in this chapter. What other contexts of injustice, pain and brokenness are significant for the mission work of your church?

In what ways is your church addressing the worldwide HIV and AIDS pandemic? What is your church's ministry to individuals infected with and affected by HIV and AIDS?

Do the two challenges mentioned at the end of this chapter restrict your church's full participation in God's mission in the Anglican Communion? What other limitations do you face?

CHAPTER 6

MISSION AND THEOLOGICAL EDUCATION

With all wisdom and insight, God has made known to us the mystery of his will, according to his good pleasure which he set forth in Christ, as a plan for the fullness of time, to gather up all things in him, things in heaven and things on earth.

Ephesians 1:8b–10.

THEOLOGICAL EDUCATION: NEW DIRECTIONS AND RICHER RESOURCES

Until quite recently, little attention was given to mission studies, the formal study of mission and mission theology. Conventional programs of theological education have separated mission from the whole Gospel and the whole church. Past approaches to the study of mission have not equipped the church to grow in our knowledge of the biblical and theological bases for mission, both local and worldwide.[67]

The post Enlightenment pattern of theological formation, which was exported all over the world in the missionary expansion of the 19th and early 20th centuries, was based on a view of knowledge which separated knowing from doing. The curriculum stressed the different branches of study, rather than their interconnections as part of a living whole. This coincided with a time when the church in Europe saw itself as "sending" rather than "receiving" through the instruments of mission. Mission, if it was studied at all, was considered as practical theology, alongside the other three separate streams of theological study: biblical studies, church history, and systematic theology. As part of the fourth stream, the emphasis in mission studies was on practical application and technique.[68]

This customary pattern has radically changed in recent times, as a mission focus and foundation asks new questions about the bases and priorities of theological education. The Commission is aware that other work is being undertaken around the Communion with respect to theological education. As part of its mandate to provide a facilitating and co-ordinating role with respect to mission and evangelism, IASCOME, at each of its meetings, has been engaging in reflection on the implications of a mission focus for theological education and leadership development. This is being expressed in different ways in the theological colleges, dioceses and churches of the Communion.

The mandate given to IASCOME by the Anglican Consultative Council at its meeting in Dundee, Scotland in 1999, notes the expanding diversity of mission connections within the Communion. It also affirms the priority given to mission and evangelism by the Decade of Evangelism proposed by the 1998 Lambeth Conference.[69] IASCOME seeks to encourage the Anglican Communion to see mission and evangelism as a Gospel imperative, not an optional activity. Some of the implications of this commitment are suggestive for theological education.

MISSION IS THE MOTHER OF THEOLOGY AND OF THE CHURCH

While the change is not everywhere, and not consistent, a new understanding is emerging. Theologians of many schools of thought are coming to increasingly agree that mission lies at the very heart of the theological task, and therefore at the heart of theological education. Martin Kahler's dictum is often quoted and is well known, Mission is the mother of theology. In 1908 his was almost a lone voice. Now a century later, both within the Communion and ecumenically, a vision has grown for the foundational nature of God's mission to underlie all theological work.

The practical implications of this are very significant for the church and for those delivering theological education and leadership formation at all levels. No longer is mission studies simply one separate and distinctive theological or practical subject. Rather, for a mission formed church, a mission framework and orientation needs to be integrated with biblical studies, church history, systematic theology and the other disciplines of practical theology. At the same time, mission studies have distinctive contributions to make within the theological curriculum and to the wider theological tasks facing the Communion and its constituent faith communities.

A mission framework for theological education is a keystone. It is a mission purpose and a mission orientation which support shared action in proclamation of the Gospel, reconciliation, action for justice and economic and social sustainability. We belong to a Communion held together through our mission relationships. It is mission relationships, which undergird, support, and reorient our shared accountability and interdependence.

A MISSION FRAMEWORK IS A PRIORITY AND A FOUNDATION

Concern for leadership formation for mission was evident in the work of MISSIO[70], the predecessor to IASCOME. IASCOME too has expressed its interest in supporting theological education across the Anglican Communion since our first meeting in South Africa in May 2001. A member of the Commission was named to the original Theological Education Working Group that was convened in October 2001. Further, the Anglican Consultative Council, at its 12th meeting in Hong Kong in 2001, encouraged IAS-COME to develop its work in the area of leadership training and formation for mission.[71]

IASCOME has consulted during the life of our Commission with the Anglican Communion task group on theological education and its successor, TEAC (Theological Education for the Anglican Communion). TEAC now exercises some specific responsibilities and tasks with respect to theological education. In all our work and conversations, IASCOME has had an abiding concern that leadership at all levels of the church needs to be equipped for mission. For reasons made clear in this chapter of our report, it is our view that a mission framework is a priority and a foundation for theological education in the Anglican Communion today.

Both IASCOME and the Theological Education for the Anglican Communion task group are aware that theological education for mission is now wide ranging. It is also too diverse and too full of life to be contained in any single structure.

Early in our work, the Commission identified the need for a renovated framework for understanding leadership formation. This framework identifies mission formation, theological education, and ordination training as interconnected elements with interconnected relationships. It is a mission intention which links the elements of this framework together in the preparing, forming and empowering of the people of God in the mission of God for the life of the world.

Mission formation

Mission formation is understood as the empowering of the people of God in holiness, truth, wisdom, spirituality and knowledge, for participation in God's mission in Jesus Christ through the Holy Spirit. In our vocation as Christians, all are called and all are sent. Thus mission formation includes leadership training across all levels of the church—in parishes and dioceses, in voluntary organisations, and for church-wide agencies and their leaders.

Mission formation is also understood in terms of fulfilling the baptismal vocation of all believers. Formation in mission, and the ongoing education and training of all Christians being built up into maturity, is a key part of the upbuilding of the church.

These dimensions of education and equipping require us to look beyond clerical preparation as the only horizon for theological education and formation. An understanding of the whole Gospel for the whole world asks new questions about theological education. This is because mission formation is for the whole people of God in diverse contexts, and is not exclusively linked to the three orders of ministry of the church.

Theological education

Theological education is an overarching term to describe the study of God, and it includes the study of the scriptures and the service of the church. Such intentional inquiry, study and reflection are conducted within the academy, within the church, and in and for wider public discourse.

The Commission has observed that theological education within the Communion is now less oriented to the structures of the church itself and increasingly takes place beyond the bounds of the academy. A key theme of this report is that it is in and through our relationships that we find and experience communion. But it is also true that our mission relationships provide opportunities for theological education and the advancement of our understandings of God, the scriptures and the service of the church.

The Primates, in their recent Communiqué, have recognised that theological education can be developed and improved by sharing resources across the Communion[72]. IASCOME agrees wholeheartedly, and points to our existing mission relationships as an important way in which this sharing of resources is already happening.

Educational resources are already being shared in a variety of ways, which reflect mutual accountability and mutual learning and benefit. Specific examples include the sharing of print and video resources, the sending and hosting of personnel, short term visits both formal and informal, pilgrimages, ecumenical collaboration and diocesan companionships. Companion diocesan links are one of the most important mission relationships of our time. This shared enterprise of many, which is widespread throughout the Communion, gives new dignity and potency to individuals, to churches and to dioceses in a web of shared life. All of these ways of relating result in transformative learning for participants, and underline our common need to grow in our knowledge of the biblical and theological bases for mission, both local and worldwide.

Ordination training

Ordination training is the specific training of the current and future ordained ministers of the church (bishops, priests and deacons). It includes pre-ordination training and supervision, and also life long learning and development.

These three orders share a servant leadership role, as a sign and witness to the church and beyond. Ordained leadership also encourages and organises shared action for the mission of the people of God, by the people of God, for the life of the world. *The church exists by mission as fire exists by burning.*[73] The vocation of the church is not to live for itself, but to live with and for the other. The mission of God calls the church to live with and for others in the life of the world.

The Commission acknowledges that there are a range of models in the Anglican Communion today for ordination training. While the European model of residential seminary training continues in most places, other models such as extension courses and one-on-one mentoring are also widespread. These models need to be supported and encouraged.

We note the work of TEAC in this regard in developing resources and guidelines with respect to what constitutes the Anglican Way and providing accessible documentation on Anglican history, theology, liturgy and pastoral practice. We support and appreciate this work. However, in the assessment of the Commission, it is clear that this approach does not fully prepare the whole people of God for mission. Nor do fixed and habitual patterns prepare and equip the church for contextual and local understandings and applications of mission and mission practices which convert and transform the people of God. We would seek to be included as a partner and companion in the work and deliberations of TEAC, to inform and encourage a mission dimension.

It is the view of this Commission that ordination training, and other forms of theological education, need to reflect a commitment to mission. Mission is at the heart of our shared life and our companion relationships. A shared commitment to God's mission is the responsibility of every member of the Body of Christ. The implications for theological education and leadership development connect discipleship of Christ to the transforming dimensions of a missional grounding. Discipleship equipping which is isolated from a mission footing is likely to be a deficient discipleship, with loss to the church.

The Primates, in their recent Communiqué of February 2005, have issued their own strong commitment, as leaders of our Anglican Communion, to God's mission in world.

> *Indeed, in the course of our meeting, we have become even more mindful of the indissoluble link between Christian unity and Christian mission, as this is expressed in Jesus' own prayer that his disciples should be one that the world may believe (John 17.21). Accordingly, we pray for the continuing blessing of God's unity and peace as we recommit ourselves to the mission of the Anglican Communion, which we share with the whole people of God, in the transformation of our troubled world.*[74]

THE VOCATION OF ALL BELIEVERS
FOR KNOWLEDGE AND LEARNING

We all share a common vocation sealed by baptism. What follows are examples of how theological education and leadership training take many forms in the life of the churches of the Communion. These includes Sunday Schools, children and youth, adult education, the work of Mothers' Union and local churches. Missionary presence and work continues to occur through a host of educational and medical institutions, including schools and hospitals. Diocesan schools, and medical institutions including those staffed by mission organisations, play an important role in health and education provision in many countries.

The stories which follow describe a variety of ways to strengthen the capacity of the church through a more broadly based understanding of theological education informed by a mission mandate and a mission priority. They describe leadership formation, theological education and ordination training all of which are grounded in the priority of mission. This gives a fuller Gospel approach and a wider variety of opportunities at all levels. In our work and reflection on leadership development and theological formation across the span of the Communion, IASCOME has sought to build in a mission dimension and a mission intention.

What the greater diversity of service in the life of the Communion is clearly pointing to is that leaders equip others. As the servant people of God in Christ, it is incumbent on the leadership of the church to be equipped *and* to provide for the equipping of others. This includes, but is not limited to bishops, clergy and lay leadership who work alongside those designated as theological educators.

Ministry and lay training

Materials made available to the Commission informed us of creative and intelligent work happening in many local contexts. These include training manuals for evangelists and lay pastoral assistants in the Solomon Islands which have been well received in the Pacific. In Melanesia, educational and development processes are the responsibility of the whole community. Everybody's efforts, be it in training or learning, are all a socialisation process both for the benefit of the community and the individuals.

Locally developed theological education and methods in Papua New Guinea also connect Christian formation and mission with community living in local contexts. An example is discipleship training for young adults, including parenting training. Particular ministries, especially those of teachers and leaders, need to be integrated into the church's overall vision and planning for mission and evangelism.

In the dioceses of Manicaland (Zimbabwe) and Accra (Ghana), lay training centres have been established with great effect. Their main function is to equip the laity with theological education and so create effective members of the church. Training is provided for evangelists, lay readers, and newly elected members of Parish Councils and Synods to equip them in their respective roles. In addition, continuation and enrichment training is provided for those engaged in baptismal preparation, confirmation training, teaching Sunday School, organising stewardship campaigns, leading Mothers' Union groups, serving as special chaplains in schools and counselling those infected and affected by HIV and AIDS. Such lay training, once established, soon becomes crucial to mission and evangelism within the life of the church.

The Anglican Church of the Central American Region provides formal training to students seeking ordination through the Anglican Centre for Higher Theological Education. Students come from the various countries which form the Province. The students who come together for formal ordination training are already doing mission work in their own dioceses, for example in charge of a mission centre or establishing a new one. The training program includes regular coming together to reflect on experience, to share resources and learnings from different contexts, and to grow in pastoral effectiveness and biblical literacy. This is an experiential learning process, where those appointed to ordained office also have the confidence of the Christian communities where they serve, or the ability to plant new communities of mission.

Attention to a holistic understanding of theological formation and education develops and promotes cohesion between the community, the person, and the vocation of all believers. Such training seeks the development of personal character, in engagement with the community. It is through the equipping of the saints in their gifts and skills, that the body of Christ is fed, clothed, encouraged-in-hope and built up.

Growth in numbers in the South and growth in discipleship training for all

This Mission Commission and other Commissions over the past two decades have rejoiced that in the Global South the Anglican Communion is growing rapidly. The numbers of new people coming to Christian faith bring both challenges and opportunities for discipleship development, leadership formation and theological education. We heard concern from our African members about how this rapid growth has resulted in a gap in discipleship training, and also in a shortage of trained clergy.

However, the Commission also heard that the report *Anglicans in mission: a transforming journey,* received by the ACC at its meeting in Edinburgh Scotland in 1999, has filled a gap and a need.[75] Its linkages of mission to Anglican settings, and the impact of its stories, have been widely appreciated. We are aware that the report has been widely used in a variety of educational settings. For example, we heard how the *Anglicans in Mission* report was used with students preparing for ordination at a seminary in Tanzania. Through reading and reflecting on the stories in the report, students, many of whom had never left Tanzania, were introduced to Anglican life in other parts of the Communion. They were also invited to compare the narrative accounts with Christian community life as they experienced it in their own settings. Stories like this one from Tanzania have informed the way the Commission has prepared this report.

Theological colleges and seminaries have significant roles to play in the provision of a range of programs alongside other diocesan initiatives and programs. Seminary training can and does range from degree programs at University level, to accredited diplomas or certificate training programs. Auditing of courses, the development of programs at local levels in response to need, and theological education by extension (TEE) have also been very valuable in many places to equip and sustain mission.

New networks have emerged

The forms of relational connections are now very diverse within the Communion. These includes personal links, and formal and informal networking now made possible for those with access to electronic resources. Some new examples of more formalised networks are important and relevant to theological education and its intersections with mission and evangelism. Recent developments include a network of parish theologians and the Anglican Contextual Theologians network (ACTs).

The following example is illustrative. The Anglican Contextual Theologians network came into being at the initiative of a group of theologians from around the Anglican Communion who saw the need for ongoing theological conversations across the Communion that wrestle with, and celebrate the richness of the many and diverse cultural and geographic contexts of contemporary Anglicanism. An initial consultation was held in the USA in May 2003[76]. Following this, with the leadership of the African Network of Institutions of Theological Education Preparing Anglicans for Ministry (ANITEPAM), a second consultation was held in South Africa, with most of the participants on this occasion from Africa. The primary value of the consultations was the building of relationships across the Communion, across cultural and theological frontiers, such that weak bonds of affection were strengthened. IASCOME sees such networks as rich resources for the building up of relationships in mission across the many and diverse contexts of the Anglican Communion.

Other examples of networking are given throughout this chapter, as the ways of theological formation multiply and the shape of discipleship formation becomes more diverse.

Outcomes-based learning rather than inputs-based teaching

In many places in the world, new systems of accreditation now link theological education institutions to new and more rigorous criteria for curriculum development and assessment. For example, in South Africa, post apartheid educational standards require education and training at all levels, to integrate knowledge and understanding with skills and values/attitudes. This outcomes-based approach has reshaped the curriculum for theological colleges. It places stricter requirements on demonstrating outcomes-based assessments. This means close attention is given to what learners value and can do, as well as what they know. In South Africa, theological colleges seeking accreditation were required to decide what outcomes they sought in properly equipped learners of theology and ministry. In designing the curriculum, they made a mission focus foundational to the qualifications.[77]

These mandated changes impact not only South Africa, but also those outside South Africa who were previously linked in an ecumenical body set up by the South African Council for Theological Education, who now face being less resourced. At the same time, South African educational institutions, if they are to achieve accreditation, must revise their curricula and justify their standards to more rigorous criteria. As a result many South African theological colleges are closing, amalgamating or exploring different options.[78]

Restructuring, new partnerships and ecumenical linkages

In England a major reform of theological training is underway. The church has 11 theological colleges for residential training of its clergy, and a larger number of non-residential courses. These are being amalgamated into a series of Regional Training Partnerships (RTPs) spread across the country, to make better use of resources of money and people. The intention is that these Regional Training Partnerships will provide pre- and post-ordination training as well as Continuing Ministerial Education for clergy and lay readers (and other accredited ministries). A new syllabus and curriculum is under consideration, with a greater stress on the mission calling of the church and of the clergy. There is a particular focus on training for clergy and evangelists who are called to be church planters and pioneers.

In Australia a key trend has been for theological colleges to link with university partnerships for accreditation. National (and international) distance education has entered theological education through one such partnership, based in Canberra. Thus a wide variety of degree levels and programs and subjects are offered by extension. These cover both Anglican clergy training and ecumenical theological education for lay leadership, both in and beyond the church.

Theological education by extension (sometimes referred to as TEE) is now an important way that teaching and learning are delivered in many parts of the world. It is common to most parts of Africa, including, Ghana, Nigeria, Sierra Leone, Gambia, and is also widely used in Canada.

In South America, co-operation to achieve workable networks of students and resources operates at provincial levels, linking dioceses in different countries.

Theological cross fertilisation across the Communion

Together what these stories indicate is that creative new linkages have emerged within the Communion. For example, in the past few years the African Network of Institutions of Theological Education Preparing Anglicans for Ministry (ANITEPAM) has managed to arrange a South-to-South program in which theological tutors were exchanged. Some examples of this cross fertilisation include Ghana and Zimbabwe, Uganda and South Africa, Tanzania and Zambia, Uganda and Tanzania. Funds are presently being sought to run parallel programs for student exchanges.

Initiatives like these have brought some key theological issues, which cut across the Continent to the attention of the Council of Anglican Provinces of Africa. Cross linkages have assisted in the development of syllabi on HIV and AIDS, for Theological Education by Extension (TEE), and to provide resources for colleges which have not been in a position to develop their own. Support for New Bishops Training Courses has emerged, and joint efforts makes lecture programs and the publication of journals possible. These raise consciousness about key African theological issues and concerns. Discussion has also raised the need to support African heads of institutions as well as women involved in theological education. Networking and support for those facing crisis situations (e.g. Rwanda, Sudan and Congo) has also been strengthened for mutual benefit.

Such initiatives are not confined to regional groups. Creative cross fertilisation also occurs regularly across the Communion. For example the Anglican Church of Canada has a theological student internship program that places students for three months in some other part of the Communion. The participating theological colleges accept overseas placements as credits in the overall training of students.

Aboriginal clergy in Canada can earn a Master of Divinity degree by attending summer courses in Native Ministries at the Vancouver School of Theology. Similar in-service training is provided in several dioceses by bringing lecturers and students into rural centres in isolated northern areas.

Particular programs of enrichment and empowerment for indigenous people are also provided in New Zealand and Australia.

In the United States, the Seminary Consultation on Mission (SCOM) operates as a network of seminary faculty and deans of Episcopal seminaries in the United States. The network is dedicated to supporting American seminary faculty and students who participate in cross cultural mission internships and experiences in other churches of the Anglican Communion. Over the last twenty-five years SCOM has supported over four hundred faculty/students in their learning in other parts of the Communion. It also encourages the development of missiology and mission studies in American seminaries and across the Communion. For example, ANITEPAM grew out of a consultation that SCOM sponsored in Zimbabwe.[79]

At its December 2003 meeting, IASCOME discussed the idea of 'floating faculties' to support theological education across the Anglican Communion. We imagined such a 'floating faculty' as a list of current or former seminary and university professors and teachers from around the Anglican Communion who might make themselves available for short-term teaching assignments as mission partners in under-resourced theological education institutions in the Communion. However, we also noted that such faculty members should be sensitive to the local contexts, perceiving themselves as "learning missiologists" (not as exporters of particular national theologies), who can later assist their home churches to look beyond local boundaries. IASCOME is aware of the survey of theological education institutions being undertaken by Colleges and Universities of the Anglican Communion (CUAC). Such a survey could be most useful in determining both the faculty resources for the imagined 'floating faculties' as well as the needs of seminaries and theological institutions around the Anglican Communion.

Ministry to young people and families: Ministry through schools

A growing emphasis across the Communion on the vocation of all baptised believers has led to many forms of Christian service and training, both within the church and associated with it.

A ministry with and for children, families and youth is a key area of concern in many places. Women and children can be among the most vulnerable groups in many contexts, and the incorporation of young people into the life of the church is a key, and frequently challenging issue. The Commission is aware that from the early 20th century, work with children and youth in many places was conducted separately from the main body of the church. The result in some of those contexts that adopted this model, has been that over the long term, children and youth became socialised out of church. Adherence has dropped and churches are now working hard to re-incorporate families and young people back into the life of the Body of

Christ. IASCOME recognises that youth work and its importance is recognised in different ways. In the North, detached, fringe and/or integrated approaches apply.

The varied linkages of formation and training set out in this chapter are illustrated in Papua New Guinea. Here community development and cohesion is aided by trained pastoral work by the church with families. The curriculum in an Anglican secondary school includes training with respect to HIV and AIDS, with partnership links to schools and programs being developed in Zimbabwe. Environmental sustainability is modelled and taught through the school's farm and vegetable garden. Linkages in terms of personal contacts, and support by outside mission institutions and dioceses were reported both from Australia and across the Pacific.

Given the diversity of ministry and service offered by local churches and dioceses, the Commission endorses the principle that appropriate training be provided for specialised ministries (for example chaplaincies) wherever practicable. In addition we note that particular practices, training, supervision and safeguards with reference to working with all vulnerable groups need to be implemented, respected and observed.

Recommendation

We recommend that IASCOME continue to co-operate with Theological Education for the Anglican Communion so that mission and evangelism can become an integral part of its work.

Questions for Discussion

This chapter argues that all ordained and lay leadership formation in the church should have a mission orientation. What do you think of this idea?

What types of leadership formation are you aware of in your church, and to what extent do these have a strong mission orientation?

Discuss the difference between outcomes-based learning and inputs-based teaching. What outcomes would improve the training of clergy in your church?

CHAPTER 7

Inter Anglican Standing Commission on Mission and Evangelism (II) and Anglican Communion Office Mission and Evangelism Desk

Inter Anglican Standing Commission on Mission and Evangelism II

IASCOME is thankful to the Anglican Consultative Council for its mandate and support during the five years of our term together. We are convinced that the Anglican Communion must stay focused on mission and evangelism in these difficult times. For it is in our common service to God's mission of reconciliation that our unity with God and each other in Christ is more fully realised. IASCOME thus recommends the following for the second Inter-Anglican Standing Commission on Mission and Evangelism (IASCOME II).

1. Mandate

That the Inter-Anglican Standing Commission on Mission and Evangelism (IASCOME II) be appointed by and accountable to the Anglican Consultative Council or its Standing Committee.

2. Tasks and Functions of IASCOME II

a. Covenant for Communion in Mission

foster and co-ordinate study and application of the Covenant for Communion in Mission across the churches of the Anglican Communion;

monitor the responses and evaluate the effectiveness of the Covenant across the churches of the Anglican Communion;

co-operate with the bodies of the Anglican Communion tasked to continue consideration of covenants for the Anglican Communion.

b. Relationships in Mission and Evangelism across the Anglican Communion

assess the feasibility of, and begin to plan for: a second consultation of provincial co-ordinators of mission and evangelism and a third conference of mission agencies and organisations in the next decade;

facilitate Companion Diocese and other companionship links throughout the Communion, in accordance with the Guidelines for such links;

address the question of the colonial and postcolonial past and present of Anglican mission, and consider how Anglicans might be helped to explore such issues in mission relationships.

c. Mission in a Blessed but Broken and Hurting World

reflect on the missiological implications of the Anglican Communion's commitments with respect to the various ways Anglicans effect healing and reconciliation in the world;

liaise with the various networks of the Anglican Communion as to the missiological significance and contributions of their portfolios;

co-ordinate a Mission Consultation for Network Representatives to better understand and co-ordinate pan-Anglican information and action in service to God's mission.

d. Mission and Theological Education

engage in theological reflection on mission with a goal to advancing commitments to mission and evangelism across the Anglican Communion;

co-operate with Theological Education for the Anglican Communion to promote mission and evangelism in its work

e. Anglican Gathering

assist the proposed Anglican Gathering Financial Development Task Group in developing fundraising options for Anglican Gathering of 2013;

work with the staff and leadership of the Anglican Communion Office in planning for the 2013 Anglican Gathering to facilitate and advance its mission focus.

f. Accountability to the ACC

receive tasks from the Anglican Consultative Council related to mission and evangelism in the Anglican Communion;

report to ACC-14 and 15 on the work of the Commission.

3. Membership of the Commission:

Membership of the Commission shall be appointed by the ACC Standing Committee with intention to include a mix of the following factors:

expertise in missiology

gender balance

clergy/lay balance

7 members from Voluntary Mission Agencies and Synodical Mission Boards from both North and South with at least 3 from the South

knowledge of or involvement with Province/Region/Anglican Communion

continuity with IASCOME I of up to 6 continuing members

18 members appointed from nominations submitted by the Provinces of the Communion with two members from each of the nine regions of the Anglican Communion: North America, the Caribbean and

Mexico, Central and South America, Europe, East Africa and the Indian Ocean, West Africa and Nigeria, Southern and Central Africa, Middle East and the Sub-Continent, Australasia, East Asia.

members-at-large, these to be appointed to balance the factors listed above

Chairman to be appointed by the ACC, either from among the provincial members or as a member-at-large

rotating membership by province within a region to ensure variation in membership is desirable.

4. Modus Operandi of the Commission:

The Commission shall meet 4 times during its 5-year term of office, with meetings lasting for approximately 10 days plus travel time.

Members are expected to undertake tasks between meetings.

It is recommended that the Chairman appoint an advisory group of 3 or 4 members who can function as a decision-making executive between meetings.

Mission and Evangelism Desk at the Anglican Communion Office

It is recommended that the Director of Mission and Evangelism at the Anglican Communion Office be maintained with the following leadership functions:

ensure that the Inter-Anglican Standing Commission on Mission and Evangelism II receives the staff support needed to accomplish its work

offer leadership and suggest new initiatives for the work of mission and evangelism in the Anglican Communion, as appropriate.

serve as the mission liaison/connector with the appropriate Anglican Communion networks

liaise with Provincial Mission Officers/Secretaries, Synodical Mission Boards and Voluntary Mission Agencies

ensure good communication and the sharing of information around the Communion regarding mission and evangelism experiences/stories/resources.

oversee the development of various kinds of companion links within the Anglican Communion.

ACC RESOLUTION—This Anglican Consultative Council:

Supports the mandate for the next Inter-Anglican Standing Commission on Mission and Evangelism (IASCOME II)

Encourages the Standing Commission in its work over its next term

CHAPTER 8
STORIES

CAPA—HIV AND AIDS

Over the last few years Anglicans from around the world have begun to join together in new ways to address the needs of individuals living with HIV and AIDS and those who are ministering with them. In August of 2001, the first-ever All Africa Anglican Conference on HIV and AIDS was held in Johannesburg, South Africa to address how the Church could be more effective in combating the pandemic. Over 130 delegates from 34 countries attended the conference including church, business and government leaders. By the end of the four day meeting, church and secular leaders alike had dedicated themselves to a multipoint 'planning framework' for: 'securing the human rights of those infected by HIV and AIDS, and giving unconditional support; improving the health and prolonging the lives of infected people; accompanying the dying, those who mourn and those who live on; celebrating life; nurturing community; and advocating for justice.'[80] The co-operation of many agencies and churches to address AIDS in Africa resulted in new relationships in service to God's healing mission. Included at the Conference were representatives from every Anglican province in Africa as well as a variety of other Anglican churches and non-governmental agencies including: Christian Aid, UK, Episcopal Relief and Development from the United States, the Mothers' Union, the Compass Rose Society, The United Society for the Propagation of the Gospel, The Anglican Church of Canada, The United Nations Agency for International Development, Tear Fund, Africa Alive, and the World Bank.

The ambitious plans and early hopes of the All Africa Anglican Conference on HIV and AIDS have been owned and implemented in varying degrees across the Anglican churches in Africa and new relationships in mission continue to be forged to fighting the pandemic. Co-operation between many African Anglican churches and the Episcopal Church in the United States continues in life-affirming relationships in mission. Dr Douglas Huber, a specialist in women's health and HIV and AIDS prevention who is Principal Medical Officer for the International NGO Management Sciences for Health, has been a special Volunteer for Mission from the Episcopal Church helping the CAPA AIDS Board to plan and implement its programs. He is supported in his work for CAPA and other individual Anglican churches such as Uganda and Nigeria, and by the Diocese of Massachusetts Jubilee Ministry. The Jubilee Ministry is an organisation of the Diocese of Massachusetts in the Episcopal Church that receives and disburses funds for development and relief related to HIV and AIDS, particularly in Africa, and also provides technical support to Church groups engaged in HIV- and AIDS-related activities.

On September 26, 2003, a major conference was held by CAPA in Nairobi, in conjunction with the 13th International Conference for AIDS and Sexually Transmitted Infections in Africa (ICASA) to evaluate and plan CAPA's next steps in addressing the HIV and AIDS pandemic. In addition to CAPA's leaders, the consultation was attended by representatives of the Diocese of Massachusetts Jubilee Ministry, Episcopal Relief and Development, the United Thank Offering, Trinity Church Grants Program in New York, The Episcopal Church Centre in New York, the Diocese of Washington DC, the Anglican Communion Office, and a host of individuals from Communities Responding to the HIV and AIDS Epidemic Initiative, known by its acronym the CORE Initiative. CORE is a non-governmental organisation working with CAPA that is funded by the United States Agency for International Development, and working in partnership with CARE International, the World Council of Churches, the International Centre on Research on Women and the Johns Hopkins Bloomberg School of Public Health. All of these individuals and agencies met to consider how, drawing on their own particular strengths, they could work together more effectively to advance African Anglican efforts to overcome HIV and AIDS. The 'Conference Proceedings with Recommendations' emphasised that: "Working together, CAPA and the Provinces of the Anglican Churches are demonstrating how the Church in partnership with donors, local and national authorities, and other faith groups, can presents new opportunities for communion in mission relationships."

LIVING POSITIVELY WITH HIV AND AIDS

This is a story about Neama Adili Eliardo who is a Person living with AIDS (PWAs). Neama is 44 years old and a mother of three children. She was married to Eliardo Lasn a soldier in the Sudanese Government army, who worked in Morobo town which borders on the Democratic Republic of Congo (DRC) and Uganda. Morobo was a trading town that gathers people of different moral behaviours from the Sudan and the neighbouring countries.

When the Sudanese Peoples Liberation Army (SPLA) overran both Morobo and Yei town in 1992, Neama's family fled to Juba. In 1993, Eliardo was transferred to Mangala, 34 miles from Juba. Soon after their arrival Eliardo fell sick with a lot of complicated diseases and unusual marks on his body. He died on 22nd November 1995 as an AIDS victim.

Because of the lack of awareness about HIV and AIDS among the soldiers and the entire community, Neama was brutally mistreated. She was chased out of her house and her belongings were thrown out. She was not allowed even to sleep under anyone's veranda. She was isolated and finally she was strongly advised by the military authorities to leave Mangala immediately. She was refused a lift to Juba and told not to climb aboard any vehicle going to Juba. By then Neama had two children and she was seven months pregnant with her third child.

Neama was able only to take a few bed sheets, clothes and a little dry food for their trip to Juba. Five months later Neama began to experience sickness on and off and general body weakness. She took courage and went to Juba Teaching Hospital where a blood-screening test showed that she was HIV positive. She was then directed to us, in the Episcopal Church of the Sudan, for post test counselling. This is where Neama received the moral and spiritual counselling that made her feel strong in body as well as spiritually. She grew in confidence and is able to speak boldly today in front of different groups of people about HIV and AIDS. She has become an educator as well as counsellor.

When the military authorities realised that Neama was playing a greater role in HIV and AIDS, raising awareness among communities in and around Juba, she was allowed to go to Mangala to get the death certificate and other documents needed to receive the pension of her late husband. Now nine years later, Neama is living positively with the virus and worry about the future of her children. The Church in Sudan is facing a very big financial crisis. But Neama remains strong in faith and in her hope that God will take care of her children when she dies.

SYSTEMIC INJUSTICE—
ABUSE OF POWER AGAINST THE POOR

This article illustrates the level of injustice being experienced by many people in Zimbabwe. This is only one of many. The denial of food, which is a human right, to a starving citizen is one among many other unjust acts being experienced by many people in Zimbabwe. These acts of injustice are committed against some citizens who are supposed to be supporters of the opposition party. Thousands of people are faced with starvation and yet the government does not feel responsible for them.

Misuse of authority, power, wrong understanding of democracy (totalitarianism), lawlessness, disregard of human rights are some of the factors that have created the unjust system we have today in Zimbabwe. The goal of injustice is to kill or eliminate those people who are considered undesirable elements in the society. Indeed the church whose missionary mandate it is to condemn injustice cannot turn a blind eye against such an evil whereby food is denied to a 79-year-old man. Mupinda—79 years old—is left to starve because he is suspected of supporting the opposition. The only way for him to survive is to collect leaves.

The hallmark of an unjust regime is that it is not accountable to all its citizens but only to the few who support it for their selfish ends. It is sad though, even in a country like ours, where glaring examples of injustice are committed, that you still have a few co-opted voices from the church saying: There is peace and justice in Zimbabwe. But such voices are familiar in the history of the church. The British church did not say a word to condemn the so-called pioneer column in the early 1890's when thousands of black Zimbabweans were killed. "German-Christians" supported Hitler. Some individual church leaders in the USA supported their government in Vietnam killing and maiming of the indigenous population. We see this being repeated in the Burundi/Rwanda massacres and in the Sudan and in many other places around the world. The church has to live with some of its members who totally misunderstand the teaching of Jesus, that is to preach the Gospel of peace, justice and love. In spite of all this, those voices which have refused to be co-opted have to continue to speak against injustice.

The Rt Revd Sebastian Bakare
Bishop of Manicaland

HOW ZIMBABWE'S LEADER IS USING THE STATE GRAIN MONOPOLY AND UN FOOD AID FOR POLITICAL ENDS

Sitting dejectedly on a wooden stool, Anderson Mupinda, 79 and blind, leans his head against a walking stick. "The hunger makes me weak. From six in the morning to six at night we don't have anything to eat. I haven't eaten a proper meal for more than a week." He lifts his ragged T-shirt to show the folds of skin across his stomach. "There is nothing there. We only have leaves to eat. We dry them and then boil them with salt, but there is no salt. We eat them anyway." In April, the Mupinda family were given food by the UN World Food Programme. "The food lasted for a month. We were supposed to get more, but when the trucks came the war veterans chased them away," Mr Mupinda said. "They said the food came from whites overseas who support the MDC [the opposition Movement for Democratic Change]." He makes a clicking sound with his mouth to show disgust. "What rubbish. They are keeping food away from us because we support the MDC. They are starving us. The only way we can survive is to get this man out and get a new government."

The government does not even deny that it is discriminating. Last weekend the deputy foreign minister, Abednico Ncube, told a crowd in Matabeleland that anyone who voted for the MDC could not expect to get food aid from the government. "Maize is in abundance but very soon it will be available only to those who dump the opposition and work with Zanu PF," the Zimbabwe Standard quoted him saying. "The party will start feeding its children before turning to those of MDC." Living in the arid Hwange district in western Zimbabwe, Mr Mupinda is one of the thousands of Zimbabweans already hungry because of the food shortage. His plight is made worse by the fact that the area voted for the MDC leader, Morgan Tsvangirai. By September the famine will affect nearly six million Zimbabweans, by the government's own estimates. Many may be denied food because they are suspected of supporting the opposition.

In Binga, on the shore of Lake Kariba, Mr Mugabe's self-styled war veterans have stopped distributing food to school children. "We have 115 tonnes of fortified porridge which should be delivered to 28,000 students in all the schools in this district," an official of the Catholic Commission for Justice and Peace said. "But since May 25 the war veterans have prevented us from distributing that food because they say it comes from the UK and it is being used to support the opposition. How can five-year-old children know anything about politics? Our food is just sitting in the warehouse and it is beginning to rot. That food was the main meal for most schoolchildren in Binga district and now they are not getting it. It is a crime." Binga district hospital has recorded 27 deaths this year in which malnutrition was a factor. "Most of those deaths were from malaria, but if the children had enough food, many of them would have survived," a hospital official said. "The situation is getting worse, not better."

It has taken only 30 war veterans with stones and wooden clubs to stop the food being distributed, but the police refuse to take action against them. "A small group of fanatics is holding this entire district hostage because the police will not arrest them," Joel Gabbuza, the local MDC MP said. The state grain marketing board (GMB) has a monopoly on imports and wholesale trade in maize and wheat. Its depot in Binga sells maize at a relatively affordable controlled price, but only to residents with membership cards for Mr Mugabe's party, Zanu PF. "The war veterans buy most of the maize meal from the GMB and then they sell it at much higher prices," Mr Gabbuza said. Many believe that Binga has been singled out for starvation because its people voted overwhelmingly for Mr Tsvangirai in the presidential election in March, giving him 27,000 votes: the most he won in any constituency. Mr Mugabe got 5,000. "The government wants to punish us for that vote," Mr Gabbuza said. Political violence has continued, he added. "My shop in Senga was destroyed two weeks ago. Another shop was looted and burned last week. One of our party officials was beaten and police do nothing to protect us. We do not feel safe."

Binga is not unique. In Mberengwa, central Zimbabwe, the MDC says government officials are preventing its members from getting food from the

WFP. Much of the food comes from the British government, and British offi-cials in Harare say they are investigating the complaints. The High Commis-sion in Harare said: "It is a fundamental principle for the British government, as it is for the World Food Programme and the non-governmental organisa-tions with whom we work, that humanitarian assistance is apolitical, tar-geted at those most in need. It is our collective responsibility to ensure that this principle is adhered to on the ground and we are all working to fulfil that responsibility. We believe that this approach is working. If there are any allegations of politicisation related to our assistance, both we and WFP want to know about them. They will be investigated promptly."

Judith Lewis, WFP's Regional Director, says there is "an army of food monitors" to ensure that all the needy get food, not those with a ruling party card. "We have conveyed to the government our zero-tolerance pol-icy for food aid abuse." But Britain and the UN cannot assure fair sales of maize by the GMB. First-hand reports have come from Harare, Bulawayo, Murehwa, Mutoko and Chiredzi that people must produce Zanu PF cards to buy maize. Others say that people pointed out as MDC may be beaten in the queue or have their maize seized. Despite numerous reports in the inde-pendent press the government has not said it intends to change the policy. In Hwange, Anderson Mupinda rises from his stool and adroitly uses his walking stick to locate a basket of dried leaves. "I am sorry for you to see me like this. I only have these leaves to offer you. The life that we are living here is like being in handcuffs and in jail. It is hard to look at the future because we are so hungry."

The Rt Revd Sebastian Bakare
Bishop of Manicaland, 2002

WAR IN THE DEMOCRATIC REPUBLIC OF CONGO

We are seeking for lasting peace, justice, reconciliation and to fight the silent enemy HIV and AIDS in the Democratic Republic of Congo. The war in the Democratic Republic of Congo (formally Zaire) began in 1996 when a group of rebels led by Laurent Kabila opposed President Mobutu Seseseko and eventually took over in May 1997. Kabila became president of the D. R. Congo and Mobutu Seseseko took refuge in Morocco where he died in September 1997.

In 1998, another group started a new rebellion against President Lau-rent Kabila. This second rebellion was begun by five small groups from dif-ferent regions in the country, each group having its own leader and its own army. Also the neighbouring countries Uganda, Rwanda, Angola, Namibia, Zimbabwe and Burundi used this opportunity to send their troops and armies into the D. R. Congo to help the rebels. They came not only to fight but also to loot the resources of the D. R. Congo. In January 2001, President Laurent Kabila was shot by one of his guards and he died. Then his son Joseph Kabila took over power and he is the present president of the D. R. Congo.

Some consequences of this war:

About 3.5 million people have died. More than 500,000 people are displaced in the country after their goods were looted and their houses burnt. About 25,000 women have been raped by soldiers. The number of orphans and widows is unknown but the number is very considerable. Many church properties have been looted (vehicles, motorbikes, instruments). Church houses were burnt.

Most of the people are severely traumatised. People do not have enough food because they usually live by growing their own food but during this long period of war and insecurity people are not working in the fields. Many children are not at school because their parents do not have money to pay school fees for them. Corruption is everywhere in the country. Because of poverty, many women are selling their bodies in prostitution. Because of this, and rape by soldiers, HIV and AIDS is spreading rapidly.

What is the church doing through these sufferings?

The church is preaching the message of God's love through his Son Jesus Christ, the message of repentance, forgiveness, reconciliation and peace. The Church is praying for the political leaders and encouraging them to stop the war. The Church is teaching strongly about HIV and AIDS and how to help people who are already victims and also orphans and widows. But the Church has its limitation because of the lack of financial resources. As a consequence of what the Church is doing, God is answering our prayers and today all rebel leaders have decided to stop the war. They are now in the process of reconciliation and peace-building in the country. There is a transitional government and after two years there will be elections. We thank our brothers and sisters in Christ in other countries who are with us and have wept when we have wept. Once the war comes to an end in the D. R. Congo, Congolese people will need to be supported by other people for the reconstruction of the country in different ways, particularly the work of the Gospel because it is the first priority in the D. R. Congo.

The Ven Muhindo Ise-Somo
Provincial Co-ordinator of Evangelism Sept 2003

THE COST OF MISSION IN THE CHURCH OF MELANESIA

The Church of Melanesia has once again recorded in its history books the names of seven Melanesian Brothers who were martyred between March and April 2003.

In 1871 the Church recorded the martyrdom of its first missionary bishop. In the past there were lay evangelists, priests, even Brothers who were martyred in the process of bringing the Gospel of peace to the people. It was the seed of these martyrs which has helped to Christianise the whole of the Solomon Islands, the only Anglican dominated nation in the small nations in the Pacific Ocean. Sometimes we describe ourselves as 'the liquid Continent'. Perhaps nowhere else will you find that the leaders of the nation are Anglicans. Currently our Governor General is an Anglican priest, the Prime Minister is an Anglican, as are many in the Parliament.

The Solomon Islands continued to enjoy peace until the last two or three years when ethnic tensions broke out. The Government was not able to bring the warring parties together. It was the work of all the churches, and especially the Anglican Church, which took the lead through the work of the four religious communities: (the Melanesian Brotherhood of 300 members; the 150 Sisters of Melanesia; 100 Franciscans; and the Sisters of the Church, numbering 120). Together with the Mothers' Union, the clergy and Christian people who helped to negotiate for peace between the two warring parties.

At the height of the tension, the Melanesian Brothers and the other religious orders stood together between the two warring parties, trying to bring peace to the two sides. What was outstanding was that the religious communities remained faithful to their vows and did not side with either of the warring parties. Finally a peace agreement was signed in Townsville, Australia. However, one of the war-lords who was not a signatory to the Townsville Peace Agreement, continued to harass people. He burned villages and killed more than fifty innocent people, including a Catholic priest who was also the Member of Parliament for Harold Keke's constituency. A Seventh Day Adventist pastor was also killed, together with innocent people, including women and children who were living in fear, hunger and hopelessness.

The Government then decided to once again send the Police Force to hunt and capture Keke, but he was more powerful than they were. The situation could not be controlled. Keke was more indignant than ever, treating everyone as spies and the Government was powerless to control him.

The other ex-militants saw the situation as advantageous, to get what they wanted, and from time to time they entered the Treasury Department and threatened the workers with guns. Corruption in the Government, within the ministries and the Police Force could not be controlled. The economy was at the verge of collapse. Schools closed. Clinics and hospitals were without medicines so that doctors, teachers and others sought job opportunities elsewhere. Economically, no industries had opened since the tensions, apart from fishing and logging, leaving many people jobless. The country was in a desperate situation.

It was in the midst of this chaos that Br Nathaniel Sado met his death.

Br Sado was a frequent visitor to Harold Keke during the tension. He was the chief negotiator between Harold Keke, the Church and the Government. It was on one of these missions, when he went alone to visit Keke to tell him that the killing of innocent people should be stopped, that Keke branded him a spy for the Government and Police, and brutally murdered him in March 2003.

News about Br Nathaniel Sado's death was a shock to the nation, and especially to the Melanesian Brotherhood. His death prompted six of the Brothers to go to see Harold Keke on 23 April. They wanted to find out if the news was true, and if it were, to find out the reason for his death and to bring his body back to Tabalia, their headquarters, for proper burial.

The six Brothers did not return. They were thought to be spies also. Three were killed on 23 April, while the other three were killed three days later. When the six Brothers did not return there was already concern among Church members, who continued to pray for their release in vain.

Harold Keke and his supporters continued to tell lies, saying that the Brothers were still alive and being well looked after. The Church continued to pray for them. But it was taking too long for the Government and the people to find out what had happened to them so the Prime Minister, himself an Anglican, sought foreign assistance to bring an end to the hopeless situation that we had in the Solomon Islands.

In response the Regional Assistance Mission to the Solomon Islands (RAMSI) was sent from Australia, New Zealand, Tonga, Fiji, Cook Island, Papua New Guinea and Vanuatu to put an end to these criminal and corrupt activities and restore order, peace and justice to our nation and especially in the areas where the criminals ruled.

It was as a result of the work of the Foreign Intervention Force who interviewed Keke, that the Police Commission released the news on 9 August that the six Brothers were confirmed dead. As well as the six Brothers, Harold Keke also took four Novices and two other Brothers from a nearby household as hostages, but after four weeks they were released.

In June 2003 an Anglican village was burnt down and two youths who opposed Keke were tortured in front of their families. Fr Lionel Longarate, an Anglican priest from the area, was taken hostage, tied hand and foot and left on a sand beach for three days, but was later released.

The Regional Assistance Mission to the Solomon Islands (RAMSI) came in with full force, collected guns and arrested the criminals. Harold Keke and his men were arrested and put into custody, awaiting the decision of the courts. All former militant commanders of the two sides have now been arrested and one by one the senior police officers who were involved in criminal activities have been put in prison. The RAMSI police officers have now taken control of policing the city, with the local police.

RAMSI also dug up the remains of the seven Brothers and on 26 October, during the great conference of the Melanesian Brothers, the remains of six of the Brothers were taken to Tabalia by RAMSI. About 10,000 people attended the burial service. The nation once again shed tears with the families and friends of the late Brothers. People who attended included the Governor General, Ministers of the Crown, the Police Commissioner, the Australian High Commissioner, the British Commissioner, members of RAMSI, nine bishops, 30 priests, and representatives of the other three communities. Together they paid their last respects to the Brothers.

One of the seven Brothers who was from Papua New Guinea and who was also the assistant Head Brother and the leader of the Mission, was buried a week later as his relatives had to be flown to the Solomon Islands. His burial again was attended by the Governor General, the Prime Minister, Papua New Guinea's High Commissioner, members of Parliament and about three thousand people, including eight bishops, 29 priests and representatives from other religious communities.

Brothers and sisters, the Church of Melanesia has gone through a very painful time this year. The result of the death of the Brothers has been peace for the nation of the Solomon Islands. There is much acknowledgement and appreciation for the work of RAMSI. On behalf of the Church of Melanesia I would like to thank the whole of the Anglican Communion for your prayerful support throughout this year. More than 300 condolence messages were recieved, including those from Archbishop Rowan Williams, many of the Primates, Canon John Peterson, and others.

The Rt Revd Richard Naramana
December 2003

THE ANGLICAN CHURCH OF CANADA'S CONTINUING STRUGGLE WITH ITS COLONIAL HISTORY

For more than a decade, the Anglican Church of Canada has been struggling with the legacy of its own participation in the attempt by European colonisers to assimilate the Indigenous Peoples of Canada. Early Christian missionaries in Canada established schools for Indigenous children, but by the mid-nineteenth century, these schools were seen by the government as the main vehicle to implement the government's policy of assimilation. Indigenous children were forcibly placed in residential schools, were forbidden to speak their own languages, and were taught the cultural practices and values of the colonisers. The Anglican, Presbyterian, Roman Catholic and United churches continued their involvement with the residential schools, acting as agents, sometimes willingly and sometimes not, of the government's assimilation policy. With hindsight, this mission endeavour is viewed as an example of the cultural arrogance of the day and of the confusion of Gospel and culture. The Europeans believed their cultures to be superior to the cultures of the First Peoples of North America. In addition, they failed to recognise the ethnocentricity of their own particular interpretations of the Christian Gospel.

In the late 1960's, the churches withdrew from the government's assimilation project and began to advocate on behalf of Indigenous Peoples, who by this time were demanding the recognition of their inherent rights and the return of their traditional lands. In the 1990's, the churches began seeking ways to address the damages caused by assimilation policies and by the physical and sexual abuse suffered by many students during their boarding school years. The Anglican Church of Canada established a residential school's Healing Fund in 1991 to assist community groups to implement programs of healing. In addition, in 1993 Archbishop Michael Peers made a formal apology to Indigenous Anglicans for the church's participation in the running of the residential schools.

However, despite apologies, program funding and advocacy support from the churches, overall in Canadian society atonement was muted and financial compensation to individuals was not forthcoming from government or churches. In 1996, the Royal Commission on Aboriginal Peoples released its lengthy report containing over 600 recommendations for addressing the many injustices suffered by Aboriginal Peoples. Government response to this report was delayed for over a year and was then widely criticised, as was a less-than-adequate formal apology issued by the Minister of Indian Affairs in 1998. Former students of the residential schools, disheartened by these responses and encouraged by their lawyers, began to bring lawsuits against the Government of Canada and the four churches, which had run the residential schools. These lawsuits multiplied rapidly so that by the end of 2001, the Anglican Church of Canada faced impending bankruptcy, and was struggling to reach an agreement with the government which would relieve it of some of the costs of litigation. Other churches were similarly affected, lacking the "deep pockets" of the government, which was able to use public tax funds to meet these costs.

The Anglican Church of Canada stated its goals in this process as follows:

To continue to work at its ministry of healing and reconciliation with Indigenous Peoples;

To continue to survive as an institution in order to continue its ministry.

To seek an accommodation with the federal government in order to be able to accomplish its first and second goals.

To this end, the church spent over a year in negotiations with the Government of Canada, which eventually resulted in an agreement signed formally in March of 2003. The main elements of the agreement are as follows:

The Church will contribute 30% of the settlements for all validated claims of sexual and physical abuse, up to a maximum Church contribution of $25 million, with the Federal Government covering all additional settlement costs.

All Anglican dioceses will be invited to contribute to the payment of compensation.

The Anglican Church will continue its work dedicated to the healing of individuals and reconciliation with all parties.

Each of the Anglican dioceses in Canada ratified this agreement and accepted responsibility for contributing a percentage of the $25 million over the following 5 years. Despite the significant financial burden that this presented to many of the dioceses, all saw themselves as members of the church family and saw this as one way to begin to atone for the past and move forward towards eventual reconciliation. Their willingness to accept responsibility was at least in part a result of 30 years of effort by a relatively small number of Indigenous and non-Indigenous Anglicans to raise awareness of Canada's colonial history and to address deep-seated racist attitudes.

However, in the terms of the agreement, the government has insisted that victims be compensated only for physical and sexual abuse. The Anglican Church has agreed to abide by this requirement, while at the same time supporting the government's promise of funding for programs of recovery of language and culture. Many Aboriginal people are angry, insisting that the greater danger to their continued existence and identity is the loss of their distinctive languages and cultures, for which they deserve compensation. Thus they feel betrayed, and have accused the church of placing its own institutional existence ahead of its stated ministry of healing and reconciliation. Furthermore, despite the government's announcement of its intention to fund programs of language and culture recovery, few details of these programs have been provided thus far, and so this promise has been dismissed as an insufficient response or worse, as a disguised attempt to continue the project of full assimilation. Through its willingness to sign the agreement, the Anglican Church is viewed as once again complicit in the assimilation project, particularly due to the fact that the agreement was negotiated under conditions of strict confidentiality which prohibited adequate consultation and information sharing with the church's Indigenous Council. Within the church, relations between Indigenous and non-Indigenous Anglicans are severely strained, with a feeling that much of the progress of the past decade towards right relationships has been lost. Some have gone so far as to say that the signing of the agreement has negated the Primate's apology.

This story continues to unfold, and those of us on the journey, both Indigenous and non-Indigenous, are now challenged to continue to seek ways of establishing new relationships of trust and love. We must remind ourselves that our calling is to be people of hope, not to give in to cynicism, anger or despair. The Spirit will guide us if we do not harden our hearts. Reconciliation is our vocation since Christ came to show us the way to be reconciled with God and with each other. We continue to make mistakes and our steps falter, but we cannot turn away or give up. Our only choice is to go forward, in trust and hope. The most recent sign of hope has been the establishment of a special Indigenous Commission charged with the task of proposing how Indigenous Anglicans can achieve the highest possible level of self-determination within the Anglican family in Canada. This will undoubtedly mean changes to the canons and structures of the church. The Commission continues its work, with a commitment to bring preliminary proposals to the next national gathering of Indigenous Anglicans in August, 2005, with a further hope that a final proposal will be ready in time for the General Synod of 2007. We sincerely believe that the Spirit will be with us and guide us all in these next steps of our common journey.

Dr Ellie Johnson
January 2005

KENYAN CHURCH THRIVES AT HEART OF NAIROBI SLUM

Kibera slum is home to one million Kenyans on the outskirts of Nairobi. There are no legal water or electricity supplies, the sewers run through the middle of the mud "streets", and when it rains, the corrugated iron shacks— single rooms that sometimes house more than ten people—flood with garbage and human excrement. Every few months, fires destroy large numbers of these shacks, killing and injuring their inhabitants. "This is an illegal settlement, it doesn't exist," said the Revd Richard W Mayabi, the priest of St Jerome's Anglican Church in Kibera to the delegates of the Council of Anglican Provinces of Africa (CAPA) Mission and Evangelism Conference last week. "Because Kibera doesn't exist, its people also don't exist."

The Revd Mayabi works amongst some of the world's most impoverished people. Despite the shocking surroundings, his work is thriving, his congregation growing, and he has high hopes and a vision for the future. St Jerome now holds two Sunday services (English and Swahili) and hosts a Sunday School—the only schooling some of Kibera's children receive. It also has an enthusiastic choir that has recorded a collection of African hymns and songs. He is the only pastor for the two Anglican Churches in the slum area.

"I have only been here since January of this year, but I have already made major changes," he said. "We have expanded the Church building [an iron-walled shed tucked down an alley and surrounded by washing lines] . . . we removed the office and moved the back wall and the toilet out as far as we could from behind the altar. What do we need with an office? I need to be out with my parishioners."

He has also taken over the running of the community/mission centre—set up with the help of Church Army Africa—which although without electricity, acts as a school, a centre for mission and evangelism, and a general meeting place for the Mothers' Union—which runs all of the Kibera activities with boundless enthusiasm.

"We hope to increase the role of the centre too in the future. Already we teach people discipleship—to go out and bring more hope to people—but I have a vision of offering even degree teaching for people from this building," he said. "Outsiders think that because these people are dispossessed they are non-people, but that simply isn't true. Some who live here are university graduates, some are skilled professionals, but because of a lack of work they have been reduced to life in Kibera."

The Revd Mayabi is also about to start a micro-finance project and classes to teach people how to deal with money. The classes will again be run from the community/mission centre.

"Sometimes it gets to me," he continued. "I go to a diocesan meeting and the things I have seen are still banging in my head so I can't always concentrate. It's difficult to get through to people what we are dealing with here, and that is often dispiriting too." But, he said, he had to carry on because the Church was bringing hope to Kibera's people. "I must carry on with God's work. There are many ways in which God is working through lives in Kibera and my helpers—Church Army Africa and the Mothers' Union—trying to unlock this in people, and I thank God for his presence in our lives."

The congregation's daily reality in Kibera is hard to take in. There is no law in Kibera. Murders are commonplace and when the police come they come only to remove the bodies. Kibera's fires are sometimes started by officials to encourage people to move on. Settlements are torn down and people thrown out without any warning. And the people themselves have no official voice. "If they speak, they do not know what the consequences will be," he said.

The Revd Mayabi added that people's expectations from a priest were basic, but with only one Anglican priest for a million people it put endless demands on the parish. "The most important requirement for the people of Kibera is that a priest is there when someone dies. Though it is important to just be there—ever present in the community. Part of my work is to visit people and show my presence all over the slum, and this really helps," he said. "When I arrive it adds something to their day and they are always so generous despite the poverty." His main problem, he said, was drinking too much tea. "I can't refuse it! And in a slum with more churches than toilets this can become quite a problem!"

The delegates of the Council of Anglican Provinces of Africa's Mission and Evangelism Conference visited the Revd Mayabi with Church Army Africa. The visit was made for delegates to see some of the good work undertaken in Kenya with some of the continent's least empowered people. It also demonstrated how mission and evangelism works in many different aspects of the Church's life.

"Another church will be needed soon in Kibera," he said. "God bless these people."

Anglican Communion Office
©2004 Anglican Consultative Council

HELPING THEM TO LIVE AGAIN

Shelter is not merely having a roof above one's head, it is also an expression of an individual's concept of life, it reflects his ambitions and hopes.

In the morning of the 26th of December 2004, when the fatal waves suddenly struck the southern and eastern coasts of Sri Lanka with the unimaginable ferocity that only nature can unleash, our people were physically, mentally and psychologically unprepared to meet the consequences of that calamitous event. It was holiday time in Sri Lanka. The seaside hotels were full. People were strolling on the beach. Traffic was active on the coastal road. A packed train with a thousand passengers was speeding to its destination. Fishermen had returned with their night's catch, their boats tethered on shore. Tens of thousands were engulfed, crushed and drowned. Buildings were swept aside, roads torn up, railway tracks uprooted and mangled, bridges destroyed, that unfortunate train was derailed and suspended. The bodies of little children were found on trees. The dead number 30,196. The injured number 15,683, those missing number 3,846. 88,022 houses were totally demolished. 212,223 families have been affected and 834,849 persons have been displaced. 789 camps have had to be opened to accommodate the displaced persons.

While the material needs are being looked after, only a tiny fraction of these displaced persons have had access to one of their most urgent needs. It is ironic that the emotional scars caused by seeing their homes and loved ones being swept away by the sea should now be compounded by an additional threat of being preyed upon by sex vultures who roam these camps, targeting the most vulnerable, at a time when they most need to be comforted and protected.

The worst affected by emotional and physical abuse in these overcrowded camps are of course women and children. The National Child

Protection Authority, the Social Services Department, the Protection and Child Care Services, UNICEF, and the Provincial Councils in each of the affected areas are working round the clock. While the biggest challenge facing all those currently compiling data on child survivors of tsunami is to actually locate them, identifying them and their families poses an equally daunting task. Once they are located answers will have to be found to equally important questions such as: Who are these children? From where have they come? Where are their homes? Who are their relatives? How many of them are languishing in camps? How many in homes of friends and relatives? How many have been forcibly taken on the pretence of adoption? And most importantly, where will they go from there? We have to put our first priority towards the orphaned children because they are the most vulnerable. Also we must ensure that children are protected from exploitation. In a tumult like this, when families are broken apart, when incomes are lost, when dignity and hope are in short supply, children are more vulnerable to abuses. Our relief efforts must be conceived and carried out in a way that reduces these vulnerabilities and helps restore children's trust. Also we must help them to cope with their traumas by getting them back to school, as quickly as possible.

Our task today more than ever before is to rebuild the country which was destroyed by the tsunami. We are fortunate to have received a large amount of foreign aid for emergency relief and for the reconstruction of the shattered areas. Shelter is not merely having a roof above one's head, it is also an expression of an individual's concept of life, it reflects his ambitions and hopes. Our people have shown their commitment and willingness to forge ahead to build a nation. They now have to be given dedicated and committed leadership.

After a very prayerful consideration, we Sisters of St Margaret came together as a team by the name of 'HEN'—Health, Education and Nurture. Our target is to help twenty-five families without any religious barriers. We came together as a team in order to facilitate ways to bring love and care to those who are affected. Our aim is to create a new society where justice prevails. God is indeed so powerful as to draw good out of evil and it is our hope and prayer that our Land will emerge stronger from the tsunami disaster and be a 'Dharmadveepa' for all her citizens in the years to come.

Sister Chandrani Peiris, January 2005

CHURCH PLANTING IN EGYPT

The Anglican Church in Egypt, in the past, was known as the English Church. The early colonialists worshipped in this church and also set up schools and hospitals that were given over to the government in

1953–1954. The government also gave some of the churches to the evangelical churches.

The situation changed for the Anglicans in Egypt with the appointment of the first Egyptian Bishop. He started with just three Egyptian priests. After him came the Rt Revd Ghais Abdel Malik and the churches increased to nine. Although the dioceses includes North African, Ethiopia and Somalia, this story is only about Egypt. The Church has continued to grow under the leadership of the present bishop, the Rt Revd Dr Mouneer Hanna Anis, and there are now over 19 churches and we thank God for that.

The work I am involved in for the diocese is church planting. I first started in Alexandria where I stayed for six months. An Australian priest was leading an English speaking service and when he left I was alone and my English is not very good. I started an Arabic speaking service that has grown today to a large Arabic congregation. In the Cathedral there are four or five services including Sudanese and Ethiopian services. I have planted three other churches in four years.

The Bishop sent me to Suez where there is a very beautiful church built by the English. There had been no services there for many years. The church building was in very bad condition. The wall was broken, the roof was broken and nothing had been repaired. When I arrived I went to see the government and I told them I am the new priest, they said, "Ah, ah the old damaged building in the middle of the town? I said yes. But thanks be to God, now we have rebuilt the walls around and after this will be renovating the roof.

The Church started with my wife, myself and my daughter. We prayed and prayed. I was looking for someone with whom I could work and God sent a young man and we began by praying together. Then we met a group of young people who first met in the Coptic Church and then moved to a room in the Catholic Church. The group got too large and needed to move again. I went to see this group, they were all young people worshipping and serving God. They asked me if they could meet in my Church and I said yes. I thought, Congregation!!! without any communication, thanks be to God. All these people come along to the church and belong to the church, and now we have three prayer meetings.

These are very important prayer meetings, believe me, this is the foundation of the church. A lot of problems were coming but all were solved in God's hands when we brought them to the cross. Hallelujah. Our style of worship is a blend of traditional Anglican liturgy with free worship. You bring tradition and free worship together and people are very happy and feel free in their worship.

I have a Bible study group, a women's meeting, and a Sunday school. There are 70 children in the Sunday school and there is also a youth meeting. The Bishop leads the diocese in mission and it is growing. He provides very vital leadership for his priests and encourages us in mission which is so very important. All of us are human beings, all of us need encouragement, all of us need a very nice word and when we encourage each other we open up new life and inspiration which I think will be very good for us.

The Revd Hany Shenouda, May 2002

A MISSION IN THE GUATEMALA HIGHLANDS

This is a story of a mission started in July 2002 in a departmental capital named Sololá. That area is predominantly Mayan and the language spoken by the peoples is Zutuhil.

The whole story began with a call made by some Christians, not committed to a particular Christian denomination, to the Anglican Church in the area (not in that town). They requested pastoral assistance because they felt that they were in the process of losing their faith because of the strong work of the Mayan religion followers amongst them. They made their call to the nearest Roman Catholic parish but they were neither interested nor ready for calling an evangelical group. So they approached the Anglican Church.

A couple of weeks after they called the Anglican Church, a group of 12 representatives of the community plus the priest in charge of the work in the area, paid a visit to the bishop some 250 kilometres away from their home town. During the visit, the bishop questioned their reasons for calling on the Anglican Church to accept the challenge to do mission with them. Very briefly the bishop explained to them the living process of becoming Anglican, which he explained was not to accept a number of belief but to share a common life and hope in Jesus Christ as Saviour. He told them that it might require a long process of learning and living together the faith, and after that, the next step would be communicating to others the Good News of salvation.

They accepted the terms set by the bishop and designed an educational program and a date to be received as faithful Anglicans (about a nine months process). The whole process was left in the hands of the priest in charge of the area and four lay readers from the nearby mission. Nine months later the community invited the bishop to receive the people (in most cases to be confirmed) into the Church. That day the bishop received and confirmed 60 adults and officially commissioned them to evangelisation and outreach ministries.

One month later the leaders of the new Anglican community came to see the bishop to request the status of an organised mission within the diocese. The bishop accepted them and heard their plans for mission and evangelism. The plan consisted of the establishment of two new congregations in the nearby area.

This story is just one example of many other such instances happening in the diocese of Guatemala.

The Rt Revd Armando Guerra-Soria, Sept 2003

A STORY OF CREATIVE MODEL
OF REACHING OUT EVANGELISTS

This story might not sound traditional in the way we know as the regular mode of reaching out to people in evangelism. First of all, the method recognises the fact that there is a desperate need to bring labourers into God's vineyard. The second fact that the method recognises is that there are a number of people from other Christian denominations willing to serve the Lord as evangelists who have not received a call from their own church. The third fact, and it might sound awkward, is that the very high rate of unemployment in the area encourages people to take a job that will help them to feed their families, and even more importantly, a job that comes from God.

Here is the story. One of the dioceses in the Province of Central America became very concerned, on one hand about the great need for outreach among the peoples of the country and on the other about the tremendous shortage of personnel willing to serve as evangelists. The bishop therefore decided to put an advertisement in the local newspaper saying that the Episcopal Church was hiring people to be evangelists.

It said that payment was not high but enough, and that the requirements were:

proof of their Christian baptism

a sense of having been called or being called to serve in the spreading of the Good News

proof of godly life (letters, note from their pastor, recommendations from former employers)

a written biography tracing their spiritual journey

proof of under graduate studies,

proof of theological or biblical studies if any and willingness to get involved in an intensive course of preparation.

More than one hundred persons (men and women) applied, and the diocese made a careful selection of candidates, interviewed them and signed a three years term contract. At present, ten of the applicants have embarked on their training and are working on the design of their strategic plan for the diocese in the years to come.

The program will need a lot of resources and a great deal of prayer.

The Rt Revd Armando Guerra-Soria, Sept 2003

CONGREGATIONAL BUILDING

Something is happening in the Episcopal Church. It started as a restlessness some of us began to notice that doing and being the church was not the way it used to be. For some it was the plight of a small congregation worried about being able to continue to afford a full time priest. For others it was an awareness that we Episcopalians have got old, that our own children were not a part of the church we love. For another group it was an awareness of how our world, locally and globally, has and is changing. As a church we are becoming uncomfortable; it is an anxious restlessness. It is exactly the kind of discomfort that often leads to a change of behaviour.

That restlessness began to be addressed. The restlessness became focused in a goal of radically growing the Episcopal Church. The General Convention in Denver in 2000 adopted a resolution that became known as "20/20-Doubling the Episcopal Church by the year 2020." That resolution asked for a task force to be appointed to create a plan for realising that goal. The task force reported to Executive Council in October 2001. That report was not so much a plan as it was a vision of the Episcopal Church seriously engaged in mission, God's Mission of restoring all people to unity with God and each other in Christ. It is a healthy and robust vision, faithful to God's calling of us to be engaged in God's mission, work and purpose for the world. Our Presiding Bishop has helped us understand the mission is God's, not the church's. It has been said that it is not that the church has a mission, it is that God's Mission has a church.

So, a restlessness became a goal that requested a plan that became a vision. Vision always challenges the present. Vision calls us to that which is better and truer. But vision comes in a present moment which is connected to the past. Vision does not deny where we are and where we have been. Vision asks us to examine our calls, our work, our ministries in light of the vision. Vision asks us to make our own plans in the light of the truth that the vision evokes in us. When I look at where we are as a church and where we have been, I am able to see progress. It has never been as quick as I wanted, and it often takes decades to see it. When one looks at some of the issues we Episcopalians have been concerned about in the last twenty-five or thirty years, three stand out:

Outreach to the poor
Inclusion of diversity
Personal faith and spirituality.

Recent research shows that 97% of the congregations in the Episcopal Church are engaged in a feeding program of some description. That is a dramatic contrast to the situation when I was ordained in 1968. When the outreach ministries of the Episcopal Church are examined in light of the mission vision of 20/20, some are asking why we kept those we fed safely at a distance? Why did we not offer them the Gospel food that truly nourishes? What if we offered those we feed and shelter a place in a faith community? Over half of our dioceses are using demographic data to receive a truer picture of the people in our geographic communities. What we are discovering is that we live in dynamically diverse communities. We are expanding our definitions of diversity to include racial/ethnic, gender, age, sexual orientation, and socio-economic diversity. What does it mean to reach out in mission to all people? What would our congregations look like if they looked like the communities in which they are located?

Personal faith and spirituality are a high priority for us. We have learned to pray, we have sought out spiritual directors, we have tended ourselves as spiritual beings. In a world where increasing numbers of people do not know how to name God and do not know Jesus Christ, perhaps our inner work now has an outward focus. Is it time to learn how to share our personal faith with others-even with our children, even with strangers? While we are open to new visions when we are somewhat dissatisfied, while visions challenge what we know and are comfortable with, ultimately visions give us hope, energy, and direction. The Episcopal Church In Mission: 20/20 is such a vision.

Builder Newsletter Archived Articles, January 2002
buildchurch@ecbf.org

OUT OF THE FIRE: HOPE EXISTS FOR
A LASTING PEACE IN BURUNDI

Burundi—While hope exists for a lasting peace through the coming elections in October 2004, the Church of the Province of Burundi has been working extensively with the country's communities to ensure that the hope remains strong through a Christian spirit of co-operation.

Talking with the Rt Revd Martin Blaise Nyaboho in Nairobi earlier this year at a Mission and Evangelism Conference, the Bishop highlighted the challenges that the church has faced. "The Church has been working and growing, despite going through fire," said Bishop Nyaboho. "The civil war, which has been ongoing for many years has caused incredible damage to the country's infrastructure, eroded trust among its people, and displaced millions. In such an environment, you would expect the church to crumble; but through the constant efforts of its congregations and leaders the Anglican Church has been at the forefront of many social initiatives, given people reasons to stay together, and offered opportunities for reconciliation."

The current crisis—which is now nearing its end with some 97% of Burundi enjoying peace—started in October 1993 with the death of the country's president. The Anglican Church, which numbers 500,000 out of the country's seven million population, lost many of its parishioners, with large numbers fleeing to neighbouring countries. The effect could have been catastrophic. "Initially, the Church felt paralysed. Its building were destroyed, its members killed or fled, to say nothing of the feeling of hopelessness caused by the conflict," Bishop Nyaboho continued. "But despite the fear and despair the Church remained and persisted with its message." At the height of the war, Bishop Nyaboho even held Church services in the road, bringing people together in the middle of the countryside because the towns and villages were sometimes too dangerous.

"Ironically, the trauma that Burundi has gone through has started to show positive effects. The refugees have evangelised those to whom they fled, new churches are springing up as those previously shattered communities restore meaning to their lives—we will even create a new diocese next year," he continued. "But one of the major aspects of the revival has been the new energy that Church members have given to theological education." He stressed that education was vital to train priests not only to lead the reconciliation process, but also to go beyond this to meet the challenges that Burundi had so far not been able to tackle—such as the HIV/AIDS pandemic and the successful propagation of Islam from religious scholars from abroad. "We now see young people responding to God's call to these challenges, and taking evangelism into new territory. And they are supported—as ever—by the valiant work of the Mothers' Union. There are school, hospital, and home visits, with a strong emphasis on community care."

The Episcopal Church of Burundi had its origins in the 1930's through the success of missionaries from Uganda and Rwanda, with its first converts in the country's rural areas. Initially scattered, the 30-year missionary work, which centred on medical assistance and education, led to the creation of the first diocese, Buye, in 1965 with a Burundian as Bishop. The second diocese was created in 1975. As the province reached five dioceses by the early 1990's the Church was given provincial status. It now has more than 150 parishes and some 170 clergy. Its Primate is the Most Revd Samuel Ndayisenga, who is also the Bishop of Buye diocese.

Currently the Arusha Peace Agreement is being implemented with ex-combatants being progressively reintegrated into a national army. The interim government is gearing itself up for formal elections whilst endorsing local political consultations and negotiations on the new constitution, electoral procedures, and on the structure of the first post-transitional government. "The Church in Burundi wishes to thank everyone who gave us support, whether moral or material, and we also thank God for that," Bishop Martin concluded. "I ask all of you to keep the Episcopal Church of Burundi on your prayer lists and at the forefront of your thoughts."

by Michael Craske
Anglican Episcopal World Trinitytide 2004

THE WITNESS OF THE CHURCH, ZANZIBAR

The creating of the new Diocese of Zambia and the presence of the Bishop on the Island strengthen the Church in their witness. In a predominately Muslim society the visible presence of a church building is a significant witness to Christ and the Church. The mission strategy of the Diocese in evangelism is to plant churches in areas were there is no Christain witness. This begins with building some form of meeting place where a handful of Christians meet. This gives a visible presence in the area and a place where people can come with their questions and needs. In the early years of the Diocese four small churches were planted and although there was persecution with one church being burnt, the young Christians persevered and the church began to grow.

Another strong witness on the Island is the Anglican Cathedral. The Cathedral is built on the site of the slave market that traded with North Africa. The very spot where the slaves were tied to a pole for 'auction' is now clearly marked in the nave near the altar. Winding down some stone steps that lead under the Church, the rooms where the slaves were 'stored' before moving on to another place tell their story today. A memorial has been built in the grounds of the Cathedral below ground level that portrays the suffering, humiliation and oppression faced by those early slaves. The Cathedral is firstly a place of Christian Worship, discipleship and training. It is also a place of evangelism as the story of the slaves is remembered and told, by evangelists, to the many tourists and visitors who come daily to learn of the past. They also hear the story of the One who also suffered to bring freedom to a sinful world.

Marjorie Murphy
Director for Mission and Evangelism

ACC-13 Resolutions
(Nottingham, England, June 2005)

Resolution 26: Inter-Anglican Standing Commission on Mission and Evangelism

The Anglican Consultative Council:

- (a) receives the report from the Inter-Anglican Standing Commission on Mission and Evangelism (IASCOME) entitled "Communion in Mission"
- (b) expresses its appreciation to IASCOME and thanks its members for their work and dedication
- (c) adopts as the mandate for the next IASCOME the text set out in their Report
- (d) encourages IASCOME in its work over its next term.

Resolution 27: The Covenant for Communion in Mission

The Anglican Consultative Council:

- (a) commends the *Covenant for Communion in Mission* to the churches of the Anglican Communion for study and application as a vision for Anglican faithfulness to the mission of God
- (b) forwards the *Covenant for Communion in Mission* to those bodies of the Anglican Communion tasked to consider an Anglican Covenant as commended by the *Windsor Report* and the Statement of the February 2005 Primates' Meeting
- (c) requests the next Inter-Anglican Standing Commission on Mission and Evangelism to monitor responses to the *Covenant for Communion in Mission* and evaluate its effectiveness across the Communion.

Resolution 28: Resolution on recommendations from IASCOME

The Anglican Consultative Council:

- (a) receives the *Guidelines for Evangelism Co-ordinators* and recommends them to the Provinces for their use and guidance
- (b) gives thanks for the Consultation of Provincial Co-ordinators of Mission and Evangelism held in Nairobi, Kenya, in 2002, and the Second Anglican Conference for Mission Organisations held in Larnaca, Cyprus, in 2003, and asks IASCOME to give consideration to holding further consultations of this kind in the future

(c) asks IASCOME to address the question of the colonial and post-colonial past and present of Anglican mission in its future work, and advise on how Anglicans may be helped to explore such issues in mission relationships

(d) receives the recommendations of IASCOME for a Mission Consultation for Network representatives, and asks the Standing Committee to explore how best to take forward this suggestion

(e) encourages IASCOME and TEAC to discern together ways in which their work may be integrated and mutually supported.

Resolution 13: The Anglican Gathering

The Anglican Consultative Council:

(a) remains enthusiastic about the concept of holding an Anglican Gathering

(b) thanks the Design Group for the proposed Anglican Gathering in 2008, and all others involved, for their work for the proposed gathering in association with the Lambeth Conference

(c) acknowledge that they have followed the advice of the Joint Standing Committee in October 2004 and acted responsibly with their decision that plans for the Anglican Gathering should be cancelled

(d) offers sincere thanks to the Archbishop of Cape Town and the South African team for all their work in preparation for the Gathering, and are sorry that it was not possible to proceed

(e) asks the Standing Committee to consider the viability, concept and funding for a future Anglican Gathering.

Section II
Interim Report to ACC-12
Travelling Together in God's Mission

Foreword

It is a great pleasure and privilege for IASCOME to present to ACC-12 our interim report.

This interim report comes to you as a result of our recent IASCOME meeting in St. Andrews, Scotland where we were warmly welcomed by the Scottish Episcopal Church, the host province.

Travelling together in God's mission is only possible if all those who are travelling together share a common vision. As you read through this interim report, you will soon recognise our approach to mission and evangelism in its multi-faceted global challenges and opportunities. Our goal in this report is to share with ACC some medium and long term tasks for the Communion as it seeks to responds to issues which challenge the very nature of the Gospel and its liberating message. It is our hope as a Commission that this report and the recommendations therein will stimulate discussions and suggestions which will assist the Commission in its respective studies for further work, not only to be proactive but relevant in its approach to mission and evangelism. The Commission requests prayers from the Communion to help it to carry out its mandate faithfully.

The Commission would like to wish ACC-12 a successful meeting in Hong Kong.

+Sebastian Bakare, Bishop of the Diocese of Manicaland
IASCOME Chair

A Introduction

The Inter Anglican Standing Commission on Mission and Evangelism (IASCOME) is unique in that its 21 members are drawn from the nomination of provinces from all regions of the Communion, according to detailed criteria and provide a very wide range of experience of mission and evangelism as well as life within Church and Society. There has been a depth of understanding and fellowship as well as, at times, frank but loving differences of opinion among the members that has proved greatly enriching and supportive—a microcosm of life in communion.

The following report summarises work undertaken at the two meetings held so far—in Johannesburg (South Africa) and St Andrews (Scotland). In each place we have been warmly welcomed by our host provinces and given vital experience of the life and witness of the Churches through weekend and other visits. We endorse the view of the previous Mission Commission that such on the ground experience is essential to the Commission's work.

In our report,

> we give an account of how we have addressed our mandate and report on tasks remitted to us,
>
> we report on three important conferences to which we have contributed or organised,
>
> we highlight our concern about the mission focus at the heart of theological education
>
> we identify a number of areas of concern and continuing work,
>
> we list in *bold italics* our interim recommendations for comment and endorsement by the ACC-12 and resolutions for consideration.

In particular we would draw attention to the reflection that is developing on being a 'Communion in Mission' (Section F2) and our concern to see the thinking found in other documents of the Communion (e.g the Virginia Report) developed in a more grounded and mission direction.

B. Our Mandate and Summary of Action so far

In this section we list our Mandate (**in bold type**) and provide a summary of action taken since the last ACC meeting (ACC-11, 1999, in Dundee, Scotland).

B1. Reporting

To report to and receive reports and tasks from the Anglican Consultative Council.

We table this interim report.

We received a report from the Primates' Special Working Party on Theological Education established by the Primates, on which two of our members sit. Action arising from this is reported below (Section E).

B2. To oversee mission relationships.

To facilitate companion diocese and other companionship links throughout the Communion, in accordance with the guidelines for such links.

> We affirmed the value of this program and appointed our member from Canada to organise a more intentional promotion and facilitation of this program, in support of the 1998 Lambeth resolution and in accordance with the guidelines for such links.

To work with Anglican networks for mission and evangelism as they currently exist or might emerge in the future.

> See section below on 'Tasks remitted to IASCOME' (Section D).

To facilitate the sharing of resources, both human and financial, throughout the Communion.

> Conferences that have either taken place or will do so enable connections to be made and complement resource lists published and on the worldwide web.

To link, share and critique experiences of capacity-building for mission and evangelism.

> The main contribution has been made through conferences.

B3. Reflection

To engage in theological reflection on mission.

> See the sections below on Justice-Making and Peace-Building, Wholeness and Fullness of Life, Islamisation, Money and Power (Section F).

To be a forum where the provinces and the voluntary and synodical agencies of the Communion share and reflect.

> IASCOME meetings themselves are such forums. In addition we have convened one conference for Provincial Mission and Evangelism Co-ordinators, with a conference for Mission Organisations to be held in February 2003. One other conference is under consideration.

B4. Priority of Mission & Evangelism

To continue the momentum of the Decade of Evangelism.

> We have convened a conference for Provincial Co-ordinators of Mission and Evangelism[81]. We intend to reflect further on the nature of evangelism and its place within the mission of the church.

B5. New Structures

To encourage the emergence of new and appropriate structures for mission and evangelism.

We have encouraged the Global Episcopal Mission (GEM) proposal, and received reports from Network for Anglicans in Mission and Evangelism (NAME) (Sections D2 and D3). IASCOME has also been in correspondence with the International Fellowship of Parish Based Missiologists and a Consultation of the Anglican Contextual Theologians Network (ACTs).

To liaise with the South-to-South Movement.

We have discussed a report from our member from Singapore.

B6. Ecumenical Expression

To encourage, monitor and learn from ecumenical expressions of mission.

Our Canadian member sits on the Commission for World Mission and Evangelism of the WCC, and reports on and circulates the documents from that body. Our Indian member brings perspectives from the united Church of North India (CNI). The WCC staff person for Evangelism, Carlos Ham, was a theme speaker at our Nairobi Conference (see below). Our members from Ghana and Sudan are employed by ecumenical councils of churches in their own countries. Other members of IASCOME are involved in a myriad of ecumenical conversations and memberships in their own countries.

C. Major Meetings and Conferences held and forthcoming

In this section we report on major Communion-wide events organised by the Commission, or in which members have contributed to planning.

C1. 'Encounters on the Road': Nairobi, Kenya, 6–13 May, 2002

Sponsored by IASCOME this was the first ever **Consultation of Provincial Co-ordinators of Mission and Evangelism** within the Anglican Communion. It brought together forty representatives from provinces in Asia, the Pacific, Australasia, the Middle East, Central, West, and Southern Africa, North America, the Caribbean, Britain and Ireland. Over two-thirds had never attended an international Anglican Communion consultation before. It was a deliberate follow-up to the Decade of Evangelism. The Conference was funded by special gifts from individuals, congregations, agencies and provinces of the Communion.

There was much exchange of stories, ideas and encouragement in a conference that was full of energy and vitality. A full report of the Consultation is in preparation but a summary of the report and a listings of the major findings and recommendations are in Appendix 4. These have been circulated to Primates, Provincial Secretaries etc. They have also been considered by the Commission which has agreed how the recommendations should best be taken forward.

An email network has been established to pursue the connections made at the Consultation. Participants have expressed a strong desire to maintain momentum by meeting again and plans are being put forward for a second meeting early in 2004.

C2. 'Transformation and Tradition in Global Mission': Cyprus 12–18 February 2003

This Conference was recommended by the previous Commission and will be the first gathering of representatives of mission organisations of the Communion since Brisbane 1986. Its aim is to explore new dimensions of our common mission. This Conference is being arranged and organised by IASCOME.

Objectives of the Conference

To bring together diverse forms of Anglican mission agencies and organisations that express the comprehensive nature of world mission today;

To bring together the current generation of lay and ordained mission leaders in the worldwide Anglican Communion, to share their experiences;

To gain a better understanding of contemporary mission issues and changing patterns in mission (for example, outreach to immigrants and web-based evangelism);

To renew our vision for mission through biblical and theological reflection, worship and prayer;

To be challenged by new church models in mission and evangelism;

To encourage the development of new networks among mission organisations, dioceses and parishes in the Communion.

The planning group has prepared a detailed program. Speakers have accepted. Invitations to mission organisations are in the process of being sent out. It is anticipated that about 150 representatives of voluntary mission agencies, organisations and synodical boards of the Anglican Communion will be present both to look back, learning and reflecting on the past and consider the emerging mission movements and organisations.

The Conference is self-funding but because of problems of funding in parts of the world, a program of bursaries will be offered.

C3. All-Africa HIV/AIDS Consultation: Johannesburg, South Africa, August 2001

Along with many other parts of the Communion, the Commission, at its first meeting in Johannesburg on 2001, identified the HIV/AIDS pandemic as one of the major challenges to the mission of the Communion and so strongly supported the Primate of Southern Africa's initiative, supported by the Primates, to call a conference in South Africa in August 2001 on HIV/AIDS. A member of IASCOME was a member of the planning committee of the conference as well as representing IASCOME at the conference. The report of the conference was tabled at our meeting and discussed.

The Conference had two distinct tracks. Track One was for Anglican Communion representatives from all levels of the Anglican Communion across Africa, as well as a delegation of People Living With Aids (PWAs) from a number of African countries.

Delegates participated in sessions to:
Focus on their own experiences of the HIV/AIDS pandemic
Articulate a vision around key issues facing their church communities in relation to HIV/AIDS
Indicate how they believe the worldwide Anglican Communion can best intervene and contribute to addressing the unfolding pandemic.

Track Two was for representatives from partner organisations and included international donor agencies, AIDS service organisations, civil society groups and representatives from government departments. They too were asked to:

Focus on their own experiences of the HIV/AIDS pandemic
Articulate a vision of key issues facing their church communities and church partners in relation to HIV/AIDS
Indicate how they believe that the worldwide Anglican Communion can best intervene and contributed to addressing the unfolding pandemic.

The main purpose of the Conference was to engage the Anglican Communion in a process of strategic planning to guide its response to HIV/AIDS in Sub-Saharan Africa. The outcome of this process was a model of planning that the delegates could adapt and use at parish, diocese or provincial level.

At the end of this conference the Primates from Africa met and commended the work done and resolved to create an AIDS Board in the Council of Anglican Provinces in Africa (CAPA) with the Archbishop of Southern Africa, as chair to ensure that the strategic planning process is implemented in all the dioceses in Africa.

Strategic planning workshops have been run in every diocese of the Church of the Province of Southern Africa. Appendix 8 consists of the Statement 'Our Vision, Our Hope, The First Step' made by the Conference.

D. Tasks Remitted to IASCOME

We list here our actions on particular issues remitted to the Commission in its Mandate or by the ACC, Primates' Meeting or Joint Standing Committee.

D1. 'Mission 21'

This program has been developed by the Scottish Episcopal Church to encourage the growth of existing congregations. It has been in use in that Church since 1995. It differs from catechumenal courses like Alpha and Emmaus, which are basic introductions to the Christian faith. One of its unique features is that trained facilitators accompany, support and encourage congregations as they develop programs of welcome and implement them. The program was warmly welcomed by ACC-11. It is being piloted in the Church of Ireland and there are plans and funding for it to be used in Uganda. The Commission has received presentations about Mission 21 at both its meetings.

D2. Proposal from the GEM Network

The Global Episcopal Mission [GEM] network is a voluntary network of dioceses of the Episcopal Church in the USA committed to international (global) mission. The Joint Standing Committee referred to the Commission a proposal from the Network to accept in principle that a network of dioceses committed to global mission ('Anglican Network of Dioceses in Global Mission') be formed as an official network of the Communion. It also made proposals about acting as the 'enabling agent' for a number of possible initiatives.

The Commission noted that the GEM network is currently a network solely of American dioceses. It encouraged the network to act as an 'enabling agent' to take soundings among the dioceses of the Communion (e.g. by holding a Consultation) to see whether there was wider support for such a network and what dioceses across the Communion might set as an agenda, to see what might develop and to keep in touch with the Commission.

Official recognition as a network of the Communion might be considered at a later date.

D3. Network for Anglicans in Mission and Evangelism (NAME)

NAME was formed initially by bishops in Section Two (Mission) of the 1998 Lambeth Conference to seek to support and resource each other in diocesan mission initiatives. Although it applied to ACC-11 for recognition as a formal network of the Communion, ACC-11 decided to defer a decision until a more worked out proposal came forward and the Commission was asked to remain in touch with NAME in the interim.

The Commission at its first meeting received a formal report from NAME and subsequently informally through connections between some of its members and members of NAME. The network has now bedded down and carries out significant practical initiatives with a number of provinces and dioceses, for example, assisting the Council of Anglican Provinces in Africa (CAPA) in its conference with the World Bank on 'The World Bank and the Churches'.

The Commission will continue to remain in touch with NAME.

D4. The South to South Movement

The Commission keeps in touch with the 'South to South Movement' through the Bishop of Singapore (a member of the Commission). The movement came out of the 1986 Brisbane Conference to enable representatives of mission work in churches of the Global South to encourage and support each other. Two meetings ('Encounters in the South') have been held—Nairobi (1992) and Kuala Lumpur (1997).

The officers of the Movement have changed and in December 2001 the Chairman (the Most Revd Peter Akinola, Primate of Nigeria), the Treasurer (the Rt Revd Dr Mouneer Anis, Bishop in Egypt) and the Secretary (the Rt Revd John Chew, Bishop of Singapore) led a review meeting of the movement in Cairo.

The meeting reviewed the two 'Encounters in the South' and noted the positive opportunities for those from the 'non-Western' world to interact. It also noted the organisational inadequacies in terms of follow up and implementation. It was unanimously agreed to broaden contact with Primates and diocesan bishops of the South to gain their views on the continuance of the South-South Encounter and whether to hold a third meeting in 2003 or 2004. After these soundings have been taken a more definite vision and objectives of the South-South movement will be drawn up and presented.

D5. The Anglican Gathering

The Commission has received regular reports of developments in thinking about the Anglican Gathering proposed for 2008. It has reiterated its concern that the mission of the Communion be the theme of the Gathering. It welcomed the Nairobi Mission and Evangelism Co-ordinators affirmation of the Commission's call for inclusion of mission representatives on the design group.

Recommendation

IASCOME Recommends:
that two of its members be members of the Planning Group of this Gathering.

D6. CWME—Conference for World Mission and Evangelism

One of IASCOME's members is a member of the Standing Committee of CWME and keeps the Commission briefed on ecumenical developments in mission as seen through CWME. In particular the Commission has received the draft statement on *Mission and Evangelism in the Modern World* the successor statement to the seminal document *Mission and Evangelism: an Ecumenical Affirmation* of 1982. It has also heard of plans for the CWME Conference (the latest in the line of world Conferences on Mission since Edinburgh 1910) in February 2005 and will ensure that Anglicans who are invited to that Conference meet together during its course.

D7. The Partners in Mission process—a comment

PIM Consultations—their preparation and their follow up—were important practical bonds of holding together and developing the relational life of the Communion during the 1970s, 1980s and early 1990s until overtaken by the Decade of Evangelism.

The previous Mission Commission commented that 'the Partners in Mission process of consultations appears to have slowed to a virtual halt' and provided some reasons for that development. It stressed that the lessons learned should be developed and carried into the new context of the twenty-first century. [82]

That slowdown has continued. There has not been a formal provincial Partners in Mission (PIM) Consultation since 2000, although a few informal consultations on specific issues or around specific areas of work have been held.

We observe that new forms of association for mission are beginning to emerge which while not taking over the role of the Partners in Mission process do, in fact, provide networks of connection that flesh out the principles of partnership and companionship identified in previous Mission Commission reports. These networks and consultations are distinct from the 'official' networks of the Communion and do not have nor necessarily require the formal endorsement of the ACC, but the Council needs to be aware of them. The Commission is in touch with them all.

1. **Networks and Consultations initiated through ACC Mission Commissions**

    The South to South Movement

    The Provincial Mission and Evangelism Co-ordinators Consultation (2001)

    The Mission Organisations Conference (2003)

2. **Initiatives independent of the Commission, but with which the Commission is in touch**

    Network of Anglicans in Mission and Evangelism (NAME)

    Emerging networks of Anglican Communion Mission Agencies

    International Fellowship of Parish Based Missiologists

    Global Episcopal Mission (GEM) network proposal to develop a network of dioceses in mission

    Network of Anglican Contextual Theologians (ACTs)

    The Global Anglicanism Project (GAP)

D8. Companion Diocesan Links

The development of formal links between two or more dioceses has been a major feature of the developing *koinonia* in mission of the Communion over the last twenty years. IASCOME has taken note of the 1998 Lambeth Conference Resolution II:3 on Companion Dioceses particularly the encouragement to all dioceses to have another diocese as a companion by the time of the next Lambeth Conference. Through its staff in the Anglican Communion Office a list of companion links is maintained and advice offered to dioceses. The Commission has observed that better briefing on companion diocese links could be provided to new bishops and appointed our member from Canada to organise a more intentional promotion and facilitation of this program, in support of the Lambeth resolution and in accordance with the guidelines for such links.

E. Equipping and Formation for Mission

At the first and second meetings of IASCOME, significant attention was paid to the concerns of equipping and forming God's people for God's mission. We reviewed the background and the work of past mission commissions that referred to theological education and the work proposed in the Action Plan of the Primates' Meeting (Kanuga 2001). We believe that IAS-COME has a significant contribution to make to inter-Anglican conversations concerning theological education.

At our first meeting in South Africa (May 2001) we sought clarification about what is meant by theological education, mission formation, and clerical preparation. To assist the Primates' Special Working Party on Theological Education, called for in the Action Plan, we articulated the following definitions:

Theological education as an overarching term to describe the study of God in service to the church, the academy and also for public discourse.

Mission formation as the empowering of the people of God in holiness, truth, wisdom, spirituality, and knowledge for participation in God's mission in Jesus Christ through the Spirit. As such mission formation includes leadership training.

Clerical preparation as the specific training of the current and future ordained ministers (bishops, priests, and deacons) for service in and for the church.

IASCOME rejoiced that the Anglican Communion is growing rapidly and changing, especially in the Global South. Anglican Mission and other Commissions over the last two decades have noted that this change has brought about challenges and opportunities for theological education. These realities have led us to ask questions about changing paradigms in theological education that force us to look beyond clerical preparation towards mission formation. This Commission is prepared to ask hard questions about church and theological education because God's mission is larger than promoting Anglicanism.

The Commission recognised that there are a range of theological education models in the Anglican Communion today that are specifically orientated towards the preparation of clergy, often in difficult circumstances. These models need to be supported and encouraged as an important contribution to theological education. Whilst appreciating this tradition, we recognise that this approach does not prepare the whole people of God for mission. And even within the preparation of clergy, the emphasis on contextual and local theological understandings of mission and mission practice are rarely present or fully embraced.

We can imagine that some of the current theological education centres and models could be broadened to be centres for mission formation primarily for all God's people including the ordained. And secondarily these centres could offer preparation specifically for the clergy for the furtherance of mission. If this is to happen effectively, theological education needs to be refocused around a formation that is more than just in-formation. Theological education for mission formation is grounded in and shaped by local contexts, and must be about both personal holiness and the affirming of life in wider society and the world. Such centres might form mission educators who could then advance other formation models. We learned of similar mission educators in such diverse contexts as Scotland (Mission 21) and Papua New Guinea.

We heard about emerging efforts across the Communion to advance theological education committed to mission formation. The Commission commented on and encouraged the development of the consultation for Anglican Contextual Theologians Network (ACTs) and the International Fellowship of Parish Based Missiologists. We believe that these and other ventures across the Anglican Communion will advance theological education with strong missiological commitments. We will be inviting others to inform the Commission about similar initiatives.

At our second meeting in Scotland (June 2002) we reviewed recent developments in the Anglican Communion's concern for theological education with particular attention to mission formation. We noted the following:

> Mid-point Review of the Decade of Evangelism held in Kanuga USA in September 1995. Their report to MISSIO, *The Cutting Edge of Mission,* contains a major section on ministry to the whole church, ministry of laity and empowering the whole people of God.
>
> MISSIO, (the Mission Commission of the Anglican Communion) in their final report to the Anglican Consultative Council 11, 1999, *Anglicans in Mission: A Transforming Journey*, acknowledged that the Decade of Evangelism highlighted the need for training and formation for leaders in mission and called for a Communion-wide review of such.
>
> Anglican Consultative Council 11 (Dundee, 1999) accepted the recommendation from MISSIO in their resolution 11.
>
> In September 2000 the Chair's Advisory Group to the new Inter-Anglican Standing Commission on Mission and Evangelism suggested a process for the new Commission to follow in fulfilling the MISSIO generated ACC resolution.
>
> The Primates' Meeting at Kanuga, (March 2001) called for a Special Working Party to analyse and give advice to the Primates on theological education around the Communion. IASCOME was noted as a resource for this work.
>
> IASCOME produced a communication to the Primates' Special Working Party on Theological Education of its priorities for mission formation at its meeting in South Africa (May 2001).

The Primates' Special Working Party met in October 2001 and a report was produced for the Primates' Meeting that proposed five recommendations on theological education.

IASCOME sponsored the Anglican Communion's Provincial Mission and Evangelism Co-ordinators Consultation in Nairobi (May 2002) that noted the strategic priority for training in evangelism.

IASCOME at its meeting in Scotland (June 2002) heard reports from affiliated networks and projects with related interest in mission formation including: the International Fellowship of Parish Based Missiologists, The Anglican Contextual Theologians Network (ACTs), and the Global Anglicanism Project (GAP).

Concern for mission formation will be given top priority at the Mission Organisations Conference in Cyprus (February 2003) sponsored by IASCOME.

On the basis of this review and consideration of the report of the Primates, the Commission made a number of proposals to the Primates' Special Working Party on Theological Education about an additional term of reference on Mission Formation and membership of the Action Groups.

Recommendation

IASCOME therefore recommends:

that ACC-12 re-affirms IASCOME's mandate to continue fulfilling the initiatives begun with MISSIO and ACC-11 with respect to leadership training and formation for mission.

F. Some Areas of Concern and Continuing Work

In the course of our work and the reports we have received from across the Communion we have identified a number of mission issues on which we have begun to reflect. We list them below as an interim summary comment on what we hope to include in our final report. The sections contain a number of recommendations.

F1. Islam and Islamisation

In our review of relations with people of other faiths, the issue of relations with Muslims was the most widely expressed concern. We heard from the Philippines, Indonesia, Malaysia, Tanzania and in particular Nigeria and Sudan of how Christians experienced their relations with the Muslim community and in particular the effects of growing Muslim presence and Islamisation, often funded from Saudi Arabia, Libya or Iran. The events of 11

September 2001 and evidence of international networks of radical Islamist groups, often with strong political, economic and violent agendas, has changed the scene very significantly.

We recognised that the situation is complex and contexts vary greatly. For example in the West where Islamic communities are in a minority the situation is very different from parts of the Middle East where the Christian Church is very small and often overlooked. Situations in Africa where Christianity and Islam often seem to be in competition significantly differ, for example, from Pakistan and South East Asia, where Christian communities are much smaller than the churches in Nigeria and Sudan.

Care needs to be taken to consider each situation on its own terms rather than generalising or drawing universal principles from very particular experiences.

We heard that examples of the practical expression of Islamisation included the increased building of mosques, social and economic institutions; restrictions on the construction of churches; discrimination against Christians in employment and in legal cases; and the forced marriage of Christian girls by Muslims. There was particular tension for Christian communities in situations where Shariah law has been imposed. There was also reference to political radical Islamist movements and expressions among them of desire for domination of the Christian world—particularly in Africa.

At the 1998 Lambeth Conference the first guideline recommended by the bishops on the approach of Christians to relations with people of other faiths was:

Commitment to working towards genuinely open and loving human relationships even in situations where co-existence seems impossible.

We have heard of situations in which the possibilities of dialogue (a word which those in such situations found increasing difficult) were severely constrained by the nature of the Muslim presence. Dialogues at the national or international level, important and welcome as they are, seemed often to have little effect at grassroots level.

We give two examples.

Nigeria. The process of Islamisation has continued since we last met with more states declaring Shariah law. Churches have been burnt and people killed. The introduction of Shariah law is evidence of an on-going process of Islamisation in spite of repeated calls for dialogue, tolerance and peaceful co-existence.

Sudan. The question of Islam and Islamisation in the Sudan has been a serious concern to Sudanese Christians for over four decades ever since Sudanese independence.

It is believed that there is a deliberate effort to Islamise and Arabise Sudan. This is seen in the consistent trends undertaken by successive Sudanese government policies of Islamisation and Arabisation of the Sudanese populace at all costs. Islamic schools and Islamic universities have been set up. Arabic is enforced as the official language of the country, and there is a comprehensive program of what is known as Islamic orientation. The whole educational curriculum for the Sudan has been Islamised. The media, especially radio and TV, are used as tools of Islamisation. The country has been declared an 'Islamic country' with Arabic as the official language. Shariah Islamia (Islamic Law) has been introduced and the whole constitution of the Sudan is Islamic in complete disregard of the non-Muslims in the Sudan.

As if all these were not enough, Islam has taken a prominent and almost central place in the civil war that has lasted over four decades in the Sudan. 'Jihad' has been invoked by Islamic leaders as a way of perpetuating the cause of Islam in the Sudan.

This leaves the Sudanese Christians with very limited or no options for dialogue. Sudanese Christians see Islam as being used by the government as a threat. They feel a very high sense of persecution. Is there a way for others to share their pain and agony?

Recommendations

In responding to such situations IASCOME recommends:

that the priority of appropriate witness and service among Muslims be raised to a higher place on the Primates' and ACC agendas.

that there be gatherings of people living in situations of Muslim presence to share accounts of Christian living and witness for encouragement and learning. We heard with appreciation that one such gathering sponsored by USPG and CMS had already been held, but we recommend others to be planned in which the active participation of women and men; lay people and clergy alongside bishops be ensured.

that particular attention be paid to ensuring children are included in gatherings and their voice and their hopes are heard.

that there be such a gathering specifically for those living under Shariah law.

that we recognised there needs to be action on many fronts, for example the Archbishop of Canterbury's Al-Azhar initiative is to be greatly welcomed. We encourage all such initiatives at all levels.

that out of the gatherings clear guidelines be prepared on how to respond to Islamisation in a Christian way.

that the cry and pain of those Christians and Churches suffering or under pressure in the face of Islamisation be acknowledged with great sensitivity and understanding.

The Commission discussed and warmly welcomed the report of the 'Agreement for dialogue between the Anglican Communion and al-Azhar al-Sharif'[83]. It placed on record its warm support for the initiatives taken, the visits made and the commitment given by the present Archbishop of Canterbury in developing relations with leaders of Muslim communities in many parts of the world.

F2. Developing Anglicanism: A Communion in Mission

The Anglican Communion has grown out of the vision for world mission. The Decade of Evangelism highlighted this founding perspective and encouraged Churches of the Communion to explore what this might mean for a new era. Today we see signs of many different kinds of mission in the Communion leading to growth and developments in terms of both the size and nature of Anglicanism.

One way of expressing this emerging perspective is to say that we are a family of Churches who find their Communion in Mission. Within this Communion we find structures which express our unity, marks which identify our mission, and relationships which create our fellowship. We are a Communion in Mission in so far as our identifiable mission is relational and our structures serve those mission relationships.

As a Communion in Mission, being led forward by the Holy Spirit, we acknowledge (with other sister Churches) that we are God's pilgrim people, and therefore whilst affirming the patterns and traditions of our past we realise that these are provisional and that our Communion is developing as it is being transformed in Christ.

Indicators of Mission

The various issues addressed in this report can also be seen as indicators of mission. We have identified a number of these:

> The Missio Dei, the mission of God, is grounded in the Trinitarian affirmation of a Communion in Mission (see above). One way of understanding the mission of God, in which the church is called to participate, is "to restore all people to unity with God and each other in Christ".

> The Church finds its vocation as it expresses and serves a restored, reconciled and redeemed creation.

> The new creation brought forth by the mission of God embodies wholeness and life abundant in the pains and possibilities of our daily experiences.

A Communion in Mission is characterised at one and the same time by a celebration of commonality and difference. Our commonality and difference is sustained by apostolic truth and the promise of the unity of all things in the worship of God.

The evangelistic imperative draws the Church into a movement to both proclaim and live out a restored, reconciled and redeemed new creation.

These indicators of mission challenge us to see Anglican identity as developing historically over time through an engagement with a variety of contexts. The variety of contexts push us to give priority to relationships as fundamental to a Communion in Mission.

The Quality of Mission Relationships

A Communion in Mission is characterised by the quality of its relationships engendered by God's own relational life in mission (koinonia). These characteristics include:

interdependence
integrity
honesty
transparency
laughter
acceptance
openness
vulnerability
sharing
brokenness
compassion
solidarity in pain

Structures of Communion

The structures of a Communion in Mission express God's mission when they:
seek to serve and not to be served
offer effective leadership
nurture relationships
effect reconciliation, freedom, justice and peace
are alive and dynamic
are flexible, available and accessible

Recommendations

ACC-12 is asked to affirm IASCOME's concern to give priority to the development of and reflection about Anglicanism as a Communion in Mission.
And specifically to:

support ventures in the Church that serve relationships in mission, e.g. the Anglican Gathering and the emergence of new networks;

lift up and celebrate the stories of mission relationships across the Communion;

live more deeply into the local-global nature of the Anglican Communion today;

address questions of authority and truth in relation to the life of the Church as a Communion in Mission.

The Commission recognises that there is still further work to do on new ways of being Church and new forms of evangelism.

F3. The Journey towards Wholeness and Fullness of Life

Listening to reports from many parts of the world we are aware of so many serious threats to life—not just of individuals, communities and nations, but also to the life of the planet. For example we heard accounts of:

The unfolding consequences of the HIV/AIDS pandemic on families and, in particular, children across sub Saharan Africa.

The traumatic effects of exploitation of children, child soldiers, internal displacement of families and child abuse in countries like Sri Lanka and parts of Africa on the emotional growth and social development of children from whom leaders of the future are likely to emerge.

The effects of environmental degradation in situations of war and conflict, for example in the Sudan, which have brought about desertification caused by the cutting down of trees and the effects of the oil industry.

The internal displacement of millions of people in the Sudan and many more becoming refugees outside the country divides families and deprives children of education and development of skills for the future quite apart from the emotional impact upon them.

War between nations and within countries (for example the thirty-six year war in the Sudan, conflict in Sri Lanka, Democratic Republic of the Congo, Israel/Palestine) has lasting physical and emotional effects on those involved and tears the social fabric of civil society apart.

Poverty in many areas has a crippling effect.

Slavery and the terrible physical abuse of captives in war situations, forming part payment for unpaid government troops.

In northern nations where material wealth might be greater than in other parts of the world there are many areas of poverty and the effects of dysfunctional families and relationships, the pressures and stress of life can all prove wounding and death dealing.

So many of the tragic situations in the world today are evidence of the forces of death and destruction that contradict the desire of God expressed in Jesus' words that 'all people should have life, life in all its fullness' (John 10:10).

It is the calling of all Christians to witness that God is a God of Life expressed in the working of God's Spirit throughout the created universe, to bring life and to counteract the forces of death. The universal life-giving work of God's Spirit is focused in human form in the person of Jesus—'In the beginning was the Word . . . in him was life, and the life was the light of all people . . . the Word became flesh and lived among us' (John 1:1-14). Jesus is described as 'the Bread of Life'; 'the Way, the Truth and the Life'; 'the Water of Life'. Through his death on the Cross Jesus entered into the pain and evil of the world, taking on the forces of death and destruction and rising after they had done their worst into a new resurrected life.

The Bible speaks of the Spirit of Jesus carrying on his ministry of bringing life and encouraging all people to join in the journey into life which will culminate in the new heaven and new earth.

Our response to the forces of death is to analyse causes, develop preventative programs, provide alternatives and to heal; in other words to pursue Jesus' Nazareth Manifesto (Luke 4:18–19). In this section we focus specifically on the call to heal, to make whole those wounded physically and emotionally as individuals and communities by the death dealing trends in the world. The prophet Isaiah speaks of God's servant not breaking 'the bruised reed' and not quenching 'the flickering flame', but of binding up and healing wounds and helping all people on the journey to wholeness that is God's calling and all people's need.

In relation to HIV/AIDS there is a ministry of care, counselling and support both for People living with AIDS and for their families and those who support them, both before and after their death—a ministry of support, accepting and holding.

Destruction of the environment calls for a healing of the wounds inflicted on the earth.

Communities that have suffered trauma and displacement need reconciliation and healing.

The ministry of healing, which takes the form of prayer, the laying on of hands and anointing with oil, is frequently practised in some and being rediscovered in other parts of the Communion as a form of ministry to Christians and those outside the Christian faith alike.

The healing of children who have suffered abuse and need emotional and social healing is a skilled and demanding work of love.

Recommendations

IASCOME therefore recommends:

that Liturgies for cleansing and healing in communities where terrible things have happened be researched, and listed/collected for sharing more widely.

These should include liturgies for environmental healing.

Connection with representatives on liturgical committees or on the International Anglican Liturgical Consultation.

Liturgies from Anglican and other Churches.

New liturgies for healing and the laying on of hands that are being developed in some parts of the Anglican Communion.

Any reports on healing produced within member Churches of the Communion.

Examples of the work of circles of prayer, healing and reconciliation.

that the ways in which the ministry of healing and reconciliation, including its psychological elements, are part of the theological and ministerial formation of Church and youth leadership be researched.

that some assessment be made of how the Church in each country plays an important role in the preparation of leaders for the future in the light of the huge threats posed by HIV/AIDS and the consequences of war to the present and next generation of leaders within many countries.

that stories be collected and shared (in an appropriate way) of the effects of the forces of death and of life-giving responses being made as the basis for analysis. People's stories have proved valuable in awakening awareness.

ACC-12 is asked to affirm the Commission in undertaking these tasks and encouraging others to do so.

F4 Mission as Justice-Making and Peace-Building

At both the first and second meetings of IASCOME, we listened to members describe the mission work of their various churches, and were struck by the powerful stories of committed Anglicans challenging injustices in their own contexts and also working to bring about peace and reconciliation in areas of conflict. In many parts of the Anglican Communion the mission focus of the church at this time is justice-making and peace-building in contexts of poverty, abuse of power and violence.

We noted **two types of violence:** firstly, visible and spectacular violence against individuals and communities; and secondly, systemic, structural violence.

These are characterised as follows:

Visible and spectacular violence:

Wars arising from ethnic, religious or political conflicts and from socio-cultural practices that are funded through external sources and often fought using outside personnel.

Domestic violence within the family.

Violence against children, including child trafficking, child labour and child soldiers.

Systemic and structural violence:

Poverty perpetuated by oppressive and exclusionary systems.

The abuse of power in and by both secular and religious institutions.

Globalised capitalism, including unethical biotechnology practices.

Based on the stories we heard, we make the following observations about how Christians in mission behave:

Christians in mission live out the values of the Gospel: love, justice, peace and the preferential option for the poor, powerless and weak. They respect and affirm the dignity of each person, looking for and honouring Christ in each child of God.

Christians in mission affirm those structures and value systems that are life-giving, and seek to transform cultural practices that oppress, discriminate and are contrary to the Gospel.

Christians in mission have a richness of spirit that leads them to repent, forgive, reconcile and restore.

Christians in mission are engaged in the political and economic life of the/their world in a non-partisan way. They challenge unjust structures and value systems in institutions, especially the church, and in groupings in society such as tribes, clans and social movements, and in the economic and political systems at local, national and international levels.

Christians in mission are prophetic risk-takers.

Christians in mission are actively involved in peace-making as part of building a safe world. They find ways to hold safe spaces where opposing forces can listen and talk to each other.

We believe the imperatives for this behaviour are firmly grounded in the teaching of Scripture and the faith of its practitioners, which we heard articulated as follows:

Jesus said, "Love one another as I have loved you." His life is the example of how we are to love.

Jesus said, "Love your enemies." The challenge is to hold our enemies accountable in the hope of bringing change, without destroying them.

All people are created in the image of God, irrespective of race, class, gender, age and sexual orientation.

God continues to redeem humanity, and Christians in mission are called to be instruments of this redemption in their own cultures.

IASCOME affirms the good work done by the Anglican Peace and Justice Network (APJN) and encourages provinces to support those in their midst engaged in the mission work of justice-making and peace-building.

Recommendations

To expand and strengthen this work, IASCOME makes the following recommendations:

that provinces examine their health and educational institutions to ensure that there are appropriate policies and monitoring mechanisms to protect the vulnerable, and as much as possible, to guarantee fair access to services.

that provinces examine their cultural practices, affirming those that liberate, and transforming those that contradict and deny the liberating message of the Gospel.

that provinces, dioceses and parishes include in their various cycles of prayer, prayers for peace-makers and those involved in the work of reconciliation.

that provinces gather and submit to IASCOME resources being used in peace-building, so that these can be made available to assist in the training of peace-makers.

F5 Money, Power and Christian Mission

During the course of our first two meetings, the members of IASCOME have listened to stories of the benefits which a healthy local economy, financially self-sufficient churches, and the compassionate exercise of power can bring to the furtherance of Christian mission. But we have also heard how poverty, financial dependency, and financial corruption coupled with the abuse of power can obstruct and distort God's mission. Based on these stories, we make the following observations:

Jesus came to offer abundant life to everyone (John 10:10). This means the material basis of life as well as the spiritual. The Good News has no credibility if people remain poor and powerless while the rich thrive.

Love of God is false unless there is a genuine love of neighbour evidenced through mutual respect and service. We are accountable to God for the gifts we have received and for the welfare of our neighbours (Matt. 25).

Wealth is a gift from God requiring honesty, transparency and vigilance in financial management and accountability. Financial scandals tarnish the image of the church and diminish the credibility of the Gospel.

Power must be exercised in the service of the powerless, as exemplified by Jesus. Failure to follow Jesus' example of empowering the powerless makes a mockery of the liberating message of the Gospel.

Those engaged in Christian mission need to include the following tasks in their work:

- **Economic analysis.** People need to be equipped to seek answers to their concerns about their local economic situations. This means paying attention to the economy at the global as well as the local level, since the two are so closely intertwined. Information and basic tools of analysis need to be provided so that people can make informed economic decisions.

- **Sharing financial resources.** Financial resources need to continue to be shared across the Communion, but capacity must also be built in wealth generation and financial management. The sharing of resources should be seen as a stepping stone to financial self-sufficiency. To this end, we need good ethical teaching in Christian stewardship that leads to accountability and tithing.

- **Participation in civil society.** People need help to become positively involved in civil society. This requires building dignity and self-confidence, and teaching organisational skills, as well as finding ways to both share power and exercise it in compassionate and responsible ways.

- **Ethical financial behaviour.** Christian values apply at all levels, local, and global. Financial corruption and mismanagement need to be challenged, as do unethical investment practices.

It is important that Christians in mission challenge the abuse of power and financial corruption and mismanagement in the wider society. At the same time, these sins continue to be present within the church and need to be corrected.

Recommendations

IASCOME recommends:

- that provinces examine their entire investment portfolios, including pension funds, to ensure that they meet the Global Reporting Initiative Standard[84] (www.globalreporting.org), especially in relation to the arms trade and the environment.

- that provinces examine their governance structures to ensure transparency in decision-making processes and financial management.

- that provinces seek ways to train creative administrators who are also strategic thinkers.

- that provinces put in place measures to deal with corruption in the church at all levels, and make these measures known to the membership.

- that each province affirm its commitment to the Anglican Communion by a renewed endeavour to fulfil its financial obligation to the Inter-Anglican Budget.

F6 Evangelism

Evangelism has run as a theme through many of the Commission's discussions and presentations, but a sustained reflection on evangelism across the Communion has been identified as a major piece of work for future Commission meetings. We look forward to continuing to encourage and support the significant efforts in evangelism that are emerging in the Communion.

G. ACC-12 Resolution

The following resolution was suggested to ACC-12 and passed by them. Resolution 12 entitled "Inter Anglican Stranding Commission on Mission and Evangelism" resolved.

to receive with thanks the Interim Report 'Travelling Together in God's Mission' from the Inter Anglican Standing Commission on Mission and Evangelism (IASCOME);

to give thanks for the successful Nairobi Consultation for Provincial Mission and Evangelism Co-ordinators 'Encounters on the Road'; to receive the report of that Consultation; to encourage dissemination of its report and to support plans for a follow-up conference, funded outside of the budget of the ACC;

to look forward to and pray for the mission organisations Conference planned for February 2003;

to take note of action taken on matters remitted to the Commission;

to note that comments on the Primates' Strategic Working Party on Theological Education have been sent direct to that working party;

to encourage the Commission to develop its mandate, reflection and work particularly in the areas of

- Leadership Training and Formation for Mission
- Islam and Islamisation
- Developing Anglicanism: A Communion in Mission
- The Journey to Wholeness and Fullness of Life
- Justice Making and Peace Building
- Evangelism

to circulate the interim report to provinces, other Commissions and networks and more widely for comment and discussion.

Section III

Appendices

APPENDIX 1

THE JOURNEY SO FAR

The first meeting of the Anglican Consultative Council in Limuru in 1971 identified four themes for its work—Unity and Ecumenical Affairs; the Church's role in society; Order and organisation in the Anglican Church (i.e. its internal life) and Mission and Evangelism.[85]

Those themes have run as threads through successive meetings of the Council (and indeed of the Lambeth Conference). The Inter Anglican Standing Commission on Mission and Evangelism (IASCOME) is the latest instrument for providing communion-wide reflection and action on mission and evangelism issues. It is the heir to a distinguished history.

Partners in Mission Process

Following the first ACC Meeting the Partners in Mission process was instituted as the first Communion-wide program to enable the sharing of people, funds, ideas, insights, experience, prayer and information across the Churches of the Communion, with the intention of providing mutual support in engagement with wider society in each locality where the Anglican Church was set. Lasting from 1974 to the early 1990s it has proved one of the longest most extensive and deep rooted programs with a Communion-wide focus. A senior ACC staff member was appointed as Secretary (Director) for Mission and Evangelism with responsibility for encouraging and developing this program.

The process was based on the principle that the Church in each place took lead responsibility for mission in that place, but that the wider Church could provide both insight and resources to assist with that mission. At the same time, churches in the wider Communion, had lessons to learn from the gifts and experiences from each local Province and Church. The process was focused around consultations at which a province would invite representatives of partner Churches and organisations to assist it in identifying priorities for its mission and ministry; provide support for its work on those priorities: and through those who participated in the consultations, take back lessons and insights to the Churches from which they came.

Reports on the different consultations held during the second half of the 1970s were made to successive meetings of the Anglican Consultative Council but by 1981, the process had reached such a stage that the fifth ACC meeting set up an international advisory group on Mission Issues and Strategy *(MISAG I)*. Its remit was to review mission issues and strategy; identify exceptional needs for mission and development calling for a Communion-wide response; and find ways and means of collaborating with other Christian bodies in mission and evangelism.[86]

MISAG I (1981–1986)

MISAG I challenged the pastoral model of mission inherited from the experience of England as being inadequate in situations where the majority of people were not Christian. It reviewed the progress of the PIM process thus far, identified lesson learned and provided detailed guidance for the process and for the organisation of consultations. It recommended a data-gathering process to enable a more transparent and open statement of the resources of people and money being exchanged across the Communion. It called for a gathering of representatives of mission boards (predominantly from what today is termed the 'North') together with representatives from the Churches of the 'global South' to consider the data gathered, to build trust and to provide for a more co-ordinated strategy

The Brisbane Conference (1986)

That Conference was held in Brisbane in 1986 following some data collection (which identified a number of problems in actually doing it). Its purpose was 'to assist the Mission Agencies and Churches of the Communion to have a better understanding of current mission issues, Agency policies, practices and resources with a view to more faithful stewardship in God's mission today'. It identified three particular issues to be addressed—the places of evangelism, development and ecumenical sharing in mission.[87] Alongside a substantial review of the PIM process it provided a brief report on each of these issues and set up a Mission Agencies Working Group (MAWG) specifically to co-ordinate *mission agency* responses to PIM consultations; to assist the ACC in organising effective and meaningful data collection; to prepare guidelines for companion diocese relationships throughout the Communion; to investigate establishing a loan fund for the Communion and to prepare guidelines on development. This group was made up of mission agency representatives i.e. those who had some specific control over programs of exchange of people and money. It met from 1987–1992.

The Conference also recommended that there should be a meeting of representatives of Churches from the 'global South' independent of the 'North' to discuss the issues they were facing.

MISAG II (1987–1992)

The Singapore Meeting of ACC (ACC-7, 1987) established a second 'Mission Issues and Strategy Advisory Group' with wider participation (from 14 Provinces and including five mission agency nominees from the Brisbane meeting) than the first. Whereas MAWG was looking at the practicalities of data-gathering, the PIM process and the developing Companion Diocese links, MISAG-II took up wider issues—evangelism in a pluralist society; theological issues emerging from the partners in mission process; ecumenical concerns; and theological education.

Its final report *Towards Dynamic Mission* contained an extended theological reflection on mission in contemporary contexts, and major assessments of the Partners in Mission process (including identification of ten Principles of Partnership to undergird partnership relations); theological education for mission and exchange and encounter.

MISAG II also encouraged a conference for representatives of churches from the 'global south' and recommended the establishment of MISSIO, a Standing Commission for Mission for the Anglican Communion, made up of representatives of provinces and mission agencies (combining both those engaged in running programs and representatives from the wider Church).

Although it passed on the data-gathering task from MAWG to MISSIO—that task proved impracticable and was dropped.

The Decade of Evangelism

Resolution 43 of the 1988 Lambeth Conference recognised that 'evangelism is the primary task given to the Church' and asked 'each Province and diocese . . . in co-operation with other Christians, to make the closing years of this millennium a 'Decade of Evangelism' with a renewed and united emphasis on making Christ known to the people of his world'. This was to prove one of the most uniting, influential and far-reaching of any Lambeth Conference resolutions with responses taking place in every diocese of the Communion. One of the tasks of the successor to MISAG II was to encourage and produce an overview of the Decade.

MISSIO (1994–1999)

ACC-9 meeting in Cape Town (1993) set up MISSIO—the first Standing Commission of the Anglican Communion. The Commission continued the work of previous groupings (a forum for provinces to review the mission of the Church; encourage the partnership of Churches and agencies; assessment of the PIM process etc.) but significantly, had the development of the Decade of Evangelism added to its mandate.

The major achievements of the Commission included a mid-point review of the Decade of Evangelism (Kanuga 1995), the most widely representative gathering of the Communion between the 1988 and 1998 Lambeth Conferences, which produced the influential report *Evangelism: The Cutting Edge of Mission*—with its ten priorities for mission in the Communion—and a range of practical suggestions.

South to South

1994 also witnessed the long awaited gathering of representatives of Churches from the South. Taking place in Limuru, Kenya, in January, the Anglican Encounter in the South produced a statement *'Trumpet from the South I—Maturity, Its Challenges and Responsibilities'*, encouraged connections from south to south, and established a continuation group to maintain links and prepare for a second such Anglican Encounter. This subsequently took place in Kuala Lumpur in February 1997 and produced *'A Second Trumpet'*.[88]

MISSIO concluded its work in 1999, producing its report *Anglicans in Mission—A Transforming Journey*[89]. This contained a theological reflection on mission, emphasising mission as transformation. It drew out a number of lessons from the Decade of Evangelism. It highlighted the importance of theological training and formation in mission including calling for a Communion-wide review of leadership training to identify trends, needs and problems and how they could be addressed—a recommendation that has now come to fruition in the task group on Theological Education in the Anglican Communion (TEAC).

By 1999, the PIM process had virtually come to an end and new expressions of partnership and collaboration were emerging. *Anglicans in Mission* suggested that the term companionship in mission would be a more fitting expression to describe the journey of Anglican Christians in their Churches, provinces and agencies as they sought to reach out to the wider world. The report identified structures for collaborative working that had emerged within Churches and made proposals for pan-Communion structures in the form of the next Mission Commission and the work of a Director for Mission and Evangelism.

In 1999, the Anglican Consultative Council, at its 11th meeting in Dundee, Scotland, accepted the recommendation from MISSIO to establish a successor body, the Inter Anglican Standing Commission on Mission and Evangelism, IASCOME, to continue the work.

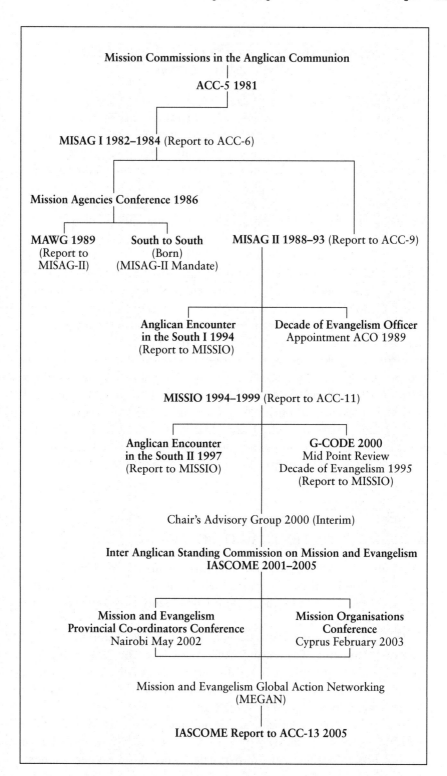

Mission Commissions in the Anglican Communion
ACC-5 1981

MISAG I 1982–1984 (Report to ACC-6)

Mission Agencies Conference 1986

MAWG 1989
(Report to
MISAG-II)

South to South
(Born)
(MISAG-II Mandate)

MISAG II 1988–93 (Report to ACC-9)

Anglican Encounter
in the South I 1994
(Report to MISSIO)

Decade of Evangelism Officer
Appointment ACO 1989

MISSIO 1994–1999 (Report to ACC-11)

Anglican Encounter
in the South II 1997
(Report to MISSIO)

G-CODE 2000
Mid Point Review
Decade of Evangelism 1995
(Report to MISSIO)

Chair's Advisory Group 2000 (Interim)

Inter Anglican Standing Commission on Mission and Evangelism
IASCOME 2001–2005

Mission and Evangelism
Provincial Co-ordinators Conference
Nairobi May 2002

Mission Organisations
Conference
Cyprus February 2003

Mission and Evangelism Global Action Networking
(MEGAN)

IASCOME Report to ACC-13 2005

APPENDIX 2

ANGLICAN CONTEXTUAL THEOLOGIANS NETWORK (ACTs)

The Anglican Contextual Theologians network (ACTs) came into being at the initiative of a group of theologians from around the Anglican Communion who saw the need to engender ongoing theological conversations across the Communion that wrestle with, and celebrate the richness of, the many and diverse cultural and geographic contexts of contemporary Anglicanism. The first consultation of Anglican Contextual Theologians (ACTs1) gathered thirty-four people for five days of conversation in Cambridge, Massachusetts, USA in May 2003. (see ACTs Communiqué, below)

The Cambridge consultation recommended that another consultation should take place and members of the African Network of Institutions of Theological Education Preparing Anglicans for Ministry (ANITEPAM) offered to host such a meeting if it was held in Africa. With the leadership of ANITEPAM, the second consultation of Anglican Contextual Theologians (ACTs2) was held in Durban, South Africa, in August 2004, with eighteen participants, fourteen of whom were from Africa. The Co-ordinator of ACTs2, Mike McCoy, summarised the consultation with the words: 'My hope is that the value of this gathering—and of others like it—will be shown in the building of relationships across the Communion, across cultural and theological frontiers, so that our rather stretched bonds of affection may be strengthened.' IASCOME sees networks as ACTs and ANITEPAM as rich resources for the building up of relationships in mission across the many and diverse contexts of the Anglican Communion.

COMMUNIQUE
FROM A CONSULTATION OF
ANGLICAN CONTEXTUAL THEOLOGIANS

A consultation of Anglican contextual theologians was held from 13th to 16th May 2003 at the Episcopal Divinity School, in Cambridge, Massachusetts, USA. Thirty-four theologians from twenty-two countries participated in the consultation.

The aim of the consultation was to establish a voluntary network of Anglican Contextual Theologians (ACTs network). The network will provide a forum for multiple theological voices within Anglicanism to be heard and acknowledged and will advance resources for theological education and leadership formation for the Anglican Communion.

The consultation took the form of group and plenary discussions around definitions and methodologies of contextual theology. The consultation identified death-dealing issues of particular concern to members' contexts and their relevance for theological education. Four key issues were discussed including: the dehumanising effects of poverty, globalisation and its marginalising effects on small nations states, the HIV/AIDS pandemic, and war and violence. Challenges of interfaith realities were also considered.

The participative and open process adopted by the consultation itself reflected an evolving theological method, resulting in a broad conversational agenda for the group. To this end, the consultation sought to develop a working understanding of the nature of contextual theology and its potential contribution to the life of the Anglican Communion.

The overwhelming majority of participants in the consultation agreed that contextual theology emerges out of an engagement with economic, political, and social realities that deeply inform issues of identity and culture. Contextual theology is rooted in a critical and communal reading of the Bible that seeks to discern the presence of the life-giving God in a suffering world. It affirms and uplifts the role of women in the theological enterprise. It is a reflection on God's transforming action in an increasingly globalised world. It is prophetic and critical, hopeful and life affirming. It participates in Jesus' solidarity with the marginalised and privileges their voices. It is a theology that fosters engagement and action.

The consultation believes that our Anglican Contextual Theologians network can provide a valuable resource for the churches of the Anglican Communion. It will encourage contextual theological reflection among other bodies of the Anglican Communion (such as but not limited to: the Inter Anglican Standing Commissions on Mission and Evangelism, Theology and Doctrine, and Ecumenical Relations, the Anglican Consultative Council and the Primates' Meeting), and will help to foster theological conversations and reflection within and between provinces and at local levels. The network will seek to engage further discussions with, and supply resources for, theological education institutions across the Anglican Communion.

Participants in the consultation offered personal and institutional commitments to further the work of contextual theology locally and globally.

APPENDIX 3

THE GLOBAL ANGLICANISM PROJECT REPORT TO THE IASCOME, MARCH 2005

Summary

A report on the Global Anglicanism Project (GAP) was presented to IASCOME at its meeting in 2003. It described the GAP pilot-phase and prospects for expanded research. The pilot-phase of GAP is now complete and a written report will be released after Easter 2005. This report outlines the current status of the GAP and commends it to the Standing Commission as a resource for the Communion, grounded in grassroots research about Anglican identity and leadership for mission.

The GAP Pilot Project

The purpose of the Global Anglicanism Project (GAP) is to learn who we are as Anglicans in all our complexity, diversity, brokenness, and wholeness in order to more genuinely witness to the transforming life in Christ, and with other Christian communities offer ourselves as a thanksgiving to God. The GAP pilot phase was launched in June 2002 by a group of 22 Anglican leaders from around the Communion. The Archbishop of Canterbury is fully informed about the GAP and in 2004 he endorsed the project. He underscored the importance GAP offers for strengthening the relationships that bind and unify the Communion at the grassroots.

Field research was carried out at the local congregation level in four pilot sites: Brazil, North India, New Zealand and Polynesia, and Tanzania. Focus groups and individual interviews concentrated on seven thematic areas that will be reflected in the 60-page pilot report: (1) Spirituality and Worship, (2) Community Life, (3) Leadership Development, (4) Conflict Resolution, (5) Inter Religious and Inter Denominational Relations, (6) Mission Outreach, and (7) Identity Formation. Stories of local vitality will be evidenced through case studies and local stories. It is anticipated that a CD with video footage will be widely disseminated as part of the pilot report to every diocese in the Anglican Communion. Additional copies of the report can be obtained from the Episcopal Church Foundation which serves as the Secretariat for GAP.

Pilot Phase Findings

The pilot study encompassed over 200 interviews with some 1000 leaders in congregations and the wider community. Patterns and practices of leadership in the four pilot sites uncovered the unique contribution Anglicans are making to both religious and secular life. Some of the findings include:

Anglicans are translating Christian expressions of worship and spirituality into local culture

Evangelism is central to the life of the local congregation

Young people forge new patterns of spiritual practice and mission

The Anglican Church is growing

Anglicans are innovative leaders who effect renewal and change in society

Anglicans are creating social capital in their communities

The Anglican Church is equipping and empowering lay and clerical leadership

Anglicans are mobilising against injustice and poverty in their society

Leaders in the Anglican Church are influential leaders in civil society

Anglicans are succeeding in resolving conflict and in peace making

Anglicans are at the forefront in combating HIV/AIDS pandemic and other crises

Anglicans make a unique contribution to fostering relationships with other faith groups

Second Phase of the Project

It is estimated that a wider study will cost approximately US$1.5 million. This next stage will conclude in 2008 and focus on cross-regional research around the major themes, incorporating learnings from the pilot-phase. Approximately a dozen additional sites will be the focus of field research at the local congregational level. The six themes identified are: (1) Indigenisation of spirituality and worship; (2) Dynamics of evangelism and conversion; (3) Leadership development and theological education; (4) Community organising for social justice, economic development, and public policy; (5) HIV/AIDS ministry and humanitarian interventions; (6) Inter-religious, Inter-denominational and intra-Anglican relations. Once funding has been secured further fieldwork will commence.

GAP and the IASCOME

The Global Anglicanism Project is a resource to the entire Anglican Communion and will contribute to the strengthening of mission relationships and networks throughout the Communion. GAP research remains the only current source of grass roots information about patterns and practices in the Communion. Actions that the Standing Commission may wish to consider:

IASCOME commends the pilot-phase of the GAP, and the ongoing GAP research, and encourages members of the Anglican Communion to participate in the broader study;

IASCOME commends the pilot phase of the GAP and the ongoing GAP research to the Anglican Consultative Council for consideration at its next meeting;

IASCOME invites the GAP researchers to make a presentation to the next meeting of the Standing Commission on their findings of the project;

IASCOME commends the GAP pilot report, due for publication in April 2005, to the Communion as a valuable resource for engaging in mission and evangelism

This report was compiled by Maurice Seaton, GAP Manager at the Episcopal Church Foundation, 22 February 2005.

APPENDIX 4

ENCOUNTERS ON THE ROAD
PROVINCIAL CO-ORDINATORS—MISSION
AND EVANGELISM CONSULTATION

RESURRECTION GARDENS—NAIROBI—KENYA
6–13 May 2002

Mission at the Heart of the Church

'Mission is at the heart of the life and calling of the Church. God's mission of love and life is universal in scope- to all people in all situations' (John 3:16)

This was the central affirmation of the first-ever Consultation of Provincial Co-ordinators of Mission and Evangelism within the Anglican Communion meeting in Nairobi, Kenya from 6–13 May 2002.

Representatives from Anglican provinces in Asia, the Pacific, Australasia, the Middle East, Central, East, West and Southern Africa, North America, the Caribbean and Britain and Ireland met for the first major gathering on mission and evangelism in the Anglican Communion since the end of the Decade of Evangelism.

They were joined by representatives from the world mission agencies—the Mothers' Union, Church Army (Africa), Church Mission Society (CMS) and United Society for the Propagation of the Gospel (USPG).

(Mr.) John Clark, Chief Secretary for Mission of the Church of England, chair of the Consultation commented: 'This has been an invigorating and spiritually refreshing experience. I sense a great energy and vitality amongst those present and within the Communion, and a renewed commitment to make evangelism and mission a priority within the life of our church. The Consultation has helped us appreciate the rich variety of the Communion and to be deeply challenged by those amongst us who are seeking to forward the Gospel in situations of great suffering and hardship.'

The majority of those attending had never participated in an international Anglican Communion gathering before. So there was much sharing of accounts of how the churches from which they had come were carrying out God's call to mission. Churches are growing often in situations of conflict and poverty, among displaced people, in many cases threatened by HIV and AIDS. The challenge of life and witness in Islamic contexts and under Shariah law was identified as a major concern. Co-ordinators also shared their experience on how best to carry out their jobs and began to prepare a list of guidelines for new co-ordinators.

There was a particular focus on church planting, evangelism in the context of affluent nations, (like the USA) co-operation between provincial structures and mission agencies, and work with other denominations. Dr Carlos Ham, Executive Secretary for Evangelism in the World Council of Churches, challenged the consultation with insights drawn from beyond the world of Anglicanism.

Archbishop David Gitari, Primate of the Anglican Church of Kenya, spoke on the role of a bishop in mission and evangelism, drawing from his years of experience in Kenya and emphasising the bishop's role as a missionary, called to lead in the work of evangelism.

Particular attention was given to the importance of the witness of lay people and the provision of training for evangelism. Clergy and bishops in particular were challenged to exercise their role of leadership and encouragement in mission and evangelism.

Co-ordinators exchanged details of how they carried out their work and agreed to form an email network as initial step in continuing to support, challenge and stimulate each other.

Daily worship beginning with a Eucharist and including mid-day, evening and night prayers drawn from liturgies across the world enriched the meeting and provided a framework for discussion. A half night prayer vigil was held during which all Churches within the Communion were prayed for.

Bishop Mano Rumalshah, former Bishop of Peshawar, Pakistan, and now General Secretary of the United Society for the Propagation of the Gospel (USPG) presented daily Bible studies on encounters that Jesus had with people during his ministry and the lessons they provided for mission and evangelism today.

The Rt Revd Michael Nazir-Ali, Bishop of Rochester (England) provided a theological and historical framework for the Conference with a presentation on 'Evangelism and the Wholeness of Mission'.

Much of the work of the Consultation took place in group discussion. Conclusions laid stress on the importance of prayer and worship and the Christian community in mission and evangelism. The importance of local contexts leading to a diversity of approaches to mission and evangelism was emphasised but attention was also drawn to the influence of global trends e.g. globalisation, urbanisation, HIV/AIDS and the growth of Islam.

Training in mission and evangelism was identified as a priority. The role of bishops and clergy not just in setting a lead but also in encouraging others was stressed. There was a call for greater sharing of ideas, experiences, people and finance across the Communion and for all provinces and dioceses to appoint a mission and evangelism co-ordinator.

The Conference, hosted by the Anglican Church of Kenya (ACK), concluded with Sunday visits to parishes and congregations in and around

Nairobi to give participants an inspiring experience of the Church in Kenya at worship.

The Consultation was an initiative of the Inter Anglican Standing Commission on Mission and Evangelism (IASCOME), which will hold its second meeting in St Andrews, Scotland, from 16–25 June 2002. There is to be a similar consultation for mission agencies of the Communion in Cyprus in February 2003.

NOTES OF THE CONSULTATION
CONCLUSIONS AND RECOMMENDATIONS

The following points were prepared immediately after the Consultation as a report of the major findings, to remind Consultation members of the basic findings and to report to the Inter Anglican Standing Commission on Mission and Evangelism.

These notes list basic principles in **bold** text with recommendations in *italics*.

I. FOUNDATIONS

1. **There are many ways of describing and expressing God's mission.**
2. **All mission is fundamentally God's mission, most clearly expressed in the sending of Jesus Christ and the Holy Spirit.**
3. **The Church is called to participate in God's mission and so has an essentially missionary character. ("As the Father has sent me, even so send I you." John 20:21)**
Mission is universal in scope—to all peoples in all situations. (John 3:16)

1. *The Anglican Communion needs a renewed vision for mission and evangelism.*
2. *This requires continual, deliberate, prayerful and intentional reflection on how the Communion is both engaging and called to engage in mission.*

II PRAYER AND WORSHIP

1. **The Anglican Communion is part of a living Church in which the Spirit of God is moving.**
2. **We need always to be open to how the Spirit is working in the Church and the world.**
3. **We must remain in touch with God.**
4. **In mission and evangelism we particularly need to take seriously the call to prayer:**
   - **for each other**
   - **for guidance**

• for inspiration
• following the example of Jesus

We often spoke of the importance of worship as a way of sharing the Gospel and making Christ known.

1. *All our practice of mission must be rooted in prayer, worship and reflection on scripture.*
2. *Provincial mission and evangelism co-ordinators need to connect with the liturgical committees and groups of their provinces to ensure that liturgy is rooted in God's call to mission.*

III CONTEXTS

1. All mission must fit local situations and contexts. Therefore mission and evangelism will be expressed differently in different places.
2. We need to know and understand the different contexts in which we do mission and evangelism, and formulate appropriate strategies and ways of working.
3. We recognise and accept that this will lead to a diversity of approaches and models in our Communion.
4. In each situation, mission and evangelism needs to relate to the particular context, culture and people.
5. In looking at situations/context we need to take account of:
   • the historical context
   • the socio-political situation
   • the internal context of the Church
   • global concerns and pressures

We need to celebrate and learn from the diversity of approaches to evangelism and mission within the Anglican Communion, as we have at this Consultation.

1. *The Consultation identified a range of specific situations and issues. Those involved in these situations need opportunities to share together their stories, experiences and insights so mission and evangelism might be taken forward. We call for opportunities to be created for that sharing.*
2. *Situations and issues include:*
   Islam and Islamisation (particularly living under Shariah Law)
   conflict and war
   youth
   poverty and abundance
   trade
   marginalised peoples
   HIV/AIDS

people who do not yet know Christ
globalisation and urbanisation

IV. PARTNERSHIP

1. If all mission is God's mission, then mission must always be in partnership with God.
2. In the same way, all mission should be open to partnership with all others in God's mission.
3. In many situations, particularly of conflict and poverty, solidarity is one way in which partnership is expressed.

1. *We encourage an openness to partnership in mission:*
   * *among provinces, dioceses, individuals*
   * *with mission agencies*
   * *with other Christian Churches and Communions*
   * *with all who share our common purpose*
   * *through international mission teams going from and to each diocese*
2. *We commend the Anglican Communion's 'Ten Principles of Partnership' [found in 'Anglicans in Mission: a Transforming Journey' p. 126; and in the booklet "Guidelines and Principles for Mission and Evangelism" available at the Consultation.]*

V. THE MINISTRY OF THE WHOLE PEOPLE OF GOD

1. All Christians are called to be witnesses to Christ and to share in his mission and ministry.
2. The Church is missionary by its very nature because this is the nature of God.
3. All ministry, lay and ordained, shares in the missionary task. We have a shared ministry, and must have a shared vision of mission.
4. It is vital to help and encourage lay people to be effective in witness and mission.
5. We recognise the important role of clergy and bishops in leading and encouraging the witness and mission of all Christians.
6. Clergy and lay people need to work together in the mission task.

Bishops have a particularly important role in affirming the priority of mission and evangelism through their leadership, example and encouragement of others.

1. *We call for each province and diocese to review training in mission and evangelism and ensure that it fits the local situation.*
2. *We call for mission and evangelism co-ordinators to ensure that there is effective lay training in mission and evangelism in their provinces.*
3. *We encourage the development and sharing of lay training programs across the Communion.*

4. *We call for a rethinking of the orders of ministry and their role in the light of our missionary calling and situation. This includes:*
   * *the role of the bishop in mission (see 1998 Lambeth Conference Report, Section II)*
   * *the role, ministry and mission of priests and deacons*
   * *the role and recognition of other ministries/orders e.g. evangelists, catechists, readers etc.*
5. *We call for bishops to reflect on how they are leading in mission and evangelism, and encouraging others.*
6. *We call for the priority of mission and evangelism to be considered when making appointments at provincial, diocesan and parish level.*

VI. RESOURCES FOR MISSION AND EVANGELISM

1. Resources do not just mean money. They include people, ideas, experience, prayer, spiritual gifts and insights, and practical materials (e.g. literature, pictures, films etc.).
2. Since mission is at the heart of the Church, resources are held in trust for mission.
3. Across the Communion there is a rich diversity of these resources.
4. But there is also a disparity and inequality in sharing resources across the Communion. There are often limited financial resources for mission and evangelism.

We need to find ways of sharing resources (particularly money) to support mission needs and opportunities within the Communion.

1. *We call for provinces and dioceses to examine their budgets and funding for mission and evangelism to ensure that it reflects the priority of mission and evangelism.*
2. *We call for guidelines to help in sharing finances for mission across the Communion.*
3. *We call for practical action to direct resources to those in frontier situations of conflict, oppression and poverty (particularly Sudan, Myanmar, Congo, Palestine).*
4. *We encourage greater sharing of people, ideas, materials etc across the Communion, in order to assist and strengthen mission and evangelism. We ask for practical ways to enable this to happen (for example, through a regular video documentary and/or through printed news about mission and evangelism).*
5. *..We call for creative use of the internet to help share resources (for example, an internet site and web editor for Anglican mission and evangelism).*
6. *We recommend that every diocese have a diocesan evangelist and/or evangelistic team.*

VII. TRAINING

1. We identified training and encouragement as an important priority.
2. Telling our faith story is a vital way of witnessing, but people may need help to know and tell their story.
3. Training is important, but effective witness depends much on the integrity, Christ-likeness and authenticity of Christians.

1. *We call for a greater sharing of what is actually happening (courses, ideas, stories, materials and insights) in training for mission and evangelism, and for practical ways to enable this to happen.*
2. *We affirm the work of organisations like the Church Army, the Mothers' Union and others in equipping people for evangelism.*
3. *We call for the further development of programs and training centres to equip lay people and evangelists.*

VIII. MISSION AND EVANGELISM CO-ORDINATORS

Mission and Evangelism Co-ordinators in dioceses and provinces have a vital role in sharing information, encouraging people and parishes, training others, advising bishops and clergy, co-ordinating action, and developing initiatives and strategies in mission and evangelism.

1. *Every Church/Province/Diocese of the Communion should be encouraged to appoint a Co-ordinator for Mission and Evangelism.*
2. *We recommend that guidelines be developed for the work of Mission and Evangelism Co-ordinators. These will include an outline of their roles and tasks (our Consultation already has begun a list).*

IX. NETWORKS

1. Meeting and sharing in mission is vital for exchanging news and ideas, developing initiatives, for prayer and worship, and for encouraging each other.
2. Networks need to include provincial structures, mission agencies and other denominations.

1. *We recommend that the network of those at this meeting (and their regional equivalents) continue to work and meet. We intend to set up an email network among ourselves as part of this process.*
2. *We recommend that opportunities (conferences and consultative meetings) at various levels (diocesan, regional and world levels) be organised on a regular basis.*
3. *We encourage the development of diocesan mission teams to work across boundaries (geographical, cultural etc).*

4. In particular we encourage development of networks to share insights about mission and evangelism in multi-faith situations and in the area of church planting

X. ANGLICAN CHURCH STRUCTURES

The structures of the Church should be orientated towards mission as the Church's first priority.

1. *We recommend that provinces rethink their provincial, diocesan and local structures in the light of the mission and evangelism priority. We recommend that mission and evangelism co-ordinators assist in this process.*
2. *We call on provinces to continue the process of consultation we have so valued at this meeting.*
3. *We affirm the importance of maintaining a Co-ordinator for Mission and Evangelism for the Communion within the Anglican Communion Office (see tasks listed in 'Anglicans in Mission: A Transforming Journey').*
4. *We strongly re-affirm the Mission Commission's call for the inclusion of mission representatives on the design group for the proposed 2008 Anglican Gatherings. We affirm the Mission Commission's call for "mission" to be the theme of the Gathering.*

APPENDIX 5

TRANSFORMATION AND TRADITION IN GLOBAL MISSION

MISSION ORGANISATIONS CONFERENCE
LORDOS BEACH HOTEL—CYPRUS 12–18 FEBRUARY 2003

Conference Statement

From: 110 mission practitioners and advocates from 40 countries representing mission organisations, voluntary agencies and synodical bodies.

To: The Churches of God in the Anglican Communion. Grace to you and peace from God our Father and the Lord Jesus Christ.

We have come to the Anglican Communion Mission Organisations Conference in Larnaca, Cyprus, to take counsel, learn and explore how to be more faithful to God's mission in the world today.

Our theme: Transformation and Tradition in Global Mission. Transformation stands at the heart of mission. Tradition is dynamic, the body of faith we have received and are called to 'hand on' to others in the same spirit in which Jesus 'gave himself up' on the Cross.

Our setting: Cyprus offered important resonances. Our host diocese, Cyprus and the Gulf, serves a region that has always been a crossroad in mission. Here Paul and Barnabas launched their mission to the gentiles. The diocese includes Iraq, so the threat of war is felt deeply. Separation between the peoples of northern and southern Cyprus continues.

Through our Bible studies, particularly, we have reaffirmed that:

> God's grace *(charis)* has been poured out in order that we should be united with the whole world in a sacrifice of service, praise and thanksgiving *(eucharistia)*. The Church thus exists for and by mission in the world
>
> the incarnation is the supreme model for our mission engagement
>
> we are called to live out our faith on the fault lines of a divided world
>
> faithfulness to God's mission is the principle from which the unity and strength of the Church is derived.

We thank God for:

> the chance to meet globally, learn from one another and be inspired by the stories of risk and sacrifice for the Gospel we have heard
>
> the Inter Anglican Standing Commission on Mission and Evangelism (IASCOME), its role in fostering mission and evangelism, and developing and hosting this conference, the second in 18 years.

We commend:

> hosting another such conference by IASCOME within the life of its next five year term
>
> the proposal for a global gathering of Anglicans in 2008, for bishops, clergy and laity, to discern God's will for the renewal of the Church in mission.

We pledge ourselves to:

> ongoing transformation and renewal of our mission structures
>
> closer sharing between mission organisations and to seek new ways of working together in mission.

We challenge the Provinces of the Anglican Communion to:

> appreciate the diverse cultures and contexts in which we live, work and witness, and find new ways to use these positively in our mission
>
> recognise that nurturing fellowship is more important than transaction of business

greater understanding of how mission and evangelism is to be conducted in a post-colonial Communion, and taking seriously the communication needs of non-English speaking contexts

seek new models for mission engagement and being Church alongside traditional ones

undertake conscious and sustained engagement with the other faiths

encourage renewal in prayer and fresh approaches to fostering international chains of prayer and intercession

work for justice, peace and reconciliation in places torn apart by war, violence, poverty and human misery

strengthen work on behalf of refugees and displaced persons

raise up a new generation of children free from the scourge of HIV and AIDS

renew commitment to God's mission by providing sufficient resources for the task.

APPENDIX 6

GUIDELINES FOR MISSION AND EVANGELISM CO-ORDINATORS

The Decade of Evangelism stimulated mission and evangelism in the provinces of the Anglican Communion. Many, if not all the provinces, were challenged to shift their thinking and strategies from a maintenance mode to active mission. In many provinces a new position was created that of a Provincial Evangelism Co-ordinator, during the Decade.

These guidelines are a result of a discussion of the participants at the Conference of Provincial Mission and Evangelism Co-ordinators, held in Nairobi, Kenya 6–13 May 2002. The guidelines contain:

Questions to help clarify job expectation.
Advice from newly-appointed co-ordinators.

These guidelines can assist both provincial and diocesan co-ordinators of mission and evangelism.

QUESTIONS TO HELP CLARIFY THE JOB EXPECTATIONS

Definitions

What are the locally understood definitions of "mission" and "evangelism"? What are the differences between these two?

What are the various aspects of mission and evangelism that the job will entail in practice?

What are the commonly quoted biblical imperatives for mission and evangelism locally?

Strategies and Planning

What strategies are currently employed in mission and evangelism in your province?

How effective have these been?

What other strategies need to be implemented?

Is there an overall strategic plan for the work of mission and evangelism?

What needs to be done to strengthen this plan and improve the strategies?

Social, Cultural and Environmental Challenges

What are the particular social challenges facing people locally?

What cultural beliefs and customs will be challenges to the mission and evangelism work?

What environmental challenges are you aware of?

Skills, Talents and Gifts Needed

What special skills, talents and gifts are needed for the tasks of mission and evangelism in your context?

Where can the co-ordinator expect to find help in securing all the necessary skills, talents and gifts?

Is there general recognition of these skills, talents and gifts as ministries within the local church? If not, what can be done to affirm the legitimacy of these talents?

How will a team ministry be created and/or strengthened for the work of mission and evangelism?

Ecumenical Links

What ecumenical partners can be identified who are already at work in mission and evangelism in the area?

What needs to be done to strengthen these relationships and avoid unhealthy competition?

Formation Processes for Mission and Evangelism

Mission and evangelism is an imperative for all Christians. Is this commonly understood, and if not, what needs to be done to teach this?

What programs are needed to prepare lay people for the work of mission and evangelism?

What programs are needed to prepare ordained people for the work of mission and evangelism?

Part of the ministry of the church should be to prepare people for mission and evangelism. It should be part of the formation ministry of the church—catechumen, youth, women and men ministry, ministerial formation processes for both the ordained and lay ministries. These formation processes should not only be academic but pragmatic as to ignite in the participants a zeal for mission. It should focus on highlighting the fact that mission is about doing our Father's business—not an option but a must.

SUGGESTIONS FOR EVANGELISM CO-ORDINATORS

Clear Goals

Have a clear understanding of what the role of the Evangelism Co-ordinators involves for your province.

Understand this role in the light of the overall ministry of the province and the individual dioceses.

Concentrate on co-ordination of evangelism in the province and not the doing of evangelism yourself.

Evangelism is for the whole people of God not just for those with special gifts.

Know your context

a. Province

Where are the dioceses geographically?

Where are the gaps in the province?

What is the nature of the dioceses—rural, urban or metropolitan?

What are the needs?

b. Diocese

Where are the churches and congregations?

Where are the gaps where there is no Christian witness?

What other Christian churches are in the area and is it possible to link with them?

What are the social needs in the dioceses?

Where can the church have the most effective witness?

Know your people

What dioceses have Evangelism Co-ordinators?

In what ways can you invest in good relationships with the diocesan Co-ordinator of each diocese?

What are their gifts, strengths and particular role(s)?

What training do they needed? Where can they get the training?

What support do they needed? Where can they get the support?

Know your church

Visit parishes as often as possible and learn about the local communities, including their problems.

Get to know the parish lay leaders.

Get to know the clergy.

Seek support from the bishop.

Plan on paper then get the bishop's approval.

Teamwork

One major role of Evangelism Co-ordinators is that of providing leadership alongside others especially the diocesan co-ordinators. Leadership includes developing positive relationships in the team and showing interest in team members as subjects and not objects of the task to be accomplished. A sense of humour and the ability to laugh at oneself is part of these skills. Having appropriate gifts is helpful in participation and co-ordination but a well-co-ordinated people will be more effective than working alone. The ability of the position holder to be a team player is therefore vital for effective mission work. It is the Holy Spirit who imparts these gifts and graces. People in mission should therefore strive to have a special relationship with the Holy Spirit and should be most sensitive to his bidding and presence.

Teamwork is important. The Evangelism Co-ordinator should therefore:

Develop networking skills; connect and link groups together.

Develop good and open relationships with your team; be interested in them as people.

Encourage contacts and connections.

Think through problems with your team before you consider action.

Listen to people, share the vision and set apart a team.

Set up a public relations program.

Create an enabling environment.

Develop networks, so that co-ordinators can meet regularly and foster partnership.

Tell people they are doing a good job. (Some people never hear that from anyone else.)

Training

As evangelism is the task of every Christian, training will be on every level. During the Decade of Evangelism retraining in evangelism for bishops clergy and laity was recommended. The involvement of the diocesan bishop in the support of the evangelism co-ordinator and evangelism in the diocese is a priority and is often the key to effectiveness.

Areas of training

Training for a co-ordinators before their appointment is important.

Personal training for the diocesan co-ordinators in the area of their specific gifts is also advantageous.

The training of the laity in faith sharing.

Consultations

We are living in a day of consultations on varying aspects of mission and these have proved very effective in straightening relationships, networking, sharing of information and learning from one another. Consultations should be encouraged on the following levels.

Diocesan Evangelism Co-ordinators—it is important to learn from one another and to exchange ideas, strategies, successes and failures. It is also important for mutual encouragement and visioning.

The same kind of consultation could be done on a diocesan level for parish evangelists.

Mission is of God and from God. Therefore in order for an effective co-ordination in mission engagement to be possible, there should be an intimate relationship with God both by the faith community and by the mission practitioner. Evangelism and Mission should be the first priority in all church group activities

APPENDIX 7

ANGLICAN GATHERING

As a mission and evangelism commission for the Anglican Communion, IASCOME has monitored developments related to a proposed Anglican Congress over the length of our term. The brief for such monitoring was given by our predecessor commission, MISSIO: The Mission Commission of the Anglican Communion. MISSIO's report to the 1999 Anglican Consultative Council stressed that Anglican Congresses, as global gatherings of Anglican lay people, priests, and bishops from around the world, have been important vehicles for focusing the Anglican Communion on God's mission. MISSIO stated that: 'We believe that a fourth congress offers the promise of an equally fruitful summation of the mission of God in our time, into the service of which we are each commissioned by baptism.' MISSIO thus committed its successor commission (IASCOME) to assist in 'making the next Anglican Congress a reality and success,' and offered to make some of its own members available for the task of planning the next congress.[90]

The 11th meeting of the Anglican Consultative Council in Dundee, Scotland in September 1999 endorsed the idea of an Anglican Congress 'in association with the Lambeth Conference' in Resolution 14: Anglican Congress. With the help of the staff of the Anglican Communion Office and the then General Secretary of the Anglican Communion, the Revd Canon John L. Peterson, feasibility studies and initial planning for the 2008 Anglican

Gathering and Lambeth Conference were undertaken. During this initial planning stage, the name of the Congress was changed to that of an Anglican Gathering to emphasise the missiological and celebratory nature of the congress rather than a legislative, resolution driven agenda. Also, during this initial stage of planning and development Cape Town, South Africa was identified as a possible venue for the two events. In July 2003, the Archbishop of Canterbury, the Most Revd Rowan Williams, named a Design Group for the combined 2008 Anglican Gathering and Lambeth Conference. Consistent with both the 1999 MISSIO Report as well as the interim report of IASCOME "Travelling Together in God's Mission" to ACC-12 in Hong Kong in 2002, a member of IASCOME was named to the Design Group to help advance the mission orientation of the Gathering.

At the third meeting of IASCOME in Jamaica in December 2003, the Commission encouraged the Group to begin its work as soon as possible. At IASCOME's final meeting in Larnaca, Cyprus in March 2005, the Commission received a report on the work of the Design Group from its member who serves on the Group. The Commission learned that a primary agenda for the Design Group's activities in 2004 was securing adequate financial resources to support the global gathering of Anglicans for mission since there are no funds available for Anglican congresses within regular budgeting procedures in the Anglican Communion. The Design Group, however, was working under severe time constraints to secure the funding for the Gathering. Financial guarantees for the Gathering needed to be in place by December 2004 as contracts with the hospitality industry in Cape Town, South Africa, for events planned in July 2008 needed to be signed by the end of 2005. Despite the hard work and sustained efforts of both the Design Group and staff of the Anglican Communion Office, there was not sufficient time to put in place an acceptable funding plan before the contract deadlines came due. Thus in December 2005 the Design Group had to recommend to the Archbishop of Canterbury, that it would not be possible to hold an Anglican Gathering in association with the 2008 Lambeth Conference.

IASCOME was disappointed by the news that it would not be possible to hold the Anglican Gathering in 2008. Acknowledging that the Gathering will not happen in 2008, the mandate and ongoing planning for a broadbased mission oriented gathering of Anglicans from around the world nevertheless remains within the purview of the Anglican Consultative Council and its mission commission IASCOME.

IASCOME believes that it is crucial that a Gathering of Anglicans to celebrate and encourage our relationships in mission, be held in the not too distant future. Such a Gathering would help to build understanding across the Anglican Communion in these strained times while encouraging new friendships in God's mission. More specifically IASCOME proposes to

ACC-13 that an Anglican Gathering be held in the year 2013. The year 2013 represents both the midpoint between Lambeth Conferences as well as the fiftieth anniversary of the last Anglican Congress held in Toronto in 1963 that gave the Anglican Communion the far-reaching mission vision 'Mutual Responsibility and Interdependence in the Body of Christ'. As an immediate next step, IASCOME proposes that the ACC call for an Anglican Gathering Financial Development Task Group that will bring before ACC-14 in 2008 a clear and well-developed fundraising plan to ensure that the Anglican Gathering of 2013 will occur.

ACC RESOLUTION: This Anglican Consultative Council:

1 Thanks the Design Group of the Anglican Gathering and Lambeth Conference and the staff of the Anglican Communion Office for their faithfulness in seeking funding for the 2008 Anglican Gathering;
2 Appreciates that funding constraints prohibited the Anglican Gathering from taking place in association with the 2008 Lambeth Conference;
Remains committed to an Anglican Gathering to celebrate and encourage relationships in God's mission;
Calls for an Anglican Gathering to be held in the year 2013
Proposes that an Anglican Gathering Financial Development Task Group bring before ACC-14 clear and well-developed fundraising options to ensure that the Anglican Gathering of 2013 will occur.

APPENDIX 8

'Our Vision, Our Hope, The First Step': Statement from the All Africa Anglican HIV/AIDS Planning Framework

Johannesburg—August 2001

1. Our Vision

We, the Anglican Communion across Africa, pledge ourselves to the promise that future generations will be born and live in a world free from AIDS.

2. God's call to transformation

We are living with AIDS. As the body of Christ, confronted by a disaster unprecedented in human history, we share the pain of all who suffer as a result of AIDS. Faced by this crisis, we hear God's call to be transformed. We confess our sins of judgement, ignorance, silence, indifference and denial.

Repenting of our sin, we commit ourselves to:
- Breaking the silence in order to end all new infections
- Educating ourselves at every level within the Church
- Confronting poverty, conflict and gender inequalities
- Ending stigma and judgement, and
- Holding ourselves accountable before God and the world.
- Only then can we live out the Good News of the all-embracing love of Christ.

3. Our mission

Our mission is to respect the dignity of all people by:
- Securing the human rights of those infected by HIV/AIDS, and giving unconditional support
- Improving the health and prolonging the lives of infected people
- Accompanying the dying, those who mourn and those who live on
- Celebrating life
- Nurturing community, and
- Advocating for justice.

We acknowledge that we cannot do this alone. We are sustained by the love of God and emboldened by the Holy Spirit. We are inspired by the compassionate efforts of the faithful in attending to those affected by HIV/AIDS. We accept the responsibility of our leadership. We invite the wider community into creative, life-giving partnership.

4. Our commission in the context of AIDS

We believe we are created, in the image of God, as physical and spiritual beings. We are created to be in relationship to God, the community and ourselves. We believe that we are given the freedom to make choices, to love, to celebrate, to live in dignity and to delight in God's creation. We believe that suffering and death are neither punishment from God nor the end of life and that we are called to an eternal union with God.

Stigma is a denial that we are created in the image of God. It destroys self-esteem, decimates families, disrupts communities and annihilates hope for future generations. We commit in all our efforts—personal and corporate, programmatic and liturgical—to confront it as sin and work for its end.

Given who we are, and who we are called to be by God, we have defined and embraced a six-fold commission of ministry in response to AIDS.

These six calls in our commission are:

4.1 Prevention

The Church's commitment to prevention recognises that all life is sacred. Because we love our children, we speak and act to protect them from infection. Sex is a gift from God. We are accountable to God and one another for our sexual behaviour. Christian communities have a special responsibility and capacity for encouraging and supporting loving, just, honest relationships.

4.2 Pastoral Care

Pastoral care supports spiritual growth with the aim of sustaining whole and holy relationships with God, each other and community. This is achieved by affirming the dignity and worth of each human being and making clear the claim of God in our lives.

4.3 Counselling

Christian counselling equips people to live into God's invitation to wholeness, freed of the burdens of the past, and capable of moving in freedom toward the perfection promised in Christ's example with confidence and determination.

4.4 Care

In caring for all who suffer, we fulfil God's purpose by restoring dignity and purpose to people's lives. Christian care, therefore, seeks the fullness of life, in the context of the community, by the restoration of body, mind and spirit.

4.5 Death and dying

Death is a rite of passage in our spiritual journey and into eternal life. The call of all Christians is to uphold the dying by our love, as well as those who live on and those who mourn.

While death brings suffering and loss, our faith can make it a time of enhanced relationship and growth for individuals and communities. We are a resurrection people and our relationship with God does not end with the death of physical bodies.

4.6 Leadership

All authority is accountable before God. All people of the church are stewards of God's creation. We have a unique responsibility to speak truth to power, to act without fear, and to embody Christian values of love, compassion and justice.

5. Our Response

5.1 Prevention

Out of love for our children, one another and our communities, we commit to speak openly and with moral authority about responsible sexual behaviour, and to support one another, embracing and adopting behaviours that avoid the transmission of HIV.

5.2 Pastoral Care

As the embodiment of the merciful Christ in a suffering world, we commit to equip our clergy and laity to support all people, especially those living with HIV, in life-sustaining relationships with their God and their community.

5.3 Counselling

We commit to promote voluntary counselling and testing for HIV by our own examples and as a ministry of the Church. We call for the establishment of support groups and other counselling services for those who are orphaned, ill, afraid, dying or bereaved.

5.4 HIV Care

We commit to being central to networks of community support, to meet the health care and basic needs of those who are orphaned, ill or excluded due to HIV, freeing them to productive life as long as their health permits.

5.5 Death and Dying

As death transforms the body, AIDS calls us to transform those traditions and practices, by which we care for the dying and honour our dead, that consume scarce resources and contribute to denial.

We commit to:
   Training the Church to provide holistic care for the dying and prepare families for living on.
   Offering rituals that honour the dead and promote the well-being of those who survive.
   Training the clergy to counsel and protect the rights of those who survive, especially women and children.

5.6 Leadership

Silence permits inaction and is the breeding ground of stigma. We call for bold, compassionate community and institutional leadership at every level, to prevent infection and care for the ill and dying. We invite similar leadership by government, and all sections of society and international partners.

Because leadership must address power, culture and morality, we call on our government leaders to be accountable for health expenditures and to declare an 'HIV state of emergency', in order to combat AIDS and mobilise resources. We further declare that all people have the right to health, which includes access to basic health care.

HIV calls for bold and creative approaches by our leaders, which recognises the reality of power and gender patterns at community levels, to mobilise resources and facilitate development of new models of leadership, particularly among laity and women.

5.7 Education and training

Nothing in our educational systems equips us to deal with this catastrophe. In achieving the strategies outlined in this document, it is essential to assess needs and establish education and training capacity, in order to assure that sufficient numbers of clergy and laity:

- Have current and accurate basic information on the science of HIV, standards of home-based care, and the rudiments of treatment.
- Have both the technical information and the interpersonal communication skills to effectively teach and counsel regarding human sexuality.
- Are knowledgeable of local laws and practices regarding inheritance and equipped to impart that information.
- Receive practical training in community organisation and development, so that they may assist in establishing care and support which is needed.
- Are trained and available to meet exploding demands for pastoral care necessitated by HIV/AIDS

5.8 Theological reflection

As the Church, it is uniquely our task to gather for study, for prayer and for worship. Therefore we must engage in constant theological reflection, seeking discernment on the issues of sin, guilt, grace, judgement and forgiveness. To this we commit ourselves, our families and our friends.

APPENDIX 9

Mission Focus Expressed by Commission Members

Commission Members have been asked to summarise the mission focus of their Church, province or mission agency. This list is provided for the interest of ACC members.

1. The Church in the Province of the West Indies is committed to be and to become more and more God's agent of reconciliation within the complex network of relationships in the Caribbean Society. (Harold Daniel)

2. The focus of the Province of South East Asia is to equip and mobilise the whole people of God in our diocese/province through total mission and evangelism to make Jesus Christ known and confessed as Saviour and Lord in our region and beyond. (John Chew)

3. The Mission of God is the mission of the Episcopal Church in the Philippines. It is the proclamation of Jesus Christ and what he has done for us in his passion, death and resurrection.

This is expressed in various mission programs, such as,
   • children's ministry
   • nurture of members, etc.

The most prominent program where this mission is expressed is in the prophetic ministry of the church in relation to poverty, which is endemic in the country. This is based on the ministry of Jesus, which was actively a ministry in favour of poor people.

Our struggle, therefore, is how to do the Mission of God in a country that is suffering from hunger, unemployment and other social evils resulting from poverty and its causes. (Edward Malecdan)

4. The Scottish Episcopal Church carries out its mission through Mission 21, which is an emphasis of all seven dioceses. We aim to increase the spiritual vitality of the congregations through helping congregations to discern their vocations and God's future plans for them. In doing this, the Church seeks to serve God's reconciliation with creation in Scotland. (Pat McBryde)

5. In the Anglican Church of Tanzania, there is a constant challenge to rethink and re-evaluate the traditional "Empire-like" parishes, deaneries and dioceses. The cry of many is to have ministry brought as close to the grass-root peoples as possible. There is a need to create and re-create smaller more "manageable" parish churches, deaneries and dioceses. (Fareth Sendegeya)

6. The mission of the Church of the Province of Southern Africa is to actively witness and be God's presence in the ministry of healing and reconciliation, to speak Truth to Power and continue to challenge injustice. (Shirley Moulder)

7. The mission focus of the Church of Central Africa is to preach the Gospel and uphold its values of justice, peace and love in an environment that is hostile to human dignity and freedom. (Sebastian Bakare)

8. The mission focus of the church in Sri Lanka is on our solidarity in our common humanity and faith in Jesus Christ, and the renewal of our commitment to share the Good News of Jesus Christ to our fellows in the region and beyond. Encouraging practical encounters and people exchange programs in order that churches in the Province can move into closer partnership in mission and evangelism and bring healing to our nations. (Sister Chandrani Peiris)

9. The focus of the mission of the Church in Brazil includes three challenges: service, transformation and celebration. (Mauricio Andrade)

10. The Church in Papua New Guinea is focusing on the training and equipping of church leaders, as well as the whole body of Christ in building up a strong healthy church based upon small Christian (faith) communities. (Joseph Kopapa)

11. The mission focus of the Anglican Church in Central America is the consolidation of the work and planting of new congregations in the main cities of its five countries. (Armando Guerra-Soria)

12. The mission focus of the Church in the Province of Melanesia is justice-making and peace-building—reconciliation, transformation and nurturing. (Richard Naramana)

13. The focus of the Church of Nigeria is on evangelism and church planting, with investment in projects that are of great benefit to the people, and to be self-sustaining. (Josreph Akinfenwa)

14. The focus of the Church of North India is to make Jesus and his gifts of forgiveness and everlasting life to be known through witness, service and unity. (Pearl Prashad)

15. The Church in the Province of West Africa is focused on the need to reflect on and to design strategies to minister to people in the context of

   • conflict and civil strife amidst political instability;
   • increasing presence of HIV/AIDS;
   • increasing rate of abuse and neglect of the vulnerable; and
   • newly emerging structures and their leadership requirements (Joseph Kofi deGraft Johnson)

16. The current mission focus of the Anglican Church of Canada is to work towards building right relationships between Indigenous and non-Indigenous people in our church and in our nation within the wider of goal of working for healing and reconciliation between all the various groups in Canadian society. (Ellie Johnson)

17. The Church of England seeks to be **outward-looking** (sharing in the mission of God for the world and working for God's justice and peace for all); **united** (growing together in the love of God); and **confident** (living and proclaiming the Good News of Jesus Christ). This will be reflected in four priorities—all undergirded by worship and the call to the visible unity of all Christians:

    • Engaging with social issues
    • Equipping to evangelise
    • Welcoming and encouraging children and young people
    • Developing the ministry of all. (John Clark)

18. The mission agencies of the Church of England (as in other provinces), have developed and enacted a world mission mandate for the Church. These agencies have acted on behalf of, and as part of, the Church in seeking to share the Gospel with all peoples that all may be drawn into fellowship with Christ. This mandate now consciously includes mission to the European context. (Tim Dakin)

19. The mission of the Episcopal Church, USA, especially in light of the horror of September 11, 2001, is to participate in God's project of reconciliation, seeking to restore all people to unity with God and each other in Christ. (Ian Douglas)

20. The focus of the Church in the Democratic Republic of Congo is to seek lasting peace, justice and reconciliation and also to fight the silent enemy, which is HIV/AIDS. (Muhindo Ise-Some)

21. In Sudan, where the context is dominated by conflict, civil war, Islamisation, poverty, uprootedness and displacement, the main aim of the Church is to bring about the reconciliation of all the peoples of the Sudan (the different tribes and races) under the Cross of Jesus, to preach the message of the Good News of Jesus Christ, and to work for justice, peace and reconciliation. (Joy Kwaje Eluzai)

APPENDIX 10

The Global Reporting Initiative (GRI)— A Background Overview A Common Framework for Sustainability Reporting

Overview

Timely, credible, and consistent information on an organisation's economic, environmental, and social performance is a key element in building sustainable societies. Communities, investors, governments, and businesses need reliable information to effectively address the development challenges of the 21st century.

The Global Reporting Initiative (GRI) was established in late 1997 with the mission of developing globally applicable guidelines for reporting on the economic, environmental, and social performance, initially for corporations and eventually for any business, governmental, or non-governmental organisation (NGO). Convened by the Coalition for Environmentally Responsible Economies (CERES) in partnership with the United Nations Environment Programme (UNEP), the GRI incorporates the active participation of corporations, NGOs, accountancy organisations, business associations, and other stakeholders from around the world.

The GRI's Sustainability Reporting Guidelines were released in exposure draft form in London in March 1999. The GRI Guidelines represent the first global framework for comprehensive sustainability reporting, encompassing the "triple bottom line" of economic, environmental, and social issues. Twenty-one pilot test companies, numerous other companies, and a diverse array of non-corporate stakeholders commented on the draft Guidelines during a pilot test period during 1999–2000. Revised Guidelines were released in June 2000.

By 2002, the GRI will be established as a permanent, independent, international body with a multi-stakeholder governance structure. Its core mission will be maintenance, enhancement, and dissemination of the Guidelines through a process of ongoing consultation and stakeholder engagement.

A Steering Committee with a membership drawn from a diverse mix of stakeholders has guided the GRI thus far.

Vision

The GRI seeks to make sustainability reporting as routine and credible as financial reporting in terms of comparability, rigour, and verifiability. Specifically, the GRI's goals are to:

- Elevate sustainability reporting practises worldwide to a level equivalent to financial reporting;
- Design, disseminate, and promote standardised reporting practises, core measurements, and customised, sector-specific measurements;
- Ensure a permanent and effective institutional host to support such reporting practises worldwide.

A generally accepted framework for sustainability reporting will enable corporations, governments, NGOs, investors, labour, and other stakeholders to gauge the progress of organisations in their implementation of voluntary initiatives and toward other practises supportive of sustainable development. At the same time, a common framework will provide the basis for benchmarking and identifying best practises to support internal management decisions.

Opportunity

Improved disclosure of sustainability information is an essential ingredient in the mix of approaches needed to meet the governance challenges in the globalising economy. Today, at least 2,000 companies around the world voluntarily report information on their economic, environmental, and social policies, practises, and performance. Yet, this information is generally inconsistent, incomplete, and unverified. Measurement and reporting practises vary widely according to industry, location, and regulatory requirements.

The GRI's Sustainability Reporting Guidelines are designed to assist organisations publish reports:

In a way that provides stakeholders with reliable and relevant information that fosters dialogue and inquiry;

Through well-established reporting principles, applied consistently from one reporting period to the next;

In a way that facilitates reader understanding and comparison with similar reports;

In a form that provides management across different organisations with valuable information to enhance internal decision-making.

Learning

A broad array of stakeholders interested in sustainability reporting came together to fashion the March 1999 exposure draft Sustainability Reporting Guidelines.

Twenty-one companies, representing diverse countries and multiple industry sectors, tested and provided comments on the draft Guidelines. At the same time, hundreds of additional comments were provided by external stakeholders, representing perspectives from human rights, accountancy, government, business, labour, and multi-lateral, international, environmental, and religious organisations.

Reflecting the feedback gathered through this process, the June 2000 Sustainability Reporting Guidelines incorporate the following:

- Flexibility in the order in which reporters present information, while assuring information is easily located by users;

- Guidance to reporters on selecting generally applicable and organisation specific indicators, as well as integrated indicators that span multiple aspects of sustainability;

- Incremental application of the Guidelines (e.g., "environmental only "reports, or "headquarters country" reports);

- Forward-looking indicators; including strategy, management indicators, trend information, and targets for future years;

- Articulation of reporting principles adapted from financial accounting.

The Future

The GRI vision is bold. It has brought together disparate reporting initiatives into a new multi-stakeholder, global process with long-term implications for disclosure, investment and business responsibility. Its success will lead to:

- Expanded credibility of sustainability reports using a common frame work for performance measurement;

- Simplification of the reporting process for organisations in all regions and countries;

- Quick and reliable benchmarking;

- More effective linkage between sustainable practises and financial performance.

On the basis of this vision, the United Nations Foundation awarded a $3 million partnership grant to CERES and UNEP to support GRI activities. From 2000–2002, the GRI will pursue:

- Creation of a permanent, independent host institution for the GRI;

- Continued periodic revision of Sustainability Reporting Guidelines developed through the efforts of a global, multi-stakeholder process;

- Extending the reach of GRI to all regions of the world to enlarge its reach and ensure continual feedback to enhance the quality of the Guidelines.

The Global Reporting Initiative is uniquely positioned to bring standard reporting guidelines to a global audience. The GRI's engagement of multiple stakeholders across regions and nations distinguishes the GRI from numerous other reporting initiatives. At the same time, the GRI continues to build bridges to such initiatives in pursuit of its vision of a generally accepted sustainability-reporting framework.

See website for further information: http://www.globalreporting.org

APPENDIX 11

An agreement for dialogue between the Anglican Communion and al-Azhar al-Sharif

We affirm the importance of building on the excellent relations between the Anglican Communion and al-Azhar al-Sharif.

We acknowledge the brotherly relations between the Grand Sheikh of al-Azhar, Dr Mohamed Sayed Tantawy and Dr George Carey, the Archbishop of Canterbury and the President of the Anglican Communion.

We believe that friendship which overcomes religious, ethnic and national differences is a gift of the Creator in whom we all believe.

We recognise that both sides need to accept each other in a straightforward way so as to be able to convey the message of peace to the world.

We believe that direct dialogue results in restoration of the image of each in the eyes of the other.

Continuing from the visit of Dr Carey to al-Azhar al-Sharif in October 1995 and the visit of Dr Tantawy, the Grand Sheikh of al-Azhar al Sharif, to Lambeth Palace in 1997 and the return visit of Dr Carey to al Azhar al-Sharif in November 1999,

and because of our common faith in God and our responsibility to witness against indifference to religion on the one hand and religious fanaticism on the other, we hope that we may contribute to international efforts to achieve justice, peace and the welfare of all humanity,

resourced by the positive experiences in our long history as Christians and Muslims living together both in Egypt and the United Kingdom and many other parts of the world.

In consequence of this, Dr George Carey, the President of the Anglican Communion, has appointed the following members to the Interfaith Commission:

- The Revd Canon Dr Christopher Lamb
- The Rt Revd Mouneer Hanna Anis,
    Bishop in Egypt with North Africa
- The Rt Revd David Smith,
    Bishop of Bradford, UK

The members of the Permanent Committee of al-Azhar al-Sharif for Dialogue on Monotheistic Religions are:

- Sheikh Fawzy El Zefzaf, President
- Dr Ali El Samman, Vice President
- Ambassador Dr Ahmed Maray
- Dr Mustaffa Al Shukfah
- Sheikh Abu Agour
- Ambassodor Nabil Badre

Representatives of both sides met in al-Azhar on 10 and 11 September 2001 and discussed the proposal for the dialogue between the Anglican Communion and al-Azhar al-Sharif with the hope of achieving the following goals:

- To encourage Anglicans to understand Islam and to encourage Muslims to understand the Christina faith.

- To share together in solving problems and conflicts that happen sometimes between Muslims and Christians in different parts of the world, and to encourage religious leaders to use their influence for the purpose of reconciliation and peace making.

- To work together against injustice and the abuse of human rights among different nationalities and to spread the good teaching of both Islam and Christianity.

- To encourage institutions on both sides to play a positive role in development.

- To achieve these goals the following decisions were taken:

- A Joint Committee will be established from both sides composed of a Chairman and two members from each side already appointed. it may be possible in future to ad new members but each side will inform the other about membership.

- This joint Committee will meet at least once a year in Egypt and the United Kingdom alternately. Each delegation will cover its expenses for travel and accommodation and could meet more than once a year if necessary.

- At the end of each meeting a Press lease will be issued. The text of the communiqué must be agreed by the Joint Committee before publication. No information about papers presented to the Joint Committee will be released outside it without the agreement of both sides.

Signed by:

The Most Revd and Rt Hon Dr George Carey
Archbishop of Canterbury

The Rt Revd Mouneer Hanna Anis
Bishop in Egypt with North Africa

The Revd Canon Dr Christopher Lamb

His Eminence Sheikh Mohamed Sayed Tantawy
Grand Imam of al-Azhar

Sheikh Fawzy El Zefzaf
President, Permanent Committee of al-Azhar for Dialogue with the Monotheistic Religions

Dr Ali El Samman
Vice President, Permanet Committee of al-Azhar for Dialogue with the Monotheistic Religions

APPENDIX 12

MISSION 21

Since 1995 Mission 21 has been the primary mission strategy of the Scottish Episcopal Church. It has proved to be a powerful agent for change in the Church's understanding and practice of mission. In particular, its focus on congregation and community has demanded that ministry and mission are no longer seen as separate entities and the preserve of the few. They are the task of all the baptised.

To give a brief overview, Mission 21 resources congregations as they respond to the invitation to discern God's call to them in the context in which they are set and the ministries they will need to live out that call. Recognising that all mission is worked out contextually, and so what is appropriate for one congregation may not be right for another, Mission 21 seeks to enable a variety of approaches for growth and development, recognising that the congregation is the primary focus for mission.

Mission 21 aims at:

- increasing the spiritual vitality of individual congregations in their context
- numerical growth overall, lived out through training, facilitation, publications and other resources, and undergirded by prayer

Making Your Church More Inviting (MYCMI)

This programme is a foundation phase of Mission 21 and has up to 15 units, depending on the congregation's needs. It looks at the basics of congregational life—size and style of congregations, history, norms, role of volunteers, children's work—and encourages the setting of goals. The following are the title of each session.

Session I	Building the team
Session 2	Changing sizes of congregations
Session 3	The wisdom of newcomers
Session 4	Listening to our newcomers
Session 5	The history that is our journey
Session 6	Norms—discovering the rules by which we live
Session 7	Who is welcome in our congregation?
Session 8	Becoming more inviting to children
Session 9	Inviting friends and family to church
Session 10	The power of an effective visitor follow-up
Session 11	The faith-shape of the congregation
Session 12	Managing and caring for volunteers
Session 13	The overall process of incorporating newcomers
Session 14	Re-structuring for growth
Session 15	Putting it all together

This lays the foundation on which the church can grow and build. It identifies the needs of the individual congregation and using specially devised programmes, workshops, materials etc the church can move into congregational development. The aim is to enable a congregation to look at its life and mission, to build on its strengths and to look to the future. Mission 21 is a continuing programme that is based on the foundation of discovery, goals, development, growth etc, in the life and mission of the church.

Mission 21: from Scotland to Uganda

At the 11th meeting of the Anglican Consultative Council (ACC-11) in Dundee in 1999 the Scottish Episcopal Church presented Mission 21 as their provincial strategy for evangelism. Some of the representatives from other provinces expressed the desire to adopt Mission 21 for their own Province. Financed by the Scottish Episcopal Church and gifts raised by the ACO, a pilot scheme was set up in the Diocese of Kumi, Uganda.

The project began with the Revd Johnson Ebong-Oming, the Provincial Mission Co-ordinator for the Church of Uganda, and Canon John Omagar, Archdeacon of Kumi, visiting some of the parishes in Scotland to see how Mission 21 had changed the life of the church. A team of three people from the Scottish Episcopal Church, the Revd Dean Fostekew, Mission 21 Co-ordinator; Ms Pat McBryde, former Deputy General Secretary; Ms Gill Young, Mission 21 Training Officer together with Marjorie Murphy, Director for Mission and Evangelism, Anglican Communion Office; made a return visit to Uganda to learn more about her people, culture and faith in preparation for the pilot scheme.

Kumi Diocese is the second youngest diocese in the Church of Uganda (3 years old) and is in the Teso region of Uganda, which is amongst the three poorest regions in the country. The Diocese has a number of projects reaching out to those in need, especially among the children of HIV and AIDS victims. Anglicans in Kumi are large in number but their request for Mission 21 is to help them discover new ways of taking the faithful deeper into spirituality and prayer; to enable them to put deep roots down into their faith and then to put their faith into action. They also hope to explore new ways of worshipping that does not rely on the prayer book alone. While they want to maintain both the English and Ateso services they hope to develop more hymns and prayers in their local language and to encourage the wider use of native instruments but as of yet they have only just begun to explore alternatives.

The Training

Twenty-one lay and ordained leaders from the Diocese of Kumi, plus the Diocesan Secretary, Diocesan Treasurer and the Provincial Mission Co-ordinator met for three days at Green Top Hotel and Conference Centre, in Kumi.

The purpose was to introduce to the Mission 21 philosophy, the foundation material of MYCMI (Making Your Church More Inviting) and to train the delegates in basic facilitation and consultancy skills. This would enable them to implement a 'Ugandanised' version of Mission 21 into Kumi Diocese as a pilot project for the Church of Uganda as a whole. The training went well and the participants said that they felt well prepared for the task and that they were able to translate the training/skills to different aspects of their lives as well as to Mission 21. One facilitator, a teacher, said that he was going to train his colleagues before anyone else, as the skills he had gained were very appropriate to his role in the classroom. The translators also said they could see how the training related to the foundation materials and how they paved the way for a greater understanding of MYCMI.

The Translation

The translation team said that they had found the experience of translating MYCMI challenging, not just because of the material and its concepts but in the fact that meeting together had been problematic due to distances to be travelled and work/home commitments.

The following are some of the comments made by the translation team:
- It was very exciting work. I liked the content very much and although some bits were not fully appropriate to Kumi we found discussing the replacements stimulating.
- The translation encouraged great co-operation and working together.
- The MYCMI material helped in the translation, as it reminded them that they were a team and working through the exercises built them as a team.
- The material inspired us. One member is now exploring a vocation to the priesthood because of the experience.
- A big challenge was breaking the Mission 21 sentences into shorter Ateso ones.
- The material is very relevant to us.
- The translators felt that they had gained an insight into the church in Scotland and that Mission 21 will bring a change in Kumi; especially in involving others in ministry and encouraging lay ministry. The section on encouraging and caring for volunteers was important learning.
- It was not a literal translation but a translation that kept the meaning. Not a transliteration which was good.
- This is the first draft and we will revise it as we use it in response to what people say about it.
- Felt that ones own knowledge of English grew as we learned new words.

Implementation

The next step is for the facilitators to identify other facilitators who will in turn train in facilitation skills. The Ateso version of MYCMI will be shared and congregations identified to be the pilots. Within the next month or so the foundation of course of MYCMI will begin to be used in congregations. Some of the congregations have already been identified for the training. Each congregation will work out their own priorities for mission with their own facilitator as they work through the 15 sessions using the material in the most appropriate way. The facilitators, local co-ordinators and translators will continue to meet together in the future

Future Development

Those trained as facilitators will act as co-ordinators in their local areas for Mission 21, identifying individuals to train as facilitators and to prepare congregations for MYCMI. The original facilitators for Mission 21 will continue to meet as a group to chart the progress of Mission 21 in the Diocese of Kumi and will be supported by the regional archdeacons and the diocesan and provincial missioners.

Conclusions

The training week was intense but rewarding. The responses of the facilitators to the MYCMI material and the facilitator training were positive and encouraging and their comments on the relevance of the ethos and materials in relation to Ugandan culture led us to believe that we had 'got it right'. MYCMI and Mission 21 are now in another continent and, God willing, it will spread and develop in appropriate cultural ways.

Adapted from the report of:
The Revd Dean JB Fostekew
Provincial Mission 21 Co-ordinator
Scottish Episcopal Church

Appendix 13

Anglican Communion Publications on Mission

TITLE	COST
Giving Mission its Proper Place *Mission Issues and Strategy Advisory Group (MISAG I) Report 1984*	£2.50
Progress in Partnership *Report of the Mission Agencies Conference Brisbane 1986*	£2.50
Renew our Vision for Mission *Mission Issues and Strategy Advisory Group II Interim Report*	£2.50
Towards Dynamic Mission *Mission Issues and Strategy Advisory Group II (MISAG II*	£2.50

Report 1993)

TITLE	COST

Guidelines and Principles for Mission in the Anglican Communion   £1.50
Includes. Companion Relationship Guidelines, Development,
  Partnerships, Networks Evangelism etc

Partners in Mission: Consultations and Process   £1.00
Guidelines for PIM's

Current Companion Link Relationships List   £1.00
A list of current Companion Relationships around the Communion

The Cutting Edge of Mission   £4.99
The report on The Mid-Point Review of the Decade of Evangelism
  Conference, Kanuga, USA 1995 (G-CODE 2000)

Vision Bearers   £4.99
Conference Stories, lessons and challenges drawn from G-CODE
  (1995)

Anglican in Mission: A Transforming Journey   £8.00
The report of the Anglican Communion Mission Commission
  1999 (MISSIO)
A practical handbook for mission and evangelism (1999)

Encounters on the Road Books I and II   £3.00
Report of the Provincial Mission and Evangelism Co-ordinators
  (2002) including Bible studies and worship book

Travelling Together in God's Mission   £2.50
The interim report of the Inter Anglican Standing Commission
  on Mission and Evangelism (IASCOME) 2002

Communion in Mission
The full report of the Inter Anglican Standing Commission
  on Mission and Evangelism (IASCOME) 2005

Available from:
Angican Communion Office, St Andrew's House, 16 Tavistock Crescent,
London W11 1AP, UK

Notes

1 For a details of this history, see Appendix 1, *The Journey So Far.*
2 *Travelling Together in God's Mission.* Interim Report to ACC-12. Inter Anglican Standing Commission on Mission and Evangelism. 2002.
3 The Windsor Report 2004. London: Anglican Communion Office, 2004,

pp. 62–64.

4 To proclaim the good news of the Kingdom of God; To teach, baptise and nurture new believers; To respond to human need by loving service; To seek to transform unjust structures of society; To strive to safeguard the integrity of creation and sustain and renew the life of the earth.

5 Relatório Windsor.

6 Proclamar as Boas Novas do Reino de Deus; ensinar, batizar e nutrir os crentes; atender às necessidades humanas no serviço de amor; transformar as estruturas injustas da sociedade; salvaguardar a integridade da criação e sustentar e renovar a vida sobre a terra.

7 Windsor Report pp. 62-64.

8 Kutangaza habari vyema ya ufalme wa Mungu; kufunza, kubatiza na kulea waamini wapya; kutumika katika mahitaji ya kibinadamu, kutafuta kubadilisha hali zisizo haki katika jamii , kufanya bidii kulinda vyote alivyoviumba Mungu na kustawisha na kuboresha maisha ya dunia.

9 Stephen Neill's classic, *Anglicanism* (London: Mowbray, 1977. 4th ed.), offers an account of this development in chapters 12 and 13.

10 For an extraordinary meditation on this theme see W. H. Vanstone: *The Stature of Waiting* (London: Darton, Longman & Todd, 1982).

11 Christopher Duraisingh reminded participants of this during the opening presentation of the 2003 Anglican Mission Organisation Conference held in Cyprus.

12 That introductions to Anglicanism often miss out the role of mission relationships in the formation of the Communion needs to be corrected. But see T. E. Yates *"Anglicans and Mission"* for one of the few introductory surveys, in S. Sykes, J. Booty & J. Knight (eds): *The Study of Anglicanism* (London: SPCK, 1998 2nd ed.). See also the recommendations in chapter six about incorporating a mission focus and dimension to educational materials on The Anglican Way as proposed by the Theological Education for the Anglican Communion working group.

13 This musical image was recently used by Bishop Tom Wright and the Archbishop of Canterbury when the Windsor Report was debated in the General Synod of the Church of England (Feb. 2005). For a stimulating 'stop-press' article reflecting on the Instruments see A. Goddard: *"Walking Together? The Future of the Anglican Communion"* in ANVIL (Vol 22 No 1. 2005, pp. 81–88).

14 MRI was proposed at the Anglican Congress of 1963 as a way of expressing the growing equality of relationships between the churches in the Communion. For reflections on MRI in the context of mission developments in the Communion see Anglican Congress (Anglican Book Centre, Canada 1963 pp. 117) in this report.

15 See D. Doyle: *Communion Ecclesiology* (Maryknoll: Orbis, 2000) for a review of developments. See also N. Sagovsky: *Ecumenism, Christian Origins and the Practice of Communion* (Cambridge: CUP, 2000), chapters one and two, for a discussion about communion as 'koinonia' and some of the joys and struggles of the practice of 'koinonia' in the Anglican Communion. For recent work on "communion" by an Anglican Commission see the *Six Propositions on Anglicans and Communion* from the Inter-Anglican Theological and Doctrinal Commission:

www.anglicancommunion.org.uk.

16 N. M. Healy: *Church, World and the Christian Life: Practical-Prophetic Ecclesiology* (Cambridge: CUP, 2000) p. 45. Healy reviews the use of the concept of communion by six theologians each coming from different traditions: Roman Catholic, Orthodox, Liberationist, Feminist, Liberal and Free Church.

17 It should be noted that this Report does not deal in any depth with relationships between Christians and those of other faiths. Any understanding of communion in mission would need to include an understanding of relating to those of another faith. Exploration of this issue needs to be taken to another level by appropriate inter-Anglican discussions and initiatives, bearing in mind colonial, postcolonial and neo-colonial sensitivities, whilst not succumbing to the rhetoric of either the clash within or between cultures. See M. Barnes: *Religions in Conversation* (London: SPCK, 1989) for one approach to this question.

18 Two key texts that expressed and helped propagate the partnership paradigm were S. Neill: *Christian Partnership* (London: SCM, 1952) and M. Warren: *Partnership: The Study of an Idea* (London: SCM 1956).

19 E. Johnson and J. Clark: *Anglicans in Mission: A Transforming Journey* (London: SPCK, 2000), p. 80. One way in which partnership has been positively reframed in order to describe mission relationships has been in the emerging new approach of business as mission; another positive reframing has been provided by new interdenominational groupings of organisations and churches.

20 For some thoughts about going beyond partnership see Colin Marsh: "Partnership in Mission: To Send or to Share?" in the *International Review of Mission* vol. xcii No 366, July 2003, pp. 370–381.

21 J. Loder: *The Transforming Moment* (Colorado Springs: Helmers & Howard, 1989 2nd ed.), chap. 4.

22 J. Kapolyo: *The Human Condition: Christian Perspectives Through African Eyes* (Leicester: IVP 2005) p. 130. Kapolyo does also recognise some tension between family and church, see p. 142.

23 During the Middle Ages in Europe friendship was rehabilitated as a way of describing the relationship with God. Human friendship, as a way of knowing God's love, was also newly emphasised. For a detailed survey see Elizabeth Carmichael: *Friendship: Interpreting Christian Love* (London: T&T Clark 2004).

24 See Brian Stanley: *The Bible and the Flag: Protestant missions and British Imperialism in the Nineteenth and Twentieth Centuries* (Leicester: IVP, 1990) for a study which broke new ground on this issue.

25 Interview for *The Christianity Century* August 2000.

26 Walls, Andrew: *The Cross-Cultural Process in Human History* (Edinburgh: T&T Clark, 2002, p. 78)

27 With the break up of Christendom the possibility of discovering the Jesus of other cultures emerged. See W. Dyrness: *Emerging Voices in Global Christian Theology* (Grand Rapids: Zondervan, 1993). For an exploration of new and inter-cultural/contextual understandings of Jesus see V. Kuster: *The Many Faces of Jesus Christ* (London: SCM, 2001), P. Pope-Levison & J. R. Levison: *Jesus in Global Contexts* (Louisville: Westminster, 1992) and A. Wessels: *Images of Jesus: How*

Jesus is Perceived and Portrayed in Non-European Cultures (London: SCM, 1990). For the challenge now facing Northern Christianity see C. Greene: *Christology in Cultural Perspective* (Carlisle: Paternoster, 2003).

28 For example, see how this approach is used in an ecumenical way in a British context by the Building Bridges of Hope learning process sponsored by the Churches Together in Britain and Ireland. The seven values used in the learning process are as follows: focusing vision; building local partnerships; sharing faith and values; nourishing daily living; developing shared leadership; becoming communities of learning; being accompanied. See http://www.ctbi.org.uk/bbh/old.htm.

29 See S. Escobar: "The Global Scenario at the Turn of the Century" in W. D. Taylor: *Global Missiology for the 21st Century* (Grand Rapids: Baker, 2000) pp. 25–47 for a summary of changes and challenges. See also S. Escobar: *A Time for Mission* (Leicester: IVP, 2003) for a more extensive but accessible exploration.

30 For example, see (in date order) the work of Lamin Sanneh: *Translating the Message: The Missionary Impact on Culture* (Maryknoll, New York: Orbis, 1993); I. T. Douglas & K. Pui-Lan: *Beyond Colonial Anglicanism: The Anglican Communion in the Twenty-First Century* (New York: Church Publishing, 2001); R. S. Sugirtharajah: *The Bible and the Third World: Precolonial, Colonial and Postcolonial Encounters* (Cambridge: CUP, 2001); R. S. Sugirtharajah: *Postcolonial Criticism and Biblical Interpretation* (Oxford: OUP, 2002) Andrew Porter (ed): *The Imperial Horizons of British Protestant Missions, 1880–1914* (Cambridge UK/Grand Rapids, Michigan: Eerdmans, 2003); Brian Stanley (ed): *Missions, Nationalism, and the End of Empire* (Cambridge UK/Grand Rapids, Michigan: Eerdmans, 2003 Cambridge UK/Grand Rapids, Michigan: Eerdmans, 2003); and Andrew Porter: *Religion versus Empire?* (Manchester: Manchester University Press, 2004).

31 See, for example, Joerg Rierger: *"Theology and Mission between Neocolonialism and Postcolonialism"* (Mission Studies 21.2, 2005), pp. 201–227.

32 The 50th Anniversary of Ghana's independence from Britain (2007) is being used to educate people about past slavery and raise awareness about contemporary forms of slavery.

33 *The Windsor Report 2004* (Anglican Communion Office: London, 2004) p. 21.

34 Surveys and assessments of the Partners in Mission process and of the Decade of Evangelism can be found in *Towards Dynamic Mission* (London: Anglican Communion Office, 1992) pp. 21–29 and in E. Johnson and J. Clark (ed.) *Anglicans in Mission: A Transforming Journey* (London: SPCK, 2000) pp. 63–67.

35 'Official networks' are those which have gained formal recognition by the Anglican Consultative Council.

36 See Appendix 2 for more details.

37 *Mission-shaped Church* (London; Church House Publishing, 2004), p. 7.

38 Migration movements and the discovery of God form a major theme in the Bible including Adam and Eve's migration from the garden of Eden; Abraham's journey from Ur to Canaan; Joseph to Egypt; the Hebrew people out of Egypt et al.

39 This represented the re-discovery of the role of missionary bishops first contributed to the Communion by the Episcopal Church in the USA (ECUSA) in the

first half of the nineteenth century. See Timothy Yates," The Idea of a 'Missionary Bishop' in the Spread of the Anglican Communion in the Nineteenth Century," Journal of Anglican Studies Vol. 2. No. 1 (June 2004): 53–54.

40 The first such chaplain was sent by the Bishop of London to St Petersburg with the Muscovy Company in the reign of Elizabeth I (1558–1603).

41 See Appendix 12.

42 See Appendix 3 for more details on the Global Anglicanism Project.

43 For a longer discussion of co-ordinating structures and examples in practice see *Anglicans in Mission: A Transforming Journey* pp. 61–62 and p. 78.

44 Refer to Chapter 4 and Appendix 5 for details.

45 For the Ten Principles of Partnership see *Towards Dynamic Mission* (pp. 25–28).

46 See Chapter 7 for more details.

47 See Appendix 1 for full details.

48 See Appendix 7 for more details.

49 Study document *"Mission and Evangelism in Unity Today"*, adopted by the CWME in Morges, Switzerland, 2000, p. 2.

50 *"Mission in a Broken World"*. Report of ACC-8, Wales.

51 Fung, Raymond, *Evangelism in the Anglican Communion: An Ecumenical Perspective*. In *The Cutting Edge of Mission*: A Report of the Mid-Point Review of the Decade of Evangelism, Cyril C Okorocha, ed. 1996, pp 145–152.

52 See Chapter 8 for the full story, Out of the Fire.

53 See Chapter 8 for the full story, Church Planting in Egypt.

54 See Chapter 8 for the full story, Congregational Building.

55 See Chapter 8 for the full story, The Cost of Mission in the Church of Melanesia.

56 Full reports of these conferences are available from the Anglican Communion Office.

57 See Appendix 4.

58 See Appendix 6.

59 See Appendix 5.

60 See Appendix 6.

61 *"Guidelines and Principles for Mission and Evangelism in the Anglican Communion"* available from the ACO.

62 See Chapter 8 for the full story, Helping Them Live Again.

63 Eluzai, Joy Kwaje. "Religious Structures and the Role of Women in Peace Making: Hope For the Oppressed and Marginalised". Paper delivered at the International Conference on Tools For Peace: The role of Religion in Conflicts. Sweden, November 2004, p. 5. Used with permission.

64 See Chapter 8 for the full story, The Anglican Church of Canada's Continuing Struggle with its Colonial History.

65 'Our Vision, Our Hope: The First Step: All Africa Anglican AIDS Planning Framework,' Anglican Communion News Service #2601, 22 August 2001, http://anglicancommunion.org/acns/acnsarchive/acns2600/acns2601.html.

66 CAPA Report Nairobi.

67 See Bosch, David J. Theological education in missionary perspective. *Missi-*

ology X/1 (January 1982), 13–34.

68 Farley, E. *Theologia: The Fragmentation and Unity of Theological Education*. 1983. (Philadelphia, Fortress Press)

69 See Chapter One for the IASCOME mandate.

70 See *Anglicans in Mission: A Transforming Journey,* Chapter 5, *Training Leadership for Mission.*

71 See the report of ACC-12, Resolution 12, p. 465.

72 Paragraph 21 of the *Primates' Communiqué* of February, 2005 states: "Two whole sessions of our meeting were devoted to the important work of the discernment of theological truth and the development and improvement of theological education through the sharing of resources across the Communion. The Archbishop of Canterbury has identified this as a priority concern during the period of his leadership."

73 Emile Brunner, citation will be found in bibliography of D Bosch, *Transforming Mission.*

74 *Primates' Communiqué,* February 2005, paragraph 22.

75 MISSIO, *Anglicans in Mission: a Transforming Journey,* London, SPCK: 2000.

76 See Appendix 2.

77 McCoy, Michael. Restoring mission to the heart of theological education: A South African perspective, p. 4. Unpublished paper provided to IASCOME Cyprus meeting, 2005. Used with permission.

78 Ibid., pp. 2–4.

79 The recently published vision statement *Companions in transformation: the Episcopal church's world mission in a new century,* presented by the Standing Commission on World Mission to the 2003 General Convention of ECUSA, proposes an increase in support for such cross-cultural mission internships and experiences.

80 'Our Vision, Our Hope: The First Step: All Africa Anglican AIDS Planning Framework,' Anglican Communion News Service #2601, 22 August, 2001, http://anglicancommunion.org/acns/acnsarchive/acns2600/acns2601.html.

81 See Appendix 4.

82 Clark, John Johnson, Ellie (ed) *Anglicans in Mission: A Transforming Journey* London, SPCK, 1999, pp. 66–67.

83 See Appendix 11.

84 See Appendix 10.

85 *The Time is Now* (report of the first meeting of the ACC: Limuru, Kenya 1971)

86 *Giving Mission Its Proper Place* (report of MISAG I) (London: ACC, 1984, p. 5.

87 *Progress in Partnership* (Report of the Mission Agencies Conference), London: ACC, 1987), pp. 5–6.

88 The Place of Scripture in the Life and Mission of the Church in the 21st Century.

89 Clark, John; Johnson, Ellie, (ed) *Anglicans in Mission—A Transforming Journey* (London: SPCK, 1999).

90 MISSIO, The Mission Commission of the Anglican Communion, *Anglicans in Mission: A Transforming Journey* (London: SPCK, 2000), 118–120.

Department of Telecommunications

The Revd Clement W.K. Lee

The work of the Anglican Communion Instruments of Unity is significantly impacted by the way telecommunications is used across the Church by leaders, congregation members and also by many others in society. The Anglican Consultative Council, through *ad hoc* telecommunication projects, has for many years provided both the capability to begin using online communication to facilitate the work of the Instruments of Unity and also to demonstrate at meetings and international consultations of Anglican bishops and other leaders how telecommunications can enhance the work of ministry across geographic and church structure boundaries.

The ACC has endorsed and embraced the value of telecommunications for ministry and has been grateful for the unique telecoms funding support of the Parish of Trinity Church, New York City, has generously offered for almost 20 years. But at the same time it must be pointed out that the ACC has not yet found it possible to include even a modest amount for telecommunications costs in its core budget. Fortunately, Trinity Grants awards to the ACC have been substantial enough that professional consultation and online publishing efforts have made a good and well received beginning. Here are some highlights:

- An official Anglican Web Portal was launched at ACC-2. It is a "website of websites", combining and increasing the web pages of the Anglican Communion Office ministry departments and ministry networks with several new sections that presently include websites produced with and on behalf of Anglican Provinces and Dioceses, especially in parts of the global south, so they can share their news, information and educational resources, with the rest of the Anglican Communion.

- The ACO Communications Department has benefited from the new telecommunications infrastructure (which uses state of the art web server technology and hosting that enables, among other innovations, database driven page preparation and delivery) and has been able to use its own communications departmental staff to professionally program and maintain a website section for Anglican Communion News Service, a site for the Anglican Cycle of Prayer, and a site being developed to present current Anglican statistical data. And it developed a web section for Windsor Report related information.

- The Telecoms Department provides public and private email services for either the distribution of information or for officially related discussion groups. Anglican Communion News Service uses such an email "listserv" to distribute its news around the world and as of this month more than 8,000 individuals receive their ACNS stories this way. The ACNS listserv refers readers to the ACNS website to see news photos. The Anglican "Francophone" network and the Anglican Communion Environmental Network are examples of private email discussion groups, which serve participants from many parts of the world.

- Trinity Funding has made it possible for the ACC to establish an Inter-Anglican Commission on Telecommunications Ministry. An initial meeting was held at Canterbury Cathedral in 2003. It is expected that its work will be done using telecommunications, meaning that periodic in-person meetings of the commission will be opportunities for planning and review but the major part of its work will be done using online services, including telephone, fax, email, web enabled conferences, etc. This work will resume as the new Secretary General further shapes the work of his administration.

- The Telecoms Commission encouraged the development of "primary source news release pages" (official releases written and distributed, without external editing) by Anglican Provinces, after receiving a report from John Allen, a professional church journalist, who described the way the portal planned to work with provincial offices to enable their own posting of news. Also, those provinces which already are or will be publishing their own news web sites have links on the portal to their own pages of news releases. This official news releases section of the portal began operation earlier this year under Mr Allen's management. The primary source releases include those that are published in French, Portuguese, Chinese and Spanish, as well as English.

- TEAC, Theological Education in the Anglican Communion, an initiative of the Archbishop of Canterbury, with staff at the Anglican Communion Office, is using telecoms to broaden its survey of theological education and for sharing the results of its research. The TEAC website has begun the development of an annotated bibliography of theology publications.

The Telecommunications Department operates, because of limited funding, only with a part-time Director of Telecommunications who manages the work of freelance web development and graphics professionals who are geographically disbursed across the Communion. The director administers the work of contracted telecoms vendors and Internet service providers and also serves as the staff liaison with the Telecoms Commission.

While the telecoms work has consistently been seen as immensely useful to the life and work of the Anglican Communion and its Instruments of Unity, a serious review both of its current offerings, not to mention the potential for enhanced use of these tools for ministry, shows that funding and staffing need to be stabilized and not dependent, as now, solely on non-budgetary funding. The volume of material departments want published, the increased need for inter-communication among leaders, and the growing expectations of Anglicans who want reliable and accurate information and ready access to resources are clear evidence of legitimate demand for an integral and permanent ACC telecoms operation.

Already at Lambeth 1988, bishops sensed the growing importance of online communication and resolved that the Anglican Consultative Council should begin development of an Inter-Anglican "network". Simultaneously, military, academic and industry specialists were speeding development of what has become known variously as the Internet, worldwide web, email, digital media, e-commerce, public and private networks. Collectively these communication methodologies are referred to as telecommunications.

I look forward to a comprehensive exploration with the Secretary General and the Telecoms Commission of ACC telecommunications ministry potential, as well as a thorough review of telecoms work to date and its working relationships with the communications, public media, interpretation and educational work of the ACC and the ACO. Current tensions are another prompting that the Anglican Communion requires the best possible cooperative and coordinated telecoms and communications efforts, both at the ACO and across the Communion. And that wider usage can be modelled and facilitated by the ACC as one of the significant ways that it serves as an "instrument" of unity.

The telecoms department is pleased to acknowledge the work of the following colleagues: The Revd Canon James G Callaway Jr, Trinity Church, NYC; the Very Revd Oge Beauvoir, Trinity Church, NYC; the Revd Dr Philip Sallis, chairperson of the Telecoms Commission; the Revd Canon

Richard Marsh, Canterbury Cathedral International Study Centre; Michael Ade, ACO database manager and communications staff member; John Allen, Anglican News Releases website manager; Joey Fan, telecoms associate, chief operating officer, Internad Ltd.; the Revd John Rollins, telecoms associate, JARdigitalworks; and the Revd Michael Graham, telecoms assistant and Telecoms commissioner.

The Anglican Consultative Council United Nations Office (ACCUNO)

Nottingham University, 25 June 2005

The presentation of the report by the Anglican Observer to the United Nations, included testimonies, singing and participation of ACC members, especially those involved with the global gatherings of women from around the Communion, that are held in New York.

PART I

1. GREETINGS & PREAMBLE:

1.1. Talofa lava. I greet you all in the mighty Name of Jesus Christ, He who loved his mother most profoundly and, who greatly respected as well as acknowledged the ministry of women during His time on Earth. I bring you also the greetings of the Ecumenical Working Group at the United Nations, members of the Advisory Council of ACCUN Office under the Chairmanship of The Rev Canon Don Brown, the members of the ACCUN Office committee in Europe and, of course the Staff of your office, namely The Rev Canon Douglas Renegar (Volunteer Executive Director), Br. William F. Jones, the full time Secretary and Office Assistant and, The Rev Canon Dr. Jeff Golliher, the Programme Associate for Environment and Sustainable Development (a Parish priest working for us on a part-time basis).

1.2. It is again a great privilege to address this august gathering of honourable members of the Anglican Consultative Council (ACC) as well as the members of the Primates Standing Committee. Thank you for this opportunity to express to you my sincere gratitude to the ACC for its support of your office at the United Nations, especially the President for his guidance and personal interventions on many occasions on International/ Foreign policies especially those impacting the work of the United Nations; the Chairman, whose advice, support and friendship had always been a tower of strength for my ministry; and of course some of you my brothers and sisters (you know who you are) who offered advice and useful information to assist ACCUN Office to make appropriate interventions and especially for giving us those useful contacts both at UN, the Government missions, as well as other Non Government Organizations (NGOs) and Civil Society Organizations (CSOs).

1.3. I also owe a lot as well to my colleagues and friends at the Anglican

Communion Office (ACO) at St. Andrew's House—thank you for your support in our combined services for the common good of our Communion. I have not interacted as much as I wanted to with The Rev Canon Kenneth Kearon. The two occasions of being with you Ken were very useful opportunities to learn about your rich theological and academic background and to share your initial thoughts about your plans for the future. I am confident that you are a blessing to the Anglican Communion 'for such a time as now.' I am looking forward to continuing to work with you in the remaining 11 months of my tenure of office as the Anglican Observer at the United Nation.

1.4. Please allow me this opportunity to also pay a special tribute to the former Secretary General, Revd Canon John Peterson, from whom I received the greatest support for more than 3 years. Right from day one of my assignment, Canon Peterson made sure that I had settled in well in New York, got people in the USA to support my ministry and was very sympathetic towards my personal needs during a lonely period of my assignment so far away from home and familiar surroundings. I wish to thank him also for the financial support he vigilantly sought for the costs of the office which has over the years been operating on a "hand to mouth" basis. Again it was through John and for John that people willingly assisted to fundraise for the office. John as he reported at ACC12 greatly assisted me in establishing a committee of retired Anglican Volunteers in Geneva to support the ministry of the office. I will forever be indebted to John for many things and especially his valuable advice on how to handle the politics in the Church, the United Nations and especially the people of the USA, including the US government. I did not have the courage to say goodbye to John before he left the position of Secretary General, but found solace in the knowledge that since he is a new member of the Advisory Council for ACCUN Office I still have time to apologise to him for that and for not sharing some important personal news with him.

1.5. Since ACC12 in 2002, I have reported annually to the Joint Standing Committee of the Primates and ACC. Nevertheless, we wish to capture those details and more for your information and for the report of ACC13 since this is the very last time that I get to address you as your Anglican Observer at the United Nations. Furthermore, this report is presented to you in two parts. The second part will concentrate on the United Nations Commission on the Status of Women (UNCSW) for which specific mention is made in the programme.

2. HISTORY AND FOCUS OF ACCUN OFFICE WORK:

2.1. As you may be aware this office was established in the late 1980s and was accredited to the United Nations as a partner in 4 specific areas. These areas of focus were for Development; Disarmament; Freedom of Faith and Religion; and, Environment. Over the years these were further broken down to cover many areas of the United Nations work and since 2001, to focus on the UN Millennium Development Goals (MDGs).

2.2. The ministry of the Anglican Observer is to knock at the doors of the United Nations and of government missions regarding the concerns of the Anglican Communion. Essentially this requires working together in partnership with appropriate Non Government Organizations (NGOs), Civil Society Organizations (CSOs) and UN agencies. On the other hand the office needs to keep the Communion informed about United Nations initiatives and how they could benefit from the UN Resources, or on how they could be effective partners to UN programmes.

2.3. During the tenure of the first Anglican Observer, the focus of the office was on Human Rights, the Environment and the Rights of Indigenous People. The Second Observer concentrated on Human Rights, Environment and Women and in addition worked on Land Mines as well as International Debt. The interim Observers also continued some of this work on a part time basis.

2.4. A month after my appointment and 6 months before I took over the position, the former Archbishop of Canterbury and Lady Eileen Carey, passionately recommended to me that I should focus my attention on the needs of Women and Children. They had witnessed their plights and vulnerability during their travels, especially to Africa, Asia and the Middle East. That request stayed with me as a woman and as a mother of 11 children and 21 grandchildren. (I inherited two more children when I got married again in November last year and my wonderful companion and husband Afioga Mata'utia Pau Elesio (Sio) Leota took special leave from his work in New Zealand to accompany me to ACC13).

2.5. During my tenure of office and due to limited resources (financial & personnel), the office chose to concentrate on six main areas of focus for its work. They were carefully chosen in response to:

    2.5.1 the areas for which the office was originally established and received accreditation to the United Nations;

    2.5.2 the last 3 points of the ACC Mission Statement. That is: to respond to people's needs through loving services; to break down unjust structures to maintain peace and justice; and, to safeguard the integrity of God's creation and to sustain and renew the earth; and,

2.5.3 to continue the remarkable work established by highly esteemed predecessors.

2.6. The six areas as fully described in our ACCUN Office flyer are:

2.6.1. Women—to make sure that the policies of the UN governments do include a strong gender perspective;

2.62. Children—as an integral part of the Christian Family and the United Nations Decade for a Culture of Peace and non-violence for children (2001 to 2010);

2.63. Sustainable Communities (Development), especially on environment issues (but also trade, poverty and international debt). We are committed to educating and organizing leaders to advocate for sustainable values as this critical debate continues at the Untied Nations;

2.64. Human Rights—a cross-thematic area to ensure all policies adhere to the Universal Declaration of Human Rights for the protection of the dignity of the rights of every individual in the world;

2.65. The Rights of Indigenous People and Issues especially those who are living as minorities in their own countries of origin; and;

2.66. Economic & Social Security with a special focus on Countries under Conflicts.

2.7. A coalition of NGOs has a stronger voice at the UN. ACCUN Office therefore works very closely and maintains close cooperative relationships with many NGOs and CSOs at the United Nations, both informally and through active participation in NGO Working Groups some of which include the following:

2.7.1. the Working Group on Israel and Palestine;

2.7.2. the Working Group on Iraq;

2.7.3. the NGO Human Rights Committee;

2.7.4. the Committee for the Commission on Sustainable Development;

2.7.5. the NGO support Group for the UN Development Fund for Women (UNIFEM);

2.7.6. the NGO Committee for the Status of Women;

2.7.7. the NGO Board on Disarmament, Peace and Security;

2.7.8. the United Nations Ecumenical Working Group;

2.7.9. the Working Group on the International Year of the Family;

2.7.10. the NGO Committee on the Decade for Indigenous Peoples;

2.7.11. the Subcommittee on Older Women; and,

2.7.12. the NGO Working Group on HIV and AIDS (the Observer is an Executive Member).

The Observer as a Life member of the UN Association of Former International Civil Servants (AFICS) works closely with members and their personal contacts on issues pertaining to the 6 areas of focus for ACCUN Office.

3. ACTIVITIES UNDER THE AREAS OF FOCUS

3.1. Environment and Sustainable Communities (Development):
(ACC Mission Statement (5)—Committing Anglicans *"to safeguard the integrity of God's creation and to sustain and renew the earth."*) We firmly believe that all initiatives for the common good of all should be sustainable otherwise it is not "development," and thus we preferred to work towards Sustainable Communities, taking into account the personal values of the peoples in the communities.

3.1.1. There was much to be done following the Global Anglican Congress on the Stewardship of Creation and the UN World Summit on Sustainable Development (WSSD) in August 2002. The UN Commission on Sustainable Development (that we work very closely with) was charged with immediate follow-up on the urgent issues for **WEHAB**—Water and Sanitation, Energy, Health, Agriculture, and Biodiversity (and Environment), the main thrust of the World Summit.

3.1.2. A lot of time was devoted throughout 2003 and the first 6 months of 2004 to finalize the proceedings of the Global Anglican Congress on the Stewardship of Creation. I am glad to note that some of the provinces including the USA have adopted resolutions supporting the Millennium Development Goals (MDGs) and have made determined efforts to implement appropriate undertakings in response to the Congress statements adopted by ACC12. There is still a lot more that requires the attention of every Anglican.

3.1.3. I'm very glad to report on the publication of our book entitled "Healing God's Creation," which was one outcome of the Global Anglican Congress on the Stewardship of Creation in 2002. In many, very real ways, this book represents the work and concerns of the whole Communion about our love of God and God's magnificent creation, which has been put at great risk. As Anglicans, as Christians, as human beings made in God's image, we know we must take action now to reverse the present destructive course. The Global Anglican Congress was a step in the right direction. The very first book published by the office aimed to make this work more widely known to many people including all of you, and together we can be witnesses to God's call to stewardship, to faith and justice, to building sustainable communities, and to the love which makes us one people. You will be glad to share our pride in having in our book the excellent presentation (The Beauty of Empowerment) by Dr. Wangari Maathai, who last year won the Nobel Peace Prize for her work on Environmental matters. I should also say that "Healing God's Creation" has received very favorable reviews, and its sale has even brought in some needed funds for the Office. Furthermore, it has been well recognized by many Anglicans and Episcopalians that the book is a very good resource for Christian teaching. I recommend this book to you all as a wonderful resource for your ministry in compliance with the Fifth Mark of the ACC Mission Statement. It is available from Morehouse at the cost of only US$16.

3.1.4. ACCUN Office work on the Congress represented an expansion in the previous goals of the Office of the Anglican Observer. We wanted to have a positive impact in two ways: The first of our goals is to have an impact on the deliberations at the United Nations, by working with the diplomats and ambassadors of member States and NGOs who are represented there. In other words, we wanted to bring our voice to them. Second, we want to bring the resources, insights, and work of the UN to the Anglican Communion, particularly with regard to the deepening environment and development crisis.

3.1.5. The Congress was a first step in that direction and our follow up activities have been undertaken to strengthen these efforts. Specifically, our Program Associate for the Environment and Sustainable Development, Rev Canon Jeff Golliher, PhD., has been working with the Convener of the Anglican Environmental Network (ACEN), which had its first official meeting recently in Canberra, and he will continue to support the work of the network. ACCUN Office was entrusted by the former Secretary General with making the appropriate arrangements for the meeting of ACEN and to make sure that an appropriate structure was established for the Network for its work. We are glad to report that this was successfully achieved.

3.1.6. We are also developing new educational materials in the area of the environment and sustainable development for the Provinces. These materials will include a series called "Study Papers on the Environment, Poverty, and Sustainable Development." We are giving you a gift of two (2) examples of Study Papers Numbers One and Two. These are:

3.1.6.1. "The Web of Life, The Body of Christ: Our Shared Life and Moral Responsibility"

3.1.6.2. "The Water of Baptism, the Water of Life."

3.1.7. To make our ministry more effective, we also need to take our relationship with the Provinces a step farther than it already is. We need your assistance in identifying official liaison/focal persons within your Province so that communications pertaining to these issues at the United Nations can be channeled directly to us. Many of the ongoing projects and opportunities for involvement from the churches relate to several of our Anglican Networks. Although we have linkages with all the Networks, more direct communication with the Provinces in these matters would make our overall ministry at the UN Office run more smoothly and effective and efficient.

3.1.8. In the last three years—since the meeting of the 2002 Global Anglican Congress in Johannesburg which was the same year and the same location of the UN Summit on Sustainable Development—the UN's Commission on Sustainable Development (CSD) has given a great deal of attention to the Millennium Development Goals (MDGs). As mentioned before, this has been particularly true in the areas of water and sanitation (for WEHAB). Our work at the Anglican Observer's Office has also focused on these goals, and it will continue to do so into the foreseeable future. The MDGs of eight principal areas are: (1) eradicate extreme poverty and hunger; (2) achieve universal primary education; (3) promote gender equality and empower women; (4) reduce child mortality; (5) improve maternal health; (6) combat HIV/AIDS, malaria and other diseases; (7) ensure environmental sustainability; and, (8) develop a global partnership for development. These are fully described in our other special gift to each of you in the form of a UN pocket size flyer.

3.1.9. It is hoped that by 2015, all 191 Member States of the United Nations will have joined together to meet these goals; however, we are way behind where we need to be. One specific goal is to reduce by half the proportion of people without sustainable access to safe drinking water. Already, drought conditions associated with climate change are making the accomplishment seem remote. Our Office works with the UN's Commission on Sustainable Development on these issues, as well as with our ecumenical brothers and sisters in the NGO community. Yes, as I have already stated in this report, it is absolutely necessary that we work more closely together as brothers and sisters in the global Anglican Communion.

3.2. Human Rights:
*All human beings are born with equal and inalienable rights and fundamental freedoms (the UN booklet on the Universal Declaration on Human Rights—is another gift to you ACC sisters and brothers. **Learn about your Rights**).*

3.2.1. Our church calls us to "respect the dignity of every human being". The teachings of Jesus tell us to love our neighbour. This certainly falls under the category of "Human Rights", a very important focus of the ACCUN Office. The Office of the High Commissioner for Human Rights is based in Geneva, Switzerland therefore much of our human rights ministry is undertaken by our Geneva based ACCUN Office Committee of devoted volunteer Anglicans. Most of the United Nations Agencies, the World Trade Organization and the World Council of Churches (WCC) have their headquarters in such cities as Geneva, Vienna, Paris and Rome. The ACCUN Office Committee also participates with the Chair of the Conference of Non Government Organizations (CONGO) in pursuing human rights issues during the meetings of the Human Rights Commission. I wish to record here my sincere and special thanks to Mr. Trevor Davies and

Revd Michael French for the wonderful work they do in representing ACCUN Office in Europe along with many other volunteers.

3.2.2. The Human Rights Commission meets annually and the 61st Human Rights Commission was held there in March and April of this year. The Geneva office represented us very well in attending many of these meetings. They are also setting up networks of Anglicans that can be used in the future as we continue to expand the important ministry of human rights.

3.2.3. Whilst ACC (through ACCUN Office) is a member of the NGO Committee on Human Rights, much of the work in this area was approached through the plight of Women (including the aged and those with disabilities) and Children. In fact Human Rights issues on Gender and those concerning Children were annually dealt with in the Third Committee of the General Assembly, where interactions with government delegates were made. Government representatives gave accounts of their own domestic achievements and obstacles in pursuing the Universal Declaration on Human Rights. Last year, Robert Picken, a retired professor and parishioner of St. Mary's the Virgin at Time Square in New York City, assisted us in covering the issues at the Third Committee sessions.

3.2.4. It can be truly said that almost everything we do in our New York office and through our Geneva based committee of volunteers deals with human rights. We would all agree with the opening statement in the UN Preamble on Human Rights established over 50 years ago: "Whereas recognition of the inherent dignity and of the equal and inalienable rights of all members of the human family is the foundation of freedom, justice and peace in the world". There could be no doubt that our Lord himself would say "Amen".

3.3. Economic & Social Security with special focus on Countries under Conflicts:

3.3.1. Since 2002, the ACCUN Office hosted the meetings of the NGO Working Groups on Security Issues especially those concerning the Israel/Palestine issues and Iraq. This promoted not only the visibility of the office but also the need for worshipping together and lighting prayer candles with our partners for Peace in the World. Prayer vigils periodically held at the Chapel were well attended by many people of different faiths. Unfortunately, we could not continue with these arrangements in 2005 due to the present reconstructions of the Episcopal Church Centre.

3.3.2. Your ACCUN Office is very much concerned with Economic and Social Security. This comes from good stewardship, sustainable development, generous sharing and security from conflict. One of the critical areas of our current world status is the area of world disarmament and conflict resolution. The scriptural promise is that as the peoples of the world we can turn our spears into pruning hooks and our swords into plowshares. The ACCUN Office has been active in the Gospel imperative of being a peacemaker. During the past years we have taken an active part in the following actions:

3.3.3. As a commitment to the ACC Resolutions and Anglican Communion's concerns, the ACCUN Office joined and became a member of the Israel/Palestine working group during the fall of 2001. This Working Group meets monthly and sometimes with other NGOs and Faith bodies to focus on the injustice in this part of the world. The group brings in speakers, promotes news items and advocates with a united voice to help bring an end to this tragic situation. Because of its work over the past two years, the Working Group earned great credibility with the UN Department of Political Affairs (UNDPA), which has depended on the group for programmes concerning the Rights of the Palestinians.

3.3.3.1. ACCUN Office wrote and made direct advocacy concerning the bombing of our Saint Philip's Church and the Ali Arab Hospital in Palestine in January 2003. Our correspondences were acknowledged by the US and Israeli Missions. The Israeli Mission responded 'almost', and with no denials about American Missile having being used. The NGO Working Group also wrote to request a session with the Israeli Mission but this was not successful either. Advocacy for the same issue was also made by NGO partners in Washington.

3.3.3.2. ACCUN Office was fully involved in the campaign to stop the construction of the separation wall built by the Israeli government dividing Palestinian settlements from the rest of the country. An extensive display was put up in the UN Visitors lobby and was later transferred to the General Assembly hall to promote awareness of the reality of what is happening in the land of the Holy One. We have tried to bring the attention of the world onto the Israeli occupying forces and the terrible injustice placed upon the Palestinian people by the dividing wall, by contributing to the printing and wide distribution of post cards showing the picture of the wall (a copy of which is our gift to each delegation of ACC so that you too can advocate further for the plight of the Palestinians). The Israel/Palestine working group was pursued by the UN organizations to continue to advocate for the demolition of the wall for peace and development in that area.

3.3.3.3. At the invitation of the Anglican Peace and Justice Network, I visited Israel and Palestine in 2004. It was during this visit that I was privileged to meet the then President of the Palestinian people His Excellency Yasser Arafat. This year (2005), two volunteer staff members also visited the area and brought back information on the continuing tragedy of the terrible barricade known as "the wall". Information gathered from these visits was shared with the Working Group and subsequently the Division for Palestinian Rights in the UNDPA.

3.3.3.4. As part of an ecumenical group of clergy, the ACCUN Office Executive Director also visited Lebanon and met with President Emile Lahoud. Our support for the peace process was relayed to him as well as hopes for Christians and Muslims to continue to work in harmony and peace.

3.3.4. The office has been a member of the Iraqi working group since the fall of 2001 in support of other Ecumenical Partners who had personnel suffering under the old regime.

3.3.4.1. As you may be aware, we advocated for peace and not war in Iraq based on the ACC12 resolutions. Br. William represented the office in the Working Group delegation that handed a statement to the UN Secretary General on March 2003 to advocate for Peace and not War in Iraq. An ACCUN Office statement approved by the Archbishop of Canterbury and ACC Chairman was also issued in May during a press conference at UN and was sent to members of the Security Council and UN Staff, advocating for the post war reconstruction of Iraq under the supervision of UN. (Copy of Statement attached)

3.3.4.2. On the very day we learnt of the tragic death of UN staff in Iraq, ACCUN Office, on behalf of ACC quickly sent a letter of condolence to the Secretary General with our promise that as a global church we will be vigilant in pursuing appropriate protection of UN staff everywhere. (Copy each of letter and response from UN are attached). Again any useful advocacy on Iraq has to be pursued with the Super Power through ECUSA.

3.3.4.3. The Working Group continues to encourage the UN to become more involved in helping to bring peace to this troubled region and also encourages NGOs to become active participants in the reconstruction process. We keep up with the true situation on the ground by numerous reports that are brought to us by fellow Christians who are still working in that country.

3.3.5. ACCUN Office contacted the Primate of Sudan, the UN Ambassador from Sudan and the US Ambassador to advocate for the peace process in Southern Sudan especially the recently (January 2005) signed agreement.

3.3.5.1. The Anglican Observer on behalf of the UN Ecumenical Working Group chaired a meeting with Rev Dr. Haruun Ruun, the Executive Secretary of the New Sudan Council of Churches. This meeting was an Ecumenical Conversation on what was the truth about Sudan and was also attended by United Nations Staff and Staff of government missions. The Executive Secretary supported by the Ecumenical partners advocated for the general strengthening of the Peace Keeping Forces of the African Union in Sudan. The representative of the UNDPA promised to look into this matter.

3.3.5.2. Concerted efforts to advocate for our brothers and sisters in Sudan will continue with UN DPA and during the present conversations in preparation for the UN Summit in September 2005.

3.3.6. The Observer discussed appropriate interventions concerning the Democratic Republic of the Congo with the Primate and members of his delegation to the Francophone Consultation in Mauritius in July 2003. Since then ACCUN Office has been awaiting their advice on data and facts so we could pursue reinstitution from UN on the occupation of the Theological College by the French Peace Keeping Forces. I could sense some caution on pursuing advocacy on this matter, as at first they were enthusiastic but were non-committal towards the time I left the consultation. Since March 2005, we noticed that working through the link women of the International Anglican Women's Network (IAWN) and especially the Mother's Union, we maybe able to get some trustworthy information as basis of any meaningful advocacy/interventions in the future.

3.3.7. ACCUN Office also advocated for peace in West Africa and prepared a brief for the Archbishop of Canterbury before he visited West Africa in 2003. We celebrated along with the Liberians when the former president Mr. Taylor left the country to live in exile elsewhere. It was also a great privilege to meet last year the Hon. Chairman Bryant (the interim leader of the country and devout member of the Episcopal Church of Liberia), who was very committed to maintaining the resilience of his people to withstand the trauma of war.

3.3.7.1. In June 2003 I wrote a letter to my own Prime Minister about Samoans joining the UN Peace Keeping Missions. I am glad to note that by January 2004, Samoa sent her first contingent (about 20 members) of the Police Force to Liberia—they were members of the Police Force in Timor Leste but this was the first time Samoans got to join the UN Peace Keeping Forces. For a nation with a population of 160,000 people this is a major contribution. Since then, more Samoans have been joining UN Peace Keeping Forces in Liberia and elsewhere. Unfortunately, several Samoans joining the US Arm Forces through neighbouring American Samoa have been killed in Iraq as well.

3.3.8. A coalition of NGOs has a stronger voice at the UN and so ACCUN Office needed to depend on other Ecumenical partners to advocate for many other security issues and we are kept well informed on areas relevant to our mission by our involvement with them. The NGO/Committee for the Security Council is chaired by the Head of the Quaker office with members from the Mennonites, United Methodist, the Presbyterians and the Lutherans, who enlist our support for interventions.

3.3.9. As a committed member of the NGO Committee on Disarmament, Peace and Security, ACCUN Office attends meetings of the First

Committee of the UN General Assembly dealing with disarmament and conflict resolutions. Mrs. Nancy Colton (a good friend of the office and secretary of many NGOs) made sure that ACCUN Office is represented at the meetings and that we signed onto interventions that we would support as a Church. We also get to attend some Security Council meetings on appropriate areas of concerns and we follow issues such as children soldiers as well as arms agreements. In February 2005 at the meeting of the ACCUN Office Advisory Council at Lambeth Palace we reported to the Archbishop of Canterbury about our hope and advocacy for a unified agreement to mark all small arms ammunition so they could become traceable when crimes are committed with them.

3.3.9.1. As a member NGO of the Disarmament Group we also advocated for the Nuclear Non-Proliferation Treaty (NPT). We resourced and supported the statements issued by two Representatives of the Church of England, Ms. Caroline Gilbort and The Rev Liz Griffith of St. Martins in the Fields in London who attended the Review Conference for NPT last month (May 2005). The latter represented the Clergy Against Nuclear Arms (CANA). The ACCUN Office was the contact point for the two women to prepare interventions and to solicit assistance for the prayer vigil at the Isaiah Wall outside of the UN during the session of the review meeting. Archdeacon Mike Kendall who was one of our delegates reported that the main concern expressed at the meeting was that while the UN Protocols on non-proliferation are the right course, some nations do not comply or admit they have nuclear weapons and there is, so far, no action to enforce the protocols. There was no consensus reached for a final political statement. The States of the world have much work yet to do concerning nuclear disarmament.

3.3.10. Jesus says "my peace I bring you". It is the fervent hope of this ministry and of every Christian person and every person of faith that peace to the world's nations may someday prevail. We will continue to work towards that glorious vision.

3.4. The Rights of Indigenous Peoples and Indigenous Issues:

3.4.1. The ACCUN Office has been deeply involved with the ongoing struggle of indigenous peoples since the beginning of the ministry in the early 1990's. Among other activities, the ACCUN Office actively participated in the Working Group on Indigenous Peoples (now the Working Group for the Decade for Indigenous Issues), which is the primary vehicle for NGO representation at the UN. As an indigenous person from Samoa, I was recently quoted on the website of the Anglican Indigenous People's Network (AIN) in saying that indigenous minority issues at the United Nations are one of it's priorities.

3.4.2. Although indigenous peoples have been making their voices heard at the UN for over 75 years, their concerns became especially prominent in 1993, in which year the UN proclaimed as the "International Year for the World's Indigenous People." The purpose of that designated year was to create a "new partnership" between the UN, its member States, and indigenous peoples. However, as the Working Group aptly insisted, the correct term should not have been "people," but "peoples" in order to express accurately the tremendous diversity among the millions of indigenous peoples living in all parts of the world. This concern was about much more than the meaning of words. It was about continuing attempts to silence their voices and to deny their basic human rights, sometimes leading to genocide. As one member of the Working Group put it, "we are human beings living today; we do not live in a museum; we are not a thing of the past." This statement summarized well, as it still does, the many obstacles faced by indigenous peoples everywhere and everyday.

3.4.3. The Working Group on Indigenous Peoples and other NGOs representing them at the UN have effectively brought to the UN the severe problems of Indigenous Peoples, but various forces still continue to work towards destroying them and their homelands. The goal of the "new partnership," which was to create a post-colonial relationship between indigenous peoples and member states, has not been achieved. Archbishop Sir Paul Reeves, the first Anglican Observer, described this situation by saying indigenous peoples are not seen "as citizens, but as subjects" in a colonial dynamic that has not essentially changed over several centuries. Part of the reason for this is that tribal territories are not usually given legal status by the countries in which they geographically exist. At the UN, "sovereignty" applies to the citizens and laws of member states, rather than to people who exist either outside or at the margins of those states. This situation creates ambiguity in the official identification of indigenous peoples, who live as minorities in their own countries, but do not receive full rights to make decisions for themselves about their own lives. The concept of sovereignty employed by most states both deprives indigenous peoples of fundamental religious, economic, and political rights and supports exploitative economic development strategies, which destroy ecological systems. In other words, indigenous peoples are marginalized in the most severe sense of the word. The testimony of their experience calls into question the effectiveness of the Universal Declaration of Human Rights as truly "universal." It is for that reason that the ministry of the Anglican Observer has taken a special interest in them and the issues they bring to the UN.

3.4.4. In recent years, the struggle of indigenous peoples has often been directed toward the legal recognition of their "intellectual property" in its many forms, including cultural knowledge, which has diverse practical and sacred uses. Examples of this intellectual property are the medicinal and ecological knowledge of plants, animals, and land usage practices in the ecosystems in which indigenous peoples live. The question of adequate and equitable financial compensation is crucial here, as well as the basic human right of preserving that knowledge as part, their own cultural tradition. Also, the preservation of this cultural knowledge and the vitality of the people who hold it are crucial to the sustainability of those ecosystems.

3.4.5. The ACCUN Office takes the position that indigenous peoples and the issues they bring to the UN are anything but marginal. They should be at the center of policy-making in virtually all matters pertaining to human rights, sustainable development, and the environment. They are at the heart of the ongoing struggle for all humankind to become more humane at a critical time in human history.

3.4.6. I thought it appropriate that I get to share with you an intervention made at the UN on your behalf last year on May 18th by the ACCUN Office intern. It was done in the manner that all interventions at the UN are generally made:

> "My name is Robert Bergner. I am from the office of the Anglican Observer at the UN which represents 75 million Anglicans in 164 countries. In keeping with the title of our office, I would like to share a few observations with this Forum.
>
> First, I wish to commend the UN for establishing the Permanent Forum on Indigenous Issues; I wish to commend the Forum itself for its efforts to bring indigenous issues to the attention of the world community; and, I wish to commend the indigenous peoples, especially the indigenous women, who have had the strength and the courage to make their voices heard.
>
> Second, we spoke at length last week about the importance of indigenous languages, their preservation and their degradation. We must also be aware of the use and misuse of European languages. We need to take notice when new terms of suspect intent enter our discourse. One in particular that I will mention here is the term "eco-system services" which I have now read in several documents available at this Forum. Using the term "eco-system services" to refer to things like fresh water, clean air and fertile soil can only perpetuate the incorrect and destructive perception that nature exists for no other reason than to service the needs of people. The Anglican Communion believes, and I think that this would be the view of most, if not all, indigenous peoples, that humanity's proper role is to be a steward of nature rather than its overlord.
>
> Third, as we discuss the environment this afternoon, I would like to remind the Forum that we do not have to look any further than outside the east-facing windows of the UN to observe a case of near total ecological devastation. What was once an estuarial environment overflowing with luxurious vegetation, thousands of sea and shore birds, innumerable aquatic species, and animal life of all kinds is now an alien realm of toxic water,

smokestacks, garbage, concrete and rusted metal where one is as likely to see an airborne helicopter as an airborne bird. I was at the southern tip of Manhattan island last Saturday where, attached to the fence over which several people were fishing, a sign read: **"Warning: pregnant women and children under fifteen should not eat fish caught in these waters."** And, more generally, **"Eating fish caught in these waters may be hazardous to your health."** Some fishermen had laid out a few scraps of fish for the birds to take. There was just one problem: there were no birds. Not even one, single seagull. Either the birds were too wise to eat poisonous fish, or, more likely, they already had.

Finally, in planning future meetings, I wonder if the Forum would like to consider architectural environments and meeting structures other than those employed presently. Although, certainly, having this Forum at all is a great achievement, it seems fairly incongruous to me, and several indigenous delegates have concurred, that a discussion of indigenous women's issues is taking place in an environment and according to a format that is so overwhelmingly European and male. Perhaps, the Forum could consult with various indigenous groups to establish a context for future meetings that is more appropriate to the topic under consideration.

Thank you. Merci. Gracias."

3.4.7. Mr. Bergner (who is here as at ACC13 as a volunteer for the Communications Team) also represented ACCUN Office as one of its delegates to the Fourth Permanent Forum of Indigenous Issues last month. He prepared our statement (attached) which was widely distributed during the two week meeting. It was not very easy to get Anglican delegates from AIN to attend the Forum meetings and so we depended on Anglicans of the First Nations around New York apart from Robert Bergner. One of the delegates, 'Ms. Janine Tinsley-Roe, was appointed soonest after the Third Permanent Forum last year, as the Director for the Episcopal Indigenous Ministries and is anticipating studying for a law degree to assist with the legal rights of her people. Janine with a few other women also participated in the Fourth Permanent Forum last month.

3.4.8. The ACCUN Office participated in all the meetings of the Permanent Forum to date. Most of the issues dealt with at the meeting were land rights; preservation of sacred sites, knowledge and culture; and, the needs for education as well as other social services. The Indigenous Peoples also stressed that the UN should deal directly with Indigenous people on issues concerning poverty, development, and human rights.

3.4.9. As ACC Staff focal point for the Indigenous Network, I will continue to pursue the rights of the indigenous peoples at UN. In this same connection, I responded to an invitation of the Network to attend their meeting in New Zealand (30 March–4 April) to also be the facilitator for their Wahine (Women) Caucus. It was the very first time the women were allowed to deliberate on their issues which highlighted violence against women, their being kept uninformed on church policies impacting their lives and their not being involved in decision making.

3.4.10. The year 2004 was the final year for the First Global decade for Indigenous Issues and although our interventions were based on what we already know and my own conscious as an indigenous people (who is blessed to belong to a race that holds the majority rule in my own country), we found it most unfortunate that issues were never received from AIN nor the provinces for our work in this area. However, it is a real joy to report to you that the UN General Assembly in adopting resolution 19/174 on 20 December 2004, proclaimed a second International Decade of the World's Indigenous People to commence on 1 January 2005. The goal of the Second Decade is for the further strengthening of international cooperation for the solution of problems faced by indigenous people in such areas as culture, education, health, human rights, the environment and social and economic development, by means of action-oriented programmes and specific projects, increased technical assistance and relevant standard-setting activities. The ACCUN Office is committed to working towards the goals of the decade once the plan of action is released from the United Nations during the 60th Session of the General Assembly this fall.

3.5. Children:

3.5.1. It is meet and right that the United Nations and ACCUN Office continues to be fully committed to pursuing the requirements of the resolution ACCUN Office promoted at ACC12 in 2002—"A World Fit for Children" in connection with the UN Decade (2001 to 2010) for a Culture of Peace and Non-violence for Children. I commend the Anglican Consultative Council for approving that resolution. Why? It is because the world continues to be a troubled place for far too many of our children. It is because children are our most precious resource. It is because we have no trust more sacred than ensuring their safe-keeping and their future. It is also because the child is the key to the kingdom of heaven. Matthew 18— "Then Jesus called a small child and said unless you are transformed and become as little children you will by no means enter the kingdom. Therefore whoever humbles themselves as this little child, whoever receives this little one in my name, receives me".

3.5.2. Children continue to be at the forefront of every war and conflict, as innocent victims and as soldiers pressed into fighting. Children continue to suffer immensely, and in the case of young girls, often the most, in the scourge that is HIV/AIDS, and children continue to be trafficked and preyed upon all over the planet for purposes of sex and cheap labour. Due to the focused efforts of many, through diplomatic missions and hard work on the international level, the situation has improved, somewhat, since we last reported to the Standing Committee. In some countries under conflict, such as Liberia, fewer children carry arms. In some countries devastated by HIV/AIDS, such as Burkina Faso, infection rates among young persons, especially young girls has decreased dramatically. And in some countries, such as Ghana, more children are receiving proper education, and the rate of boys vs. girls is incrementally improving.

3.5.3. Of course there is still much more to be done. I have endeavoured to address the concerns of young people wherever and whenever I was given the opportunity during my travels across the Communion. I also raised the awareness of, and advocated for the Convention for the Rights of the Child (CRC). With every opportunity I got, I have encouraged Permanent Missions representatives to support the CRC, especially since some countries, such as the United States, have yet to become signatories of the Convention. ACCUN Office continues to encourage proactive-ness on all UN issues pertaining to children among all UN stakeholders.

3.5.4. The main UN advocate for the Decade of Peace and Non-violence for Children, Ambassador Anwarul Chowdhury (Special High Level UN Representative for Least Developed Countries, the Land Locked Countries, and the Small Island Developing States) became a very good friend. When a recent UN display entitled "Building a Culture of Peace" was opened to the public, he asked that I attend the event with him. He told a profound story that I will never forget, about once seeing the children of men at war playing together in a garden not far away from where their fathers were shouting at each other at a meeting. Their innocent minds will remain innocent and know no violence until influenced by adults—a great role for the church to undertake and for nurturing men for their role for gender equality

3.5.5. The UN started in December 2003 a campaign towards celebrating the 10th anniversary of the International year of the Family (1994). The NGO Working Group on the Family (in which ACCUN Office is a member) was fully involved in activities leading up to the celebration of the 10th Anniversary of the event.

3.5.5.1. The NGO working group on the Family since 2003 hosted several panels—most of them promoted the importance of two-parent families (specifically the involvement of the father in raising the children who will learn to curb their anger and perhaps reduce the crime and other acts of violence); the relationship between the family and international organizations; the education of the girl child (mostly neglected in many cultures and religions); the problems facing children of migrant families; and the United Nations commitment to strengthening families and recognizing the role of the family as the foundation of society and culture in the world.

3.5.5.2. Children, like women, are the most vulnerable in all forms of crisis. I shared with the NGO groups and during discussions with government personnel, the reflections and commitments made by the Consultation of the Inter Anglican Family Network that I chaired in June 2003 and was publicized in the Anglican World.

3.5.5.3. In 2004 the UN commemorated the 10th Anniversary of the International Year of the Family (1994). ACCUN Office joined the celebration activities and we were greatly encouraged to see the family being affirmed by the UN as "the foundation of society."

3.5.6. Through its Volunteer Associate for Human Rights, Gary Ryan, the ACCUN Office has recently become associated with Vandy Kanyako, a Task Force member of the UN General Assembly/Civil Society Hearings, and Conference Coordinator for Global Partnership for the Prevention of Armed Conflict. A former child soldier in Sierra Leone, Mr. Kanyako has advocated effectively against the use of child soldiers in areas of conflict, and against the use of anti-personnel landmines. Mr. Vandy Kanyako's experience and knowledge will doubtless prove helpful as ACCUN Office continues to chart a plan of action and advocacy relevant to this very important issue.

3.5.7. The ACC Resolution 1 calls for actions by the provinces to be reported to ACC13. I am looking forward to reading the Provincial reports on what has been done so I could include this in my report to the United Nations as soon as I return to New York.

3.5.7.1. The Director for ECUSA Youth Ministries, Mr. Thomas Chu, continues to receive a UN pass through ACCUN Office to cover issues concerning youth and children. During the ECUSA General Convention in 2003 I addressed the children/youth gathering and as a result about 50 young people signed up for a programme related to the UN's activities. We hope that a suitable programme will be established for them during summer 2006. Our volunteer Gary Ryan will be working closely with Mr. Chu and the design team for this event in the next few weeks. It is our hope that some young people from other Provinces could also join this programme, funds permitting of course.

3.5.7.2. In response to the ACC Resolution, ECUSA brought together in February 2003 a variety of Christian educators, Christian education networks and faith formation leaders for an exceptional event, "Will Our Faith Have Children—Faith Formation from Generation to Generation." Over 600 persons from a record 91 dioceses participated, including participants from Canada, England, and Ireland. A video featuring the voices of children, youth, and adults in their faith premiered at the event and an educational video with teaching from the event may be made available for use by other Provinces. Full details can be viewed through a link from our Website.

3.5.7.2.1. Furthermore, the ECUSA children's mission magazine, "Treasure," featured the Special Session on Children and the UN Convention on the Rights of the Child. This publication was widely distributed throughout the USA and neighboring countries. The text is available online and I have brought for display a few of our office copies, as this work is directly linked to the work of ACCUN Office.

3.6 Women:

3.6.1. I have a special passion for women's issues and especially those issues affecting "the family" today. I am therefore committed to making sure that the policies of the UN states do include a strong gender perspective, and are based upon universal Human Rights.

3.6.2 In most countries, Women remain "the invisible and unrecognized backbone of agriculture (and of the church too), and remain hostage to the feudal traditions. Administrative structures have not shown adequate sensitivity to rural women's needs, and as a result, women's programs are still peripheral," as documented by the United Nations.

3.6.3. ACCUN Office therefore started participating at the meetings of the UN Commission on the Status of Women (UNCSW) since 2002 to start networking with other delegates for gender issues. In 2003 Dr. Pauline Muchina from Kenya, and former Coordinator of an ECUSA project on HIV/AIDS, chaired a side Event for the Anglican Communion to highlight some of the areas in which women were marginalized through culture and religion. She also assisted me in sending a strong statement to the Conference of NGOs criticizing the inability of the UN Commission to adopt the appropriate language enforcing policies on the reproductive rights of women due to the boycott by USA and other Islamic governments.

3.6.4. In our efforts to establish a Working Group to support the office in Gender issues, ACCUN Office hosted on June 30th, 2003 an event for the top women in UN and the NGO Conference (CONGO) as well as a Nigerian spokesperson from the UN Fund for Populations Activities (UNFPA), to address the Episcopal women on the themes for UNCSW in 2004, namely—The Role of Men and Boys in achieving gender equality; and, the Women's equal participation in the prevention, management and conflict resolution, and in post-conflict peace building. The women of ECUSA were committed to advocating for the ratification of the Convention for the Elimination of all forms of Discrimination against Women (CEDAW), yet to be ratified by their own government and especially for the release of much needed funds (about US$34 million) due to UNFPA but withheld by the Government of the USA. The ECUSA sisters were also committed to facilitate the participation of women from other provinces in the CSW meetings in 2004 and 2005 and if at all possible assist me and

Jolly (of the Joint-Standing Committee as well as the newly appointed Coordinator, Revd Alice Medcof), in revitalizing the dormant International Anglican Women's Network (IAWN).

4. ANGLICAN NETWORKS:

4.1. In the Terms of Reference (TOR) for the Anglican Observer, the incumbent is required to work where appropriate with the Anglican Networks. During my tenure of Office, I made sure that the Networks were given due attention and also tried to make them join the UN as other International Anglican NGOs for the specific issues they chose to pursue. The underlying reason was that some Ecumenical Partners including the Roman Catholic Church have several members in the NGO fora. Almost every Order has a representative accredited to the ECOSOC (Economic & Social Commission) and hold the same status as the Anglican Observer at the United Nations. You would find at the UN a Roman Catholic representative for each of the Roman Catholic Orders and organizations such as the Franciscans International, the Dominican Sisters, the Sisters of Mercy, the Passionists, CARITAS and many more. For the United Methodists, they are represented not only by their main representatives, but they are also represented as United Methodist Women, United Methodist Indigenous People, and many other representatives of church bodies.

4.2. During my 3 years and 9 months as your representative at the United Nations, ACCUN Office has worked very closely with the Peace & Justice Network (APJN), the Migrant & Refugees Network (which unfortunately may have ceased to exist already), the Inter Anglican Family Network (IAFN), the International Anglican Women's Network (IAWN) and the Anglican Communion Environment Network (ACEN).

4.3. As mentioned before, I attended the IAN meeting in Aotearoa/NZ in March 2003 and chaired the Women's Caucus of the network; I also chaired the very first Regional Consultation for the IAFN in Nairobi in June 2003— a task I did with much pleasure and joy since I chaired the very first meeting in Singapore (1987) that established the network; attended, spoke and contributed to the inaugural meeting of the Anglican Francophone Network meeting in Mauritius; attended and contributed to the Executive meeting of the APJN as an ex-officio member in the fall of 2003; attended and contributed to the special Task Force of the Primates for Trade and Poverty immediately following the APJN Executive Meeting; and, I also attended the meeting last year of the APJN in Jerusalem.

4.4. Much of the ACCUN Office work in the past two years and to date was dealing with Women's issues. The main aim was to sensitize the women to gender balance issues and their rights as human beings; and, to revitalize the dormant Anglican Women's Network. I am pleased to report that I conducted the induction of the first steering committee members for IAWN in March this year and the network appears to be thriving since then.

4.5. The Anglican Communion Environment Network (ACEN) you will recall, was established through a resolution in connection with my ACC12 report. The former Secretary General got ACCUN Office to pick up the arrangements for the inaugural meeting of the Network when Revd Canon Eric Beresford changed jobs last year. We are pleased to report that the meeting resulted in adopting an excellent structure for the Network and already we have yet another Network of committed Anglicans that is thriving with regular exchanges of information. The ACCUN Office will continue to assist the Network with information from the United Nations.

4.6. Except for the ACEN meeting all other Networks paid the full costs of the Observer's participation at their meetings due to the very limited travel budget of the office.

5. UN REFORM & "IN LARGER FREEDOM: TOWARDS DEVELOPMENT, SECURITY AND HUMAN RIGHTS FOR ALL"

In March 2005, the UN Secretary General issued a report proposing actions that according to him "are achievable in the coming months." This report is potentially the primary document for the Heads of State and Government preparation for the High-Level summit in September 2005, which will not only celebrate the 60th anniversary of the organization but it will also be a 5 year review of the Millennium Declaration (Millennium +5 summit). The Secretary General is asserting that Larger Freedom "encapsulates the idea that development, security and human rights go hand in hand," and "accordingly we will not enjoy development without security, we will not enjoy security without development and we will not enjoy either without respect for human rights." The report highlights four main thematic areas namely (I) Freedom from Want, (II) Freedom from Fear, (III) Freedom to Live in Dignity, and (IV) UN Reform.

5.1. Whilst drawing heavily on the reports of two important independent advisory panels, the High-Level Panel on Threats, Challenges and Change and the Millennium Project Taskforce, the Secretary-General's report does not seek to be simply a consolidation or restatement of these reports. Rather, the approach has been taken of distilling from these reports, from other reviews and the experience of the SecretaryGeneral himself, key principles, urgent challenges and actionable strategies for dealing with them. The Secretary-General himself states in the report that it is limited to "items on which I believe action is both vital and achievable in the coming months."

5.2. Of special interest to me as Your Observer and I believe to you as ACC members, is the Secretary General's proposal to update the structure of the UN. At present the UN is comprised of the Security Council (which is often overly assertive), the Economic and Social Council (which is too often marginalized and has no enforcement powers), and the Trusteeship Council (which is now mostly symbolic). However, it is hoped that rhetoric on reforms will not take away the more important issues concerning the development of sustainable communities and the funding of such programmes through the Overseas Development Assistance (ODA) of 0.7% by the wealthy countries toward the international development budgets for poorer nations.

5.3. Three whole days this month (22nd, 23rd and 24th) have been dedicated to intensive discussions related to the preparations for the High Level summit and main discussions will be centred around the Secretary General's report.

5.3.1. The Conference on Interfaith Cooperation For Peace on 22 June 2005 is a tripartite dialogue between the Government Representatives, the United Nations Agencies and the Religious NGOs on the Theme of "Enhancing Interfaith Dialogue and Cooperation Toward Peace in the 21st Century." The two different sessions for the dialogue will focus on the sub themes of "The role of religions in promoting intercultural understanding towards sustainable peace" and "Exploring strategies to enhance interfaith cooperation for sustainable peace."

5.3.1.1. My ecumenical colleagues were very keen to have the Archbishop of Canterbury to address the conference as they were quite impressed with His Grace's wisdom and well publicized vision concerning the areas highlighted in the United Nations Millennium Declaration as well as the reforms at the United Nations. At the time of writing this report, I have not seen a response from His Grace, the Archbishop of Canterbury to the invitation. I have therefore assigned Dr. Pauline Muchina from Kenya to represent the office at the meeting and to make appropriate interventions in accordance with Anglican interfaith dialogues and the Archbishop of Canterbury's speeches on United Issues. In additional to Pauline our volunteers and other associates in New York as well as some members of the Advisory Council will be attending this conference at the United Nations.

5.3.2. The Informal Interactive Hearings of the General Assembly (GA) with non-governmental organizations, civil society organizations and the private sector are scheduled to be held on 23rd and 24th of June 2005 to be presided over by the president with the GA president. The four sequential sessions over the two days will cover the areas mentioned above as the four clusters of the Secretary General's report "In larger freedom: towards development, security and human rights for all."

5.3.2.1. The United Nations gave us a very short notice with a speedy turn around for inputs and nominations for active participation at the Hearings. The Ecumenical Working Group nominated 10 representatives including Anglicans as members of the WCC Ecumenical team to represent 24 Churches and Christian Organizations, as per the attached list. We will post onto our website the GA president's summary of the Hearings which will be a GA document prior to the High-level Plenary Meeting in September 2005.

5.4. The report of some 62 pages can be viewed on the UN website and few hard copies are being displayed for your information. However, I thought it important that a Review of the Secretary General's report by our intern Ms. Louise Gleich, is attached in its entirety for your further studies and if at all possible, to use as basis for your own ministries and most importantly for discussions with your respective governments on issues raised and on how the Church could be an effective partner in promoting the issues of the MDGs; especially raising the 0.7% for development issues especially in feeding the poor and hungry amongst us.

6. THE ANGLICAN CONSULTATIVE COUNCIL UN OFFICE (ACCUNO)

6.1 The ACCUN Office has an Advisory Council comprising of 25 members and 6 ex-officio members. The Ex-Officio members are the Chairman of ACC, the Vice Chairman of ACC, a representative of the Archbishop of Canterbury, the Bishop of New York, the representative of the Presiding Bishop of ECUSA and the Secretary General of ACC.

6.1.1. Since my tenure of the office, there has been a concerted effort to make the membership of the Council more representative of the Communion. So far we have been successful in having the Bishop of Barbados and, the International President of the Mother's Union will join the Ex-Officio members as soon as the Archbishop of Canterbury signs her letter of appointment hopefully in the next few days. Invitations have also been extended to other friends in Hong Kong and elsewhere to join the Council.

6.1.2. The Advisory Council was established to fund raise for the office, which has been an annual obligation since the ACCUN Office was established. Members of the council are required to raise at least US$1,000 annually to cover the operational costs. These funds were either made as a personal donation or raised by the individual members themselves. Since September 11th, 2001, pledges from traditional donors decreased substantively, resulting in the office operating at a deficit over two years until June last year. A major fundraising event last June 2004 was most successful that the payments for deficits of two years were met. A group of very dedicated Anglicans & Episcopalians also worked vigilantly last year to finalise the Fund Raising Case Statement to raise a US$6 million Endowment for the office.

6.1.3. Since 2003, the Advisory Council took up other tasks to assist the ministry of the office. The members established task teams for: Development and Endowment; Communications; Liaison between the ACCUN Office & UN Agencies & ACCUN Office and counterparts; and, Policies and Networks. The latter Task Team has been reporting regularly to the Advisory Council on Anglican/Muslim roundtables on civil society and common issues for these faiths. The Communications team has been very effective in updating our website and producing documentation including publicity material—thanks to Peter Ng and Mission Graphics, the publishing ministry of the Jubilee Community Center at The Episcopal Church of Our Savior (Chinese) and Ms Neva Rae Fox of the Cathedral of St. John the Divine.

6.1.4. Members of the Council especially the Secretary, The Very Venerable Mike Kendall, have been covering some of the important UN meeting for ACCUN Office. We were fortunate to get reports on those meetings from them to add to our resources for appropriate interventions at the United Nations.

6.1.5. The success of the fundraising activities for ACCUN Office over the years depended largely on the dedicated efforts of Mrs. Marion (Marnie) Dawson Carr and her husband (ACCUN Office Treasurer) Mr. James (Jim) G. Carr. And in 2004 we wish to acknowledge with much gratitude our special thanks to His Grace the Archbishop of Canterbury for coming to America to address the friends of Canterbury who gathered in Greenwich, Connecticut for a Fund Raising Dinner. We raised approximately US$400,000 at this event. ACCUN Office is most grateful too to the Development & Endowment Team comprising of Mr. & Mrs Carr, Mrs Anita Timmons, The Rev Canon Doug Renegar, Archdeacon Mike Kendall and The Chair of the Council, The Rev Canon Don Brown for their hard work and substantial financial contributions towards the costs of the office.

6.2. The ACCUN Office staff comprises of two full time employees, the Anglican Observer and the Office Assistant. Br. William Francis Jones (BSG) joined the office in October 2002 to replace Ms. Yasmeen Granville who left to start a family as soon as I returned from ACC12. We were blessed that The Rev Canon Doug Renegar joined us in November last year for a period of 12 months, and The Rev Canon Jeff Golliher who has been with the office since its inception, continues to work for the office on a part time basis. A month ago, Mr. Gary Ryan joined us as a volunteer who wanted to work with Human Rights issues and those concerning children and so far he has worked for us for at least two days a week. ACCUN Office is well known at 815 Second Avenue for working long hours and sometimes Br. William would accompany me on my speaking engagements after hours or during the weekends or when I am invited to preach at a church on Sunday. All this work was done free of charge and was really a labour of love on Br. William's part and I thank him most sincerely for this.

6.2.1. We therefore welcome offers received from interns and volunteers who would join us for specific issues and durations. All in all since 2002, we were joined by 19 volunteers as per the attached list: Robert Bergner, Lavern Cameron, Jacquiline Carroll, Claire Dezotell, Phoebe Gallagher, Louise Gliech, Ranjit Mathews, Lyndon Metembo, Andrew Othieno, Sam Peabody, Robert Picken, James Plowden-Wardlaw, Marie Poyet, Elizabeth Renegar, Gary Ryan, Anna Salick, Bryan Starer, Anthony Townsin, William Zhong. We greatly benefited from their assistance and free labour. They enjoyed the work at the United Nations for exposure to international affairs and making valuable contacts whilst attending meetings and activities of the UN as well as the NGOs and CSOs. We wish to thank the Rt. Rev Tom Shaw who jointly financed the costs of our first intern together with "Witness" publication; as well as the Church of Southern Africa which co-shared the costs of Lyndon Metembo's costs; and, the Church Missionary Society (CMS) of the Church of England for sending us Ms. Louise Gleich following her stint for a year with Sabeel in Jerusalem.

6.2.2. Office space and most of much needed support services have been provided by ECUSA over the year. However, at the end of the year 2003, ACCUN Office together with other offices independent of ECUSA were given notices indicating changes in office space and the likelihood that we may be charged for the services we have enjoyed free of charge in the past. In calculating the annual costs of the office, it was discovered that ECUSA has paid about 85% of the office expenses. There was no way that the ACCUN Office could pay for about US$130,000 per annum for such costs. After a direct appeal to the Episcopal Church Center Administration, I am happy to advise you that we received in July 2004 a letter from the Executive Council of ECUSA that it had resolved to continue to provide office space and support services for the Anglican United Observer, and this be reflected in the budget as an additional annual contribution to the Anglican Consultative Council as a gift in kind. I wish to record here my sincere gratitude to Presiding Bishop Frank Griswold and ECUSA and especially our friends/colleagues in the staff of the Church Centre who advocated for us to receive this kind and substantial gift.

6.2.3. The office receives an annual contribution (about 16% of its budget) from ACC. ACCUN Office also applies and receives an annual grant from the Archbishop of Canterbury's Fund and sometimes directly from the Anglican Investment Agency (AIA). We therefore wish to record here our sincere thanks to ACC for its financial assistance, the Chair and Trustees of the Archbishop of Canterbury's Fund for the Anglican Communion, AIA and of course Mrs. Marnie Carr one of the benefactors for both AIA and the Archbishop's Fund. The office also applied and received over the past three years a grant of US$30,000 each year from Trinity Church Wall Street for the support of our Sustainable Communities work especially the costs related to work to Canon Jeff Golliher's role in this area. We are most grateful to the Rector of Trinity Church and especially The Rev James Callaway and staff of his department for this great assistance.

7. OTHER ACTIVITIES

ACCUN Office tried with much limited resources to undertake many tasks as described in this report.

7.1. Other activities expected of the Anglican Observer included full attendance of the Primates' annual meetings to report to them and to interact with the Primates on issues requiring the attention of the Observer. The Anglican Observer was also required to attend and report to the Joint Standing Committee meetings and was also required to report to the committee on the Anglican Indigenous Network.

7.2. Since 2001 the ACCUN Office was represented at all the meetings of the Advisory Council by the Observer, Jeff Golliher, the Office Assistant, and was joined at the November 2004 meeting by The Rev Canon Doug Renegar as the new Executive Officer for the Office. In February this year the Coordinator & Chairman of the ACCUN Office committee in Europe joined us at the Lambeth Palace meeting. The Council meets annually before Lent at Lambeth Palace and during the fall a day prior to an Office Evensong and Reception (hosted by Presiding Bishop Frank and Mrs. Phoebe Griswold) for UN Mission staff, UN personnel, and NGO and CSO representatives as well as the friends of ACCUN Office.

7.3. I also attended the ECUSA General Convention in 2003. It was an opportunity to discuss the Ministry of the Office the role of the United Nations in global issues, interacted with Episcopalians to promote appropriate resolutions related to the work of the office and to personally thank those, especially the Bishops who contributed substantially to the costs of the office. It was also an opportunity to discuss the IAWN with the Coordinator (who was a guest of the Episcopal Church Women and Mrs. Phoebe Griswold who readily agreed to be a Patron for the Network). My interview during my participation was publicized by ENS on August 7th 2003.

7.4. I addressed the gathering and said a prayer during the Event held at the Dag Hammarskjold Plaza to observe the International Day for Peace on 21st September 2003, which was well attended by Mission Representatives, UN Staff and NGOs.

7.5. I have attended and interacted with Heads of Government Delegations and Permanent Missions to the United Nations during the General Assembly as an official of the Samoa delegation in September/October. I wish to acknowledge with much gratitude the valuable assistance received from my own government in this respect and when I needed to attend meetings closed to NGOs and the fact that I travel on a diplomatic passport from the Independent Government of Samoa.

7.6. On 12th November 2003 I delivered a Reflection at the Service of Repentance and Renewal the Dag Hammarskjold Plaza. The event was to mark the anniversary of the Kyoto Protocol on Climate Change and Global Warming. I highlighted the commitment of the Anglican Communion to the fifth mark of its Mission statement to safeguard and renew God's Creation. That we also resolved as a Communion to write letters to apologize to our children for damaging the environment—which was a recommendation of my group at ACC9 in Wales. At the same event, I was also given the task to introduce the Ambassador of Tuvalu, who highlighted the fact that his country was losing its atolls to rising sea level due to global warming. The event was followed by deputation and meeting with many Permanent Missions and some Corporate Businesses whose activities contribute to global warming. I joined the group that visited the US Mission, the representative of which advised us that everything is determined and decided in Washington and they were only in New York to convey what had been predetermined. We emphasized that for many people like Tuvalu global warming was a critical issue.

7.7. Invitations to a few receptions during the GA Committee meetings provided additional opportunities for further interactions with Delegates and Mission staff.

7.8. On the International AIDS day on 1 December 2003 I was accompanied by the Chief Executive Officer of the Anglican Communion Office (ACO), Mr. Mark Pellew and Br. William to hand over to the Secretary General, a letter from the Secretary General, Canon John Peterson on ACC's programme on HIV/AIDS especially in Africa. The Secretary General was happy to acknowledge this wonderful work of his Anglican Communion.

7.9. In October 2004, we arranged and I spoke at the launching of the Micah Challenge at the United Nations. The Micah Challenge is the Church's response to the Millennium goal to reduce poverty by 50% by the year 2015 and the key note speaker was Archbishop N. W. Ndugane, the Primate of the Anglican Church of Southern Africa. In my reflections as one of the speakers I highlighted the environment crisis that the world is facing—yet some governments responsible for greatest percentage of harmful gas emissions, were not ratifying the Kyoto protocol for climate change and global warming. I also referred to the billions of dollars spent in arms, yet a mere tiny fraction of that will completely eradicate poverty in the whole world. I also made reference to the Anglican response to the Environment Crisis as publicized in the first book produced by your Anglican UN office "Healing God's Creation." (A copy of the Address is attached)

7.10. I was invited to preach at different churches in the USA especially around New York and to address their adult/education forums as well. At each occasion, I made sure that the ministry of the ACCUN Office as well as the importance of the United Nations are mentioned and understood. I also preached at a parish in Canada whilst attending the Provincial Synod last year. Twice I was invited to preach at the First Moravian Church in New York City. Last June, I had the privilege of addressing the Mother's Union General Meeting at the Isle of Man on the "International Year of the Family—Building Relationships" and I was also made a General member of the Organization immediately after my speech. A list of speaking engagements is attached with a copy of my address as one of the three Keynote speakers at the opening of the 25th conference on 31st May at the conference of professionals of the International Association for Impact Assessment.

8. ACKNOWLEDGEMENT AND THANKS

8.1. The work as reported would not be possible without the assistance from many sources for which we are most grateful. I have already mentioned some of them. However, I wish to say a special thank you to Mrs. Nancy Colton who has been a sincere friend of the office since I became the Observer. Nancy does not just contribute annually to our costs, but she also paid our annual subscriptions to some of our NGOs, supplied us with UN information on all the meetings she attended and since the beginning of last year agreed to represent us at most meetings of the NGO working groups on Disarmament, Sustainable Development, and the Committee on Human Rights to name a few.

8.2. Being your Anglican Observer at the United Nations has been a time of great opportunities for learning about the UN from a different angle from being a UN employee. Despite being very homesick for my family so far away in Samoa, I found it most rewarding to experience many opportunities to interact with people of many faiths, people from many cultures and educational backgrounds, people of diplomatic status and I got to appreciate the many images of the loving Christ in my work to serve you all.

8.3 My Wonderful Anglican Church of Aotearoa, New Zealand and Polynesia, has been supporting my ministry both financially as well as praying for me. I therefore wish to also record in this report my sincere gratitude to the Leadership and people of my church.

Thank you, Kia Ora, Faafetai lava, Vinaka Vaka Levu, Bahu Dania But, Malo Aupito, Fakaaue lahi, Metakima'ata. I also wish to pay a special tribute to the Bishop of Polynesia, the Rt. Rev Jabez Bryce, the new Assistant Bishops, the Standing Committee and people of my beloved Diocese of Polynesia—I hope I have lived up to your expectations—thank you for your prayers and especially for your annual contribution towards the costs of ACCUNO. I know you could hardly afford it but you gave ACCUNO top priority for Development funds and your 0.7% for such a goal. Faafetai lava.

8.4. I wish to avail myself of this opportunity to also thank my dearest friends and colleagues at ACCUN Office. They have been dedicated and hard working partners in our work. I wish to pay a special tribute to my hard working and prayer partner, Br. William Jones who was a tower of strength ever since he joined the office on October 14th, 2002. I honestly feel that any success of my work as your Anglican Observer at the United Nations was due to my hard working staff and especially Br. William. Although it will be joy to return home for good next year, it is the thought of not having you around that will make it hard to leave ACCUN Office and you all.

8.5 Our work may have fallen short of your expectations as ACC employees, but I will strive to do the very best I could whilst walking towards the sunset of my term of office. I promise you that I will make sure that your next Observer will not go through what I experienced by not having proper office records (thanks to our wonderful volunteer, Mrs. Elizabeth Renegar), as well proper furniture and fittings for an office environment conducive of serving the Anglican Communion effectively and efficiently. We have been assured of getting the best of the second hand furniture and equipment that ECUSA will not require when we move to our designated office in accordance with the new configuration of the Church Centre. In the next few months we will try to be better stewards of the resources and to effectively serve you, the rest of the Anglican Communion and God's people.

8.6 May God repay you ACC a thousand fold for your kind assistance to ACCUN Office. May God grant you peace and tranquility within yourselves, your families and loved-ones. Please also pray for the United Nations and for Peace in the World.

PART II
THE UNITED NATIONS COMMISSION ON THE STATUS OF WOMEN (UNCSW)

1. INTRODUCTION:

1.1. The UNCSW was established in 1946 at the request of the UN Economic & Social Council (ECOSOC) in order that women's rights in political, economic, civil, social and educational fields and, emerging issues could be tracked by the United Nations. The object of the Commission is to promote implementation of the principle that men and women shall have equal right. Its membership is comprised of 45 member states of the UN on the basis of: 13 from African states; 11 from Asian states (including the Pacific /Oceania); 9 from Latin American and Caribbean states; and, 8 from Western European and Other States. The present Bureau of the Commission elected this year for the 50th and 51st Sessions (2006 and 2007) comprises of Chairperson from El Salvador, four Vice Presidents from Nigeria, Hungary, the United Kingdom, and Indonesia. The UNCSW meets annually and is a time within which organizations that are accredited to the UN can also participate together with civil society.

1.2. As alluded to in Part I (Section 3.6.), ACCUN Office started participating at the UNCSW sessions in February 2002. ACC however was represented in 1995 at the Fourth World Conference on Women in Beijing under the leadership of The Rt. Rev James Ottley, the Second Anglican Observer at the United Nations. It was at that conference that 189 governments (the full membership of the United Nations then) adopted by consensus the Beijing Declaration with full commitment to the implementation of the Beijing Platform for Action. The declaration clearly linked the equal rights of women to other instruments of human rights, in particular the Convention on the Elimination of All Forms of Discrimination against Women (CEDAW), the Convention of the Rights of the Child (CRC), the Declaration on the Elimination of Violence against Women and the Declaration on the Right to Development. The UNCSW was mandated by the General Assembly to play a central role in monitoring, within the UN system, the implementation of the Beijing Platform for Action (BPfA) and report annually to the ECOSOC.

1.3. Since 1996 the UNCSW met on specific areas as follow up on the Beijing conference and the implementation of the BPfA. The UN General Assembly (GA) in its special session of June in 2000 adopted a "Political declaration" and Resolution for "Further actions and initiatives to implement the BPfA (referred to as the "outcome documents"), The UNCSW for its Multi-year progamme of work 2001 to 2006 therefore concentrated on the Implementation of Critical Areas of Concerns in compliance with the outcome document.

1.4. The two themes for the 46th Session in 2002 were (1) Eradicating poverty, including through the empowerment of women throughout their life cycle in a globalizing world, and (2) Environmental management and mitigation of natural disasters: a gender perspective. ACCUN Office was represented at this session by Mrs. Marge Christie of ECUSA, who paid for her own personal expenses and Ms Martha Gardner of the ECUSA Peace and Justice Ministries who attended the Session on a part time basis. Marge's report on ACC12 was part of the International Anglican Women's Network (IAWN) reports.

1.5. In 2003, three (3) women (Mrs Christie, Mrs Elizabeth Loweth from Canada and Dr. Pauline Muchina of Kenya working for ECUSA) offered to represent ACC at the 47th Session of the Commission at their own expenses. This specific session dealt with (1) Participation and access of women to the media, and information and communication technologies and their impact on and use as an instrument for the advancement and empowerment of women, and (2) Women's human rights and elimination of all forms of violence against women and girls as defined in the BPfA and the outcome documents. I referred to the tensions experienced at this particular conference under section 3.6.3 of Part I above. As reported by Ms. Angela King on 6 March 2005, many women were very disappointed but through skillful negotiations and compromise, the 58th GA was able to adopt a very comprehensive resolution later that same year.

2. PARTICIPATION UNDER THE ANGLICAN CONSULTATIVE COUNCIL OFFICE AT THE UNITED NATIONS (ACCUNO)

2.1. ACCUN Office has long recognized the critical importance of establishing and strengthening the links between the various instruments of the United Nations and as many 'agencies' of the worldwide Anglican Communion as possible. Of particular concern has been the desire to promote and facilitate the participation in and empowerment of Anglican women through involvement in UN activities. Furthermore, as a former UN employee I was exposed to the UN programmes and objectives to improve the status of women in a changing world. I was fully aware of the Beijing Declaration which affirmed and reflected my own personal life story, that Women's empowerment and their full participation on the basis of equality in all spheres of society, including participation in decision-making process and access to power, are **fundamental for the achievement of equality, development and peace.** It is for these reasons and many more that following ACC12, I was determined to give priority to an annual commitment to securing the presence and contributions of a strong and influential ACC delegation of global Anglican women at the UNCSW gatherings.

2.2. Furthermore it was also the intention of the office for concentrating on the UNCSW in order to: (a) sensitize the ECUSA sisters (especially those around New York) about gender issues as promoted at the UN so they could be bridge builders for UN issues blocked by the US government (eg. the ratification of CEDAW and for releasing funds for UNFPA work); (b) to promote awareness of the plight of the women and gender issues worldwide; and (c) to empower the Coordinator of the International Anglican Women's Network (IAWN) as well as the Director of the ECUSA Women's Ministries to be more involved in implementing the BPfA.

3. THE ACCUNO SUPPORT GROUP FOR UNCSW

3.1. Working with Ecumenical partners I became aware of and greatly envied their capability to finance delegates to attend the UNCSW meetings. By March 2003, ACCUN Office was already in the red and there was no way we could do this. But it was a blessing, when Phoebe Griswold told me that if I could convince her that it was for a good cause she would consider helping me in fielding an ACC delegation in 2004. Following several meetings and with some educational programmes one of which is mentioned under 3.6.4 above, as well as a special meeting with Alice Metcof in Minneapolis, I managed to convince Phoebe about the value of exposing the ECUSA women to UN work and networking with other Anglican sisters overseas that greatly needed help. It was also a blessing that ECUSA decided to re-establish the position of Director of Women's Ministries and Margaret Rose joined as the incumbent in June 2003 and offered to help us in pursuing our goals. Marge Christie greatly assisted me in the process of convincing Phoebe to be involved. I am pleased to say that once convinced, there was nothing stopping this wonderful woman leader in pursuing what she believed in. I thank her most sincerely for being the driving force for our work in this area of focus.

3.2. It was in the Fall of 2003, that many women contacted by Phoebe and some of the friends for ACCUN Office, that we were able to establish a strategy team (later became the design team) as well as a special commission of about 20 dedicated Anglicans/Episcopalians to plan and make the necessary arrangements for the delegation to the 48th Session of the UNCSW.

3.3. Should you wish to search for information on UNCSW through "Google" the very first item you will find will be: "Anglican Delegation to the UNCSW." If you care to open the item, it talks about "Anglican Women's Empowerment and the UN Commission on the Status of Women." It succinctly describes the ministry of the ACCUN Office support group which has graduated from being an Anglican Women's Empowerment Team (AWET) to AWE, Anglican Women's Empowerment and they do exactly that including the empowerment of ACCUN Office as well. They are a group of AWEsome Women

3.3.1. AWE was formed in 2003 under the leadership of Mrs. Phoebe Griswold to provide direct assistance to ACCUN Office for Anglican Women's participation at UN activities especially the UNCSW. AWE was greatly assisted and resourced by the Episcopal Church of USA (ECUSA) to fulfill its role in supporting the ACCUN Office. In order to be more focused in its work, AWE adopted the following Statement of Purpose for its Ministry: "We are women of the Anglican Communion gathering to build a movement whose commitment to the gospel propels us to speak and advocate for the dignity of every human being in our churches and the world by participation as Anglican Consultative Council delegates to the UNCSW sessions through the Office of the Anglican Observe at the UN."

3.3.2. The AWE membership of committed women volunteers includes African Americans, Women of colour, Africans as well as Asian women. The members did their work under task groups for Education (Issues and Advocacy), Funding, Events, Publicity and Hospitality.

3.3.3. For UNCSW 2005, AWE was responsible for planning and organizing a comprehensive programme of social activities, public events and a wide range of significant occasions where wonderful hospitality was accorded the Anglican delegation. The members of AWE Hospitality Team to whom a huge debt of gratitude is nevertheless owed include, Christina B Hing, Blandina Salvador, Inez Saley & Alice Ogwal. The AWE was very ably assisted by Kim Robey and Janis Rosheuvel of the ECUSA Women's Ministry as well as the ACCUN Office staff Br.William Jones, Phoebe Gallagher (High School Intern) and Louise Gleich (CMS Intern from England). Ms. Ednice Baerga of the Presiding Bishop's Office was also a member of the secretariat who greatly assisted AWE in its many roles.

4. THE ACC DELEGATION TO THE 48TH UNCSW SESSION IN 2004

4.1. In 2004 ACCUN Office was able to invite and host 55 Anglican women and two men from 12 of the 38 Provinces of the Anglican Communion to participate at the 48th UNCSW session. It was the largest delegation present at this UNCSW. The Provinces represented were Aotearoa, New Zealand & Polynesia, Canada, Central Africa, England, Jerusalem and the Middle East, Kenya, North India, Papua New Guinea, Philippines, Southern Africa, Uganda, and the Episcopal Church of the United States of America.

4.1.1. Other Anglican Women included The Mothers' Union, itself an UN Accredited NGO, which had a delegation of 3 women from England and 1 from Canada. Many other Anglican women were present, as delegates, as members of delegations, and as members of a variety of NGOs. The highest profile Anglican was Ms. Angela King, UN Assistant Secretary-General and Special Advisor on Gender Issues and the Advancement of Women to Kofi Anan, Secretary-General of the UN. Ms King retired from her position on 30 April 2004 and at the ACCUN Office fund raising dinner in June 2004, and in the presence of the Archbishop of Canterbury, was recognized and was the first to receive the Anglican Observer's Award as an Anglican living out her faith globally.

4.2. In preparation for participation at the 48th Session ACCUN Office sent out from August 2003 to February 2004, a steady stream of information, via email, to each delegate. AWE raised a substantial sum of money to finance representatives from around the world. They also organized an easy transition for those who came from outside of the USA to enter the bustle of New York City by supplying hospitality, subway passes, telephone cards, and, most importantly, a buddy system so each visitor had a friend from the very first day. In the words of one out-of-country delegate: "It would have been so much more difficult if they hadn't taken such good care of us".

4.2.1. The women of the Anglican Delegation went specifically as women of faith. They linked with other women of faith through Ecumenical Women 2000+, with a membership comprising of representatives from the ACCUN Office, Church Women United, Methodist Church, Lutheran World Federation, Presbyterian UN Office, National Council of Churches of Christ, the Young Women's Christian Association and ECUSA. The Ecumenical Women 2000 Plus conducted a training day on 28 February which women of the Anglican Delegation found very helpful.

4.3. The 48th Session focused on the following two major items for it's work:

"The role of men and boys in achieving gender equality" and "Women's equal participation in conflict prevention, management and conflict resolution and in post conflict peace building". As it was done in the past, Expert group meetings were held throughout the year to discuss the status existing in most countries, good practices, constraints and to formulate a draft agenda for the forthcoming CSW Session and a draft statement for delegates to adopting at the Session.

4.4. In advance of the Session, each NGO sent its statement to the UNCSW. The Anglican statement prepared by members of AWE with inputs from the provinces is attached:

Statement of the Anglican Consultative Council
to the 48th Session of the Commission on the Status of Women
New York, 1–12 March 2004

The Anglican Communion

The Anglican Communion is comprised of 75 million Christians from 164 countries reaching from England to Southern Africa, from Australia to the Southern Cone, from the United States to the Philippines. Many Anglicans, mostly in Africa and the Middle East, experience conflict affecting mainly Women, Children and the Aged.

A Theological Statement

As Christians we believe that all humanity is made in the image of God; as Anglicans we live in the creative tension of differing experiences and viewpoints; as Women we are called to respond to the brokenness of the world. This is at the heart of our theology.

We firmly believe the two areas of critical concern for this year are important ones and pray that this gathering can help give insight, direction and inspiration to those who daily face gender inequality and conflict.

The Role of Men and Boys in Gender Equality

We concur with the statement of the Beijing Platform for Action, Paragraph 41, which comments on the Critical Areas of Concern stating that, "the advancement of women and the achievement of equality between women and men are a matter of human rights and a condition for social justice and should not be seen in isolation as a women's issue."

The achievement of gender equality is a responsibility of the whole society and should fully engage women, girls, men and boys. At the root of our faith is a commitment to justice and peace in the world. Unequal power relations and gender stereotypes in education and socialization processes, in health and HIV/AIDS, violence and harassment pose serious challenges to the achievement of gender equality. We welcome the systematic evaluation of the role of men and boys in achieving gender equality at this 48th session of the United Nations Commission on the Status of Women and we fully support the Millennium Development Goals and their commitment to promote gender equality and empower women. For example we applaud the efforts of our sisters in South Africa as they initiate talks within the church on gender equality.

We therefore call upon this commission to:

a).support the work of the partnership of government and the NGO community in the implementation of policies and programmes which will create gender harmony;

b) urge United Nations agencies to formulate programmes dealing with education and re-socialization of women and men for gender equity;

c) urge governments to apply gender budgetary analysis to overseas development aid, as recommended in the Financing for Development consensus;

d) advocate for those marginalized by gender injustice, and to work in a collaborative way in order to bring about changes in all institutions including faith communities and society; and,

e) encourage governments to promote a better understanding of issues around Gender Justice, recognizing that the achievement of gender equality is a responsibility of everyone and that national policies should fully engage women, girls, men and boys.

Women as Peacemakers and Conflict Reconcilers

We believe peace is possible on a global scale. However, it will take a new way of acting—for too long national leaders have led the human race into wars and violence in the name of justice, religion and revenge. In modern day warfare, civilians are 90 per cent of the casualties, and the vast majority of the casualties are women and children. We know that when human rights and gender equality reinforce each other, the level of violence decreases, not only within countries but globally as well.

The Beijing Conference in 1995 saw more than 180 governments commit themselves to the goal of equal participation of women and men in decision making to provide the necessary balance to strengthen democracy. On average on a global scale, only 14 per cent of the seats in national parliaments are held by women.[1] Almost ten years later women remain significantly under represented in national and local assemblies. We therefore encourage the Commission to pursue the adoption and implementation by all governments of the General Assembly Third Committee Resolution on Women and political participation (Agenda 110 adopted on November 6th 2003). Furthermore we also urge the Commission to ensure full implementation of the Security Council Resolution 1325.

Women of The Episcopal Church (the Anglican Communion in the United States) are particularly distressed that their country remains one of the very few which has not signed the Convention on the Elimination of all forms of Discrimination Against Women. The decision of the US government leadership not to ratify this UN convention underscores and helps to explain the paucity of women in decision-making roles. Because CEDAW has not been ratified in the US, women in that country have not been able to record whether or not gains have been made in the participation of women in conflict management and peace making. The Episcopal Church, through its legislative procedures, has expressed its commitment to CEDAW by continuing to urge ratification. The signing of the Convention would enhance the authority of the United States as an advocate for the seating of women at the peace table.

In conflict and post-conflict arenas women's exclusion is even more pronounced. Despite their experiences as casualties of war, women are rarely seen in peacekeeping, peace-building, pre and post-conflict prevention, post-conflict resolution and reconstruction of their societies. We are confident this will change as around the world women rise up to proclaim that violence is never the answer, it only leads to more violence. Circles of women for peace are rising up across the globe and in that context, special attention should be given to identifying and working with local women who represent an influential voice for peace.

We hear from our Anglican sisters in other parts of the world of efforts underway in peace movements. From India comes "It is not enough to talk about peace, one must believe in it; it is not enough just to believe, one must work at it." The church women are committed to actions for peace-building in their country. In Eastern Zimbabwe such work takes the shape of sending women to Capetown for training at the Centre for Conflict Resolution. In Nigeria, dismantling the barriers of poverty and illiteracy are a priority. As in many countries, a male-oriented work culture and a hostile police force restrain women from taking their place in public office and in conflict resolution.

Conclusion:

We commit ourselves to the areas of concerns of this gathering—the role of men and boys in achieving gender equality and women's equal participation in conflict prevention, management and conflict resolution and in post-conflict peace-building.

We present our 2004 statement remembering with dismay that in 2003 the Commission on the Status of Women was unable to adopt a statement of Agreed Conclusions condemning the epidemic of violence against women. The delegation from the Anglican Communion, committed to respecting the dignity of every human being, decries the ways in which religion—and custom and tradition—are used in the oppression of women. We are committed to listening to all points of view on the issues, understanding differing cultural and religious contexts but speaking and working particularly to identify when and where faith empowers and enhances women's lives. As Christians, Anglicans and Women, we are called to be peacemakers. We yearn for a new creation and the realization of God's promise to make all things new.

A Prayer for Gender Equality and Peace

We therefore wish to offer you the following in words paraphrasing a prayer written expressly for Beijing:

O God, Creator of the heavens and the earth, we pray for all who gather at the United Nations to uncover the role of women as peacemakers and participants in conflict resolution as they also address the role of men and boys in achieving gender equality. Open our ears to the cries of a suffering world and to the healing melodies of peace. Amen

---

4.5. ACCUN Office sponsored several side events during the 2004 UNCSW Session. We also invited the Mothers Union (MU) delegates to work together with our delegation and to attend all the events hosted by ACCUN Office as well.

4.5.1. ACCUN Office sponsored a main event "Blessed are the Peacemakers: Anglican Women as Peace Builders through Service and Action" at the Synod Hall of the Cathedral of St. John the Divine, New York City, on Sunday afternoon 7 March 2004.

4.5.1.1. The Rt Rev Cathy Roskam, Bishop Suffragan of New York, offered prayer to God on behalf of those assembled, and then everyone was welcomed by Phoebe Griswold, Lead Delegate of the 2004 UNCSW and wife of the Presiding Bishop of the United States. The Anglican Observer at the United Nations, Archdeacon Taimalelagi Fagamalama Tuatagaloa-Matalavea introduced the panelists and moderated the discussion.

4.5.1.2. The featured speaker was Jane Williams, Theologian, lecturer in Doctrine and Modern Church History—Trinity College, Bristol and wife of the Archbishop of Canterbury. Mrs. Williams' speech is attached.

Responses were offered by the following delegates who, in the process talked about how their faith as Anglicans informed their work:

- Dr. Jennifer Plane Te Paa, Te Ahorangi/Dean of Te Rau Kahikatea, constituent of St John's Theological College, Auckland, New Zealand.
- Nema Aluku, HIV/AIDS Programme Coordinator, Council of Anglican Provinces in Africa (CAPA)
- Clair Ghais Abdel Malik Barsoum, Director, Deaf Unit, El Malek el Saleh, Cairo, Egypt.

- Jyotsna Rani Patro, President Synodical Women's Fellowship for Christian Service Church of North India, and President All India Council of Christian Women Unit IV of the National Council of Churches of India and
- Rev Margaret Rose, Director of Women's Ministries, Episcopal Church USA

4.5.1.3. Discussions focused on the hope of the Anglican delegation for the CSW to highlight the need for peaceful solutions to conflicts and urged member states of the United Nations to support the full implementation of United Nations Security Council Resolution 1325 Women, War, and Peace. The proceedings of this well attended event was publicized and telecasted and can still be viewed on the worldwide web at http://www.episcopalchurch.org/uncsw.htm.

4.5.2. ACCUN Office also sponsored, with several other co-sponsors, six other workshops:

4.5.2.1. "The Cross-Generational Spread of HIV/AIDS in Sub-Saharan Africa and its Effect on Girls". Two of the speakers were Anglican delegates: Dr Pauline Muchina and Nema Aluku.

4.5.2.2. "The Role of Rural women—Conflict resolution or Conflict? In the Home . . . in the Community . . . in the World".

4.5.2.3. "Women's Stories of Inclusion and Exclusion from the Abrahamic Traditions' Sacred Texts: Their Application to Contemporary Issues". (A very popular event held at the Episcopal Church Centre Chapel)

4.5.2.4. "Teaching Boys to be Men: Youth Push for Gender Equality in efforts to Combat HIV/AIDS".

4.5.2.5. "Indigenous Perspective on Gender Equality & the Media— A Discussion of the Creation Myth of the Whangara Peoples of New Zealand as portrayed in the book & film 'The Whale Rider'". The speaker was Anglican delegate, Dr Jennifer Plane Te Paa.

4.5.2.6. "War is not Good". Discussion of ways of advocating for a peaceful world.

4.6. Final Documents:

4.6.1. Prior to the beginning of the 48th Session, a document was prepared for each of the two topics. The NGOs altered and added to the documents and then the UN government delegations carefully reworked them. NGOs monitored the reworking, suggested new wording, kept in touch with their country's delegation, lobbied, and did what they could to make the final document as strong as possible for the benefit of all women.

4.6.2. The final document for "The role of men and boys in achieving gender equality" is attached.

Commission on the Status of Women
48th session
1–12 March 2004

The role of men and boys in achieving gender equality
Agreed conclusions

1. The Commission on the Status of Women recalls and reiterates that the Beijing Declaration and Platform for Action encouraged men to participate fully in all actions towards gender equality and urged the establishment of the principle of shared power and responsibility between women and men at home, in the community, in the workplace and in the wider national and international communities. The Commission also recalls and reiterates the outcome document adopted at the twenty-third special session of the General Assembly entitled "Gender equality, development and peace in the twenty-first century", which emphasized that men must take joint responsibility with women for the promotion of gender equality.

2. The Commission recognizes that men and boys, while some themselves face discriminatory barriers and practices, can and do make contributions to gender equality in their many capacities, including as individuals, members of families, social groups and communities, and in all spheres of society.

3. The Commission recognizes that gender inequalities still exist and are reflected in imbalances of power between women and men in all spheres of society. The Commission further recognizes that everyone benefits from gender equality and that the negative impacts of gender inequality are borne by society as a whole and emphasizes, therefore, that men and boys, through taking responsibility themselves and working jointly in partnership with women and girls, are essential to achieving the goals of gender equality, development and peace. The Commission recognizes the capacity of men and boys in bringing about change in attitudes, relationships and access to resources and decisionmaking which are critical for the promotion of gender equality and the full enjoyment of all human rights by women.

4. The Commission acknowledges and encourages men and boys to continue to take positive initiatives to eliminate gender stereotypes and promote gender equality, including combating violence against women, through networks, peer programmes, information campaigns, and training programmes. The Commission acknowledges the critical role of gender-sensitive education and training in achieving gender equality.

5. The Commission also recognizes that the participation of men and boys in achieving gender equality must be consistent with the empowerment of women and girls and acknowledges that efforts must be made to address the undervaluation of many types of work, abilities and roles associated with women. In this regard, it is important that resources for gender equality initiatives for men and boys do not compromise equal opportunities and resources for women and girls.

6. The Commission urges Governments and, as appropriate, the relevant funds and programmes, organizations and specialized agencies of the United Nations system, the international financial institutions, civil society, including the private sector and nongovernmental organizations, and other stakeholders, to take the following actions:

a) Encourage and support the capacity of men and boys in fostering gender equality, including acting in partnership with women and girls as agents for change and in providing positive leadership, in particular where men are still key decision makers responsible for policies, programmes and legislation, as well as holders of economic and organizational power and public resources;

b) Promote understanding of the importance of fathers, mothers, legal guardians and other caregivers, to the well being of children and the promotion of gender equality and of the need to develop policies, programmes and school curricula that encourage and maximize their positive involvement in achieving gender equality and positive results for children, families and communities;

c) Create and improve training and education programmes to enhance awareness and knowledge among men and women on their roles as parents, legal guardians and caregivers and the importance of sharing family responsibilities, and include fathers as well as mothers in programmes that teach infant child care development;

d) Develop and include in education programmes for parents, legal guardians and other caregivers information on ways and means to increase the capacity of men to raise children in a manner oriented towards gender equality;

e) Encourage men and boys to work with women and girls in the design of policies and programmes for men and boys aimed at gender equality and foster the involvement of men and boys in gender mainstreaming efforts in order to ensure improved design of all policies and programmes;

f) Encourage the design and implementation of programmes at all levels to accelerate a socio-cultural change towards gender equality, especially through the upbringing and educational process, in terms of changing harmful traditional perceptions and attitudes of male and female roles in order to achieve the full and equal participation of women and men in the society;

g) Develop and implement programmes for pre-schools, schools, community centers, youth organizations, sport clubs and centres, and other groups dealing with children and youth, including training for teachers, social workers and other professionals who deal with children to foster positive attitudes and behaviours on gender equality;

h) Promote critical reviews of school curricula, textbooks and other information education and communication materials at all levels in order to recommend ways to strengthen the promotion of gender equality that involves the engagement of boys as well as girls;

i) Develop and implement strategies to educate boys and girls and men and women about tolerance, mutual respect for all individuals and the promotion of all human rights;

j) Develop and utilize a variety of methods in public information campaigns on the role of men and boys in promoting gender equality, including through approaches specifically targeting boys and young men;

k) Engage media, advertising and other related professionals, through the development of training and other programmes, on the importance of promoting gender equality, nonstereotypical portrayal of women and girls and men and boys and on the harms caused by portraying women and girls in a demeaning or exploitative manner, as well as on the enhanced participation of women and girls in the media;

l) Take effective measures, to the extent consistent with freedom of expression, to combat the growing sexualization and use of pornography in media content, in terms of the rapid development of ICT, encourage men in the media to refrain from presenting women as inferior beings and exploiting them as sexual objects and commodities, combat ICT- and media-based violence against women including criminal misuse of ICT for sexual harassment, sexual exploitation and trafficking in women and girls, and support the development and use of ICT as a resource for the empowerment of women and girls, including those affected by violence, abuse and other forms of sexual exploitation;

m) Adopt and implement legislation and/or policies to close the gap between women's and men's pay and promote reconciliation of occupational and family responsibilities, including through reduction of occupational segregation, introduction or expansion of parental leave, flexible working arrangements, such as voluntary part-time work, teleworking, and other home-based work;

n) Encourage men, through training and education, to fully participate in the care and support of others, including older persons, persons with disabilities and sick persons, in particular children and other dependants;

o) Encourage active involvement of men and boys through education projects and peerbased programmes in eliminating gender stereotypes as well as gender inequality in particular in relation to sexually transmitted infections, including HIV/AIDS, as well as their full participation in prevention, advocacy, care, treatment, support and impact evaluation programmes;

p) Ensure men's access to and utilization of reproductive and sexual health services and programmes, including HIV/AIDS-related programmes and services, and encourage men to participate with women in programmes designed to prevent and treat all forms of HIV/AIDS transmission and other sexually transmitted infections;

q) Design and implement programmes to encourage and enable men to adopt safe and responsible sexual and reproductive behaviour, and to use effectively methods to prevent unwanted pregnancies and sexually transmitted infections, including HIV/AIDS;

r) Encourage and support men and boys to take an active part in the prevention and elimination of all forms of violence, and especially gender-based violence, including in the context of HIV/AIDS, and increase awareness of men's and boys' responsibility in ending the cycle of violence, inter alia, through the promotion of attitudinal and behavioural change, integrated education and training which prioritize the safety of women and children, prosecution and rehabilitation of perpetrators, and support for survivors, and recognizing that men and boys also experience violence;

s) Encourage an increased understanding among men how violence, including trafficking for the purposes of commercialized sexual exploitation, forced marriages and forced labour, harms women, men and children and undermines gender equality, and consider measures aimed at eliminating the demand for trafficked women and children;

t) Encourage and support both women and men in leadership positions, including political leaders, traditional leaders, business leaders, community and religious leaders, musicians, artists and athletes to provide positive role models on gender equality;

u) Encourage men in leadership positions to ensure equal access for women to education, property rights and inheritance rights and to promote equal access to information technology and business and economic opportunities, including in international trade, in order to provide women with the tools that enable them to take part fully and equally in economic and political decision-making processes at all levels;

v) Identify and fully utilize all contexts in which a large number of men can be reached, particularly in male-dominated institutions, industries and associations, to sensitize men on their roles and responsibilities in the promotion of gender equality and the full enjoyment of all human rights by women, including in relation to HIV/AIDS and violence against women;

w) Develop and use statistics to support and/or carry out research, inter alia, on the cultural, social and economic conditions, which influence the attitudes and behaviours of men and boys towards women and girls, their awareness of gender inequalities and their involvement in promoting gender equality;

x) Carry out research on men's and boys' views of gender equality and their perceptions of their roles through which further programmes and policies can be developed and identify and widely disseminate good practices. Assess the impact of efforts undertaken to engage men and boys in achieving gender equality;

y) Promote and encourage the representation of men in institutional mechanisms for the advancement of women;

z) Encourage men and boys to support women's equal participation in conflict prevention, management and conflict resolution and in post-conflict peace-building;

7. The Commission urges all entities within the UN system to take into account the recommendations contained in these agreed conclusions and to disseminate these agreed conclusions widely.

1 Report of the Fourth World Conference on Women, Beijing 4-15 September 1995 (United Nations Publication, Sales No. E.96.IV. 13). A/RES/S-23/3, annex.)

The final document for "Women's equal participation in conflict prevention, management and conflict resolution and in post-conflict peace-building" is also attached.

Women's equal participation in conflict prevention, management and conflict resolution and in post-conflict peace-building

Agreed conclusions

1. The Commission on the Status of Women recalls and reiterates the strategic objectives and actions of the Beijing Declaration and Platform for Action, the outcome document of the twenty-third special session of the General Assembly entitled "Gender equality, development and peace for the twenty-first century"(*Report of the Fourth World Conference on Women, Beijing, 4-15 September 1995* (United Nations publication, Sales No. E.96.IV. 13), chap. I, resolution 1, annexes I and 11. 2 General Assembly resolution S-23/3, annex E/1998/27) and its agreed conclusions on women and armed conflict adopted at its forty-second session in 1998. It recalls the Convention on the Elimination of All Forms of Discrimination against Women. It also recalls Security Council resolution 1325 (2000) on women, peace and security. It further recalls all relevant resolutions of the General Assembly, including resolution 58/142 on women and political participation.

2. The Commission calls for the full respect of international human rights law and international humanitarian law including the four Geneva Conventions of 1949, in particular the Fourth Geneva Convention relative to the protection of civilian persons in time of war.

3. The Commission calls for the promotion and protection of the full enjoyment of all human rights and fundamental freedoms by women and girls at all times, including during conflict prevention, conflict management and conflict resolution and in post conflict peace building. It further calls for the protection and security for women and girls under threat of violence and their freedom of movement and participation in social, political and economic activities.

4. The Commission recognizes that the root causes of armed conflict are multidimensional in nature, thus requiring a comprehensive and integrated approach to the prevention of armed conflict.

5. International cooperation based on the principles of the United Nations Charter enhances women's full and equal participation in conflict prevention, conflict management and conflict resolution and in post-conflict peace building and contributes to the promotion of sustainable and durable peace.

6. To **achieve sustainable and durable** peace, the full and equal participation of women and girls and the integration of gender perspectives in all aspects of conflict prevention, management and conflict resolution and in post-conflict peace-building is essential. Yet women continue to be under-represented in the processes, institutions and mechanisms dealing with these areas. Therefore, further effort is needed to promote gender equality and ensure women's equal participation at all levels of deci-

sion-making, in all relevant institutions. Further effort, including consideration of adequate resourcing, is also needed to build and consolidate the capacity of women and women's groups to participate fully in these processes as well as to promote understanding of the essential role women play. In this regard, the international community should use lessons learned from actual experience to identify and overcome barriers for achieving women's equal participation.

7. The Commission recognizes that while both men and women suffer from the consequences of armed conflict, there is a differential impact on women and girls who are often subject to, and affected by, particular forms of violence and deprivation. The Commission calls for measures to prevent gender-based violence, including sexual violence against women and girls, as well as trafficking in human beings, especially trafficking in women and girls, arising from armed conflict and in post-conflict situations, and to prosecute perpetrators of such crimes.

8. The Commission encourages the collection and dissemination of sex-disaggregated data and information for planning, evaluation and analysis in order to promote the mainstrearning of a gender perspective in conflict prevention, management and conflict resolution and in post-conflict peace-building.

9. Peace agreements provide a vehicle for the promotion of gender equality and the participation of women in post-conflict situations. Significant opportunities for women's participation arise in the preparatory phase leading up to a peace agreement. The content of a peace agreement likewise offers significant scope for ensuring that the rights, concerns and priorities of women and girls are fully addressed. Finally, once a peace agreement has been concluded, its implementation should be pursued with explicit attention to women's full and equal participation and the goal of gender equality.

10. Women's full and equal participation and the integration of gender perspectives are crucial to democratic electoral processes in post-conflict situations. A gender-sensitive constitutional and legal framework, especially electoral laws and regulations, is necessary to ensure that women can fully participate in such processes. Political parties can play a crucial role in promoting women's equal participation. Steps are also necessary to ensure that women participate fully in, and that a gender perspective is incorporated throughout, the design and implementation of voter and civic education programmes, and in election administration and observation.

11. Governments in particular, as well as the United Nations system, especially those United Nations entities having a mandate on peace and security, and other relevant international, regional and national actors, including civil society, have a responsibility for advancing gender equality and ensuring women's full and equal participation in all aspects of peace processes and in post-conflict peace-building, reconstruction, rehabilitation and reconciliation, where they are participants in these processes.

12. In regard to conflict prevention The Commission on the Status of Women calls on Governments, as well as all other relevant participants in these processes, to

a. improve the collection, analysis and inclusion of information on women and gender issues as part of conflict prevention and early warning efforts;

b. ensure better collaboration and coordination between efforts to promote gender equality and efforts aimed at conflict prevention;

c. support capacity building, especially for civil society, in particular women's organizations, to increase community commitment to conflict prevention;

d. continue to make resources available nationally and internationally for prevention of conflict and ensure women's participation in the elaboration and implementation of strategies for preventing conflict.

13. In regard to peace processes

The Commission on the Status of Women calls on Governments, as well as all other relevant participants in these processes, to

a. promote women's full, equal and effective participation as actors in all peace processes, in particular negotiation, mediation and facilitation;

b. ensure that peace agreements address, from a gender perspective, the full range of security aspects, including legal, political, social, economic and physical, and also address the specific needs and priorities of women and girls;

c. ensure, in the implementation phase of a peace agreement, that all provisions concerning gender equality and the participation of women are fully complied with, and that all provisions of the peace agreement, including demobilization, disarmament, reintegration, and rehabilitation, are implemented in a manner that promotes gender equality and ensures women's full and equal participation;

d. promote women's full and equal access to public information related to peace processes;

e. review, on a regular basis, their contributions to the promotion of gender equality and the full and equal participation of women, and to fulfill their monitoring, accountability and reporting obligations in the implementation of peace agreements;

f. with regard to gender mainstreaming, ensure and support the full participation of women at all levels of decision-making and implementation in development activities and peace processes, including conflict prevention and resolution, post-conflict reconstruction, peace making, peacekeeping and peace building, and in this regard, support the involvement of women's organizations, community-based organizations and non-governmental organizations;

g. develop and strengthen the provision of gender advisory capacity and gender sensitive training programmes for all staff in missions related to armed conflicts;

In this regard, the Commission takes note of the report of the Secretary-General

14. In regard to post-conflict peace building

The Commission on the Status of Women calls on Governments, as well as all other relevant participants in these processes, to *concerning elections:*

a. ensure equal access of women in all stages of the electoral process including to consider the adoption of measures for increasing women's participation in elections through, inter alia, individual voter registration, temporary gender-specific positive actions and access to information, representation in bodies administering elections and as election monitors and observers, as well as encouraging political parties to involve women fully and equally in all aspects of their operations;

b. ensure equal access for women to voter and civic education, provide women candidates with full support, training and financial resources, and eliminate discriminatory practices hampering women's participation either as voters or candidates.

concerning reconstruction and rehabilitation:

a. ensure the full participation of women on equal bases, in the reconstruction and rehabilitation process;

b. ensure the equal access of women to social services, in particular health and education, and in this regard, to promote the provision of adequate health care and health services and assistance for women and girls in conflict and post-conflict situations and counseling for post-conflict trauma;

c. facilitate equal employment opportunities for women to achieve their economic empowerment.

15. The realization and the achievement of the goals of gender equality, development and peace need to be supported by the allocation of necessary human, financial and material resources for specific and targeted activities to ensure gender equality at the local, national, regional and international levels as well as by enhanced and increased international cooperation.

16. The Commission on the Status of Women requests the Secretary-General to disseminate these agreed conclusions widely including to the high level panel on global security threats and reform of the international system.

4.7. Highlights of UNCSW 2004:

The four significant UN documents impacting women's lives are:

a) The Beijing Platform for Action (BPFA) adopted at the Fourth World Conference on Women (Beijing, 1995),

b) The Outcome of the 23rd Special Session of the General Assembly (2000),

c) The Millennium Development Goals and Targets (2000) (MDGs)

d) The Security Council Resolution 1325 (Women, Peace and Security), adopted at its meeting on 31 October 2000.

4.7.1. The members of the Anglican delegation are committed to urging their governments to live up to the commitments made when they signed these documents.

4.7.2. An assessment of the UN instruments in 4.7. was planned for the year 2005. The Division for the Advancement of Women (DAW) sent a questionnaire, known as the DAW questionnaire, to all governments for completion. NGO's were asked to prepare an alternative report on their own governments and submit these to DAW, thereby including women's voices in the reporting system.

4.7.2.1.The members of the Anglican delegation approved, in principle, the redesign of the DAW questionnaire specifically for the use of the Anglican Church worldwide. It was our hope that, by asking some specific questions regarding women's participation in church structures and activities, the Anglican Communion will be better able to organize its life to include women in all aspects of church life.

4.8. Men and Boys:

4.8.1. Historically, the subject of Men and Boys has not been discussed in depth at CSW meetings. Many new ideas emerged in 2004. The word "patriarchy", formerly whispered by only a few brave delegates, was used routinely this year to describe cultures which value men over women; as most cultures do. Patriarchy is particularly evident in the major religions of the world: in their sacred writings, theologies and structures.

4.8.2. It was agreed that men should be challenged to redefine masculinity, and to teach boys how to be masculine without assuming they can control women. Such a redefinition would take a long time, however it must begin NOW. The HIV/AIDS pandemic makes it imperative. Women must have control over their own bodies if the pandemic is to be reversed.

4.9. It Wasn't All Work: We Had Fun, Too.

4.9.1. By Saturday 28 February 2004, most of the out of country women had arrived. We knew ourselves to be colleagues/working partners/sisters with a cause: but we were strangers. Virginia Davies and Willard Taylor (friends of Alice Metcof) opened their beautiful home to us. During an evening of peace, overlooking the New York skyline, and nourished with good food and drinks, we met and bonded into a dedicated group of friends.

4.9.2. On Saturday 6 March we waited in the lobby of the ECUSA Church Center for the arrival of Mrs. Jane Williams, having just learned a traditional welcome ceremony taught to us by Rita Simeni, of Papua New Guinea. As Jane walked in we greeted her with song, dance, and a shower of flower petals. Then we enjoyed the gracious hospitality of Phoebe Griswold in her home.

4.10 Our Logos:

Each woman was presented with a Compass Rose pin: a treasured keepsake of our time together. A bronze sculpture entitled: "He's Got the Whole

World in His Hands", designed by Anne Mimi Sammis, was pictured on some of the Anglican advertising materials used at the UNCSW. The sculpture consists of God's hand holding the earth from which a celebratory circle of people—young and old, men and women—springs forth.

4.11. Feedback from the Anglican delegates:

Many of the delegates submitted feedback forms which were analyzed and three categories were excised and gathered as:

Hopes and dreams for the Anglican UN Observer's Office.

Commitments to enhance the place of women in church and society.

Messages to the Anglican Consultative Council.

4.11.1 Hopes and Dreams for the Anglican Observer's Office to the United Nations: Anglicans are called to take their faith perspectives into all aspects of their lives, which includes secular (or civil) society. The primary way that civil society can engage in conversation with the United Nations is through ECOSOC. The interface between the Anglican Communion (75,000,000 Anglicans in 164 countries) and ECOSOC is the UN Anglican Observer. The delegates felt that the person holding this office has an awesome responsibility as she/he enables the voices of Anglicans to be heard at the UN. Adequate funding must be raised if Anglicans are going to be able to fulfill their mandate of taking their message of justice and peace to UN deliberations.

4.11.2. The Anglican women of the ACC delegation were unanimous in their praise of the Observer, Archdeacon Taimalelagi Fagamalama Tuatagaloa-Matalavea. Her understanding of the cultural backgrounds of peoples of the world, her ability to interpret all the varying voices into "UN language", her concern for each one as a person, her total commitment to Anglican involvement in the UN process, her Samoan charm, and her faith, endeared her to all the delegation. They fully supported the ACCUN Office and requested that adequate funding be provided to continue her work.

4.11.3. Commitments to enhance the place of women in the church and society: The ACC Delegates were committed to continuing the work started at UNCSW 2004. The delegates were committed to urging their governments to live up to the commitments made when they signed UN documents. Each pledged to do her part in teaching her constituency about the BPfA, the MDGs, the Outcome Documents and Security Council Resolution 1325.

4.11.4. Recommendations from the Anglican delegates to the Anglican Consultative Council:

4.11.4.1. The women of the ACC delegation were enriched by the UNCSW 2004 experience. For some it renewed their commitment to work for justice and peace for all peoples and particularly the advancement of women, for others it was life-changing, and others committed themselves to the steep learning curve that complete engagement in the process demands.

4.11.4.2. Some snapshots of opinions

- From Canada: women are the last great resource to be developed on this planet. We are, I believe, standing at the entrance to a whole new era in the church, when women will be seen as the glue of our societies domestically, socially, economically and politically.
- From Papua New Guinea: the role of women in the Anglican Consultative Council is very important and ACC should include more women in the Council.
- From the USA: I am sure that our perilous 21st century will continue the spiral of violence we have seen in these first four years unless a fundamental inequality is addressed, the inequality of men and women which impoverishes the whole world, and contributes to its instability. This meeting of CSW was an affirmation of women's gifts and roles in creating a more peaceful future. Indeed, it was a pivotal year because it links work from the Security Council with the General Assembly and ECOSOC.
- From Uganda: Continue to support the work of the International Anglican Women's Network. Try to address the Millenium Development Goals from the Christian perspective.

4.12. The closing statement from the Anglican delegation & Note of thanks:
4.12.1. The Closing statement is attached:

The Anglican Consultative Council (ACC) delegation to the 48th Session of the United Nations Commission on the Status of Women (CSW) meeting in New York, 1–12 March, 2004 examined two themes from the 1995 Beijing Platform for Action, "Men and boys in gender equity" and "Women's equal participation in conflict prevention, management, resolution and post-conflict peace building." The delegation comprising members from 11 provinces claimed the Anglican Communion as an unbreakable bond. The 55 Anglican delegates experienced communion as the reality of women working together for justice and peace in the name and power of Jesus Christ. Women rejoice in God's gift of the Anglican Communion and claim their call to strengthen that Communion.

We are convinced that women hold society together during times of natural disaster, illness and war. Women's experience of holding, healing and sustaining families and communities will not be relegated to the private sphere but will become a public voice heard and acted on in places of power and decision making in the Church and around the world. Just as the United Nations calls for women's presence in all processes of conflict resolution and peace building, so should the Church seek women's participation at every level.

We were proud to participate under the auspices of the Anglican Observer to the United Nations and are privileged to carry forth the work of the ACC and its commitment to preventing and eradicating HIV/AIDS (Resolution 2 of ACC 12). The ACC delegation hosted a public forum on "The Cross-Generational Spread of HIV/AIDS in Sub-Saharan Africa and its Effect on Girls", recognizing the feminization of the disease in the faces of the young girl, the wife and the widow.

Therefore:

We call on the Anglican Consultative Council to continue its affirmation of the International Anglican Women's Network and we challenge the ACC to adopt the goal of a 30% representation of women in all decision-making bodies in our Anglican Communion.

We commit ourselves to communicating with women at the grass roots level, the empowering learning of this gathering established in the Beijing Platform for Action and the Millennium Development Goals (MDG). We embrace and work to implement those goals particularly 3) "Promote Gender Equality and empower women." We deplore all forms of violence against women, and commit ourselves to expose and correct these violations of human rights: war, sexual abuse, poverty and trafficking. We invite boys and men to join us in this critical work.

We commend those provinces who sent delegates to the 48th Session and challenge all 38 provinces to send delegates to the 49th Session of the CSW meeting in March of 2005, where we will join with women of faith to be an even stronger voice for women's empowerment.

We affirm our love and passion for the work of Jesus Christ and invite our sisters and brothers to a life of mission in Jesus' name. "Glory to God whose power, working in us, can do infinitely more than we can ask or imagine" Ephesians 3:20

4.12.2. Thanks to:

- Mrs. Phoebe Griswold for her dream of including Anglican women from around the world in the Anglican Communion's NGO team for the UNCSW 2004 and for her hospitality at lunch on Friday 27 February and dinner on Saturday 6 March;
- Archdeacon Tai for her gracious leadership and for her confidence in the ability of Anglican women delegates to make a difference on the world stage;
- The Rev Margaret Rose, for her companionship, love and support but especially for the major funding, without which our participation at this event could not have happened;
- The Rev Maryetta Anschutz for boundless energy to coordinate much of the events, for her excellent record keeping and for the impressive publicity material plus media coverage of the events;

- Mrs. Jane Williams for her excellent presentation Sunday 7 March at the Cathedral;
- Jacqueline Carroll for her many, many hours of volunteer work in preparing the Anglican delegation;
- Virginia Davies and Willard Taylor for hosting the dinner on Saturday 28 February;
- Jacqueline Plumez and Anne Herman for hosting a social evening on Thursday 11 March;
- The Church of the Ascension and Hondi Brasco for hosting a social evening on Sunday 29 February;
- The women who came from near and far to add their wisdom to the proceedings; and last but not least,
- Br. William F. Jones of ACCUN Office, Kim Robey of the Women's Ministries and Ednice Baerga of the Presiding Bishop's office for their valuable assistance in providing many secretarial/administrative tasks for the delegation.

Glory to God whose power, working in us, can do infinitely more than we can ask or imagine: Glory to him form generation to generation in the Church, and in Christ Jesus for ever and ever. Amen. Ephesians 3:20–21.

5. THE ACC DELEGATION TO THE 49TH SESSION OF THE UNCSW

5.1. The 49th Session of the United Nations Commission on the Status of Women (UNCSW) was held at the United Nations (UN) in New York from 28 February to 11 March 2005. Entitled as the Follow-up to the Fourth World Conference on Women and to the special session of the General Assembly entitled "Women 2000: Gender Equality, Development and Peace for the 21st century", its major objective was the 10-year review and appraisal of the Beijing Platform for Action (BPfA).

5.1.1. The major themes for the meeting were:

- Review of gender mainstreaming in entities of the United Nations system;
- Emerging issues, trends and new approaches to issues affecting the situation of women or equality between women and men;
- Implementation of strategic objectives and action in the critical areas of concern and further actions and initiatives;
- Review of the implementation of the Beijing Platform for Action and the outcome documents of the special session of the General Assembly entitled "Women 2000: gender equality, development & peace for the 21st century, the Millennium Development Goals (MDGs) and Resolution 1325;" and,

- Current challenges and forward-looking strategies for the advancement & empowerment of women and girls.

5.1.2. The review and appraisal by the Commission focused mainly on implementation at national level and identifying achievements, gaps and challenges and to provide an indication of areas where actions and initiatives, within the framework of the Platform for Action and the outcome of the special session (Beijing+5), are most urgent to further implementation.

5.2. Participation under the Anglican Consultative Council Office at the United Nations (ACCUNO)

5.2.1. At the conclusion of 48th Session in 2004 it was decided that the ACCUN Office would participate again at the 49th session of the UNCSW in 2005.

5.2.2. This year saw a spectacular rise in the number of Provinces represented, from just 12 in 2004, to 25 in 2005. The ECUSA delegates, about 40 (self-funded) women and girls, were also accredited and got registration under ACC. The Anglican delegation this year was by far the single largest NGO delegation present at UNCSW.

We also wish it noted that the Mother's Union (MU) which is accredited to the United Nations and shares the same status as ACC was represented at the meeting by two young women of Mary Sumner's House, Ruth Lee (Social Policy Officer) and Rachel Barber (Social Policy Researcher). Mrs. Marigold Seager-Berry the official MU Representative at the UN was an official ACC delegate representing the Anglican Church of England. The MU delegates were invited to all ACC events and they gladly joined us in addition to being NGO members of the official delegation of the United Kingdom.

5.3. Statements to the UNCSW

5.3.1. In accordance with Item 3(a) of the provisional agenda as printed in E/CN.6/2005/1, the ACC statement attached was submitted to the Division for the Advancement of Women (DAW) in January 2005. Again this statement was put together by Mrs. Marge Christie with a few inputs from the Provincial delegates.

5.3.2. The Mother's Union statement, which was duly shared in January with the ACC delegation, is also attached.

5.4. Sponsorship/Funding

5.4.1. The ACCUN Office acknowledges with much gratitude the financial contributions made by the Friends of the Office, the generous grant from Trinity Church at Wall Street, the ECUSA Women's Ministries and other ECUSA individuals and institutions that believed in the ministry of the Anglican Observer at the United Nations. These contributions made it possible for the 41 provincial delegates to attend UNCSW and to be accommodated at the Crowne Plaza Hotel at the United Nations. Support was also given by various groups, including the Anglican Peace and Justice Network, Asian Ministries, Latin American Ministries, Anglican and Global Relations, the Global Anglican Programme and many other institutions and individuals.

5.4.2. The ACCUN Office was also able to support this work through the contributions received from the Anglican Investment Agency (AIA) in London and the Archbishop of Canterbury's Fund for the Anglican Communion.

5.4.3. The ACC delegates remain indebted to all those, whose fundraising and advocacy efforts secured necessary funding to enable so many women to attend UNCSW. This appreciation is especially strong from women who came from those Provinces where support for women's issues, let alone women's ministries, is still negligible or insufficient.

5.5. Preparation prior to New York

From late 2004 logistical information regarding the UNCSW was sent to each delegate.

They were also asked to provide biographical information about themselves and to answer a questionnaire on the implementation of the Beijing Platform for Action in each of their countries and identify gaps and challenges as opportunities for additional work. In making these responses delegates were also required to identify any positive changes in their churches especially with regards to the role of women in decision-making and to describe something of how the work of the church interfaced with the government vis-à-vis the pressing social ministry issues of poverty alleviation, peace, armed conflict and justice.

5.6. Orientation for the UNCSW

5.6.1. Two events were held in order to familiarise delegates not only to the very specific issues arising from the Beijing Platform for Action but also to the complex processes of the United Nations, including the role and purpose of UNCSW. For most delegates it was a first time experience of both the UN and being in New York City and so the carefully planned orientation was of critical importance to enabling them to do their work as delegates with efficiency and confidence.

5.6.2. The first event was held jointly with the Ecumenical Women 2000 Coalition. For this occasion the ACC delegates joined other ecumenical women for an orientation to UN processes. Discussion focused in particular, on how the ecumenical women's movement could form a more effective group to lobby both individual governments and within the UN system itself. After much discussion on how to strengthen the ecumenical women's lobby, consensus was reached on the following:

- The ecumenical coalition is a faith based organization and is an added dimension to gender perspective;
- Governments are to be lobbied to affirm the Beijing Platform of Action; and,
- Governments to be lobbied not to accept the proposed amendments to the Draft Declaration by the US government (this was specific to the 2005 gathering and was successful as a result of the ecumenical women's lobby together with a wide range of equally outraged NGO and government representatives. The ECUSA delegates were very effective in this work).

5.6.3. The second orientation event was entitled NGO Consultation: From Mexico City to Beijing and Beyond: Realizing the Vision. This consultation was organized by the NGO Committee on the Status of Women (NY) and was held at Barnard College on Sunday 27 February. Both events were of enormous assistance to enabling each member of the ACC delegation appreciate the comprehensiveness of UNCSW activities and responsibilities.

5.7. The Beijing Platform for Action & Millennium Development Goals

5.7.1. In accordance with the major themes of the 49th Session of the CSW delegates were to ensure implementation of the Beijing Declaration, the Beijing Platform for Action (BPfA), the Millennium Declaration, the Millennium Development Goals (MDGs) and Resolution 1325. The year 2005 marked the 10 year milestone since the Fourth World Conference was held in Beijing, China. This milestone period provided an opportunity for Member States to describe in detail how fully and successfully they have each implemented the twelve goals of the BPfA. It also opened a window for members to strategize for ways in which the BPfA could be integrated into the MDGs in order to make them explicit in terms of quantitative commitment to gender equity. Members of the ACC delegation are committed to working through their respective national churches to urge their governments to honour the commitments made when they each ratified the UNCSW documents.

5.7.2. As early as 24th February, the delegates got to attend two events at the United Nations Headquarters. In the morning they attended an event "Hoping and Coping: How Women in Least Developed Countries (LDCs) response to HIV/AIDS." The event was moderated by the UN High Representative for LDCs, Land Locked Countries and Small Island Developing States (SIDS), and was co-sponsored by UNAIDS as well as the United Nations Development Programme (UNDP). They also attended in the afternoon a Round Table discussion on "Beijing + 10: Review, Appraisal and Implementation." This was the delegates' first exposure not only to the United Nations itself but also to the work ahead of the official start of the 49th session for UNCSW.

5.7.3. On 25th February, the Provincial delegates brainstormed in groups on the BPfA and their countries and their churches. The AWE members were the scribes to listen and take notes for issues that could be further discussed for future actions by the delegates. Some of these issues were dealt with during the March 5th exercise at St. Bartholomew's Church.

5.8. The Declaration

5.8.1. Prior to the beginning of the 49th Session, a draft Declaration reaffirming the Beijing Platform for Action was prepared by the Bureau of the Commission on the Status of Women. All Member States indicated their willingness to adopt the draft Declaration, with the exception of the United States who attempted to impose amendments which were clearly antagonistic to women's human rights. After a week of intense and often outraged lobbying from member states the US was finally persuaded to withdraw its proposed amendments thereby allowing the Declaration to be adopted by consensus. Many NGO caucuses—including one formed by Marge Christie for United States Women—participated in convincing the United States to withdraw its amendments.

5.8.2. The Declaration is appended attached under the cover of the letter dated 18 March 2005 from Ms. Carolyn Hannan of the UN Division for the Advancement of Women (DAW) with a report on the proceedings of the High Level Roundtable mentioned in section 5.10 below.

Declaration issued by the Commission on the Status of Women at its forty-ninth session:

We, the representatives of Governments gathering at the forty-ninth session of the Commission on the Status of Women in New York on the occasion of the tenth anniversary of the Fourth World Conference on Women, held in Beijing in 1995, in the context of the review of the outcomes of the Conference and of the twenty-third special session of the General Assembly, entitled "Women 2000: gender equality, development and peace for the twenty-first century", and the contribution of the Commission to the high-level plenary meeting of the Assembly on the review of the United Nations Millennium Declaration, to be held from 14 to 16 September 2005;

1. *Reaffirm* the Beijing Declaration and Platform for Action adopted at the Fourth World Conference on Women and the outcome of the twenty-third special session of the General Assembly;

2. *Welcome* the progress made thus far towards achieving gender equality, stress that challenges and obstacles remain in the implementation of the Beijing Declaration and Platform for Action and the outcome of the twenty-third special session of the General Assembly, and, in this regard, pledge to undertake further action to ensure their full and accelerated implementation;

3. *Emphasize* that the full and effective implementation of the Beijing Declaration and Platform for Action is essential to achieving the interna-

tionally agreed development goals, including those contained in the Millennium Declaration,[1] and stress the need to ensure the integration of a gender perspective in the high-level plenary meeting on the review of the Millennium Declaration;

4. *Recognize* that the implementation of the Beijing Declaration and Platform for Action and the fulfilment of the obligations under the Convention on the Elimination of All Forms of Discrimination against Women are mutually reinforcing in achieving gender equality and the empowerment of women;

5. *Call upon* the United Nations system, international and regional organizations, all sectors of civil society, including non-governmental organizations, as well as all women and men, to fully commit themselves and to intensify their contributions to the implementation of the Beijing Declaration and Platform for Action and the outcome of the twenty-third special session of the General Assembly.

5.9. ACC Delegates participate in UNCSW Caucusing

5.9.1. During the two weeks of the UNCSW many personal interventions were made by individual ACC delegates. Some delegates participated in their NGO Regional Caucuses and lobbied their Mission Ambassadors for support of the Declaration and the goals of the BPfA. Some delegates were fortunate to be either included in their government delegations or given close associate status as in the case of New Zealand, Canada and the United Kingdom. Some of the delegates received passes to be full members of the government delegations for the Solomon Islands, Papua New Guinea, Fiji and Madagascar.

5.9.2. ACCUN Office also arranged for all the delegates to call on their permanent missions to the United Nations whilst in New York and a few of the delegates managed to do this depending on the availability of appropriate staff and being able to spare the time from our busy programme.

5.10. High-level Roundtable

I was selected by the UN to participate at a High-level Roundtable on Innovations in Institutional Arrangements for Promoting Gender Equality at National Level on Monday 28 February. Speaking as a woman of faith, a Christian and an Anglican I emphasized the need for the BPfA to be a living document just as the Holy Bible is. Since I was specifically asked to speak on behalf of the Pacific region, I had to acknowledge the unique working relationship and partnership between NGOs and governments.

1 See General Assembly resolution 55/2. 2 *Report of the Fourth World Conference on Women, Beijing, 4-15 September 1995* (United Nations publication, Sales No. E.96.IV.13), chap. I, resolution 1, annexes I and II. 3 Resolution S-23/2, annex, and resolution S-23/3, annex.

That close relationship has contributed a great deal to the advancement of women in that region.

5.11. Youth representation

A small number of younger women joined the ACC delegation for the UNCSW. High school students Kristi Koltiska, Katie Keeney Mulligan and Phoebe Gallagher, and ECUSA Young Adult Service Corps member Ann Figge attended various sessions of the Commission and side events. They also participated in the NGO caucus on the girl-child and the young women's caucus. Along with provincial delegate Lisbeth Barahona and ACCUN Office intern Louise Gleich they shared their experiences of attending the UNCSW as young women with the rest of the delegation during an evening forum. Many delegates expressed their appreciation of the opportunity to share experiences across generations and across cultures as well as the hope that more young women be invited to join the future delegations.

5.12. Parallel & Side Events

5.12.1. The CSW has always been characterized by the many parallel events happening at the UN itself organized by various UN agencies and member states and side events organized by NGOs. This year was no different and delegates had a rich selection to choose from.

5.12.2. This year the ACCUN Office sponsored and co-sponsored only two events compared to seven in 2004. This decision was taken so that the ACC delegation would focus their energy on the CSW itself and its many parallel events and also have quality time to form together as a strong and coherent Anglican delegation.

5.12.2.1. "African Women Making a Difference: A Hopeful Story of Women's Leadership in Rwanda" was the first ACC sponsored event.

5.12.2.1.1. This documentary video event was held at the UN Church Centre on Wednesday 2 March. "Ladies First" was produced by WIDE ANGLE and it highlighted the leadership of women in the aftermath of the Rwandan genocide, focusing on their roles in government, business, education and reconciliation. The video provided compelling profiles of those women on the forefront of change. It revealed the challenges still facing Rwanda as it struggles to build a sustainable peace between the majority Hutus and minority Tutsis just ten years after the genocide that killed an estimated 800,000 people in just 100 days. Following the rebuilding and restructuring of the nation the country passed legislation allowing for 30% of seats in parliament to be reserved for women. In 2005 women's membership of parliament is actually 48% since women are also eligible for other seats. This event had a major impact on all who attended, providing as it did an example of profound hope and healing which can arise out of a situation of extraordinary brutality and violence.

5.12.2.1.2. This very popular event was moderated by Dr. Pauline Muchina of Kenya and currently working in the United States and according to Pauline, showcased what "the brave women of Africa could do." The event was also attended by the film makers who contributed to the lively discussion on the film.

5.12.2.2. "Repairing the World: Anglican Women's Faith in Action" was the second ACC sponsored event and it took the form of a keynote address followed by an international panel of contributors and was attended by more than 400 women and men of all ages. The youngest was Miles Brooks, 3 month old son of the Rev Theodora Brooks (Liberia), an AWE member and also a member of the Advisory Council for the ACCUN Office.

5.12.2.2.1. This event was held at the Synod Hall, Cathedral of St John the Divine on Sunday 6 March and was moderated by Archdeacon Taimalelagi F. Tuatagaloa-Matalavea. The keynote address was given by Marian Wright Edelman, Founder and President of the Children's Defense Fund. Panelists were Ms Angela King (mentioned in 4.1.1. above) Reverend Sereima Lomaloma (Diocesan Secretary & Registrar of Polynesia, Fiji), Dr Esther Mombo (Dean of Academic Studies, St. Pauls Theological College, Limuru, Kenya), Dr Pauline Sathiamurthy (Provincial Secretary of the Church of South India) and Mrs Amelia Ward (an Activist from Liberia).

5.12.2.2.2. Ms. Edelman, founder and president of the US-based Children's Defense Fund spoke of the need for solidarity in prioritizing the needs of children as well as the eradication of poverty and violence. Statistics showed that an American child is neglected every 30 seconds and one is born into poverty every 60 seconds. "After we talk of 'speaking truth to power' we need to redefine and grab back morality". Ms Edelman said, "the test of morality in a society is how we treat our children". Referring directly to the US she added, "We are the wealthiest and also the most militarily powerful nation and somehow we can't protect our children".

5.12.2.3. Jamaica-born Angela King spoke about violence against women and the role of women in peacemaking. She said that, "We know that violence against women is increasing all over the world and the UN has very firmly come out and said that violence cannot be tolerated." "We need to collect data at the national level and adopt zero tolerance campaigns". She insisted that women are better at negotiating and reconciliation because they are perceived to be 'less threatening.' Ms. King's full address is attached as reference material for ACC.

5.12.2.4. The Reverend Sereima Lomaloma said that "God calls each one of us at a particular time for a particular purpose. When I was ordained it was very significant because it was indicative of how barriers can be broken." She said that she left a high status position within the public service to work for the Church because she believed that that was where God was calling her to serve. "I was not interested in how much it paid. I know that God had prepared me for that time. Over the years God had shown me in very practical ways that this God is a God of abundance, of miracles and a God therefore who always provides."

5.12.2.5. Dr Esther Mombo sees her job as ensuring that students are equipped to be critical thinkers and servants of God and humanity. In her work with women and children who live with HIV/AIDS, she said that her faith is challenged daily. "My role is to help my students to break the silence of the church, to make the church accommodate those who are affected and to stand with them in times of need. My role is to help my students to be able to empower women wherever they are". She concluded by saying that "the church has a moral obligation to make sure the treasures of theological education are available to all women who wish to participate".

5.12.2.6. Dr Pauline Sathiamurthy, General Secretary of the Church of South India, describes her context as "a patriarchal male-dominated society" and she is proud to be working in a man's world. Pauline said that "women are marginalized but the Church of South India has launched a massive campaign against discriminatory practices." A major issue is that of the caste system and she indicated that the church is working hard to advocate that the same privileges that are offered to the small minority high caste are also offered to the lower caste and to all Christians irrespective of caste.

5.12.2.7. Amelia Ward, a Liberian widow and activist and a leader of the Mano River Peace Process in West Africa, described how after fourteen years of civil conflict, 750,000 people became refugees and 1.2 million became displaced. She said, "Of these rendered homeless most are women and children. Women are raped or murdered and forced into marriages. The emotional and psychological costs are high as we try to rebuild our lives." Speaking of her compassion and faith Ward emphasized her strong belief in God, "In God everything is possible. Together we can bring peace to our world. And God is bringing Anglican women together here today to repair the world."

5.12.3. ACC delegates as Panelists at other side events

Two members of the ACC delegation participated at other side events. The Reverend Margaret Rose was a panelist on the topic of "Women's Voices: Contested Territories" held on Wednesday 2 March.

Mrs. Priscilla Julie of the Seychelles was a panelist on "Religion and Women's Human Rights" on Monday 7 March. Priscilla stressed the importance of the Church speaking to civil society, especially related to debt cancellation.

5.13. Delegates Daily Activities

5.13.1. The AWE programme for the delegates started as soon as they arrived in New York. This programme was later changed when a Steering Committee was set up to assist AWE plan the daily activities for the ACC delegates. These were of necessity interspersed between the UNCSW and side/parallel events but were intentionally planned in order to ensure the highest level of personal and group interaction possible among all members of the ACC delegation.

5.13.2. The day's programme would normally begin and end with morning and evening prayers under the leadership of Rev Bellina Mangena with different provincial delegates leading the services. This was a very important component of the daily activities as it provided a much needed opportunity for quietness and peace in the endless bustle of New York.

5.13.3. Briefings were held daily too so that critical information could be disseminated to the delegates before they went off to attend the various daily UN sessions. As a strategy for maintaining inter-connectedness it was very useful, functioning as a 'homing device' for a group that was essentially scattered throughout the day in the numerous meetings and side events that were taking place in many different venues.

5.14. Hopes & Expectations

5.14.1. A focused session for the Anglican delegation on hopes and expectations not only dealt with the delegates personal ministry hopes, but also their dreams for their church. Many shared the hope that through the privilege of being present at UNCSW they would learn from one another's experiences. They also felt confident that from all the new information gathered they would find renewed inspiration and strength to continue with their commitment to bringing about peace, improvements in living standards and social transformation.

5.14.2. Many felt that their identity as Christian women in a rapidly changing world continued to be challenged and the search and hunger for spirituality, faithfulness in an increasingly pluralistic and secular materialistic world was a paramount consideration. Solidarity with sisters from Palestine and other areas where there was political upheaval was of critical importance. A group of women are already planning to travel to Palestine in August to prove their solidarity with Palestinian sister Mrs. Eliane Abd El Nour and to join the programme of the "Women in Black," of both Israeli and Palestinian descent.

5.14.3. As far as the institutional church is concerned there was agreement that although many individual Provinces and local churches had made a lot of progress in certain areas, there remains much yet to be done especially in respect of ordaining women to the priesthood, increasing the numbers of women in key decision-making roles, intentionally addressing patriarchy and removing all institutional barriers to women's participation and progress in any area of church life.

5.15 Priority areas in the BPfA for the ACC delegations

Time was also allocated for delegates to discuss the most critical areas of concerns in the BPfA to the delegates. Based on earlier meetings, the first one was the one held 25th February, the four (4) areas identified were Education, Healthcare, alleviating Poverty and countering Violence with Peace. A Biblical Reflection led by Dr. Jennie Plane Te Paa set the scene for these discussions and is attached for your information.

5.16 Hospitality

5.16.1. One of the most exciting and invigorating aspects of the two weeks was the atmosphere of community that flourished. From Morning Prayer, to lunch time caucuses, to pizza dinners and late night conversations, a spirit of camaraderie and community-building permeated. The community that was built between the delegates was palpable because it represented more than simply conference attendance, but suggested the potential for this group of women to build bridges across the Anglican Communion. It was the spaces between the official events that seemed to count most.

5.16.1.1. The 4th floor conference room of the Episcopal Church Center was a prime example. Here, the delegates exchanged ideas about the roles of women in their countries, the future of the church, and the vital role women do and must play in transforming the world. Indeed, it was in these moments of debate, laughter, and sharing that the vitality and notion of faith as action most came alive. Moreover, in all of their interactions, large and small, public and private, these sisters nurtured lasting bonds that helped to further galvanize an active movement for peace and justice within and beyond the bodies of the Anglican Church.

5.16.1.2. The generous hospitality extended to the delegates by various departments within the Episcopal Church Center and by the entire ECUSA-NYC family was a memorable component of the community-building atmosphere that triumphed during the two-week period. While many hospitality efforts were spearheaded and collaboratively organized by the AWE, the ACCUN Office and the Office of Women's Ministries, the delegates were made to feel at home with receptions sponsored by Anglican and Global Relations and Episcopal Relief and

Development. These events sought to build on the momentum of the gathering by facilitating partnerships that would support the work of the delegates at the conference and in their home dioceses.

5.16.1.3. Another element in the development of a worldwide sisterhood of Anglican women was the informal intercultural exchanges that took place. Though the delegates were vigorously engaged in these exchanges on many levels, a prominent example of this was the evening tour, evensong, and supper hosted by Church of Our Savior in New York's historic Chinatown district. This outing was an extraordinary chance for the delegates to gain a glimpse of how parts of the ECUSA interact in the community, and build bridges across cultures that strengthen the Church in the process. The ease of exchange and interpersonal communication offered the delegates a hospitable welcome and promoted the development of bonds of affection among this group of Christian sisters.

5.16.1.4. A great deal of thanks must be extended to all of the individuals and organizations whose hospitality helped to foster a community of faith, fellowship, and activism. These included Mrs. Phoebe Griswold, Anglican and Global Relations, Episcopal Relief and Development, Church of Our Savior-Chinatown, The AWE Hospitality Team under the Leadership of Christina B. Hing (Philippines/Asia), St. Bartholomew's Episcopal Church, Virginia Davies and Willard Taylor, Cathedral of St John the Divine and the Diocese of New York.

5.17. International Anglican Women's Network (IAWN)

5.17.1. The delegates were given an opportunity to discuss the future of IAWN. The IAWN is an historic creation of the ACC. It was doubtlessly created in response to pressure from Anglican women to have a distinctive forum for discussing women's concerns and for strategizing on best ways for advancing Anglican women's interests. The discussions started on 4th March with a conversation led by Esther Mombo and Jennie Te Paa on a proper structure for the network. Jennie challenged the delegates that the network should be based on 3 Rs. It should be Relevant, Radical to ensure good practice and Responsive to women's needs.

5.17.2. In recognition of the strategic role IAWN plays by being the direct link for the women of the Anglican Communion to ACC, it was unanimously agreed that IAWN should be invigorated by having a Steering Committee comprising of women from the regions who will work with the provincial link members and will assist the International Coordinator maintain the network. The Steering Committee members for IAWN comprise of the International Coordinator and representatives from Latin America & Caribbean, South America, North America & U.K., Africa, Jerusalem &

Middle East, West Asia, Oceania, Far East and the International President of the Mother's Union or her nominee.

5.17.3. The official commissioning of the IAWN Steering Committee into existence was conducted by Archdeacon Taimalelagi F Tuatagaloa-Matalavea and the Reverend Alice Medcof at the closing meeting held on the International Women's Day Tuesday 8 March at the Episcopal Church Centre Chapel.

5.18. Closing Statement & Commitments

5.18.1. At the closing meeting the delegates unanimously endorsed the Closing Statement which captures their vision of having a shared and equal voice in the decision-making of the church. As a short-term goal the delegates are calling for 30% representation of women at all levels of decision-making bodies of the church and a long term goal of 50% representation by 2010. In response to the attached statement each delegate made a commitment on how they will promote the goals of the Statement and how they will continue to work towards the establishment of a truly inclusive church. A Spanish translation of the closing statement was received from Ms. Lisbeth Barahona during the third week of March thus fulfilling part of her commitments.

5.18.2. The ECUSA Delegation also wrote a statement for the meeting of the Executive Council meeting scheduled for second week of June 2005.

5.18.3. As affiliated members of the Ecumenical Women 2000 Coalition, the ACC delegations also signed into the attached Statement by this group of Christian women.

5.18.4. A Video capturing some of the voices and part of the rich experiences of the times shared by the ACC delegation is being processed. The full Video to be used for several purposes especially for Education includes individual interviews with the Provincial delegates. A tiny part of this Video has been captured on DVD; a copy is given to you as a gift from your sisters that represented ACC in New York.

5.19. Plans for 50th session of UNCSW 2006

5.19.1. As previously mentioned, AWE was instrumental in bringing together delegates from the Provinces to the UNCSW. In recognition of this they have been mandated by the ACCUN Office to plan for the participation of Anglican women at the 50th session of the UNCSW in 2006. In anticipation of the 2006 gathering the membership of AWE has been expanded to incorporate the members of the 2005 Steering Committee. This makes the ACCUN Office support group one which is credibly globally representative of the whole Anglican Communion. The membership of the group now includes Ann Skamp of Australia, Shigeko Yamano for the Far East, Clair Malik for Jerusalem & Middle East, Joyce Ngoda for Africa,

Bellina Mangena for Southern Africa, Marigold Seager-Berry for North America & UK, Pauline Sathiamurthy representing West Asia and Christina Winnischofe for South America.

5.19.2. AWE goals for 2006 are to identify key individuals from among the 2005 delegates-to act as a satellite advisory board; to achieve 100% representation of the Provinces of the Anglican Communion for the 2006 UNCSW and to facilitate on-going ECUSA participation.

5.19.3. The theme for 2006 are again two-fold. These are (a) Enhanced participation of women and development: an enabling environment for achieving gender equality and the advancement of women, taking into account, inter alia, the fields of education, health and work; and, (b) Equal participation of women and men in decision-making processes at all levels.

5.20. The UN organized Panel Discussions

These Six Panels were:

- Panel I: "Synergies between national-level implementation of the Beijing Declaration and Platform for Action and the Convention on the Elimination of All Forms of Discrimination against Women."
- Panel II: "Addressing the linkages between the implementation of the Beijing Platform for Action and the outcome document of the twenty-third special session of the General Assembly and the internationally agreed development goals, including those contained in the Millennium Declaration: Progress, gaps and challenges."
- Panel III: "Presentation of the review and appraisal processes at regional level—achievements, gaps and challenges."
- Panel VI: "Remaining challenges in relation to statistics and indicators, building on the discussions at the High-level round table organized in the 48th session of the Commission 2004 as well as available data from the World's Women: Trends and Statistics (2005) and the World Survey on the Role of Women in Development (2005)."
- Panel V: "Future perspectives on promotion of gender equality: Through the eyes of young women and men."
- Panel IV: "Integration of gender perspectives in macroeconomics."

The reports on the discussions did not quite capture the richness of the discussions and interventions during the sessions.

5.21. The Resolutions adopted at the 49th Session

The 2005 UNCSW adopted 10 Resolutions. These resolutions were for: Gender Mainstreaming; HIV/AIDS; Women in Afghanistan; Women in Palestine: Indigenous Women; Women and Natural Disasters; INSTRAW; Trafficking; A proposal for appointing a Special Rapporteur on Laws that Discriminate against Women; and, Economic Advancement of Women. The debate on the latter resolution stretched the time of the final session well beyond closing time that a formal closure for the 49th Session and the Opening of the 50th Session had to be abandoned until March 22nd.

5.22. Reflections & Gratitude

5.22.1. Reflections

5.22.1.1. Some of the women attended the Linkage Caucus religiously and their reflections were fully accepted by the ACCUN Office delegates. Their Statement highlighted some of the important issues to be followed and publicized for future actions. It referred specifically to the linkage between the BPfA and the Millennium Declaration which will be reviewed in September. Throughout the CSW, the governments recognized that the MDGs, the time bound targets for eradication of poverty and implementing the Millennium Declaration, **cannot be achieved without advancing the human rights and empowerment of all women in all their diversity.** All of the caucuses which took place during the two weeks had input into the government declaration and ratification of the same. It conveys the difficulties and interruptions of the agenda created by the U.S. government, but it also speaks to the good work done by the almost 6,000 NGO delegates in attendance.

5.22.1.2. It was also important that some of the governments specifically referred to the role of faith-based organizations such as the ACC in the positive outcome. One example is the Pacific Islands Forum Group which said, "We acknowledge that since religion and tradition play such an important role in our communities, there is a need for faith-based organizations to use their influence to take a leadership role in promoting gender equality." This is a clear challenge to the Anglican Communion and an assurance that Anglican women continue to present themselves as women of faith.

5.22.2. Expressions of Gratitude

5.22.2.1. There are many people to thank and express gratitude to for their efforts at assuring a successful and productive Anglican Consultative Council Delegation during the UNCSW. I have already acknowledged some of them. However, we wish make special mention and sincere gratitude to Phoebe Griswold and the AWE members for their valuable assistance; All at the Episcopal Church Center for the use of meeting rooms and the chapel; Church of our Saviour in Chinatown for a tour, dinner and entertainment and for their gift of red tote bags; Virginia Davies and Willard Taylor for hosting a lovely dinner for delegates in their home; Hondi Brasco and Karen Chane for arranging the special side events: Repairing the World and Women of Rwanda; Constance Beaven for arranging filming to create a documentary and keeping our 'home away from home' in the fourth floor conference room filled with flowers; The Communications Office for filming the event at the Cathedral; St. Bartholomew's Church for providing the meeting space, lunch and the use of their chapel where we celebrated our commitment to the work of justice encompassed in the Beijing Platform; Jennie TePaa for her several offerings of theological reflection; The ECUSA women who created a U.S. NGO caucus; and of course The Primates who identified excellent women from their Provinces as delegates.

5.22.2.2. Last but not least, I wish to extend on behalf of AWE and ACCUN Office, our sincere gratitude to all of the global and local women who trusted that their trip to New York, the Episcopal Church Center and the United Nations would be a valuable and fruitful experience.

6. CLOSING REMARKS

6.1. I referred above (Part I: 5.18.1) to the final Statement of my sisters that capably represented ACC at the UNCSW. With much respect for you all, I wish to beg for your indulgence, that you study this very carefully. Please note that your sisters in Christ are addressing each of you directly in that statement.

6.2. The same women also sent me the following recommendations to be presented to ACC13. I will be failing them if I do not read this out for your information and support. These recommendations read as follows:

The Women found encouragement in what Archbishop Desmond Tutu said at the United Nations last year when he spoke on "God's Word and the World of Politics" as a lecture for the UN Secretary General. And I quote:

> "How do you educate for peace? Any mother who says I want war to see my child die is a most unnatural mother. Most ordinary people, away from the politicians want peace."

He further stressed that he would support, and even start, a women's movement of women. That one of the things they learnt at the Truth and Reconciliation Commission in South Africa was that, they would not have gained their freedom without the women. "Women," he said, "have an extraordinary capacity for nurturing life. Most women say, 'How could I carry a baby for 9 months and then go and turn them into canon fodder'."

Kofi Annan, the UN Secretary General, when speaking at the Trinity Institute in May 2004 said,

> "If you are going to reconcile at the national level, you need to bring in the women. They have a different attitude to men. Their influence and voices are extremely important. They bring equality and a dimension to the discussion that men cannot."

The Pacific Islands Forum Group speech, at the 49th Session of UNCSW specifically said, and I quote,

> "We acknowledge that since religion and tradition play such an important role in our communities, there is a need for faith-based organizations to use their influence to take a leadership role in promoting gender equality."

The World Council of Churches meeting at its 50th anniversary Assembly in Harare in 1998 commended to member churches the adoption of the Beijing Platform for Action. The Anglican Communion, however, continues to lag behind in the full inclusion of women.

Recognizing the need for all voices to be at the decision making tables of government, civil society and the Church, these leaders and governments called for the equal participation of women and men. The United Nations in 1995, through the Beijing Platform for Action ratified by all member governments, called for 50% participation of women in all decision making bodies. Among the official instruments of unity (The Archbishop of Canterbury, the Lambeth Conference, members of the Anglican Consultative Counsel, the Primates) women comprise only 3.5%.

The Anglican Provincial delegates to the United Nations Commission on the Status of Women therefore respectfully calls on the ACC to adopt the following recommendations in response to the plea of the above mentioned leaders and the WCC, the membership of which is dominated by a large number of (if not all) Anglican Provinces.

6.3. Recommendations to the Anglican Consultative Council (ACC)

From the (ACC) Provincial Delegation to the 49th United Nations Commission on the Status of Women (UNCSW)—2005

6.3.1. We, the ACC Provincial Delegates present at the 49th United Nations Commission on the Status of Women, strongly recommend that the ACC continue to affirm the International Anglican Women's Network (IAWN) as it works to forward the full flourishing of God's creation through the Beijing Platform for Action (BPfA) and the Millennium Development Goals (MDGs).

6.3.2. We call on the ACC to affirm the advancements our governments have made regarding the status of women in the BPfA and the MDGs and encourage them to continue in this work.

6.3.3. We call again on the ACC to adopt the goal of 30% representation of women in decision making bodies at all levels of our Anglican Communion. We believe that this goal can be achieved by:

> 6.3.3.1. making sure that the 14th meeting of the ACC to be held in 2008 reflects the ACC's commitment to this goal by having 30% women in the membership of the ACC and other bodies appointed by the ACC.

6.3.3.2. making sure that the Standing Committee of the ACC makes an appropriate constitutional change that reflects these goals in the membership of the ACC and its Standing Committees

6.3.4. We are grateful to the Provinces who participated this year in the 49th UNCSW. We recommend that the ACC encourage those provinces not represented this year to demonstrate their solidarity with the women of the Anglican Communion by sending delegates to the 50th UNCSW (2006) in order that 100% of the Provinces will be represented.

6.3.5. We recommend that the ACC promote a study on the status of women in the structures of the Anglican Communion as well as in the missions women undertake. This survey will be overseen by the Office of the Anglican Observer at the United Nations in conjunction with the Anglican Women's Empowerment group, an inter-provincial planning team for the UNCSW. This is consistent with Object (i) of The Constitutions of the Anglican Consultative Council. *"To keep in review the needs that may arise for further study, and, where necessary, to promote inquiry and research."*

6.3.6. In order to ensure that the above objectives are met, the Provincial Delegation requests that the ACC encourage the establishment of a Women's Desk in each of the 38 Provinces of the Anglican Communion.

6.4. On behalf of all Women of the Anglican Communion I wish you all a wonderful and successful meeting. We want to be your effective agents for the good of all of God's creation including the birds, the bees, the insects and the whole web of life in our global village.

6.5. For the vulnerability of the women & children and for the ACCUN Office ministry, we sing to you with much Alofa, Aroha, Haloha and love the ACCUN Office song which reminds us all about the danger of the senseless consumerism in our world.

REDUCE, REUSE, REPAIR, RECYCLE,
RETHINK, REPENT, REJOICE

Words by Archdeacon Tai Tuatagaloa-Matalavea and Robert Bergner
Music by Robert Bergner

Refrain:
People of God, Children of God, Household of God Reduce
People of God, Church of God, Disciples of God Reuse
People of God, Servants of God, Apostles of God Repair
Reduce, Reuse, Repair, Recycle, Rethink, Repent, Rejoice

Everyone is hoppin' in their car to go shoppin';
　　no one has enough
They're usin' up their debit, stretchin' out their credit,

loadin' up with stuff
Nothing fills the void, time's never been better employed
    than goin' out to shop
Once you're down that road, even when your home is owed,
    you won't be able to stop

Planet Earth, she's the gang's home turf;
    she's given it the best she's got
But you know she's gettin' weary, even kind of teary,
    when every field becomes a parking lot
The water's risin' higher; we're sinkin' in a mire
    of non-biodegradable trash
The air is smellin' rotten; it seems that we've forgotten,
    life can't be bought with cash

All around the world, every woman and every girl
    has got something to say
Bearers of the Word, their voice has gotta be heard
    if we're gonna waken to a brighter day
They're speakin' of connection, of spiritual reflection,
    of inter-relatedness
They're teachin' about love, about that heavenly, heavenly love
    that's gonna lead us out of this mess

6.6. Soifua ma ia Manuia.

1 Linda Wirth, "Breaking Through the Glass Ceiling"; International Labor Organization, Geneva

Ecumenical Greetings

Ecumenical Greeting Delivered by the Representative of the Baptist World Alliance, The Revd Professor Paul S. Fiddes on behalf of the General Secretary, Dr Denton Lotz and from the President, Dr Billy Kim

Brothers and Sisters in Christ!

We are grateful for the recent world-wide conversations between Anglicans and Baptists, which have shown in a new way the unity we have in Christ. These bi-lateral conversations were unique in that they were held in five different continents which helped all of us appreciate the spectrum of God's grace and of our common witness to Christ's love and salvation in very different settings.

The leaders of the Baptist World Alliance are always pleased to meet with Anglican representatives during the annual meeting of the Christian World Communions. Baptists have always appreciated the 'bridge' that Anglicans have formed between the Free Church tradition and the more liturgical churches. We rejoice at the increasing unity that we have with one another, particularly in Africa, Asia and Latin America. In the third world setting where hunger, war and poverty dominate, denominationalism tends to fall away and our unity in Christ and working together becomes more important.

We are grateful for the strong Biblical and ethical positions that the worldwide Anglican communion adopts on many issues, which are an encouragement to Baptists and the rest of the evangelical world.

Our President, Dr. Billy Kim from Korea, joins me in wishing God's blessings upon you. Many greetings from the community of 80 million Baptist believers worldwide. May the Christ of All Joy be your strength and encouragement!

—Denton Lotz

To this greeting I would like to add a special greeting from the Baptist Unions and Conventions who helped to host the Anglican–Baptist conversations in the six regions where they were held over the past five years.

That is, greetings from the Baptist Convention of Myanmar-Burma; the Baptist Convention of Kenya; the European Baptist Federation; the Union of Evangelical Baptist Churches of Chile; the Canadian Baptist Ministries; and the National Baptist Convention of the Bahamas.

As I have met with members of these conventions over the past year, I have been very aware that they have excellent memories of the times spent in conversation with Anglican Christians, and especially of the periods of sharing worship and eucharist together. I know that they want to be especially mentioned in these greetings, as you gather in faith and hope from all parts of the world. Grace be to you, and peace from our Lord Jesus Christ.

Ecumenical Greeting Delivered by Bishop Kallistos of Diokleia of behalf of the Ecumenical Patriarch Bartholomew

Dear Brothers and Sisters in Christ,

It is with great joy and love in our Lord that his All Holiness, the Ecumenical Patriarch Bartholomew, wishes to respond to your kind invitation to send a message to the 13th meeting of the Anglican Consultative Council. The Ecumenical Patriarchate and the Orthodox Church in general have always valued highly their relations with the Anglican Communion, with which they have been engaged in theological dialogue and fraternal contacts for many decades now.

Your meeting takes place at an important moment in the history, not only of your own Church, but of the Christian Church as a whole. After having devoted a great deal of effort and work to the restoration and further deepening of the unity of the Church of Christ, we who bear the name of Christians realise that we are now faced with new challenges coming from the world in which we live and to which we are called by God to proclaim the Gospel. These challenges oblige us to strengthen and deepen our ecumenical relations and our unity in Christ 'so that the world may believe' (John 17: 21).

In order to respond to these challenges it is necessary for us, in the first place, to avoid or overcome any divisive tendencies within our own Churches. Anglicans and Orthodox have in common a tradition of Church polity which values highly the autonomy of each ecclesiastical province to which the Orthodox have given the name of 'autocephalous Church'. Although the Orthodox structures of autocephaly and the Anglican provincial system are not identical in all respects, both of them present the same problems with regard to the unity of the Church. Decisions made at the level of a province or an autocephalous Church sometimes create tensions within the whole Church. The problem of the relation between the local church and the Church at the universal level is one of crucial issues we face today, both within our own particular Churches and in our ecumenical relations.

The Orthodox feel strongly that these problems can be properly solved only in the spirit of an ecclesiology of communion. We are pleased to see that this is the view taken also by the Anglican Communion in the *Windsor Report* which has been read carefully and with appreciation in the Ecumenical Patriarchate. It is our view too that decisions of major importance can be carried into effect in a constructive manner only after consultation and agreement with the rest of the local churches. This calls for a careful study of the levels of primacy within the Church and more particularly of the manner in which such primacy may be applied, so as to respect the right balance between local autonomy and universal unity.

We believe that the same principle of consultation and consensus should govern also our ecumenical relations. It is for this reason that the Orthodox would have hoped that decisions on major matters affecting deeply our ecumenical relations, such as the ordination of women to the priesthood, would have been made with deeper consideration of their ecumenical repercussions. We are pleased, however, that such important questions have been receiving full consideration and deep examination in the official Theological Dialogue between the Anglican and the Orthodox Churches. It is with great satisfaction that we note that the Commission on this Dialogue is now completing its present phase of work and will soon approve for publication the agreed statements that it has drawn up.

The challenges that the Church of Christ receives from the world today call us to extend our pre-occupation beyond matters concerning our internal problems. We are called to face the dangers arising from the use of religion as a source of conflict and fanaticism, and to work together in order to combat, alike at a national and an international level, all forms of hatred and discrimination.

We are also asked to work with all the spiritual means at our disposal for the overcoming of poverty throughout the planet, and to foster the protection of God's creation at this critical time of severe ecological crisis. In all these and other areas we can and must join forces, never losing sight of the vision of one Church visibly united, as our Lord wills her to be.

With these thoughts and feelings His All Holiness, the Ecumenical Patriarch, wishes to greet this meeting of the Anglican Consultative Council on behalf of the Ecumenical Patriarchate, and assure you of his prayers for the success of your work, for the benefit of the Church of Christ and her unity.

Ecumenical Greeting Delivered by the Revd Esme Beswick MBE, President of the Churches Together in England

I would like to begin by thanking God for enabling me to stand here today in the presence of my fellow brothers and sisters, many of whom have travelled many miles.

However, we must be reminded that it is our duty as Christians, here in the presence of the Anglican Communion, to maintain the unity of the Spirit in the bond of peace, a requirement of God our Father and part of the covenant as president of the Churches Together of England, whom I represent.

As acknowledged, there has been widespread exploration of the meaning of the word 'ecumenical', which has Greek origins—meaning 'the whole inhabited earth'. As I look around me I see representatives from most of the whole inhabited earth and the richness of our diverse previous culture from which we can learn.

Ecumenism is therefore far more than Church unity. It is about the culmination of our traditions through faith for disseminating the gospel to the whole world.

National

There are 23 member Churches Together in England (CTE) including most if not all the major world confessions. A major shift in 1990, from being the British Council of Churches to a new 'Churches Together' model enabled the Roman Catholic and several Black Majority and Pentecostal Churches to join CTE and the umbrella body connecting the four nations, 'Churches Together in Britain and Ireland'.

The thinking behind the changed name and procedures was to ensure that decision making remained within the Churches rather than being presumed by a Council, which might become remote from the Churches. Authority has remained within the Churches.

This has increased the sense of ownership, though it means that decision-making can be more laborious. Public statements are rare and this reflects the diversity within Churches as well as between Churches. The Churches speak 'with one voice' less than some people would hope; this can mean that voluble non-representative voices satisfy a thirsty media.

Much of CTE's work is through 'Co-ordinating Groups', which bring together those in the Member Churches who have responsibility for a particular are of work—Evangelisation, Health Care, Family Life, Ministerial Training, Gathering Statistics, Education. A Theology and Unity Group monitors developments and dialogues: it reflects on, for example, the notion of 'Covenant, it is currently looking at *Mary: Grace and Hope in Christ*.

Though most work is co-ordination, sometimes tasks are undertaken on behalf of all the Churches at their request, the most recent example of which is preparation to mark the Bicentenary of the Abolition of the Slave trade Act in 2007.

Intermediate/County/Diocese/Major Cities

There are around 50 intermediate bodies in England, roughly the size of a Church of England diocese. In the intermediate bodies the leaders of the Churches—bishops, chairs, moderators—meet and have the opportunity to reflect on the Churches' response to the life and social situation of their communities, to plan Church life, and to supervise local ecumenical partnerships [for example, joint congregations].

This is an emerging form of shared oversight, which is usually facilitated by a 'County Ecumenical Officer', full or part time.

Local

There are about 2000 local ecumenical groups of 'Churches Together'. Also some 800 formalised Local Ecumenical Partnerships, where there are substantial agreements about the use of buildings, forms of shared worship and pastoral care The Church of England participates in about 500 of these.

However, I would like to acknowledge the importance of this gathering for Christian consultative purposes that can only help to foster the body of Christ, Church leaders, Theologians and Church historians, to engage in the process for bringing into context from experience, the subjects that will be discussed here this week.

Ecumenical Greeting Delivered by the Representative of the Churches of the Union of Utrecht, The Revd Canon W.B. Van Der Velde, on behalf of the Archbishop of Utrecht, Dr Joris A.O.L. Vercammen

Dear Sisters and Brothers,

When in 1871, the Church Congress of the Church of England met here in Nottingham, it adopted a vote of sympathy with the young Old Catholic Movement in Central Europe. The resolution affirmed, among other things, the Church of England's concern to maintain the catholic faith as it is expressed by the Ecumenical Councils of the Universal Church and to be united *upon those principles (. . .) in the bonds of brotherly love with all churches in Europe.* There was clearly a recognition between the Old Catholic Movement and the Anglican longing for unity among the churches. Both were convinced that only the strong fundaments of the Ecumenical Councils would offer the opportunities to grow in unity.

But the Anglican and the Old Catholic churches are not only partners on this point of view. Both traditions did face the modern developments as they influenced western society since the Age of the Enlightenment. Anglicans and Old Catholics are holders of "fellow-traditions" since both have opened themselves to the challenge of secularization. Both are rooted in the confrontation between reason and belief.

Therefore, thinking about Anglicans and Old Catholics, one of the most important characteristics that comes into our mind, is that we both are Bridge-churches. Our churches built bridges between modern secularized culture and Christian belief. They want to build bridges between the great Christian traditions. And, since both are convinced religion should contribute to peace, both want to build bridges between the religions that are seen as—to some extent—bearers to human wisdom and divine inspiration.

We want to express our gratitude towards the Anglican Consultative Council for all the work that is already done by it in respect to building bridges among all those aspects of our world we mentioned above. We want to encourage the Council and to express our hope that it will become more and more that opportunity for exchange and reflection that will enable all of us to grow in Unity.

This Unity is a condition for the reliability of the churches and their witness in our societies.

Encouraged by—among others—your council, next year we will celebrate the 75th Anniversary of the Agreement of full communion between the Anglican and the Old Catholic churches of the Union of Utrecht. In the resolution of the previous meeting of your Council, that agreement is called *a milestone in our ecumenical relations*. To put it that way expresses precisely our great esteem for the agreement that was certainly trendsetting in a time that ecumenical contacts were just beginning.

We will celebrate the Bonn Agreement, as our agreement of full communion is called because of the place where it came into being, during the next Old Catholic Congress that will be held in Freiburg (Germany) from August 7th until 11th 2006. The theme of the congress has to do with Anglicans and Old Catholics together on the way in Europe. We are very grateful that His Grace the Archbishop of Canterbury plans to attend the celebration during the congress Wednesday the 9th. He will be invited to address the congress as well. We do hope a lot of Anglicans will not only attend the celebration with the Archbishop, but will also stay for the whole of the congress.

Anglicans and Old Catholics have some important work to do on the European Continent as well. Nevertheless our agreement of full communion, Anglicans and Old Catholics built their own ecclesiastical structures on the continent. There is a clear lack of links between those. In addition there is still the problem of the overlapping jurisdiction as a crucial point within the challenge of organizing our common witness. We do hope this Council will support our efforts to solve this anomaly in our ecclesiastical structure.

Concluding this short address, we again want to express our gratitude for the opportunities for collaboration already created by the Anglican Communion and we do hope and wish the sisterhood between our communions will be strong enough to witness of the hope our world is waiting for.

God bless you all!

Dr Joris A.O.L. Vercammen
Archbishop of Utrecht
Utrecht, 21 June 2005

Ecumenical Greeting Delivered by the Representative of the Lutheran World Federation, Bishop Walter Jagucki, on behalf of the Secretary, The Revd Dr Ishmael Noko

Most Honoured President, Chairperson and Secretary General, dear friends,

It is a privilege and joy for me to send you a word of greeting through Bishop Walter Jagucki of the Lutheran Church in Great Britain, representing the Lutheran World Federation at your meeting. I do this as I gratefully remember the time I spent with you in Hong Kong three years ago. Since then, the relationship between the Anglican Communion and the Lutheran World Federation has remained close and stable. We are in so many ways sister communions, with family bonds of many kinds binding us together.

The strongest ties between us are the committed forms of church communion that Anglican and Lutheran churches have entered into in Europe and North America. It remains a major opportunity and challenge to stimulate similar agreements in other parts of the world.

But we are also bound together in many other ways. One of them is the strong commitment we share for the inner unity of our communions. There are those who see our efforts to uphold the integrity of our communions as a form of confessionalism. I believe, as I know you do also, that nothing could be farther from the truth. Our commitment to unity within our families is one very important way in which we participate in, and contribute to, the ecumenical movement. This is, of course, on the basis that we are at the same time ecumenically open and ready to recognize other churches as true churches of Christ and enter into communion relations with them whenever possible.

I have been graciously invited by the Anglican Communion to be an ecumenical participant in the Reception Reference Committee pertaining to the *Windsor Report*. This is also one expression of the way we are involved in each others' life and each others' concerns as world communions.

Secretary General John Peterson and I enjoyed a close and trusted relationship and I am confident that such a relationship will continue also with Secretary General Kenneth Kearon. Let me take this opportunity to wish you once more, Canon Kearon, God's blessing in his new, present calling.

The Anglican Communion and the LWF can always rely on each other to be represented at important ecumenical meetings and events. We look to each other as do siblings, for mutual comfort and joy.

We meet annually in Joint Staff meetings, where we usually process quite a long agenda of ecumenical issues of common concern and interest. It is this Joint Staff Meeting that also decides, with approval of our governing bodies, on matters concerning the official dialogue between our two families. A new Anglican-Lutheran International Commission (ALIC) will begin its work in January 2006 with a meeting to take place in Moshi, Tanzania. The mandate agreed on for this commission is an interesting and promising one. We shall also do what we can to ensure that the All Africa Anglican-Lutheran Commission can continue its work with a view to reaching a communion agreement between the Anglican and Lutheran churches on the African continent.

Let me assure you of my sincere good wishes and prayers to God for this meeting of the ACC. May the Holy Spirit be your strength, your guide and your hope—for each one of you, for your Council, and for your Communion. In Christ Jesus, our Lord.

Ishmael Noko
General Secretary

Ecumenical Greeting Delivered by the representative of the Mar Thoma Church of Malabar, The Rt Revd Dr Euyakim Mar Coorilos, on behalf of the Metropolitan Dr Philipose Mar Chrysostom and the Diocese of North America and Europe

Respected Archbishop, the Most Revd Dr Rowan Williams, revered Bishops, clergy and members of the Consultative Council; I deem it as a privilege to be invited to this Consultative Council to represent the Mar Thoma Church. I consider this as a noble ecumenical gesture. At the outset, let me bring you all greetings from the Mar Thoma Church, especially on behalf of our Metropolitan Dr Philipose Mar Chrysostom and the Diocese of North America and Europe.

We cherish and thank God for the relationship between the Anglican Communion and the Mar Thoma Church. In an age of fragmentation, autonomy and divisive trends at various levels, what it to be underscored is interdependence and joint witness in words and deeds.

The Mar Thoma Church has always been in the forefront of ecumenical endeavours in India. In the light of the joint witness in various fields in order to give more visible manifestation to our common concerns, the Joint Council of the Church of South India-Church of North India and the Mar Thoma Church is now known as 'The Communion of Churches in India' (CCI). The Church is active in the Tsunami relief activities in collaboration with CASA.

As you are well aware, the Church is understood in a variety of ways: as the people of God, Communion of the faithful, Community of faith, Movement of the Kingdom, the Wider family of God and so on. While acknowledging the theological content of all these concepts, the one that seems to be more relevant in the light of the contemporary realities is the 'Wider family of God' (Eph. 3:14). Here God is the ultimate home maker.

Ever since the creation of this world, He is in the process of making His home on earth. He makes His home so inclusive so that all will have space in it. Hence all our projects and programs are to be assessed in the light of our proximity to or estrangement from this 'Wider family of God'. Though there is a gap between the ideal and the actual in the life of the church, rather than making truth claims for ourselves, the question is whether we can make our Christian presence more meaningful. There are commonalities and divergences in our ecclesial polity and historical predicaments; yet let us continue to cherish our ecumenical concerns and commitment: unity in essentials and diversity in non-essentials.

Mission is both being and doing. As the Nairobi Assembly statement rightly points out: Our concern should be the proclamation of "the whole Gospel, for the whole person, through the whole church, in the whole world". As we are gearing up for the upcoming Assembly of W.C.C. to be held in Porto Alegre, Brazil under the theme "God, in your grace, transform the world"; rather than giving a mandate to God, let us make ourselves agents of transformation.

Our calling is to make a difference in our times. This is definitely swimming against the current. The emergence of the new is always a painful process which involves struggles and sufferings. The authenticity of our decisions is to be measured in terms of our preparedness to listen to the promptings of the Holy Spirit who always opens up new possibilities and challenges before us as a community of faith.

I hope and pray that the Anglican Communion would usher in new decisions which would enrich and transform the life and ministry of the Church at all levels. "Our task is to make the message of Jesus Christ intelligible in our times and a choice for or against him inescapable." (M.M.Thomas) Let us resolve that our actions will be dictated by convictions and not by convenience. Let the discussions and deliberations in this Consultative Council enable us to make our witness more credible and our journey of faith more significant.

Thank you and may God bless us all.

Ecumenical Greeting Delivered by
The Revd William R. Morrey, President
of the Methodist Church Conference

Mr President, I have looked forward to the opportunity to be able to address the Archbishop as Mr President, so it is one President to another, and members of the council. It does give me great pleasure to bring greetings to you on behalf of the Methodist Church in Britain and as far as anyone can speak for the Methodist Church world-wide communion on their behalf as well. I am not quite sure about the wisdom of asking a Methodist minister to bring brief greetings on the longest day and when you have set your clock such as to give us an extra hour. However, I am aware that Anglican ways and Methodist ways can be a little different and I shall probably always remember the rather novel way in which having been welcomed, 10 minutes later, I was asked to respectfully withdraw for a little while.

If you look at your agenda you will find that actually I have been asked to speak on a particular subject to you in bringing greetings. I have been asked to particularly share with you about the Methodist/Anglican Covenant which is the Covenant between the Methodist Church in Britain and the Church of England. The Covenant was signed two years ago and there is an interim report on the Covenant that comes to our Conference and to General Synod this year. Two years in church time is actually rather quick and I have been asked to share with you something of that experience.

As I travelled around England this year I have been aware that in many places there are times when Methodists and Anglicans are sitting down together to do their thinking about ministry and mission together. To do their planning and to look at their sharing of resource in a way which will work for the Kingdom and so there are many hopeful signs because of the Covenant we have signed together. In one sense the Covenant is a child of its time. It has been signed at a point in our histories where we are very conscious of living in post modern and as some would call it, post Christian Britain, and we have come together to commit ourselves to a journey. The impact of that coming together is noticeable in localities. What I thought I would do is to share with you something of the feel of the Covenant by sharing from the report that is coming to us, something of what it says about good covenanting, and I think you will hear in what I say resonances of some of the things we heard in the Presidential Address and that we have heard in some of the other contributions so far during the consultation. Thinking of covenanting we observe that vows are for living. Making a covenant is similar to taking religious vows but vows taken at a wedding or by a novice in a religious community mark the beginning of a journey of a life within a committed relationship. We are not called simply to implement an Anglican Methodist Covenant but to learn what it means to live it so we are discovering what it means to be in a special relationship together. Covenanting is both deeply rewarding and also costly. Covenant is about living in a way that involves a dynamic tension. A tension between being where we are and where we believe we should be, knowing what it is that we are trying to actually embody whilst also being aware of our failures to express our unity together.

We note that we are in this for the long term. It isn't about a quick fix between two churches. The Welsh experience, to which Rowan alluded, where five churches have been in covenant for thirty years is that change is often slow but there is no going back on the commitment made in relationship together. So patience is essential and change is inevitable. We are learning, I think, to cherish appropriate diversity and to sense where the spirit is speaking to us through our difference. Without wanting to make one like the other but rather to recognise that the Spirit speaks in that very diversity. And then I read to you a little more fully this passage:

Our Covenant will be shaped by a purpose beyond itself. Only God can make a covenant with a known ultimate destinational purpose. Without a sense of purposefulness rooted in God's purpose of the unity of all creation in Christ our relationship will just drift. Inside some scripture may yet challenge our two churches to express more clearly how our Covenant commitment serves God's Kingdom purpose beyond ourselves. Clues may lie in the language of reconciliation, of healing, of self emptying, and of hospitality. Because it will always point to a purpose beyond itself a mutual covenant commitment will be neither self righteous nor inward looking. If our purpose is too narrowly focused on ourselves and on the future of our two churches our journey will not lead to a deeper unity in Christ but only to a self conscious defensiveness, a fractiousness which will make us less serviceable within God's reconciling purposes in this land. Only by looking to God and beyond ourselves can we hope that our covenant commitment will bring about what God wants to achieve. So I offer to you that sense of journeying from the English context.

I am also aware that I stand as a Methodist and if the statisticians are correct then the Methodist world-wide membership is a little under 70 million and so for all of you there are likely to be Methodist congregations of various sizes in the countries from which you have come. I would hope that in each of those settings it was possible to look at the ways in which covenant or some other commitment to working together is possible. Methodist history is such that most of our autonomous churches came about because of missionary movements from Britain. Some subsequently came about because of missionary movements from America. We have a whole series of autonomous conferences. I won't bore you with trying to explain how they are in some way related together. What we do find is a very rich sense from our sharing together, when we come together to sense what God is saying to us from our different perspectives. It is our hope and our prayer as Methodists that you will find as you come together from the wide variety of contexts from which you come that you will also sense the way in which God's spirit is speaking to you about the richness of the diversity of God's love. Thank you for the opportunity to share some of that time with you. I am afraid I will have to leave you at the end of this day in order to go to a Methodist Conference that will be meeting in what is described as the English Riviera of Torquay. Thank you.

Ecumenical Greeting Delivered by the Representative of the Pontifical Council for Promoting Christian Unity, The Revd Canon Donald Bolen, on behalf of the President, His Eminence Cardinal Walter Kasper

Your Grace, dear members of the Anglican Consultative Council, dear friends in Christ,

I send warm greetings to you as you meet to reflect on aspects of the life and mission of the Anglican Communion and, in particular, on the *Windsor Report* and its various recommendations.

Over the past four decades, the Catholic Church and Anglican Communion have made sustained efforts to clarify and overcome the causes of our separation, seeking always to the next step which we can take towards greater communion. Five years ago, in Mississauga, Canada, Anglican and Catholic bishops took stock of what we had achieved to that point and noted that our partial communion should 'no longer be viewed in minimal terms . . . but is even now a rich and life-giving, multifaceted communion.'

As you know, last month we sought to take another step towards the goal of full communion, with the launch of ARCIC's most recent agreed statement, *Mary: Grace and Hope in Christ.* While at this stage the document remains the work of ARCIC and is not an official statement of the Anglican Communion or the Catholic Church, it has nonetheless been a moment to give thanks to God for having brought us this far. As we now invite a wide-ranging reflection on the text, it is our hope that it will serve as an instrument of reconciliation, providing further theological foundations upon which our relations can be strengthened.

As a result of our growing relationship and an increased awareness of our common calling, we have come to learn as dialogue partners that the actions and decision of each of us has a significant impact on the other. Two years ago, developments in the Episcopal Church USA and in the Anglican Church of Canada raised serious questions, from both moral and ecclesiological perspectives, regarding the degree of faith we share. In December, 2003, the decision was taken to put on hold the principal project of IARCCUM—work towards a common statement attempting to identify our common faith on matters addressed by ARCIC documents.

During the period that followed, we were encouraged by the attentiveness to ecumenical concerns which has characterized the Anglican Communion's discernment of a way forward. Close communication and friendly relations have been maintained between the Pontifical Council for Promoting Christian Unity and Lambeth Palace, the Anglican Communion Office and the Anglican Centre in Rome. As well known, at the initiative of the Archbishop of Canterbury, we jointly established a sub-commission of IARCCUM which prepared a document—submitted in due course by the Archbishop to the Lambeth Commission — reflecting on the current ecclesiological situation in the Anglican Communion in the light of the work of ARCIC over the past 35 years. When the *Windsor Report* was published, again the Archbishop of Canterbury invited written reflections on its possible ecumenical implications, and asked that I lead a PCPCU delegation to meet him and Anglican Communion staff at Lambeth Palace to carry forward the discussion.

We have been able to speak with an openness and directness which in the past would have been impossible. In our communications, I have stressed my appreciation for the ecclesiological foundations set forward by the *Windsor Report,* noting that they are largely consistent with the *koinonia* ecclesiology articulated in the agreed statements of ARCIC. The consequences which the Report draws from these foundations are also helpful to our ecumenical relations, notably the interpretation of provincial autonomy in terms of interdependence, thus 'subject to limits generated by the commitments of communion' (n. 79). This is consistent with the *Gifts of Authority's* understanding that maintaining and strengthening the *koinonia* and a commitment to interdependence are constitutive aspects of the Church and vital for its unity.

When reflecting on what would help our relations to flourish, I find it useful to think of the *Windsor Report* and the communiqué of the most recent Primates' Meeting as a starting point rather than a point of arrival. We believe that the *Windsor's* principal recommendations would have a positive ecumenical impact if received and implemented. I would like to assure you, as I did the Archbishop of Canterbury, 'in a spirit of ecumenical partnership and friendship, we are ready to support this process in whatever ways are appropriate and requested.' Above all, it would be the reception of the *Windsor's* ecclesiology, concretized by tangible decisions to give it an authoritative character, which would enhance our understanding of the Anglican Communion precisely as a communion, which is the premise on which we have proceeded in our dialogue since the Second Vatican Council. Any strengthening of the bonds of communion which are consistent with the apostolic faith as witnessed in the Scriptures, the early councils and the patristic tradition, is bound to draw us more closely together.

In affirming the traditional understanding of marriage and endorsing the ecclesiology of the *Windsor Report,* the communiqué of the February

Primates' Meeting has given us an indication of the direction the Anglican Communion wishes to move, and has encouraged us to believe that our dialogue can continue to make progress. Work on the IARCCUM common statement project is scheduled to resume with a drafting meeting in September, and it is hoped that this will provide us with a constructive means to receive important elements from the corpus of ARCIC II texts. Meanwhile, discussions have begun towards a third phase of theological dialogue.

As you meet in Nottingham, it is the hope and prayer of the Pontifical Council for Promoting Christian Unity that the Holy Spirit will strengthen the bonds of communion among you, and that renewed by this same Spirit, we will all be able to join increasingly in living out our calling to be light for the world and salt for the earth.

Walter Cardinal Kasper
President

Ecumenical Greeting Delivered by the Representative of the World Council of Churches, Ms Teny Perri-Simonian on behalf of the General Secretary, The Revd Dr Samuel Kobia

Your Grace, President of the Anglican Consultative Council, Brothers and Sisters in Christ,

Grace and Peace to you. I am sure that your prayers, deliberations and resolutions at this 13th meeting of the Consultative Council will help you continue your Christian vocation as a living communion. By so doing, you will also strengthen the fellowship of churches within the World Council of Churches (WCC) on their way towards *koinonia,* in response to their common calling to unity, mission and service.

Recently I had the opportunity to visit the Archbishop of Canterbury and President of the Anglican Consultative Council. During out meeting the Archbishop reconfirmed the commitment of the Anglican Church to the fellowship of churches within the World Council of Churches. Our cooperation has been has been fruitful for the ecumenical movement. I reminded him of the visits of his predecessor His Grace Robert Runcie and invited him both to our 9th Assembly to be held 14–23 February 2006 in Porto Alegre, Brazil, and to the World Council of Churches in Geneva after the Assembly. I use this opportunity to reiterate my invitations. We shall continue walking together according to the prayer of Jesus Christ *that all may be on in order that the world may believe* (cf. John 17:21).

In 1998 the Eighth Assembly of the WCC adopted the policy stated: "Towards a Common Understanding and Vision". The document called for the strengthening and deepening of relationships with and among member churches. It encouraged the WCC to widen its relationships to include non-member churches. And, not least, it recognized the important relationship between the WCC and the Christian World Communions, stating that

> "these relationships should be marked by mutual accountability and reciprocity, and the Council should seek ways to share tasks and resources with these partners in the ecumenical movement. Such sharing is particularly important for ... world-wide communion of churches of which most if not all members are also member churches of the WCC" (CUV, Chapter 4).

I therefore extend my greetings to the representatives of the Anglican Provinces, which are also members of the World Council of Churches. A strong relationship between the WCC and the Anglican Consultative Council through our common member churches will be enriching for both of us. It will strengthen the Anglican member churches' sense that they are part of the worldwide fellowship of Christians, and it will remind all the churches in the World Council that ecumenical commitment can be nourished by rootedness in an ecclesial tradition (CUV, Chapter 4).

Driven by this spirit, I would like to identify four areas of work that are on the agenda of the WCC and will also impact the life of the Anglican Consultative Council:

Bilateral Dialogues: Although bilateral dialogues and theological and ecclesiological discussions have been successful, they will contribute to visible unity only when they are discussed in a multilateral context. The bilateral forum of the Faith and Order Commission has served as the place for such conversations. Only by strengthening Faith and Order will we be able to bring together the results of these dialogues and also identify new issues for discussion in bilateral dialogues.

The Special Commission on Orthodox Participation in the World Council of Churches was created in response to questions raised by Orthodox member churches. The work of the commission demonstrated that the issues raised by the Orthodox also reflected the concerns of other member churches. On the basis of the final report of the Special Commission, the Central Committee added a theological criterion to the WCC membership requirements and proposed a new category of membership, "members in association with". This new category will enable smaller churches to join the Council, and, in other cases, will allow churches in difficult situations to withdraw from the Council temporarily and yet remain in association with the Council until the period of difficulty has passed.

The Special Commission also proposed that WCC governing bodies adopt consensus decision-making as an alternative to voting. This concept is not new for the WCC; certain member churches live this experience based on their theology and ecclesiological self-understanding: for example, 'conciliarity' in the case of Orthodox churches, and 'suspending judgement' in the case of the historic peace churches.

Difficult questions: Like the Anglican Communion, the WCC finds itself facing sensitive issues which challenge both individual churches and churches in their relations with each other. Many of these issues relate to fundamental questions of anthropology and ethics. Today, member churches of the WCC do not speak with one voice on a number of new sensitive issues; indeed, in some cases they have not yet found the language to talk constructively with one another about them. We have begun using a methodology of "listening to one another", especially in the area of human sexuality. In February 2005, the Central Committee adopted an aide-mem- oire to help churches journey together towards mutual understanding in these areas. Can we learn together how to shape a common response to dif- ficult questions?

Ecumenism in the 21st Century: Since 2003 the WCC has undertaken a study process in order to respond to the changing Christian landscape, and to the need to revitalize the ecumenical movement. Statistics reveal that Christianity is thriving in the South, and new churches are springing up in all regions and challenging the ecumenically committed historic churches. Ecumenical organizations seeking Christian unity at the global, regional and national levels have multiplied, and this brings new questions regard- ing their financial sustainability and the role within the one ecumenical movement.

Being the Church and serving the one ecumenical movement are central ecumenical issues today. A consultation held in December 2004 proposed the establishment of a Continuation Group convened by the WCC, to which Christian World Communions are also invited. This group will take up the reflection on the new configuration of the ecumenical movement. I would wish that the plurality of the Anglican Church as it has enriched the World Council of Churches, and the experience of the Anglican Consulta- tive Council as a world communion, will contribute to this process.

The areas of concern I have tried to identify have no "expiration date". They will remain with us as we prepare the 9th Assembly of the World Council of Churches. At the Assembly we shall pray, celebrate and reflect on the basis of the theme **"God, in your grace, transform the world."**

I pray that this theme will not only help us draw lessons regarding the areas of concern mentioned above, but will also help us move together in building spirituality based on our respective ecumenical treasures. Only through prayer and spirituality may we respond to the devastating prob- lems of the world and to the changing ecumenical scene. Nor may we for- get that the youth of today will inherit our legacy and, therefore, we are responsible to prepare them as active participants in building the household of God.

In conclusion, I would like to ask our member churches in the Anglican Consultative Council to help strengthen the fellowship of the World Coun- cil of Churches in its proclamation of our common faith, prophetic witness, mission and service so that our unity may be visible and the world may believe.

Yours in Christ,

The Revd Dr Samuel Kobia
General Secretary

Provincial and
Network Reports

PROVINCIAL REPORTS

Report of the Province of the Anglican Church of Congo

BISHOP ISINGOMA KAHWA HENRI AND THE REVD JOYCE MUHINDO
24 June 2005

We want to start by greeting you all in the name of the Lord Jesus Christ and to thank the Chairperson of this Council and the committee for this opportunity. The Province of the Anglican Church of Congo is a minority church in the country and in the Anglican Communion. She regards the Communion as at once a gift from God, and also as a force which helps her take her place among the large Protestant churches of Congo and particularly the Roman Catholic church. She only has a sense of playing a worldwide role through the historical and doctrinal connection that she has with the other Anglican Churches in the world.

Nevertheless, she is a church which is operating in a special cultural context and enduring social tensions which keep her in a particular and very unhappy situation. Language difficulties do not allow her adequately to share her story in the councils of the Communion nor to make the most of Anglican writing, resources and documentation which is mostly in English.

As far as the national political context goes, The Anglican Church of Congo has not been spared the consequences of the terrible civil war between eight national armies and many other armed rebel groups over six long years. This war has caused the disappearance of over three million people (UN figures); villages have been ravaged and wholesale pillage of the astonishing natural resources of the country has taken place. The church has lost many members including some of the clergy, notably Revd Canon Henri Basimaki, who was cruelly assassinated while he was on his way to the ACC-12 meeting in Hong Kong.

Churches and schools have been burnt down in Ituri and North Katanga. A huge population including many Anglicans has been internally displaced; many others have gone into exile in neighbouring countries (Uganda, Rwanda, Burundi) sometimes for reasons of ethnicity. Even the Theological College (Institut Supérieur Théologique Anglican—ISThA) has been obliged to go into internal exile moving from Bunia to Aru.

We have recorded very many cases of people traumatised by the war; above all women and girls; children separated from their parents and orphans, and old people. Ex-combatants who have laid down their arms are without work; some who have stopped fighting but who retain their arms constitute a permanent threat to the population.

As we meet here, even though there are still centres of significant instability and tension in north Katanga, South Kivu and Ituri, a precarious calm has returned to the country thanks to the formation of a transitional national government which includes all the principal former belligerents. Peace is kept by the troops of the United Nations. South Africa has helped us very much by maintaining dialogue between the parties formerly in conflict.

The task of this government is to prepare a new constitution which will define a new political order and to prepare for the first democratic and independent elections since Congo gained her independence in 1960! There is very widespread and significant corruption which keep the country in extreme poverty. What a paradox for a country with such extraordinarily abundant natural resources!

The country has an estimated population of about 60 million of which 80% are Christian. The Roman Catholic Church is the largest. The Protestant churches and the Anglicans constitute about 35% of the population. Islam is present but doesn't constitute a threat. The Anglican church numbers about 250,000 members and is growing rapidly; for this reason theological formation is a particular priority to help us help these Christians to put down strong roots. Each diocese fulfils its ministry according to the following general departmental structure; Evangelisation; Theological formation for lay people and clergy; Christian youth (including Sunday Schools, Boys Brigade, Scouts etc); Mothers Union and women's department; Development, Community Health and Education (with state-recognised primary and secondary schools).

This year an eighth diocese, Aru, will be inaugurated following the diocese of Kinshasa which was founded last year. Kinshasa includes missionary work beyond the national frontier in Congo Brazzaville.

The Anglican Church participates actively with other churches and NGOs working in Congo to bring about a variety of projects that will confront the challenges posed by poverty and internal conflicts; these include; conflict-resolution programmes; reconstruction of schools and health centres; the fight against HIV/AIDS and malaria and other dangerous diseases; women's development and her contribution to society; the provision of apprenticeships in various trades for unemployed young people; agricultural development and so on.

As far as the great ethical and doctrinal questions facing the Communion go, the Province of the Anglican Church of Congo, while taking the Scriptures as the basis of her faith and doctrine, also adheres to the resolutions of CAPA, the ACC, the Primates' Meeting, and the Anglican Consultative Council. She therefore remains passionately committed to a Communion which is a spiritual reality coming from God in answer to the prayer of Our Lord in John Chapter 17.

We wish you the blessing of God.

We also propose the following resolutions:

1. ACC-13 warmly welcomes the report of the Province of the Anglican Church of Congo.
2. The Council recognises that the Province of the Anglican Church of Congo faces a great social crisis that deserves the particular attention of all the churches and organisations of the Anglican Communion in particular those of the ACC networks.
3. The Council encourages the Province of the Anglican Church of Congo to continue its evangelisation of Congo Brazzaville as a new stage in the expansion of the Anglican Church in the Francophone world.

Presentation by the
Melanesian Brotherhood

I. INTRODUCTION

The following brief report covers the life of the Melanesian Brotherhood, its primary evangelism work/mission, and its involvement in the effort for peace during the ethnic fighting that broke out on the island of Guadalcanal from 1998 to 2000 as well as in the continuing and ensuing work of disarmament and reconciliation (following the cessation of hostilities after the signing of the Townsville ceasefire agreement) from 2000 onwards, till the arrival of The Regional Assistance Mission to Solomon Islands (RAMSI) in 2003. And, of course, the future ministry of the MBH—what will it be like?

In the preparation of this report, the Brotherhood was greatly hampered by three things. First, the invitation to attend this meeting was received by our former Head Brother who was released late last year, and we did not get our hands on the documents pertaining to this invitation, from him, until only about two weeks ago. Secondly, confusion arose in the past week as to who will be responsible for preparing the Melanesian Brotherhood report and we were only informed at the last minute that we have to do it ourselves. Third, we are without our most resourceful persons for this task and who would have compiled a better report than the one being presented. Former Brother and Chaplain, Revd. Richard Carter, left the Brotherhood in April this year and is in England leading a combined COM Religious Communities mission team to Chester and Exeter Dioceses as well as here in London. Current Spiritual Advisor and Tutor, Revd Dr. Brother John Blyth is away in Canada to attend the funeral service of a long time friend of his as well as great supporter and companion of the Melanesian Brotherhood, the late Fr. David Reetter.

II. BACKGROUND TO THE FOUNDING AND FORMATION OF THE MELANESIAN BROTHERHOOD.

The Melanesian Brotherhood was founded by a remarkable man named Ini Kopuria, a Solomon Islander born on the island of Guadalcanal in 1900.

After being educated at the Anglican Church schools of Pamua and later in Norfolk Island he joined the British Protectorate native armed police constabulary. But in 1924, when he was recovering in hospital from an injury sustained to his leg during an effort to arrest an escaped felon in the inland jungles of Guadalcanal, he received an experience which he believed to be a vision from Christ that was to change his life. He believed that Christ spoke to him and told him that he was not doing the work that Christ wanted him to do. He began, with the encouragement of Bishop John Manwaring Stewart, to realize that God was calling him to start a community of native Solomon Islands men who would take the Gospel of Christ to all who had not received it.

Much of the population of the Solomon Islands lived on remote islands and villages high up in the hills and bush or coastal villages with no easy access either by sea or land. Ini Kopuria believed the Gospel was for all people and just as he had visited remote villages as a policeman now he would visit as a missionary.

On St. Simon and Jude's day 28th October 1925, he made his promises renouncing possessions, marriage and freedom of action. He gave away all his property and a large area of his family's land at Tabalia, west Guadalcanal, to the Brotherhood. The following year the first six Brothers joined him.

The Melanesian Brotherhood has since grown from these humble beginnings and now serves in Vanuatu and Papua New Guinea where it has a regional headquarters in each country overseeing a network of Brotherhood households, and, in the Missionary Diocese of Palawan of the Philippine Independent Church. It has also served for a time in Fiji (especially the Wailoku area) and Australia (Diocese of Carpentaria, Northern Territory), and has carried out short overseas missions both to New Zealand and the United Kingdom in 2000 and in Australia in 2004. A more recent mission of this nature by the Melanesian Brotherhood is currently being undertaken (May to August 2005) in the United Kingdom together with members of the other three religious orders in the Church of Melanesia: the Communities of the Sisters of Melanesia and the Sisters of the Church, and the Society of St. Francis; in the Dioceses of Chester and Exeter, as well as in London. Requests for such missions continue to be received from all over, including an invitation to send a missionary team from the Melanesian Brotherhood to Jerusalem with the possibility of more permanent arrangements in the future.

Ini Kopuria also founded the Companions of the Melanesian Brotherhood in 1930, whose work it was to support the Brotherhood through prayer, material support and follow up ministry on the work of the Brotherhood when the Brothers moved on to other villages and communities.

There are now companions of the Melanesian Brotherhood in the Solomon Islands, Papua New Guinea, Vanuatu, New Caledonia, Australia, New Zealand, United Kingdom, Philippines, United States of America, Canada, Netherlands and Sweden. In 2004, the Archbishop of Canterbury, the Most Revd and Rt. Honourable Rowan Williams and his Secretary, Canon Herman Brown, were admitted as Companions by Revd Br. Richard Carter in the Chapel at Tabalia, Headquarters of the Melanesian Brotherhood.

III. LIFE OF THE BROTHERHOOD.

Ini Kopuria's vision for forming the Melanesian Brotherhood was to build up a Brotherhood of Men who has answered the call of God to give themselves, under the threefold promise of poverty, chastity, and obedience, completely to his service by:

1. Taking the message of the Good News to the heathens / pagans—he unchurched;

2. Bringing back and strengthening those who have fallen away from the Church; and

3. Working their calling in great humility after the example of the Lord Jesus who said to his Apostles, "I am among you as one who serves", and offering themselves in that spirit of humility to the service and love of God and those to whom they are sent.

In order to give ourselves more fully to this calling, the members of the Brotherhood give up and offer to God for the sake of the Kingdom of Heaven, those things which though right for other people, would keep us from serving with our whole hearts and wills while we are in the Brotherhood. As long as we Brothers remain in the Brotherhood, we will dedicate ourselves to the Lord under the vows of poverty, chastity and obedience.

These conditions stand for the ideas of a Christian's baptismal promises, when agreeing to give up the world, the flesh and the devil—three great enemies of the spiritual life.

(1) Poverty

Our Lord willingly accepted a life of poverty in this world. "Rich as he was, he made himself poor for our sake" (2 Cor 8:9). In the same way he calls those who would follow him, to a life of poverty, "Whoever wants to serve me must follow me" (Jn 12: 26). "No one can be my disciple unless he gives up everything he has" (Lk 14:33).

As Brothers therefore, we seek to be poor in Spirit and to resist love for the things of this world, wanting only to possess the wonderful riches of

Christ. As in Acts 4:32 where the group of believers were one in heart and mind, and shared all they have with one another, we Brothers also share with other Brothers around us. In all our households we live as a family sharing all things together and receiving for our personal use, only the simple needs in life and wanting only to have those things which we really need for our life and work. Yet we must see that those things which we receive do not belong to us personally, but belong to the Brotherhood and are only lent to us for a time.

As Brothers we are all equal, except that our leaders have special duties because of their office. They have no special things for themselves though, but share in the common life in the household. The Brotherhood aims at simplicity of life, living simply and adopting a simple way of life of the kind that will allow us Brothers to have good health and work hard and well. In all things, we try to show true simplicity. We aspire not to seek the things of this world, because we see ourselves as pilgrims on this earth, and must set our hearts only on that spiritual home where our true treasure is to be found (Lk 6:45).

(2) Chastity

Like all Christians, Brothers are in a constant battle to overcome the temptations of the flesh, in an effort to live lives of purity and self-discipline so essential for our mission and ministry. We realize though, that we cannot do this in our own strength. It can only be done through God's Grace. As Brothers we willingly accept the calling of the single life whilst remaining in the Brotherhood, so that we can give ourselves fully to the Lord Jesus and his work. Whilst in the Brotherhood, we are to be "married" only to Jesus Christ.

We are to remain single, not because we think that the single life is a higher state than the married life but because we believe this is how God has called us to serve him. We look to him alone to give us the grace to live that life. When we choose to stay single for the Kingdom of Heavens sake, we are careful not to fall into the temptation of thinking only of ourselves, or to be unloving and uncaring towards others. Our union with Christ allows us to love more deeply with his love all those whom we meet, and minister to. "Let us love one another, help one another, show love and do good" (cf: Heb 10:24).

(3) Obedience

As Brothers, we strive to surrender and give our wills to God in the Spirit of perfect obedience. In doing so, we believe we will be following the way of Christ, who came into the world not to do his own will but the will of the one who sent him. Also when we freely accept the Rule of the Brotherhood, we agree to live by it. We also agree to accept the decisions of the Great Conference, the Regional Conference, and other lawful meetings of the Brotherhood because it is through these conferences and meetings that the common mind of the Brotherhood is expressed.

Our leaders within the Brotherhood try to ensure that the rules are being kept and to see that the decisions of the conferences are put into action. Their directions are happily and obediently carried out by all of us except where we think some may be against the rules or sinful. Each Brother put in charge of a particular department or work is obeyed in that department. Like other members of the Brotherhood, Brotherhood leaders are themselves under obedience to the Rule, the lawful conferences, and meetings of the Brotherhood. When exercising their lawful authority they do not show favouritism or act in a spirit of pride and selfishness but offer equal care for all.

The obedience that we Brothers willingly accept within the life of the community is not something different from the obedience that we see ourselves giving to God. We believe that if God has called us to the Brotherhood, then whilst we are in the Brotherhood and living under the Rule, we will be truly obeying him when we faithfully carry out duties of that life. We believe we can overcome the sin of pride and deepen our giving of ourselves to others by happily and willingly accepting all that the Rule expects of us.

THREE WAYS THE BROTHERHOOD TRIES TO SERVE CHRIST.

The Brothers try to serve our Lord in three ways:

(1) By living a life of Prayer
(2) By sacred study
(3) By works

These three ways of life, by God's grace, must be found in the life of each Brother. This does not mean that we will all be able to give ourselves equally to each of these three ways of service. The ways in which we serve best will depend on the gift that God has given us. Yet all of us Brothers must give some of our time to all three.

(1) Prayer

God is Spirit, and those who worship him must worship him in Spirit and in truth. (Jn. 4:25)

As Brothers we recognise that a strong personal and corporate prayer and worship life is absolutely essential and the root of everything that we do. Prayer as far as is possible in the life and work of the Melanesian Brotherhood is not negotiable as this is the very heart and power of its existence.

We try to develop our prayer life so that we are living in a constant remembrance of, and contact with, God's presence and indeed "pray at all times". (1 Thess. 5:17). As a group, be it at Tabalia or at any other household, the Brothers pray seven times a day beginning with First Office at 5:30 am, followed by Matins and then a Eucharist around 7:00 am. A Morning Office follows after the Eucharist. Then there is a Midday Office at noon and an Afternoon Office at 1:30 pm. Evening Prayer begins at 5:30 pm, and the Last Office at 9:00 pm, after which silence is kept in the household until breakfast the next day. Personal meditation and prayer in the chapel and elsewhere forms part of this spiritual formation emphasis.

(2) *Sacred Study*

"True knowledge is the knowledge of God." The first place in the Brothers work of study will always be given to the study and practice of personal communion with God. The study of Sacred Scriptures, as well as the Spiritual life, is a chief help to this personal communion.

All Novices of the Melanesian Brotherhood undergo various training courses in their three years of training which is capped by a five to six months practical training in the Mission field, before their admission as Brothers (or "Tasius") under vows. Their first year of training takes place in the various section headquarters and their second and third years, at Tabalia Headquarters. In Vanuatu and Papua New Guinea, second and third year novices are trained at their respective regional headquarters. Upon admission, Brothers serve for an initial period of three years after which they can renew their vows or ask for release having honourably served in the Brotherhood for a time. It was the founder's vision that vows for young men wishing to join the Melanesian Brotherhood should not be life-long unless wished for, since the Melanesian culture places a great emphasis on the married life and the support of grown up children for parents in their old age.

A yearly two-semester syllabus for Novice training is constantly revised and updated to adequately equip and prepare them well for the demanding missionary and evangelistic work of the Melanesia Brotherhood, and which also recognises the need to be relevant in today's changing contexts for mission and evangelism.

(3) *Works*

Our Lord Jesus Christ who became a servant for our sake said that he did not come to be served but to serve (Mk.10:45). He went about doing good, healing the sick, preaching the good news to the poor, strengthening the down hearted. As Brothers therefore, who claim to be his servants, and follow him, we must be faithful in ministry to others. The active works by which we seek to serve Christ begins within the house, the gardens and the farm. House and manual work is seen as part of earning our own living and all of us must be able to do some sort of manual work in addition to our own work as far as possible. There is no place for a lazy person in the Brotherhood.

In our evangelistic work outside the special works of service to the Brotherhood itself, the most important form of ministry and service we can offer others is the effort to show all people to Christ, who is the strength and joy of our own lives. We do not force ourselves on them or look down on the beliefs they already hold, but rather share with them the great treasure of living with Christ himself, who has the power to save from sin and give new life.

We are aware though, that in this work of showing Christ to others, the witness of our own personal and corporate life speaks louder than words.

As Brothers we try to be willing at all times to help those who come to us for help or counsel, and be ready to lay aside other work if such service is immediately required. We believe that giving urgent attention to this ministry is pleasing to "The Servant" of all people.

THREE QUALITIES THE BROTHERHOOD ASPIRES TO

As Brothers we strive to ensure that the three qualities of Humility, Love, and Joy may be found at all times in our lives. It is our belief as well as experience that the absence of these qualities from our lives renders weakness in the life and work of the Brotherhood.

(a) Humility

Jesus Christ emptied himself, taking the form of a servant. On the last night of his life he washed his disciples' feet as though he was a servant or slave. As Brothers we try to always remember to clothe ourselves with Christ's humility and serve one another. In our dealings with other people we try to show Christ's humility and will welcome any acts of humble service without expectation of praise or reward. We are careful not to fall into the trap of thinking that we are better off than others because we have given ourselves to God's service in the Brotherhood, but instead help others to build up self esteem and confidence in them by our humble service, love and care for their spiritual well being.

(b) Love

Jesus said, "if you have love for one another, then everyone will know that you are my disciples" (Jn. 13:35).

The Brotherhood recognises that love should be the greatest quality of all Christian disciples and strives to maintain this as the greatest quality of the Brothers, especially being dedicated as we are, to the servantship of Christ. We seek to love all who are united within our family of the Brotherhood, praying for and aspiring to grow in love for everyone. We believe this is not a natural expression of love but a love which God gives us in our union with Christ. In our relationship with those outside the community and with those whom we work, we try to show the same Christ-like love to all, Christian or not.

(a) Joy

As Brothers we always rejoice by the grace of the Lord, in the beauty of his divine joy. This joy, a divine gift of God because of our union with him in Christ, is carried with us as an inner secret of happiness and peace at all times as we work and relate with other people to help rid sorrow and bring joy into their lives in times of discouragement, sickness, hopelessness and suffering; and also as we relate to the rest of God's creation. Because of this we will easily accept weakness, insults, hardships, persecutions, and difficulties for Christ's sake believing that when we are weak then we are strong.

In our service as Brothers we seek to empty ourselves from self and be totally surrendered to God so that he will use us to further his kingdom here on earth. For us, faith is indeed a risk because we literally depend on God for sustenance and power for our very own lives and for the work he has called us to carry out for him.

Yet we find great joy and an inner peace and satisfaction whatever our circumstances—in times of hunger when the households run out of food and we miss two meals a day; when we walk barefoot for miles to help people in need even if our own need seems so much greater; when we lie down for days stricken by Malaria and often remember with fondness the love of parents and relatives left behind at home; when people seem to look down on us from their noses as if we are inferior and losers; when we cross mountainous regions and interiors of the jungles of our islands for days amidst swarms of insects and with hardly any food in the bush (and sometimes wearing down a night of torrential rain as best as we can under trees), to reach the coast. In all of this we are living the gospel in the Melanesian context.

IV. THE MISSION OF THE BROTHERHOOD

When Ini Kopuria began the Melanesian Brotherhood with the help of Bishop John Manwaring Stewart, it was at a time when heathenism and paganism was still rife and cannibalism only recently outlawed and banned with the declaration of the islands as a British Protectorate in 1899, still an uncertain factor. As a Police Constable, he had been sent to collect taxes from people of the required age, many of whom lived in hostile inland villages situated in inhospitable and inaccessible territory. Now as a missionary he envisioned taking the gospel to these places which cannot be reached by the foreign missionaries, evangelising in a Melanesian way in what would seem to be a community and contextual approach.

To get through to the people and communities they go to with the message of Christ, the Brothers had to literally live and share the life of the people in all things. They lived with them as equals yet always in the spirit of humility and love and as servants to those they minister to. In this the greatest things in their favour was that they did not force the people to convert and, more especially, they were prepared to stay with the people for as long as it took to help them be rid (through prayer and the exorcism ministry) of the fear of devils, ghosts/spirits, and ancestral gods. In the process the gospel message was preached in word and very much lived among the people in action, people became converted, leaf houses were built which became church houses for the Brothers and the new converts to worship God in those places, temporary catechists were trained, and in many instances basic reading and writing in the Mota language (and later in English) was taught.

Before long the Brothers reputation as being fearless of devils and spirits, as well as being men filled with the undefeatable spiritual mana or power of God, grew. They converted many heathen villages and communities and gained the love and respect of many people. Their purpose and work therefore was primarily primary evangelism—that is, breaking new grounds and making inroads into heathen and pagan areas. In some places secondary evangelism work by the church through its priests, trained catechists and others, could not adequately catch up on and consolidate the Brothers initial work resulting in other denominations taking over after the Brothers when they moved on.

While the more common conversion strategy among native and indigenous peoples by western churches in these early times were usually accompanied by, to a substantial extent, western material goods, superior tools and medicines to be found at the mission stations on the coasts, the Brothers by comparison had nothing material to offer and their success in similar situations was largely due to an unmovable faith in the power of God at work through them, and their great humility, obedience and servant-like manner to all people, friend or enemy alike. They depended on God alone for everything and their very own lives, in the face of hostile pagans who did not want them in the first place. "If we live, we live to the Lord or if we die, we die to the Lord. If we live or die, we are the Lord's."(Romans 14:8).

What the Brothers had to offer was a refreshing joyful and peaceful change in the power of God to a new life free from: spiritual bondage to demanding ancestral spirits, constant fighting and feuding between rival tribal and island groups, an oppression to fear and despotic rulers. In their presence people felt safe, peaceful, loved and useful.

In a reciprocal way, because of the simplicity and seeming physical vulnerability of the Brothers people felt that these young men who have given so much of themselves for them, need looking after and caring—much as parents would feel responsible for looking after the needs of their own children. By their life of poverty and vulnerability they showed forth a sense of needing to be looked after, raising parental instincts in people to look after and care for them. By their obedience they are an example of what parents and the community would wish their children to be like, and hence came to be greatly loved. By their life of chastity, they reflect a holiness and purity of character, a trait greatly respected by the people who have had a long history of respect for holy pagan priests in their traditional religion. It was, and still aspires to be, contextual evangelistic ministry at its best.

Today the Melanesian Brotherhood's evangelistic mission seems to be taking on a new phase. It's no longer a primary evangelism mission to traditional heathens and pagans as it was in the last sixty to seventy years but more a secondary evangelism work of helping to encourage and build up the faith of many who are still Christian but only in a very nominal way. Perhaps the primary evangelism nature of the Brothers mission can still be found and seen today in that we are now faced with the need to breakthrough and make inroads into the world of the modern and educated heathen/pagan. Notwithstanding this though, the mission field for primary evangelism in the rest of the world is far from being exhausted. Problems abound today in a new way and with a new face providing a new mission field for the Melanesian Brotherhood: The HIV and AIDS pandemic, prostitution, alcohol and drug abuse, gambling, increased divorces and broken homes, child abuse, secularism and the loss of Christian values, and ethnic hatred and enmity leading to civil war, amongst many others.

V. THE MELANESIAN BROTHERHOODS INVOLVEMENT IN THE ETHNIC TENSION

The ethnic tension between Guadalcanal people and Malaitans flared in late 1998 with the emergence of the militant Guadalcanal group known unofficially as the 'Guadalcanal Revolutionary Army', later known as the Isatambu Freedom Movement (IFM).

The IFM demanded that all Malaitan settlers living on Guadalcanal return to their own island of Malaita and made good their demand by chasing out and forcibly evicting at gunpoint Malaitans living on Guadalcanal soil outside Honiara, and burning down numerous settlements. More than 20,000 Malaitan settlers were displaced and escaped to Honiara where they were sent back to Malaita, though some resettled in squatter areas on the edges of the city.

The IFM quickly surrounded the eastern, western and southern outskirts of Honiara and initially engaged in sporadic fighting with the Royal Solomon Islands Police Force (RSIP), who managed to keep them out of the city. Road blocks manned by both the RSIP and the IFM within a hundred or so metres from each other on the outskirts effectively closed Honiara to Guadalcanal people, as well as Malaitans from moving beyond Honiara City edges.

The displaced Malaitans were to later form their own military group called the Malaita Eagle Force (MEF) which raided the Central Police Armoury at Rove, Honiara (with the help of the Malaitan members of a Malaita-dominated Police Force) on June 5th 1999, and effected a coup removing Prime Minister Bart Ulufa'alu (a Malaitan who they see as not doing enough to protect Malaitan interests and bring the insurgent IFM under control). A new Prime Minister was elected by the Solomon Islands Parliament under, as it may have seemed, MEF influence.

A mass exodus of foreign diplomatic, business and specialist personnel took place and economic development underwent a reverse plunge towards rock bottom with the closure of major export companies operating in the Guadalcanal Plains and in the Western Solomons, as well as several prominent foreign-owned business houses in Honiara. The situation in Honiara deteriorated rapidly as militia-men roamed the capital breeding a culture of intimidation and fear, extortion, violence, abduction, rape and suffering. In IFM held Guadalcanal, the situation was no different and innocent women and children suffered the most. The scene was set, as it may seem, for the darkest chapter in Solomon Islands modern history.

The first response of the Melanesian Brotherhood and other religious communities was a humanitarian one. We had to do something to help those who were suffering. All the Anglican religious communities have their headquarters in the area of rural Guadalcanal controlled during the conflict by the IFM but also households in Honiara which was virtually controlled by MEF. Thus we found ourselves bridging the war zone, divided by bombed bridges, road blocks and checkpoints of the two opposing militant groups. Throughout the conflict, when schools, colleges, villages, and even families were divided against each other on ethnic lines, in contrast each one of us in the religious communities managed to maintain our unity:

Malaitan Brothers and Sisters living side by side with Guadalcanal Brothers and Sisters on both Guadalcanal and Malaita. What is more, most of the militants themselves did not seem to discriminate against or judge us according to island or tribe. We were considered first and foremost religious brothers and sisters with an allegiance to God and to all Melanesians. This was an astonishing recognition in such an ethnic conflict where the opposing island groups were treated often with hatred and suspicion.

Our headquarters and households in both rural Guadalcanal and Honiara became places of refuge where people felt safe and trusted us to remain helpful and impartial to both sides. We were able to help displaced Malaitans get safely past IFM roadblocks to Honiara preventing some of the violence that could have developed, and also provided sanctuary to fleeing Guadalcanal villagers and families whose homes were threatened and burned down by MEF coastal raiding parties, and who were unable to get medicines and important supplies through the Honiara roadblocks.

Before long, hundreds of requests reached the religious communities and Brothers and Sisters were stretched to the very limits. People needed and asked us to search for relatives, reunite separated families, look for children, pick up property and possessions left behind in the displacement, protect the threatened, transport family members to safety, and help reconcile divisions and disputes among many families and marriages divided by tribe or island.

Eventually the Melanesian Brotherhood, as well as the other religious communities, decided to become more directly involved to prevent further violence, killing and suffering. At the Melanesian Brotherhood Great Conference at Tabalia in October 1999 we elected a Malaitan HeadBrother and an Assistant HeadBrother from Guadalcanal. In the middle of this ethnic tension it was an important and symbolic move. This new Brotherhood leadership expressed the belief that the community and ethnic unity of the Brotherhood must move out from Tabalia and be taken into the conflict zone. In May 2000 the Brothers chose and commissioned a team of Brothers to work directly for peace; these Brothers moved into the no-mans land between the roadblocks of the opposing militants and spread out to visit and try to pacify those directly involved in the growing violence.

The Brothers went with a simple message of appeal in the name of Jesus Christ to stop the killing, hatred, payback, and suffering caused to a lot of innocent fellow Solomon Islands country men and women. It was an appeal to stop bloodshed which will lead to more blood shedding, hatred which will result in greater hatred, and the imprisoning of all to the evil that we continue to perpetuate. The Brothers continued to camp between enemy lines for the next four months moving backwards and forwards and were often caught between cross-fires of the militant groups, talking to them, trying to calm them, praying with them, and trying to lessen false stories and suspicion which generates between factions in such a context.

Similarly the Brothers visited both MEF and IFM camps where training was taking place and prisoners were being held and tortured. By their words and presence they sought and were often successful in reminding the militants to use peaceful ways and to awaken Christian conscience to stop torture and violence. The Melanesian Brothers also became involved in negotiating the successful release of hostages taken by rival factions. Brothers and Sisters worked bravely trying to get supplies through road blocks to families and children, and also carried the displaced, the wounded, and the dead. Brothers carried the corpses of victims across the checkpoints to grieving relatives for proper burial and investigated the deaths of those missing, even digging up the bodies so that they could be identified and their remains returned. It was indeed very hard and painful work. We Brothers actually involved have described how, as the conflict developed, there was no glory; we have been left with painful memories we find difficult to forget.

The signing of the Townsville Peace Agreement on October 15, 2000 was accompanied by much celebration but we were soon to learn that the problems were far from over. The Melanesian Brotherhood was asked to work with the Peace Monitoring Council (PMC) but we withdrew after only three months as we found the way of life we were drawn into did not fit our religious way of life or our life as a community. In 2001 we were increasingly called upon to become the security for commercial property and people, a role that depleted our manpower.

Those who felt threatened requested Melanesian Brothers to stay at their homes. It would seem that the Melanesian Brotherhood had become too involved in protection and security of people and property but at the time there was no one else for people to turn to.

Later in 2002 approaches were made to the Melanesian Brotherhood to become involved in the disarmament process. On Pentecost 2002 it was decided in a meeting of the Brothers at Tabalia that the Melanesian Brotherhood must help in the collecting of guns for these were causing such injustices and social unrest in the nation. The Melanesian Brotherhood decided with one mind that there could be no chance of true peace in the nation unless the guns were destroyed. During the next five months the response to the Brothers call for guns to be returned was so great. It seemed that people trusted the Brothers with the proper disposal of the guns more than Police, some of whom may later decide to use the guns for their own ends as evidenced during the coup, and before the ceasefire agreement. The Melanesian Brotherhood worked to disarm all sides and this included guns held illegally by members of the Police Force, Malaitans, Guadalcanal or anyone else holding weapons. The many guns, bullets, bombs handed over to the Brotherhood were taken out to deep sea and sunk in the presence of the Police Commissioner, so that they can never be used again.

By 2003 it was increasingly obvious that the situation on the Weather coast of Guadalcanal was growing worse. Harold Keke (the Guadalcanal Liberation Front leader and his followers—an original warlord in the IFM who broke away and led his own rebel faction because he did not agree to the terms of the Townsville Peace Agreement) based on the Weather Coast of Guadalcanal, had not given up his guns and many Malaitans used this as an excuse not to hand over theirs. There was a culture of fear in which few were brave enough to speak out but rumours of the atrocities taking place on the Weather Coast reached Honiara including the murder of Fr. Augustine Geve, a retired Roman Catholic Priest. Many of those who Keke suspected of complicity with the government or betrayal of his cultish cause were tortured or executed including his own followers. The Solomon Islands Police Force were ill equipped and without the trust to deal with the Weather Coast situation and had enlisted the support of Keke's opponents and this joint operation was causing its own problems. There were accusations of burning down of villages and human rights abuses on both sides. The majority of the Weather Coast people including women and children were confused and afraid, caught between Harold Keke's militants and a joint operation militia which many did not trust.

Br. Nathaniel Sado, the first of the Melanesian Brothers to be murdered, had gone to visit Keke in February 2003 with two other Brothers. They took with them a letter from the Anglican Archbishop Ellison Pogo to try and open up dialogue for peace and bring an end to the atrocities in which so many innocent people were suffering. It was obvious at this stage that the Royal Solomon Islands Police did not have the numbers, capability, or support to re-establish the rule of law and order. Brother Nathaniel knew Keke well and had worked with his brother during the disarmament period. He naively believed that he could help to bring peace.

When the other two Brothers, unable to meet with Keke, returned, Br. Nathaniel, against their advise decided to stay. He made the mistake of believing Keke would not harm him. On Easter day one of Keke's followers who had escaped from him and run away to Mbabanakira station, several miles from Keke's stronghold, reported on the national broadcaster, SIBC, that Br. Nathaniel Sado had been murdered.

When the Brothers heard the news of this death they were deeply shocked and unsure whether it was true. While the Melanesian Brotherhood had always tried to advocate for others now there was no one to advocate for them.

More than two months later on April 23rd, 2003, six Bothers led by the Assistant HeadBrother Robin Lindsay, who was responsible for the welfare of the Brothers in the Solomon Islands Region left Honiara by canoe for the Weather Coast. Their mission, as authorised by the Archbishop, was to visit the Brotherhood Households on the Weather Coast to find out what had happened to Br. Nathaniel and if his death was confirmed, to try to bring his body back for burial at Tabalia. The other five Brothers who went with him were Brothers Francis Tofi, Tony Sirihi, Alfred Hilly, Patteson Gatu and Ini Paratabatu.

The Brothers arrived on the Weather Coast and walked inland towards Keke's village. They came upon a group of Keke's followers (Keke was not with them) who attacked them and killed Brothers Robin Lindsay, Francis Tofi and Alfred Hill when they refused to lie face down on the ground. The other three Brothers were taken back to Keke's camp where after a night of humiliation and torture they were lined up in front of a single grave and shot in the chest falling in the grave. Those who were later arrested for their murders told that they were killed because they were considered to be government spies who had come without permission from Keke.

When the Brothers did not return, three months of waiting, vigil, and prayer began in which negotiations with Keke for their release continued. Keke claimed all these hostages were still alive and were being held as prisoners of war. In the meantime, Keke took more Brothers and Novices hostage. For more than a month he held another five Novices and two Brothers. These seven were all released unharmed. In fact Keke had asked them to pray with him and to preach to his men. He sent them back with gifts of shell money and pigs for the Melanesian Brotherhood. A week after their release, and in a meeting with the just arrived Regional Assistance Mission To Solomon Islands (RAMSI), Keke announced that the seven Brothers originally believed by many to be still his captives and hostages were dead and killed on arrival. He also agreed to an unconditional surrender and the laying down of arms of his followers. So came the hope of peace but for the Melanesian Brotherhood at great cost.

VI. TODAY AND THE FUTURE

Our seven young martyrs (probably among, if not, the first Christian Martyrs of the 21st Century) will continue to live on in the hearts and minds of our community and the whole Church in Melanesia. Their sacrifice seems so great and hard to believe but we are slowly coming to terms with the enormity of their, and our, loss in the past two years. There has been a lot of trauma and its still here with us but there is great peace too in the knowledge that these young colleagues of ours lived Christ's Gospel to the full and gave us a true paradigm for our own faith, life and mission/ministry through their life and sacrifice: one of complete dedication—of faith, hope and love — for God's glory, and the good of his church and people.

They showed us the way forward. To keep on witnessing, proclaiming and living out the Gospel beyond the confines and safety of our homes, communities and churches. For when such real life issues are so much at stake in our world, this is what the Gospel should be. In a world disfigured by violence, suffering and brutality, the Melanesian Brotherhood must continue to be as *salt of the earth* and *light to the world*. We are to continue getting our hands dirty for the sake of (the kingdom of) peace, joy and love, in the here and now and moving towards the final consummation of all things. By God's grace we will endure.

And indeed by God's grace, and contrary to widely held speculations especially over the death of our Seven Brothers, the Melanesian Brotherhood continues to thrive today as never before. More applications than we can handle continue to flood in from young men all over who wish to join the Brotherhood. Some say the temporary nature of our vows as Brothers appeals strongly to young men who feel called to serve God for a certain period of time as missionaries; after which they can continue on in life as witnesses for Christ's Gospel in other capacities in their own communities. The work of secondary evangelism beckons strongly to us but we are ever more aware today that we need to reassess what we are doing now by looking at the past and then planning ahead for the most appropriate evangelistic direction in the future. The mission field for primary evangelism on a global scale remains overwhelming as if to remind us that such was, and still is, the Brotherhood's original purpose of existence as envisioned by its founder, Ini Kopuria. However as it is now, both primary and secondary evangelism seem inseparable in the mission and ministry of the Brotherhood today.

Grounding in theological education has become an issue of importance to the Brotherhood as we find ourselves more and more called to suggest solutions to complicated problems in an era of an options explosion and where the Church has seemed to become boring. We have since sent several Brothers to undergo theological training in various institutions locally and overseas and their input will be invaluable towards helping the community direct its future mission and ministry.

Finally, perhaps the strength of the Brotherhood's evangelistic mission is that we belong to the people. We become part of their culture, eating the same food, respecting their customs, understanding their way of life, entering into a real relationship with the people and in the process really living the gospel in their midst. People feel it is their community and the young men, their sons and it is true. No discomfort is too much for us as long as we know that we are doing the will of the Almighty Creator and bringing joy, peace and love to all. But it is not that we inflict punishment and hardship on ourselves; when there is plenty we will feast like there is no tomorrow and when there is little or nothing we will also famine with the community. We communicate not only in words but also in symbol and action. The future remains to be seen but we are confident that wherever the wind of God's Spirit blows there too we shall follow, humbly and simply as servants to do the will of God and of his Son Jesus Christ our Lord. *Amen.*

Our acknowledgements and thanks to Revd Richard Carter, former Melanesian Brother and Chaplain of Melanesian Brotherhood from January 1992 to April 2005, whose works form the bulk of material used in this report. Thank you.

Brother James Tata, MBH, Tabalia. Guadalcanal, Solomon Islands.

NETWORK REPORTS

Report of the Anglican Indigenous Network

Member nations have met formally and networked their ministries between meetings over the last eight years.

THE BEGINNING

In the early 1980s discussions began on the development of a network of relationships among indigenous peoples. These discussions took place during the meeting of the General Assembly of the World Council of Churches in Vancouver in 1983 and in the context of setting procedures for the election of an Aborigine Bishop. From this discussion further meetings were held which included indigenous delegates from Australia, Canada, Hawai`i, Aotearoa and the United States. But during the remainder of the 1980s the matter of a formal network never went beyond the discussion stage.

During the 1991 General Convention of the Episcopal Church in Phoenix, Arizona the first step was taken toward forming a network of indigenous Anglicans. It was here that the Anglican observer to the United Nations, the Rt. Rev. Sir Paul Reeves, convened a meeting of indigenous Anglicans and/or their representatives: Dr. Owanah Anderson, the Rev. Dr. Martin Brokenleg, Bishop Steven Charleston and Dr. Carol Hampton of the Episcopal Council of Indian Ministries; Bishop Wakahuihui and Doris Vercoe from Aotearoa; the Rev. Charles G. K. Hopkins from Hawai'i; Archbishop Michael Pierce representing native Canadians. The idea of an indigenous network to coincide with the United Nation's International Year of the World's Indigenous People was presented and the countries represented at the meeting agreed to participate in it. It was further decided that one person from each country meet as a steering committee with Sir Paul Reeves to develop a plan for networking among American Indians and Alaska Natives, Canadian Natives, Native Hawaiians and Maori. Father Hopkins' offer of his Mission, St. John's By-the-Sea in Kahalu`u, Hawai'i, as the site and host of the meeting was accepted with appreciation.

HAWAI'I [USA] 1991

The steering committee, consisting of Sir Paul Reeves, chair, Dr. Owanah Anderson, Mr. Charles Bellis, the Rev. Laverne Jacobs, the Rev. Charles Hopkins, Professor Pua Hopkins, and Bishop and Doris Vercoe, met on December 10 through 12 in Hawai'i where each one expressed the concerns of their people and identified the areas of mutual concerns. They were: 1) Self-determination, 2) Indigenous Ministry, 3) Spirituality, 4) Liturgy and Worship, 5) Church Self-examination and Transformation, 6) Church's Role in Society, 7) Funding and Resources. The steering committee also adopted the following Statement of Consensus:

This Anglican Indigenous Peoples' Network Steering Committee:

1) Adopts the statement of our areas of concern; 2) recommends to our constituencies that there be a representative gathering to consider these mutual concerns in November 1992 in Hawai'i; and that the representatives invited be persons of expertise in one or more areas of mutual concern; 3) agrees to take advantage of important events happening in our respective churches for the purpose of further networking, for example:

Auckland, NZ—1/92 Ministry Summer School
Rotorua, NZ—3/92 Ordination of Bishops
Christchurch, NZ—8/92 Partners in Mission
Washington DC, USA—10/92 Celebration of Survival
Vancouver, Canada—7/93 International Youth Gathering
Ontario, Canada—8/93 Native Convocation;

4) and conveys to our respective constituencies the significance of networking among indigenous peoples within the Anglican Communion.

Native Hawaiians and American Indians who were in Aotearoa for the consecration of three Maori Bishops in Rotorua in March 1992 attended a Network meeting called by Bishop Vercoe at which a consensus was reached on the following matters: 1) the dates for the November network meeting were set for Nov.12–15; 2) the meeting would be held in Hawai'i at St. John's By-the-Sea, and members of the congregation would host fifteen out-of-State delegates; 3) each constituency in the Network would be entitled to five delegates at the November meeting; 4) each member of the delegation would be selected for his/her expertise in one or more of the "areas of mutual concern,"; 5) each delegate must be an indigenous person (no non-native expert) and a resident of the country he/she represents; 6) because of the number of "mutual concerns," each constituency would review the "mutual concerns" and forward a prioritized list to Bishop Reeves or Owanah Anderson by August 15 along with a list of five delegates and the area of expertise of each; 7) for the time being membership in the Network would be kept as is: Native American, Native Canadian, Native Hawaiian, Maori.

HAWAI'I [USA] 1992

Network delegations met at St. John's By-the-Sea in Kahalu`u, Hawai'i on November 12 -15: Native Canadians Mr. Charles Bellis, Mr. Gordon Crow Child, the Rev. Laverne Jacobs, Ms. Vi Smith, Ms. Esther Wesley; Maori of Aotearoa Ms. Jenny Kaa, Professor Whatarangi Winiata, Ms. Francis Winiata, Ms. Doris Vercoe. Bishop Wakahuihui Vercoe; Native Americans Dr. Owanah Anderson, the Rev. Dr. Martin Brokenleg, Bishop Steve Charlston, Ms. Ginny Doctor, Bishop Steve Plummer; Native Hawaiians the Rev. Darrow Aiona, Mr. Malcolm Chun, the Rev. Charles Hopkins, Professor Pua Hopkins, Ms. Linda Sproat.

At this meeting the Anglican Indigenous Network was adopted as the official title of the network along with the following Mission Statement:

We are indigenous minority peoples living in our own lands. We are committed to the Anglican tradition while affirming our traditional spirituality. We have discovered that we have many things in common: a common spirituality, common concerns, common gifts, common hopes. We believe that God is leading the Church to a turning point in its history and that the full partnership of indigenous peoples is essential. Therefore we pledge to work together to exercise our leadership in contributing our vision and gifts to transform the life of the Christian community.

Presentations were heard and discussed on the mutual concerns of self determination, indigenous ministry, liturgy and worship, and development of resources which resulted in identifying goals and objectives for 1993–94. It was agreed that AIN would next meet in Aotearoa (New Zealand) in March 1994, that Bishop Reeves would represent AIN at the events of the UN International Year of the World's Indigenous People, and that an AIN report be made at the meeting of the Anglican Consultative Council at Cape Town in January 1993. A calendar of events in the four constituencies in 1993 was formulated for networking between meetings.

AOTEAROA [NEW ZEALAND] 1994

From February 28 through March 6, 1994, AIN met at St. John's Theological College, Auckland, the home of Te Pihopatanga's Te Rau Kahikatea and at St. Faith Parish in Rotorua. At this gathering an indigenous delegation of Aboriginal Anglicans from Australia was added to the Network, which helped to make it the largest gathering (43) of delegates and observers: Aotearoa 19, Australia 5, Canada 5, Hawai'i 8, Continental US 6.

After hearing comprehensive reports on the plight of Maori in their home land and in the Anglican Province of New Zealand, and in response to hearing of the same plight by other delegations, and after hearing reports on indigenous training programs developed by the Commission On Native

Hawaiian Ministry (CONHM) and by the Episcopal Council On Indian Ministry (ECIM), there was a shift in the AIN's goals from formulating a sense of identity to building a viable interacting network. This was evident in the ideas from participants which were readily adopted: a proposal to increase membership in AIN by considering the inclusion of Latin Americans; the offer of scholarships and lectureships for other AIN constituencies at Te Rau Kahikatea; the production of a directory of human resources for their exchange within AIN; the production of a newsletter and video to interpret and promote AIN; the coordination of internal communications to keep constituencies linked; and a proposal to place women's concerns on the agenda of each meeting.

Following an agreement on these steps toward a solid network, there was a discussion on the effect of rotating delegates on preserving continuity from one meeting to the next. As a result it was agreed that it is the responsibility of each constituency to update new delegates on the current status of AIN so that unnecessary backtracking can be avoided. Because of the loss of Bishop Reeves as convener, it was decided that the constituency responsible for the next meeting would act as coordinator for AIN until that meeting is held. The American Indian delegation offered to host the next meeting of AIN in September 1995 somewhere in the continental US.

ALASKA [USA] 1995

The period between AIN gatherings in Aotearoa and Alaska was a time of mixed pain and gladness for the five constituencies. The bad news included the turmoil over financial matters in the Diocese of Hawai'i and the Episcopal Church Center in New York. In Hawai'i the diocesan budget was to be scaled back sharply in order to pay the interest on a foreclosed $4,000,000 loan the Diocese had guaranteed. In an atmosphere of accusations and mistrust Bishop Hart, who had met with the Network in 1992, resigned. This financial turmoil seriously reduced CONHM's funding and delayed the approval of its Native Hawaiian Ministry Study Program until December 1995.

While this was happening in Hawai'i, the US delegates returned home to an ECIM meeting in San Jose, California where, in the spirit generated in Rotorua, they welcomed CONHM as a partner in the ECIM network and instructed the staff to invite the chair of the Commission On Native Hawaiian Ministry to the next ECIM meeting. This action was in response to CONHM's request in July 1993 for a liaison relationship with the Council with voice, vote only on issues of mutual concern, funding for liaison travel if available, and to be inclusion in the Staff Officers' portfolio. But later on in 1994 internal conflicts moved the Executive Council to approve a restructuring of the Church Center that would eliminate ECIM along with the other ethnic commissions and have 3 persons from the constituencies of the four ethnic desks appointed by the Presiding Bishop to a single advisory committee. Later that summer at General Convention, Bishop Charleston's pleas for the restoration of ECIM resulted in a truncated ECIM, reduced from 13 members to 5, only one of whom was a reappointment. Hawai'i lost its seat after only two ECIM meetings in 1995.

Unfortunately that was not the only setback for Native American ministry. Out of a renewed sense of self determination at the 1995 Winter Talk there emerged a Statement of Self Determination as a Native effort towards cohesiveness and unity. The larger Church, in its upheaval over the discovery in May of the embezzlement of $2.2 million by the Church Center's treasurer, regarded the statement as further separation and divisiveness in the Church family. With not much to smile about, Ginny Doctor was quoted as saying, "But we have not given up."

On a happier note, there was gladness in AIN over the optimism just north of the US border and in the faraway South Pacific. The First Nation peoples of Canada returned home from Rotorua and took bold steps toward self-determination in April by calling for a new relationship with the Anglican Church in Canada, resulting in a public apology from Archbishop Peers for the past behavior of the Church and the beginning of a process towards a real partnership. Bishop Charleston of Alaska went south to assist the USA's Canadian AIN partners to the north with their initiative.

Reporting for AIN's newest constituency, Australian Bishop Malcolm said that ideas from AIN had been put to use by Anglican Aborigines and Torres Strait Islanders through the National Aboriginal Anglican Council (NAAC). As a result of this cross fertilization within AIN, they were looking forward with optimism to a synod after returning home from Alaska that could well provide an additional Aboriginal bishop in North Queensland, a new Native bishop for the Torres Strait Islands and the possibility of an all-indigenous theological college.

This mixed note prevailed at the AIN gathering from September 11–13 at Meier Lake Conference Center led by a "down-sized and down-cast" but not down-and- out American Indian and Alaska Native delegation. After delegates reported on the status of their constituencies, took care of old business and were treated to an Alaska Native Potlatch, the gathering took on a positive note cued by the personal statement of Bishop Charleston:

"In the last few days I have begun to see again through the glass darkly; I have again felt the passion, and begun to recapture the vision I thought I had lost."

Consequently, a second Statement of Consensus was adopted which renewed our pledge to support each other with specific references to the

First Nation's Covenant Statement of Self Determination adopted in Canada, the appointment of indigenous bishops in the Carpentaria and North Queensland Regions in Australia, the Statement of Self, Determination adopted at the U.S. Natives' Winter Talk in 1995, the development of an indigenous training center in North America, and the newly established Native Hawaiian Community of Faith, Ka Papa Anaina Hawai'i O Kristo. The Statement also reflected the desire to enlarge the AIN circle by inviting two new members. It included the adoption of the Anglican Consultative Council's five-point Statement as AIN's guiding principles. Finally, this Statement was to be distributed throughout the Anglican Communion, as high up as "Canterbury, and even to the Queen, herself."

LETHBRIDGE [CANADA] 1997

On the campus of the University of Lethbridge, the Canadian delegation convened the 1997 assembly of AIN. After hearing a brief history of AIN, the five delegations reported at length on their ministries since the gathering in Alaska; one of the items from the U.S.A. was the establishment of the Indigenous Theological Training Institute. The description of local developments and concerns set the agenda for the remaining sessions.

The apparent "second class" status of Bishop Malcolm in the Anglican Province of Australia raised the issue of a bishop's jurisdiction, especially as it applies to indigenous bishops. Are the jurisdictions, defined by geographical boundaries within a national church or by the location of indigenous people and the need for one of their own kind, no matter where they are in the Anglican Communion? After a lengthy discussion and suggestions for the Australian situation, it was decided that a position paper was needed regarding the authority, jurisdiction and role of bishops in their episcopate among indigenous people. Mark MacDonald was given the responsibility for the position paper to be presented at the next AIN gathering.

Native Spirituality, one of the priority mutual concerns, was the next matter taken up by the assembly. Discussion centered on what native spirituality means in each delegation's constituency: beliefs and practices, authenticity, expressions, role in the Church, place in the lives of the young, etc. Delegations were asked to present a paper on their understanding of native spirituality at the next AIN gathering in Hawai'i.

Other matters covered were 1) indigenous theological training where those who head institutions within the Network were asked to establish an ongoing working group to support and assist one another; 2) the need for indigenous input on local churches' policies and plans to combat racism in church institutions in preparation for the WCC meeting in 1998; and 3) the need for Anglican Consultative Council's official recognition of AIN as the voice of Anglican indigenous people utilizing those in the AIN constituencies who sit on the Council.

HAWAI'I [USA] 1999

Five delegations representing the People of the Land in Aotearoa (NZ), Australia, Canada, the continental United States, and Hawai'i gathered on September 8, 1999 on Kaua`i, fourth largest of the Hawaiian Islands, for the seventh meeting of AIN. After an opening Eucharist, the host delegation, the Commission On Native Hawaiian Ministry, convened the Network's three day formal meeting on the morning of September 9 at All Saints' parish in Kapa`a, where each delegation reported on the ministry of their constituency since the previous 1997 gathering in Canada. The afternoon session was given over to reports on matters carried over from 1997; which included reports from the working group of heads of native theological training institutions, the group working on the development of native theology and the bishops in the Network on the jurisdiction of indigenous bishops. This was followed by the presentation of papers on the native spirituality of the constituents of each delegation.

In the remaining sessions, the mode shifted to the future of AIN. Where do we go from here? What tasks do we need to undertake in the upcoming direction of AIN? It was agreed: 1) to appoint Whatarangi Winiata of Aotearoa as AIN's voice at the upcoming ACC meeting in September 1999, when AIN will seek recognition as an Anglican Indigenous Network with observer status and support in funding; 2) to establish of the following working groups: prayer and support, communications, youth participation, women's concerns; 3) to distribute Bishop Macdonald's paper on the authority and jurisdiction of bishops for discussion in the constituencies and to appointment a working group to follow up; 4) to expand participation in the Network by inviting other minority indigenous people to participate as observers at the meeting in Cairns in 2001; 5) to have Bishop Vercoe coordinate AIN administration in collaboration with member constituencies until our next meeting in 2001; 6) to encourage each delegation to make contributions as their budgets allow to a special AIN account in Bishop Vercoe's office to help with administrative expenses until 2001.

After a tour of the East side of the Island on Saturday afternoon, the gathering concluded that evening with a closing Eucharist, dinner, Hawaiian entertainment and farewells.

The 8th Anglican Indigenous Network (AIN) gathering (31 March–5 April) began with a traditional Maori welcome near the shores of Lake Rotorua, Aotearoa (New Zealand). A young Maori man dressed in traditional warrior's apparel came forward before the entering delegations with a traditional club-spear to test the delegations' intentions of either peaceful or warlike. By picking up the green fern leaf branch left upon the ground, the Secretary General of AIN, Mr Malcolm Naea Chun, gave the Maori host of the Bishopric of Aotearoa, that the delegations came in peace. A few moments later he would reaffirm this by invoking a traditional Maori saying that the gathering was to "sew the threads of humanity together so they could never be broken." Even at the end of the formal welcome traditional cultural elements were seen in the appearance of a double rainbow.

CAIRNS [AUSTRALIA] 2001

Duress and the difficulty of international travel after the tragic events of 11 September in the United States of America, delegations from Canada, Aotearoa (New Zealand, Hawai'i and Australia (including representative of the Torres Strait Islands) met in Cairns, Australia for gathering of the Anglican Indigenous Network (AIN). The delegation from Hawai'i was delayed for four days before they reached Cairns and the Canadian delegation comprised of two members, Donna Bomberry, staff officer and Todd Russell, Vice-Chair of the Indigenous Council. Greatly missed was the entire American delegation, although they were represented by proxy through Episcopal Council on Indigenous Ministry member, Malcolm Naea Chun, head of the Hawaiian delegation.

Before the meetings began, members who arrived early were able to witness the consecration of the new Aboriginal Bishop the Rt. Rev. James Leftwich at St. Albans in the Aboriginal community of Yarrabah, and the retirement of Bishop Arthur Malcolm. With the arrival of the Hawaiian delegation, the meeting began on Wednesday 19 September with cultural activities and fellowship that helped the delegations to recognize and appreciate the diversity of the Aboriginal tribes and the uniqueness of the Torres Strait Islanders.

With the arrivals of the delegation from Aotearoa (Maori) and Donna Bomberry of Canada their status reports since the 1999 AIN meeting in Hawai'i were given. The Maori delegation reported on education and mission and the Canadian focused upon the present situation regarding the Church/Crown litigations, impending bankruptcy of the National Church, a new document entitled 'A New Agape': a plan for justice, healing and reconciliation of our relationships. Also noted was of Bishop Beardy's resignation as diocesan bishop, and a presentation of the video of Sacred Circle 2000 'Walking a New Vision' was attended by Bishop Arthur Malcolm. This was all followed by discussion, questions and answers. Each delegation will be forwarded a copy of the video from Canada.

Official business was commenced on Thursday, 20 September at St. Alban's Church in Yarrabah, the home community of Bishop Arthur Malcolm, retiring Aboriginal Bishop.

The original agenda hoped to focus upon particular issues such as youth, women's concerns, and land; however without full delegations to provide information and discussion, the venue was changed to an open plenary on the future of AIN.

Bishops Arthur Malcolm and Hui Vercoe, Bishop of Aotearoa (New Zealand); and Malcolm Naea Chun each brought out the concerns for the continuation of AIN, its past history and accomplishments and challenges for AIN to be effective and viable in the near future. In particular the discussion focused upon reviewing AIN's mission statement and the need for budget and financing.

Bishop Malcolm in his welcome to the delegations introduced the delegations to the Aboriginal spiritual concept of the dreamtime, "to be one with creation, the land and the people" so that all could bring the creativity to vision for the future of AIN and to help the Aboriginal and Torres Strait Islanders to become full partners in their own homelands and among the indigenous peoples of the world.

Bishop Vercoe set forth the new agenda calling for this AIN meeting to consider "Where are we going with our theological education centres? We need to pull together what those programmes really mean to us. We are caught up with the agenda of the national churches and we need to get away from that. The form and order that we talk of and use is way too dependent upon dominant culture and church. The process we use for work and ministry among youth is a process of the church that is still living in the past. We must enable and empower our laity to be an equal part of the leadership of the church, not just priests and bishops. They are the ones who elect or should elect their bishops."

Aboriginal delegate, the Rev. Di Langham emphasized the need for constant and reciprocal communication among the members of AIN. This was supported by Hawaiian delegate Malcolm Naea Chun who called for better communication remembering that there are still places that have no access to electronic communication and hence the continued need and responsibility for "regional, local and person to person communication; in whatever form is necessary and appropriate be it a website, emails, faxes, printed and recorded materials, and by voice."

Canadian First Nations delegate Donna Bomberry reiterated the need for AIN as it had given tremendous support and inspiration for the indigenous peoples of Canada when they were in need of new thinking in the church. "AIN has supported the Canadian church. Maintaining who we are is terribly important for the indigenous people in Canada. We need the lifelines and linkages and communication with others sharing our common issues. This relationship has been very valuable to us and will remain high in our agenda."

There were several other resolutions and actions taken to ensure the work of AIN by formalizing its operations.

BE IT RESOLVED THAT;

AIN reaffirms its commitment to the mutual concerns of the indigenous peoples within the Anglican Communion for self-determination. AIN encourages the establishment of national indigenous bishops for indigenous ministry. AIN will support these efforts through advocacy, education, development of strategies and other means of support.

AIN strongly supports the Gwich'in Nation of Alaska in their opposition to the exploration and drilling for natural resources in the Arctic National Wildlife Refuge of Northeastern Alaska. The threat and potential destruction of their lifeline—the Porcupine Caribou—means the destruction of the life of Gwich'in traditions and their fundamental human rights. It is inexcusable to extinguish the livelihood of a people.

We call upon our brother and sisters of the indigenous peoples of the world to formally voice their opposition to the US Senate and the President of the USA, to the Canadian government and other affected nations.

AIN pledges its support in mutually sharing forms of indigenous ministries as expressed in liturgical worship and liturgy, training, theological education and social justice issues.

AIN resolves to establish the Office of General Secretary to the AIN.

It is further resolved to establish a Sub-Committee of the AIN chaired by Mr. Malcolm Naea Chun and consisting of at least one person from each member, nation. selected before the end of 2001. This Sub-Committee will be authorised by the AIN to establish the office of the General Secretary including the establishment of terms of reference, functions, staffing, budgeting and established protocol.

The Interim Secretariat will help to organize a gathering of the leadership of the theological educators to be held in the next six to twelve months in the United States of America (Hawai'i) for the purpose of introduction of programmes for leadership and ordination, the sharing of curriculum and resources, the exchange of faculty and students, and other issues of concern.

The next AIN meeting is scheduled for late autumn (March–April, 2003) and is to be held in Rotorua, Aotearoa (New Zealand)

The member host Aotearoa has asked each delegation to be prepared to have a delegation that can focus and work on specific issues and therefore each delegation should consist of a priest, woman, youth, educator, and elder. The gathering will involve small groups and plenary, and each delegation should be prepared to offer a form of liturgical worship for either morning and evening that is reflective of their traditions so members can experience the liturgical diversity and gifts that each has to offer the Church.

It was also agreed upon that at least two observers would be invited from other Anglican indigenous minorities such as Taiwan, Japan, Mexico, and Belize to attend the next AIN meeting. Each of these groups would be responsible for their air expenses and for providing their own translation services.

ROTORUA [NEW ZEALAND] 2003

The host for this gathering, the Rt. Rev. Whakahuihui Vercoe, in his sermon at Eucharist on the morning of the first day of business, called for the delegations to be "storytellers, value bearers, community builders and spiritual journeyers" whose voices and work more than ever needs to heard and seen in the Anglican Communion. He implored the delegates, "This is our heritage and to act on this heritage is our ministry. It is a ministry of listening, of healing, and of caring."

Further words of encouragement and greetings came from the Secretary General of the Anglican Consultative Council, the Rev. Canon John L. Peterson, who wrote, "As you reflect on how you are able to grow into the fullness of the purpose of your network, we, too, will be reflecting how we as a Communion can be more effective in our support of your ministry. Together might we be able to use our common gifts and our common spirituality 'to transform' the life of the Christian community."

The Presiding Bishop and Primate of the Episcopal Church of the United States of America, the Rt Rev. Frank T. Griswold, wrote, "A gift of our Anglican Communion is that we are able to come together to share in one another's realities and contacts, and therefore have a better understanding of how Christ moved throughout the world." He further wrote, "I hope that the time you spend together is fruitful, and that you find a strengthening of faith through community. I pray that you will all grow in your awareness of the strengths that can be found by being attentive to the movement of the Holy Spirit in our lives. This comes with my very good wishes and blessings for you all. Yours in Christ."

Before the delegations broke out into their representative groups, they listened to a special guest, Archdeacon Taimalelagi Tuatagaloa Matalavea, the Anglican Observer to the United Nations. She reported on the nature of her office and work and stressed that indigenous minority issues at the United Nations are one of her priorities. She also pointed out the tenuous nature of the office due to the lack of funds, but also how important the office is by letting groups like AIN know of forthcoming world gatherings like the next meeting in late May of the Permanent Forum of Indigenous Peoples, whose topic is children and youth.

Among eight resolutions passed by AIN, the most encompassing one called for: *the "creation of a non-geographic Province of the Anglican Communion for the Indigenous Peoples of the Pacific Rim." It was noted in the deliberations that unlike other Anglicans in the world who have sought to have their religious expression outside being in relationship and dialogue in the Communion, the membership of AIN continues to fulfill its mission statement in being "committed to the Anglican tradition while affirming our traditional spirituality. We believe that God is leading the Church to a turning point in its history and that the full partnership of indigenous peoples is essential. Therefore we pledge to work together to exercise our leadership in contributing our vision and gifts to transform the life of the Christian community."*

Each of the delegations also introduced resolutions of regional concerns for mutual support. The following resolutions were adopted and passed by the membership:

AIN supports the concept presented by Te Pihopatanga o Aotearoa for a "Primatial Leadership Team," for the purpose of exercising collaborative leadership among the three Senior Bishops of the Anglican Church in Aoteoroa, New Zealand and Polynesia.

AIN as a formal body of the Anglican Consultative Council supports and recognizes the Episcopal Commission on Indigenous Ministry as a formal body representing the needs and concerns of the indigenous peoples of the United States.

AIN supports the establishment of a Native Hawaiian Area Mission; the establishment of an office of the co-ordinator for Native Hawaiian indigenous ministry; the increase of numbers of indigenous Native Hawaiian clergy; the training of our indigenous aspirants to ministry through our Native Hawaiian Study Curriculum.

AIN strongly supports the efforts for a true and meaningful Covenant between the Anglican Indigenous people of Australia and the Church.

AIN express support for the position of the Anglican Council of Indigenous peoples in relation to the Settlement Agreement between the Anglican Church of Canada and the Federal Government of Canada.

AIN express continual support for the Gwich'in Nation and for the establishment of a permanent natural reserve and refuge from the exploitation of natural resources.

It was also moved formally that:

AIN supports the development of the Anglican Indigenous Youth Network to assist the Anglican Indigenous Network in meeting and addressing the needs of the youth and young adults within the Anglican Church and our home communities.

On a more informal level the groups representing women, elders and indigenous theological educators will also continue to organize themselves and to meet before the next AIN gathering in 2005. The women and elders have indicated their interim gatherings are in 2004 to be held in Hawaii. They also, following the call of the AIN Secretary General, found the need for dialogue between groups and this was initiated by the elders and youth with designated leaders. In this dialogue they began to explore the need for better interaction among the generations especially as means for church and community growth, with the youth calling to their elders to get more involved.

A special proposal for funding of AIN was presented by the Secretary-General for the establishment of a $300,000 (US) operating endowment fund set up under the Anglican Consultative Council (ACC). It is hope that the fund will provide an annual budget of $15,000 (US). Members will be asked to explore individual donors and other sources to help establish this badly needed fund. This proposal is part of the ACCs "Endowment Fund Campaign for the Anglican Communion" to ensure that the Church's programs have a secure future. Those wishing to contribute to this special fund should contact The Rev. Canon John Peterson, Secretary General of the Anglican Consultative Council (ACC).

Continuing the rotation of hosting AIN gatherings, the next gathering will be held in the United States of American in early spring of 2005 and with the venue in Oklahoma. [coverage from AIN website (www.ainetwork.org), Anglican Communion News Service (www.anglicancommunion.org)]

PALA [USA] 2005

The ninth gathering of the Anglican Indigenous Network (AIN) was held on the reservation of the Pala Indian Mission in Pala, California and was hosted by the Episcopal Council on Indigenous Ministry (ECIM) of the Episcopal Church of the United States, from 10–15 April, 2005.

This gathering was successful from the start, having almost full delegations from all the members. This increased participation by the members signaled a revitalization and invigoration since the events of September 11, 2001. It also is the result of the changing leadership of all the members as none of the participating delegations had attended the initial meetings that created and established AIN.

The gathering began with a morning Eucharist service led by members of the host nation, ECIM. They represented the diversity of the indigenous peoples of the United States of each regional area: Alaska-Northwest,

Northeast, Midwest, Southeast, and Hawai'i. Several indigenous traditional rites and symbols were interwoven into the service with many indigenous songs of praise, traditional and modern. The homily was given by Mr. Robert McGhee, Vice Chair of ECIM and a member of the Poarch Creek Nation. The service was led by Native American bishops, the Rt. Rev's Carol Gallagher (Southern Virginia), a member of the Cherokee Nation, and Michael Smith (North Dakota), a member of the Potawatomi Nation.

The delegations and guest heard greetings from the Archbishop of Canterbury, Rowan Williams, who called upon the gathering as "an opportunity to affirm the role and gifts you have to offer the world-wide Anglican Communion, to give thanks and to celebrate all that you have achieved, and to plan and build for the future." The Presiding Bishop and Primate of the United States, Frank Griswold, also sent his greetings saying, "I support your mission wholeheartedly 'that God is leading the Church to a turning point in its history and that the full partnership of indigenous peoples is essential.' The whole Church looks forward to your partnership at this important moment for us all." With these inspiring words, the delegations heard AIN's Secretary General, Malcolm Nāea Chun call upon all AIN members to use the time to determine the implementation of AIN's programmes for elder and youth, women, theological education, and the development of a church with borders and an indigenous province.

All the member delegations turned in printed reports updating their own work and concerns and of particular note were the development of a covenant in Australia for indigenous peoples in the church and the collaborative efforts of the Native Americans and indigenous Canadians to define an indigenous church and develop one without political and geographic borders.

The gathering was also inspired by the presentation of a newly released video entitled, "Topahdewin: The Gladys Cook Story." It is the real life story of an indigenous woman who uplifts herself from boarding school sexual abuse to using love and reconciliation to heal herself and others.

Interviewed by the Episcopal News Service, Secretary General was quoted, "Cook's story resonates for everyone in this room. It was a very heavy and challenging day. Some of us have been kept silent for a long time. It reminded us that, beyond the celebratory things, beyond the rejoicing and coming together, that we struggle yet both within and without the church."

Delegates included representatives of the Maori people of New Zealand, Torres Strait Islanders from Australia, native Hawaiians, Native Americans from the continental United States, as well as Canada. A frequent theme discussed was incorporating traditional rites into worship services and cultivating indigenous male and female clergy and leaders.

"There are many people who can't worship the way they would like to worship, Chun said. "They don't have priests who look like them, who talk like them. As a result, the church loses people."

After several days and evenings of deliberation in the programme working groups, the following resolutions were adopted by all delegations.

Resolutions

Indigenous Urban Ministry

Acknowledging that the urban migration of indigenous peoples often results in their disconnection from their home lands, people and traditions resulting in the consequent need for ministry and outreach among indigenous peoples living in urban areas;

BE IT RESOLVED THAT: We at AIN PALA 2005 urge our respective Provinces and Dioceses to help encourage and resource urban ministry and outreach among indigenous peoples.

Archbishop of Canterbury

Acknowledging the role of Rowan, the Archbishop of Canterbury for appointing an indigenous person, Dr. Jenny Te Paa of Aotearoa, to serve on the Lambeth Commission on Communion, we express our desire to remain members of the Anglican Communion and to work in unity for the advancement of indigenous mission and ministries.

BE IT RESOLVED THAT: We at AIN PALA 2005 commend the Windsor Report as a way forward together, despite our differences of opinion over matters of justice and morality.

Indigenous Ministry and an Indigenous Province

Acknowledging the need to enable minion and ministry to the indigenous peoples, and that the AIN Rororua 2003 resolution called for the establishment of an Indigenous Province in the Pacific basin, and the vision of our AIN elders calls for a "Church without Borders;"

BE IT RESOLVED THAT: We at AIN PALA 2005 wish to develop an enablement plan for indigenous world mission and ministry in the Pacific basin. We intend to exercise our right to self-determination, by considering stories, structures, processes, visions, mission and values appropriate for indigenous peoples, and we will appoint a working group to begin work on developing a plan, and who will report back to the AIN 2007 gathering in Canada.

World Mission

Acknowledging that indigenous ministry has a mission not just to itself, but to the whole world, and the Archbishop of Canterbury's letter inherently encourages the AIN to share its gifts, and Bishop Carol Gallagher's recommendation of sending an indigenous evangelism mission to England during the 2007 commemoration of the Jamestown Covenant as "the roots of our Faith stories;"

BE IT RESOLVED that we at AIN PALA 2005 wish to send a team to England in 2009 comprising all of the AIN membership, and we will appoint a working group to finalize a draft mission plan for discussion at the AIN 2007 gathering in Canada.

Healing Ministry

Acknowledging the need for appropriate forms of healing ministry among colonized indigenous peoples;

BE IT RESOLVED that the AIN PALA 2005 wish to develop appropriate forms of indigenous ministry for prayer, the sharing of healing stories, reconciliation and restorative justice seeking wholeness, and a working group will be formed to develop and to implement this ministry.

Gwich'in Nation and the Arctic Drilling

Acknowledging the sacred connection of Land, Language and Culture is a gift from God, receiving its authority from God; that authority has been recognized by churches and nations for centuries, most recently in the United Nations Draft Declaration of the Rights of Indigenous Peoples; the threat of the development of oil in the Arctic National Wildlife Refuge is a threat to the Aboriginal usage, right, and life of our brothers and sisters in Christ, of the Gwich'in Nation; AIN affirms our aboriginal rights rooted in the truth of God and in the inherent rights of all people; in the God ordained living connection of the peoples of Mother Earth, our environments; and the living connection of the Arctic National Wildlife Refuge, the Porcupine Caribou Herd, and the Gwich'in Nation;

BE IT RESOLVED that AIN PALA 2005 supports the Gwich'in Nation of North America in their opposition to oil development in the Arctic National Refuge, and urges the churches and nations of this earth to protect us all by looking to protect the Refuge.

Youth Ministry and Concerns

Acknowledging that indigenous youth have an active voice at all levels, such as the development and practice of liturgies and programs, that meaningful relationships with elders include mentoring through the sharing of stories to provide guidance support and growth so to develop a meaningful dialogue through sharing and listening;

BE IT RESOLVED that AIN members support and provide resources, particularly funding, for an annual indigenous youth gathering of United

States Youth and the AIN youth delegates to maintain a continuity of youth participation;

AND BE IT FURTHER RESOLVED that we reaffirm the resolutions and reports of the previous AIN Youth meeting in ROTORUA 2003.

Concerns of Indigenous Elders

BE IT RESOLVED that the Elder group of AIN PALA 2005 calls for the support of meaningful dialogue and programs with indigenous youth of AIN, to put forth an action plan for change, ministry and growth which includes funding and logistical support for an annual gathering of both the United States indigenous youth and the youth delegates of AIN,

AND BE IT FURTHER RESOLVED that the progress of this plan will be supported and monitored by AIN Elder Delegates Frank Oberly and Gloria Moses for a report to the AIN 2007 gathering in Canada.

Church without Borders

Acknowledging that AIN has for several years held intense discussion concerning the concept of a "church without borders" as a means of bringing the message of reconciliation and forgiveness, of unity and hope, and a future for indigenous members of the churches of Canada and the United States of America, we have witnessed recent events in both our churches that call out for this concept to be seriously considered and discussed on greater and deeper levels of our churches for all people and members of our churches;

BE IT RESOLVED that, AIN calls upon the House of Bishops of the churches in Canada and the United States of America to recognize this concept of a church without borders as a viable means of bringing reconciliation, forgiveness, unity and hope for a future for the indigenous peoples and all members of our churches, and will expand the depth of discussion of this concept at the national and diocesan levels of the churches in Canada and the United States.

Indigenous Theological Issues and Concerns

Acknowledging our belief that the following will enrich our traditions and relationship with the Trinitarian aspects of a 'Living God' who was, and is, always among us;

BE IT RESOLVED that we need to develop a living pedagogical model that will enable indigenous communities to articulate the diverse theologies that are grounded within those communities; develop these tools and or models that enable indigenous communities to create liturgies that express their unique spiritualities; develop a "gospel lens" that is appropriate to each of our indigenous languages, cultures and life experiences; strongly urge the non-indigenous church to also develop a "gospel lens", develop through the text and traditions of the Anglican communion a post-colonial and post-modern critique, that transforms the colonial legacy that has been imposed upon us; to believe that we have a responsibility and obligation to the future, to those generations who are children now and those yet to be born, not to repeat the destruction, damage and cultural genocide of our colonial past; to assist the wider church to be sensitive of the pressures upon indigenous leaders, both lay and ordained, who walk the path between the two worlds, i.e., the world of the church and their own respective worlds; to urge the Anglican Church, in all of its Anglican ministry units throughout the world, to establish clearly defined and accessible resources, including financeing from national churches, to undertake effective professional and curriculum development and to enable appropriate exchanges of indigenous educators and students within the Anglican Communion, and to urge the Anglican Communion to honestly and seriously engage in cross-cultural exchange with their respective indigenous communities.

In Support of Mr. Michael Tamihere, Youth Representative to the Anglican Consultative Council

Acknowledging the appointment of Mr. Michael Tamihere from the Province of New Zealand and a member of the Pihopatanga o Aoteroa as a youth representative to the Anglican Consultative Council;

BE IT RESOLVED that AIN PALA 2005 congratulates, recognizes and supports Mr. Michael Tamihere as a voice for indigenous youth at the Anglican Consultative Council and as a liaison for the Anglican Indigenous Network.

AIN has applied in the United States for a non-profit, tax exemption status to establish a working endowment fund for its programmes. The working group on women anticipates holding a meeting in mid fall of 2005 in Hawai'i, and the church leadership group would like to hold a similar meeting in 2006. The next AIN gathering is planned for Canada in 2007.

Anglican Peace and Justice Network 1985–2005

A report of its deliberations in Jerusalem
September 14–22, 2004

ANGLICAN PEACE AND JUSTICE NETWORK PARTICIPANTS

Host: The Right Reverend Riah Hanna Abu El-Assal
Anglican Observer at the UN: Taimalelagi F. Tuatagaloa-Matalavea
APJN Advisor: Naim Ateek
Aotearoa/New Zealand & Polynesia: Jenny Te Paa
Australia: Chris Jones
Brazil: Luiz Osorio Prado
Burundi: Pie Ntukamazina
Canada: Cynthia Patterson
Central America: Lisbeth Barahona
Congo: Beni Bezaleri Bataaga
England: Charles Reed
Japan: Nathaniel Makoto Uematso
Japan (for the Steering Committee): Samuel Koshiishi
Jerusalem: Elian Abdelnour
Jerusalem: Suzanne Khayo
Jerusalem: Naim Ateek
Kenya: Gideon Ireri
Korea: Jeremiah Guen Seok Yang
Myanmar: Saw Wilme
North India: Prem Masih
Philippines: Andrew A. Tauli
Rwanda: Geoffrey Kayigi
Scotland: Alison Simpson
South India: Pauline Sathiamurthy
Southern Africa: Delene M. Mark
Sri Lanka: Kumara Illangasinghe
Tanzania: Kuwayawaya S. Kuwayawaya
Uganda: Nalwoga Jessica Sanyu Alexandra
USA—ECUSA: Brian J. Grieves

Also invited:
Anglican Women's Network: Jolly Babirukamu
USA—ECUSA (for *The Witness* magazine): Ethan Vesely-Flad

SECTION I

THE LOCAL CONTEXT OF THE MEETING

2005 marks the Anglican Peace and Justice Network's 20th anniversary and its meeting in Jerusalem in September 2004 brings it full circle to its first full meeting which also took place in the City of Peace in 1985. Invited by the Right Reverend Riah Hanna Abu El Assal, APJN convened 23 Provinces of the Anglican Communion under the leadership of Dr. Jenny Te Paa of Aotearoa, New Zealand and Polynesia, and was graciously hosted by Bishop Riah and the diocese at St. George's College. During the course of the meeting, the group traveled through the West Bank, the Jordan Valley, the Galilee area, Nazareth and Israel's central valley. The group requested and received permission to visit Gaza, but because of delays and stalling on the part of the Israeli army, they were not able to enter and support the local Christian community there.

At the outset, we salute Bishop Riah and his colleagues the Latin Patriarch of Jerusalem and the Bishop of the Evangelical Lutheran Church in Jordan and the Holy Land. They reminded the world in a statement released April 2, 2005 that "In contrast to 10 years ago our community now represents less than 2% of the population and continues to decrease at an alarming rate. This is largely due to emigration. Many Palestinian Christians are leaving as a result of the ongoing conflict. We are writing to you as Palestinian Christian leaders concerned for the dramatic situation of the Christians in the land of the Holy One. The Israeli illegal occupation has made it impossible for Christians, indeed for the whole Palestinian people of whom we are an integral part, to live with dignity, freedom and security. Palestinian Christians like all Palestinians want to live in peace and justice. We yearn for freedom and life abundant." This message brings home the urgency for the international community, including the Anglican Communion, to address the conflict we encountered.

APJN was both nurtured and shaken during its visit, the former by the warmth of the people of the diocese (virtually all of them Palestinian), and the latter by the conditions of Occupation under which most Palestinians live. Sitting in the beauty and tranquility on the hillside overlooking the Sea of Galilee where Jesus preached, listening and reflecting on moving readings from Scripture led by Canon Naim Ateek, contrasted sharply to the high tension of being held in the dark of night at an Israeli checkpoint by cocky young soldiers brandishing their weapons. The comfort of St. Margaret's guest house in Nazareth and the hospitality of congregations in Shefa Amr and Raineh where worship, music, fellowship and food filled the hearts of the APJN participants, again contrasted with the sight in Hebron of the Star of David painted on the shops of Palestinian businesses. Placed there by right wing settlers, they praise the massacre of several dozen Muslim worshippers a decade earlier as an act of heroism.

APJN participants were grateful to hear and meet both Israeli and Palestinian voices for a just resolution to the current conflict. Knowing that people of good will exist on both sides of the conflict is the surest sign of hope that peace may prevail, that Palestinians will rightfully obtain a viable and sovereign state, and that Israelis will realize security and both sides will live in cooperation and with mutual respect.

It was greatly hoped during the last APJN meeting in New Zealand in 2001 that by this meeting, there would be a viable, sovereign and independent state of Palestine based on the authority of United Nations resolutions 242 and 338.

In this meeting however, it was realized that there have been no significant positive steps towards the creation of the state of Palestine. On the contrary, the state of Israel has systematically and deliberately oppressed and dehumanised the people of Palestine as shown by:

- The construction of the 'security' wall as referred to by the Israeli government but in reality is an apartheid/segregation wall judging from its effects on the lives of the Palestinian people, built on Palestinian land and ruled illegal by the International Court of Justice.
- The ongoing illegal establishment of exclusively Israeli settlements on Palestinian land. These settlements (actually towns) continue to marginalize the people of Palestine and gravely reduce the possibility of a viable state of Palestine through appropriation of land and critical resources and violate international law (4th Geneva Conventions).
- The construction of a steadily expanding web of by-pass roads to which access is denied to non-Israeli Palestinians. These roads are constructed to connect the settlements with Israel, while cutting off communication/access between Palestinian villages in the vicinity.

The three-part strategy of the wall, the settlements and the by-pass roads have the combined effect of minimizing Palestinian lands, resources and general cohesion. The emerging reality makes it impossible or difficult to conclude other than that the Israeli government seeks to push the Palestinians into isolated cantons. Credibility must be given to observations by journalists and other international visitors, including members of APJN, that the situation bears a dismaying resemblance to the bantustans of South Africa.

We recognize that the Israeli people have endured attacks and suicide bombings causing great suffering, loss and agony, and that the fear of further suicide bombings continues. We also recognize and lament the historical context of the experience of persecution and genocide by the Jewish people. However, the extent to which the Israeli government has gone in annexing Palestinian land and pushing the Palestinians into cantons and denying this people both dignity and self-determination is unjustifiable. If Israel continues with its actions in the name of security (as is often argued) then their hope for life without fear is diminished as the Palestinian people will continue in their struggle for nationhood.

We quote Bishop Riah and his colleagues: "We believe that the churches can and must do more to recognize their duty towards the Holy Land and act together to sensitize their governments, their people and the international community. Our communities ask your help so that justice will prevail and so that Palestinian Christians will flourish in the Holy Land and be strengthened to carry out our mission in the power of the Resurrection.

With St. Paul we affirm: *"That if one member suffers all suffer with it. If one member is honored all rejoice together with it.—*I Cor. 12:26"

MORAL RESPONSIBILITY IN INVESTMENTS

In the recommendation section, APJN calls upon the ACC to support morally responsible investments, including challenging corporations to divest from any part of their business that supports the occupation or violence against innocent Israelis (suicide bombings). Two important international ecumenical organizations have addressed this subject and excerpts are noted here to assist the ACC in deciding an appropriate response:

From the World Council of Churches:

"The Central Committee takes note of the current action by the Presbyterian Church (USA) which has initiated a process of phased, selective divestment from multinational corporations involved in the occupation. This action is commendable in both method and manner, uses criteria rooted in faith, and calls members to do the 'things that make for peace' (Luke 19:42).

The concern here is to abide by law as the foundation for a just peace. Multinational corporations have been involved in the demolition of Palestinian homes, and are involved in the construction of settlements and settlement infrastructure on occupied territory, in building a dividing wall which is also largely inside occupied territory, and in other violations of international law being carried out beyond the internationally recognized borders of the State of Israel determined by the Armistice of 1949.

In 1995, the Central Committee established criteria for economic actions in the service of justice, namely, that these must be part of a broader strategy of peacemaking, address flagrant and persistent violations, have a clear and limited purpose plus proportionality and adequate monitoring, and are carried out transparently.

In 2001, the WCC Executive Committee recommended an international boycott of goods produced in illegal settlements on occupied territory, and the WCC-related APRODEV agencies in Europe are now working to have Israeli settlement products fully and properly identified before shipment to the European Community in accordance with the terms of the EU's Association Agreement with Israel.

Yet illegal activities in occupied territory continue as if a viable peace for both peoples is not a possibility. We are not blind to facts and must not be complicit in them even unwittingly. The Central Committee, meeting in Geneva 15-22 February 2005 therefore:

- *encourages* member churches to work for peace in new ways and to give serious consideration to economic measures that are equitable, transparent and non-violent;
- *persuades* member churches to keep in good contact with sister churches embarking on such initiatives with a view to support and counsel one another;
- *urges* the establishment of more and wider avenues of engagement between Christian, Muslim and Jewish communities pursuing peace;
- *reminds* churches with investment funds that they have an opportunity to use those funds responsibly in support of peaceful solutions to conflict. Economic pressure, appropriately and openly applied, is one such means of action."

[WCC Central Committee—Geneva, 21 February 2005]

From Sabeel:

"Sabeel calls on churches to exert pressure on companies and corporations to discontinue business activities that:

a. provide products, services or technology that sustain, support or maintain the occupation;

b. have established facilities or operations on occupied land;

c. provide products, services, or financial support for the establishment, expansion, or maintenance of settlements on occupied land or settlement, related infrastructure;

d. provide products, services or financial backing to groups that commit violence against innocent civilians; or

e. provide finances or assist in the construction of Israel's separation wall or settlement infrastructure.

(adapted from the criteria set by the Presbyterian Church USA)

When such pressures fail to yield positive results, Sabeel calls on churches to divest/disinvest from companies and corporations that do not respond and comply with morally responsible investment and business practices."

HONORING A PEACEMAKER

The Reverend Dr. Naim Ateek has been a member of APJN since its founding in 1985. He has been a champion for peace and justice for many causes around the world, but is especially known for his work for justice for the Palestinian people, whom he has served as pastor and prophet over the many years of his ministry. He is the founder of Sabeel, an ecumenical organization based in Jerusalem that witnesses for a non-violent, just resolution to the Israeli/Palestinian conflict. APJN was touched to visit Naim's boyhood home from which his family was expelled by the new State of Israel. An Israeli bank now sits on the site of the former home. APJN stopped and picnicked at a nearby park to reflect on the injustice done, not only to Naim's family, but to hundreds of thousands of Palestinians who were also expelled from their villages. As a way to honor all of them, APJN elected Naim to be a member emeritus of the Network, joining Emma Mashinini of South Africa and Michael Hare Duke of Scotland in that honored company.

APJN STATEMENT ON PALESTINIAN/ISRAELI CONFLICT

What follows is the statement that was released on the closing day of the meeting.

ANGLICAN PEACE AND JUSTICE NETWORK STATEMENT ON THE ISRAELI/PALESTINIAN CONFLICT

SEPTEMBER 22, 2004

Give Sight to the Blind and Freedom to the Captives

We, as members of the Anglican Peace and Justice Network, representing 23 Provinces of the worldwide 70,000,000 member Anglican Communion, have visited the Episcopal Diocese of Jerusalem over these last 10 days, and during that time, have been inspired by the faith of the people in the diocese, while also being exposed to the draconian conditions of the continuing Occupation under which so many Palestinians live. We have heard from Israeli Jewish voices, and from Palestinians, both those who reside in Israel and those who live under Occupation. We note the continuing policies of illegal home demolitions, detentions, check-points, identity card systems and the presence of the Israeli military that make any kind of normal life impossible. We have seen the effects of the overwhelming presence of settlements or colonies in the West Bank, including East Jerusalem, and in Gaza, and the bypass roads and highways that connect them while disconnecting Palestinian villages, one from another. And we have been exposed to the separation barrier that violates international boundaries, disrupts Palestinian daily life and further defines Israeli intentions to appropriate land from the Palestinians.

We conclude from our experience that there is little will on behalf of the Israeli government to recognize the rights of the Palestinians to a sovereign state to be created in the West Bank—which includes East Jerusalem—and Gaza. Israel, with the complicity of the United States, seems determined to flaunt international law, whether they are the Geneva Conventions, United Nations resolutions or the most recent decision of the International Court of Justice in declaring the separation wall illegal. In fact, we note that this latter decision is based on building the wall on non-Israeli territory, which once again demonstrates the illegality of the Occupation itself.

We deeply respect and honor those Israelis who are prepared to end this miserable Occupation and recognize a Palestinian State, people courageously committed to justice and who work against home demolitions, who promote human rights and oppose settlements, bypass roads and the separation wall. We also deplore the unwillingness of their government to implement United Nations resolutions 242 and 338.

We want to assure the Israeli Jewish community of our concern for their security and safety, to be able to live without fear of reprisals arising from the long and tortured history of the last century, especially since 1948. We deplore the unbroken cycle of violence which has claimed too many innocent lives on both sides. We condemn violence whatever the source. We reach out to Palestinians and Israelis of good will, assuring both of them of our love and support in ending this long and troubled conflict. We embrace all those who have lost loved ones in the violence and extend our deepest sympathies.

We offer not only our solidarity for a just peace, but also our observation that it is the Occupation in its many facets that foments the violence and fuels the conflict. Collective punishment of the Palestinian people must be brought to an end. We therefore urge the following steps in order to achieve a sovereign and independent Palestine living alongside a secure Israel recognized by and at peace with her neighbors:

- The withdrawal of Israeli armed forces from all occupied areas in accordance with 1967 borders and a complete halt to settlement building, both new or expanded, to be followed by a process of phasing out settlements altogether

- The immediate dismantling of the separation wall in compliance with the ruling of the International Court of Justice wherever the wall violates West Bank land
- The introduction of an international peacekeeping force under the auspices of the United Nations into the Occupied Territories charged with maintaining security so that both sides may be free from further attacks
- A humanitarian effort led by the United Nations to provide relief to the suffering Palestinian people
- The immediate resumption of negotiations involving Israel and the Palestinian Authority under the umbrella of the United Nations, European Union, Russia, the United States and the Arab League (while we support the withdrawal of settlements in Gaza, we urge negotiations over unilateralism)
- That negotiations be based on United Nations resolutions 242 and 338 that results in a viable and sovereign Palestinian state with Jerusalem as its capital as well as the capital of Israel, and assures the right of return for Palestinian refugees

The unconditional recognition of the state of Palestine must be hastened if peace is to prevail in the Middle East. As an aside, we are deeply troubled by the use of U.S. made weapons and aircraft provided to Israel and being used for attacks on civilian targets which occur with increasing frequency. We urge a moratorium on the use of such weapons which violate U.S. law.

And we address a word to the wider conflict in the Middle East. The war in Iraq further fuels anger and hatred during these already volatile times. We urge the withdrawal of U.S. forces to be replaced with an international presence led by the United Nations. Further, we believe that a much more constructive course for President Bush and Prime Minister Blair would be to intervene and resuscitate the peace process as a direct action of healing and reconciliation for the global community.

Finally, we call upon the faith communities, and especially the Anglican Communion, to a time of focused and intentional prayer for peace in the Holy Land. We also call on the leadership of the Abrahamic Faiths from around the world to exercise a ministry of presence in the region as a gesture of solidarity with the people. We urge that they exercise their authority and influence on the political leadership among the several nations who carry the responsibility for making a just peace.

SECTION II
VOICES FROM THE COMMUNION

REGIONAL CONFLICTS—SEEKING CONFLICT TRANSFORMATION

An APJN working group looked at conflict and war especially in the Middle East and the Great Lakes region of Africa. However, the discussions included general conflict and war issues around the world.

CONFLICT IN IRAQ

While the APJN acknowledges the reality of global terrorism, and also notes with great concern the campaign against it led by the United States of America and the impact this campaign has had globally, especially on the people of Afghanistan and Iraq.

The admission by the Bush and Blair governments that the claims of the presence of weapons of mass destruction in Iraq (upon which the invasion was based) were in fact not there, casts doubts about the real reasons, so important, as to why America and her allies invaded Iraq after ignoring the UN security council and the Secretary General of the UN.

We conclude that the struggle against violent forces will be better waged through programs of development that alleviate poverty and promote the well being of people.

GREAT LAKES REGION AND HORN OF AFRICA CONFLICTS

For a long time, peace has eluded and continues to elude the people of the Great Lakes and Horn of Africa. There are violent conflicts in Somalia, Sudan, Uganda, Burundi and the Democratic Republic of Congo.

Numerous peace initiatives have been embarked upon to bring peace in these regions and we note with hope the recent peace agreement in Sudan. But still very little is being achieved as long as crises keep breaking out. For example, the violence in the Sudanese western region of Darfur has resulted in thousands of people being killed by both the militia and government forces.

Burundi is now heading toward the end of a three-year transitional period. The new president of Burundi has been elected and installed as called for in the peace accord signed in August 2001 in Arusha, Tanzania. But there continue to be hot political discussions over power sharing that should include ethnic and gender issues. Drawing a new Constitution has also been an endless debate, based on a lack of agreement over acceptable percentages of ethnic groups to represent people in the Executive, the Legislature and in the Judicial institutions.

Jacob Zuma (South African Deputy to the President) as the Mediator who replaced Nelson Mandela, together with President Museveni of Uganda (the Chairman of the Great Lakes Region on the Burundi issue), have been trying to help implement this peace accord, but thus far without any visible success. This lack of progress is making it more difficult for the government to function effectively and some Cabinet Ministers have even boycotted meetings.

The continuing war

Mediation and a series of negotiations have been giving hope to Burundians that a cease-fire is at hand, but there is still one rebel group among the five which has not yet signed the peace agreement. The same group of rebels is now declared by the UN to be one of the terrorists in the region, since it claimed to be responsible for the massacres of the Congolese Refugees (Banyamulenge) which took place in Bujumbura, Burundi on 13th August 2004, at Gatumba, 7 miles from Bujumbura, the capital city of Burundi, and 5 miles from its western border with the Democratic Republic of Congo. Armed people who have been identified as Mai-Mai of Congo and Interahamwe of Rwanda slaughtered 163 Congolese refugees (Banyamulenge). Many of the victims were women and children. Among the men killed were 5 pastors from different Christian denominations. More than 200 people were seriously injured and were evacuated to nearby hospitals and clinics in Bujumbura. The slaughter took place around 10 p.m. and lasted until midnight. Guns, bombs, grenades and knives were used during the attacks.

Refugees Returning

Refugees are returning to Burundi, one of the few positive signs of progress in peace negotiations. But at the same time more Congolese refugees are fleeing because of fighting taking place in the eastern part of Congo.

The international community has still failed to effectively intervene in conflict situations in the entire region, leaving the people at the mercy of their corrupt, arrogant and often dictatorial governments with their incompetent and worn-out armies.

Justice through love and reconciliation is the only bedrock for successful development and prosperity of all people worldwide. The enigma of the people of the Great Lakes and Horn of Africa Regions who are wallowing in the quagmire of poverty, disease, war, and ignorance in a region so richly blessed with material, mineral and agricultural resources continues to challenge those committed to working for justice in the region. Therefore, the Anglican Communion is being called upon with great urgency to support, implement and encourage appropriate life-giving interventions in the Region.

The United Nations

The United Nations organization originally established to ensure the promotion, achievement and maintenance of world peace has in recent times been undermined by some of its own member states, especially the United States of America and Israel. The currently very complex organization and insufficiently representative composition of the UN has also made it vulnerable to countries making war under the guise of patriotism and security.

The UN peacekeeping forces have, in some instances, been reduced to being guardians of injustice and oppression. A good example is Rwanda, where, in 1994, more than 800,000 people were massacred in the world's worst genocide in recent times and the UN simply watched even though it had peacekeeping forces stationed in Rwanda.

A further example of UN impotence to act in a situation of obvious injustice is the case of Palestine. APJN found it impossible to reconcile how the UN could simply stand by and watch as the state of Israel continues illegally to annex Palestinian land thereby openly defying UN resolutions, especially 242 and 338 which recognize the right of Palestinians to a sovereign state.

The Anglican Communion together with all peace loving institutions and people, be they sacred or secular, must courageously and actively support the UN in implementing resolutions that promote peace, justice and development in the world. Left in isolation to deal with violence and injustice, the UN cannot be or become the globally influential body envisaged at its creation. The relevance and effectiveness of the UN will be measured in successes achieved and failures permitted as it struggles to nurture and protect the marginalized, to make peace, to promote policies of conflict resolution and to advocate for the just and responsible stewardship of this world's resources.

The UN left in isolation to deal with the forces of oppression and injustice cannot be the globally influential body it was created to be. The evidence of the successes and the failures of the UN will be in its struggle to relieve the oppressed and marginalized of this world and make development accessible to all.

GLOBALIZATION / TRADE AND POVERTY

"Deliver the poor and needy: deliver them from the hand of the wicked. They know not, neither will they understand: they walk in darkness; all the foundations of the earth are out of course." —Psalm 82

The Working Group on Globalization focused on reviewing what had been accomplished since the last APJN meeting in 2001, analyzing the current international context and developing a detailed plan for work in conjunction with the ACC Task Team on Trade and Poverty* over the next twelve months, with broader goals set for the following two years.

The group was encouraged to note the expansion of civil society's social forum events and international campaigns for just trade which include, among broad ecumenical engagement, many Anglican participants. The WCC has also contributed to building a growing body of theological reflection on globalization, research and analysis through an international series of regional consultations on trade and justice. APJN members have participated in and monitored this process. Of particular note is the world-wide growth of farmers' and indigenous peoples' movements which provide the church with critical experiential and statistical information, as well as a place to engage in such issues as the just sharing of land and water, sustainable development and sustainable communities. One example provided us by an APJN member is the work of the Anglican Church of Kenya in taking part in the initiative to form the Kenya Small-Scale Farmers Association in 2003 and in playing an instrumental role in the creation of campaigns for fair trade. As a Mexican *campesina* movement says, "This is globalization from below which globalizes hope, creativity, intelligence, imagination, life, memory and the construction of a world with room for many worlds."

We were deeply distressed, however, by the relentless advance of what that same *campesina* movement describes as "the globalization of death." This was starkly laid before the world in September 2003 when Lee Kyang Hae, president of the South Korean Federation of Farmers and Fishers, took his life by stabbing himself at the opening of the 5th Ministerial World Trade Organization Conference held in Cancun, Mexico. Mr. Hae's action was that of a disturbed person: a person disturbed not by mental illness, but by the evidence of his own experience and that of the farmers and fishers he lived beside, worked with, and represented. Mr. Hae's action was a desperate means of focusing public attention on the devastating impact on

---

* The Working Group on Globalization was provided a rich opportunity to deepen its work and to act on recommendations made at our 2001 meeting, with the appointment in 2003 by Archbishop Rowan Williams of a Task Team on Trade and Poverty which included several members of the APJN. Mandated by a Lambeth Resolution of 1998, *to develop an action plan for the ACC in response to the challenges of globalization in the context of Trade, Poverty and Debt, recognizing the role of the HIV/AIDS pandemic in the process*", the seven-member team is chaired by the Most Rev. Njongonkulu Ndungane and facilitated by Hellen Wangusa, of Uganda. The team met in Canterbury in 2003 where the broad themes were shaped into work for two sub-committees: Theological Reflections and Advocacy. This work continues to move forward with participation from APJN's globalization group. A separate report from the Task Team on Trade and Poverty is available.)

farmers and rural communities of WTO practices and policies and of the International Monetary Fund's structural adjustment programs.

According to physicist Vanadana Shiva's Research Foundation for Science, Technology and Ecology, located in India, some 20,000 farmers world-wide have taken their lives in recent years because of the attack on small-scale, family farms by the policies of globalization. The Foundation also raises concern over the growing practice by Indian farmers of selling their organs (mainly kidneys) to avoid starvation.

A report to APJN from the Anglican Church of Kenya's Justice and Peace Commission lists among the numerous harmful impacts of economic globalization on Kenya, and on all of Africa, serious environmental degradation caused by agribusiness; shut-downs of local industries, increases in poverty and unemployment; devastation of small-scale agriculture; and the loss of diverse cultures, languages and community-rooted values. "We are raising a generation that is not in touch with its heritage and which is not concerned with this loss." The report describes as "unfair" and "biased in favour of rich northern corporations" current trade policies which rely on heavy agricultural subsidies in the north and tariffs designed to keep out southern products. The fact that a long struggle was necessary to win the right for African countries to manufacture generic drugs to be used to treat HIV/AIDS illustrates the extent of the injustices perpetrated by northern governments and corporations.

In Africa, Asia, India, Latin and South America the links between the practices and effects of colonialism and those of globalization are clear and disturbing. We also note the growing numbers of marginalized and economically displaced people in the north. While India, Brazil and numerous other southern countries refused to capitulate in Cancun to further demands on agriculture (despite pressure tactics that can only be described as threats and bribery), the economic interests of the north have continued since then to pursue their agenda through bi-lateral treaties and by proposed regional trade agreements (e.g. with Central and South America).

The group observed the correlation between economic injustice and war, other types of violence, poverty and environmental degradation. Economic injustice is without doubt the common factor. We observed also that it is the earth's most vulnerable who suffer most deeply: indigenous peoples, children, women, our elders, the land and water.

Members were deeply moved and strongly challenged by meeting in Jerusalem and the Land of the Holy One. Visits to churches associated by long oral tradition with holy sites and scriptural events elicited prayer, awe and reflection. At least one member was troubled by the evidence of centuries of disputed claims and ownership of these sites in what could be termed attempts at "privatization of the Holy Spirit." The separation wall also provoked many responses as comparisons were made with other walls, actual and metaphorical: walls of class and income; walls of racial and gender discrimination; tariff walls; walls of intolerance. "We don't have concrete walls," said a member from the Congo, "but we have walls of hatred." And this post-meeting reflection came from a member who traveled direct to Germany from Israel: "The concrete walls of Palestine, the barbed-wire fence of the Buchenwalt camp and the 155 mile borderline between North and South Korea, on these three walls I am still looking for my way." Guen Seok Yang's conclusion, while still in process, offers an insight important for all committed to justice work:

> "I have learned that suffering is the source of self-transcendence and liberation, but I think we are living in a world where the experiences of suffering become the source of antagonism. This is the situation when experiences are betrayed by interpretations. So, we have to ask why such betrayals have continued in history. My answer is the lack of our solidarity in the suffering. I believe that the problem is not suffering itself but the suffering that is excluded, isolated and abandoned by us. Solidarity is the way to heal the world."
>
> "If one member suffers, all suffer together with it" —Corinthians 12:26

CONFLICT TRANSFORMATION
By Bishop Pie Ntukamazina

(Bishop Pie, long time member of APJN, has been a leader for a just peace in his country as Bishop of Bujumbura. In August of 2004, after a day spent confirming hundreds of new members, he was taken prisoner along with 23 members of his staff by a rebel group while they made their way along a well travelled road outside Bujumbura. Only a tip off from a Catholic priest to the local authorities who saw what was happening prevented Bishop Pie and his colleagues from being slaughtered at dusk. As government soldiers arrived and fighting broke out, Bishop Pie and his colleagues fled for safety. Bishop Pie was separated from his colleagues and in darkness sought refuge in a tree, from where he was rescued hours later. He begins this report from that context.)

The world is facing a culture of violence and terrorism caused by conflicts of all sorts. As I found myself in the bush in fear of my life, after a blessed Sunday service, I had more than one question to ask God. I had confirmed 221 people that day. If God would spare my life and the lives of the 23 people I was with, what would now be the focus of my ministry? The answer, which came to my mind, was to continue working for peace and justice. Yes, perhaps I had been spared for that purpose.

Making peace and justice is an active role, and active ministry; it is not sitting idly by, waiting for something to happen or for events to take place. It is neither observing from the sidelines, nor is it talking about peace. It is making peace. Making peace and justice is doing conflict transformation. Making peace is promoting the activities that will render justice possible, feasible and practical.

Conflict transformation, like making peace, is bringing people together—especially those who call themselves "opponents" or "enemies." Once they are together, sooner or later they will better see that they share a common humanity and have similar needs and hopes in their lives.

In June, 2004, I spent a week at Eastern Mennonite University, USA, at the Summer Peacebuilding Institute (SPI) which is designed to provide specialized, intensive training in conflict transformation, peace building, trauma healing, and restorative justice to secular and faith-based practitioners from the U.S. and from around the world. 180 participants from 45 countries attended SPI. The Institute is an innovative experiment in "education-in-community". It is participatory in its approach in order to draw from the experiences, not only of the faculty, who are experienced practitioners and scholars in their fields, but also of the diverse groups of participants attending the sessions.

The conflict in Burundi

Since 1998 the official peace process has been framed in a series of meetings in Arusha, Tanzania, led by the late president Julius Nyerere of Tanzania, then since mid-1999 by former South African President Nelson Mandela and more recently by Deputy President Jacob Zuma of South Africa. This peace process has been seen as the key to future peace in Burundi, but may in practice legitimize the continuation of the war, since no cease fire has ever been completely implemented. The content of the agreement was worked out in five committees, chaired by international experts, on: 1) the nature of the conflict; 2) democracy and good governance; 3) peace and security; 4) reconstruction and economic development; and 5) guarantees for implementation of the peace accord. The challenge that the Church is facing today is how this Peace Accord can be implemented not only by politicians without good will but include civil society, with church participation, which would lead to the gospel of peace and conflict transformation.

Where is the Church in all of this?

If the Gospel we preach is not responding to the here and now problems we are facing, then how will we convince people that faith in Christ is the answer to all human needs at all times? In response to this two decades old conflict, and with help from international partners, our diocese inaugurated a four story Peace Centre in January 2004.

The Peace Centre in Bujumbura is looking into this challenge to try to respond to some of the sensitive issues, such as: 1) Prevention for HIV/AIDS and care for the victims; 2) Fighting poverty by assisting street children and families in difficulties; 3) Listening Orientation (to avoid "counseling and trauma healing" as professional terms); 4) Communication and Advocacy; 5) Dialogue and Conflict Resolution..

This new Centre forces us to review our church strategies in propagating the Gospel we preach from our pulpit. How relevant should be the transforming Gospel which we bring to our communities?

Conflict transformation has a place in the Church

Referring to what the APJN has been doing throughout these past years, it is time to move ahead and implement what we have been stating in our declarations, recommendations and resolutions. To make the Gospel relevant, we need to put into practice what we preach, locally and throughout the Anglican Communion, especially in those countries where political, economic and religious conflicts are raging.

Conflicts are inevitable in human relationships though in the Church we tend to cover them up. For example, a culture of violence based on ethnic conflicts has been largely ignored for two decades in the Great Lakes Region. The ethnic violence and the cover up are both evidence of sin. No pastor or priest would dare to preach against ethnicity until recently after the political uprising was boiling and the consequences ended up in a series of genocides in the region.

Conflict Transformation has to start from within

The Anglican Peace and Justice Network have been tackling different issues raised up by members from different provinces of the Anglican Communion. Pastoral visits have been paid to a few countries, including Burundi and Sri Lanka, but one wonders how well we, as a Church, are focusing on our own internal conflicts, such as ethnic and racial tensions, the generation gap, gender issues, human sexuality, and so on. These internal issues must also become part of our theology of conflict transformation along with war and civil conflict. The Church itself is to be an instrument of transformation, not just civil society. We need to address these internal issues with care and in full authority of the Gospel in order to be truly authentic.

We are called to promote Community transformation

Christ was right when He commanded us to "go and make disciples . . ." Matt. 28:18–20. We are called to consider revising our strategies on how we proclaim the Gospel of peace and reconciliation to our communities in which we live.

Submitted by Bishop Pie Ntukamazina, Bishop of Bujumbura

ENVIRONMENTAL JUSTICE

"We know the whole creation has been groaning in labour pains until now." (Romans 8:22)

Since APJN's last meeting in 2001, a new, fledgling Anglican Environmental Network (AEN) has been created. We take heart in this encouraging news for our worldwide Communion, and pledge to work collaboratively with the AEN to address environmental issues and sustainable development in our communities. We commend to the Communion the new book *Healing God's Creation*, published by the Anglican UN office on behalf of the AEN just prior to our APJN meeting in Jerusalem. This book is a very valuable resource for our international church.

Nowhere is the groaning of God's creation, as suggested in the passage from Paul's letter to the Romans, more evident than here in the historic "Land of Milk and Honey." As we meet in Palestine/Israel, and have traveled to Christ's birthplace and throughout the land in which he ministered, we have seen how the natural environment has been the victim of unjust treatment. Confiscated land, uprooted trees that are centuries old, controlled water resources, pollution, and nuclear waste—all of these issues are evidence that Power and Oppression affect human and ecological systems together. While Psalm 24 tells us "The earth is the Lord's, and everything in it," we are distressed to find evidence here in the Holy Land of the ways that throughout our globe the earth and its resources have instead become commodities for human ownership and abuse.

LAND

We know that colonialism was motivated by economic pressures. These economic activities encouraged land degradation without the consideration of their environmental impact. Our report from the APJN meeting in Auckland (2001) put it clearly that: "In the modern context, the impact of colonialism continues not through political colonization but through economic pressures that lead to unsustainable exploitation of land through the method of agribusiness. The use of intensive farming in many contexts can leave the land unproductive and its people landless." In this case, we must look at these issues in three ways:

First, during colonialism the environmental matters were not considered, and unbearable and unsustainable land policies were used that did not look forward to the generations to come. Activities like mining were initiated, which not only took resources out of the ground, making those areas unfit for sustaining living creatures, but also used chemicals in the processing of those resources, creating further environmental problems. When mining projects were completed, ditches were left uncovered, sometimes several kilometers in width and depth.

Neo-colonialism is a second concern. In the region of the Galilee here in Palestine/Israel, we were deeply moved by information about the impact of the ways that Palestinians have been alienated from the land by Israeli governmental policies. Israel, through building settlements and making "security" decisions, has removed Palestinians from their historic lands through unilateral decisions. There are two particular concerns here. First, confiscation of this land has made many Palestinians landless, leading to millions of refugees and related environmental problems, such as health problems in increasingly congested communities. Second, the construction of massive bypass roads and settlements has been done in ways that damage the earth, introduce chemicals into the ecology, and destroy historic agriculture lands.

The final concern relates to post-colonial activities. It is apparent now that, worldwide, the lack of proper education in the farming arena, through the use of chemical fertilizers and pesticides, has rendered those lands unsustainable in the long run. Those chemical substances drain into water sources, destroying all sorts of living organisms in those ecosystems. Plants are affected, and the poisonous substances are passed through plant and animal species. Humans, who have introduced these destructive chemicals into the environment, must answer the scriptural question:

"Where were you when I laid down the foundation of the earth? Tell me if you have understanding." (Job 38:4) A generous articulation of this scriptural reference is that God is creating the earth. God had anticipated that the earth is sacred. Thus people should enjoy the creation without any kind of discrimination or dis-harmony.

WATER

We have been blessed in our meeting to travel through the biblical region of the Jordan River valley and the farmlands by the Mediterranean Sea. We have bathed in the Sea of Galilee, and drunk from the nourishing spring that once led to Mary's Well in Nazareth. Yet water, on which human life depends (as well as other animal and plant life), is tragically becoming scarce and is no longer considered a human right. Across the globe, water is being privatized and sold at a profit by for-profit corporations to impoverished communities. Access to water is becoming the privilege of the rich and powerful, which is an injustice.

Here in Palestine/Israel, for example, we have seen and heard evidence of the stark divisions in access to water. In Gaza, where some 9,000 illegal Israeli settlers are to be evacuated, they have lived among a congested Palestinian population of 1.4 million. In the midst of one of the most densely populated areas on earth, that tiny group of extremist settlers—which represents less than one percent of the population—controls more than one-third of the land and more than 50% of potable water resources. This grave injustice reflects broader disparities between Israel and the occupied territories vis-à-vis Israel's control of access to the Dead Sea, the Galilee, and the Jordan River, among other water sources.

APJN members, especially from Africa and the Americas, have similarly highlighted concerns regarding water from their geographic regions. Pollution of primary water sources, such as lakes and rivers, is a growing problem throughout those regions. As Latin America rivers disappear or are rendered useless to pollution, our Brazilian representative raised concerns about defending his country's vast clean water sources against multinational interests. In Africa, the challenges are interconnected with those of war and armed conflict, and with the rise of agribusiness and pollution based on chemical and garbage dumping. The rapid growth of Hyacinth, an invasive weed that has come to suffocate water sources in central Africa (which is described in the essay "How Good Intentions Go Wrong: An African Case Study" in the book *Healing God's Creation*) is a particular concern. Nuclear-based pollution—which was noted as a key concern in the Jordan valley as emerging from Israel's Dimona nuclear reactor—will be an emerging problem for developing countries around the world that similarly rely on nuclear energy.

POLLUTION

Every day we find issues to complain about in our communities around the world. It may be too hot, or cold; too populated or isolated; too dry or rainy; too dirty; and so on. But are we really aware of our surrounding natural settings, or are we just thinking about our daily comfort? To what extent are our very human lives the cause of such climate conditions?

There is no question that development is necessary for human communities, but we need to consider to what extent it can be done sustainably in order to not damage our natural habitat, which is indeed the very source for life. Economic growth is crucial, but we often seem to forget that all natural resources were created by God so that we could make just and proper use of them. While walking down the beautiful streets of the Old City of Jerusalem, and touring some of the other historic sites of the Holy Land, for instance, we have seen pollution from garbage dumping as well as the unhealthy environmental conditions typical of impoverished communities around the world.

The increase in transportation and industrial processes, in relationship to economic growth, has simultaneously led to increased air pollution. Additional problems include soil erosion and chemical runoff into underground water sources. These concerns combined with increased deforestation have led to an imbalance in weather conditions, according to most scientific research, and consequently have diminished agricultural activities in regions where farming is a critical part of the economy.

Environmental awareness and education is very limited so wealthier regions of the world have been able to enjoy better environmental conditions. Pollution is a reality and can be analyzed from different perspectives: air, soil/earth, water, and landscape view. Even the geography of countries has changed. Original natural sites have been obliterated by construction and "development."

Environmental assessment and economic growth, together with training and education in preserving and protecting the environment, is a priority. This must include the issue of how waste is transported between communities, and in some cases between countries. The control of natural resources is a major concern, as is the misuse of chemicals in underdeveloped countries. We depend more and more on "bottled water," yet we see plastic bottles littering our land and water sources.

We need to be awakened to the fact that we human beings require air, space, water, land and healthy communities to live in peace. Social discrepancies are also polluting our earth, changing the natural and wise equilibrium of nature. Some countries around the world are rich in terms of the environment, yet most of them are deprived of sound environmental conditions. We should look forward and support laws that will reduce, control, mitigate and compensate the damages caused by pollution.

If we think about the phrase "everyone has a right to a healthy environment," then we realize that we are still far away from achieving sound acceptable and fair worldwide environmental actions.

THEOLOGICAL EDUCATION AS FOUNDATIONAL TO PEACEMAKING

The APJN working group on Theological Education recognizes that there are widely different levels of commitment to the provision and the resourcing of theological education and ministry formation among and between the Provinces of the Communion. In some Provinces only those being prepared for ordination are given priority or even the opportunity to participate in theological education. This practice unjustly excludes lay people and mostly always also excludes women and young people. In many Provinces there is no specific priority given to peace and justice studies within either theological education or as part of ministry formation. We consider this omission unacceptable for the preparation of anyone involved in contemporary mission and ministry activity.

The group notes also the urgent need to prepare lay and ordained people for all aspects of the Church's mission and ministry and not simply for church based administrative tasks. We note the need for distinctive and specialized training for both lay and ordained people and we urge the provision of quality theological education and ministry formation for both groups.

The group further notes the systematic diminution of Anglican Studies across the Communion. It was made aware of the very uneven levels of commitment and delivery among and between Anglican Theological Colleges throughout the Anglican Communion. The group was apprised of the shared concerns on this issue of the Archbishop of Canterbury's Commission of Theological Education (TEAC). We believe it is timely for the APJN to stand in solidarity with other Commissions such as TEAC in calling for a strengthening in the teaching of Anglican Studies across the Anglican Colleges of the Communion.

The group discussed the vexed question of Anglican teaching on human sexuality and in particular the Churches, commitment to continue with the "theological study of sexuality in such a way as to relate sexual relationships to that wholeness of human life which itself derives from God..." (Lambeth 1978 Resolution 10). We further discussed the 1988 Lambeth Resolution 64 which called all provinces to undertake, "deep and dispassionate study of the question of homosexuality, which would take seriously both the teaching of scripture and the results of scientific and medical research." We do not believe the Church universal honoured its commitment to undertake such intentional and necessary studies. We further believe that the resolutions passed in 1998 at Lambeth simply obfuscated the Churches' existing albeit unfulfilled commitment to the theological study of human sexuality. This action has resulted in further entrenching injustice against those who "experience themselves as having a homosexual orientation." (Lambeth1998, Resolution 1.10). The APJN working group believes that in light of the events leading up to the production of the Windsor Report the theological educational implications, especially for those preparing for ordained ministries are rendered both stark and urgent.

The APJN working group on Theological Education welcomed the reports of the work of the newly forming Anglican Contextual Theologians Network. The Network met first in May 2003 at the Episcopal Divinity School in Cambridge, Mass., under the guidance and leadership of Ian Douglas, Sathi Clarke, Jenny Te Paa and Denise Ackermann. It held a second meeting in Durban South Africa under the leadership aegis of ANITEPAM, a network serving African Anglican theological education. The network is fluid and dynamic matching the inherent nature of contextual theological education as it evolves its own identity/ies and ultimately its own contextualized methodologies, delivery and evaluation systems and accreditations.

INTERFAITH RELATIONS AS A TOOL FOR JUSTICE

Having met in Jerusalem, the city of Peace, sacred to the three Abrahamic faiths, APJN was confronted by both the failure and hope of interfaith relations in resolving conflicts. Clearly, at this moment in history, failure is more evident as Christianity, Judaism and Islam are a cause of the Israeli/Palestinian conflict rather than agents of a just peace. But there are voices for reconciliation and justice in all three communities, and that is a sign of hope to build upon.

We were particularly struck by the witness of the Christian community in Israel and Palestine. First, we noted the disturbing decline in the number of Christians, now making up less than 2% of the population after having been 12% before the 1967 war. Israel and its policies have been a source of frustration to Palestinian Christians both in Israel and in the Palestinian areas under occupation. But we also noted the vigorous witness for justice in the ecumenical community, including our own Anglican diocese, and were heartened by the determination to build a just peace for both Israeli Jews and Palestinians.

Bishop Kumara of Sri Lanka notes the challenge of being a Christian minority in his country: "When considering the means and the effectiveness of our mission, we must consider the multi-faith context and the plurality in which we are placed as a minority community. In a country that has been bleeding for almost two decades due to ethnic civil conflict, people do not want another conflict among religious groups."

Worldwide, Christians need to engage in intense interfaith dialogue as a direct means of promoting reconciliation and justice among all people. The family of God includes every human being, and that is a fundamental premise for doing mission.

In pursuing interfaith relations, Bishop Kumura reminds Christians, "We believe that people of different faiths are the concern of God's eternal love and should not be treated as targets to be won or 'annihilated' or doomed. There is no need to condemn their faiths and practices or destroy their faith objects, as the task of mission is to reveal in word and deed the love of God and to assist people to experience that love. We need to avoid references to doctrines, practices and objects of worship in other religions. Let us not forget that human beings are tools in God's hands. The mission is God's, and God alone will determine the end result of fragile human action. Target numbers, dates and operational plans in respect of converts are unnecessary and counter-productive to God's mission. Public demonstrations by those who have accepted our faith and other arrogant proclamations can invite criticism and even violence."

We refer as a reference point to the Lambeth Conference of 1988 on developing a coherent approach to interfaith dialogue:

This conference commends dialogue with people of other faiths as part of Christian discipleship and mission, with the understanding that:

1. dialogue begins when people meet each other;
2. dialogue depends upon mutual understanding, mutual respect and mutual trust;

3. dialogue makes it possible to share in service to the community;
4. dialogue becomes a medium of authentic witness.

Acknowledging that such dialogue, which is not a substitute for evangelism, may be a contribution in helping people of different faiths to make common cause in resolving issues of peacemaking, social justice and religious liberty, we further commend each province to initiate such dialogue in partnership with other Christian Churches where appropriate.

APJN also commends this recommendation, not just because it promotes interfaith understanding, but as a tool for peacemaking.

MORDECHAI VANUNU
A Dialogue with the Anglican Peace and Justice Network

September 20, 2004 (submitted by Ethan Vesely-Flad from the *Witness* Magazine)

Mordechai Vanunu was imprisoned for 18 years in an Israeli jail for informing the world of its nuclear weapons program. An Israeli Jew, he converted to Christianity as an Anglican before his incarceration. Here are some of his comments and his interaction with members of APJN. APJN salutes him as a courageous witness for truth.

I am a nuclear scientist. Nuclear weapons technology was developed by Israel in secrecy, but with support from abroad. Israel received its "Dimona" nuclear energy reactor from France. The U.S. administration knew this could lead to further efforts toward nuclear weapons, and President John F. Kennedy tried to prevent the Israeli government from developing nuclear weapons.

I began working as a technician at the Dimona reactor in 1976. Most workers at the reactor don't know what they are doing there—they simply work on an assigned task. I knew what was happening because I took physics courses while attending university.

In 1982, Israel invaded Lebanon. It is mandatory for all Israeli men to serve in the military, but I refused to serve in Lebanon.

During that stage of the conflict in Lebanon, I helped establish a group of Jews and Palestinians to advocate for peace. The Israeli secret service called me and warned me to not be active in university politics. They called me a few times, and sought to get me to sign a piece of paper saying that I would not meet with Palestinians. I refused to sign.

The only way to publish these nuclear secrets was to get out of Israel.

I had all the information in my head, since I had worked at the reactor for nine years. I was working in a building that was underground: there were seven floors underground that went down 23 meters. I took photos of the structure for proof, since it can't be seen from the air.

Then I traveled the world. In Sydney, Australia, I contacted a journalist who made copies of the photos I had taken. He went to London and met with the Sunday Times. They told me to come meet with them there. I knew that it would be very dangerous because England is close to Israel, and has many Israeli spies there.

I was in England, and the Sunday *Times* waited three weeks to publish their article. I decided to leave England because it was too dangerous. An American woman invited me to come with her to Italy. I did, and was kidnapped there by Israeli agents.

They took me away in a car. I wrote "Kidnapped Rome Italy" on my hand and put the hand up against the car window.

My worst moment was hearing that I was sentenced to 18 years as a spy and traitor. I didn't believe I had done anything wrong. I made a vow: I would let them see I would speak out when I came out from prison. My focus was to help destroy nuclear weapons and make peace.

For my first two years in prison, I was kept in a cell that was 2 meters by 3 meters, with a light on all the time. The constant light was a form of torture; and the guards would disturb my sleep throughout the night. I was given no razor to shave. All of this was an attempt by the prison authorities to put in one's head the idea: "Go commit suicide."

The only people who could visit me in prison were my immediate family, every two weeks, and security agents. The prison was filled with several hundred Palestinian prisoners and me. That was my life for eleven and a half years.

Every criminal in Israel is released after two-thirds of their sentence is completed, but not me. However, after I had served about 12 years, they did finally let me be in contact with other prisoners.

What I am doing now is not in accordance with the terms of my release. I am not allowed to speak to foreigners.

I have decided to stay here, at St. George's College in East Jerusalem. It feels good to be among Palestinians, among Christians, among foreigners. I am doing interviews, which is also considered illegal by the Israeli government. But there is nothing I am saying that is not already known.

I don't have the possibility of changing Israeli policies regarding my status; it will only happen if a foreign state gives me asylum and helps to arrange my release from Israel.

Jessica Nalwoga, Uganda: How did you stay strong?
Mordechai Vanunu: I decided they could hold my body, but not my spirit and my mind. I kept this freedom of spirit in my head. And for five years, every day I used to read from the Bible in English. Also, I would listen to opera music.

Chris Jones, Australia (Tasmania): What would you estimate Israel's nuclear arsenal is now?
Mordechai Vanunu: I don't know now. We used to produce 30-40 kg of plutonium each day. My estimation in 1986 was that Israel had more than 200 atomic bombs. It does not cost much money to produce more plutonium.

Charles Reed, England: What is your focus now, and what is happening with the Dimona reactor?
Mordechai Vanunu: It is important to continue to build up the network of solidarity and support the work of peace that we do together. My message is to stop the development and use of nuclear weapons.

All of the issues of environmental destruction connected to the Dimona reactor have already come out. The reactor has created environmental damage all around it: there is now a badly polluted area around Jordan. The reactor is also operating well beyond its lifetime: nuclear reactors are supposed to be shutdown after 25–30 years, and it has been in operation for 40 years. This is dangerous.

Pie Ntumakazina, Burundi: Once you depart Israel, what will be your dreams for this country?

Mordechai Vanunu: What I want for Israel is for it to be a real democracy, not just a democracy "by the Jews and for the Jews." It should be a secular democracy, not a religious democracy.

Beni Bataaga, Congo: What are your connections to your family, and how will you manage to travel from this country?

Mordechai Vanunu: I received the "Yoko Ono Award" of $50,000, which will help to support me. My family is living in Israel. They are religious Jews, and I have no connection to them anymore.

Ethan Vesely-Flad, The Witness: What do you think is the hope for ending nuclear weapons?

Mordechai Vanunu: On the one hand, you can see hope now. When I was arrested in 1986, only a few countries had nuclear weapons, but others were developing them and nuclear energy was widespread. Since then, some countries have ended their efforts to develop nuclear weapons. And the reality now is that no state is developing them in secret: much more is known publicly. On the other hand, the technology is there. It is much easier for a state or group to develop weapons. So that is a real problem. But in general, people are more aware, and are rejecting nuclear energy and weapons.

Charles Reed: What do you think about the efforts by North Korea and Iran to develop nuclear programs?

Mordechai Vanunu: In Asia, there is a widespread concern about the need for energy. Millions of people need access to energy throughout Asia, and this need will translate to an increase in the use of nuclear energy. Israel doesn't like me to talk because I tell the truth. They make it a question of the Holocaust, (which is not right).

Kumara Illangasinghe, Sri Lanka: Why did they not seek to take your life?

Mordechai Vanunu: Some did say I should be killed. They thought that by putting me in prison, they could silence the case, but they did not realize the effect that this story would have on the whole world.

When I was in prison, they tried to do all they could to lead me to death through poor nutrition. After five years in prison, I asked my brother to give me a book on nutrition.

I am only one human, though; they assassinated the prime minister [Yitzhak Rabin, in 1995].

Charles Reed: What is your view of the Israeli peace camp?

Mordechai Vanunu: I am very disappointed in the Israeli peace community. You cannot be Zionist and for peace! And how can people say they want peace, and not be against nuclear weapons? For example, the well-known Israeli peace organization Gush Shalom has not taken a nuclear stand. Israeli peace activists have a big problem: they need to respect the Palestinian people, and they need to act against nuclear weapons.

Pie Ntumakazina: Do you think that the Christian community could bring the gift of conflict transformation here?

Mordechai Vanunu: When I was in prison, I found myself reading the New Testament and the letters of St. Paul. The way of Jesus Christ is a way of peace, of nonviolence. I think that is the role that Christianity can play here. This is the reason I became a Christian.

It is not the way of Hamas. We follow the way of Christ, the Prince of Peace. This is what Christianity can teach the Jews and the Muslims. We can even influence the Muslims to follow the way of nonviolence.

Since June 2004, after my release from prison and arrival at St. George's, every day I go up to the cathedral tower and ring the bell. I encourage many Christians to come here, to visit here, to experience here, and to be in solidarity. There are Christians visiting Hebron, and supporting the people there. The Christian world is very large; it can send a lot to the community here.

Jenny Te Paa, Aotearoa New Zealand: What would be the one special thing that you would ask us to share with people in our home countries?

Mordechai Vanunu: Christianity is still alive after 2,000 years. My message, my mission here, is to help proclaim peace. From here we can spread that message to all the world—to New Zealand and everywhere. We don't want nuclear weapons anywhere in this world.

Jeremiah Guen Seok Yang, Korea: I really appreciate your message of nonviolence. But most Christian countries are supporting violence around the world.

Mordechai Vanunu: Those practicing violence are not really following the way of Jesus Christ. In spite of all the mistakes that people around the world—and Christians, specifically—have done, we are surviving.

SECTION III
APJN RECOMMENDATIONS TO THE ANGLICAN CONSULTATIVE COUNCIL

APJN recommends the adoption by the ACC of the following:

Recommendations on conflict transformation

A. To accept as its own the September 22nd statement on the Israeli/Palestinian Conflict;

B. to commend the Episcopal Church USA's resolve to determine appropriate action where it finds that its corporate investments support the Occupation of Palestinian lands and violence against innocent Israelis, and commends such a process to other Provinces having such investments, and to encourage investment strategies that support the infrastructure of a future Palestinian State;

C. to request that the Office of the Anglican Observer at the United Nations, through or with the UN working committee on peace in the Middle East, as well as through the Anglican Consultative Council, support and advocate the implementation of UN resolutions 242 and 338 towards peace, justice and co-existence in the Holy Land as a priority of that office;

D. to ensure support that Burundian refugees returning from Congo and Tanzania, along with displaced persons within Burundi, be assisted and cared for in their time of rehabilitation and integration through agencies of the United Nations, the European Union, Organization of African States, and other appropriate government and non-government organizations, and calls for Congolese refugees gathered in Burundi and Rwanda border areas to receive the care of the international community including shelter, food and medication, and implores (through a letter from the General Secretary of the ACC) so called "freedom fighters" to stop killing innocent civilians who have nothing to do with fighting;

E. to encourage pastoral visits by members of the ACC to regions of conflict, especially the Great Lakes, Sri Lanka, West Africa, Sudan, the Korean Peninsula and the Middle East so that churches in those regions feel empowered to carry on the mission of peacemaking, until there is lasting peace and good governance;

F. to make training trainers for peace and justice and conflict transformation throughout the Anglican Communion a priority theological educational project for all church leaders today and tomorrow;

Recommendations on Theological Education

G. that all Provinces be requested to ensure the widest spread in terms of accessibility to quality theological education programs and opportunities at all levels of scholarship is made available to all people in the Church who wish to undertake such educational studies. It particularly urges the intentional inclusion of women, lay people and youth in all theological educational and ministry formation activities. (The APJN recognizes the need for the whole people of God to have access to quality theological education and ministry formation.);

H. that every Anglican Theological College in the Communion be requested to ensure the inclusion of a significant component of both Anglican Studies and Peace and Justice Studies in their required courses of studies for all students prior to their admission into any form of lay or ordained ministry for the Church. (The APJN recognizes the urgent need for all Anglican theological educational teaching institutions to strengthen their teaching of Anglican Studies and we further recognize the need to strengthen the teaching of Peace and Justice studies within all curriculum offerings.);

I. that each Province of the Communion undertake to commit itself to ensuring that all of its teaching institutions immediately and intentionally include theological studies of human sexuality in accord with Lambeth Resolutions of 1978, 1988 and 1998 respectively. We further recommend that each Province commit themselves to the ongoing studies called for in the Windsor Report, and that each Province report back to the next ACC meeting on their progress. (The APJN recognizes a very significant curriculum comission in most Anglican Theological Colleges is that of human sexuality. Given the urgings of all three of the most recent Lambeth Meetings for the `theological study of sexuality' to be undertaken within the Communion and especially given the current situation of extraordinarily heightened tensions among and between Provinces arising from vastly differing understandings of human sexuality (which in turn has given rise to the production of the Windsor Report), then these theological studies are seen by APJN as being of the highest priority);

J. that the TEAC be encouraged to maintain dialogue with APJN to ensure mutual support for each other's theological educational endeavours and to provide mutual support and resourcing where possible. (APJN applauds the initiative of the Archbishop of Canterbury in establishing the TEAC and wishes to be as supportive as possible in contributing to curriculum development and in any other theological educational activity particularly to do with peace and justice studies for the Communion.)

K. that the Anglican Contextual Network ensure the inclusion of Peace and Justice Studies and studies in Human Sexuality in all the theological education and ministry formation activities of the Network. The APJN affirms and supports the work of the Anglican Contextual Theologians Network. (While we recognize the Network is still relatively small and is not yet fully globally representative we do acknowledge its importance as a fledgling yet vitally important new and 'organic' theological educational initiative.)

Recommendations on interfaith relations

Anglican Provinces ensure:

L. That they are aware of what other Christian churches and organisations are doing in their regions and are encouraged to participate in any existing inter-faith forums, meetings and similar gatherings;

M. that models of mission be developed that are transparent and respectful of others;

N. that education be provided to those in training for ministry, lay and ordained, on the basic beliefs of other religions, especially those that have adherents in the local area. Resources should be developed, either independently or ecumenically, that would enable parishes to better engage with their neighbours;

O. that Anglican church leaders are encouraged to develop their relationship with the leaders of other religions in their area. The strategies to accomplish this include inviting other religious leaders to our major festivals and seeking invitations to the festivals of other faiths. Such involvement should be viewed as a ministry opportunity and a long-term engagement;

P. that in those areas where there are particularly complex issues, an Inter Religious Commission to monitor what happens be established;

Q. that consideration be given to having joint programs to respond to issues of social justice, such as employment creation opportunities for marginalised groups and education programs about human rights.

Recommendations on the Environment

R. That there be collaboration between the Anglican Environmental Network and APJN on intersecting issues of justice and peace;

S. that Anglican provinces promote more training programs and educational resources about environmental issues, in ways that are broadly accessible, so as to increase environmental awareness;

T. that the distribution of *Healing God's Creation,* the new book from the Anglican UN office, be promoted throughout the Communion as a resource for local discussion and action on environment and sustainable development.

SECTION IV
NETWORKING, BUSINESS, AND
NOTE OF APPRECIATION

APJN was fortunate to have present at its meeting members from several other networks of the ACC whose concerns relate to the broad areas of peace and justice. Reports were heard from:
- The Anglican Indigenous Network
- The Youth Network
- The Women's Network
- The Urban Network
- The Environmental Network

Reports were also heard on the work of HIV/AIDS by the Provinces of Africa and its partners.

In addition, a report was received from the Poverty and Trade Task Team. This group is made up of APJN members and others and appointed by the Archbishop of Canterbury at the request of the Primates. The Most Reverend Njongonkulu Ndungane is chair and Hellen Wangusa of Uganda is facilitator. The Team is charged with developing a Communion wide response to globalization, and has been a priority of APJN from its inception. A separate report from the Team is available.

The Business of the Network

During its business session, the Network accepted the invitation to hold its next meeting in the Great Lakes Region under the hospitality of the Province of Burundi, most likely in 2007.

The following members were selected to serve on the Steering Committee by the various regional representatives: Sam Koshiishi for Asia and the Middle East, Jenny Te Paa for the Pacific, Pie Ntukamazina for Africa, Brian Grieves for North America, Charles Reed for Europe, Luiz Prado for Latin America and the Caribbean, Tai Matalavea, ex officio, UN Observer's Office. In addition, the following members were appointed by the Steering Committee: Delene Mark (Southern Africa), Nalwoga Jessica Sanyu Alexandra (Uganda), Lisbeth Barahona (Central America).

Finally, but by no means least, all the participants of the APJN meeting in Jerusalem extend profound gratitude to Bishop Riah and his wife Suad,

Ms. Nancy Dinsmore, Canon Naim Ateek and his wife Maha, the staff of St. George's College, Palestinian representatives Elian Abdelnour and Suzanne Khayo, the staff of St. Margaret's in Nazareth, the headmaster of Bishop Riah School, Hanna Abu El-Assal, the Board and staff of Sabeel (especially Cathy Nichols), Jeff Halper, Suheil Dawani, the Honorable Dr. Azmi Bishari, Dr. Mustafa Barghouti, Mordechai Vanunu, Kids 4 Peace Jerusalem led by Dr. Henry Carse, Jad Ishaak of the ARIJ, and our hosts in Shefa Amr and Raineh led by Father Fuad, and so many more. These good people, and countless more unnamed but equally appreciated, made our time in the land of the Holy One an experience none of us will ever forget. We also want to mention the honor of meeting the Presiden of the Palestinian Authority, the late Yasser Arafat, who so warmly welcomed us in what turned out to be one of his last days among us.

We only hope that in some small way, our visit will have lightened the burden of occupation on the Palestinians we visited and bring hope to Israelis living in fear, and more importantly, contribute and lead to some measure of justice for all the people of that sacred land. Our solidarity and advocacy will continue in the days, months and year ahead. For as long as it takes, until God's justice reigns.

Statement to the Anglican Communion from the Anglican Communion Environmental Network

We send greetings from the environmental network conference of the Anglican Communion meeting in Canberra, Australia, April 2005. This second global Anglican Conference on the environment was the first meeting since becoming an official network of the Anglican Communion. The focus of our meeting was the challenge posed by global climate change. We have met in the name of Jesus, the incarnate word of God, whose coming amongst us compels us to take seriously the whole created order made sacred in Christ.

"He is the image of the invisible God, the first born of all creation; for in him all things in heaven and earth were created . . . all things have been created through Him and for Him" (Col. 1:15-17)

The Faith that Moves Us

Holy Scripture reminds us that, "the earth is the Lord's and everything in it" (Psalm 24:1). All of creation belongs to God, not to human beings. We are part of the created order and our first calling by God is to be stewards of the earth and the rest of creation (Genesis 1:28–29).

God has called us to stewardship of the world to ensure that it remains fruitful for the future. We are becoming increasingly aware that the world is being harmed by us and we know how to eliminate the harm we are doing. This is a breaking of the most fundamental commandments known to us, in that we are knowingly causing the degradation of the world's ecosystems out of our greed and selfishness, rather than living with and protecting the design that issues from the Creator's generosity. Adam (humanity) is explicitly told to be content with what is rightfully allocated (Gen 2:8) and not be tempted to take that which is appropriately denied. Ignoring this injunction continues to be our abiding sin. It is one matter to act out of ignorance, it is quite another to act out of willingness. Willfully causing environmental degradation is a sin.

It is clear from the reports of the represented Provinces, and the presentations of the scientists who spoke during the conference, that humanity has failed to fulfil God's will for creation. The earth and everything therein now face perilous and catastrophic environmental destruction, often as a result of human activities. The Archbishop of Canterbury has warned that our continued failure to protect the earth and to resolve economic injustices within and between societies will lead not only to environmental collapse but also to social collapse.

We met in the joy of Eastertide, celebrating our hope in the Risen Lord, a hope that makes us claim, "If anyone is in Christ, there is a new creation, everything old has passed away, see everything has become new" (1 Cor. 5:17). The mystery of His Creation is still unfolding and, watching and waiting in hope, we call on the whole Church to respond. What is now needed is that the stewardship given to us by God be proclaimed and acted upon, for "all this is from God who reconciled us to himself for Christ, and has given us the ministry of reconciliation" (1 Cor. 5:18–19). We must take the lead from the Holy Spirit to be instruments in the renewal of that "whole creation" which has been "groaning in labour pains until now" (Rom. 8:22).

We confess that the Anglican Communion as a whole has failed to promote its mission priority, "to strive to safeguard the integrity of creation and sustain and renew the earth." We commend our Anglican/Episcopal brothers and sisters worldwide who are contributing to the protection of the environment in response to the call of our baptismal covenant to serve Christ in all creation. "Just as you did it to one of the least of these . . . you did it to me" (Matt. 25:40 c.f. 45).

The Realities that Concern Us.

We gathered to reflect on the current impact and threat posed by climate change both globally and locally noting that current global CO_2 levels have not been experienced for over 400,000 years and average global temperatures rose by nearly 1° C during the twentieth century, which represents an unprecedented rate of change in human history. These temperature changes are already causing severe environmental stress to vulnerable populations and fragile ecosystems. We also heard that the current scientific consensus predicts significantly increased CO_2 levels by 2100 with locally catastrophic consequences.

Climate change impacts are already being registered across the world and can be illustrated from the experience of the communities whose stores we heard at our meeting:

Sea level rise in the Pacific

Our delegates from Polynesia and Melanesia described how low-lying atolls in Tuvalu and Kirabati are experiencing coastal flooding and contamination of fresh water. Kiribati has lost one island already. Current sea-level is rising at 6cm per decade and by 2100 this could increase to 4–11cm per decade, presenting an even greater threat to other island nations.

Global warming and health

Our delegates from Kenya and the Philippines reported an increase in the range of mosquitoes, resulting in more widespread malaria. This is attributed in part to rising temperatures. Projected further increases of 1.5° C to 5.8° C by 2100 with further exacerbate this trend.

Melting of glaciers, ice sheets and frozen ground

Our delegate from Kenya reported melting snows on Mt Kenya mirroring the well-known reduction in glaciers on Mt Kilimanjaro. Projected further melting of the tundra in Canada's frozen north could release catastrophic amounts of methane—an even more potent greenhouse gas than CO_2

Enhanced climatic variability

Our delegates from Australia and Africa reported longer and more severe droughts, which, in the case of Kenya, are also coupled with uncertainty over the length and timing of the rainy season. Prolonged droughts across Africa are already affecting local food security, causing increased poverty and suffering. This trend is set to intensify under projected temperature rises.

Increased Storms and Floods

Our delegates from the US, Canada, Oceania and the Philippines reported increased storm activity severely affecting vulnerable coastal populations. Further increases in atmospheric and sea level temperatures will intensify this trend throughout the century. In Scotland and Wales (along with much of northwest Europe) widespread and severe flooding has occurred since 2000. Projected increases in rainfall by the end of the century will substantially increase current losses.

Many of these impacts on vulnerable populations are also being experienced by fragile ecosystems upon which the whole of humankind depends for food, shelter and well-being. Ecosystems in the Brazilian Amazon and in the Philippines are changing more rapidly and extensively than at any time in human history, resulting in an irreversible loss of the diversity of life. Degrading ecosystems locally increases poverty but also poses a major threat to future generations and to the achievement of UN Millennium Development Goals. Climate change will further intensify these threats.

The Responses We Propose

We see hope and rejoice in progress made. We heard at our meeting that:

- The Kyoto Protocol is now legally binding in 128 nations.
- Many provinces, dioceses and parishes within the Anglican Communion are actively pursuing actions towards environmental sustainability.

- Task forces within the Anglican Communion are addressing inter-related issues, such as trade and poverty, and women's issues.
- Parishes in some provinces have begun to use programs to help them reduce the environmental footprint of their activities (Eco-congregations/Footprint Files, etc.)

In the light of these hopeful signs, we encourage all Anglicans to:

- recognise that global climatic change is real and that we are contributing to the despoiling of creation.
- commend initiatives that address the moral transformation needed for environmentally sustainable economic practices such as the Contraction and Convergence process championed by the Archbishop of Canterbury [ii].
- understand that, for the sake of future generations and the good of God's creation, those of us in the rich nations need to be ready to make sacrifices in the level of comfort and luxury we have come to enjoy.
- expect mission, vision and value statements to contain commitment to environmental responsibility at all levels of church activity.
- educate all church members about the Christian mandate to care for creation.
- work on these issues ecumenically and with all faith communities and people of good will everywhere.
- ensure that the voices of women, indigenous peoples and youth are heard.
- press government, industry and civil society on the moral imperative of taking practical steps towards building sustainable communities.

There are specific steps which we believe must be undertaken urgently:

- include environmental education as an integral part of all theological training.
- take targeted and specific actions to assess and reduce our environmental footprint particularly greenhouse gas emissions. Such actions could include energy and resource audits, land management, just trading and purchasing, socially and ethically responsible investment.
- promote and commit ourselves to use renewable energy wherever possible.
- revise our liturgies and our calendar and lectionaries in ways that more fully reflect the role and work of God as Creator.
- press for urgent initiation of discussions leading to a just and effective development beyond the Kyoto Protocol, which includes all nations.

---

ii Rowan Williams in the Independent, Sunday April 17th, 2005.
http://www.archbishopofcanterbury.org/sermons_speeches/050417.htm

- support the work of the World Council of Churches Climate Change Action Group.
- bring before governments the imperative to use all means, including legislation and removal of subsidies, to reduce greenhouse gases.

We express our gratitude to His Grace, the Archbishop of Canterbury, for his outstanding leadership and his championing of this vital aspect of our Christian commitment. And call on Anglicans everywhere to follow this example.

We commit to pray for one another, especially our sisters and brothers who courageously set standards in developing countries, knowing that in the short term these very standards may slow the process of development.

We commit ourselves to maintain this global network, to share resources with each other, and to lift the Anglican Communion to new levels of both awareness and commitment to these aspects of our Gospel imperative. We call on all provinces to become involved in the work of the network.

Report of the International Anglican Family Network

Although based in the UK, the work of the International Anglican Family Network (IAFN) is international—drawing on resources of information and practical expertise from throughout the Anglican Communion. Since 1992, IAFN has regularly produced 3 newsletters per year on topics affecting families. The articles are written by contributors from a wide range of countries, most of them working at the "grass roots" of family issues. The newsletters are published in *Anglican World,* giving them a wide international circulation. There is also a small separate print-run of 500 copies. These are sent free to authors and potential contributors, are printed on strong paper so they can be widely distributed and are clearly valued in many parts of the Communion. The text of the newsletters is now published on the Network website (www.iafn.net) so the information is available to those with electronic communication as well as those without.

The three most recent newsletters published are:

1. *The International Year of the Family: Ten Years On: Problems and Progress* (June 2004).

2. *Moving Families* (Christmas 2004) covering issues of displacement through war and economic migration.

3. *Families at the Frontiers of Faiths* (Easter 2005) showing how families deal practically with crossing faith barriers, often developing new areas of understanding and witness.

These three newsletters contain articles from a total of 31 different countries from Africa, Asia, Australasia, America and Europe, with 43 different contributors writing about their work and experience. The database of international contacts built up by the Network now numbers over 1,500. It is hoped the latest newsletter on the theme of *Women and Poverty* will be available for ACC members at Nottingham. The newsletters tell of the many projects linked with churches working to help families in the light of the Gospel. They provide a voice and encouragement for a large number of Anglicans whose struggles and successes are often unknown. Special newsletters were produced for the 1988 and 1998 Lambeth Conferences and the Bishops strongly affirmed the work of IAFN and urged that it should be supported.

The Chair of the Management Committee is the Rt Revd Khotso Makhulu, formerly Archbishop of Central Africa, and the international mission societies of CMS and USPG are represented on the committee, with field officers able to give important input about their areas.

With one part-time member of staff, administrative costs are kept to a minimum.

The work of the Family Network was greatly strengthened by a consultation on *Violence and the Family* held in Nairobi in June 2003. This was made possible by a generous private donation which covered all the travel costs and so enabled key workers to attend rather than only those who could afford to do so. Thirty-two delegates participated representing 17 African countries. A full report of the consultation is available. The meeting engendered both mutual support and great enthusiasm for action. A main recommendation was that the Church should endeavour to break the silence on issues such as violence between couples (including marital rape) and against children, women and the elderly. The delegates have subsequently been running workshops and training days in their own Provinces. Copies of the report were sent to all of the Bishops and many other church leaders in Africa, to the Archbishops worldwide and to all of the co-ordinators internationally for the WCC Decade to Overcome Violence. A newsletter was subsequently produced on this theme, using material from the conference and with the addition of articles from other parts of the world. Such was the success of the consultation that the Network is trying to raise funds for another such regional meeting, possibly to be held in Korea with delegates from this region.

But the future work of the Family Network, including its production of newsletters, is under serious threat because of lack of funding. If further resources are not identified it may have to cease operation by the end of this year.

Report of the Global Anglicanism Project (GAP)

Foreword

The title of this report "The Vitality and Promise of Being Anglican" is singularly appropriate to our life together as a Communion at this moment. The empirical, grassroots research being undertaken by the Global Anglicanism Project offers much needed factual information about the life and faith experience of our Anglican Churches. How little we know of the rich tapestries that make up the stories of vital Anglican communities in Brazil, North India, Aotearoa New Zealand, and Tanzania, or other parts of the Anglican Communion for that matter!

The narrative presented in the GAP pilot-phase report offers inspiration to Anglicans everywhere and underlines that Anglicans are making a difference in their local situations. This report successfully avoids taking positions on ideologically or theologically divisive issues, yet relates conflict situations in a neutral way where they exist.

The Global Anglicanism Project points toward the need to build new networks of relationships between individuals and communities who, though separated by geography, share much in common because they are Anglican. For this reason I look forward to the next phase of GAP when field research will be extended beyond the four pilot sites to a wide cross-section of our global Anglican family.

I commend this report to all members of the Churches of the Anglican Communion. It is my hope that through sharing the stories that GAP brings to light, we might learn the depths of God's gifts to his churches and be renewed to pray for one another and enter relationship with each other with increased enthusiasm. The wisdom and compassion that comes from understanding the experience of 'the other' holds profound promise for being Anglican.

The Rev. Canon Kenneth Kearon
Secretary-General of the Anglican Communion

The Global Anglicanism Project

1. The Global Anglicanism Project is the only grassroots study to identify and explore the diverse and concrete manifestations of vitality in
   the Anglican Communion. It lifts up ordinary people's stories of leadership and ministry as a source of hope, and a challenge to the
   Church's endeavors.

2. The project's key goals are to:
   a. Identify and shape best leadership practices from around the globe;
   b. Identify leaders who are making a difference;
   c. Strengthen Anglican identity and mission at the local and global
      levels;
   d. Foster networks for collaborative action, and for the sharing of
      resources and leadership expertise.

3. The GAP is governed by a Global Reference Group composed of 22
   Anglican leaders from 14 countries around the world. The Episcopal
   Church Foundation, an independent, yet affiliated agency of the Episcopal Church functions as the Secretariat for GAP. A Management
   Committee oversees policy decisions required. For the pilot-phase a
   team of six researchers from four countries contributed to data gathering in the field in collaboration with local partners in each site.

4. The pilot phase of GAP research has concluded and a report will be
   issued in late 2005. The pilot study focused on local congregational
   and community life in four sites: Brazil, North India, New Zealand,
   and Tanzania. Two hundred focus groups and individual interviews
   were conducted with over 1000 persons between 2002 and 2004.

5. Stories of Anglican mission in action uncover the work of people
   who have overcome great odds and made a difference in both reli-
   gious and secular life. Some of the the learnings the GAP has identi-
   fied include:
   • Anglicans are translating Christian expressions of worship and
     spirituality into local culture.
   • Young people forge new patterns of spiritual practice and mission.
   • The Anglican Church is growing.
   • Evangelism is central to the life of the local congregation.
   • Anglicans are innovative leaders who effect renewal and change in
     society.
   • Anglicans are creating social capital in their communities.
   • The Anglican Church is equipping and empowering lay and cleri-
     cal leadership.

- Anglicans are mobilizing against injustice and poverty in their society.
- Leaders in the Anglican Church are influential leaders in civil society.
- Anglicans are succeeding in resolving conflict and in peace making.
- Anglicans are at the forefront in combating HIV/AIDS pandemic and other crises.
- Anglicans make a unique contribution to fostering relationships with other faith groups.

6. This next phase of the project begins in 2005 and concludes in 2008. A report will be issued to coincide with the Lambeth Conference of Anglican Bishops that meets every ten years.

7. Additional sites will be selected for field research at the local congregational level and additional researchers will be recruited. The six thematic areas of focus will be: (1) Indigenization of spirituality and worship; (2) Dynamics of evangelism and conversion; (3) Leadership development and theological education; (4) Community organizing for social justice, economic development, and public policy; (5) HIV/AIDS and humanitarian interventions; (6) Inter-religious, Inter-denominational and intra-Anglican relations.

8. List of GAP Reference Group Members
   * Denotes member of the GAP Management Committee
   + Denotes member of the GAP Research Team

   1) The Rev. Canon Naim Ateek, Director of Sabeel, Jerusalem
   2) The Rt. Rev. Mauricio Andrade, Bishop of Brasilia, Brazil (*)
   3) The Rt. Rev. Terry Brown, Bishop of Malaita, Solomon Islands
   4) The Rev. Sathi Clarke, Wesley Seminary, Washington DC, Church of South India (*)(+)
   5) The Rev. Ian Douglas, Episcopal Divinity School, Cambridge, USA (*)
   6) Dr. Eleanor Johnson, Anglican Church of Canada, Toronto, Canada
   7) The Rt. Rev. Maternus Kapinga, Bishop of Ruvuma, Tanzania
   8) The Rev. Bruce Kaye, Editor, Journal of Anglican Studies, Anglican Church in Australia
   9) The Rev. Sipho Masemola, Diocese Christ the King, South Africa
   10) Dr. Don Miller, Center for Religion & Civic Culture, Univ. of Southern California, USA(+)
   11) Lorna Miller, All Saints Episcopal Church, Pasadena, USA
   12) Raj Patel, Asdal Institute, Oxford, United Kingdom (*)
   13) The Very Rev. Titus Presler, Dean: Episcopal Seminary of the Southwest, USA(+)

14) The Rt. Rev. Mano Rumlshah, Bishop of Peshawar, Pakistan
15) Canon Maureen Sithole, Diocese of Highveld, South Africa (*)
16) John Martin, Church Mission Society, United Kingdom
17) Dr. Jenny Plane Te Paa, Dean, College of St. John the Evangelist, New Zealand (*)(+)
18) William Andersen, Executive Director, Episcopal Church Foundation(*)
19) The Rev. William Sachs, Director of Research, Episcopal Church Foundation(+)
20) Maurice Seaton, GAP Manager, Episcopal Church Foundation(+)
21) Vacancy
22) Vacancy

For additional information about GAP contact:
Maurice Seaton (GAP Manager)
Episcopal Church Foundation
815 Second Avenue
NY, NY, 10017, USA
E-mail: maurice@EpiscopalFoundation.org
Tel: (212) 697-2858
Fax: (212) 297-0142

Report of the International Anglican Women's Network

The International Anglican Women's Network (IAWN) links all Anglican women: it is a Network which cooperates for action. Via email and web site (www.iawn.org) information is shared, common needs emerge, and, by consensus, action is planned.

1.0 Organization of IAWN

The Anglican Communion is divided into 8 Regions. A Representative from each Region and a Representative from the Mothers' Union serve on the IAWN Steering Committee.

1.1 Regions and Regional Representatives

Latin America & Caribbean	Rev'd Canon Emily Morales
South America	Christina Winnischofer
North America & United Kingdom	Rev'd Nancy Acree
Africa	Priscilla Julie
Jerusalem and the Middle East	Eliane Abd El Nour
West Asia	Prabhjot Masih, Jyotsna Patro
Oceania	Janet Hesketh
East Asia	Esperanza Beleo
Mothers' Union	Marigold Seager-Berry

1.2 Work of the Steering Committee

This group of 10 women forms the IAWN Steering Committee and will guide the evolution of IAWN as it links Anglican women, reports the challenges and joys of bringing Jesus' reconciling love to a troubled world, and advocates for justice for all. The future work of the Steering Committee includes fund-raising, writing of a Mission Statement, setting out the process by which decisions are made, and describing the position of the International Coordinator. All work is done by volunteers.

1.3 Request to the Anglican Consultative Council

27 Provinces have Link women, or Link Teams. When 41 of these women were together in New York to take part in the UN Commission on the Status of Women, they spoke with united voice: it is time for the Communion to embark on a process for including more women in decision-making. They call on the Anglican Consultative Council to work towards 30% representation of women on the Council and on its Committees, and to encourage Provinces, Dioceses and Parishes to do likewise.

Summary of Regional Reports

2.0 Reports from the 8 Regions and the Mothers' Union

When disaster strikes, such as drought, environmental degradation, floods, disease and conflict, women work heroically to provide for their families. In cultures that are excessively patriarchal women struggle to maintain their dignity, and work creatively to ameliorate the problems. Through it all, their faith sustains them. The Regional reports speak compellingly of the huge difference that exists between the vision of God's Kingdom on earth, and the present reality.

The reports, in their entirety, are appended to this report. A brief summary, perhaps better described as a mere snapshot, appears below.

2.1 Region of Latin America & Caribbean

2.1(a) *Puerto Rico, The Episcopal Church in the USA, Province IX*

Puerto Rico stands out as a pioneer in Latin America and the Caribbean in the adoption of government policies on women's rights in various areas that deal with the protection and advancement of women, thus creating better conditions for their life and their development.

2.1 (b) *El Salvador, Iglesia Anglicana de la Region Central de America.*

The situation of women in Central America can be summarized as a constant struggle to reach a quality of life with the dignity that every human being should have at all levels of life: personal, within the family, professional, economic status, etc. We have yet to achieve a complete education system, a less violent culture, more work opportunities where gender equity is the norm, and where international laws and covenants are applied.

2.1 (c) Costa Rica, Iglesia Anglicana de la Region Central de America.

It was a blessing and a privilege for me to represent the Region of Central America at the United Nations 49th Session of the Commission on the Status of Women.

Exchanging experiences with committed people is necessary for the betterment of women, children, youth, men, and the family as a whole. The event also strengthened the network of Anglican women all over the world.

2.2 Region of South America,

Igreja Episcopal Anglicana do Brasil

Although in the Igreja Episcopal Anglicana do Brasil there are clear advances for women — for example, ordination is open in the three orders, the General Secretary is a woman, and there are women sitting on the Executive Council, the Diocesan Council, and other committees — women are present in insufficient numbers to influence the decisions. Nevertheless, in April 2005, the Executive Council and the House of Bishops endorsed the Statement of the Anglican Consultative Council delegates to the 49th Session of the United Nations Commission on the Status of Women, which calls on the ACC "to adopt the goal of 30% representation of women in decision-making bodies at all levels in our Anglican Communion".

In Brazilian society, the reality is still one of inequality between women and men. Domestic violence is of great concern, and indicates the lack of respect for women.

Anglican women in Brazil believe that education is the key to helping people understand that justice, peace and equality are in the hands of women. Persistence will be necessary. Within the Church, they are committed to the task of ensuring that women achieve 30% representation in all decision-making bodies.

We acknowledge the importance of the IAWN in empowering women throughout the Anglican Communion by strengthening the bonds of sisterhood among them through prayer, and by sharing ideas, experiences and needs. Also, it is important that the Anglican Communion become aware of the suffering women experience, of their hope for a better life grounded in divine grace, and their God-given abilities to influence the world for good.

2.3 Region of North America and United Kingdom

2.3 (a) The Episcopal Church of the United States of America

In the United States of America the church is needed as never before. There is a growing sense of isolation and anxiety. The tragic events of September 11, 2001, commonly known as 9/ll, have changed us as a nation. Fear seems to be the motivation for many personal and corporate decisions. One report says that one in six children in the USA lives in poverty. Many people lack basic health insurance. Gender equality in the work place has not been achieved. This is the richest country in the world and yet still has the second highest rate of infant mortality. In other words, far too many here suffer for and from the same causes as the other nations in the world. Much of the energy of the church has been spent being "against" whatever the local issue is. As the church, as the women of the church, we can be "for" the common good and IAWN offers us a platform from which to speak.

The Office for Women's Ministries of the Episcopal Church USA encourages and empowers the work and ministry of women within the church and beyond. It serves as a resource and staff support for domestic and global initiatives which seek justice for women in society and the inclusion of women at all levels of church life. The Women's Ministries Office collaborates in the work of the UN Anglican Observer, the Episcopal Church Office of Government Relations and all other relevant program clusters of the Church. The Office for Women's Ministries works ecumenically and seeks increasing interfaith partnerships. www.episcopalchurch.org/women

2.3 (b) The Anglican Church of Canada

The Anglican Women's Network–Canada (AWN–CAN) was formed in 1996 as the Canadian component of IAWN. In 2003, when the Rev'd Canon Alice Medcof was asked to coordinate the IAWN as a volunteer, women of AWN–CAN volunteered to assist her in the coordinating tasks, and an executive body for IAWN was formed.

AWN–CAN communicates with the Canadian Mothers' Union, Anglican Church Women of Canada, Evangelical Lutheran Women of Canada, Anglican Aboriginal Women and, through the members of the board, theological schools and artisans. We have contributed to dialogue at the United Nations Commission on the Status of Women in 2000, 2003, 2004 and 2005, on behalf of the Anglican Church of Canada and the ACC.

2.3 (c) The Scottish Episcopal Church

The establishment of the Scottish Parliament in 1998 with devolved powers has led to a more accessible form of government and consultation papers are released to allow the public to respond before a Bill comes to Parliament. This allows Christians to have a voice and express an opinion and there is often a collated response from the Mothers' Union (MU) members.

The Make Poverty History campaign is gaining momentum as many propose to attend the rally in Edinburgh on 2nd July just prior to the Gleneagles G8 summit. There are vigils and prayer groups organised to support these events.

MU members continue to work ecumenically in various community projects—they run a Family Contact Centre, play schemes at several prisons and mother and toddler drop-in groups. Prayer is important and Lady Day services and Quiet days are held.

A highlight of the year is the Provincial Retreat held at the monastery in Perth.

This year women from different churches in the UK will be meeting in Scotland at the 4 Nations women's conference and the WISE women's synod and the Sec and the MU will be represented at both of these.

2.3 (d) The Church of England

For women in ordained ministry in the Church of England, 2004 was a very significant and special year as it marked the 10th anniversary of the first women to be ordained as priests in the church. In February 2005, the General Synod of the Church of England debated the Rochester Report, "Women Bishops in the Church of England?" At the end of a very lengthy debate synod accepted the report on a take-note motion and proceeded to look at ways in which legislation can be drawn up to allow those women with the right skills and gifts to fulfil their calling to serve as Bishop in the church.

2.4 Region of Africa

The Vision of our Region is "To be the Voice of the Voiceless". It is rooted in Scripture: "Speak up for those who cannot speak for themselves, for the rights of all who are destitute". (Proverbs 31.8)

Our Mission is to enable gender concerns to be voiced through churches, theological institutions, faith based organizations and any other available platforms. We have for our objectives the following:

1. Strengthen the church-life application of gender issues.
2. Encourage the progression of gender within the church
3. Promote health issues in the church and communities
4. Educate the church in gender mainstreaming and gender budgeting in all activities
5. Promote networking within our region

Africa has been the scene of much tragedy:
Tribal warfare, genocide, and millions of refugees.
HIV/AIDS pandemic
Drought and starvation
Poverty exacerbated by inflation, unemployment, collapsing government systems.

Cultural norms and patriarchy adversely affect women.
Professional women need to be vigilant about sexual harassment at work.
Widows have little respect and may be distanced from their children.
Men, having paid bride price, may sometimes treat his wife with little respect.
Incest is often not reported.
Marital rape and rape during war needs to be talked about openly.

At the grassroots level, faith-filled women work to alleviate these problems.
The Mothers' Union of Katanga Diocese, Congo, is teaching women about:
Peace and conflict resolution,
Gender justice,
Violence against women,
Micro-credit for those who want to do business,
Skills such as sewing and needlework.

In Uganda, discussions continue on the issues of:
Female poverty and economic empowerment;
The causes of domestic violence and on how to deal with the perpetuators;
Personal development, self-esteem, life skills and counseling skills;
How to access free legal aid from FIDA;
Home-based care services for families that are affected with HIV/AIDS.

2.5 Region of Jerusalem and the Middle East

The Anglican Peace and Justice Network held a meeting in Jerusalem. The APJN report stated: "We note the continuing policies of illegal home demolitions, detentions, checkpoints, identity card systems and the presence of the Israeli military that make any kind of normal life impossible."

In search of a normal life, many Christians have emigrated. The population of Israel/Palestine is now less than 3% Christian.

2.6 Region of West Asia

2.6 (a) The Church of North India (United)

The Church Council of Asia is enabling women and men to reflect on the challenges of building communities of peace. However, CCA can do more and go beyond the commonplace. CCA is urged to continue to expand its concern over the impact of patriarchy and globalization on the lives of women and children in Asia. We call on the churches to repent its complacency and complicity to different forms of violence, and endeavor to end violence against women and children. We urge men to be truly our partners in the struggle for just and peaceful communities for women and children. Let the churches' practice of genuine solidarity with women be an embodiment of our faith in Jesus the Christ who showed us the Way to build communities of peace.

2.7 Region of Oceania

Women of the Anglican Communion in Oceania continue to work actively both in their churches and their communities. The major issues and challenges are:
- The rising cost of living & increasing impoverishment—costs of food, medicines, schooling, housing, are all rising.
- AIDS/ST is on the rise and churches are not actively promoting prevention.
- Violence & abuse against women & children is increasing and is frequently considered to be normal behaviour.
- In many countries there is ethnic tension, political instability and armed uprisings. Women have been active in the promotion of mediation and peaceful resolution.
- The tension between raising of children within traditional cultural values and modern western values. This is a source of major tension between younger and older generations.
- Churches are losing congregations to Pentecostal churches.

2.8 Region of the East Asia

2.8 (a) The Episcopal Church in the Philippines

The common concern that we would like to present to the ACC is the approval/affirmation and implementation that women within the worldwide Anglican Communion have at least a 30% representation in all decision-making or important Commissions/Committees of their churches and its institutions. Lest we be of just pushing women who may not be qualified for such positions or appointments, we would like to make it clear that qualified women be appointed or included in the list of nominations for memberships to the said Commissions/Committees.

It is disturbing to note that, when women share amongst themselves ideas and concerns about our churches, their voices seem to be silent. Most of the ideas that come out from such gatherings are not even relayed to the proper bodies (due to fear maybe of rejection?), or when the women do open up to their generally male leaders, they are not given the attention and importance they deserve.

2.8 (b) Hong Kong Sheng Kung Hui

There is no structure, neither explicitly in constitutional provisions nor in implicit practice, to prescribe or encourage the participation of ordained, or lay, women in Church decision-making bodies such as vestry member-ship, diocesan committees, or provincial committees, despite election to these organs through a democratic process. Since the Beijing Platform for Action aims at equal participation between genders in government and NGOs, and the Millennium Development Goals have set 2015 as the target date, a mere 10 years from now, we have to hasten our process and we have a long way to go.

Even though Hong Kong was the forerunner in women's ordination, statistics show that women priests are in a marked minority. More active effort, it seems, needs to be put towards identifying, nurturing and preparing suitable candidates for such calling.

Social issues affecting women are:

Domestic Violence is so serious in some cases that wives commit suicide.

New Immigrant-wives from Mainland China are overwhelmed with culture shock.

Overseas Domestic Helpers, mostly from the Philippines, Indonesia and Sri Lanka, are increasingly reporting physical abuse by employers.

Care for the Aged is a great concern.

2.9 Mothers' Union   www.themothersunion.org

Report from The Mothers' Union for the past three years, printed here in its entirety.

The Mothers' Union members throughout the world continue to look to the needs of their communities and reacting to them. Engaging with the communities in which we live is one of the keys to growth in the church, and it is because of this that we have seen spectacular growth in Mothers' Union membership during the last few years.

Many of our members are Anglicans but some belong to ecumenical groups linked to the Anglican Communion. A particular example of this is the recent formal affiliation to membership of the Women's Fellowship in the Church of South India. There, the Protestant Churches are united and their women have now followed the example of North India and rejoined the Mothers' Union. Women's groups in Peru have also become members through affiliation. The MU in the USA has been officially inaugurated and is growing fast. This means that we have now reached over 3.6 million members in some 76 countries all united in prayer, fellowship and Christian service and a common link of concern and care for family life worldwide.

The major projects initiated from our Centre in London, Literacy and Development, Parenting Group Facilitation, and Relationships and Marriage continue to move ahead strongly. The Literacy and Development Project in Burundi, Malawi and Sudan has now enabled over 16,400 learners to become literate and numerate.

We continue to support/employ more than 300 indigenous MU workers—they are the backbone of our work overseas. We have recently employed two field workers in the UK. This initiative recognises the very real growth in numbers of members wherever a worker is operating—workers are able to make clear links between the needs of the community and our programmes.

The Mothers' Union Social Policy Unit under the umbrella of Prayer and Spirituality is a way of welding policy and spirituality together. Over the last few years the team at the Centre has encouraged the voluntary membership and we have responded to numerous government consultations as well as working on, under our own accreditation, statements for the UN Commission on the Status of Women. This year has been particularly encouraging with MU having representation with the ACC on this Commission in New York. This has enabled the MU, the Anglican Observer and the ACC delegates to unite with a common voice on world issues which affect women and families. They unanimously reaffirmed the Beijing Platform for Action.

The MU has joined a mass mobilization of church groups, development agencies and civil society, generally, to declare 2005 the year to MAKE POVERTY HISTORY. Throughout the year, members of the coalition are challenging Tony Blair and other world leaders to tackle poverty through real policy change.

As the leaders of the world's richest countries gather in Scotland for the G8 Summit, MU members will join tens of thousands of others in Edinburgh in July to demand trade justice, debt cancellation and more and better aid for the world's poorest countries.

Our Worldwide President, Trish Heywood, has a full programme of visits around the world, which unites and encourages the membership. She sees ordinary people doing extraordinary things, bringing ministry and mission into their families and communities.

3.0 In Gratitude

3.1 IAWN thanks the Archbishop of Canterbury, the Most Reverend Rowan Douglas Williams, for his kind words of support, and the Rev'd Kenneth Kearon for including IAWN in the roster of Networks.

3.2 The Anglican delegation to UNCSW 2005 were thrilled to see themselves on the cover of Anglican/Episcopal World. Thank you, Jim Rosenthal.

3.3 Thanks to the Rev Joan Fraser, of the Diocese of Long Island, New York, USA, FrasJ6@aol.com, for volunteering to administer the web site.

3.4 We note, with deep appreciation, the work of Mrs. Liz Barnes, of South Africa, International Coordinator of IAWN, 1997—2003.

3.5 Communicating via internet technology lacks one important factor: personal, face to face conversation. Whenever link people are together, enthusiasm for the network rises, organizational details can be worked through, and plans for the future proposed, as happened when 41 women from 25 Provinces attended the United Nations Commission on the Status of Women, 2005. We thank Phoebe Griswold and the Anglican Women's Empowerment Team of ECUSA for making it all happen.

3.6 Archdeacon Taimalelagi Fagamalama Tuatagaloa-Matalavea, Anglican Observer at the United Nations, has been unwavering in her insistence that women be included in the Councils of the Church. Thank you, Tai. We share your vision and count it a privilege to work with you at the Commission on the Status of Women.

Respectfully submitted,

IAWN Steering Committee
Emily Morales, Christina Winnischofer, Nancy Acree, Priscilla Julie,
Eliane Abd El Nour, Prabhjot Masih, Jyotsna Patro, Janet Hesketh,
Esperanza Beleo, Marigold Seager-Berry

Jolly Babirukamu, IAWN Link to the Joint Standing Committee and the Anglican Consultative Council.

IAWN Coordinator, Alice Medcof, amedcof@national.anglican.ca

Regional Reports

2.1 Region of Latin America & Caribbean

2.1 (a) Puerto Rico, The Episcopal Church in the USA, Province IX

Puerto Rico stands out as a pioneer in Latin America and the Caribbean in the adoption of government policies on women rights in various areas that deal with the protection and advancement of women, thus creating better conditions for their life and their development.

One of the biggest problems in our island is the high incidence of domestic violence and violence with children and aging. Even though women are educating themselves and graduating from college in a higher percentage than men, we have yet to achieve the goal of equity in the areas of employment.

The church, through Episcopal Social Services, Episcopal Health Services and Parochial Schools, is working in areas and issues concerning child care, health and education. The church has organized training for clergy and laity at diocesan and local levels to deal with these issues.

The list of link women from the different dioceses is growing.

2.1 (b) El Salvador, Iglesia Anglicana de la Region Central de America.

The situation of women in Central America can be summarized as a constant struggle to reach a quality of life with the dignity that every human being should have at all levels of life: personal, within the family, professional, economic status, etc. We have yet to achieve a complete education system, less violent culture, more work opportunities where gender equity is the norm, and where international laws and covenants are applied.

The number of non-governmental organizations (NGO's) has increased as well as women's associations. Activities undertaken by women have a positive impact in the development of our country, making the empowerment of women the key for better conditions of life and a more just society.

Women outnumber men on the parish roles. The Anglican Church is actively developing programs with, and for, women.

2.1 (c) Costa Rica, Iglesia Anglicana de la Region Central de America.

It was a blessing and a privilege for me to represent the Region of Central America at the United Nations 49th Session of the Commission on the Status of Women.

Exchanging experiences with committed people is necessary for the betterment of women, children, youth, men, and the family as a whole. The event also strengthened the network of Anglican women all over the world.

2.2 Region of South America,

Igreja Episcopal Anglicana do Brasil

Although in the Igreja Episcopal Anglicana do Brasil there are clear advances for women — for example, ordination is open in the three orders, the General Secretary is a woman, and there are women sitting on the Executive Council, the Diocesan Council, and other committees — women are present in insufficient numbers to influence the decisions. Nevertheless, in April 2005, the Executive Council and the House of Bishops endorsed the Statement of the Anglican Consultative Council delegates to the 49th Session of the United Nations Commission on the Status of Women, which calls on the ACC "to adopt the goal of 30% representation of women in decision-making bodies at all levels in our Anglican Communion".

In Brazilian society, the reality is still one of inequality between women and men. Domestic violence is of great concern, and indicates the lack of respect for women.

Anglican women in Brazil believe that education is the key to helping people understand that justice, peace and equality are in the hands of women. Persistence will be necessary. Within the Church, they are committed to the task of ensuring that women achieve 30% representation in all decision-making bodies.

We acknowledge the importance of the IAWN in empowering women throughout the Anglican Communion by strengthening the bonds of sisterhood amongst them through prayer, and by sharing ideas, experiences and needs. Also, it is important that the Anglican Communion become aware of the suffering women experience, of their hope for a better life grounded in divine grace, and their God-given abilities to influence the world for good.

2.3 Region of North America and United Kingdom

2.3 (a) The Episcopal Church of the United States of America

In the United States of America the church is needed as never before. There is a growing sense of isolation and anxiety. The tragic events of September 11, 2001, commonly known as 9/ll, have changed us as a nation. Fear seems to be the motivation for many personal and corporate decisions. One report says that one in six children in the USA lives in poverty. Many people lack basic health insurance. Gender equality in the work place has not been achieved. This is the richest country in the world and yet still has the second highest rate of infant mortality. In other words, far too many here suffer for and from the same causes as the other nations in the world. Much of the energy of the church has been spent being "against" whatever the local issue is. As the church, as the women of the church, we can be "for" the common good and IAWN offers us a platform from which to speak.

The Office for Women's Ministries of the Episcopal Church USA encourages and empowers the work and ministry of women within the church and beyond. It serves as a resource and staff support for domestic and global initiatives which seek justice for women in society and the inclusion of women at all levels of church life. The office convenes the Council for Women's Ministries, a consortium of women's organizations in the church and serves as staff support for the ECUSA Committee on the Status of Women. New program initiatives involve Internet Conversations seeking to listen to and engage the voices of young women in shaping the church today. The Women's Ministries Office collaborates in the work of the UN Anglican Observer, the Episcopal Church Office of Government Relations and all other relevant program clusters of the Church. The Office for Women's Ministries works ecumenically and seeks increasing interfaith partnerships. www.episcopalchurch.org/women

2.3 (b) The Anglican Church of Canada

The Anglican Women's Network–Canada (AWN–CAN) was formed as the Canadian component of IAWN. In 2003, when the Rev'd Canon Alice Medcof was asked to coordinate the IAWN, women of AWN–CAN volunteered to assist her in the coordinating tasks, and an executive body for IAWN was formed. Although still in its infancy, the potential for IAWN continues to grow, as does the necessity for such a powerful communication tool in the Church.

AWN–CAN currently communicates with the Canadian Mothers' Union, the Anglican Church Women of Canada, the Evangelical Lutheran Women of Canada, the Anglican Aboriginal Women and, through the members of the board, theological schools and artisans. We have circulated prayer requests, conference information, dates and locations of events of interest to Christian women as well as supporting campaigns such as "Sisters in Spirit", and "Make Poverty History". We have contributed to dialogue at the United Nations Commission on the Status of Women in 2000, 2003, 2004 and 2005, on behalf of the Anglican Church of Canada and the ACC.

2.3 (c) The Scottish Episcopal Church

In Scotland fewer people are attending Church services on a Sunday but more of the population are seeking a spiritual dimension to their lives this is set against a background of fears about increased consumerism and debt, local violence and unruly teenagers. As fewer candidates are coming forward for ordination the Church is moving to a more developed and structured Lay Ministry and the Scottish Episcopal women feature in this trend and are involved in raising social awareness and engaged in many projects at local level.

The establishment of a Scottish Parliament which includes devolved powers on health, education, women's issues and voluntary sector, has led to a more open form of government. When a Bill is proposed, a consultation paper is released and made available for the public to respond with their views. It is important, in the face of so much secularism, that a Christian viewpoint is made. The Mothers' Union (MU) members in Scotland have responded over the last 2 years to the Sexual Health Strategy, the Family Matters Consultation, Work and Families: choice and flexibility (relating to Maternity benefits and time off work). They also responded recently to the proposal that Retail Trading should be made illegal on Christmas Day and New Year's Day as it could discriminate against the poorest who should be allowed this time with their families.

The MU members are also involved in the Make Poverty History Campaign and hope to have a large presence at the rally in Edinburgh in July prior to the G8 Conference at Gleneagles Hotel. This campaign seeks to put pressure on rich nations to cancel the debt of the poorest countries and encourage fair trade and justice.

The MU's involvement in social concern and welfare is balanced and enriched by our emphasis on prayer and worship. Our Provincial Retreat this year was on the theme "I am: seeking God and knowing myself". We were encouraged to discover who we were and how God was calling us. Apart from Retreats and Quiet days, the MU has regularly held events such as "Celebrating the Family"; "Looking at ways to encourage children in church"; developing our prayer life and exploring new ways to meditate. We also run training days to enable women to volunteer for project work and know their responsibilities when working with children and vulnerable adults and to ensure their own personal safety.

MU members in Scotland are involved in a variety of projects including helping in play schemes in several prisons, running a Family Contact Centre which helps maintain children's contact with estranged parents, Parenting courses and Mother and Toddler groups etc.

The MU members in Scotland are active ecumenically and seek to work with other Christian denominations on such committees as the World Day of Prayer, groups involved in such areas as prevention of domestic violence, Refugees, drug addiction, prostitution and at present the proposed extensions to the Gambling Laws.

This year women from different churches within the UK will be meeting in Scotland at two events —a 4 Nations' Women's conference and a WISE (Wales, Ireland, Scotland and England) women's Synod. The Episcopal Church and the Mothers' Union will be represented at both of these events.

We endeavour, with God's Grace, to work to his praise and glory here in the Province of Scotland.

2.3 (d) The Church of England

For women in ordained ministry in the Church of England, 2004 was a very significant and special year as it marked the 10th anniversary of the first women to be ordained as priests in the church. Each diocese marked the anniversary with a service of Holy Communion in their Cathedral, and most though not all had the support of their diocesan and Suffragan Bishop.

In February 2005, the General Synod of the Church of England debated the Rochester Report, "Women Bishops in the Church of England?" At the end of a very lengthy debate synod accepted the report on a take note motion and proceeded to look at ways in which legislation can be drawn up to allow those women with the right skills and gifts to fulfil their calling to serve as Bishop in the church.

2.4 Region of Africa

It was a wonderful experience for the Anglican women from the Region of Africa to have had the opportunity to meet and share experiences with each other. We are very thankful to everyone who made it possible to happen. This was historic, as 16 women from 9 African Provinces met (English and French speakers—Egypt joined the Arab speaking region). As a result, we unanimously decided to congregate as a Region to discuss important issues that concern ourselves, our families, churches, countries and Region.

The Vision of our Region is "To be the Voice of the Voiceless". It is rooted in Scripture: "Speak up for those who cannot speak for themselves, for the rights of all who are destitute". (Proverbs 31.8)

Our Mission is to enable gender concerns to be voiced through churches, theological institutions, faith based organizations and any other available platforms. We have for our objectives the following: -
1. Strengthen the church-life application of gender issues
2. Encourage the progression of gender within the church
3. Promote health issues in the church and communities
4. Educate the church in gender mainstreaming and gender budgeting in all activities
5. Promote networking within our region

To achieve these goals we undoubtedly have to work together, that is, the Anglican Communion in our Region in collaboration with the Anglican Communion worldwide.

Since our parting in New York in mid March 2005, we have been networking with each other within our Region, via email or post. The Anglican women of Africa are determined to realize our objectives and have planned to gather before the end of October 2005 to continue the work.

We therefore, request the ACC13 and the Primates to support our cause by providing work facilities for the Provincial representative and maintain contact with her.

2.4 (a) Zimbabwe, The Church of the Province of Central Africa.

1. **Poverty:** In the face of a deteriorating economy with a high rate of inflation (over 100%), unemployment (over 70%), a collapsing health system and recurrent droughts, poverty levels are rising at an alarming rate, and the women are the ones to bear the brunt of having to fend for their families, especially where husbands are unemployed, sick or deceased. The wife/mother often becomes the breadwinner, a role traditionally taken by the husband.

2. **Professional women** find themselves overburdened as, unlike their husbands, they also have to look after the home and raise the children in addition to often demanding jobs. Especially in previously male-dominated professions, they have to be several times better than their male counterparts to get promoted. They are also exposed to sexual harassment at the work place, and when they do rise to the top, they are suspected to have done so through giving sexual favours to men in important positions.

3. **Widows:** Widows get shunned by the late husband's family and are often accused of having killed their husband and end up being deprived of all their possessions. Even the children may be taken away from her. This is a distortion of cultural practice as traditionally the husband's family would have to take care of the widow and her children. There is also little recognition of wives who are professional and have made substantial contributions to the matrimonial home. It appears the extended family is out to gain as much as they can in material terms from the death of their son/brother. All this happens within our so-called good Christian families. Our own MU members may be the ones who are inflicting misery on their daughters-in-law. In addition, widows, no matter how young they are, are not expected to remarry, and this impacts further on the spread of HIV & AIDS.

4. **HIV/AIDS:** Poverty is directly linked to the spread of HIV/AIDS as most of those infected with the virus are not able to afford anti-retroviral drugs. Women are the victims in most cases contracting the virus from their husbands. Even where a woman is aware that her husband is HIV positive or has full-blown AIDS, the husband may not be willing to use a condom, and at the same time she cannot refuse him sexual intercourse. This issue comes up regularly at our MU gatherings.

Women end up being the caregivers to those who have AIDS including the unfaithful husband who will return to his wife once he is sick. The women also have to fend for the children whether the husband is sick, looses employment or eventually dies. She herself may also be infected with the virus. Anti-retroviral drugs are not available to those who cannot afford them. In addition, people are afraid to speak openly about their status due to stigmatisation which is still rampant. This means they cannot be given adequate counseling and medical advice.

5. **Wife-beating/abuse:** This is rampant in a lot of families if not most. It is considered to be normal by many that wives need to be beaten from time to time. She too may accept it as a token of the husband's love for her!! Generally women are not expected to speak out against such treatment and in most cases silently endure and suffer abusive relationships. Sermons rarely address such issues as they are considered too sensitive, or may be the priest himself considers wife-beating as normal. With increasing poverty and unemployment, husbands experience high levels of frustration which in turn is taken out on the family and the wife in particular. Cases of serious injury and even death resulting from husbands' assaults are not uncommon.

6. **Rape:** Rape too is on the increase especially during times of political tension like elections campaigns. If women are raped, they often do not dare to report it to the police lest they be thrown out by their husband suspecting them of having an affair. This also makes women easy victims to contracting HIV. Rape within marriage is hardly talked about at all or recognized as an issue. Again many women suffer in silence. At our MU gatherings women have complained about the increase in fathers raping their own daughters and granddaughters. Their mothers may not dare report such cases to the police.

7. **Migration of women to other countries:** Many women, especially those with skills like nursing leave Zimbabwe to work abroad. While they will all give economic reasons for their migration, in some cases they are trying to escape from an HIV positive husband, or indeed they are already HIV positive themselves and hope to get easier access to medication abroad. They often leave behind their husbands and children which is not conducive to stable family life, and in itself compounds the spread of the virus.

8. **Absence of ordination of women in the Province of Central Africa:** Our women would benefit a great deal if we had women priests as women do not find it easy to confide in male priests, especially concerning very private and sensitive issues. They have often expressed their desire to see women ordained to the priesthood, especially since

women are in the majority in the church and in the rural areas are often leaders of congregations. It appears that the special gifts women could bring into the priesthood as complementary to those of men would go a long way in offering a more wholistic ministry to our people. While our diocese voted in favour of women's ordination, to date the issue has not received majority support in the Province.

2.4 (b) Province de L'Eglise Anglicane Du Congo

Greetings in the name of our Saviour Jesus Christ. I thank God for giving me the opportunity to share with you the difficulties we are facing.

In the Democratic Republic of Congo people are living in extreme poverty causing hunger and starvation because of the political and economic instability. Armed conflicts aggravate the situation because of displacement, loss of properties, burning of farms and villages, and sexual violence. Women and children are the victims of conflict: they are suffering without end.

In Congolese society women bear all the responsibility for caring for the family. Poor women work hard to ensure family survival. She must leave home early to get her goods to market, and return late in the night, having left her children alone at home. Meanwhile the husband plays cards, until his wife comes back. He expects her to work hard for him because he bought her from her family. Sometimes she becomes a prostitute in order to earn money. HIV/AIDS is often an inevitable consequence.

The Mothers' Union of the Diocese of Katanga is working to alleviate the problems. The initiatives include teaching women about:

Peace, and conflict resolution,
Gender justice,
Violence against women,
Micro-credit for those who want to do business,
Skills such as sewing and needlework.

With these initiatives we will achieve our four objectives in order to alleviate the poverty that affects our sisters in the Diocese of Katanga.

We need to explain our situation to the International Anglican Women's Network. If our voices are heard and if we give the information about women from the Democratic Republic of Congo, IAWN will be able to share with us and to propose ways forward.

The Network will be strengthened if we manage to spread it to UFPPS Union des Femmes pour la Paix et la Promotion Sociale, Women United for Peace and Social Promotion, throughout all the Province of the Anglican Church of Congo.

We need to organise training sessions and conferences in the various dioceses to explain what the Network means and to establish a representative in each diocese. Through the representatives, women in different dioceses can learn about their Anglican sisters around the world, and we, in turn, can share with the IAWN.

Please, we need your help

2.4 (c) *The Church of the Province of Uganda*

The goal of the organization known as Family Empowerment and Development is to create and restore family values and sustain a stable family life. It is addressing the issues of:

Domestic Violence.
Parenting skills and styles.
HIV/AIDS.
Poverty eradication.

In rural areas, women are victims of HIV/AIDS because of economic dependence on their husbands. They have no sexual bargaining power. Husbands, who have paid bride price, believe that the words "marital rape" do not exist in marriage. The Domestic Relations Bill has yet to be passed by Parliament.

Discussions continue on the issues of:

female poverty and economic empowerment;
the causes of domestic violence and on how to deal with the perpetuators;
personal development, self esteem, life skills and counseling skills;
how to access free legal aid from FIDA;
home-based care services for families that are affected with HIV/AIDS.

With minimal resources, the workers have not given up hope that God will provide the funding at His timing.

2.4 (d) *Province of the Episcopal Church of the Sudan*

Extreme disappointment has been expressed by Sudanese Church leaders at the needless deaths and injuries incurred in the Khartoum suburb of Soba Aradi in May, 2005, as police attempted to evict internally-displaced residents of the area by force.

The Bishop of Khartoum, Rt Revd Ezekiel Kondo, visited Soba Aradi and consoled residents still traumatized by the incident.

"The deaths of civilians and police like this is a terrible thing at any time, but is completely wrong at the present moment as concrete progress is being made towards peace," decried Bishop Kondo. He expressed condolence to all the bereaved.

Soba Aradi is a well-established area for internally-displaced Sudanese on the South East edge of Khartoum. Over the last twenty years, war-displaced people from Southern Sudan and Nuba Mountains have made their homes there, being joined more recently by displaced people from Darfur. Schools and churches have grown up to serve the local community. However, in September 2004, bulldozers were sent in to destroy some 7,500 homes in that area in the name of town planning. Land was to be re-allocated to residents through a process of registration, while schools and places of worship were left standing.

With the lack of subsequent progress on land allocation, residents who have remained in the area were recently instructed to rebuild one room each for protection against the heavy rains due in the coming months. Many had begun to do so when police arrived unannounced to evict them.

Residents awoke on the morning of Wednesday 18th May 2005 to find the entire area surrounded by the army, including three tanks. Armed police then moved in to evict people from their homes. As no advanced warning had been given, many residents determined to resist forced eviction. In the ensuing violence, both civilians and police were killed and many more injured. Official figures set the number of police killed at 14 while the number of civilian deaths is unconfirmed. State authorities announced only 3 civilian deaths while reports from media and local communities have put this figure at between 15–22, including several children.

The Constitutional Review Commission, tasked with creating a new national Constitution under the terms of the Sudan Peace Agreement, was meeting as these events took place and suspended discussions for the day out of concern. The UN Secretary General's representative on the human rights of internally displaced persons has also expressed serious concern and called for any relocation not to be undertaken in an atmosphere conducive to violence and only to be carried out in full consultation with those affected.

2.5 Region of Jerusalem and the Middle East

The Anglican Peace and Justice Network held a meeting in Jerusalem. The APJN report stated: "We note the continuing policies of illegal home demolitions, detentions, checkpoints, identity card systems and the presence of the Israeli military that make any kind of normal life impossible."

In search of a normal life, many Christians have emigrated. The population of Israel/Palestine is now less than 3% Christian.

2.6 Region of West Asia

2.6 (a) *The Church of North India (United)*

The Church Conference of Asia (CCA) held its 12th assembly. The theme was Building Communities of Peace. Prior to that, in Chaiangmai Thailand, the Pre-assembly Women's Forum was held. Before reading the message from the women's forum in the General Assembly, women entered the hall with banners held high while the singing:

> "Women are now arriving through the doors and through the windows,
> From the streets and from the alleys,
> Women are now arriving, women are now arriving."

Truly we are still in the process of arriving. There is so much that we have yet to do towards building communities of peace in Asia. But as we dream, pray, study and work together, our dreams will come true.

Women of Asian Churches said that we are expected to build Communities of Peace in the Midst of Suffering.

Women in Asia struggle against the day-to-day hardships standing at the crossroads of different forms of violence and discrimination, namely: sexism, heterosexism, race, class, caste, religious violence and ethnocentrism. We deplore the complicity of the church in inflicting violence on the vulnerable and those it deems as "the other" by using the Bible and religious and theological traditions to legitimize such cruelties. We deeply understand that women's experience of violence is profoundly connected with the degradation of the Earth. One has to have a deep sense of justice to be able to see the forces that cause the extreme poverty and suffering of the vast majority of Asian people, especially women and children.

We believe that it is not God's will for women and children to suffer any form of violence. We are created in God's image; therefore we claim our place as equal partners with men in the task of building communities of peace. We have the potential and gifts to offer to the church to promote justice, peace and to make community life flourish in its fullness. We are endowed with God's gift of dignity and human rights to experience the fullness of life (John 10:10) and to be the salt of the earth (Mark 19:50b). Women are able to experience the abundant life that Jesus the Christ has spoken of, only when we commit ourselves to choose life rather than death (Deuteronomy 30:19). This demands that we continue to resist the evils that denigrate life, and to affirm our potential to build communities where justice, love and peace flourish. We condemn all forms of violence inflicted on women and children as sin. Even as we nurse our own pains, we are called to be agents of healing and bind the wounds of others.

The contributions of Asian women in doing theology are still not taken seriously. Our method is not only contextual and transformative; it is also integral and inclusive. Asian theologies have emerged, but still the voices of women are rarely listened to. We women are called by our faith to condemn patriarchy and empire. In this light, we commit ourselves to collectively transgress the boundaries of structures set by patriarchy and the hegemonic control in church and society.

It was recommended that the Church Council of Asia General Assembly should:

- Re-affirm and strengthen its commitment to gender justice and ensure full participation of women in the church.
- Endeavor to bring an end to all forms of violence against women and children in church and society.
- Continue to encourage resistance to the forces of globalization that denigrate the dignity of women and children, and of the Earth.
- Guarantee support for women victims of abuse and violence, especially in situations of conflict and war.
- Engage in serious study on the broader issue of human sexuality.

The participants acknowledged the efforts of the Church Council of Asia in enabling women and men to reflect on the challenges to build communities of peace. However, we challenge CCA to do more and go beyond the commonplace. We urge CCA to continue to grow in its concern over the impact of patriarchy and globalization on the lives of women and children in Asia. We call on the churches to repent its complacency and complicity to different forms of violence, and endeavor to end violence against women and children. We urge men to be truly our partners in the struggle for just and peaceful communities for women and children. Let the churches' practice of genuine solidarity with women be an embodiment of our faith in Jesus the Christ who showed us the Way to build communities of peace.

The Bride School at Aurangabad teaches the girls about marriage, health, kitchen work, etc. There are 16 girls and Mrs. Sharda C. Aswale the Bride School teacher informed me that they are taking 10 year old girls and helping them till the age of 16. There's a question in my mind that India's marriage age for a girl is 18 years, so we should continue to keep these girls till the age of 18 and give them proper guidance about marriage and family. I am thankful to the teacher Mrs. Sharda Aswale and Warden of Christ Church Ms. Khare for their help for these little girls.

2.7 Region of Oceania

The Anglican Church in Aotearoa, Polynesia, and New Zealand, of Australia, of Melanesia, and of Papua New Guinea.

Women of the Anglican Communion in Oceania continue to work actively both in their churches and their communities. They do not confine this activity to their local situation, but are frequently contributing their skills nationally and internationally. In Australia and New Zealand the increasing commitments expected from women to care for their families, to be active in their communities, to be efficient and capable employees/employers, and to contribute to their church community frequently means that involvement in church activities declines even to the extent that worship becomes an infrequent activity. 'Church' is often considered to have nothing to say to the pressures of life in an increasingly secular society.

The representative from Diocese of Polynesia reports "Women's ministry has been undergoing a lot of change in the last fifteen years. With the emphasis on partnerships between the laity and the ordained, women and men, young and old, the Diocese spearheaded its awareness and training programmes to equip all the baptised for their different ministries. This resulted in creating an environment that was positive for women to pursue their own ministries. This is evident in the increased number of women in the ordained ministry, those with formal theological education, number of lay ministers and those in decision-making bodies such as vestries, issue committees, standing committee and synod. The democratization of church institutional structures, though slow in pace, is commensurate with the changes that are happening in the wider socio-political and cultural milieu."

The major issues and challenges listed from Polynesia are also those of women in the Provinces of Melanesia and Papua/New Guinea, and for groups within Australia and Aotearoa/New Zealand.

- The rising cost of living and increasing impoverishment—costs of food, medicines, schooling, housing are all rising
- AIDS/STIs on the rise and churches not actively promoting prevention.
- Violence & abuse against women & children is increasing and is frequently considered to be normal behaviour.
- In many countries there is ethnic tension, political instability and armed uprisings.
- Women have been active in the promotion of mediation and peaceful resolution.
- The tension between raising of children within traditional cultural values and modern western values. This is a source of major tension between younger and older generations.
- Churches losing congregations to Pentecostal churches.

2.8 Region of the East Asia

2.8 (a) The Episcopal Church in the Philippines

The common concern that we would like to present to the ACC is the approval/affirmation and implementation that women within the worldwide Anglican Communion have at least a 30% representation in all decision-making or important Commissions/Committees of their churches and its institutions. Lest we be misunderstood of just pushing women who may not be qualified for such positions or appointments, we would like to make clear that qualified women be appointed or included in the list of nominations for memberships to the said Commissions/Committees. Our church must acknowledge that the women comprise the biggest group in the congregations, that the women have proven their leadership skills in the various church projects undertaken (mostly with flying colours!), and that the women are now equipped and empowered to participate in major bodies affecting their local churches. We ask only for more understanding and acknowledgement of our gifts which we have been trying to extend to our churches.

The women in our churches have long stayed in the background in view of the accepted tradition of keeping to our places. There are a few women who have been recognized by the church and have been appointed to decision-making bodies but the number of such "recognized" women has not grown or increased. A significant number of these appointments have been to committees that are thought to be "for women".

It is disturbing to note that, when women share amongst themselves ideas and concerns about our churches, their voices seem to be silent. Most of the ideas that come out from such gatherings are not even relayed to the proper bodies (due to fear maybe of rejection?), or when the women do open up to their generally male leaders, they are not given the attention and importance they deserve.

2.8 (b) Hong Kong Sheng Kung Hui

A) Within the Church:

There is no structure, neither explicitly in constitutional provisions nor in implicit practice, to prescribe or encourage the participation of ordained or lay women in Church decision-making bodies such as vestry membership, diocesan committees, or provincial committees, despite election to these organs through a democratic process. Since the Beijing Platform for Action aims at equal participation between genders in government and NGOs, and the Millennium Development Goals have set 2015 as the target date, a mere 10 years from now, we have to hasten our process and we have a long way to go.

Even though Hong Kong was the forerunner in women's ordination, statistics show that women priests are in a marked minority. More active effort, it seems, needs to be put towards identifying, nurturing and preparing suitable candidates for such calling.

B) Social Issues Affecting Women

Domestic Violence is a serious matter as witnessed by a number of extremely tragic cases in which families of mother and children commit suicide after being abused.

New Immigrant-wives from Mainland China, very often young wives married to old husbands, and with very young children, experience severe problems adjusting to a highly urbanised environment.

In both of the above, government resources, to alleviate the problems, are insufficient.

HKSKH has responded promptly and pro-actively to the plight of immigrant wives by providing centres of information and assistance in Mainland China even before their departure for Hong Kong, and follow-up care and assistance after arrival.

Overseas Domestic Helpers, mostly from the Philippines, Indonesia and Sri Lanka, are increasingly reporting physical abuse by employers. There is a shelter set up in the Cathedral as a safe haven where the women can tell their stories. Betty Chan, our Chairperson of HKSKH Women's League, is planning a seminar to educate local employers about better treatment of overseas helpers and the promotion of deeper understanding, sympathy and care for these women.

Care for the Aged is a great concern. The demography of Hong Kong population is aging fast like an inverted triangle with the family structure of fewer young people taking care of aged parents, grandparents. Young people are struggling for their own livelihood and care for the aged is often neglected. Older women are overworked as they end up looking after their husbands who are ill, and tending to grandchildren. HKSKH has responded to this need by rendering all sorts of relief such as delivering meals, health care at home, centres for child-care, and centres for aged folks.

C) Participation in last 49th Session of UN Commission on Status of Women

Betty Chan and I, Fung-yi Wong, and members of HKSKH thank the Anglican Observer for organising the Anglican delegation to the UN Commission on the Status of Women, 2005, the American and Canadian sisters' and church's generosity for making this meeting possible for us, and our Archbishop the Most Revd. Dr. Peter Kwong for encouraging us to take part in this meeting.

Betty and I and hopefully, in turn, members of HKSKH, will become more sensitised to issues women face in Hong Kong and we pray we shall become God's instruments in realising the goals as set down in the Beijing Platform for Action and the Millennium Goals which our Church and the wider secular human society have endorsed as evidenced in United Nations' resolutions.

We shall communicate to IAWN our progress in the above causes and the progress of HKSKH Women's League in joining the worldwide organisation of Mothers' Union.

4.0 Region Name and Steering Committee Link for the Region, followed by a listing of the Provinces of the Region, and the extra-territorial churches (XT).

Region of Latin America & Caribbean, Rev'd Canon Emily Morales

Iglesia Anglicana de la Region Central de America
La Iglesia Anglicana de Mexico
The Episcopal Church in the USA, Province IX
The Church in the Province of the West Indies
Iglesia Episcopal de Cuba (extra-territorial)

Region of South America, Christina Winnischofer

Igreja Episcopal Anglicana do Brasil
Iglesia Anglicana del Cono Sur de America

Region of North America & United Kingdom, Rev'd Nancy Acree

The Anglican Church of Canada
The Church of England
The Church of Ireland
The Scottish Episcopal Church
The Episcopal Church in the USA
The Church in Wales

Region of Africa, Priscilla Julie

The Episcopal Church of Burundi
The Church of the Province of Central Africa
Province de L'Eglise Anglicane Du Congo
The Church of the Province of the Indian Ocean
The Anglican Church of Kenya
The Church of Nigeria (Anglican Communion)
L'Eglise Episcopal au Rwanda
The Church of the Province of Southern Africa
The Episcopal Church of the Sudan
The Anglican Church of Tanzania
The Church of the Province of Uganda
The Church of the Province of West Africa

Region of Jerusalem and the Middle East, Eliane Abd El Nour

Province of Jerusalem and the Middle East

Region of West Asia, Link Team Prabhjot Masih, Jyotsna Patro
The Church of Bangladesh
The Church of the Province of Myanmar (Burma)
The Church of North India (United)
The Church of Pakistan (United)
The Church of South India (United)
The Church of Ceylon (extra-territorial)

Region of Oceania, Janet Hesketh

The Anglican Church in Aotearoa, New Zealand & Polynesia
The Anglican Church of Australia
The Church of the Province of Melanesia
The Anglican Church of Papua New Guinea.

Region of East Asia, Esperanza Beleo

Hong Kong Sheng Kung Hui
The Nippon Sei Ko Kai (Japan)
The Anglican Church of Korea
The Episcopal Church in the Philippines
Church of the Province of South East Asia

Report of International Anglican Youth Network

After a period of quiet the International Anglican Youth Network was revived in May 2004. A meeting of nineteen provincial youth officers together with invited guests from other networks, communions and the Anglican UN Observer met April 29–May 2, 2004 at Trinity Conference Center, West Cornwall, Connecticut, USA.

A mission statement for the Network was drafted and after discussion the following was unanimously agreed:

International Anglican Youth Network

We are a network of persons involved in ministry among young people at the provincial level uniting young people within the Anglican Communion.

Our Aims:

Ministry *among* Young People

- To raise the profile of youth ministry in the Anglican Communion.
- To increase resources and support of youth ministry.

Ministry *of* Young People

- To create a communion in which young people are strengthened.
- To develop and support young people in their ministry.
- To advocate on behalf of young people to ensure participation within the Church.
- To encourage the inclusion of young people at all levels in the decision-making of the Church.

[The term 'young people' was employed to avoid confusion over the competing terms of *youth* and *young adult* where each are defined regionally by differing ages.]

A funding strategy was adopted inviting each province to contribute US$500 during every Advent to support the work of the Network.

A steering group was formed. Each of six 'regions' selected their members: The Rev'd Leite "Sam" Dessordi from Brazil (Americas); The Rev'd Samuel Barhoum from Jerusalem and the Middle East (Europe and the

Middle East); The Rev'd Feliciano Balangui from the Philippines (Asia); The Rev'd John Hebenton from Aotearoa-New Zealand (Oceania); Mr Sabelo Mashwama from Southern Africa (Africa). It was recognized that every region may not be fully present but limited resources prevent a larger contingent. Very few women were present at the 2004 Network gathering and none present wished to serve. Mr Peter Ball (England) and the Rev'd Douglas Fenton (USA) were appointed Co-Administrators.

The steering group continued its work by e-mail and has since appointed Ms Melissa Sim (Canada) to succeed Ms Delene Mark (Southern Africa) as Youth member on the Peace and Justice Network.

The first meeting of the steering committee convened in Jerusalem in February 2005. It considered nominations from the Network for the vacant ACC Youth position. Michael Tamihere (Aotearoa-New Zealand) was appointed to fill the current vacancy and Sarah Tomlinson (Scotland) to succeed Candace Payne. A request was made for Sarah Tomlinson to attend the next ACC-13 meeting in Nottingham as an observer. A response to the Windsor Report was prepared as requested by Archbishop Kwong, a plan for mutual support was developed, and discussions were undertaken to discern the next Network gathering in connection with the 2008 Lambeth Conference.

The next meeting of the steering group will be in Porto Alegre, Brazil from February 23–March 2, 2006.

Respectfully submitted,
The Rev'd Douglas Fenton
IAYN Co-Adminstrator

International Anglican Liturgical Consultation

Members of the International Anglican Liturgical Consultation held a meeting at Ripon College Cuddesdon in July 2003. There were 61 persons in attendance, drawn from 16 provinces of the Anglican Communion.

(Full Consultations are held every four years, with more informal meetings at the two-year intervals between them. An attempt is made to provide bursaries for participants who might not otherwise be able to attend full Consultations but such funds are seldom available for meetings.)

The subject of the 2003 meeting was liturgical formation, the process by which God forms *us* in worship. Paul Bradshaw, chair of the IALC, asked, "How can we effectively enable people to participate in liturgy and enable leaders to help people to grow?" He reminded the meeting that this is not an end in itself because liturgical formation is also a matter of forming people for mission in the world. He asked "What is realistic for people in many parts of the Anglican Communion?"

Presentations were made on the meaning of liturgical formation today (Juan Oliver), liturgical education and formation from an African perspective (Solomon Amusan), liturgical formation of the people of God (Mark Earey), the role of music in liturgical formation (Carol Doran), liturgical education and formation in theological education (Tomas Maddela), the continuing education and formation of clergy (Richard Leggett), and the liturgical formation of children, teens, and young adults (Ruth Meyers). The texts on which these presentations were made are now about to be edited for publication. In addition, a number of members contributed their own reflections on these and related subjects.

The meeting noted that a daily reading is now attached to the Anglican Cycle of Prayer.

A full IALC will be held in Prague in August of this year. (The IALC attempts to choose a location near the site of the biennial meeting of the international and ecumenical liturgical academy, Societas Liturgica. Anglican members of Societas Liturgica are automatically eligible for membership in the IALC and it is economical for many of them to attend both events on one travel bill. Societas Liturgica will meet in Dresden, Germany, immediately after the IALC.)

The subject of the 2005 Consultation will be liturgy and Anglican identity. A number of papers are now in circulation to enable members to prepare for the event.

The IALC has been aware for some time that in some parts of the Communion elements other than bread and/or wine are substituted for the traditional eucharistic food. A survey has suggested that deviations from the tradition may be more widespread than was at first thought to be the case. Sometimes the reason given is the need of some communicants to avoid alcohol. In other cases the reasons are cultural and relate to local laws and/or the availability of traditional elements. This was discussed in both 2001 and 2003. The 2003 Consultation, as requested, appointed a working group to consider the data that has been received and to report to the 2005 IALC.

The collection of liturgical texts housed in the ACC office to document the liturgical developments of the last 40 years continues to grow, if slowly. I would like to remind Provinces of the importance of sending new texts, whether they are formal publications (like Prayer Books) or more ephemeral drafts and testing material. Mr. David Hebblethwaite, formerly Secretary to the Church of England Liturgical Commission, lives near St. Andrew's House and has kindly offered to maintain oversight of the collection.

The Reverend Paul Gibson
Liturgical Officer, Anglican Church of Canada
Advisor to the Anglican Consultative Council on Liturgy and Worship
10 June 2005

Network for Inter Faith Concerns

Dear member of ACC,

Linked to this letter are a number of backing papers for the presentation of the Network for Inter Faith Concerns for the Anglican Communion (NIF-CON). NIFCON are privileged to be giving a presentation at the ACC which will focus on the issue of Christian-Muslim relations in the world, and particularly linked to the Anglican Communion. Given the current world situation we are very conscious that this topic is one which affects the lives of many members of the Anglican Communion. It is also an area for which NIFCON was given a very specific mandate by the 1998 Lambeth Conference.

Although we have chosen to focus on Christian-Muslim relations for this presentation, it is important to make clear that NIFCON's brief and mandate is considerably wider than the issue of Christian-Muslim relations. Our work over the past 2-3 years has also reflected Anglican involvement with the Hindu community, Buddhism and Judaism. In particular there was a key consultation held by NIFCON in Bangalore, India, which explored the relationship between Christian mission and inter faith dialogue, particularly in the Indian context. You can find out more about this consultation and the other activities of NIFCON via our regularly updated website which is www.anglicannifcon.org.

Over the past few years my colleague Susanne Mitchell and I have tried to develop NIFCON's network of Provincial correspondents. Although this is now largely complete-there are still a few Provinces where we have no official Provincial link-and we will be taking the opportunity while we are at ACC-13 to try and fill any gaps.

NIFCON's presentation will be coordinated by Bishop Michael Jackson, the Chair of our Management Group, who is also the Bishop of Clogher in Ireland. We have also drawn in and involved some members of the Management Group and associates who are based close to where we will be meeting in Nottingham. The area of Nottingham, Leicester and Derby is one of the most multi-cultural parts of England, and the issue of inter faith relations regularly affects Christians living in these cities, as they inevitably engage, on a daily basis, in an ongoing 'dialogue of life.'

With all good wishes
Clare Amos
Coordinator, NIFCON

THE LAMBETH CONFERENCE 1998
RESOLUTION FROM THE INTERFAITH TEAM

Resolution VI.1

On Relations with People of Other Faiths

This Conference:

a) having heard about situations in different parts of the world where relations between people of different faiths vary from co-operation to conflict, believes that the approach of Christians to people of other faiths needs to be marked by:

   (i) commitment to working towards genuinely open and loving human relationships, even in situations where co-existence seems impossible;

   (ii) co-operation in addressing human concerns and working for justice, peace and reconciliation for the whole human community;

   (iii) frank and honest exploration of both the common ground and the differences between the faiths;

   (iv) prayerful and urgent action with all involved in tension and conflict, to understand their situation, so that everything possible may be done to tackle the causes of conflict;

   (v) a desire both to listen to people of all faiths and to express our own deepest Christian beliefs, leaving the final outcome of our life and witness in the hands of God;

   (vi) sharing and witnessing to all we know of the good news of Christ as our debt of love to all people whatever their religious affiliation.

b) recognises that by virtue of their engagement with people of other faiths in situations all over the world, Anglican Christians are in a special position to explore and develop genuinely Christian responses to these faiths;

c) also recognises that the Network for Inter-Faith Concerns (NIF-CON) has been established by the ACC at the request of the last Lambeth Conference as a way for sharing news, information, ideas and resources relating to these concerns between provinces of the Anglican Communion;

d) recommends:

   (i) that NIFCON be charged to monitor Muslim-Christian relations and report regularly to the Primates Meeting and the ACC;

   (ii) that the ACC consider how to resource NIFCON adequately both in personnel and finance;

   (iii) that all the other official Anglican networks should be encouraged to recognise the inter-faith dimensions to their work.

NIFCON—Our Mission and What We Do

The Network for Inter Faith Concerns of the Anglican Communion exists to encourage:
- Progress towards genuinely open and loving relationships between Christians and people of other faiths;
- Exchange of news, information, ideas and resources relating to inter faith concerns between provinces of the Anglican Communion;
- Sensitive witness and evangelism where appropriate;
- Prayerful and urgent action with all involved in tension and conflict;
- Local contextual and wider theological reflection.

NIFCON does this by:
- Networking and meeting;
- The written word in its various forms;
- Gathering information through its international presidents, correspondents, and contacts support groups.

It has also been charged by the 1998 Lambeth Conference to study and evaluate Muslim-Christian relations and report regularly to the Anglican Consultative Council.

Porvoo Communion Consultation on Inter Faith Relations
Oslo, 30 November–3 December 2003

Guidelines For Inter Faith Encounter in the Churches of the Porvoo Communion

A. *Beginning with God*

When as Christians we encounter people of other faiths, beliefs and spiritualities, we do so in the name and the strength of the God whom we know as Trinity. This faith points us to some key theological principles informing our encounter:

God is no less generous in salvation than in creation

The God whom we meet in creation is generous in grace and rejoices in diversity—'O Lord, how manifold are your works! In wisdom you have made them all!' [Ps 104.24] This creator God is the same saving God who wishes to lead all to perfection.

Jesus Christ shows us God's face and opens the way to God

In Jesus we have seen 'the radiance of God's glory' [Heb 1.3]; he shows us the way to the Father and we wish to share this way with others. Our witness to this way needs to be made in such a way that it is heard as good news by all; it is not for us to proclaim limits to God's saving mercy.

The Spirit's presence is known through the Spirit's fruits

'The tree is known by its fruits', and 'the fruit of the Spirit is love, joy, peace, patience, kindness, generosity, faithfulness, gentleness and self-control.' [Mt 12.33; Gal 5.22f] When we meet these qualities in our encounter with people of other faiths, by God's grace we may discern the Spirit's presence.

B. The contexts of our societies

The societies in which our churches are called to mission and ministry are increasingly marked by a plurality of religions, beliefs and spiritualities. In large measure, this is the result of histories of migration of people from other countries who have brought their faiths and cultures with them. This has happened at different rates and over different periods: in some countries there are large and established communities of faith dating back several generations, while in others religious plurality is more recent or on a smaller scale. Moreover, the situation is constantly changing, as a result of the continuing arrival of people seeking refuge and well-being in all our countries.

Beyond the visibly and culturally identifiable communities of faith, there is also now a wider plurality and fluidity of spirituality in our societies. Many seek meaning and purpose in new or alternative patterns of spirituality. There is a growth in conversions between different religions. While some opt for loose networks within which to probe ultimate questions, others turn to clearly defined answers offered through closely organised groups. At the same time, many people look for their beliefs and values to the secular and the human without reference to transcendence of any kind.

C. The challenge of discernment

In these complex and changing situations, Christian communities are faced with the challenge of discerning God's purposes in our religiously plural societies by remaining faithful disciples of Jesus Christ open to the guidance of the Spirit. Within all our churches, there will be a variety of theological starting points, methods and conclusions in responding to this challenge. As Anglicans and Lutherans, we seek to be particularly attentive to the ways in which the Bible can challenge and guide our thinking and practice in inter faith relations. In our reading together of scripture, we have found that the interaction of its texts with our contexts can at times highlight the diversity of views among us, and we recognise that Christian reflection on inter faith encounter is likely to continue to be a contested area in both our traditions for the foreseeable future.

In these circumstances, it is essential that there should be candid and positive dialogue within our communion's churches, and with fellow Christians in our ecumenical partner churches, to complement and resource our dialogue with people of other faiths, beliefs and spiritualities. In what follows, we offer as a contribution to this intra-Christian dialogue some reflections from our own experience on twelve concrete and practical issues which have a special importance for inter faith encounter in our societies. These are offered as examples; they are not intended as a comprehensive or systematic account. Moreover, given the ever-changing nature of the contexts within which our mission and ministry is set, these pointers must be seen as work in progress, in constant need of updating and revision.

D. Twelve issues for Christians in inter faith encounter

These pointers for inter faith engagement are mostly expressed in the language of personal encounter. We have found that meeting with people of other faiths can be a profoundly transforming experience for ourselves, leading to a deepening, renewing and enlarging of faith. As Christians, though, we are never involved in inter faith situations only as individuals, but always also as members of our faith community. This representative role has a particularly high profile for ordained ministers; yet inter faith encounter is also an area of Christian discipleship where lay people have a vital role to play, and they too speak and act on behalf of the whole Church.

1. Building long-term trust

Our faith speaks of the centrality of permanent commitment to one another as the way to build stable and trustful relationships. In inter faith encounter, there can be no substitute for the patient, painstaking and time-consuming process of getting to know our neighbours of other faiths, earning their respect, and becoming their friends. We have found that it is within relationships of this kind, built up over many years, that dialogue acquires authenticity, the quest for truth can be honestly pursued, and difficult issues can be addressed.

2. Speaking truthfully about the other

Speaking truthfully requires us to avoid simplistic or homogenising language. Rather, we need to recognise the complexity and diversity of all faith communities, our own included. When we speak of the beliefs and practices of others, we must first seek good information and rely on authoritative sources to build up our knowledge, and we must talk about our neighbours in language that will enable them to recognise themselves in our descriptions. This will involve us in an imaginative and sympathetic effort to think ourselves into their situation. It is unfair to compare the ideals in our own religion with the practice of another, or vice versa. Christians and members of other communities need to acknowledge that we all face challenges in living by faith in our societies. Even in situations where we strongly disagree with others, we must make an effort to understand their beliefs and practices, to respect the faith which informs them, and to love them as our neighbours. If we feel there are times when we must be critical of others' positions, we cannot avoid the challenge of self-criticism.

3. Sharing our faith

We are called to share our faith with others in ways that are confident but sensitive. As we do so, we are ready to listen and to learn as well as to speak. We recognise that the intentions of those engaged in dialogue may differ, and it is easy to suspect one another of hidden agendas. We cannot force our beliefs on others, but we should always be ready to witness to our faith by deeds as well as by words. We must never exploit the situation of vulnerable individuals and groups, nor make our service of others conditional on their accepting Christian faith. Within our churches, we recognise that Christians differ among themselves about the relations between inter faith dialogue and evangelism. We think it is important that these differences should be discussed openly and respectfully in the light of our theology and experience.

4. Coming together before God

We acknowledge that there may be times when Christians would like to come together with people of other faiths in an attitude of prayer and worship before God. This may happen, for example, in the pastoral context of a marriage or funeral, as part of the ongoing life of a group or organisation, or at times of crisis, remembrance or thanksgiving, locally or nationally. As Christians, some of us will welcome occasions like this, while others will find them very difficult; a range of attitudes will also be found among people of other faiths. In whatever way inter faith gatherings for prayer or worship are organised, we think that it is important to be clear about the purposes of the event, to consider carefully what is an appropriate venue, and to ensure that all present can take part in what is planned with integrity and without confusion. Sharing silence can provide a valuable way of expressing our presence together before God, and we are also learning from the experience of being present as honoured guests at one another's times of prayer and worship.

5. Responding to changing societies

While we rejoice in the new vitality that religious and cultural diversity has brought to many parts of our societies, we are also aware of the confusion and pain that can be felt by long-established communities who find their neighbourhoods transformed. We emphasise the importance of maintaining a vigorous and engaged Christian presence at local level in multi-faith areas. We recognise also the need to be aware of the ethnic and religious discrimination in our societies which affect other faith groups.

6. Educating and nurturing in faith

In situations where our Churches are involved in education, we can ensure that children and young people are adequately equipped for life as citizens of religiously plural societies. As part of this, we may need to insist that Christianity is taught with an awareness of its international reach and its cultural diversity within the local situation. Within the church community, teaching needs to be shaped in such a way as to help Christians explore the inter faith implications of their faith. Experiences of educational opportunities can help to give us a proper confidence in our own faith and a generous openness to others.

7. Supporting family life

We need to be sensitive to the hopes and needs of those who are thinking of embarking on marriages across the boundaries of faith. Clergy and others with a ministry of pastoral care should be equipped to provide appropriate advice and support for such couples and for their families. They also need to have access to suitable resources for the nurture and education of children of inter faith couples, and to develop patterns of support for the families of those who have converted to or from other faiths. We sense that there is a growing need to share good practice in the pastoral care of those who experience bereavement in inter faith relations.

8. Working for the common good

We seek co-operation with people in other faith groups on practical projects where this is appropriate and possible. We believe that our Churches have a particular role to play in encouraging our national governments and local authorities to explore and to understand the complexities of faith community organisations. We recognise that people of all faiths have a concern for the whole of society, while at the same time we all need to be honest about the real differences we can experience when we try to interpret in practical terms values which may sound the same when expressed as generalities. We believe that the Churches are called to work with people of other faiths in seeking the welfare of asylum seekers and refugees.

9. Involving women and men

We recognise that in many inter faith situations there is a need to strengthen the presence and active involvement of women (though in some contexts it may be men who are under-represented). Together with people in other faith communities, we should strive to ensure that participation in inter-religious events has a fair gender balance, and to set a positive lead by insisting on this in the case of Christian representation. At the same time, we need to recognise the strength of the cultural and religious factors which may inhibit the participation of women alongside men in inter faith activities. In inter faith dialogue, we should be ready to raise issues of women's rights as human rights.

10. Engaging with international issues

We know that it is impossible to separate inter faith relations in our own countries from the effect of situations in other countries. International issues may have a very serious impact on minority faith groups, and at times of crisis in particular we should be ready to show solidarity with communities who may be feeling under threat. The situation of vulnerable minorities in other countries will often form a significant theme of dialogue, and our Churches will feel particular bonds of prayer and affection with Christian communities experiencing persecution. We need to make it clear, though, that it is unfair to hold faith communities in our countries to account for the actions of their co-religionists in other parts of the world.

11. Safeguarding the freedom to believe

The Christian commitment to love our neighbours and to seek justice for all leads us to affirm the importance of religious freedom in every society. Within our own countries, this is safeguarded by the European Convention on Human Rights: 'Everyone has the right to freedom of thought, conscience and religion; this right includes freedom to change his religion or belief and freedom, either alone or in community with others, and in public or private, to manifest his religion or belief, in worship, teaching, practice and observance.' (1950). We have a particular concern for the rights of minority communities in our own societies. We recognise the importance of the principle of equal legal protection for all our citizens; it is important that religious authority should not be abused to control or repress vulnerable individuals.

12. Changing religious commitment

Where the Spirit is at work, we rejoice that conversions of people to the way of Christ may happen. They must always be the free result of God's interaction with others, not of our own planning or persuasion. We recognise that inter faith encounter is powerful and unpredictable in the transforming effect it can have on people's lives. It may lead to people changing their religious commitment away from as well as towards Christianity. People of different faiths may also feel that inter faith encounter brings them closer to God within the framework of their own religious commitment. As Christians we need to be aware of the difficulties that can be faced by new believers, and our Churches need to be prepared to change themselves in order to welcome new members. Some converts can find the whole concept of inter faith dialogue difficult, especially if it involves them in encounter with their previous religion. Other converts may have a valuable personal contribution to make to inter faith understanding, and we think that their place in dialogue should be affirmed.

Agreement for Dialogue between the Anglican Communion and al-Azhar al-Sharif

We affirm the importance of building on the excellent relations between the Anglican Communion and the al-Azhar al-Sharif.

We acknowledge the brotherly relations between the Grand Sheikh of al-Azhar, Dr. Mohamed Sayed Tantawy and Dr. George Carey, the Archbishop of Canterbury and the President of the Anglican Communion.

We believe that friendship which overcomes religious, ethnic and national differences is a gift of the Creator in whom we all believe.

We recognise that both sides need to accept each other in a straightforward way so as to be able to convey the message of peace to the world.

We believe that direct dialogue results in restoration of the image of each in the eyes of the other.

Continuing from the visit of Dr. Carey to al-Azhar al-Sharif in October 1995 and the visit of Dr. Tantawy, the Grand Sheikh of al-Azhar al Sharif, to Lambeth Palace in 1997, and the return visit of Dr. Carey to al-Azhar al-Sharif in November 1999, and because of our common faith in God and our responsibility to witness against indifference to religion on the one hand and religious fanaticism on the other, we hope that we may contribute to international efforts to achieve justice, peace, and the welfare of all humanity, resourced by the positive experiences in our long history as Christians and Muslims living together both in Egypt and the United Kingdom and many other parts of the world.

In consequence of this, Dr. George Carey, the President of the Anglican Communion, has appointed the following members to the Interfaith Commission:

—The Revd. Canon Dr. Christopher Lamb
—The Rt. Revd. Mouneer Hanna Anis, Bishop in Egypt with North Africa
—The Rt. Revd. David Smith, Bishop of Bradford, UK

The members of the Permanent Committee of al-Azhar al-Sharif for Dialogue on Monotheistic Religions are
—Sheik Fawzy El Zefzaf, President
—Dr. Ali El Samman, Vice President
—Dr. Mustaffa Al Shukfah
—Sheikh Abu Agour
—Ambassador Nabil Badre

Representatives of both sides met in al-Azhar on 10 and 11 September 2001 and discussed the proposal for the dialogue between the Anglican Communion and al-Azhar al-Sharif with the hope of achieving the following goals:
- To encourage Anglicans to understand Islam and to encourage Muslims to understand the Christian faith.
- To share together in solving problems and conflicts that happen sometimes between Muslims and Christians in different parts of the world, and to encourage religious leaders to use their influence for the purpose of reconciliation and peace making.
- To work together against injustice and the abuse of human rights among different nationalities and to spread the good teaching of both Islam and Christianity.
- To encourage institutions on both sides to play a positive role in development.

To achieve these goals the following decisions were taken:

A Joint Committee will be established from both sides composed of a Chairman and two members from each side already appointed. It may be possible in the future to add new members but each side will inform the other about its membership.

This Joint Committee will meet at least once a year in Egypt and the United Kingdom alternately. Each delegation will cover its expenses for travel and accommodation and could meet more than once a year if necessary.

At the end of each meeting a Press Release will be issued. The text of the communiqué must be agreed by the Joint Committee before publication. No information about papers presented to the Joint Committee will be released outside it without the agreement of both sides.

Signed by:

The Most Revd. and Rt. Hon. Dr. George Carey
Archbishop of Canterbury

His Eminence Sheikh Mohamed Sayed Tantawy
Grand Imam of al-Azhar

The Rt. Revd. Mouneer Hanna Anis
Bishop in Egypt with North Africa

Sheikh Fawzy El Zefzaf
President, Permanent Committee of al-Azhar
for Dialogue with the Monotheistic Religious

The Rev. Canon Dr. Christopher Lamb

Dr. Ali El Samman
Vice President, Permanent Committee of al-Azhar
for Dialogue with the Monotheistic Religions

Communiqué for the Anglican/al-Azhar dialogue committee

14 September 2004

The Anglican-al-Azhar al-Sharif Joint Committee for dialogue met in Cairo 8–9 September 2004 and issued the following communiqué. On the Anglican side the dialogue was administered on behalf of the Archbishop of Canterbury's office by the Network for Inter faith Concerns of the Anglican Communion (NIFCON)

The Joint Committee, which is composed of a delegation from the Anglican Communion and the Permanent Committee of al-Azhar al-Sharif for Dialogue with the Monotheistic Religions, held its third annual meeting in Al-Azhar in Cairo on 23 and 24 Rajab 1425, which corresponds to 8 and 9 September 2004. This was held in accord with the agreement signed at Lambeth Palace on 30 January 2002 by the Archbishop of Canterbury and the Grand Imam of al-Azhar.

The theme of our dialogue in 2004 has been 'misconceptions'. The Joint Committee heard and discussed during these two days the following papers presented by Christian members of the Committee:
- Christianity and the West (Dr Yvonne Haddad)
- Christianity, the Crusades and western imperialism (The Rt Revd Dr Mouneer H. Anis)
- Christianity and power (The Revd Canon Dr Christopher Lamb)

The Joint Committee also heard and discussed the following papers presented by Muslim members of the Committee:
- Jihad in Islam (Dr Mustafa al-Shakaa)
- Human rights in Islam (Ambassador Nabil Badr)
- The position of women in Islam (Shaykh Fawzy el-Zefzaf)

Listening to these papers reminded us that Christians and Muslims frequently hold misconceptions about each other's beliefs and practice. Acknowledging the particular danger of generalizing about each other's faith, we commit ourselves to work seriously at counteracting inaccurate presentations of Christianity and Islam, according to the terms of the agreement signed in January 2002, which referred to the need to work towards 'the restoration of the image of each in the eyes of the other.'

It is important that religious leaders in our respective faiths have an informed understanding of the religion of 'the other'. With this in mind we were glad to hear about the time spent by Shaykh Fawzy el-Zefzaf at Ridley Hall Theological College, Cambridge. We look forward to developing a series of study exchanges between students at al-Azhar al-Sharif and those in training for the Anglican ministry, as being of significant value for our future relationships.

We were encouraged to hear reports of cooperative ventures between Christians and Muslims in both England and Egypt. We noted the decision by the Archbishop of Canterbury to help establish a national Forum in England to enable Christians and Muslims to discuss matters of common concern. We were also glad to learn about the sequence of 'Building Bridges' seminars chaired by the Archbishop which have brought together an international group of Christian and Muslim scholars.

Additionally, we appreciated the efforts by al-Azhar and the Episcopal Diocese of Egypt to give practical expression to our dialogue at the grass roots level, in a variety of ways.

Inevitably current political crises in some parts of our world received the attention of the Committee.

As regards the Holy Land, a place of particular significance to both Muslims and Christians, we expressed our regret that since we last met in September 2002 the deterioration in the situation there has increased the injustice, violence and hardship experienced by many.

In relation to Iraq, we expressed our regret for the continuing great suffering of its people and we affirmed the importance of respecting the right of the people of Iraq, with all their religious and ethnic diversity, to determine their own future.

We are aware of the enormity of the current suffering in Sudan. We call upon political and religious leaders to continue to encourage the government of Sudan and other concerned parties to ensure the security and welfare of all its citizens with impartiality.

We are conscious of meeting in the week after the dreadful events in Beslan, in southern Russia, which have been widely condemned by our religious leaders, and are deeply concerned about their potential repercussions.

We discussed several other parts of the world where the situation of vulnerable minorities, both Christian and Muslim, is of particular concern. We commend the efforts of both Muslims and Christians to work towards a greater awareness of the importance of human rights and of religious freedom. In this respect we particularly welcome the National Council on Human Rights which has been established in Egypt.

In the light of these and other such situations the importance of our continuing engagement with each other, as Christians and Muslims, is reinforced. We therefore look forward to deepening our dialogue at a further meeting in autumn 2005. We also anticipate with enthusiasm the visit of the Archbishop of Canterbury to Cairo, during which he will give a lecture at al-Azhar al-Sharif and lay the foundation stone at a new health centre in Sadat City, a project which expresses cooperation between Christians and Muslims.

In summary, we:

- Commit ourselves to use our influence in our respective religious communities to counteract misconceptions about Christianity or Islam, being aware particularly of the danger of generalization about either faith based on the actions or views of a minority.
- Commit ourselves to developing our joint study-exchange programme for students and religious leaders in training.
- Commend the initiatives undertaken by the Archbishop of Canterbury in the area of Christian-Muslim relations, especially plans for the establishment of a national Christian-Muslim Forum in England.
- Commend the cooperation of al-Azhar al-Sharif under the leadership of the Grand Imam and the Episcopal Diocese of Egypt.
- Welcome the setting up of the National Council for Human Rights in Egypt.
- Commend all international efforts to bring about security and a just peace for all in the Holy Land, particularly appreciating the role of the Egyptian government in this respect.
- Agree that the Joint Committee of Dialogue should meet again for a further dialogue in autumn 2005.

Anglican signatories
Canon Dr Christopher Lamb

The Most Revd Alexander Malik
The Moderator of the Church of Pakistan

The Rt Revd Dr Mouneer H. Anis
The Bishop in Egypt

Dr Yvonne Haddad
Muslim signatories

Shaykh Fawzy el Zefzaf
President of the Permanent Committee of Al-Azhar for Dialogue
on Monotheistic Religions

Dr Ali el-Samaan
Vice President of the Permanent Committee

Ambassador Nabil Badr

For more details please contact Clare Amos, Coordinator, NIFCON at:
clare.amos@anglicancommunion.org

A note on some current initiatives and developments linked to Christian-Muslim relations in England and Europe

1. The Christian-Muslim Forum

This is an initiative of the office of the Archbishop of Canterbury, who will be the patron of the Forum. The intention is to provide a meeting space at fairly senior level for representatives of the Christian and Muslim communities in England, primarily to discuss matters of mutual concern for the lives and well being of their respective communities. Work on the development of the Forum has been going on over the past 2–3 years, and it is intended that the Forum will be officially launched in early 2006. There will be eight Presidents formally invited onto the Forum by the Archbishop of Canterbury (four Christian and four Muslim), as well as specialist members in each of the Forum's six areas of concern. These six areas are: Community and public affairs, Education; Youth; International affairs; Media; Family. There will be a small paid secretariat.

2. 'Presence and Engagement'—The church's task in a multi faith society

This is an initiative of the Archbishops' Council of the Church of England, working through the Church of England's national inter faith advisor, and the Inter Faith Consultative Group. As a result of the national census 2001 information is now available about the specific religious demography of British cities, dioceses, parishes etc. The Presence and Engagement project is focusing on Church of England parishes where there are a substantial number of people of other faiths (than Christianity) living in the area. In many cases (though not all) these people of other faiths will be Muslims. The 'Presence and Engagement' project is seeking to explore what roles Anglican churches should play in such contexts. It has involved the systematic collection and analysis of a substantial amount of data, and has aimed to allow clergy and lay people worshipping and living in such contexts to express themselves, their vision, hopes and fears, in their own words. There will be a resolution presented to the July 2005 Synod of the Church of England developed out of the work of the 'Presence and Engagement' project which will be inviting the Church as a whole to affirm and support the work of parishes working in multi faith contexts.

3. Porvoo Guidelines

Members of ACC will of course be aware of the 'Porvoo agreement', by which a number of Anglican and Lutheran churches in North-west Europe have committed themselves to work together for more effective mission. As a result of the agreement members of Anglican churches who are specialists in a number of particular areas are meeting with their Lutheran counterparts to discuss matters of common concern. In December 2003 a number of Anglican clergy and laypeople who are involved with inter faith concerns met in Oslo, Norway, with Lutherans. The 'Guidelines for Inter Faith Encounter in the Churches of the Porvoo Communion' which is given as a separate document resulted from this meeting. It aims to help provide suggestions for inter faith encounter in the particular situations faced by Churches in North and West Europe.

Theological Education for the Anglican Communion

Monday 20 June 2005

A. Introduction

The presentation of TEAC—the Anglican Communion Theological Education Working Party—to ACC-13 was offered collaboratively by a small group of TEAC members: Canon Robert Paterson of the Church in Wales and Vice-Chair of TEAC; Ms Sue Parks, Lambeth Conference Manager and Steering Group member; Canon Mwita Akiri, of the Church of Tanzania and member of the Deacons and Licensed Lay Minsters Group; Mrs Pauline Makoni, of the Province of Central Africa and (then) Convenor of the Deacons and Licensed Lay Ministers Group; Mrs Clare Amos, Secretary to the Working Party. Archbishop Rowan Williams, who has been closely involved with the work of TEAC since its inception, also spoke as part of the presentation.

After beginning with the well-known prayer of St Augustine, requesting God for the grace of knowing him that might also love and serve him, the presentation begin with a quick-fire exchange between Pauline Makoni and Robert Paterson. Humorous and light-hearted in style, it also had a serious purpose—to challenge the often-expressed view that theological education is a luxury—a kind of optional extra—for the Church. Pauline and Robert also reminded the members of ACC-13 that they had received a document entitled 'Rationale for the work of TEAC' had been sent out in advance of the meeting (see p. 619, near the end of this report).

This led into a reflection from Archbishop Rowan who explored with characteristic profoundity—and simplicity—the positive reasons for theological education and for TEAC.

B. Reflection by the Archbishop of Canterbury

"No condemnation now I dread; Jesus and all in Him is mine; Alive in Him, my living head and clothed in righteousness divine. Bold I approach the eternal throne and claim the crown, through Christ my own." (Wesley)

Now that's theology and that's the theology most of us are aware of, that's how we mostly learn our theology. "Ere he raised the lofty mountains, formed the sea or built the sky, love eternal free and boundless forced the

Lord of life to die. Lifted up the Prince of Princes on the throne of Calvary" and that's theology.

Theology is that language which is drawn out of us, I'm almost tempted to say squeezed out of us, by the pressure, the intense reality of the new world in which we live as Christian believers. We want to find words that are, if not adequate, at least not completely wrong in order to express that world into which we have been brought.

We are exploring it, we are making some sense of it, trying to find our way and it seems to me that one of the things we have often lost in talking about theology is that sense of theology as finding a way. Theology tells us what sort of God it is we have to deal with. Theology tells us what sort of beings human beings are.

It tells us in one sense absolutely nothing but the Gospel story. But it's not so much that theology is a kind of necessary extra stage to the Gospels, it's that the Gospel overflows in theology, so that theology is perhaps first and foremost a celebration. A celebration which helps us find a way, or as you might put, it a truth that leads us into a life, a way which is specified by the gift of the person we believe in. So that's why I think we ought to be excited about theology and why good theology happens when Christians are excited about where they find themselves. About the landscape of the new creation. And theology becomes bad and stales, boring and unhelpful when we've forgotten the new world. When we are somehow trundling along with all our old ideas, our old habits, not only of thinking but of relationship with each other. Good theology in other words, comes out of let's call it conversion, that living vivid sense of a new reality. So in fact, we are doing it quite a lot of the time. We are certainly doing it when we sing hymns, as I said a few minutes ago, that's where most of us learn it, absorb it. We are doing it in bible study groups, we are doing it in catechesis, on a small scale, we are doing it when we teach our children and, perhaps even more importantly, we are doing it as our children teach us.

But how, in any church, do we create a situation where excellence in theology is something which is visibly cared about, where it's obvious that we are so profoundly committed to exploring and understanding the new world, that we are prepared to invest time and resource and imagination, energy and planning in this? And that is the challenge which this group is about.

Anglicans have had a very long and a very rich tradition of encouraging in the best sense intellectual celebration. Anglican theology has never gone in very much for producing great big summaries of doctrine, but it has always taken the human mind very seriously and expected Christians to be joyfully intelligent about their faith. That's why Anglicanism has a great heritage of poetry and hymnody, not only in English or, indeed, in Welsh, but in many other languages as well and that's the locus of theology.

How do we work then to make for a situation of excellence? Where we feel confident that we are working as hard as we can, as creatively as we can, to share the language of the new world. If we fail to do this, there's a danger that on the one hand theology becomes just the preserve of just that elite minority, whether clerical or lay, that we were hearing about a few minutes ago. On the one had, it gets hived off into specialist institutions and that's about it. Or, on the other hand, we become content with a Christian faith which is reactive, emotional, doesn't stretch the mind and doesn't regard the mind as something to be converted and transfigured. We reduce theology just to devotional noises.

In something I wrote recently, I said, "It's the polarity, if you like, between the divinity school, especially in the American model, the professional school where things are dealt with in a professional way and on the other extreme the Bible college where you learn about the faith but somehow don't connect it, explore it, historically and prayerfully in the full way that you might."

In between, I believe there really is a task for theology, true, mind stretching, heart stretching theology and of course for us as Anglicans, in some important degree, children of the Reformation, that is an activity absolutely grounded in the scriptures which are our common language. The scriptures which are the charter of our new life, which are in themselves, a map of the new country. Understanding how to use them neither as historical deposit, nor as a simple rule book, but as a treasury of God's gift in stretching our minds and hearts, that has to be of the greatest importance for us. There is no way of doing theology without scriptural authority, without scriptural, what shall I say, criteria at the very heart of it. No way at all. Because this and this alone is where we meet the newness of the new world. But we meet it as we are, hearts, minds, imaginations all at work and we seek, we hope, to make the activity of its exploration something which will genuinely give life.

So, finally, I haven't tried to answer all the questions that Pauline and Robert have put before us, but while it's certainly true that theology sometimes does seem to cause our division, promote elitism and all the rest of it, I would say when theology causes division, unnecessary division, it's bad theology, it doesn't arise out of the common celebration of the new world. Something's wrong if theology is digging ditches and where theology creates an elite, then theology is not dealing seriously with the dignity of all the baptized. Just as Moses said "Would that all the Lord's people were prophets," I think I'd be inclined to say "Would that all the Lord's people were theologians." That means, I wish that every baptised believer felt that sense of urgent delight about exploring and communicating the gift of God, which showed itself in hymns like the one I quoted in the beginning.

And, if what matters in the post-modern world as the human search for spirituality and truth is all about experience, well, the sad thing of course is that we are all completely imprisoned in the world we think we know and we are not allowing any of the robustness and the depth of truth to break in and make a difference and that's very sad. Theology proclaims not a smaller world but a larger one. A world that we are struggling to get our minds and hearts into and if we reduce it to experience or to spirituality, we shrink it to the dimension of what's in our heads or our hearts already.

And, finally, people are crying out for the story of the Gospel so they are, so they should be and we ought to be responding. But with every way in which we re-tell the story of the Gospel, we do theology and that means, on the other side of it, that of course the theological enterprise always has to be tested by the question "Is this the story of the Gospel, what's Good News about this, what's the Good News of Jesus Christ in this?" Now, if in our Anglican Communion, we can promote that kind of imagination, that kind of telling the story of the Gospel, then I think our church will be a vital, living, creative Church, the kind of Church that God has given us the capacity to be.

C. TEAC and the Seven (!) Marks of Mission

Canon Mwita Akiri and Ms Sue Parks then helped ACC to focus on the key link between theological education and mission. Their presentation was originally given in a lively dialogue format, which has now been adapted to fit the style of this written report.

A fundamental principle of the work of TEAC—the Anglican Communion theological education working party—is that concern for God's mission and good theological education belong together. Each needs the other.

Theological education is emphatically not a diversion from 'what really matters'—God's mission to a world at war, hungry, homeless and in pain. Nor is theological education, properly understood and taken seriously, a cause of elitism or even division in the Church. As members of TEAC we believe that in working to improve theological education throughout the Anglican Communion we will be helping to foster mission throughout our Churches.

So as part of the TEAC's presentation to ACC-13 Sue Parks and Mwita Akiri took as a framework the 'marks of mission' of the Anglican Communion and explored how the work that TEAC is doing links in to each of these marks.

But they had news for the members of ACC-13. The normal assumption is that there are five marks of mission. First expressed at ACC-6 back in 1984, and now widely adopted by many other Christians as well, they are sometimes regarded as a gift of the Anglican Communion to the Christian Church as a whole.

The mission of the church is the mission of God
- To proclaim the Good News of the Kingdom
- To teach, baptize and nurture new believers
- To respond to human need by loving service
- To seek to transform unjust structures of society
- To strive to safeguard the integrity of creation and sustain and renew the life of the earth.

However, TEAC's exploration of mission and theological education at ACC-13 not only looked at these 'five marks', but reflected on two others as well. They drew upon the report of MISSIO, the Anglican Communion's Mission Commission, which finished its work in 1999 and published its findings in a book called *Anglicans in Mission: A Transforming Journey*.

The members of MISSIO commended the five marks of mission as a useful checklist for churches as they move to take more seriously the demands of mission. But they went on to make some additional points—firstly that an important feature of Anglicanism is our belief that worship is central to our common life. However, worship is not something that we do alongside our witness to the good news—worship is itself a witness to the world. It is a sign that all of life is holy—and that hope and meaning can be found in offering ourselves to God. In fact our liturgical life is a vital dimension of our mission calling. So this TEAC presentation suggested that alongside the five 'traditional' marks of mission we should add the words, 'To worship and celebrate the grace of God'—as a mark of our mission as Anglican Christians.

Additionally the MISSIO report challenged people to realise that our task is not simply to 'do' mission but to be a people in mission: learning to allow every dimension of church life to be shaped and directed by our identity as a sign, foretaste and instrument of God's reign in Christ. Our understanding of mission needs to make that clear. So TEAC suggested that alongside the usual five marks we should also add the words, 'To live as one, holy, catholic and apostolic Church.'

The members of MISSIO also commented that what is often identified as the first mark of mission—to proclaim the good news of the Kingdom—is really a summary of what mission is all about, rather than simply the first of several distinct activities. It is the key statement about everything we do in mission.

Taking each of these in turn the presenters offered some pointers as to how theological education—and the vision and work of the working group—linked in to each of these marks of mission and how good theological education helps to foster the mission of God, which is the mission of Christ and his Church. This is what they suggested:

1. To proclaim the good news of the Kingdom

We believe that all mature Christians—not simply those who are called to special ministries in the church—need to be able to give a reasoned account of the hope which is in them—why it is that the gospel is good news for them—and for our world. We believe that this is particularly important when—as in many parts of our world—the shifting intellectual, political, social and religious currents mean that the Christian faith needs to be able to be expressed in a way that is intellectually and spiritually credible, and in a form which can challenge those who do not call themselves Christians to think seriously about our faith. The bottom line of the work of TEAC is that we are aiming that Anglican Christians, both lay people and clergy, should be able to give a coherent and reasoned testimony to what they believe.

2. To teach, baptize and nurture new believers

These are roles that all clergy and lay ministers need to be properly prepared to fulfil. We believe that to equip them to carry out such a task, appropriately contextual theological education and training is vital. This needs to be education and training which is concerned both with content, what needs to be learned or taught—and with helping clergy and lay ministers to become better teachers themselves. Jesus Christ has been described as the greatest teacher who ever lived—the task of theological education must include encouraging Christian ministers to model themselves on him.

3. To respond to human need by loving service

All too often the ministry of 'service' is seen as secondary to that of preaching the word. Yet if we look at the pattern of the church as it is expressed in the Book of Acts we find that it is frequently through the fact that the early Christians were willing to serve others that the gospel crossed geographical, religious and racial boundaries. It is important that in our theological education a proper consideration of the importance of service—*diakonia*—is offered. It is not an optional 'add on.' TEAC's Deacons and Lay ministers sub-group is seeking to ensure this—not least by the fact that it is addressing the question as to what is the appropriate education and training for those who feel themselves called to long term ministry as deacons.

4. To seek to transform unjust structures of society

This mark of mission reminds us quite strongly of the nature of the world in which Christians need to carry out God's mission. One of the features of the Anglican Church has been that it seeks to relate to the institutions of secular society—the political, legal, cultural world in which it lives. Sometimes it will necessarily challenge such institutions—but it is characteristic of our Anglican tradition that it does seek to challenge them—rather than to ignore them or run away from them. This can and should happen in many strands of the church's life—but perhaps it is a particular role for bishops, who are in a special way the public face of the Church. There are a number of great Anglican bishops who are honoured for their challenge to unjust structures of society and the work they have done to help transform them. Sometimes it has been very costly work indeed. We believe that in this area, as well as a number of others, bishops need training for the distinctive tasks that fall upon them as bishops—and the TEAC Bishops subgroup is making recommendations in this area.

5. To strive to safeguard the integrity of creation and sustain and renew the life of the earth

It has only been in recent years that we have become fully aware that how we care for the earth is linked intrinsically to God's mission. Yet the first covenant between God and humanity, the rainbow covenant, implies that concern for the world and creation in which we have been set is a task God has allotted to human beings—it is written into the fabric of the relationship between God and ourselves. We believe that an important task of theological education is to help us build bridges between the world as it is and the world as God wants it to be. We need special gifts, tools and skills to enable us to do this—to make sense of our stewardship at both the global and local levels.

And those two additional marks of mission:

6. To worship and celebrate the grace of God

In our Anglican history our practice of Common Prayer has helped to form us as a Church. As Archbishop Rowan said when on one occasion he was addressing the members of TEAC, through worship we as Anglicans are helped to 'inhabit our doctrine'. And given this importance of worship and celebration the members of TEAC are very much aware that training—both in the practical conduct of worship and exploring its meaning—is an essential element of theological education. This is a particular concern of a sub-group—the Anglican Way group—which has been entrusted with reflecting on the specifically Anglican components of theological education.

7. To live as one holy, catholic and apostolic church

That, too, is a mark of mission. It may be a challenging thing to be suggesting at this point in the life and history of our Communion. But if we are to live out this mark of mission in our common life we certainly believe that it will only be possible if we take with absolute seriousness the need to equip all our people, bishops, clergy and lay people theologically.

The splendid words of the Church of Sudan well express our vision:

'We affirm that all Christians are called to "learn Christ" and that theological education is one way of describing the obligation that discipleship imposes on every member of the Body. The Church should aim to provide opportunities for all its members to study the wisdom and truth of Christ in relation to their own culture, vocation, interest and capacity. Provision of theological education should therefore be multi-layered and address the needs of the whole people of God.'

At the end of this part of the presentation there was the opportunity for members of ACC-13 to 'buzz' and gather ideas to feed back to the Steering Group of TEAC.

D. What is TEAC doing?

Clare Amos, the Secretary to the Working Party, gave an overview of the work on TEAC to date, as follows:

It is my privilege to tell you something about what TEAC has been doing practically over the last two years and what it is intending to do in the couple of years or so ahead. Our remit is to have practical proposals available to feed into the discussions at the Lambeth Conference in 2008. It's good—and important—to be working to such a specific timescale.

The timeline that you have received of TEAC's work in your pre-meeting papers tells something of the story of the origin of TEAC. It stems from an initiative by the Anglican Primates around the turn of the millennium. This was given further impetus when Archbishop Rowan signalled that theological education would be a key priority of his archepiscopate. A Steering Group worked from late 2002 to devise a structure that would enable a substantial sized number of people representing most of the Provinces of the Communion to work together over the next few years—largely working by e-mail, although with occasional residential meetings. The structure that was developed has already been referred to—there are five what we call 'Target Groups'. One of these is looking at how theological education for the laity can be fostered. How we can improve what we call the general theological literacy of lay people—their mature understanding of their faith. All too often in the past the assumption has been that when people are confirmed they have learned all they need to know about the Christian faith. TEAC is aiming to encourage a process of continuing and ongoing Christian education for lay people—whether or not they are called to any specific ministry, lay or ordained within the church.

The second Target group is looking at theological education for people who are training either for lay ministries—such as the ministry of Catechist, Reader or Evangelist, or who are training to be what we have called 'vocational' or permanent deacons, in other words deacons who are not intending to seek ordination to the priesthood. It is quite a wide remit, and the connections between the different ministries with which the group is dealing has been questioned—not least by some of the group members—but they have been grouped together partly because they are all ministries for which a bishop's authorisation is necessary and for which, on the whole, people normally train for on a part time basis.

The third Target Group is looking into the question of theological education for those training for the priesthood. Its focus is much clearer than that of the two groups I mentioned previously—but it does its work in the awareness that the standard of theological training for those called to be priests is very variable and that the resources available are also uneven.

The Fourth Target group is looking in to the question of training for bishops—it has only fairly recently been recognised in the Church that those chosen as bishops have specific training needs to enable them to tackle the new wider ministry to which they have been called. Bishop Ian Ernest of the Indian Ocean who is the Convenor of that group is also a member of the Design Group for Lambeth 2008—and one of the useful results of that is that he will be able to input some of the suggestions from that group into the planning process for the Lambeth Conference.

There is also a fifth Target Group—the Anglican Way group, which is slightly different to the others. The best way to describe it might be to ask you to think of a grid—the four Target Groups I have mentioned so far can be thought of as vertical columns in the grid, and the Anglican Way group is a bit like a horizontal bar which runs across them all. It is asking what is or should be the specific Anglican component in the training for the various ministries of the Church or for Anglican laity. Perhaps it is also asking how that 'Anglican' component can—or should—be delivered. For example can you simply teach 'the Anglican Way' as a kind of intellectual activity, or is it also something that one learns in the deepest sense through praying or worshipping as Anglican Christians?

It is also intended that there will shortly be a further Target Group formed, which is provisionally referred to as the Resources group. This, like the Anglican Way Group, will be another horizontal bar running across the vertical columns of the other groups. Its brief will be to look into the question of specific resources that might be needed and which TEAC directly or indirectly could help to provide. Would a CD-ROM, for example, be a useful resource? If so, containing what material? These are the kind of questions that the Resources group will be looking in to.

Of course it's not quite all as neat and tidy as what I have said might imply. I have already alluded to the fact that one of the Target Groups covers a particularly wide range of ministries. But in reality of course the issues that we are dealing with often overlap a number of the groups—for example the question of language issues, the needs of the Francophone Anglican community, or that of whether there should be training for spouses are concerns that overlap a number of the groups. Then there is of course the way that good theological education should effectively help those training for certain ministries—such as the priesthood or episcopate—to become better theological educators of others. For example is the issue of how to improve the standard of preaching throughout and around the Anglican Communion a question for the Priests Target Group to discuss—because priests deliver sermons—or is it a question for the Laity group to look into, because listening to sermons is one of the primary practical means by which lay people can grow in the understanding of their faith? I could give other examples.

At a meeting in November 2003, which was just after I started working for TEAC one day a week, the Steering Group held a residential meeting with the Convenors of each of the Groups and the entirety of the Anglican Way Group. The main purpose of our meeting was to write briefs for each of the Target Groups—which we succeeded in doing, and you can find these briefs set out on TEAC's website, www.anglicancommunion.org/teac. In writing these briefs we took seriously the comments we had received from the Anglican Primates who had been asked earlier in the year what they felt the prime needs and concerns were regarding theological education in each of their Provinces. As you can see if you look at the briefs it is not always easy to separate out reflection on theological education needs from the nature of a specific ministry—in asking what are the theological training needs of a bishop, for instance, one inevitably finds oneself touching on what Anglicans understand the nature of episcopate to be.

Since November 2003 the Target Groups of TEAC have been working along the lines suggested in each of their briefs—with a key moment for us being last June when the entire membership of TEAC met in Bristol, England, for five days. We have one more full residential meeting planned and budgeted for—next January when we will be meeting in South Africa, which will, among other things, give us the opportunity to meet with representatives of ANITEPAM—the Association for Institutions of Anglican Theological Education in Africa. Next month, July 2005, the Steering Group and representatives of each of the Target Groups will be holding an important meeting near Oxford in England. The main task of the meeting will be on the one hand to prepare for South Africa, and on the other hand to hone and focus the work of each of the Target Groups bearing in mind that 2008—by which time TEAC has to finish its work is moving steadily closer. What I think each of the groups will be likely to be asked to address as a result of our Oxford meeting is 'what are the skills, knowledge, disposition that an appropriately theologically educated representative of each ministry or a lay person should possess'. In education jargon this is known as outcomes-based education. Robert Paterson will, in a few minutes time, be talking about such goals. I think our Oxford meeting will also be setting up the Resources Group I referred to above—and giving it its task to accomplish. It has already been good to have some conversations about potential Resources issues with people at this gathering and I look forward to having further conversations in the days ahead.

There are a couple of specific projects that the Anglican Way Group has already undertaken which I would like to draw your attention to. In itself the brief that the Anglican Way drew up, which contains a definition of what it understands the Anglican Way to be, is a significant and important document. In our covering letter that went out with the pre-meeting papers we referred to the fact that a questionnaire was sent last year to all theological education institutions in the Anglican Communion, as well as Primates, Provincial Offices, and bodies such as other Anglican Commissions and Networks. This mentioned the characteristics of the Anglican Way as defined in the group's brief and then asked questions such as 'What are the characteristics of Anglicanism which were particularly relevant today and especially important in your local context? What are the global characteristics of Anglicanism? What elements of the Anglican Way were ignored or needed to be better developed locally? What resources about the Anglican Way were already available to them and what would be useful?'

By the usual standards by which such things are measured we had a substantial response to this questionnaire, and a provisional report on the findings was sent to the Primates meeting last February. The responses we received were both affirming—with people wanting to contribute positively to what is clearly being seen as an important initiative — but also challenging-because we who are involved with TEAC feel an obligation to live up to the hopes that so many members of the Anglican Communion around the world. I quote the following paragraph from the report on the questionnaire I wrote for the Primates meeting. It gives a good flavour of the kind of answers received:

'A question was asked about the global characteristics of Anglicanism. (In response): The importance of the 'Instruments of Unity' and particularly the office of the Archbishop of Canterbury was a thread that ran through responses. The 'sharing of a common based liturgy to create a sense of global belonging' was specifically mentioned, and the possibility the Communion offered for a 'Christlike critique of global culture.' Another key positive of the Anglican Communion was its potential for building bridges of understanding and seeking reconciliation across cultures and continents. The phrase a 'collegiality between worlds' was particularly striking. The 'mistrust of clericalism' and the need for a system of balances and checks between bishops, clergy and people and the importance of the synodical structure was also affirmed. Several responses also referred to the commitment of the Anglican Church to helping the spiritual development of children in the church, and the potential for Anglicans to build bridges to other faith communities. One response argued that the notion of 'Anglicanism' should be resisted and that 'Anglican Christianity is identified by the opportunity it offers for a church of the people to emerge in each context, usually bounded by national boundaries.'

If anyone wishes to see the report on the questionnaire in its entirety I would be very glad to make copies available for them.

The same Target group has also worked on a list of key texts about the 'Anglican Way' which it believes should be available in the libraries of all theological institutions where people are training for Anglican ministry. That list is available on TEAC's website—as are a number of other resource related suggestions. As my working time allows I am trying to 'grow' that side of our website. In view of the interest which has already been expressed in this 'Anglican Way' booklist we are hoping that ways may be found to begin to finance the donation of these key texts to theological institutions where they are not currently available.

I conclude by reiterating the word 'privilege', with which I began. It is a privilege to work for TEAC. I myself have been engaged with various forms of theological education over more than 20 years and I am convinced of its importance. The story of the encounter between Jesus and the woman at the well of Samaria is a biblical story that stands at the heart of my vision for theological education. As the dialogue between Jesus and the woman made clear, in learning more about our faith intellectually and spiritually we can discover the 'living water' that can change our world. I don't think that I am the only member of the Anglican Communion who believes this. I find it remarkable that whenever TEAC sends out a press release—or for example distributes that questionnaire—I find myself literally deluged with expressions of good will for our work from Anglicans all around the globe. A very few of these were shared in the note, 'What are they saying about theological education', which we sent out with the preliminary papers. It is gratifying to feel that the work which TEAC is undertaking is seen as such a good news story in the life of the Anglican Communion. It is a privilege to be able to contribute to it.

E. What? and Why? and How?

Beginning to draw the presentation to a close Robert Paterson, TEAC's Vice-Chair, drew out some central threads:

TEAC is at the stage where a great deal of basic preparation of the ground has been done. Now we are beginning to look for possible outcomes of our work. The convenors of our five Target Groups are hoping and praying for such outcomes as:

- resources to make better lay education widely available, recognising people's varying access to education and the variety of languages we speak;
- fully appreciating the complementary ministries of lay and ordained, and training provided in a way which is appropriate to the local context;
- priests who value *koinonia* (fellowship/communion) locally and universally, calling the Church to worship and to engage with God's word;
- bishops who understand their role and responsibility as teachers and overseers in the community of faith serving the mission of God; and
- a warmer appreciation of who we are as Anglican Christians, how we worship, read the Bible and witness together, honouring unity and respecting diversity.

So, we are partly in the business of what to deliver in theological education.

But we are also going to move on to set principles—the why of theological education. All the good work any of us can do can so easily be lost if someone in authority somewhere says, "That's not for us!" or "We can't do it that way!" So, in addition, TEAC is also going to set its mind to some basic principles for theological education, and set some basic standards so that there may be, in Archbishop Rowan's words, "an even spread of quality across the Communion".

And, finally, we will also soon move on to answering the how question; in particular, looking at the provision of resources for theological education worldwide.

Rationale for the work of TEAC

The mission of God has been committed to the servant people of God in Christ. It is the privilege and duty of Christian leaders to provide for the equipping of the Church for this task. Central to equipping Christians for God's mission is education in the Holy Scriptures, in the teaching of the Church and in practical application of that education.

In the face of the countless tragedies facing the world today, the Christian commitment to God and his purposes for humanity is vital to being a reflective disciple. Theology is not simply an exercise for academics but the attempt by all Christian people to make sense of all God has given and revealed to us, in other people, in the world, in our place and time, in the Bible and, supremely, in our Lord Jesus Christ. It is the attempt to make connections between our daily life and the Christian experience of God, faith and life in the Spirit. It is the attempt to understand why trust in the Creator, Redeemer and Sanctifier makes a difference, and, in that knowledge, to be willing and eager to share God's love with others.

In many places, existing, new and renewed ventures in theological education are bearing fruit, and these examples, together with the principles on which they are based, deserve to be made more widely known.

However, there are identifiable but not insurmountable difficulties facing the Anglican Communion in the area of theological education. The degree to which each may or may not be a problem varies from place to place. The difficulties may simply be defined as:

- a general lack of theological literacy—a challenge to spiritual life and mission in increasingly secular societies and a serious hindrance to Christians in telling the gospel story and making connections between faith and life;
- inadequate engagement with contemporary thinking, culture and society—a challenge of selecting and preparing a new generation to share Christ in a world of apparently competing faiths, secularism and postmodernism;
- some confusion about the particular callings of those involved in the Church's public ministry—a challenge in particular of practising *diakonia* in a range of ministries;
- inadequately or inappropriately trained priests—a challenge of relating theological and biblical understandings to practical situations in preaching, pastoral care, evangelism and ethics, and of refreshing theology and practice;
- inappropriate practice of the particular ministry of a bishop in changing contexts—a challenge of understanding the functions of apostle-missioner, teacher, encourager, team-leader, manager, pastor, disciplinarian, public figure, example and colleague; and
- a weak or selective commitment to Christians (even of Anglicans) of other traditions and perspectives—a challenge of appreciating the positive ethos of Anglicanism and what it can contribute to and learn from others in the Christian way.

F. Conclusion

The presentation concluded with the reading by Archbishop Rowan of Ephesians 4.11–16, a text that the members of TEAC believe undergirds their work, and by the sharing of TEAC's own prayer (see below), written for the group by one of its members the Revd Colleen O'Reilly. TEAC is committed to taking seriously the needs of the Communion for good quality theological education in languages other than English and as an expression of this commitment, the biblical passage and prayer were displayed in Spanish, French and Swahili, while being read in English.

TEAC Prayer

Christ our Teacher,
you alone are the way, the truth and the life:
so lead the Theological Education group and this Council in our work,
building trust and understanding,
that, in sharing our stories, vision and resources,
all your people may grow in faith
and your whole Church built up in love;
in the power of the Holy Spirit
and to the glory of the Father.
Amen.

Christ notre Maître,
toi seul es le chemin, la vérité et la vie:
veuille conduire le travail du groupe 'Formation Théologique' et de ce
  Conseil,
approfondissant entre nous la confiance et la comprehension,
afin que, en partageant nos histoires, notre vision et nos ressources,
tout ton peuple croisse dans la foi
et que ton Eglise tout entière s'édifie dans l'amour;
dans la puissance de l'Esprit Saint
et a la gloire du Père.
Amen.

Bwana wetu Yesu Kristo,
Wewe ndiwe Mwalimu wetu,
Njia yetu,
Ukweli wetu
Na Uhai wetu.
Uongoze kikundi cha Elimu ya Kitheolojia.
Ukijenge juu ya msingi wa hekima na uaminifu.

Usaidie tushirikiane pamoja habari zetu, mafunuo yetu na uwezo wetu
Ili watu wako wote waaminifu waongezwe katika imani,
na kanisa lako lote lijengwe imara katika upendo.
Tunaomba mambo hayo yote katika nguvu ya Roho Mtakatifu,
Kwa utukufu wa Mungu Baba.
Amen.

Cristo maestro nuestro,
tú sólo eres el camino, la verdad y la vida:
rogamos que de tal manera guies al grupo de Educación Teológica
   y a este consejo en nuestro trabajo: fomentándo confianza y com-
   prensión mútua,
que compartiendo nuestras historias,
visión y recursos,
todo tu pueblo pueda
crecer en fe y tu Iglesia sea fortalecida en el amor;
en el poder del
Espíritu Santo y para gloria del Padre.
Amen.

Kanuga 2001
First TE Working Party set up

Canterbury 2002
Second TE Working Party (TEAC) set up

Gramado May 2003 Primates consulted on TE

● *Clare Amos appointed 09.03*
November 2003 Target Group Briefs finalised

June 2004 Full TEAC with Target Groups

February 2005 Report to Primates

July 2005 TEAC

*Autumn 2005 Theological Educators
at ISC Canterbury*

January 2006 Full TEAC with Target Groups

2008 Lambeth Conference

TEAC Time-line

FINANCIAL
REPORTS

Report of Financial and Administration Committee

21 June 2005

2003 and 2004 Accounts

These Accounts have been approved by both the Standing Committee and the Auditors and are laid before the meeting.

The audited Accounts for these two years are set out in the format required by the legislation governing charities registered in the United Kingdom. Copies of these detailed Accounts are available on request. If you would like a copy of these Accounts which run to over 20 pages for each year, please ask Andrew Franklin.

We changed our year-end close from 30th September to 31st December in 2003. The 2003 Accounts cover a fifteen-month period.

This paper presents the core budget figures in an abbreviated and simplified form.

Summary of Results

We have struggled with the weakness of the dollar against the sterling pound (17% depreciation over the two years) and this has substantially affected our provincial contributions from provinces and from Compass Rose Society.

A provision was made in 2003 Accounts of £189,274 in respect of a surrendered lease at Partnership House which had three years to run. This has severely depleted General Reserves which stood at only £44,010 at 31st December 2004.

Because reserves are low, it has been difficult to make further contributions to assist in the funding of the cost of Lambeth Conference in 2008. No contribution at all was made in 2004.

The contributions from provinces are fully utilised amid ever increasing demands made on the core budget. For example it cost £68,000 out of the Inter Church Conversations budget to fund the three meetings of the Lambeth Commission that produced the Windsor Report.

Thanks are due to the Compass Rose Society for their assistance in funding the core budget.

2005 Forecast

This shows that ACC should just cover its core budget expenditure without being able to give anything to Lambeth Conference 2008. I have attached a bar chart showing our total projected expenditure for 2005.

The total cost of running ACC activities is over STG £1.6 million because it should be noted that UN Observer's Office, Telecommunications and Web Costs and the costs of the Networks (e.g., TEAC, NIFCON, and Family Network) are funded outside the core budget. Thanks are due here to UN Advisory Council, Trinity Church Wall Street and others for their assistance in funding these non core activities where the provincial contributions cannot stretch.

Cash Position

The cash position shows that at the end of December 2004, cash borrowed of £215,835 from Lambeth Conference Fund, and £500,000 borrowed from Hong Kong province remains to be repaid. This money has been used to fund the alteration of our new premises at St Andrew's House.

Contributions

Details of Contributions requested and received are attached to this presentation.

Budgets

The forecasts for 2006, 2007, and 2008 are the subject of a separate presentation later in the meeting.

Andrew Franklin
Finance Director

Anglican Consultative Council

Budgets 2005-2008	2005 STG £	2006 STG £	2007 STG £	2008 STG £
INCOME				
Contributions from Member Churches	1,109,400	1,220,800	1,269,600	1,320,300
Compass Rose Society Contribution	160,000	166,000	172,000	178,000
Other Income	52,000	52,000	52,000	52,000
Total	**1,321,400**	**1,438,800**	**1,493,600**	**1,550,300**
EXPENDITURE				
Employment Costs	748,400	790,000	818,000	847,000
UN Observer's Office - contribution to costs	25,000	25,000	25,000	25,000
Meetings Council and Standing Comm	118,000	120,000	120,000	120,000
Primates	25,000	25,000	25,000	25,000
Lambeth Conference				
Inter Church Conversations	100,000	100,000	100,000	100,000
IASCOME	20,000	25,000	25,000	25,000
Panel of Reference		30,000	30,000	30,000
Listening Process		45,000	45,000	45,000
Travel and Subsistence	39,800	41,500	43,200	45,000
Office Expenses	64,800	67,000	69,400	71,800
House Expenses	39,000	40,600	42,300	44,000
Anglican World & Publications	77,000	77,000	77,000	77,000
Audit & Professional	20,500	20,500	21,000	21,500
Depreciation	27,000	27,000	27,000	27,000
TOTAL EXPENDITURE	**1,304,500**	**1,433,600**	**1,467,900**	**1,503,300**
SURPLUS/(DEFICIT)	£16,900	£5,200	£25,700	£47,000
ACC Expenditure Not in Core Budget				
UN Observer Office	145,000			
Telecomms	71,000			
Networks	84,000			

Anglican Consultative Council
Results /Forecast for 2003–2005

	2002/3 (15 Months) Budget £	Variance £	Actual Total £	2004 Budget £	Variance £	Revised Forecast £	2005 Original Budget £	Variance £	Revised Forecast £
INCOME									
Contributions from Member Churches	1,381,656	(3,997)	1,377,659	1,050,206	(2,477)	1,047,729	1,100,600	8,800	1,109,400
Compass Rose Society Contribution	180,000	6,023	186,023	150,000	(1,540)	148,460	175,000	(15,000)	160,000
Other Income	34,597	3,183	37,780	44,000	16,137	60,137	52,000	-0	52,000
Total	**1,596,253**	**5,209**	**1,601,462**	**1,244,206**	**12,120**	**1,256,326**	**1,327,600**	**(6,200)**	**1,321,400**
EXPENDITURE									
Employment Costs	782,400	22,242	760,158	720,000	8,139	711,861	780,900	32,500	748,400
UN Observer's Office - contribution to costs	31,250	(30,000)	61,250	(5,000)	-0	(5,000)	25,000	-0	25,000
Meetings Council and Standing Comm	156,250	31,250	125,000	118,000	-0	118,000	118,000	-0	118,000
Primates	31,250	-0	31,250	25,000	-0	25,000	25,000	-0	25,000
Lambeth Conference	138,000	69,000	69,000	-0	-0	-0	-0	-0	-0
Inter Church Conversations	84,485	-0	84,485	90,000	(10,000)	100,000	90,000	(10,000)	100,000
IASCOME	54,375	15,875	38,500	25,000	5,000	20,000	25,000	5,000	20,000
Travel and Subsistence	79,350	(8,560)	87,910	74,000	3,524	70,476	67,900	28,100	39,800
Office Expenses	85,500	2,601	82,899	68,250	(4,413)	72,663	74,725	9,925	64,800
House Expenses	136,925	5,682	131,243	30,300	(1,384)	31,684	38,500	(500)	39,000
Anglican World & Publications	104,000	(4,949)	108,949	78,000	(387)	78,387	82,000	5,000	77,000
Audit & Professional	20,000	(1,727)	21,727	18,000	(2,055)	20,055	17,500	(3,000)	20,500
Depreciation	12,000	(5,317)	17,317	26,000	(2,179)	28,179	26,000	(1,000)	27,000
Provision for Partnership House Lease	-0	(189,274)	189,274		-0				
Transfer from Exchange Gains A/c	-0	8,234	(8,234)		-0				
TOTAL EXPENDITURE	**1,715,785**	**(84,943)**	**1,800,728**	**1,267,550**	**(3,755)**	**1,271,305**	**1,370,525**	**66,025**	**1,304,500**
SURPLUS/(DEFICIT)	(119,532)	(79,734)	(199,266)	(23,344)	8,365	(14,979)	(42,925)	59,825	16,900
GENERAL FUND BALANCE			58,989			44,010			60,910
ACC Expenditure not in Core Budget									
UN Observer Office						145000			145000
Telecomms						71730			71000
Networks						84069			84000

AJF 16/06/05

Budget for 2002-2005	2002/3 (15 Months)		Actual Total £	2004			2005		(2/2/02)
	Budget £	Variance £		Budget £	Variance £	Revised Forecast £	Budget £	Variance £	Revised Forecast £
EXPENDITURE									
Secretary General's Department:									
Employment costs	222,000	2,613	224,613	191,600	(2,500)	189,100	224,200	(29,200)	195,000
Travel and Hospitality	30,500	(1,772)	28,728	29,000	864	29,864	25,000	(7,500)	17,500
Presentation gifts	9,750	(98)	9,652	7,000	629	7,629	6,000	(2,000)	4,000
Other costs	4,750	221	4,971	3,000	(16)	2,984	4,000	(2,800)	1,200
	267,000	964	267,964	230,600	(1,023)	229,577	259,200	(41,500)	217,700
UN Observer's Office - contribution to costs	31,250	30,000	61,250	(5,000)	-0	(5,000)	25,000	-0	25,000
	298,250	30,964	329,214	225,600	(1,023)	224,577	284,200	(41,500)	242,700
Meetings costs:									
Council and Standing Committees	156,250	(31,250)	125,000	118,000	-0	118,000	118,000	(10,000)	108,000
Primates	31,250	-0	31,250	25,000	-0	25,000	25,000	-0	25,000
Lambeth Conference	138,000	(69,000)	69,000				-0	-0	-0
	623,750	(69,286)	554,464	368,600	(1,023)	367,577	427,200	(51,500)	375,700
Mission and Evangelism:									
Employment costs	48,000	8,794	56,794	41,500	(21)	41,479	43,000	-0	43,000
Travel and Hospitality			-0				-0	-0	-0
Other Costs	2,000	1,879	3,879	5,500	(949)	4,551	5,000	(1,000)	4,000
Mission Commission	54,375	(15,875)	38,500	25,000	(5,000)	20,000	25,000	(5,000)	20,000
	104,375	(5,202)	99,173	72,000	(5,970)	66,030	73,000	(6,000)	67,000
Sub-total	728,125	(74,488)	653,637	440,600	(6,993)	433,607	500,200	(47,200)	442,700
Communications Department:									
Employment costs	114,100	(4,474)	109,626	96,200	(765)	95,435	102,800	75,100	177,900
Travel and Hospitality	21,000	6,945	27,945	16,500	(1,404)	15,096	17,100	(10,100)	7,000
Other Costs	7,600	683	8,283	6,000	1,056	7,056	5,125	(1,125)	4,000
Publications Books Journals	14,000	3,128	17,128	12,000	763	12,763	13,000	(5,000)	8,000
	156,700	6,282	162,982	130,700	1,054	130,350	138,025	58,875	196,900
Telecommunications/Database Department:									
Employment costs	83,000	(721)	82,279	74,200	60	74,260	77,400	(77,400)	
	83,000	(721)	82,279	74,200	60	74,260	77,400	(77,400)	-0
Anglican World:									
Net costs	90,000	1,821	91,821	66,000	(376)	65,624	69,000	-0	69,000

	2002/3			2004			2005		
	Budget £	Variance £	Revised Total £	Budget £	Variance £	Revision £	Budget £	Variance £	Revision £
Liturgical Co-ordinator support	9,000	(784)	8,216	7,500	936	8,436	9,000	(2,000)	7,000
Ecumenical Relations:									
Employment costs	131,700	(846)	130,854	126,600	324	126,924	133,100	2,600	135,700
Travel and Hospitality	8,000	3,710	11,710	2,500	(250)	2,250	5,000	(3,000)	2,000
Other Costs	5,000	(233)	4,767	2,500	2,176	4,676	4,200	(1,200)	3,000
	144,700	2,631	147,331	131,600	2,250	133,850	142,300	(1,600)	140,700
Meetings costs:									
Inter Church Conversations	86,575	(75)	86,500	90,000	10,000	100,000	90,000	(5,000)	85,000
Doctrinal Commission	-0	(2,015)	(2,015)	-0	-0	-0	-0	-0	-0
	231,275	541	231,816	221,600	12,250	233,850	232,300	(6,600)	225,700
Ethics and Technology	7,500	(2,307)	5,193	6,500	-0	4,775	6,500	(4,500)	2,000
Finance and Administration:									
Employment costs	174,600	(26,824)	147,776	182,400	(6,173)	176,227	191,400	(1,600)	189,800
Travel and Hospitality	600	203	803	7,000	(689)	6,311	3,300	-0	3,300
	175,200	(26,621)	148,579	189,400	(6,862)	182,538	194,700	(1,600)	193,100
Administrative Overhead:									
Office Expenses	68,150	(3,272)	64,878	56,750	1,202	57,952	61,400	(4,800)	56,600
Audit fees etc	20,000	1,727	21,727	18,000	2,055	20,055	17,500	3,000	20,500
Office rent and maintenance	136,925	(5,682)	131,243	30,300	1,384	31,684	38,500	500	39,000
Equipment depreciation	12,000	5,317	17,317	26,000	2,179	28,179	26,000	1,000	27,000
Interest Payable	-0		-0	-0	-0	-0	-0	-0	-0
	412,275	(28,531)	383,744	320,450	(42)	320,408	338,100	(1,900)	336,200
TOTAL ESTIMATED EXPENDITURE	1,717,875	(98,187)	1,619,688	1,267,550	6,889	1,271,310	1,370,525	(80,725)	1,279,500

Anglican Consultative Council
Budget for 2002-2005

	2002/3			2004			2005		
	Budget £	Variance £	Revised Total £	Budget £	Variance £	Revision £	Budget £	Variance £	Revision £
INCOME									
Contributions from member churches	1,381,656	(3,997)	1,377,659	1,050,206	(2,477)	1,047,729	1,100,600	8,800	1,109,400
Other Income:									
Interest on deposits	26,500	2,480	28,980	14,000	2,119	16,119	19,000	-0	19,000
Publications sold	-0	1,049	1,049	-0	-0	10,866	-0	-0	-0
Services other bodies	1,250	(250)	1,000	1,000	-0	1,000	1,000	-0	1,000
Donations & Misc Income	500	(363)	137	-0	3,155	3,155	-0	-0	-0

	2002/3 (15 Months)			2004			2005		
	Budget £	Variance £	Actual Total £	Budget £	Variance £	Revised Forecast £	Budget £	Variance £	Revised Forecast £
Income from Guests	6,347	267	6,614	22,000	(257)	21,743	25,000	-0	25,000
Endowment Interest	34,597	3,183	37,780	7,000	254	7,254	7,000	-0	7,000
				44,000	5,271	60,137	52,000	-0	52,000
Total	1,416,253	(814)	1,415,439	1,094,206	2,794	1,107,866	1,152,600	8,800	1,161,400
EXPENDITURE ON SEPARATE SCHEDULE	1,717,875	(98,187)	1,619,688	1,267,550	6,889	1,271,310	1,370,525	(80,725)	1,279,500
Surplus/(Deficit) before special funds	(301,622)	97,373	(204,249)	(173,344)	(4,095)	(163,444)	(217,925)	89,525	(118,100)
Compass Rose Society contribution	180,000	6,023	186,023	150,000	(1,540)	148,460	175,000	(15,000)	160,000
Special Funds towards Primates Meetings	-0		-0	-0		-0	-0		-0
Provision for Partnership House Lease	-0	(189,274)	(189,274)						
Transfer from Exchange Gains A/c		8,234	8,234						
	180,000	(175,017)	4,983	150,000	(1,540)	148,460	175,000	(15,000)	160,000
Surplus/(Deficit) after special funds	(121,622)	(77,644)	(199,266)	(23,344)	(5,635)	(14,984)	(42,925)	74,525	41,900

Anglican Consultative Council
Admin Overheads

	2002/3 (15 Months)			2004			2005		
	Budget £	Variance £	Actual Total £	Budget £	Variance £	Revised Forecast £	Budget £	Variance £	Revised Forecast £
Bank charges	2,600	(187)	2,413	2,600	(348)	2,252	2,200	-0	2,200
Faxes	1,600	161	1,761	750	124	874	1,000	(1,000)	-0
IT Maintenance	9,600	18	9,618	9,500	305	9,805	11,000	-0	11,000
Misc Expenses	4,500	(1,075)	3,425	2,200	620	2,820	3,000	(1,000)	2,000
Office equipment	9,000	2,904	11,904	15,800	2,244	18,044	13,700	-0	13,700
On-Line - Quest etc	7,000	(38)	6,962	-0	-0	-0	-0	-0	-0
Postage etc	14,000	(2,235)	11,765	7,000	(884)	6,116	10,000	(3,000)	7,000
Printing and Stationery	8,750	(896)	7,854	7,000	705	7,705	7,500	-0	7,500
Telephone	6,500	(1,074)	5,426	8,000	(562)	7,438	8,500	700	9,200
Staff Canteen	3,600	(140)	3,460	2,400	(29)	2,371	2,500	(500)	2,000
Staff Training	1,000	(710)	290	1,500	(973)	527	2,000	-0	2,000
Total	68,150	(3,272)	64,878	56,750	1,202	57,952	61,400	(4,800)	56,600
Cleaning etc	-0	-0	-0	-0	-0	-0	-0	-0	-0
Insurance (mainly on equipment)	2,900	295	3,195	14,300	63	14,363	14,600	-0	14,600
Rent & Service Charge	129,000	(3,952)	125,048	-0	-0	-0	-0	-0	-0
Rates	2,925	75	3,000	1,000	(57)	943	2,400	-0	2,400
Repairs and Maintenance	2,100	(2,100)	-0	5,500	907	6,407	12,000	-0	12,000
Gas Electricity	-0	-0	-0	9,500	471	9,971	9,500	500	10,000
Total	136,925	(5,682)	131,243	30,300	1,384	31,684	38,500	500	39,000

	2002/3 Budget £	Variance £	Revised Total £	2004 Budget £	Variance £	Revision £	2005 Budget £	Variance £	Revision £
Audit fees etc	20,000	1,727	21,727	18,000	2,055	20,055	17,500	3,000	20,500
Equipment depreciation	12,000	5,317	17,317	26,000	2,179	28,179	26,000	1,000	27,000
Travel Costs	600	203	803	7,000	(689)	6,311	3,300	-0	3,300
Total Admin Overheads	32,600	7,247	39,847	51,000	3,545	54,545	46,800	4,000	50,800
	237,675	(1,707)	235,968	138,050	6,131	144,181	146,700	(300)	146,400

Anglican Consultative Council
Budget for 2001-2004

Anglican World Estimates

	2002/3			2004			2005		
	Budget £	Variance £	Revised Total £	Budget £	Variance £	Revision £	Budget £	Variance £	Revision £
Expenditure									
Employment costs	1,500	176	1,676	1,200	(290)	910	1,200	-0	1,200
Distribution	63,750	(5,591)	58,159	44,000	2,467	46,467	50,000	-0	50,000
Printing	71,250	(203)	71,047	46,000	2	46,002	55,500	-0	55,500
Other production costs	2,500	(2,150)	350	500	(500)		500	-0	500
Advertising sales costs	6,250	(5,147)	1,103	-0	-0		-0	-0	
Advertising	1,625	874	2,499	2,000	(969)	1,031	2,000	-0	2,000
Other expenses	1,625	380	2,005	300	(300)		1,300	-0	1,300
	148,500	(11,661)	136,839	94,000	410	94,410	110,500	-0	110,500
Income									
Donations	6,000	(1,646)	4,354	4,000	1,786	5,786	4,500	-0	4,500
Subscriptions	30,000	(5,049)	24,951	17,000	51	17,051	24,000	-0	24,000
Advertising	21,250	(5,537)	15,713	7,000	(1,051)	5,949	13,000	-0	13,000
Off page sales	1,250	(1,250)		-0		-0	-0		-0
	58,500	(13,482)	45,018	28,000	786	28,786	41,500	-0	41,500
Subsidy from other Income	90,000	1,821	91,821	66,000	(376)	65,624	69,000	-0	69,000

Ecumenical Meetings Projection
Revised projection'2001/2 to 2004/5

	Actual £	2001/2 £	2002/3 £	2004 £	2005 £
Lutheran	12,782	12,431	591	2,000	10,000
Methodist		57	-0	1,000	10,000
Baptist	8,660	7,600	12,281	3,000	2,000
Oriental Orthodox	11,949	1,171	8,162	2,112	8,000
Orthodox	10,481	11,526	16,544	15,000	16,000
Roman Catholic	5,055	13,687	22,670	5,000	16,000
Old Catholic	4,382	5,378	1,048	2,000	5,000
Special Projects	2,536	3,486	1,763	4,000	6,000
Ecumenical Advisory Group/IASCER	12,537	17,251	18,637	15,000	15,000
Reformed	164				
IARCCUM		8,473	15,494	3,000	10,000
ABC Lambeth Commission				60,000	
IATDC				1,872	
	68,546	81,060	97,190	113,984	98,000
Financed by:					
Vote for Year	62,625	68,250	86,500	90,000	90,000
Publications sales	55				
	62,680	68,250	86,500	90,000	90,000
Balance (over)/underspent	(5,866)	(12,810)	(10,690)	(23,984)	(8,000)
Balance of fund brought forward	67,694	61,828	49,018	38,328	14,344
Balance of Fund carried forward	61,828	49,018	38,328	14,344	6,344

Ecumenical Meetings Projection
Revised projection'2001/2 to 2006

	Actual £	2001/2 £	2002/3 £	2004 £	Budget 2005 £	Revised 2005 £	2006 £
Lutheran	1,373	12,431	591	1,373	10,000	1,500	10,000
Methodist		57	-0		10,000	1,500	1,000
Baptist	1,756	7,600	12,281	1,756	2,000	1,500	1,000
Oriental Orthodox	2,186	1,171	8,162	2,186	8,000	4,000	10,000
Orthodox	17,337	11,526	16,544	17,337	16,000	18,000	15,000
ARCIC	4,745	13,687	22,670	4,745	16,000	4,000	1,000
Old Catholic	1,647	5,378	1,048	1,647	5,000	6,000	6,000
Special Projects	5,037	3,486	1,763	5,037	6,000	6,000	6,000
IASCER	21,100	17,251	18,637	21,100	15,000	20,000	20,000
Reformed	4			4		-0	
IARCCUM	2,802	8,473	15,494	2,802	10,000	15,000	15,000
Lambeth Commission	68,847			68,847		5,000	
IATDC						500	20,000
	126,834	81,060	97,190	126,834	98,000	83,000	105,000
Financed by:							
Vote for Year	90,000	68,250	86,500	90,000	90,000	85,000	97,000
Publications sales	10,000			10,000		3,500	
	100,000	68,250	86,500	100,000	90,000	88,500	97,000
Balance (over)/underspent	(26,834)	(12,810)	(10,690)	(26,834)	(8,000)	5,500	(8,000)
Balance of fund brought forward		61,828	49,018	38,328	11,494	3,494	8,994
Balance of Fund carried forward		49,018	38,328	11,494	3,494	8,994	994

Inter-Anglican Budget
Contributions Requests 2003-2005

	2003 Request £	Actual £	2004 Request £	Actual £	2005 Request £
Aotearoa, New Zealand and Polynesia	30,100	30,100	31,300	31,300	32,600
Australia	119,000	81,565	123,800	82,543	128,800
Brazil	3,400		3,500	2,000	3,600
Burundi	300		300		300
Canada	81,000	58,484	84,200	56,937	87,600
Central Africa	8,200		8,500	2,988	8,800
Central America	1,600	1,600	1,700		1,800
Ceylon	1,500	*500*	1,600		1,700
Congo Democratic Republic	700		700		700
England [inc Dio in Europe]	374,100	359,700	389,100	359,700	404,700
Hong Kong	23,400	23,400	24,300	24,300	25,300
Indian Ocean	3,400	3,400	3,500	3,400	3,600
Ireland	30,100	31,200	31,300	31,300	32,600
Japan	16,600	17,200	17,300	17,300	18,000
Jerusalem & M.E.	4,700	4,200	4,900	4,575	5,100
Kenya	10,200	1,995	10,600	1,995	11,000
Korea	4,500	4,500	4,700	*4,700*	4,900
Melanesia	1,500	1,500	1,600	1,600	1,700
Mexico	1,600	1,630	1,700	1,672	1,800
Myanmar	1,500	1,400	1,600	1,600	1,700
Nigeria	19,300	20,000	20,100	*20,100*	20,900
Papua New Guinea	1,500	1,238	1,600	1,238	1,700
Philippines	2,100	1,961	2,200	1,931	2,300
Rwanda	1,400	1,400	1,500	1,500	1,600
Scotland	20,300	20,300	21,100	21,100	21,900
South East Asia	4,800	4,800	5,000	*5,000*	5,200
Southern Africa	15,800	15,023	16,400	15,279	17,100
Southern Cone of S. America	3,300	3,030	3,400	2,763	3,500
Sudan	3,300	-0	3,400	-0	3,500
Taiwan		1,030		955	-0
Tanzania	6,700	3,600	7,000		7,300
Uganda	6,700	572	7,000	-0	7,300
United States of America (including Province IX)	360,000	352,231	374,400	316,653	389,400
Wales	30,100	30,100	31,300	31,300	32,600
West Africa	2,600	*2,600*	2,700	*900*	2,800
West Indies	13,300	*13,300*	13,800	*13,800*	14,400
United Churches					
Bangladesh	700	303	700		700
Church of North India	1,500	1,500	1,600	1,600	1,700
Church of Pakistan	1,500	-0	1,600	-0	1,700
Church of South India	2,100	2,100	2,200		2,300
Extra-Provincial Dioceses					
Bermuda	2,000	2,000	2,100	2,100	2,200
Lusitanian Church	700	730	700	700	700
Spanish Rfmd Episcopal Church	700	700	700	700	700
Total	**1,217,800**	**1,100,892**	**1,266,700**	**1,065,529**	**1,317,800**

ACC
Inter-Anglican Budget
Contributions Requests 2005-2008

	Request 2005 £	Request 2006 £	Request 2007 £	Request 2008 £
Aotearoa, New Zealand and Polynesia	**32,600**	**35,800**	**37,200**	**38,700**
Australia	128,800	141,600	147,200	153,100
Brazil	3,600	4,000	4,200	4,300
Burundi	300	300	400	400
Canada	87,600	96,300	100,200	104,200
Central Africa	8,800	9,600	10,000	10,400
Central America	1,800	2,000	2,100	2,200
Ceylon	1,700	1,900	2,000	2,000
Congo Democratic Republic	700	800	800	900
England [inc Dio in Europe]	404,700	445,000	462,800	481,000
Hong Kong	25,300	27,800	28,900	30,100
Indian Ocean	3,600	4,000	4,200	4,300
Ireland	32,600	35,900	37,300	38,800
Japan	18,000	19,800	20,600	21,400
Jerusalem & M.E.	5,100	5,600	5,800	6,000
Kenya	11,000	12,100	12,600	13,100
Korea	4,900	5,400	5,600	5,800
Melanesia	1,700	1,900	2,000	2,100

Mexico	1,800	2,000	2,100	2,200
Myanmar	1,700	1,900	2,000	2,100
Nigeria	20,900	23,000	23,900	24,900
Papua New Guinea	1,700	1,900	2,000	2,000
Philippines	2,300	2,500	2,600	2,700
Rwanda	1,600	1,800	1,900	2,000
Scotland	21,900	24,100	25,100	26,100
South East Asia	5,200	5,700	5,900	6,100
Southern Africa	17,100	18,800	19,500	20,300
Southern Cone of S. America	3,500	3,800	4,000	4,200
Sudan	3,500	3,800	4,000	4,200
Taiwan	1,000	1,100	1,100	1,200
Tanzania	7,300	8,000	8,300	8,600
Uganda	7,300	8,000	8,300	8,600
United States of America	389,400	428,300	445,400	463,200
Wales	32,600	35,900	37,300	38,800
West Africa	2,800	3,100	3,200	3,300
West Indies	14,400	15,800	16,400	17,000
United Churches				
Bangladesh	700	800	800	900
Church of North India	1,700	1,900	1,900	2,000
Church of Pakistan	1,700	1,900	1,900	2,000
Church of South India	2,300	2,500	2,600	2,700
Extra-Provincial Dioceses		-0		-0
Bermuda	2,200	2,400	2,500	2,600
Lusitanian Church	700	800	800	900
Spanish Rfmd Episcopal Church	700	800	800	900
	1,318,800	**1,450,400**	**1,508,200**	**1,568,300**

Inter-Anglican Budget
Contributions Requests 2002-2005

Revised Estimated Outcomes	2002	2003			2004	2005		
			15 month					
	Request	Actual	Budget	Estimate	Request	Estimate	Request	Estimate
	£	£	£	£	£	£	£	£
Aotearoa, New Zealand and Polynesia	27,800	28,625	31,200	37,325	31,300	31,000	32,600	32,275
Australia	110,000	67,813	123,400	95,400	123,800	70,600	128,800	72,200
Brazil	5,300	3,600	3,500	3,400	3,600	3,400		
Burundi	300	310	300		300			
Canada	74,900	56,255	84,000	72,000	84,200	56,700	87,600	58,900
Central Africa	7,600	8,500	6,000	8,500	4,000	8,800		
4,000	58968							
Central America	1,400	2,525	1,650	1,975	1,700	1,675	1,800	1,775
Ceylon	1,300	325	1,550	2,900	1,600	1,575	1,700	1,675
Congo Democratic Republic	600	150	730	700	300	700	300	
England [inc Dio in Europe]	345,800	356,225	387,900	449,625	389,100	359,700	404,700	359,700
Hong Kong	21,700	22,300	24,300	29,025	24,300	24,075	25,300	25,050
Indian Ocean	3,200	3,275	3,500	4,225	3,500	3,475	3,600	3,575
Ireland	27,800	28,625	31,200	38,425	31,300	31,000	32,600	32,275
Japan	15,400	15,850	17,200	21,200	17,300	17,125	18,000	17,825
Jerusalem & M.E.	4,300	1,075	4,900	8,250	4,900	4,800	5,100	5,050
Kenya	9,400	2,500	10,600	2,500	10,600	5,100	11,000	5,300
Korea	4,100	7,387	4,700	4,300	4,700	4,500	4,900	4,700
Melanesia	1,300	1,375	1,550	1,850	1,600	1,575	1,700	1,675
Mexico	1,400	1,502	1,650	1,975	1,700	1,675	1,800	1,775
Myanmar	1,300	325	1,550	1,750	1,600	1,575	1,700	1,675
Nigeria	17,900	18,425	20,000	24,650	20,100	19,900	20,900	20,700
Papua New Guinea	1,300	1,238	1,550	1,547	1,600	1,238	1,700	1,238
Philippines	1,900	449	2,200	4,000	2,200	2,100	2,300	2,200
Rwanda	1,200	2,175	1,450	1,725	1,500	1,475	1,600	1,575
Scotland	18,200	19,175	21,000	25,175	21,100	20,900	21,900	21,700
South East Asia	4,400	1,100	5,000	4,800	5,000	4,800	5,200	5,000
Southern Africa	14,600	18,922	16,400	14,000	16,400	13,500	17,100	14,000
Southern Cone of S. America	3,100	3,040	3,400	3,785	3,400	3,375	3,500	3,475
Sudan	3,100	1,500	3,400	3,400	1,500	3,500	1,500	
Taiwan	-0	1,405	-0	1,400	-0	1,400	-0	1,400
Tanzania	6,200	6,900	3,600	7,000	2,000	7,300	2,500	
Uganda	6,200	6,900	1,000	7,000	2,000	7,300	2,000	
United States of America (including Province IX)	334,800	376,113	373,400	446,000	374,400	370,800	389,400	385,650
Wales	27,800	28,625	31,200	37,325	31,300	31,000	32,600	32,275
West Africa	2,400	2,700	6,300	2,700	2,675	2,800	2,775	
West Indies	12,300	14,096	13,800	16,000	13,800	13,675	14,400	14,250
United Churches								
Bangladesh	600	685	730	875	700	700	700	700
Church of North India	1,300	1,413	1,550	1,862	1,600	1,575	1,700	1,675
Church of Pakistan	1,300	-0	1,550	-0	1,600	-0	1,700	-0
Church of South India	1,900	475	2,200	4,100	2,200	2,175	2,300	2,275

Extra-Provincial Dioceses

Bermuda	1,800	1,875	2,100	2,475	2,100	2,075	2,200	2,175
Lusitanian Church	600	698	730	912	700	700	700	700
Spanish Rfmd Episcopal Church	600	730	1,400	700	700	700	700	

	1,128,400	1,087,541	1,262,880	1,381,656	1,266,700	1,124,113	1,317,800	1,153,588
Underpayment provision	(40,859)	(142,587)		(164,212)			
	1,087,541	1,087,541	1,262,880	1,381,656	1,124,113	1,124,113	1,153,588	1,153,588

	2002/3	2004	2005
Standing Committee / IAFC Travel	8214	15000	7000
Standing Committee / IAFC Accomm	10267	16500	7000
Standing Committee Photocopy	1101	1200	1200
Standing Committee other IT/Freight	3698	3700	3000
ACC 13 Preparation		7000	
ACC12 & 13 Reports	12115		
ACC 12 & 13 Travel	3221		62000
ACC 12 & 13 Photocopy etc	1500		20000
ACC 12 & 13 Accomodation	2457		106000
ACC Meetings Rooms			17000
ACC Other Costs Freight/Gifts	1669		12000
Accommodation Ad Hoc Meetings	2755	1000	1000
Travel Ad Hoc Meetings	12126	1000	1000
	59123	45400	237200
Vote for Year	125000	118000	118000
	65877	72600	-119200
Balance b/f	1155	67032	139632
Balance c/f	67032	139632	20432

	2004 Actual £	2005 Forecast £
Anglican World Estimates		
Expenditure		
Employment costs	910	1200
Distribution	46467	50000
Printing	46001	55500
Advertising	1031	2000
Other		1800
	94409	**110500**
Income		
Donations	5786	4500
Subscriptions	17051	24000
Advertising	5949	13000
	28786	**41500**
Net Cost Core Budget	**65623**	**69000**
Telecommunications		
Salaries for Core Budget (JR MC MA IH)	**169695**	**180200**
Other Expenses		
Travel & Subsistence	12585	14500
Entertaining	2511	2600
Gifts	1605	
Publications	3432	3625
Anglican Cycle of Prayer	3624	1500
ACNS Electronic Distribution	2057	2100
Dio Europe advertising	1140	1200
Mobile Telephone	2247	2400
Other Expenses	2441	2500
Photography	3273	4800
Core Budget	**34915**	**35225**

Other Telecomms expenditure paid for by Trinity Grants

Provincial News Release Web Pages (Grant 7687)		
John Allen salary K Lee sal exp Third party costs	9872	30000
Grant runs out August 2006		
Web Site Hosting (Grant 7235)	33722	20000
Server and web production expenses		
Grant runs out March 2005		
£16000 not covered by Grant in 2005		
We need a new grant from Trinity here		
ACNS M Davies Sal +K Lee Stipend (Grant 7370)		
Expenses	14880	5300
Grant runs out March 2005 then covered by 7687 above		
Telecomms Commission (Grant 7211)		
Expenditure	16251	20000

Grant should run out in 2005 but there is enough
money to continue to end of 2006. Why not use this
for web site hosting as well ?

Extracts from 2005 YTD Figures

	Sec General	Ecum	Mission	Comms	F&AAdmin	O/H	Ang World House	Liturgy	CR /FC	Total	Estimate	Final Forecast	A World
Mobile Phone	543.59	454.33		184.32						1182.24	3546.72	4000	
Fax	202.09					200.76				402.85	1208.55	1200	
Telephone	98.04			160.01		2747.45				3005.5	9016.5	9200	
ADSL						1876.13				1876.13	5628.39	4600	
Postage	137.79		43.9	87.54	22	848.64	10291.11		194.66	11625.64	4003.92	5000	
Courier	128.49					13.78	216.02			358.29	1074.87	1000	
Photocopying	43.85					271.28				315.13	945.39	1200	
Printing &Stationery	165.47	6.99		100.8	6.99	2410.83	60.82			2751.9	3455.7	5500	
Bank Charges					212.94	251.87			18.19	483	1449	2000	
Miscelleneous	203.18				35.71	561.85			170.41	971.15	2913.45		
IT Costs					436.88	8578.88				9015.76	27047.28	19650	
Staff Canteen/Training			26.04		374.03	603.04				1003.11	3009.33	3000	
Rail Staff	113	39.7	36	89.4		604	40.4		27.5	950	2850	1000	
Air Staff	693.79	302.54		494.16		925.8		0.44		2416.73	7250.19	10000	
Taxi Staff	352.01	131.6		620.76	40.59	237.47	66.16			1448.59	4345.77	4000	
Car	3	29		5						37	111	100	
Entrertaining Hospity	442.72	167.5	124.87	726.02						1461.11	4383.33	5000	
Presentation Gifts	1005.73									1005.73	3017.19	4000	
Subsistence	115.17	48.1	8.6	7.9	18.44			217.53		415.74	1247.22	1000	
Audit/Prof					1558.07	-10816.89				-9258.82	-27776.46	20500	
Water Rates	124									124	372		
House Expenses						3124.46	23920.74			27045.2	81135.6	38600	
Accommodation	763.66							240	360	1363.66	4090.98	3500	
Books		72.65		1573.53	231	151	10631.06			12659.24	37977.72		
Photos				520.79						520.79	1562.37		
Salary	69789.6	53382.04	16368.23	67685.05	49713.4	22682.27	300	779.35		280699.939999999			
	74925.18	54634.45	16607.64	72255.28	52650.05	46669.17	21539.41	1237.32	770.76	353879.61			

Secretary General

Salaries

Gross Pay	to end of May	54158
KK LB DM	7 more months	70770
Employer NHI	to end of May	5608
KK LB DM	7 more months	7546
Pension	to end of May	7530
KK	6 months	2802
DM LB	9 months	14187
Extra Provision	Pension	3800
Temp Help		10000
		176401

Finance & Admin

Salaries

Gross Pay	to end of May	37291
AF DP CG	7 more months	52213
Employer NHI	to end of May	3311
AF DP CG	7 more months	4606
Pension	to end of May	4377
CG	12 months	2000
AF DP	9 months	13131
Extra Provision	Pension	3500
Temp Help		9000
		129429

St Andrew's House

Salaries

Gross Pay	to end of May	19800
AQ NC VR	7 more months	25900
Employer NHI	to end of May	1333
AQ NC VR	7 more months	2100
Pension	to end of May	1549
NC VR	12 months	2000
AQ	9 months	4647
Extra Provision	Pension	
Temp Help		3000
		60329

St A + Finance 189758

Ecumenical

Salaries

Gross Pay	to end of May	42331
GC CC TR	7 more months	59269
Employer NHI	to end of May	3576
GC CC TR	7 more months	4984
Pension	to end of May	6375
KK	6 months	
GC CC TR	9 months	19128
Extra Provision	Pension	5100
		-5100
Temp Help		
		135663

Comms

Salaries

Gross Pay	to end of May	54408
MA IH JR	7 more months	61852
GHH	7 more months	9786
Employer NHI	to end of May	4533
MA IH JR	7 more months	5236
GHH	7 more months	889
Pension	to end of May	8313
MC	April	600
MA IH JR	9 months	19542
GHH	Pension	1700
Robert Acomm		2000
More Temp	4 months 1 day week	4000
Temp Help	GHH 1 extra day	5000
		177859

Mission

Gross Pay	to end of May	13255
MM	7 more months	18557
Employer NHI	to end of May	1038
MM	7 more months	1449
Pension	to end of May	1997
MM	9 months	6000
Extra Provision	Pension	
Temp Help		
		42296

Salary Costs

Sec General	176401
Lambeth Rent	11000
Travel	7500
Ecum	135663
Comms	177859
Mission	42296
St Andrews finance	189758
	740477

ANGLICAN CONSULTATIVE COUNCIL
IASCOME Expenses
Department: Mission and Evangelism
** Account Number 476

IASCOME

Account summary:2002

Edinburgh
Design Group	4137	
Travel	18198	
Accommodation	13849	
	36184	

Balance in fund 1/10/01		42,169
Add Budget provision:		
Year to 30/9/02		38,500
Less Spend 2002		36,184
Balance in fund 1/10/02		**44,485**

Account summary:2003

Jamaica
Design Group	4770	
Travel	21707	
Accommodation etc	12030	
	38507	

Add Budget provision:		
Period to 31/12/03		38,500
Spend 2002/3		46,507
Balance in fund 1/01/04		**36,478**

Established provision	20000	
Add For two years 2004 2005		40,000

Provisional Budget 2004

Overprovision	-1906	
Design Group Cyprus		
deficit on Mission commission	11784	
	9878	

Provisional Budget 2005
Cyprus
Design Group
Travel	21707	
Accommodation	15000	
Report	8000	
	44707	

Less Provisional spend		54585
Balance in fund 1/01/06		**21,893**

Inter-Anglican Budget

Anglican Consultative Council
Financial Report for ACC-12

Inter-Anglican Budget Outturn 1999 to 2001

	1999 Budget £	1999 Actual £	1999 Variation £	2000 (9 months) Budget £	2000 Actual £	2000 Variation £	2001 Budget £	2001 Actual £	2001 Variation £
INCOME									
Interest on deposits	15,000	22,589	(7,589)	11,250	18,200	(6,950)	15,000	30,069	(15,069)
Publications income	5,000	6,132	(1,132)	3,750	1,708	2,042	5,000	1,062	3,938
Services to other bodies	500	500	-0	375	375	-0	500	1,000	(500)
Grants for equipment		71	(71)			-0			-0
Donations & miscellaneous income	500	563	(63)	375	152	223	500	1,421	(921)
	21,000	29,855	(8,855)	15,750	20,435	(4,685)	21,000	33,552	(12,552)
Contributions from member churches	977,636	979,934	(2,298)	763,190	763,424	(234)	1,052,000	1,060,946	(8,946)
Total normal income	998,636	1,009,789	(11,153)	778,940	783,859	(4,919)	1,073,000	1,094,498	(21,498)
Special Fund Raising	235,000	228,719	6,281	176,250	164,411	11,839		243,784	(243,784)
EXPENDITURE	1,233,636	1,238,508	(4,872)	955,190	948,270	6,920	1,073,000	1,338,282	(265,282)
Secretary General's office	196,750	182,119	14,631	154,837	153,681	1,156	215,100	141,666	73,434
Communications department	110,850	112,182	(1,332)	86,213	79,229	6,984	117,400	109,064	8,336
Telecommunications/database department	48,100	48,556	(456)	38,550	42,299	(3,749)	53,300	52,504	796
Anglican World magazine	110,000	109,630	370	82,500	27,830	54,670	110,000	83,291	26,709
Mission and Evangelism department			-0			-0		33,726	(33,726)
Liturgical co-ordinator	6,500	7,757	(1,257)	4,875	7,080	(2,205)	7,000	8,908	(1,908)
Ecumenical Relations department	86,180	84,857	1,323	70,335	70,193	142	95,300	99,250	(3,950)
Finance and Administration department	143,400	136,076	7,324	115,800	100,053	15,747	160,050	121,258	38,792
Overheads (rents, office expenses, etc)	161,500	146,726	14,774	116,198	124,341	(8,143)	162,180	160,882	1,298
	863,280	827,903	35,377	669,308	604,706	64,602	920,330	810,549	109,781
Provision for meetings etc:									
Inter-Church conversations	48,000	48,000	-0	36,000	36,000	-0	48,000	62,625	(14,625)
Missio	15,000	15,000	-0	11,250	11,250	-0	15,000	43,500	(28,500)
Council and Standing Committee	90,500	90,500	-0	93,750	93,750	-0	125,000	125,000	-0
Primates	25,500	25,500	-0	19,125	19,125	-0	25,500	50,500	(25,000)
Lambeth Conference	140,000	140,000	-0	105,000	105,000	-0	140,000	140,000	-0
UN Observer's Office	24,000	24,942	(942)	18,000	20,035	(2,035)	24,000	27,977	(3,977)
Inter-Anglican Doctrinal			-0			-0		15,750	(15,750)
Provincial Emergencies Provision	25,000	25,000	-0	18,750	18,750	-0	25,000		25,000
	1,231,280	1,196,845	34,435	971,183	908,616	62,567	1,322,830	1,275,901	46,929
Surplus/(Deficit)	2,356	41,663	(39,307)	(15,993)	39,654	(55,647)	(249,830)	62,381	(312,211)

Anglican Consultative Council
Financial Report for ACC-12

Inter-Anglican Budget Outturn 1999 to 2001
Notes on Annual Figures:

Presentation:

The audited accounts for the years 1999 to 2001 are set out in the format required by legislation.

This paper presents the core budget figures in an abbreviated and simplified form.

For the purpose of budget comparison, this presentation gives a different view from that shown in the annual accounts. This presentation gives the figures in departmental totals.

The accounting year end was changed to 30th September in Year 2000 making that accounting period one of nine months only.

General Reserve:

Resolution 49 of ACC-6 provided that the General Reserve should be maintained at a level equivalent to four months' expenditure of the Secretariat.

1999

Income:

Member church contributions were £2,298 over budget.

Expenditure:

Expenditure was lower than the budget by £34,435.

The bottom line shows a surplus of income over expenditure for the year of £41,663 .

The General Reserve stood at £146810 at the year end, £129,157 less than required.

2000

Income:

Member church contributions were £234 over budget.

In setting the budget, it was realised that substantial support would be needed in addition to the member church contributions. Compass Rose Society giving provided £164,411 mainly in support of Communications expenditure.

Expenditure:

Expenditure was lower than the budget by £62,567.

The bottom line shows a surplus of income over expenditure for the year of £39,654 .

The General Reserve stood at £186,464 at the year end, £82,294 less than required.

2001

Income:

Member church contributions were £8946 over budget.

It was necessary to supplement the contributions with support from Compass Rose Society giving. This provided £243,784 in support of Communications .

Expenditure:

Expenditure was lower than the budget by £46,929

The bottom line shows a surplus of income over expenditure for the year of £62,381.

The General Reserve stood at £248,845 at the year end, £21,338 less than required.

Anglican Consultative Council
Financial Report for ACC-12

Inter-Anglican Budgets 2004 to 2005	2,004 £	2003 £	2004 £	2005 £
Interest on deposits	19,000	20,000	20,000	25,000
Other Income	25,000			
Donations For Primates Meetings	35,000	1,000	1,000	1,000
Donations For UN Observer Office	150,000	4,500	4,500	4,500
Other Grants for Restricted Use		500	500	500
	229,000	26,000	26,000	31,000
Contributions from member churches	1,110,000	1,100,000	1,183,113	1,206,688
Total normal income	1,339,000	1,126,000	1,209,113	1,237,688
Compass Rose Society	200,000	230,000	240,000	250,000
	1,539,000	1,356,000	1,449,113	1,487,688
EXPENDITURE				
Secretary General's office	228,000	213,700	220,900	228,649
Mission & Evangelism	45,400	38,300	39,600	41,000
Communications department	132,000	128,775	130,000	133,900
Telecommunications/database department	74,200	66,300	68,600	71,000
Anglican World magazine	66,500	84,000	84,000	84,000
Liturgical co-ordinator	8,500	7,685	7,700	7,700
Ecumenical Relations department	135,600	117,885	122,500	128,000
Finance and Administration department	190,000	157,600	162,900	168,500
Overheads (rents, office expenses, etc)	133,500	183,200	185,825	188,385
	1,013,700	997,445	1,022,025	1,051,134
Provision for meetings etc:				
Inter-Church Conversations	90,000	59,750	60,750	61,750
Missio	38,500	43,500	43,500	43,500
Ethics & Technology	6,500	6,000	6,500	6,500
Council and Standing Committee	118,000	125,000	125,000	125,000
Primates	60,000	25,500	25,500	25,500
Lambeth Conference	113,000	140,000	140,000	140,000
UN Observer's Office	150,000	24,000	24,000	24,000
Other Exp paid by Grants contra				
	1,589,700	1,421,195	1,447,275	1,477,384
Surplus/(Deficit)	(50,700)	(65,195)	1,838	10,304

Anglican Consultative Council
Financial Report for ACC-12

Inter-Anglican Budgets 2002 to 2005

1999
Commentary on Budget Figures

Income

A small amount of income is expected from interest on deposits, publications sales, etc. The primary income source is **Member Church Contributions** (80% in 2002). At present these contributions do not provide sufficient income to cover the expenditure commitments. It has therefore been necessary to seek additional help through **Special Fund Raising** efforts (16% in 2002). The **Compass Rose Society** provides most of these funds .

Expenditure

The projections for the years 2003 to 2005 are based on the programmes and commitments in place in 2002.

The figures are grouped by activities. The **Secretary General's** figures includes Travel office with **Mission and Evangelism**, with one staff member dedicated to that aspect of the work is now shown separately. The **Communications** and **Telecommunications** sections deal with internal (through the computer network) and external communications issues including the maintenance of the Anglican Communion Office database. Communications department also produces **Anglican World** magazine which is widely distributed through the Communion, partly on a complimentary basis and partly to subscribers. **Ecumenical Relations** department services the Inter-Church Conversations and deals with other ecumenical matters. **Finance and Administration** department deals with the finance and accounting, office administration and much of the logistical work for meetings. The **Overheads** include the rent and other office premises costs as well as the general office expenses, audit fees, etc.

The section **Provision for Meetings, etc** includes the annual provisions for the various meetings which have to be held. Also included is a contribution to the **Office of the Anglican Observer at the United Nations**, the overall budget for which (in 2002) is about £150,000.

Anglican Consultative Council
Financial Report for ACC-12

Member Church Contributions 1999 to 2001

INCOME	1999 Request £	Actual £	Variation £	2000 (9 Months) Request £	Actual £	Variation £	2001 Request £	Actual £	Variation £
Aotearoa, New Zealand and Polynesia	34,991	24,473	10,518	27,293	17,763	9,530	27,800	26,225	1,575
Australia	101,670	74,624	27,046	79,302	53,685	25,617	110,000	68,166	41,834
Brazil	4,867	2,450	2,417	3,796		3,796	5,300	3,020	2,280
Burundi	216	424	(208)	169	169	-0	300	58	242
Canada	69,222	53,226	15,996	53,992	48,912	5,080	74,900	56,449	18,451

	(1)	(2)	(3)	(4)	(5)	(6)	(7)	(8)	(9)
Central Africa	7,030	-0	7,030	5,483	3,750	1,733	7,600	1,250	6,350
Central America	1,298	1,298		1,012	1,012	928	1,400	338	1,062
Ceylon	1,190	1,190	-0	928	-0	422	1,300	2,214	(914)
Congo Democratic Republic (formerly Zaire)	541	1,061	(520)	422		382	600	1,013	(413)
England [inc. Diocese in Europe]	319,721	319,700	21	249,382	249,000	-0	345,800	342,350	3,450
Hong Kong Sheng Kung Hui	20,000	20,000	-0	15,600	15,600	-0	21,700	21,475	225
Indian Ocean	2,920	2,920	-0	2,278	2,278	-0	3,200	3,159	41
Ireland	25,678	25,678	-0	20,029	20,029	-0	27,800	27,526	274
Japan	14,191	14,191	-0	11,069	11,069	-0	15,400	15,240	160
Jerusalem & the Middle East	3,980	3,980	-0	3,104	3,104	749	4,300	4,260	40
Kenya	8,653	8,653	-0	6,749	6,000	2,953	9,400	2,500	6,900
Korea	3,786	3,786	-0	2,953		-0	4,100		4,100
Melanesia	1,190	1,190	-0	928	928	(67)	1,300	1,285	15
Mexico	1,298	1,298	99	1,013		929	1,400	1,455	(55)
Myanmar	1,190	1,199	1,190	929	1,080	-0	1,300	4,547	(3,247)
Nigeria	16,494	16,494	-0	12,866	12,866	-0	17,900	17,713	187
Papua New Guinea	1,190	1,190	-0	929	929	3,158	1,300	1,238	62
Philippines	5,678	2,709	2,969	4,429	1,271	-0	1,900	1,771	129
Rwanda	1,082		1,082	844	844	423	1,200	281	919
Scotland	17,306	16,765	541	13,499	13,076	13,661	18,200	18,009	191
South East Asia	21,632	5,852	15,780	16,873	3,212	3,212	4,400	4,370	30
Southern Cone of South America	2,844	2,988	(144)	2,219	2,409	(190)	3,100	3,132	(32)
Southern Africa	13,498	13,498	-0	10,529	10,529	2,219	14,600	3,509	11,091
Sudan	2,844		2,844	2,219	-0	(848)	3,100	-0	3,100
Taiwan		1028	(1,028)	-0	848	-0	3,100	1,157	(1,157)
Tanzania	5,678	5,678	-0	4,429	4,429	4,429	6,200	1,476	4,724
Uganda	5,678		5,678	4,429	-0	-0	6,200		6,200
United States of America (including Province IX)	309,499	306,495	3,004	241,409	252,701	(11,292)	334,800	368,322	(33,522)
Wales	25,678	25,678	-0	20,029	19,800	229	27,800	27,450	350
West Africa	2,163	2,163	-0	1,688	1,688	-0	2,400	1,762	638
West Indies	11,357	12,182	(825)	8,858		8,858	12,300	21,036	(8,736)
United Churches:									
United Church of Bangladesh	568	568	-0	443	443	-0	600	598	2
United Church of North India	1,190	1,190	-0	929		929	1,300	2,213	(913)
United Church of Pakistan	1,190		1,190	929		929	1,300		1,300
United Church of South India	1,731	1,731	-0	1,350	1,350	-0	1,900	1,875	25
Extra-Provincial Dioceses:									
Bermuda Diocese	1,622	3,182	(1,560)	1,265	1,265	-0	1,800	1,772	28
The Lusitanian Church	541	500	41	422	422	-0	600	591	9
The Spanish Ref'md Episcopal Church	541		541	422	963	(541)	600	141	459
	1,073,636	979,934	93,702	837,440	763,424	74,016	1,128,400	1,060,946	67,454

Anglican Consultative Council
Financial Report for ACC-12

Member Church Contributions 2002 to 2005

	2002 Request £	Paid by 9/6/02 £	Unpaid Balance £	2003 Request £	Supplementary Request £	2004 Request £	2005 Request £
Aotearoa, New Zealand and Polynesia	29,450	21,400	8,050	30,100	1,100	31,300	32,600
Australia	116,600	38,885	77,715	119,000	4,400	123,800	128,800
Brazil	5,600		5,600	3,400	200	3,500	3,600
Burundi	308		308	300	10	300	300
Canada	79,400	42,656	36,744	81,000	3,000	84,200	87,600
Central Africa	8,050	-0	8,050	8,200	300	8,500	8,800
Central America	1,512	1,500	12	1,600	50	1,700	1,800
Ceylon	1,412	325	1,087	1,500	50	1,600	1,700
Congo Democratic Republic	698	150	548	700	30	700	700
England [inc Dio in Europe]	366,575	356,225	10,350	374,100	13,800	389,100	404,700
Hong Kong Sheng Kung Hui	22,975	22,300	675	23,400	900	24,300	25,300
Indian Ocean	3,350	3,275	75	3,400	100	3,500	3,600
Ireland	29,450	28,625	825	30,100	1,100	31,300	32,600
Japan	16,300	3,850	12,450	16,600	600	17,300	18,000
Jerusalem & the Middle East	4,600	1,075	3,525	4,700	200	4,900	5,100
Kenya	10,000		10,000	10,200	400	10,600	11,000
Korea	4,400	1,025	3,375	4,500	200	4,700	4,900
Melanesia	1,412	1,375	37	1,500	50	1,600	1,700
Mexico	1,513	1,500	13	1,600	50	1,700	1,800
Myanmar	1,412	325	1,087	1,500	50	1,600	1,700
Nigeria	18,950	18,425	525	19,300	700	20,100	20,900
Papua New Guinea	1,413	1,238	175	1,500	50	1,600	1,700
Philippines	2,050	449	1,601	2,100	100	2,200	2,300
Rwanda	1,312	1,275	37	1,400	50	1,500	1,600
Scotland	19,700	19,175	525	20,300	700	21,100	21,900
South East Asia	4,700	1,100	3,600	4,800	200	5,000	5,200
Southern Africa	15,500	-0	15,500	15,800	600	16,400	17,100
Southern Cone of South America	3,250	3,040	210	3,300	100	3,400	3,500
Sudan	3,250	-0	3,250	3,300	100	3,400	3,500
Taiwan		1,126	(1,126)			-0	-0
Tanzania	6,500		6,500	6,700	200	7,000	7,300
Uganda	6,500	-0	6,500	6,700	200	7,000	7,300
United States of America (including Province IX)	354,900	346,386	8,514	360,000	13,400	374,400	389,400
Wales	29,450	28,625	825	30,100	1,100	31,300	32,600
West Africa	2,550		2,550	2,600	100	2,700	2,800

	Budget £	Paid by 11/16/99 £	Unpaid Balance £	2000 Budget £	2001 Budget £	2002 Budget £	Supplementary Request £	Total
West Indies	13,050	3,446	9,604	13,300	13,800	14,400	500	
United Churches:								
United Church of Bangladesh	698	685	13	700	700	700	30	
United Church of North India	1,412	325	1,087	1,500	1,600	1,700	50	
United Church of Pakistan	1,413	-0	1,413	1,500	1,600	1,700	50	
United Church of South India	2,050	475	1,575	2,100	2,200	2,300	100	
Extra-Provincial Dioceses:								
Bermuda	1,950	1,875	75	2,000	2,100	2,200	100	
Lusitanian Church	698	698	-0	700	700	700	30	
Spanish Rfmd Episcopal Church	697	-0	697	700	700	700	30	
	1,197,010	952,834	244,176	1,217,800	1,266,700	1,317,800	45,080	
Budget "2002/3	304,970			913,350			33,810	1,252,130
Budget "2003/4				304,450	950,025		11,270	1,265,745
Budget "2004/5					316,675	988,350		1,305,025

Anglican Consultative Council

Member Church Contributions 1999 to 2002

	>>>>>>>>>1999<<<<<<<<< [Excluding paid for prior years]							
	Budget £	Paid by 11/16/99 £	Unpaid Balance £	2000 Budget £	2001 Budget £	2002 Budget £	Supplementary Request £	Total
Aotearoa, New Zealand and Polynesia	34,991	24,474	10,517	36,391	27,800	28,900	1,100	30,000
Australia	101,670	49,020	52,650	105,737	110,000	114,400	4,400	118,800
Brazil	4,867	-0	4,867	5,062	5,300	5,500	200	5,700
Burundi	216	216	-0	225	300	300	10	310
Canada	69,222	23,842	45,380	71,991	74,900	77,900	3,000	80,900
Central Africa	7,030	-0	7,030	7,311	7,600	7,900	300	8,200
Central America	1,298	1,298	-0	1,350	1,400	1,500	50	1,550
Ceylon	1,190	1,190	-0	1,238	1,300	1,400	50	1,450
Congo Democratic Republic	541	541	-0	563	600	700	30	730
England [inc Dio in Europe]	319,721	319,700	21	332,510	345,800	359,700	13,800	373,500
Hong Kong Sheng Kung Hui	20,000	20,000	-0	20,800	21,700	22,500	900	23,400
Indian Ocean	2,920	2,920	-0	3,037	3,200	3,300	100	3,400
Ireland	25,678	25,678	-0	26,705	27,800	28,900	1,100	30,000
Japan	14,191	14,191	-0	14,759	15,400	16,000	600	16,600
Jerusalem & the Middle East	3,980	3,980	-0	4,139	4,300	4,500	200	4,700
Kenya	8,653	8,653	-0	8,999	9,400	9,800	400	10,200
Korea	3,786	-0	3,786	3,937	4,100	4,300	200	4,500
Melanesia	1,190	1,190	-0	1,238	1,300	1,400	50	1,450

Mexico	1,550	50	1,500	1,400	1,350	1,298	1,199	99
Myanmar	1,450	50	1,400	1,300	1,238	1,190	-0	1,190
Nigeria	19,300	700	18,600	17,900	17,154	16,494	16,494	-0
Papua New Guinea	1,450	50	1,400	1,300	1,238	1,190	1,190	-0
Philippines	2,100	100	2,000	1,900	5,905	5,678	1,505	4,173
Rwanda	1,350	50	1,300	1,200	1,125	1,082	-0	1,082
Scotland	20,200	700	19,500	18,200	17,998	17,306	16,765	541
South East Asia	4,800	200	4,600	4,400	22,497	21,632	4,229	17,403
Southern Africa	15,800	600	15,200	14,600	14,038	13,498	13,498	-0
Southern Cone of South America	3,300	100	3,200	3,100	2,958	2,844	2,988	(144)
Sudan	3,300	100	3,200	3,100	2,958	2,844	-0	2,844
Taiwan	-0		-0	-0			1,028	(1,028)
Tanzania	6,600	200	6,400	6,200	5,905	5,678	5,678	5,678
Uganda	6,600	200	6,400	6,200	5,905	5,678	-0	-0
United States of America (including Province IX)	361,600	13,400	348,200	334,800	321,879	309,499	243,927	5,678
Wales	30,000	1,100	28,900	27,800	26,705	25,678	25,678	65,572
West Africa	2,600	100	2,500	2,400	2,250	2,163	2,163	-0
West Indies	13,300	500	12,800	12,300	11,811	11,357	11,357	-0
United Churches:	-0		-0	-0				-0
United Church of Bangladesh	730	30	700	600	591	568	568	-0
United Church of North India	1,450	50	1,400	1,300	1,238	1,190	1,190	-0
United Church of Pakistan	1,450	50	1,400	1,300	1,238	1,190	-0	1,190
United Church of South India	2,100	100	2,000	1,900	1,800	1,731	1,731	1,731
Extra-Provincial Dioceses:	-0		-0	-0			-0	-0
Bermuda	2,000	100	1,900	1,800	1,687	1,622	1,622	-0
Lusitanian Church	730	30	700	600	563	541	500	41
Spanish Rfmd Episcopal Church	730	30	700	600	563	541	-0	541
	1,219,880	45,080	1,174,800	1,128,400	1,116,586	1,073,636	848,472	225,164

Anglican Consultative Council
Reforecast 2001/2002

	Actual 2000/01	Budget £	Estimate £	Shortfall £
Aotearoa, New Zealand and Polynesia	28,900	29,450	28,625	825
Australia	114,400	116,600	68,000	48,600
Brazil	5,500	5,600	2,800	2,800
Burundi	300	308	300	8
Canada	77,900	79,400	56,700	22,700
Central Africa	7,900	8,050	-0	8,050
Central America	1,500	1,512	-0	1,512

Ceylon	1,400	1,412	1,375	37
Congo Democratic Republic	700	698	675	23
England [inc Dio in Europe]	359,700	366,575	356,225	10,350
Hong Kong Sheng Kung Hui	22,500	22,975	22,300	675
Indian Ocean	3,300	3,350	3,275	75
Ireland	28,900	29,450	28,625	825
Japan	16,000	16,300	15,850	450
Jerusalem & the Middle East	4,500	4,600	4,450	150
Kenya	9,800	10,000	4,900	5,100
Korea	4,300	4,400	4,250	150
Melanesia	1,400	1,412	1,375	37
Mexico	1,500	1,513	1,500	13
Myanmar	1,400	1,412	1,375	37
Nigeria	18,600	18,950	18,425	525
Papua New Guinea	1,400	1,413	1,238	175
Philippines	2,000	2,050	1,949	101
Rwanda	1,300	1,312	1,275	37
Scotland	19,500	19,700	19,175	525
South East Asia	4,600	4,700	4,550	150
Southern Africa	15,200	15,500	15,200	300
Southern Cone of South America	3,200	3,250	3,040	210
Sudan	3,200	3,250	-0	3,250
Taiwan	-0		1,126	(1,126)
Tanzania	6,400	6,500	6,400	100
Uganda	6,400	6,500	-0	6,500
United States of America (including Province IX)	348,200	354,900	354,900	-0
Wales	28,900	29,450	28,625	825
West Africa	2,500	2,550	-0	2,550
West Indies	12,800	13,050	13,046	4
United Churches:				-0
United Church of Bangladesh	700	698	685	13
United Church of North India	1,400	1,412	1,375	37
United Church of Pakistan	1,400	1,413	-0	1,413
United Church of South India	2,000	2,050	1,975	75
Extra-Provincial Dioceses:				-0
Bermuda	1,900	1,950	1,875	75
Lusitanian Church	700	698	698	-0
Spanish Rfmd Episcopal Church	700	697	-0	697
		1,197,010	1,078,157	118,853

Financial Report for ACC-12

Member Church Contributions 2002 to 2005

	>>>>>>>2002<<<<<<<			2003	Supplementary	2004	2005
	2002 Request £	Paid by 9/6/02 £	Unpaid Balance £	Request £	Request	Request £	Request £
Aotearoa, New Zealand and Polynesia	30,000	21,675	8,325	30,100	1,100	31,300	32,600
Australia	118,800	21,059	97,741	119,000	4,400	123,800	128,800
Brazil	5,700		5,700	3,400	200	3,500	3,600
Burundi	310		310	300	10	300	300
Canada	80,900	28,492	52,408	81,000	3,000	84,200	87,600
Central Africa	8,200		8,200	8,200	300	8,500	8,800
Central America	1,550	1,500	50	1,600	50	1,700	1,800
Ceylon	1,450		1,450	1,500	50	1,600	1,700
Congo Democratic Republic	730		730	700	30	700	700
England [inc Dio in Europe]	373,500	269,775	103,725	374,100	13,800	389,100	404,700
Hong Kong Sheng Kung Hui	23,400	22,500	900	23,400	900	24,300	25,300
Indian Ocean	3,400	3,300	100	3,400	100	3,500	3,600
Ireland	30,000	28,900	1,100	30,100	1,100	31,300	32,600
Japan	16,600	16,000	600	16,600	600	17,300	18,000
Jerusalem & the Middle East	4,700	4,500	200	4,700	200	4,900	5,100
Kenya	10,200		10,200	10,200	400	10,600	11,000
Korea	4,500		4,500	4,500	200	4,700	4,900
Melanesia	1,450	1,400	50	1,500	50	1,600	1,700
Mexico	1,550	1,500	50	1,600	50	1,700	1,800
Myanmar	1,450		1,450	1,500	50	1,600	1,700
Nigeria	19,300	18,600	700	19,300	700	20,100	20,900
Papua New Guinea	1,450	1,238	212	1,500	50	1,600	1,700
Philippines	2,100		2,100	2,100	100	2,200	2,300
Rwanda	1,350	1,300	50	1,400	50	1,500	1,600
Scotland	20,200	14,625	5,575	20,300	700	21,100	21,900
South East Asia	4,800		4,800	4,800	200	5,000	5,200
Southern Africa	15,800		15,800	15,800	600	16,400	17,100
Southern Cone of South America	3,300	3,020	280	3,300	100	3,400	3,500
Sudan	3,300	1,500	1,800	3,300	100	3,400	3,500
Taiwan	-0	1,113	(1,113)			-0	-0
Tanzania	6,600		6,600	6,700	200	7,000	7,300
Uganda	6,600		6,600	6,700	200	7,000	7,300
United States of America (including Province IX)	361,600	252,470	109,130	360,000	13,400	374,400	389,400
Wales	30,000	28,900	1,100	30,000	1,100	31,300	32,600
West Africa	2,600		2,600	2,600	100	2,700	2,800
West Indies	13,300		13,300	13,300	500	13,800	14,400

United Churches:							
United Church of Bangladesh	-0	730	-0	700	30	700	700
United Church of North India	730		1,450	1,500	50	1,600	1,700
United Church of Pakistan	1,450		1,450	1,500	50	1,600	1,700
United Church of South India	1,450		2,100	2,100	100	2,200	2,300
Extra-Provincial Dioceses:							
Bermuda	2,000	1,900	100	2,000	100	2,100	2,200
Lusitanian Church	730	730	-0	700	30	700	700
Spanish Rfmd Episcopal Church	730	-0	730	700	30	700	700
	1,219,880	746,727	473,153	1,217,800	45,080	1,266,700	1,317,800
Budget "2002/3	304,970			913,350	33,810	950,025	1,252,130
Budget "2003/4				304,450	11,270	316,675	1,265,745
Budget "2004/5						988,350	1,305,025

Inter-Anglican Budget - Income 2002

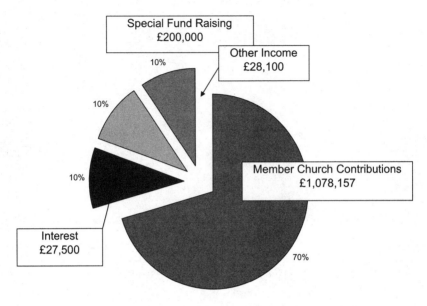

Special Fund Raising
£200,000

Other Income
£28,100

10%

10%

Member Church Contributions
£1,078,157

10%

Interest
£27,500

70%

Total Income £1,352507

Inter-Anglican Budget Expenditure 2002

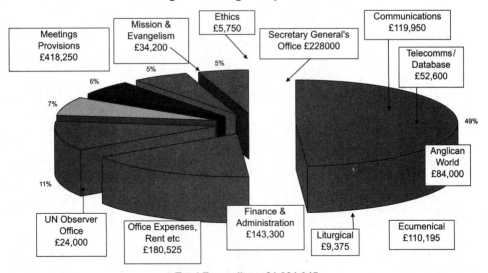

Ethics
£5,750

Mission &
Evangelism
£34,200

Meetings
Provisions
£418,250

Secretary General's
Office £228000

Communications
£119,950

Telecomms/
Database
£52,600

5%

5%

6%

7%

49%

Anglican
World
£84,000

11%

UN Observer
Office
£24,000

Office Expenses,
Rent etc
£180,525

Finance &
Administration
£143,300

Liturgical
£9,375

Ecumenical
£110,195

Total Expenditure £1,381,045

Inter-Anglican Budget 2002
Meetings Provisions

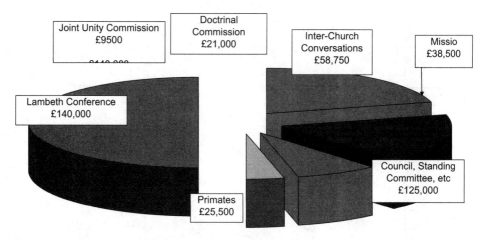

Joint Unity Commission
£9500

Doctrinal Commission
£21,000

Inter-Church Conversations
£58,750

Missio
£38,500

Lambeth Conference
£140,000

Council, Standing Committee, etc
£125,000

Primates
£25,500

Total Meetings Provisions

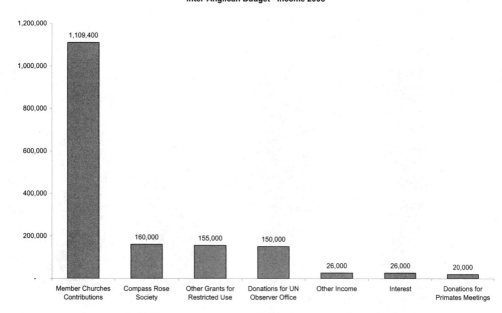

Inter-Anglican Budget - Income 2005

Inter-Anglican Budget - Expenditure 2005

Cost to run ACC   £1,629,500

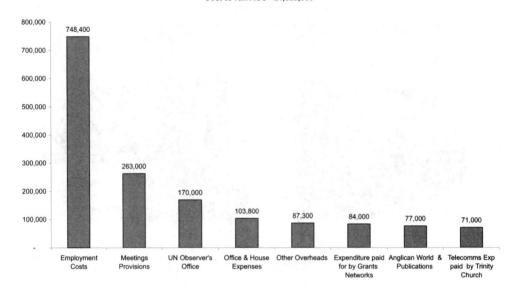

Inter Anglican Budget - 2005 Meetings

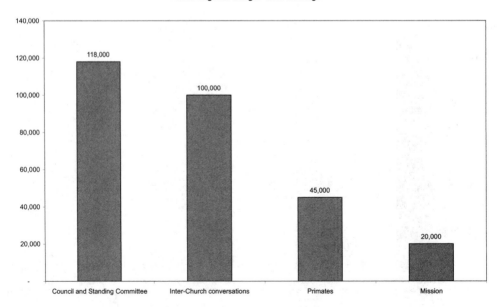

Inter-Anglican Budgets 2005

	£
Member Churches Contributions	1,109,400
Compass Rose Society	160,000
Other Grants for Restricted Use	155,000
Donations for UN Observer Office	150,000
Other Income	26,000
Interest	26,000
Donations for Primates Meetings	20,000
	1,646,400

EXPENDITURE

Employment Costs	748,400
Meetings Provisions	263,000
UN Observer's Office	170,000
Office & House Expenses	103,800
Other Overheads	87,300
Expenditure paid for by Grants Networks	84,000
Anglican World & Publications	77,000
Telecomms Exp paid by Trinity Church	71,000
	1,604,500
	41,900

Provision for meetings etc:

Council and Standing Committee	118,000
Inter-Church conversations	100,000
Primates	45,000
Mission	20,000
	283,000

THE
CONSTITUTION
OF THE ANGLICAN
CONSULTATIVE COUNCIL

The Constitution of the Anglican Consultative Council

1. Name

The name of the council is the Anglican Consultative Council.

2. Object

The object of the council shall be to advance the Christian religion and in furtherance of that object, but not further or otherwise, the council shall have the following powers:

a. To facilitate the co-operative work of the member churches of the Anglican Communion.

b. To share information about developments in one or more provinces of the Anglican Communion with the other parts of the Communion and to serve as needed as an instrument of common action.

c. To advise on inter-Anglican, provincial, and diocesan relationships, including the division of provinces, the formation of new provinces and of regional councils, and the problems of extra-provincial dioceses.

d. To develop as far as possible agreed Anglican policies in the world mission of the Church and to encourage national and regional churches to engage together in developing and implementing such policies by sharing their resources of man power, money, and experience to the best advantage of all.

e. To keep before national and regional churches the importance of the fullest possible Anglican collaboration with other Christian churches.

f. To encourage and guide Anglican participation in the ecumenical movement and the ecumenical organisations, to co-operate with the World Council of Churches and the world confessional bodies on behalf of the Anglican Communion, and to make arrangements for the conduct of pan-Anglican conversations with the Roman Catholic Church, the Orthodox churches, and other churches.

g. To advise on matters arising out of national or regional church union negotiations or conversations and on subsequent relations with united churches.

h. To advise on problems of inter-Anglican communication and to help in the dissemination of Anglican and ecumenical information.

i. To keep in review the needs that may arise for further study, and, where necessary, to promote inquiry and research.

j. To obtain, collect, receive, and hold money, funds, and property, old and new, by way of contributions, donations, subscriptions, legacies, grants, and any other lawful method, and accept and receive gifts of property of any description (whether subject to any special trust or not).

k. To assist any charitable body or bodies financially or otherwise.

l. To establish an emergency fund or funds for the support of clergy in special need and for other charitable purposes in any part of the world.

m. To assist the Inter-Anglican Finance Committee (as hereinafter defined), the Primates' Meeting, and the Lambeth Conference as and when required to do so.

n. To procure to be written in print, publish, issue, and circulate gratuitously or otherwise any reports or periodicals, books, pamphlets, leaflets, or other documents.

o. To receive and hold in custody, or cause to be held in custody, any records or legal or historical documents of any member church.

p. To arrange and provide for or join in arranging and providing for the holding of exhibitions, meetings, lectures, and classes.

q. To make bylaws, always subject to this constitution, for the better conduct of its business and to repeal or amend the same from time to time.

r. To do all such other things as shall further the objects of the council.

3. Membership

a. The Council shall be constituted with a membership according to the schedule hereto. With the assent of two-thirds of the Primates of the Anglican Communion, the council may alter or add to the schedule. "Primates," for the purposes of this article, shall mean the principle Archbishop, bishop, or Primates of each of the bodies listed in paragraphs b, c and d of the schedule of membership.

b. Members shall be appointed as provincial, national or regional machinery provides. Alternate members shall be appointed in a similar manner and shall be invited to attend a meeting if the ordinary member is unable to be present for a whole session of the council. Any appointment of a member or alternate member may be revoked by the body that made the appointment.

4. Appointment and Retirement of Members

a. Each of the appointing bodies shall have regard to the desirability of ensuring that any member appointed to represent it on the council shall be a member of its own representative structures and that such person shall be given appropriate opportunity to report the proceedings of the council to its own decision-making bodies and to convey the views of such decision-making bodies to the council.

b. The term of office for ordinary members shall be either

  i. six years calculated from a member's first attendance at a meeting of the council, or

  ii. three successive meetings of the council, whichever period shall terminate the later, or

  iii. such shorter period as the appointing body shall determine

c. On termination of his or her period of office, no member shall be eligible for reappointment nor shall he or she be appointed an alternate member until a period of six years elapses from the date when such original membership ceased.

d. Bishops and other clerical members shall cease to be members on retirement from ecclesiastical office.

e. Any appointing body as set out in the Schedule of Membership shall have power at any time and from time to time to appoint any qualified person to be a member to fill a casual vacancy to hold office for the unexpired term specified in clause 4(b).

f. Alternate members: an alternate member may be reappointed as an alternate member or appointed an ordinary member unless he or she has already replaced a member at two meetings of the council.

g. Any appointing body shall upon making such appointment notify the Secretary General of the name of the person so appointed and all relevant contact information relating to the person.

5. Advisers

The council may invite advisers, Anglicans, or others, to be present at its meetings, but not to vote.

6. Officers

a. The Archbishop of Canterbury shall always be a member of the council and its president, and not subject to retirement under the provision of clause 4(b). When present he shall inaugurate each meeting of the council. He shall be an ex officio member of all its committees.

b. The council shall elect a chairman and vice chairman from its own number who shall hold office for two meetings of the council.

c. The council shall delegate to its Standing Committee the appointment of a secretary for a specified term who shall be known as the Secretary General of the council and whose duties it shall determine. The Secretary General shall not be a member of the council. Remuneration and terms and conditions of service shall be determined by the Standing Committee [1]

[1] ACC-1, page,59 resolution 42, defined the terms of appointment as follows:

(a) to be responsible for all secretarial and other duties for the council and for the meetings of the council and of its Standing Committee; and (b) to serve the Anglican Communion and its member churches with particular regard to the stated functions of the Anglican Consultative Council and to the recommendations and reports of the Council.

ACC-8, resolution 30:
Meetings of the Primates and the Lambeth Conference
The Secretary General shall be available to serve, as the Archbishop of Canterbury shall require, as staff for meetings of the Primates and Lambeth Conference. The ACC shall not be responsible for the expenses of the Primates' Meetings or the Lambeth Conference. The Primates' Meetings and the Lambeth Conference shall be responsible for expenses incurred on their behalf by the Secretary General and his staff.

7. Standing Committee

a. The council shall appoint a Standing Committee of nine members, which shall include the chairman and the vice chairman of the council. The Secretary General shall be secretary of the Standing Committee.

b. The members of the Standing Committee shall be the trustees of the council for the purposes of the Order of the Charity Commissioners for England and Wales sealed on May 6,1994.

c. Ordinary meetings of the Standing Committee shall take place annually.

d. At least six months' notice shall be given to every member of the date and place of the annual meeting of the Standing Committee and such notice shall specify the general nature of the business to be transacted thereat.

8. Powers of the Standing Committee

The Standing Committee shall act for the council between meetings of the council and shall execute such matters as are referred to it by the council. The Standing Committee may exercise all powers of the council as are not by this constitution required to be done specifically by the council, and in particular may borrow money and mortgage or charge the council assets.

9. Meetings of the Council

a. The Council shall meet at intervals of approximately two or three years as appropriate.

b. As far as possible the council shall meet in various parts of the world.

10. Amendments to the Constitution

Amendments to this constitution shall be submitted by the council to the constitutional bodies listed under clauses b, c and d of the Schedule of Membership and must be ratified by two-thirds of such bodies provided that no amendment shall be made which cause the council to cease to be a charity at law.

11. Dissolution

If upon the winding-up or dissolution of the council, there remains after the satisfaction of all its debts and liabilities any property whatsoever, the same shall not be paid or distributed among the members of the council, but shall be given or transferred to some other charitable institution or institutions having charitable objects similar to the objects of the council and which shall prohibit the distribution of its or their income and property among its or their members.

The Schedule of Membership

The membership of the council shall be as follows:

a. The Archbishop of Canterbury

b. Three persons from each of the following, consisting of one bishop, one priest, and one layperson:

> Anglican Church of Australia
> Anglican Church of Canada
> Church of England
> Church of Nigeria (Anglican Communion)
> Church of the Province of Rwanda
> Church of the Province of Southern Africa
> Church of South India
> Church of the Province of Uganda
> Episcopal Church (United States of America)

c. Two persons from each of the following, consisting of one bishop or one priest plus one layperson:

> Anglican Church of Aotearoa, New Zealand, and Polynesia
> Church of the Province of Central Africa
> Province of the Anglican Church of Congo
> Church of Ireland
> Anglican Church of Kenya
> Church of North India
> Church of Pakistan
> Episcopal Church of the Sudan
> Anglican Church of Tanzania
> Church in Wales
> Church in the Province of the West Indies

d. One person (preferably lay) from each of the following:

> Church of Bangladesh
> Episcopal Anglican Church of Brasil
> Church of the Province of Burundi
> Anglican Church of the Central America Region
> Church of Ceylon
> Hong Kong Sheng Kung Hui
> Church of the Province of the Indian Ocean
> Nippon Sei Ko Kai (Anglican Communion in Japan)
> Episcopal Church in Jerusalem and the Middle East

Anglican Church in Korea
Church of the Province of Melanesia
Anglican Church of Mexico
Church of the Province of Myanmar
Anglican Church of Papua New Guinea
Episcopal Church in the Philippines
Anglican Church of the Southern Cone of America
Scottish Episcopal Church
Church of the Province of Southeast Asia
Church of the Province of West Africa

e. Co-opted members:

The Council may co-opt up to six additional members of whom two shall be women and two persons not over 28 years of age at the time of appointment.

f. Additional members:

When the chairman's appointment as chairman extends beyond the date at which his or her membership of the council ordinarily expires, from the time of the expiry of the ordinary membership:

  i. the body which made the appointment shall be entitled to appoint a new member of the council;

  ii. the chairman shall become an additional member of the council until the completion of the term as chairman;

  iii. the same rules shall apply to the vice chairman.

The Bylaws of the Anglican Consultative Council

(adopted pursuant to clause 2q of the constitution)

1. Meetings of the Council

a. All meetings of the council shall be called at a minimum of six months' notice in writing. Such notice shall specify the date, the place, and the general nature of the business to be transacted thereat.

b. No business shall be transacted at any meeting of the council unless a quorum of members is present at the time when the meeting proceeds to business. A quorum shall consist of members appointed by a majority of the bodies listed in clauses b, c,and d of the Schedule of Membership personally present.

c. Conduct of business at any meeting of the council shall be regulated by procedural rules adopted from time to time by the council, and insofar as any procedural matter shall arise that shall not be dealt with in the procedural rules currently in force, the chairman shall have power to determine such matter conclusively after such consultation as he shall think fit.

2. Proceedings of the Standing Committee

a. The chairman of the council may and on the request of five members of the Standing Committee shall summon a special meeting of the Standing Committee.

b. The Standing Committee may regulate their meetings as they think fit and determine the quorum necessary for the transaction of business. Unless otherwise determined, five shall be a quorum.

c. Questions arising at any meeting shall be decided by a majority of votes. In the case of an equality of votes, the chairman shall have a second or casting vote.

d. The Standing Committee may delegate any of its powers to committees as it thinks fit and any committee so formed shall, in the execution of he powers so delegated, conform to any requirements imposed on it by the Standing Committee. Any such committee may call advisers.

e. In electing members of the Standing Committee the council shall have regard to the desirability of achieving (so far as practicable) appropriate regional diversity and a balance of representation between clergy and laity and between the genders

f. Elected members of the Standing Committee shall hold office from the end of the council meeting at which they are appointed until the end of the last ordinary council meeting at which they would be entitled to attend but subject to earlier termination in the event that such elected member shall for any reason cease to be a member of the council.

3. Finance

a. The Secretary General is responsible to the council for overseeing its financial affairs and the affairs of the Inter-Anglican Finance Committee and shall ensure that proper books of account be kept with respect to:

i. All sums of money received and expended by the council and the matters in respect of which the receipt and expenditure took place

ii.The assets and liabilities of the council

and shall be responsible for presenting the council's audited accounts at each annual meeting of the Standing Committee.

b. The Standing Committee shall lay before the council properly audited annual income and expenditure accounts, balance sheets, and reports, and such documents to include full financial reports on the Inter-Anglican Finance Committee, the Primates' Meeting, and, where necessary, the Lambeth Conference. Copies of the same shall be circulated to members of the council with the other papers for the meeting at which the accounts are to be considered.

4. Inter-Anglican Finance Committee

a. The council in conjunction with the Primates' Meeting shall appoint a finance committee of at least five members, to be called the Inter-Anglican Finance Committee, which shall be responsible for coordinating the finances required by the council, the Primates' Meeting, and the Lambeth Conference.

b. The membership shall consist of at least two members appointed by the Primates' Meeting and at least three members appointed by the council.

c. Members appointed by the council shall take their place on the committee at the end of the council meeting at which they are elected, and their membership shall continue until the end of the last ordinary council meeting they would be entitled to attend but subject to earlier termination in the event that such elected member shall for any reason cease to be a member of the council. Members appointed by the Primates' Meeting shall serve as long as the Primates shall determine.

d. The Inter-Anglican Finance Committee shall appoint from its own membership its chairperson and vice chairperson.

5. Inter-Anglican Budget

The Inter-Anglican Finance Committee in collaboration with the Standing Committee shall, in consultation with member churches, be responsible for the annual Inter-Anglican budget, which will include the costs of the Inter-Anglican Finance Committee, the Primates' Meeting and the Lambeth Conference, and shall keep members of the council and member churches informed about each year's budget and about the forecast for each of the succeeding three years. In the light of those draft budgets, the council shall determine the level of expenditure and the income required to meet its purposes. The contributions to the Inter-Anglican budget shall be apportioned among the member bodies as in clauses b to d inclusive of the Schedule of Membership.

6. Casual Vacancies in the Co-opted Membership of the Council

In the event of any casual vacancy occurring in the co-opted membership of the council, the Standing Committee shall have power to co-opt a member under the provisions of clause e of the Schedule of Membership of the council to hold office until the conclusion of the next meeting of the council. Any member co-opted in this manner by the Standing Committee shall be eligible for election by the council if it so wishes.

7. Casual Vacancies on the Standing Committee

In the event of a casual vacancy occurring in the membership of the Standing Committee between council meetings, the Standing Committee itself shall have power to appoint a member of the council of the same order as the representative who filled the vacant place, and such member shall have full voting rights for the remainder of the term of service of the former member. Such member shall, subject to his or her eligibility for continuing membership of the council, be eligible for re-election to the Standing Committee at the next council meeting.

8. Common Seal

The seal of the council shall at all times be kept in safe custody and shall not be affixed to any instrument except by authority of a resolution of the Standing Committee and in the presence of the secretary or the chairman of the Standing Committee and one other member of the council, each of whom shall sign every instrument to which the seal shall be so affixed in their presence.

Guidelines for Meetings of the Anglican Consultative Council

General

1. All arrangements for the conduct of the business of the council shall be made under the general direction of the president.

Arrangements for Meetings

2.1 The Standing Committee:
   2.1:1 Shall make all detailed arrangements for meetings of the council, and
   2.1:2 Shall settle the agenda and determine the order in which business shall be considered by the council at its meetings, and

2.1:3 May delegate any of its functions relating to such matters to member(s) or officers(s) as it shall see fit.

2.2 In settling the agenda, the Standing Committee shall pay particular regard to:

2.2:1 The role of the council as one of the instruments of unity in the Anglican Communion, and

2.2:2 Specific issues referred by the Archbishop of Canterbury, by the Lambeth Conference, by previous meetings of the council, and by the Primates' Meeting, and

2.2:3 The need to inform members about the ongoing work of the council, its Standing Committee, and its officers, and

2.2:4 The finances of the council.

2.3 In its preparation for each meeting of the council, the Standing Committee shall give opportunity to members at the first business session of every meeting (which shall take place within the first three days of assembling) to comment upon the settled agenda and to request the inclusion of additional material.

2.4 The chairman after consultation with the president shall have power to direct the addition to the agenda at any time of such urgent or specially important business shall seem to them desirable.

Chairing of Meetings

3.1 The Standing Committee shall appoint persons to chair each session of the council who shall be either the president, the chairman, the vice chairman, or such other member of the council as the Standing Committee shall think fit.

3.2 It shall be the duty of the chair of each session to maintain order in debate, to ensure so far as possible that discussion of matters is broadly representative of the full range of views of members of the council as a whole, and to encourage the council to reach general assent on matters under discussion.

3.3 The chair of each session may with or without the request of any member of the council after such consultation as the chair shall think fit suspend debate on any topic under discussion for a specified period or impose any speech limit or direct that any matter under discussion shall be put to the vote or give any other direction as shall seem to the chair to be conducive to the proper despatch of business.

Speakers

4.1 In their contributions to discussion members shall pay proper respect to the chair of the session and in particular shall have regard to the duties of the chair under 3.2 above.

4.2 All members of the council shall qualify to be called upon by the chair of the session to speak in any session of the council, and Primates, ecumenical participants or other persons present at the invitation of the council may address the council at the invitation of the chair of the session.

4.3 The chair of any session may request that members wishing to speak on any particular subject be asked to submit their names in writing to the chair of the session in advance with a general indication of their particular interest or expertise in relation to the matter under discussion.

4.4 Members may not speak unless called upon to do so by the chair of the session and, if called upon to speak, shall address their remarks through the chair.

4.5 Upon being called upon to speak, a member shall first announce his or her name and province or church.

4.6 Subject to any other direction by the chair of the session, a speaker introducing a report or moving a motion may speak for up to ten minutes and all other speakers may speak for up to five minutes.

4.7 The chair of the session shall call a member to order for failure to address remarks through the chair, irrelevance, repetition of previous arguments, unbecoming language, discourtesy, or any other breach of reasonable order of debate, and may order a member to end any speech.

4.8 The person moving a motion (but not an amendment) shall have a right of reply limited to five minutes at the close of the discussion, but no member may otherwise speak more than once in the same discussion except with the express permission of the chair.

Motions and Amendments

5.1 Insofar as daily business shall not have been dealt with in the main agenda, relevant motions shall be made available in writing to members in such form as the Standing Committee shall determine as soon as possible after receipt from the person proposing the motion and in any event not later than the commencement of the session in which it is proposed to be presented or discussed, unless the chair of the session shall permit otherwise.

5.2 Motions for consideration by the council shall be presented:

    5.2:1   In the case of motions forming part of the main agenda, by a member of the council nominated by the Standing Committee; and

    5.2:2   In the case of motions formulated by a regional or other group set up for a specific purpose as part of the work of group of sessions, by a member of such group; and

    5.2:3   In the case of any other motion to be brought to a plenary session designated by the Standing Committee for such business, by any member of the council with a written indication of support; signed by ten other members;

and in the case of motions under 5.2:2 and 5.2:3 above, the full text of such a motion shall be submitted in writing not later than the time directed by the Standing Committee in advance of the relevant discussion in order that the full text may be made available for consideration by all members unless the chair of the session shall permit otherwise.

5.3 Members wishing to submit any amendment to an existing motion shall submit the full text of such motion or amendment in writing, signed by the mover and ten other members, not later than the time directed by the Standing Committee in advance of the relevant discussion in order that the full text may be made available for consideration by all members unless the chair of the session shall permit otherwise.

5.4 An amendment shall not be accepted for discussion if in the opinion of the chair of the session it repeats an amendment that has already been withdrawn or disposed or would negate the motion to which it relates.

5.5 Amendments will normally be considered in the order in which they first affect the motion under discussion but may be considered in some other order at the discretion of the chair of the session, and the order in which amendments will be taken shall be announced at the commencement of the session.

5.6 A main motion shall not be put finally to the meeting until all amendments shall have been carried, withdrawn, or otherwise disposed of, and in the event that an amendment shall have been carried, the chair of the session will read to the council the motion as amended before further discussion on the motion or any outstanding further amendment may proceed.

5.7 When all amendments shall have been dealt with, the motion, subject to any agreed amendments, shall be put to the council.

Decisions on Business

6.1 Only members of the council shall be entitled to vote on business before the council.

6.2 The chair of each session shall put the motion under discussion to the council for general assent, which may be indicated in such manner as the chair shall think fit.

6.3 If the chair of the session shall so direct, or if upon the chair requesting general assent any member shall request that a vote be taken, and such request has the support of not less than one-third of the members present and entitled to vote, then a vote shall be taken by show of hands or on ballot papers as the chair of the session shall decide.

6.4 In the event of a vote being taken, a simple majority shall be required unless the president after consultation with the Standing Committee shall direct that some other majority shall apply.

General

7.1 The chair of a session may after consultation with the Standing Committee suspend the application of these guidelines for part or all of the relevant session if the chair shall think it conducive to the better despatch of the business then before the council.

7.2 The Council may at any time with the consent of the Standing Committee revoke, amend, or supplement these guidelines or any part of them for the better conduct of the business of the council.

The New ACC Constitution Explanatory Notes

Background

- At ACC-11 it was decided to consider restructuring the ACC, to make it a company with limited liability for the members of its Standing Committee

- ACC-12 established a committee to refine the first draft: this committee met on two occasions in 2003.

- The attached draft is the result of their work, and was approved by the Standing Committee when it met in 2004.

Structure and Content

- Although the new structure is different in legal concept to the original constitution, the drafting committee has kept as closely as possible to the patterns and structures that have been established over the years.

- This document represents the "Memorandum and Articles" of a company in English law; unlike a trading company, it does not have any shares or share-holders, but is a charitable company "limited by guarantee".

- The Object of the ACC is set out more fully than in the present constitution (see page 1 clause 3)

- The company's structure consists of three elements:
  - Member-Churches (Articles 2.2 and 7; and Schedule)
  - Delegates (Articles 2.2 and 8)—the present "members"
  - Trustees, who form the Standing Committee (Articles 2.3 and 3)

- As at present, there are to be two regular sets of meetings:
  - The annual meeting of the Standing Committee (Article 4.1)
  - The Plenary Sessions of the Delegates—i.e., the present full Council meetings (Article 8)

- It is envisaged that the *Guidelines* established at ACC-11 for conduct of meetings will remain in place, with provisions for amendment as at present (Article 8.5).

Process of Adoption

- In order to give effect to this constitution, the Charity Commissioners for England and Wales will need to make a formal Scheme (to permit the new company to be substituted for the present incorporated charity).

- The proposal will need to be endorsed by two-thirds of the constitutional bodies of the member churches (under Article 10 of the present constitution).

- The British Government has announced that in the next session of Parliament, legislation will be brought forward to establish new and simplified procedures for charity companies; this may have an impact on what is being proposed.

- Some aspects of this draft may also need to be revisited in the light of recommendations in the Windsor Report.

Recommendation

- The Council is asked to note the present position, to consider the implications of the Windsor Report, in relation to this draft, and to authorise the Standing Committee and the Legal Adviser to give effect to the new structures.

Recommendations in the Windsor Report Concerning the Anglican Consultative Council

The ACC will need to discuss the comments in the Windsor Report which relate to the Council and its work. You will find a brief historical analysis at paragraph 103, and some general questions raised about the relationship of the ACC to other instruments of Unity in paragraphs 106 and 107. Appendix 1 then goes on to address some specific areas which we will want to consider together when we meet:

1. Membership

   The question is raised about each province being represented on the Council by its Primate. The proposal has been considered before, at the Lambeth Conference in 1998, and at subsequent ACC meetings. The Report notes that this raises financial issues, as well as questions of balance between the orders of laity, clergy and bishops.

Less controversially, it is suggested that the Council's voice would be more effectively heard, and its activities be more clearly accountable, if the member churches on the Council were represented only by "persons who have a voice within the highest executive body of each province". We will all be aware of cases in which ACC members felt either that they brought no particular mandate to our meetings, or that they were given no opportunity to report effectively on their return following meetings.

2. Joint Standing Committee

At present, there are informal arrangements between the Standing Committee of the ACC and the Standing Committee of the Primates' Meeting, and to an extent they deal with matters jointly. It is suggested that we might formalise this arrangement, creating a larger Standing Committee composed of members of both the present Standing Committees, to give legal effect to the informal arrangements that presently exist.

It is also suggested that the Joint Standing Committees meet on a cycle to coincide with meetings of the Primates, so that the ACC members on the Joint Standing Committee have access to the thinking of the Primates, just as the Primate members of the Joint Standing Committee have access to the thinking of the Council.

3. Anglican Communion Office

There are recommendations in Appendix 1, paragraphs (6) to (9) that the internal operation of the office be reviewed, and its management structures be strengthened. This will have particular relevance to the work of the Standing Committee, and the accountability of its individual members.

Canon John Rees
Legal Adviser
jrees@winckworths.co.uk
23 May 2005

ACC
MEMBERSHIP

ACC-13 Participants

President
The Most Revd and Rt Hon Rowan Williams (England)

Chair
The Rt Revd John Paterson (Aotearoa, New Zealand & Polynesia)

Vice Chair
Professor George Koshy (Church of South India)

The Anglican Church in Aotearoa, New Zealand & Polynesia
The Rt Revd Winston Halapua
Dr Anthony Fitchett

The Anglican Church of Australia
The Rt Revd John Noble
The Ven Kay Goldsworthy
Mr Robert Fordham

The Church of Bangladesh
The Revd Sunil Mankhin

Igreja Episcopal Anglicana do Brasil
The Rt Revd Maurício José Araújo de Andrade

The Anglican Church of Burundi
The Rt Revd Martin Blaise Nyaboho

The Church of the Province of Central Africa
The Rt Revd James Tengatenga
Mr Daniel Taolo

Iglesia Anglicana de la Region Central de America
Mr Luis Roberto Valleé

The Church of Ceylon
The Rt Revd Kumara Illangasinghe

Province de L'Eglise Anglicane Du Congo
The Rt Revd Kahwa Henri Isingoma
Miss Joyce Muhindo Tsongo

The Church of England
The Rt Revd James Jones
The Very Revd Dr John Henry Moses
Canon Elizabeth Paver

Hong Kong Sheng Kung Hui
Ms Fung Yi Wong

The Church of the Province of the Indian Ocean
Mr Bernard Georges

The Church of Ireland
The Very Revd Michael Andrew James Burrows
Miss Kate Turner

The Nippon Sei Ko Kai (The Anglican Communion in Japan)
The Rt Revd Nathaniel Makoto Uematsu

The Episcopal Church in Jerusalem & The Middle East
The Rt Revd Riah Hanna Abu El-Assal

The Anglican Church of Kenya
The Rt Revd Samson Mwaluda
Mr Amos Kirani Kiriro

The Anglican Church of Korea
The Revd Abraham Kim

The Church of the Province of Melanesia
The Rt Revd David Vunagi

La Iglesia Anglicana de Mexico
Mr Ricardo Gomez-Osnaya

The Church of the Province of Myanmar (Burma)
Mr Saw Si Hai

The Church of Nigeria (Anglican Communion)
The Most Revd Peter Jasper Akinola DD.
The Very Revd Dr David Chidiebele Okeke
Mr Abraham Yisa

The Church of North India (United)
The Revd Ashish Amos
Mr Richard Ian Thornton

The Church of Pakistan (United)
The Revd Shahid P Mehraj
Mr Humphrey Peters

The Anglican Church of Papua New Guinea
Mr Roger Baboa

The Episcopal Church in the Philippines
Mr Floyd Lalwet

L'Eglise Episcopal au Rwanda
The Rt Revd Josias Sendegeya
The Ven Damien Nteziryayo
Mrs Jane Mutoni

The Scottish Episcopal Church
Mr John Stuart

The Church of South East Asia
Dato Stanley Isaacs

The Church of South India (United)
The Rt Revd Dr Yesuratnam William
The Revd Vincent Rajakumar
Dr Mrs Pauline Sathiamurthy

The Church of the Province of Southern Africa
The Rt Revd David Beetge
The Revd Janet Trisk
Ms Nomfundo Walaza

Southern Cone
The Revd Andres Gregorio Lenton

The Episcopal Church of the Sudan
The Rt Revd Ezekiel Kondo
The Revd Enock Tombe

The Anglican Church of Tanzania
The Rt Revd Gerard E Mpango
The Revd Canon Mwiti Akiri
Mrs Joyce Ngoda

The Church of the Province of Uganda
The Rt Revd Elia Paul Luzinda Kizito
The Revd Canon Job Bariira-Mbukure
Mrs Jolly Babirukamu

The Church in Wales
The Ven Alun Evans
Miss Sylvia Scarf

The Church of the Province of West Africa
Mrs Philippa Amable

The Church in the Province of the West Indies
The Rt Revd Robert Thompson
Dr Barton Scotland

Co-opted Members

The Rt Revd Carlos López-Lozano (Spain)
Head Brother James Tata (Melanesian Brotherhood)
Mrs Maria Christina Borges Alvare (Cuba)
Ms Candace Payne (West Indies)
Mr Michael Lee Tamihere (Aotearoa, New Zealand and Polynesia)

Primates Standing Committee

The Most Revd Peter Kwong (Hong Kong)
The Most Revd Bernard Malango (Central Africa)
The Most Revd Barry Morgan (Wales)
The Most Revd Orlando Santos de Oliveira (Brazil)
The Most Revd James Terom (North India)

Following a request from the Primates Meeting (February 2005) the Anglican Church of Canada and the Episcopal Church USA have withdrawn their members from the meeting. Those members are:

The Anglican Church of Canada

The Rt Revd Susan Moxley
The Revd Canon Allan Box
Ms Suzanne Lawson

The Episcopal Church in the USA

The Rt Revd Catherine S Roskam
The Revd Robert Lee Sessum
Dr Josephine Hicks

Ecumenical Participants

Metropolitan John of Pergamon (Ecumenical Patriarchate)
The Revd Paul Fiddes (Baptist World Alliance)
The Revd Esme Beswick (Churches Together in England)
The Revd Mark Fisher (Churches Together in England)
The Revd Canon Donald Bolen (Pontifical Council for Promoting Christian Unity)
The Rt Revd Malcolm McMahon, OP (Roman Catholic Church)
The Rt Revd Walter Jagucki (Lutheran World Federation)
Ms Teny Perri-Simonian (World Council of Churches)
The Revd William R Morrey (World Methodist Council)
The Revd W B van der Velde (Old Catholic Churches of the Union of Utrecht)
The Rt Revd Dr Euyakim Mar Coorilos (Mar Thoma Syrian Church of Malabar)

SPECIAL REPORT:
HUMAN
SEXUALITY

Presentations by the Anglican Church of Canada

Primate of Canada's Letter to the Members of the Anglican Consultative Council

THE MOST REVEREND ANDREW S. HUTCHINSON

June 21, 2005

To the Members of the Anglican Consultative Council

It is a privilege for my fellow Canadian presenters and myself to gather with you at this meeting of the Anglican Consultative Council. We have been looking forward to this opportunity to meet you in person and to honour the request for consultation from Lambeth resolutions, the Windsor Report and the most recent Primates' Meeting. We hope that these critical conversations will continue throughout the Communion.

We have come among you to explain the current situation in Canada which includes: a wide diversity of views; the actions that were taken by some of our dioceses and the General Synod; the theological and biblical rationale that inform our consideration of the blessing of committed same-sex unions; and the ways in which we endeavour to remain in dialogue and communion.

We recognize that, although this matter has been before the Anglican Church of Canada for many years, some of our synodical decisions have caused distress to the wider Communion. We have not always consulted with our brothers and sisters around the Anglican Communion and we deeply regret that the bonds of our mutual affection have been strained.

We affirm our continuing membership in and commitment to the worldwide Anglican Communion. In partnership with other Provinces we remain committed to evangelism, a compassionate response to the needs of suffering humanity, and to programs of relief, justice and peace for all. With humility we seek to honour these commitments, knowing also our need to listen and learn from the experiences of our brothers and sisters in faith in other Provinces of the Communion.

We continue to affirm the Ten Principles of Partnership endorsed by the Anglican Consultative Council and the Anglican Cycle of Prayer as sources of unity in the cause of mission.

My prayer is that the Holy Spirit will guide our hearts and minds as we share together in the work that is before us.

Yours faithfully
The Most Reverend Andrew S. Hutchison
Archbishop and Primate

The Conversation in the Canadian Church: A Presentation to the Anglican Consultative Council

- **Continuing Commitment to the Anglican Communion:** We affirm and value our continuing membership in the worldwide Anglican Communion. The Anglican Church of Canada has played a strong role in the councils of the Communion. The first Lambeth Conference in 1867 was called in response to a request from Canadian bishops. In 1963, when the Anglican Congress met in Toronto, the principle of "Mutual Responsibility and Interdependence in the Body of Christ" was expressed, and this principle continues to shape the life of this church. Canadian bishop Ralph Dean was Executive Officer of the Communion during the period after Lambeth 1968 when the Anglican Consultative Council was being formed. Canadians have served as members and as staff of the various committees and councils of the Communion, and continue to support the work of the Communion in many ways. We are committed to partnership with other Provinces in serving Christ and in seeking justice and peace for all. We take seriously the call for study and dialogue, and we are grateful for the opportunities to learn from and contribute to the experiences of our brothers and sisters in faith in other parts of the Communion.

- **Church Leadership and Governance:** We are a church that is episcopally led and synodically governed. In accordance with our constitution and canons, synods composed of bishops, clergy and lay people act together to determine doctrine and practice. The recent actions of the General Synod and of diocesan synods have been taken in accordance with our understanding of these canons and the limits of the jurisdiction of these bodies, recognizing that there is a sharing of authority and responsibility at the various levels of decision-making that tests the unity of our church. The word "synod" means "a road we walk together" and we are concerned to preserve this unity as we try to discern God's will together.

- **Diversity in the Canadian Church:** Canadian Anglicans represent a wide variety of backgrounds, languages, cultures and theological opinion. Our geography covers vast distances, and our members live in all regions of Canada, each region with its own challenges and gifts to bring to the whole. Aboriginal bishops, clergy and lay people are full participants in all the councils of the church. As a church, we are committed to working in partnership with aboriginal Anglicans through the Anglican Council of Indigenous Peoples and other groups. Many of our members have come to live in Canada from other Provinces of the Communion. Like many other churches in the Communion, we have found strength in our diversity and we are hopeful that the present tensions will lead us to a deeper understanding of the ways in which we need each other. We believe that we must learn to live together with differences in order to fulfill the mission of the church.

- **The Baptismal Covenant:** In the last twenty years, much of our church has been influenced by a renewed understanding of baptism and the baptismal covenant. The presence of this covenant in the new rites of initiation, found in *The Book of Alternative Services 1985,* and the opportunity for Anglicans to renew these promises each time the rite of initiation is celebrated, shape and influence our church. The covenant reminds us of the need to "continue in the apostles' teaching and fellowship, in the breaking of bread, and of the prayers", to "seek and serve Christ in all persons" and to "strive for justice and peace among all people, and respect the dignity of every human being."

- **The Ongoing Conversation:** At present, our national church is still in the midst of a conversation, seeking discernment around issues of homosexuality. These matters will be discussed at General Synod in 2007. In the meantime, we continue to encourage discussion as widely as possible in the church.

- **Biblical Authority and Interpretation:** We believe that one of the central issues in this discussion is the question of biblical authority and interpretation. Within the Anglican Church of Canada, and indeed within the Anglican Communion, there are various ways of reading and understanding scripture. To quote our St Michael Report, 'We acknowledge that the interpretation of Scripture is a central and complex matter and that, at times in the Church's history, 'faithful' readings have led to mutually contradictory understandings, requiring ongoing dialogue and prayer towards discernment of the one voice of the gospel.' We hope, therefore, that the Communion will continue to work at questions of authority and interpretation, drawing on a variety of scripture passages, including those which call for inclusivity in the Body of Christ and for justice for all as well as those that address matters of sexual ethics.

- **Diversity in Canadian Culture:** Each Province has its own cultural context in which it tries to live out a faithful response to the gospel. We live in Canada and are committed to living out the gospel faithfully in our particular context. Canada is a country with a wide diversity of peoples, languages and cultures. It is a country that tries to be tolerant of diversity. In Canada, homosexuality was removed from the criminal code in 1969 and same sex civil marriages are now authorized in 7 of 10 civil provinces. Provincial and federal jurisdictions have legislated against discrimination on the grounds of sexual orientation. Freedom from discrimination is guaranteed by the Canadian Charter of Rights and Freedoms. As a church then, living within Canadian society, we are part of that ongoing discussion. In this, we are in conversation with our counterparts in other churches, in particular the United Church of Canada and the Evangelical Lutheran Church in Canada who are working on many of the same issues.

In communicating these key messages, we do not wish to give the impression that we are close to reaching consensus on this matter. We experience in our Province many of the deep divisions that the Communion experiences, and believe that it is only possible to grow in our mutual understanding where our disagreement has not broken our communion with one another. We continue to express regret for the way that this issue and our various responses to it have offended some members of Christ's Body. We ask for the ongoing prayers of our brothers and sisters in the Communion. Pray that our church might draw closer to Christ. Pray for God's grace to deliver us from the ignorance, fear, prejudice and self-righteousness that is manifest on all sides of this debate.

Presentations by the
Episcopal Church USA

The Right Reverend J. Neil Alexander, Bishop of Atlanta

Sisters and brothers: Grace to you and peace from God our Father and the Lord Jesus Christ. My name is Neil Alexander and I am blessed to be the Bishop of the Diocese of Atlanta of The Episcopal Church. I am grateful to Archbishop Williams, Bishop Paterson, and the leadership of the Anglican Consultative Council for making time on your agenda to listen to the experience of bishops, laypersons, and priests of The Episcopal Church. I hope this time together is a worthy contribution to the communion-wide process of listening and conversation called for by the 1998 Lambeth Conference. I remain hopeful, in fact, I am convinced, that if we take the time to listen to one another across the length and breadth of our Communion, and enter into honest, thoughtful, and holy conversation with each other, we will discover at the heart of our common life that more profound unity and solidarity in mission that is a gift of the Risen Christ.

The issues before us are quite important ones and to suggest otherwise would be unfaithful in the extreme. I do not believe, however, that holding contrasting viewpoints on some aspects of human sexuality (homosexuality in particular), the ordination of homosexual persons, or the care and nurture of the faithful relationships of persons of same-sex affection, need to be understood as matters that should ultimately divide us. I believe that we are called to remain faithful to the fundamental mysteries of our salvation in the Risen Christ that bind us together in ways far deeper than anything that may threaten to divide us. I believe—as a matter of conviction—that people of faith for whom the Scriptures are of central importance, for whom the apostolic and catholic tradition is a living framework, and for whom genuine pastoral concern for all of God's children is a core value, can live together with integrity in spite of different viewpoints on the current issues.

It is important to tell you that I gave my consent to the election by the clergy and people of the Diocese of New Hampshire that Canon Gene Robinson be a bishop of the church. I did so thoughtfully and prayerfully and with the understanding that the clear majority of the clergy and people of the Diocese of Atlanta would either support my decision or would, at the very least, be willing to walk forward together with me in mission and ministry with a generosity of spirit and commitment to our common life. It is also important to point out that my consent was a shared decision with members of the diocese I serve as it was with every bishop in the Episcopal Church. When the question of the consent to the election in New Hampshire was placed before the House of Deputies, the priests and lay deputies from the Diocese of Atlanta, in a clear decision, also gave their consent. I note this only to say that in the Episcopal Church ours is shared governance between bishops, laypersons, and priests. Although this often makes our decision making somewhat cumbersome, I have come to highly value this process of shared governance and to celebrate the fact that the Lord of the Church works not only through bishops, but also through the hearts and minds of faithful laypersons and priests in giving direction to the mission of the church.

As I have reflected upon the life of my church in these last two years, I am grateful to God for the strength and vitality of The Episcopal Church. This has not been an easy time for our church, but it is clear to me that God continues to be mightily at work among us. The decisions of the 74th General Convention have left nothing and no one unaffected. Across our church we have welcomed the Windsor Report, and it has been a rich framework for our continuing conversations. In the diocese I serve, for example, it continues to be the source from which a great deal of thoughtful interchange has emerged, and we have been particularly enriched by welcoming into our conversations friends from other parts of the Communion. We anticipate that we will continue to widen the circle of our conversations and discernment. The conversations have been hard ones, with passionate voices all across the spectrum of viewpoints, but I am pleased to report that in the midst of it all fellow Episcopalians have discovered significant common ground, if not full agreement, and perhaps more importantly, a renewed sense of those deeper realities of faith that bind us together in Christ Jesus. I believe the enabling generosity of the Holy Spirit is powerfully at work among us, calling us to venture boldly for the Gospel of Jesus and empowering our mission for the sake of God's world.

The importance of such conversations can hardly be overestimated. These are holy conversations because the Spirit of Christ is vitally present in them. We are a stronger church because of them. At the same time, one often hears language around consensus or moving towards a consensus, beating out a consensus on the anvil of holy conversation and honest exchange between persons of good will who recognize in each other the animating presence of the Holy Spirit. I believe such consensus will emerge in time, both within my church and in our larger Anglican family, as long as we continue in fellowship and holy conversation with each other. But I am convinced that the key to our life together, for the living of these days, needs to move beyond conversation and consensus to commitment. I accepted the invitation of my Presiding Bishop, for whom I have the highest regard, to be present here because of my commitment to the doctrine, discipline, and worship of the Episcopal Church, and because of my commitment to the life and work of the Anglican Communion.

As the conversations have unfolded, I am convinced that we need to claim this season as a time of renewing commitment to our life together. For me, this means several concrete things. It means that I am committed to insuring that there is a safe and honored place in the church for my dear friend and respected colleague +Charles Jenkins. That trust is mutual because we are committed to looking after each other's interests at all times, but especially at those moments in which circumstances keep us from looking after our own interests. Let me hasten to add that my relationship with Bishop Jenkins is not unique in the House of Bishops of our church. We are not in fast agreement on all things, but the level of commitment of the bishops of my church to our common life, to the mission and ministry of the Risen Christ in our own church and across the Communion is more than a conversation. It is a commitment that is deep, broad, and high, and it is a commitment that is widely shared with our laity and clergy. This suggests, perhaps, one of the differentiating qualities of life in the United States where, because of our unique history as a nation, peoples of differing nationalities, cultural roots, religious convictions, political persuasions, and economic realities, have chosen to live together amidst our differences and celebrate our God-given diversity. Such respect for the dignity of difference is also woven into the fabric of our beloved church. This means that our life together is not always as neat and tidy as some of us might desire, but the result is a family of faith whose richness and diversity are gifts of God in which we find joy and delight.

There is also the commitment to mission that drives our church at every level. In the last couple of years, much of our energy has gone into the hard but holy conversations of which I have spoken. Although this surely has been a diversion for many, I am pleased to say that the mission and ministry of the church continues apace. In my own diocese and within the Sewanee Province of The Episcopal Church, we have continued to roll up our sleeves and serve those in need in the name of Jesus. We have developed new congregations and built new or renewed facilities for our children and youth. We have expanded the scope of our work into the college and university communities which are such an important part of our evangelical outreach. We have re-energized our work of direct aid and advocacy for God's poor. Our relationships with companion dioceses around the Communion continue to be strong and vital, and we rejoice in the friendship we share with our sisters and brothers around the globe. We are grateful for and humbled by the gifts that we receive from our sisters and brothers around the Communion with whom we continue to share in mission and ministry. There is renewed energy and vigor in so many aspects of our life and ministry that one cannot help but be grateful to God for the work God is doing among us.

There is also the very real commitment of The Episcopal Church to the Anglican Communion. I know of no one in my church, whatever their position on the current issues, who does not value our relationships with our sisters and brothers in Christ across our Communion. At its heart, I believe our Communion reflects our Tradition. We are not by nature, by history, or by conviction political or juridical, but relational. Our relationships with each other, lived in response to the gracious generosity of God, are of the utmost importance. Our common life will never be dependent upon the decisions of legislative bodies or animated by institutional framework of the church, as important as those things are. Instead, we thrive in the work of the Gospel because of our passionate desire to be in fellowship one with the other. And for me, being in relationship with all of my sisters and brothers is not simply a thoughtful aspiration, but a commitment, a pledge to walk together in faith and service, in spite of our differences, if not because of them. I believe such commitment is at the heart of our vocation as God's people in mission.

Episcopal Bishop Stephen Bayne was the first executive officer of the Anglican Communion and a principal influence in the founding and shaping of the Anglican Consultative Council. In addition to being a great bishop and leader in the church, he was also a powerful communicator. I take great delight and comfort in these words from his pen:

"The mission is God's, not ours. He is the One who is at work out there. We go out to meet Him. We go out to encounter our blessed Lord, creating and sustaining and loving and forgiving and inspiring and dying and being born again even among the people of the world who do not know His name, who would even spit His name out of their mouths.

"The pain and the search and the torment and the itch of a new society being born is God at work. The new knowledge that flickers and flames into fire in these societies is His. And such grace and wisdom, as men come to know it, is His. He is at work out there and the mission of redeeming and fulfilling is His.

"And to us, less than the least of all saints, is this grace given that we are privileged to go where He is and for a minute to stand by His side."

My beloved sisters and brothers: I believe to the bottom of my heart that Bishop Bayne had it just right. I believe that the Risen Christ calls us into relationship with each other for the sake of that mission that is God's alone, that mission in which we are privileged to share by God's mercy and grace. It is to that mission that I am committed. It is to that mission The Episcopal Church is committed. And it is for the sake of that mission that we seek in all things to set our hope on Christ. To God alone be the glory!

The Reverend Dr. Michael Battle

ASSOCIATE DEAN OF ACADEMIC AFFAIRS AND VICE PRESIDENT,
VIRGINIA THEOLOGICAL SEMINARY

My theological task is to invite you into our paradox of learning to be surprised by God's communal life revealed in Christ. It is in how we are learning to be surprised by God that we seek to explain our thinking around who is eligible to lead the flock of Christ. In order to provide markers for you to understand our theological process, I have outlined three steps that lead to how we have made sense of a person in a same sex union elected to the episcopate. These three steps are:

1. Surprised by holiness (Acts 10–15; Ezekiel 4:14–15)
2. Surprised by the Bible (How we read and inwardly digest scripture)
3. Surprised by who God can make eligible

Before entering into these steps, I want to tell a story that provides the framework for how these steps build upon one another.

My two daughters, Sage and Bliss (five years old and three years old respectively), came upon a spider web in our back yard. They were extremely curious about the activity in the web—a caterpillar was caught. Now, this is a natural occurrence for many of us around the world—that is, nature's activities in which there is competition, cunning and survival. But it was what happened next that caught me by surprise. My younger daughter, Bliss, said to my wife Raquel, "Mom, that poor caterpillar needs our prayers."

Somehow, the discernment of a three-year-old put my own awareness of God to shame. A child was learning (discerning) a deeper reality in her midst—that the norm of God's creation should not be death and survival—rather, it should be cooperation and practice of God's presence. Isaiah's vision of predator and prey existing cooperatively was Bliss' vision too.

We in the Episcopal Church have also been caught by surprise in how God is being revealed among us. But this paradox of learning to be surprised is not new to us, it has existed in the very foundations of the early church. This leads me to the first step of being surprised by holiness.

1. Surprised by holiness

We notice possible analogies between the experience of the early church and our own situation. We have assumed that God's word is living and active (Hebrews 4:10–12) as they did. We have struggled with God to show us whether Christians of same sex affection are welcomed in our midst as the early church struggled with gentiles in their midst. In this struggle, we studied Acts 10–15 with great care. The inclusion of the Gentiles in the early church was of great controversy, especially to admit them without requiring them to give up certain practices and customs that seemed counter to Jewish behavior and identity. Peter was right, according to scripture (Leviticus 11), not to cross traditional clean/unclean boundaries. And yet, Peter's certainty was challenged through a vision and voice from heaven inviting him to see reality differently. Peter is not unique in learning to be surprised by God, Ezekiel 4:14–15 is another predecessor text in which a prophet's certainty of biblical prohibitions were challenged. It took Peter and Cornelius, however, a while to catch up to the fact of whom God can make holy and clean.

The rest of the church rightly called Peter into account for his new position (new vision). Peter's new story needed corroboration, criticism and a retelling. It was a strange story according to scripture, but it was not adiaphora (things that don't really make a difference). It was indeed potentially church dividing and they worked hard to avoid that outcome.

There was no discussion of rights, such as a right for Cornelius be baptized or a right to proceed contrary to the stated mind of the church. Instead, Peter and the others gave testimony which was persuasive about the gifts of the spirit manifest in Cornelius and the other Gentiles.

Acts 15 shows the church's more detailed struggle of compromise as Peter and the others decided not to add any yoke to the Gentiles that they themselves would not be willing to bear. The Gentiles were not put in the awkward position of having to list or defend their identity. Instead, church people, who were not gentiles argued on their behalf and introduced them to the part of the church that had not seen their gifts and the Holy Spirit manifest among them.

It seems to us that arguments such as: that persons of same sex affection can be ordained only if they remain celibate are rejected by implication of the working out of scriptural differences of the early Church. Celibacy is a gift given for some, not a requirement for ordination in the Anglican tradition. Going back to Peter—the primary answer that convinced so many confused Christians in the early Church was Peter's credibility as a witness (on behalf of Cornelius and the rest) that the gifts of holiness were indeed made manifest in their lives. But the church came slowly to this position.

2. Surprised by the Bible

The appropriation of scripture remains a complex matter today, as it was in the early church. How human identity is interpreted in scripture continues to be fought over today. We confess that we all assume in univocal interpretations of scripture as if all Christians could agree on complex matters (e.g., usury, slavery, just war, abortion, death penalty, contraception...). Like my daughter Bliss contemplating the complexity of a spider web, we have learned to expect deeper dimensions of Christ's saving work among us, far beyond our limited power to understand. Our salvation story told through scripture teaches us not to grow discouraged with disagreements, but to trust the Holy Spirit in our midst who will not let our differences destroy us.

So, we read the Bible in this spirit. Because biblical writers came from multiple contexts, times, places and points of view, they did not all agree with one another. We have learned that when anyone says, "the Bible says this" that our learned response is to ask, "In what book?" When was it written? What were the circumstances? What are the reasons it says that and do they apply in the same way today? For example, men were forbidden to marry foreign wives in one part of scripture (Ezra 10); and in another part, the Book of Ruth believed firmly in intercultural marriage—that Boaz acted faithfully in marrying Ruth. King David even became the fruit of their descendants from this marriage of an Israelite and a foreigner. Today, in some circumstances it may be faithful to follow Ezra, while in most situations it is faithful to follow Ruth.

The authority of scripture, as the Windsor Report reminds us (par. 54), is in fact an instrument for the authority of the triune God who speaks to us in Jesus, the living word. The Spirit gives us ears to hear such power and authority. The Spirit leads us into an encounter with the living word. Does a given biblical commandment or prohibition speak clearly to our own encounter with the living word? This question helps us with biblical passages that prohibit same sex relations. It seems very likely that there was no phenomenon of Christians of the same gender living together in faithful and committed lifelong unions which we experience today. In appropriate humility we do not think of ourselves as better than biblical writers, but that every biblical norm is discerned commensurate to every human situation. Discernment is required. There are a few references to same sex relations especially in comparison with the vast amount of biblical texts on wealth, poverty, greed and stewardship. The biblical texts focused upon are Genesis 19:1–29 (Judges 19). Both stories are more about violence than same sex relations. Most of the Bible comments on the sin of Sodom and Gomorrah pertain to greed (except Jude 7); see Ezekiel 16:49.

The two substantial texts in Leviticus that deal with same-sex relations are Leviticus 18:22 and Leviticus 20:13. Leviticus is a book about holiness, but holiness is not a private affair. The text makes clear that we can be holy in a community that welcomes God—that extends hospitality. But the world and context of Leviticus is different from ours. We no longer prohibit the cross breading of cattle, or sowing hybrid crops or different crops in same fields, or eating certain animals, or blending wool. No doubt Paul was formed by this holiness code (Romans 1:26–27), but he discerns and invites his readers to learn to discern for themselves what is natural or unnatural (1 Corinthians 11).

3. Surprised by who is eligible for ordination.

We still believe in life long committed monogamous relationships of mutual affection and respect. The experience of holiness in some same sex unions has called for and deepens our sense of lifelong unions and the manifestation of holy community. The public vows taken between persons of same sex affection commit two persons to form a life together marked by commitment and unconditional care and love. The blessing of the union does not itself constitute the union anymore than the blessing of a priest or bishop constitutes a Christian marriage. To reject what some see as the holy union between persons of the same sex often reinforces social discrimination, oppression and violence. For this reason, the blessing of same sex unions for many Episcopalians is also a call to justice.

Christians believe that ultimate justice is known only through the life, death and resurrection of Christ. To this end we also understand what makes persons eligible to lead the flock of Christ—those with the capacity to bear authentic witness to Christ's resurrection. Such capacity is the definitive mark of an apostle in the early church (Acts 1:8; 2:32). We learn from St. Paul that apostolic credentials resemble service to others, not power over others as he had once thought himself. The apostle (the one sent) now looks cruciform, like Christ. "I have been crucified with Christ; and it is no longer I who live, but it is Christ who lives in me" (Galatians 2:20). If the church had not adopted such an understanding of what it means to be sent out from Christ's death and resurrection, all the personal characteristics called for in the pastorals would have been given equal weight. This would prohibit the Episcopal election of anyone married more than once (1 Timothy 3:2) or of any with unruly children (1 Timothy 3:4) or of anyone prone to quarrel or quick tempered or arrogant. Rather than interpreting such personal qualities in isolation, the people of God understood the eligibility to be bishop as a witness to the death and resurrection of Christ. Episcopal ministry exemplifies Christ, and the qualities of purity, gentleness and holiness are not the new bishop's own possessions but can only be the outpouring of Christ who "loved us, and gave himself up for us, a fragrant offering and sacrifice to God." This means that the electing community must discern an authentic obedience to Christ in the one elected.

So, the Episcopal Church is far from thinking that eligibility criteria for being a bishop is somehow irrelevant or unimportant or consigned to the category of adiaphora (things that don't really matter). Rather the church keenly desires dialogue, discussion on these complex matters through the Anglican Communion. We do not lesson the degree of holiness or wholesomeness of our candidates for Episcopal service, rather we are often surprised by whom Christ makes eligible to lead.

Ultimately it is Christ's holiness that makes us holy and the sacrifice he accomplished in showing us the purpose of creation as being beyond death and survival. Christ's accomplishment is so profound that children can learn to refuse violent realities. In my three-year-old daughter's contemplation of predator and prey, she has discovered a new reality— namely God. She is open to the surprises of God—those surprises of not having to be enemies or participants in culture wars. Our document, *To Set Our Hope on Christ,* is just as childlike. Paradoxically, however, this childlikeness is our genius. The genius of being Anglican is in its ability to be open to God's surprises.

The Right Reverend Charles E. Jenkins, Bishop of Louisiana

My brothers and sisters in Christ, I am Charles Jenkins, Bishop of Louisiana, (See city, New Orleans), of the Episcopal Church (USA), and chair of the Bishops of the Fourth Province, sometimes known as the Sewanee Province. I am privileged to serve our Presiding Bishop as President of his Council of Advice. I am grateful for the opportunity to be here.

Amongst the presenters from the Episcopal Church from whom you hear this day, alone I stand as a Bishop who did not give consent to the recent election of the See of New Hampshire, and I remain convinced that the Divinely ordained intention for the practice of human sexuality is between a man and a woman within the bonds of Holy Matrimony. Further, I remain committed to serving Jesus Christ in the Episcopal Church, even though I think my Church made a wrong move as regards recent decisions about human sexuality. I must tell you that my presence with you is a stumbling block for some who think my willingness to even be present today is a betrayal of my theological position. I think my presence is an act of obedience to Jesus who is the Good Shepherd who calls his flock to unity and who stands with his people no matter the threats to His flock. I can do no other.

Likewise, some on the Lambeth Commission found puzzling the relationship of brotherly affection that I share with my Presiding Bishop. Though he and I are in obvious disagreement on a few issues concerning persons whose affections are directed toward those of the same gender, I must tell you that I believe with every fiber of my being that Frank Griswold would guard my interest if I could not, and I pray, with God as my strength, that I would guard and hold his interests if he could not. Such relationships of trust are not uncommon in the Episcopal Church, instead they are the rule, even in the face of serious and sometimes daunting disagreement.

My purpose in standing before you today is not an attempt to convince you of a theological position, nor am I here to justify actions by my church or inactions on my part. I obviously could not do that. Rather, I traveled here to give you a glimpse of life in the Episcopal Church and to briefly demonstrate how I, as a Bishop who voted in the minority at the General Convention in 2003, now lives and functions in the Episcopal Church. To do so, I shall of necessity relate to life in the Sewanee Province of the Episcopal Church, which consists of the southeastern United States and is, numerically, the largest of our nine provinces.

Please hear me when I affirm, in all humility, that every Bishop in the Sewanee Province, and I think the great majority of the Bishops, clergy and laity of the Episcopal Church, desire to remain part of the Anglican family, the Anglican Communion. Without false pride, but in the example of emptying of self, evident in the life of our Lord and Saviour Jesus Christ, I affirm that I am by grace, in baptism a Christian, an Episcopalian, and an Anglican. As Christians, we highly value family. I highly value my place in the Anglican family and pray that we Episcopalians may continue with integrity to be welcomed and valued as contributing members of the Anglican Communion. My affirmation is an echo of the reality and the hope of many. I do not wish to walk separately from you, and I pray that you will not choose to walk separately from me.

As my brother Bishop of the Episcopal Church and the Sewanee Province, the Right Reverend Neil Alexander, Bishop of Atlanta, will affirm, all the Bishops of the Sewanee Province remain together at the one table of our Lord Jesus Christ. Despite our difference and despite the very real pain and anguish that grips some of our Church, as well as the hopes and dreams evident in our life together, we delight to share a common mission that is based on our mutual commitment to Jesus Christ whom we affirm as Lord and Saviour. Please do not hear what I am not saying; there is hurt, there is fear, there is a sense of rejection, and there is even dread amongst some in the Episcopal Church, especially amongst those who hold a position similar to mine. I do not wish to underestimate the depth of these feelings. There are real threats to split the Church and, thus, plunge us into a generation of lawsuits what will compromise the Anglican witness in North America—you know all this. For the sake of the Christian mission, this must not happen. I think a more graceful interpretation of our existing canons, a more charitable application of those same canons, and perhaps changing canons to give more latitude, would be a good first step to provide the time, space, and safety needed to work out the issues that confront us. But, there is more to be said.

As Bishops of the Sewanee Province, we count one another as friend and we offer fellowship, support, and encouragement to one another, no matter our differences. We pray with and we pray for one another. We share in the Province's many ministries in common, such as our ministry with Youth, a strong University ministry, HIV/AIDS ministry, Christian Education, Disaster Relief, Anti-Racism and Environmental Concerns, to name a few. So, please hear what I am saying: we remain committed to evangelism and mission even in the midst of challenge and strained circumstance. Some believe that our mission is enhanced by the actions of General

Convention 2003, and others of us see those actions as a stumbling block. As Bishops, we seek to provide a safe place in the Episcopal Church, and we are willing to sacrifice for the safety and integrity of the other. We struggle with these issues; we are not good at this. Perhaps, here you would please be of help to us.

For example, let us consider the matter of Delegated Episcopal Oversight, clearly affirmed by the Windsor Report. The scheme has worked well in many places; in a few instances there have been failures. The former are hardly known, the latter much publicized. I welcome the Panel of Reference called for the Primates (15) so that our successes, as well as our failures, may be more closely examined. I would hope that we can continue the process of refining our DEPO scheme; I hope that we can hear more from those who think such to be a necessity in their situation. So, we do not yet have a final picture of what building safe space in the midst of disagreement looks like in the context of the Church Catholic and our Canon Law. I pray that you might show us examples in the Communion of how we might better live into our desire for charity, safety and integrity. I would tell you that such commitment to one another, to mission, and to the Church is not unique to the Sewanee Province. I pray that somehow we in the Episcopal Church can find a way, with integrity, to embrace the substance of the Windsor Report and remain together in our walk to God. To walk apart would wreck my Diocese as well as many others.

We are working to discover the meaning of "autonomy in communion" and "freedom held within interdependence" (par. 76). We take seriously the Windsor Report which notes: "Communion remains God's gift as well as God's command" (par. 46). Thus, do I rejoice in the rejection of a parallel jurisdiction as noted in the Windsor Report.

We are working together, committed to Jesus Christ, committed to the Episcopal Church, and committed to the "authority of the Triune God, exercised through Scripture" (par. 54). We remain committed to the Anglican Communion and to you, my brothers and sisters in Christ. May our walk together take us more and more fully into the life of Jesus, who died and rose from the grave that we might have new life.

The Reverend Susan Russell

SENIOR ASSOCIATE, ALL SAINTS EPISCOPAL CHURCH,
PASADENA, CALIFORNIA

It is a deeply humbling thing to be called to speak to you today as part of this delegation charged with the historic opportunity to witness to our larger Anglican family what we in the American Episcopal Church understand to be the Holy Spirit working in our midst. I recognize that because I am the only gay member of this presentation team I am to some degree charged with speaking not only for myself but also for countless gay and lesbian brothers and sisters in Christ who have come to faith in our Lord Jesus Christ through the mission and ministry of the Episcopal Church in the United States. It is an honor and a privilege to do so.

I carry many of their stories with me today and my deepest hope is that our conversations at this meeting of the Consultative Council will be but the beginning of a genuine listening process which will make the witness to the powerful work being done on behalf of the Gospel in the lives of the gay and lesbian faithful more widely available to the church and to the world. I recognize that the very idea of "the gay and lesbian faithful" will be received as alien by many—as incomprehensible perhaps as the idea of Gentile Christians once was to Saint Peter. Yet our conviction is that the same Holy Spirit who first brooded over the waters of creation continues to work in and through us today. We believe it is that Spirit who is the source of the vision we believe God has given us of the full inclusion of the gay and lesbian baptized into the Body of Christ—just as Peter was given the surprising vision that Cornelius and his company—those he had been taught to believe were "unclean"—were as beloved of God and as welcome in the church as he was.

Those of us who support the actions of our General Convention—who advocate for the full inclusion of gay and lesbian people into all orders of ministry and for equity between same-gender partnerships and heterosexual marriage—do so out of our deep conviction that these actions are our response to the Gospel as we receive it. I have lived my whole life in this church. I am a cradle Episcopalian who was raised to think both faithfully and critically: born at our diocesan hospital, baptized at our Old Cathedral and both confirmed and ordained in the Diocese of Los Angeles. At the ripe old age of 51, I remember a church where girls couldn't be acolytes, racial segregation was widely accepted and women were not allowed to serve as deputies to our governing conventions much less aspire to ordination. I remember well the pain and conflict—the threat of schism and the accusations that we were "abandoning the church's tradition"—that surrounded all of those steps forward. And yet, in retrospect, I count the turmoil engendered as the cost of discipleship.

For I believe the church I love has been immeasurably enriched by the ministries of women who in earlier generations would have had no place to live out their vocation. I recognize how multi-cultural, multi-ethnic and multi-racial congregations have broadened our experience of God and brought us closer to experiencing the fullness of the Kingdom. Noted biblical scholar Walter Brueggemann said in a recent interview: "[American Civil Rights leader] Martin Luther King famously said that the arc of history is bent toward justice. And the parallel statement I want to make is that the arc of the Gospel is bent toward inclusiveness." Just as I can no longer imagine a church that strives to celebrate women and people of color for all of who they are I cannot imagine a church where that same arc of history—of inclusion—does not include gay and lesbian people.

Scripture tells us that what is of the Spirit will flourish—and what is not will wither away. The witness and wisdom of the women of the church have flourished since our General Convention acted courageously and faithfully—with fear and trembling—by opening to them all orders of ministry. We believe the same will prove true with the inclusion of gay and lesbian people more fully into the Body of Christ—in fact, for many of us, that is already our lived experience. I have the privilege to serve a parish—All Saints Church in Pasadena, California—that has grown by leaps and bounds in not only numbers but in mission and ministry in the fourteen years since it began the blessing of same sex unions. We are not withering—we are flourishing.

The Gospel tells us that in our Father's house there are many mansions. St. Paul tells us that essential to the Body of Christ are its many members. And our historic tradition as Anglicans tells us that when we live into the true via media we CAN hold in tension perspectives that others find "mutually exclusive" (catholic and protestant come to mind!) To set our hope on Christ is to hope for a better way...our deepest hope is that the differences that presently challenge us will not result in divisions that will hamper our ability to address together the clarion call of our Lord to minister to "the least of these" among us on His behalf.

You have heard and will hear stories of those who understand themselves to be "healed of their homosexuality"—those who tell moving and compelling stories of God healing them of an unhealthy lifestyle—freeing them to become fully and wholly the person God created them to be. I do not doubt the sincerity of their witness and I praise God if they have found place of healing and health. I do not question their healing—I question what it is that has been healed. **It is not possible to be healed of something that is not an illness**—and we are convinced that sexual orientation itself is morally neutral—that what matters to God is not our sexual orientation but our theological orientation—that when we turn to God and ask to be healed of patterns of behavior that are destructive to ourselves or others God in God's grace will heal us...whether we are homosexual or heterosexual.

Those who have left behind lives of sexual abuse, addiction and exploitation through God's healing grace have every reason to rejoice and witness to that healing. They do not have, however, have any right to project their experience on to the lives of committed, same-gender couples who are striving to live lives faithful to each other and to the Gospel.

As a point in fact, God's love changes **all** of us—but what changes is not our sexual orientation: it is our ability to give and receive love as Christ loved us—to our partners, our families and the world.

One question I often hear is "What kind of values are we teaching our children?" We are teaching our children that no matter what their sexual orientation we expect a high standard of relationship that includes fidelity, monogamy, mutual respect and life long commitment. We are challenging all couples—gay and straight—to live their lives in relationship within the context of Christian community: both supported by and accountable to their brothers and sisters in Christ. And we are modeling to gay and lesbian young people—those so tragically at risk for self-loathing and suicide in our communities—that there is a place where they can be loved by God, embraced by a community of faith and where Jesus loves them just as they are as they grow up to be all that they can be.

Our deepest hope is that the differences that challenge us might be overcome by the power of the Gospel that unites us—that the bonds of affection that have historically linked us as members of this worldwide Anglican family will prove stronger than the temptation to say "I have no need of you" when faced with the very real challenges in front of us. Classic Anglicanism has historically focused not on having a detailed and certain knowledge of the mind of God, but on maintaining life and conversation in the faithful community. We believe that no one will ever know it all, but that the Spirit will work with us to achieve a unity that transcends uniformity and to bring us toward truth.

Verna Dozier, one of the great Biblical scholars of American Anglicanism wrote this:

> The Christian church succumbs to the temptation to know absolutely when it calls doubt the opposite of faith. Doubt is not the opposite of faith. Fear is. Fear will not risk that even if I am wrong, I will trust that if I move by the light that is given me, knowing it is only finite and partial, I will know more

and different things tomorrow than I know today, and I can be open to the new possibility I cannot even imagine today.

We set our hope on the One who is the light of world—and we move forward by the light He has given us we do so in the hope that those new possibilities include many more opportunities to share with you—our Anglican family—our witness to the hope that is in us through Christ Jesus our Lord.

Mrs. Jane Tully

CLERGY FAMILIES AND FRIENDS OF LESBIANS AND GAYS

Thank you, Bishop, and thank you all for this opportunity to speak to you about my faith, my family, and families like mine throughout the church.

I am the mother of two sons and the wife of an Episcopal priest. Our son Adam is 30, and his brother Jonah is 27.

I'm Jane Tully, and what I have to say today is from my personal experience. Because it is in personal encounters with the people God puts in our lives that we see that we are all one family in God's love.

My own mother was a woman of great faith. I remember when I was about five I said, "Mama, who is God?" And she said, "God is love." I knew what that was, because I knew that my parents loved me. I never had to doubt that.

When my own children were born, I experienced God's love in an intense new way. My children are extravagant gifts from God. I did not create them. They do not belong to me. They belong to Jesus. I see His love in their lives, and I am thankful.

Love takes so many forms. When I was about ten, I began to discover that I had a special feeling for boys. I didn't decide to feel that way. I just felt it. It was another gift from God. Later, God brought me my husband.

Growing up I thought everyone had the same feelings I had. Now I know that my grandmother's sister was different. She had those feelings for women. My mother's brother had them for other men. My aunt and uncle were both upright, loving faithful Christian people, and I adored them both.

Ten years ago, our younger son Jonah told us that he, too, is attracted to men, not women. At first I was afraid. I thought it was my fault. I was ashamed to tell my friends. I feared for his health. I worried that he would face prejudice, discrimination, and even violence because of his difference. Millions like him do every day.

I had many questions, but three things I knew for sure:

- First, I had loved Jonah since before he was born.
- Second, I knew God made him and Jesus loves him.
- And third, he was the same beautiful, funny, loving person now that I had always loved. Nothing had changed.

Now I needed to learn what it meant that his affections are drawn to men. It took time. For me, the best way to learn is to listen. So I listened to my son, because I love him. I listened to other people who have same sex affection. I listened to other families. I listened to my husband and other people in the Episcopal Church who have been studying the human reality of same sex affection for three decades. I listened carefully to the scriptures. I listened to Jesus. And I listened to my heart.

I learned that my son didn't choose to be attracted to men any more than he chose the color of his skin. I now know many people like him. They tell me the same thing—and I believe them. After all, I didn't choose my sexual attraction either, and neither did my husband or my other son, who is attracted to women. We all discover our sexuality planted deep within ourselves. I believe this is an essential and God-given part of our humanity. God makes most of us to love the opposite sex, and he makes some of us to love their own sex. Why? I have no idea. But it's pretty clear God likes variety. Just look at the world He has made!

The church and the world are full of families like mine. We are in your parish, in your diocese and in your province. Think about it. Even though only a small percentage of people worldwide are drawn to their own sex, nearly all those individuals have other living family members like me—parents, grandparents, brothers and sisters, aunts and uncles, cousins. Together, we represent a significant proportion of humanity. We family members are everywhere!

My point is, the church's discussion of the human reality of people with same sex affection personally affects a much broader group of church members and clergy than most of us realize. If you think you don't know any people like my son, or their family members, it's only because they are afraid to let you know.

Some in the church speak as if God hates what God has made. Unfortunately, this is not new. Christian scapegoating of people like my son has been going on for centuries. It is deeply hurtful to him and our family. It leads many families to reject their children, with terrible consequences for everyone.

We hear a lot of talk about sin and sinners. In my view, the real sin is not who you love. It is refusing to listen and see God's gift in the people he gave us who are different from ourselves.

We have all paid a very high price for refusing this gift, and I believe that God is leading us to a new place. My faith tells me that my son does not have to be like his father or me for God to rejoice in him. I believe God *made* Jonah different and delights in him *as he is*. So who are we to argue with his Creator?

In the Episcopal Church we have a new and growing network of families like mine—clergy families with precious lesbian and gay children and other family members. We all went through a process of learning and listening when those we love had the courage to tell us their truth. It was a difficult process, and it took some of us a long time.

Today we see church itself going through that same process. We see much the same kind of the fear and anxiety we felt when we learned the truth about our children. Some of us were angry and unwilling to accept the reality in front of us. Many of us were ashamed and afraid. Some of us weren't all that surprised. All of us had a lot to learn.

We see families break up over this. I believe this grieves the heart of God. Families who shun or banish their children with same sex affection pay a horrific price. They lose the children God gave them—sometimes even to suicide—and they diminish themselves.

But as families, we also know that this difference doesn't have to break us apart. In fact, it can make us stronger. That is my family's experience and that of other families I know. I believe it can be the Anglican family's experience too.

Loving families don't abandon each other when they differ.

Our family has embraced my beautiful gay son. He has brought us all closer to each other. He has expanded our capacity to love and shown us that what we have in common is so much more than what makes us different from each other. We love him *for* who he is, not *in spite of* who he is. After all, isn't that how God loves you and me?

Today I rejoice that God gave me a gay son. He is a precious gift to me and my family, to the church and to the world, as are all the gay and lesbian members of our church family.

PROVINCIAL
SECRETARIES

Provincial Secretaries of the Anglican Communion

The Anglican Church in Aotearoa, New Zealand and Polynesia

Mr. Robin A. I. Nairn
General Secretary / Treasurer, The Anglican Church in Aotearoa,
    New Zealand & Polynesia
PO Box 885, Hastings, NEW ZEALAND
Street Address   204N Warren Street, Hastings, NEW ZEALAND
Office   +64 (0)6 878 7902
Fax   +64 (0)6 878 7905
e-mail   gensec@hb.ang.org.nz

The Anglican Church of Australia

The Reverend Dr. Bruce J. McAteer
General Secretary, The General Synod, Anglican Church of Australia
PO Box Q190, Queen Victoria Post Office, Sydney, New South Wales,
    1230, AUSTRALIA
Office: +61 (0)2 9265 1525
Fax: +61 (0)2 9264 6552
e-mail 1   gsoffice@anglican.org.au
e-mail 2   gensec@anglican.org.au
Web   www.anglican.org.au/nco.cfm

The Church of Bangladesh

Mr. Albert Achintya Samadder
Hon. Provincial Secretary, Church of Bangladesh
St Thomas' Church, 54 Johnson Road, Dhaka-1100, BANGLADESH
Office   +880 (0)2 711 6546
Fax   +880 (0)2 711 8218
e-mail   cmcy@bdmail.net

Igreja Episcopal Anglicana do Brasil

Mrs. Christine Winnischofer
Provincial Secretary
Caixa Postal 11.510, Teresópolis, Porto Alegre, RS, 90870-970, BRAZIL

Office   +55 (0)51 3318 6200
Fax   +55 (0)51 3318 6200
e-mail   cwinnischofer@ieab.org.br
Web   www.ieab.org.br

The Anglican Church of Burundi

The Reverend Pédaçuli Birakengana
Provincial Secretary, The Episcopal Church of Burundi
C/O BP 447, Bujumbura, BURUNDI
Office   +257 270 361
Fax   +257 229 129
e-mail   eebprov@cbinf.com

The Anglican Church of Canada

The Venerable Michael Pollesel
General Secretary of the General Synod
Anglican Church of Canada, 80 Hayden Street, Toronto, ON, M4Y 3G2,
    CANADA
Office   +1 416 924 9199
Fax   +1 416 924 0211
e-mail   general.secretary@national.anglican.ca

The Church of the Province of Central Africa

The Reverend Martin Mgeni
Provincial Secretary
Private Bag 1, Chilema, Malawi
Office   +265 1 539 362
Office   +265 1 539 203
e-mail 1   cpca@zamnet.zm
e-mail 2   angus@malawi.net

Iglesia Anglicana de la Region Central de America

The Right Reverend Hector Monterroso
Bishop of Costa Rica
Apartado Postal 10520-1000, San José, COSTA RICA
Office   +506 253 0790
Fax   +506 253 8331
e-mail 1   iarca@amnet.co.cr
e-mail 2   iarcahfm@hotmail.com

Province de L'Eglise Anglicane Du Congo

The Right Reverend Molanga Botola
Suffragan Bishop of Kinshasa and Provincial Secretary,
    Province de L'Eglise Anglicane Du Congo
PO Box 16482, Kinshasa, D R CONGO
BP 798, Bunia, Republique Democratique Du Congo
CAC - Bunia, PO Box 21285, Nairobi, KENYA
Office   +256 41 273 817
Fax   +256 41 343 497
e-mail 1 eac-mags@infocom.co.ug
e-mail 2 molanga2k@yahoo.co.uk

The Church of England

Mr. William Fittall
Provincial Secretary
Church House, Great Smith Street, London, SW1P 3NZ, ENGLAND
Office   +44 (0)20 7898 1360
Fax   +44 (0)20 7898 1369
e-mail   william.fittall@c-of-e.org.uk

Hong Kong Sheng Kung Hui

The Right Reverend Paul Kwong
Bishop Coadjutor of Hong Kong Island and Provincial Secretary
1 Lower Albert Road, Bishop's House, Hong Kong,
    PEOPLE'S REPUBLIC OF CHINA
Office   +852 25 265 355
Fax   +852 25 212 199
e-mail 1 gensec@hkskh.org
e-mail 2 office1@hkskh.org

The Church of the Province of the Indian Ocean

The Reverend Samitiana Jhonson Razafindralambo
Provincial Secretary
Evêché Anglican, Lot VK57 ter, Ambohimanoro, 101–Antananarivo,
    MADAGASCAR
e-mail 1 eemdanta@dts.mg
e-mail 2 eemtma@hotmail.com

The Church of Ireland

Mr Denis Reardon
Chief Officer and Secretary
Church of Ireland House, Church Avenue, Rathmines, Dublin, 6,
    REPUBLIC OF IRELAND

Office   +353 (0)1 497 8422
Fax   +353 (0)1 497 8792
e-mail 1 denis.reardon@rcbdub.org
e-mail 2 chief@rcbdub.org

The Nippon Sei Ko Kai (The Anglican Communion in Japan)

The Reverend Laurence Minabe
General Secretary
65-3 Yarai Cho, Shinjuku-Ku, Tokyo, 162-0805, JAPAN
Office   +81 (0)3 5228 3171
Fax   +81 (0)3 5228 3175
e-mail   general-sec.po@nskk.org

The Episcopal Church in Jerusalem and the Middle East

The Venerable Ian Young
Provincial Secretary
PO Box 22075, Nicosia, 1517, CYPRUS
Office   +357 22 671 220
Fax   +357 22 674 553
e-mail   georgia@spidernet.com.cy

The Anglican Church of Korea

The Reverend Abraham Gwang Joon Kim
General Secretary, The Anglican Church of Korea
3 Chong Dong Chung Ku, Seoul 100-120, REPUBLIC OF KOREA
Office   +82 (0)2 738 8952
Fax   +82 (0)2 737 4210
e-mail 1 abgw@lycos.co.kr
e-mail 2 anck@peacenet.or.kr

The Church of the Province of Melanesia

Mr. George S. Kiriau
General Secretary
PO Box 19, Honiara, SOLOMON ISLANDS
Office   +677 20470 / 21892
Fax   +677 21098
e-mail   gkiriau@comphq.org.sb
Web   http://melanesia.anglican.org/

La Iglesia Anglicana de Mexico

The Venerable Habacuc Ramos-Huerta
General Secretary, La Iglesia Anglicana de Mexico

Calle La Otra Banda #40, San Angel, 01090 Mexico, DF, MEXICO
Office 1   +52 (0)5 550 4073
Office 2   +52 (0)5 616 2490
Fax   +52 (0)5 616 4063
e-mail 1   habacuc_mx@yahoo.es
e-mail 2   ofipam@adetel.net.mx
Web   www.iglesia-anglicana-mexico.org.mx/

The Church of the Province of Myanmar (Burma)

Mr. Kenneth Saw
Provincial Secretary
140 Pyidaungsu Yeiktha Road, Dagon PO 11191, Yangon, MYANMAR
Office   +95 1 246 813
Fax   +95 1 251 405
e-mail   cpm.140@mptmail.net.mm

The Church of Nigeria (Anglican Communion)

The Venerable Ranti Odubogun
General Secretary
Episcopal House, PO Box 212, AD CP, Abuja, NIGERIA
Street Address   Episcopal House, 23 Dovale Street, WUSE Zone 5
Office   +234 9 523 6950
e-mail   abuja@anglican.skannet.com.ng

The Church of North India (United)

The Reverend Enos Das Pradhan
Provincial Secretary
General Secretarys Office, CNI Bhawan 311, 16 Pandit Pant Marg,
   New Delhi, 110001, INDIA
Office   +91 (0)11 372 0542
Fax   +91 (0)11 371 6901
e-mail 1   enos@cnisynod.org
e-mail 2   cnisynod@nda.vsnl.net.in
Web   www.cnisynod.org

The Church of Pakistan (United)

Mr. Humphrey Peters
General Secretary
Saint Johns Cathedral, 1 Sir Syed Road, Peshawar, PAKISTAN
Office   +92 91 278 916
e-mail   humphrey@brain.net.pk

The Anglican Church of Papua New Guinea

Mr. Martin Gardham
National Secretary, Anglican Church of Papua New Guinea
Box 673, Lae, Morobe Province, PAPUA NEW GUINEA
Office: +675 472 4111
Fax   +675 472 1852
e-mail   acpng@global.net.pg

The Episcopal Church in the Philippines

Dr. Andrew Tauli
Provincial Secretary
Provincial Office, PO Box 10321, Broadway Centrum, 1112 Quezon City,
    PHILIPPINES
Office   +63 (0)2 722 8460
Fax   +63 (0)2 722 8481
e-mail 1 ecpiadmn@info.co.ph
e-mail 2 a2t2@pacific.net.ph
Web   http://episcopalphilippines.net/

L'Eglise Episcopal au Rwanda

The Reverend Emmanuel Gatera
Provincial Secretary, L'Eglise Episcopal au Rwanda
C/O PO Box 61, Kigali, RWANDA
Office   +250 5 76 340

The Scottish Episcopal Church

Mr. John Stuart
Secretary General, Scottish Episcopal Church
21 Grosvenor Crescent, Edinburgh, EH12 5EE, SCOTLAND
Office   +44 (0)131 225 6357
Fax   +44 (0)131 346 7247
e-mail   secgen@scotland.anglican.org

Church of the Province of South East Asia

Mr. Dennis Wee Khui Chew
Provincial Secretary, Church of the Province of South East Asia
65 Bampfylde Heights, Kuching, Sarawak, 93200, MALAYSIA
e-mail   denwee@tm.net.my

The Church of South India (United)

Dr. Pauline Sathiamurthy
General Secretary, Church of South India
No 5 Whites Road, PO Box 688, Royapettah, Chennai, 600 014, INDIA
Office   +91 (0)44 852 1566
Fax   +91 (0)44 852 3528
e-mail   csi@vsnl.com
e-mail   csisnd@md3.vsnl.net.in

The Church of the Province of Southern Africa

The Reverend Robert Andrew Butterworth
Provincial Executive Officer
Bishopscourt, 20 Bishopscourt Drive, Claremont, 7708, South Africa
Office   +27 (0)21 761 6071
Fax   +27 (0)21 797 1329
e-mail 1 cpsa-peo@bishopscourt-cpsa.org.za
e-mail 2 peocpsa@cpsa.org.za

Iglesia Anglicana del Cono Sur de America

The Right Reverend Miguel Tamayo
Bishop of Uruguay
Reconquista 522, Casilla de Correos 6108, 11000 Montevideo,
    URUGUAY
Street Address   Reconquista 522, 11000 Montevideo , URUGUAY
Office   +598 (0)2 915 9627
Fax   +598 (0)2 916 2519
e-mail 1 mtamayo@netgate.com.uy
e-mail 2 anglican@netgate.com.uy
Web   www.uruguay.anglican.org

Mrs Leticia Gómez Guerrero
Provincial Secretary
Reconquista 522, Montevideo, URUGUAY
Office   +598 (0)2 915 9627
Fax   +598 (0)2 915 4037
e-mail   lego@adinet.com.uy

The Episcopal Church of the Sudan

The Reverend Enock Tombe
Acting Provincial Secretary
ECS Liaison Office, PO Box 604, Khartoum, SUDAN
e-mail   ecsprovince@hotmail.com

The Anglican Church of Tanzania

The Reverend Canon Dr. R. Mwita Akiri
General Secretary, Church of the Province of Tanzania
PO Box 899, Dodoma, TANZANIA
Office   +255 262 324 574
Fax   +255 262 324 565
e-mail   akiri@anglican.or.tz

The Church of the Province of Uganda

The Reverend Aaron Mwesigye
Provincial Secretary, Church of the Province of Uganda
P.O. Box 14123, Kampala, UGANDA
Office 1   +256 (0)41 270 218
Office 2   +256 (0)41 270 219

The Episcopal Church in the USA

Ms. Margaret Larom
Director of Anglican and Global Relations, and Provincial Secretary
815 Second Avenue, New York, NY, 10017, USA
Office   +1 212 716 6224
Fax   +1 212 983 6377
e-mail   mlarom@episcopalchurch.org

The Church in Wales

Mr. John M. Shirley
Provincial Secretary, The Church In Wales
39 Cathedral Road, Cardiff, CF11 9XF, WALES
Office   +44 (0)2920 348 200
Fax   +44 (0)2920 387 835
e-mail   johnshirley@churchinwales.org.uk

The Church of the Province of West Africa

Mr. Nat N. Stanley
Provincial Secretary, The Church of the Province of West Africa
PO Box Lt 226, Lartebiokorshie, Accra, GHANA
Street Address: St Monica's Anglican Church Compound, Kaneshie,
    Accra, GHANA
Office   +233 (0)21 257 370
Fax   +233 (0)21 669 125
e-mail 1   cpwa@ghana.com
e-mail 2   cpwa_gh@yahoo.com

The Church in the Province of the West Indies

Mrs. Elenor Lawrence
Provincial Secretary, Provincial Secretariat
Bamford House, Society Hill, St John, Barbados, WEST INDIES
Office   +1 246 423 0842
Fax   +1 246 423 0855
e-mail   bamford@sunbeach.net

The Church of Ceylon

Mrs. Mary Thanja Peiris
Provincial Secretary
368/3A Bauddhaloka, Mawathe, Colombo 7, SRI LANKA
Office 1   +94 1 684 810
Office 2   +94 1 696 208
Fax   +94 1 684 811
e-mail   diocol@eureka.lk

Iglesia Episcopal de Cuba

Mr. Francisco De Arazoza
Provincial Secretary
Calle 6 No 273 Vedado, Plaza de la revolucion, Ciudad de la Habana,
    CUBA
Office   +53 7 832 1120
Fax   +53 7 834 3293
e-mail 1   episcopal@enet.cu
e-mail 2   episcopal@ip.etecsa.cu

Bermuda (Extra-Provincial to the Archbishop of Canterbury)

The Right Reverend Alexander Ewen Ratteray
Bishop of Bermuda
Diocesan Office, PO Box HM 769, Hamilton HM CX, BERMUDA
Street Address   Bishop's Lodge, 18 Ferrar's Lane, Pembroke HM O8
    BERMUDA
Office 1   +1 441 292 6987
Office 2   +1 441 292 2967
Fax 1   +1 441 292 5421
Fax 2   +1 441 296 0592
e-mail 1   bishopratteray@ibl.bm
e-mail 2   diocoff@ibl.bm
Web   www.anglican.bm

The Lusitanian Church
(Extra-Provincial to the Archbishop of Canterbury)

The Right Reverend Fernando Soares
Bishop of the Lusitanian Church
Secretaria Diocesana, Apartado 392, P - 4430 Vila Nova de Gaia,
  PORTUGAL
Street Address   Rua Afonso de Albuquerque, 86, 4430 Vila
  Nova de Gaia, PORTUGAL
Office   +351 (0)22 375 4018
Fax   +351 (0)22 375 2016
e-mail 1 bisposoares@igreja-lusitana.org
e-mail 2 ilcae@mail.telepac.pt

The Reformed Episcopal Church of Spain
(Extra-Provincial to the Archbishop of Canterbury)

The Right Reverend Carlos López-Lozano
Bishop of Spanish Reformed Episcopal Church
Calle Beneficencia 18, 28004 Madrid, SPAIN
Office   +34 (0)91 445 2560
Fax   +34 (0)91 594 4572
e-mail   eclesiae@arrakis.es

ADDITIONAL
MATERIAL

Photographs from ACC-13, Nottingham

Procession through Nottingham of ACC members before the Opening Eucharist in Saint Peter's Church. (ACNS Rosenthal)

Opening Eucharist for ACC 13 in Nottingham in Saint Peter's Church in the city centre. (ACNS Rosenthal)

Archbishop Rowan Williams celebrates the Opening Eucharist for ACC 13 in Nottingham in Saint Peter's Church in the city centre. (ACNS Rosenthal)

The Right Reverend John Paterson, Chairman of the ACC . (ACNS Rosenthal)

Archbishop Rowan Williams, with ACC members, hosted a dinner for the ecumenical partners attending the meeting in Nottingham.
(ACNS Rosenthal)

Dean Peter Elliott of the Diocese of New Westminster, Canada, speaks to the ACC. (ACNS Rosenthal)

The TEAC (Theological Education for the Anglican Communion) task group makes a presentation to the ACC. (ACNS Rosenthal)

ACC members visit Saint Mary's parish, Chesterfield. (ACNS Rosenthal)

Bishop George Henry Cassidy of the Diocese of Southwell asperses the congregation at Saint Mary's Church. (ACNS Rosenthal)

ACC members worship at Saint Mary's Church. (ACNS Rosenthal)

Rachel Maddocks lights the Paschal candle while ACC members renew their baptismal vows during the service at Saint Mary's Church.
(ACNS Rosenthal)

A recession concludes the service at Saint Mary's Church. (ACNS Rosenthal)

The Right Reverend Kallistos of Diokleia delivers the Orthodox ecumenical greeting to the ACC. (ACNS Rosenthal)

Kenneth Kearon, Secretary General of the Anglican Communion, prepares to process to Saint Mary's Church, Nottingham, for the celebratory Eucharist on the final Sunday of the ACC meeting. Immediately behind Secretary Kearon is John Paterson, Chairman of the ACC. (ACNS Rosenthal)

ACC members peruse the Compass Rose Colouring Competition entries.
(ACNS Rosenthal)

The winning entry in the Compass Rose Colouring Competition.
(ACNS Rosenthal)

Anglican Consultative Council members gathered at the University of Nottingham for ACC-13. (ACNS Rosenthal)

Prayers for the Anglican Communion

From *Parish Prayers*, Frank Colquhuon, Editor

The Anglican Communion

O Almighty God, our Heavenly Father, who hast called us to be members of the Anglican Communion and to a partnership of churches in all parts of the world: Grant, we beseech thee, that we may understand the mission which thou hast entrusted to us, and our duty to those who are separated from us; that pentitently recognising our failings in the past, we may go forward in unity and love to the fulfilment of our common work; through Jesus Christ our Lord.

—Based on a prayer of the Pan-Anglican Congress, 1908

Almighty God, our heavenly Father, who in thy providence hast made us members of a great family of churches: We pray thee to pour out thy blessing upon the Anglican Communion throughout the world. Grant that we and all its members may be faithful to the trust which thou hast committed to us, and advance thy honour in the cause of Christian unity and mission: through Jesus Christ our Lord.

To the Children of the Anglican Communion

The following letter will be sent to the children of the Communion who sent items for the Competition of the Compass Rose.

To the children of the world,

We write to you, the children of God's world today, to share with you our concerns for the future.

We pledge to you, as leaders of your church family, to pray and work for:

Justice for all people everywhere,

Peace in the world,

An end to all kinds of violence

Support for families and communities,

Fair trade and an end to poverty,

A halt to the exploitation of women and children,

Freedom and dignity for all people,

Health care and education for young and old,

And the proper use of creation.

We will strive to share the Good News with everyone we meet, and to be like Jesus in all we do and say. Some you of, although you are still young, carry huge responsibilities. Some have much in material things, while some of you have so little.

You are precious gifts to us. Be brave, know God loves you.

Help us to be like you in enjoying life and beauty of the World. Know that the church is here for you, no matter who you are or where you come from.

Worship, study and pray together, and love each other as Jesus loves you.

May God bless us all.

The winners of the Colouring Competition were announced at the ACC meeting.

Overall winner is:
Roselle Aswini Walters
11 years old
Diocese of West Malaysia

Age 11–14
Chris Arnold
11 years old
Diocese of Chester, UK

Age 8–10
Stephen Daunt
Age 9
Diocese of Cork and Ross, Ireland

Age 5–7
Anita Rooney
Age 7
Diocese of Cork and Ross, Ireland

Under 5
Jessica Malholland
Age 4
Diocese of Dunedin

The Compass Rose

The emblem of the Anglican Communion, the Compass Rose, was originally designed by the late Canon Edward West of New York. The modern design is that of Giles Bloomfield. The symbol, set in the nave of Canterbury Cathedral, was dedicated by the Archbishop of Canterbury at the final Eucharist of the Lambeth Conference in 1988. The Archbishop dedicated a similar symbol in Washington Cathedral in 1990, and one in the original design in New York Cathedral in 1992, demonstrating that its use has become increasingly widespread. The centre of the Compass Rose holds the Cross of St George, reminding Anglicans of their origins. The Greek inscription "The Truth Shall Make You Free" (John 8:32) surrounds the cross, and the compass recalls the spread of Anglican Christianity throughout the world. The mitre at the top emphasises the role of the episcopacy and apostolic order that is at the core of the churches of the Communion. The Compass Rose is used widely by the family of Anglican-Episcopal churches. It is the logo of the Inter-Anglican Secretariat, and it is used as the Communion's identifying symbol.